The Ethnic Press
in the
United States

АМЕРИЧКИ
СРБОБРАН
THE AMERICAN SRBOBRAN

VOL. XXXV, No. 7956   Уторак, 4 Новембра, 1941   PITTSBURGH, PA.,   Tuesday, November 4, 1941

ПОКОЉ СРБА У "НЕЗАВИСНОЈ" ХРВАТСКОЈ

ЗА ЧЕТИРИ МЕСЕЦА ПОУБИЈАНО ЈЕ НА НАЈЗВЕРСКИЈИ НАЧИН 180.000 СРПСКОГ НАРОДА И СВЕШТЕНСТВА

ФРАНКОВАЧКА ФУКАРА ХОЋЕ ДА ИСТРЕБИ СРБЕ ИЗ ХИТЛЕРОВЕ, МУСОЛИНИЈЕВЕ И ПАВЕЛИЋЕВЕ "ВЕЛИКЕ ХРВАТСКЕ." — СРПСКА СИРОТИЊА ЦВИЛИ ДО БОГА СЕ ЧУЈЕ, АЛИ НЕ ЧУЈУ И НЕ МАРЕ ПОДИВЉАЛА НЕБРАЋА. — ОВДЕ ДОНАШАМО ДОБИВЕНИ ИЗВЕШТАЈ, ГОЛУ И СТРАШНУ ИСТИНУ, ОВО ЈЕ ЗА ШТО СЕ ЗНА, А КОЛИКО ЈЕ ЈОШ ОНИХ ЖРТАВА ЗА КОЈЕ СЕ НЕ ЗНА!

ИЗЈАВА АРХИЕПИСКОПА ОД КАНТЕРБЕРИА О ПОКОЉУ СРБА

29 октобра Архиепископ кантерберски, поглавар Англиканске цркве у Енглеској, послао је из Лондона извештај, који долази преко Српске Православне Цркве, у коме тврди и изјављује да је до почетка августа о. г. преко 180,000 Срба масакрирано само у "независној" Хрватској.

ПОБИЈЕНИ СРПСКИ СВЕШТЕНИЦИ

ПОБИЈЕНИ ПО СРЕЗОВИМА

(Српство на 2 страни)

The American Srbobran has been published since 1906 and is currently published in Pittsburgh, Pennsylvania, by the Serb National Federation. It is the largest Serb paper anywhere in the world and is the most widely read of any Serb newspaper outside of the homeland. Courtesy of the Serb National Federation, Pittsburgh, Pennsylvania.

The Ethnic Press in the United States

A HISTORICAL ANALYSIS AND HANDBOOK

EDITED BY

SALLY M. MILLER

GREENWOOD PRESS

NEW YORK • WESTPORT, CONNECTICUT • LONDON

Library of Congress Cataloging-in-Publication Data
Main entry under title:

The Ethnic press in the United States.

Includes bibliographies and index.
1. Ethnic press—United States—Addresses, essays,
lectures.   2. American newspapers—Foreign language
press—Addresses, essays, lectures.   I. Miller, Sally M.,
1937-
PN4882.E84   1987   070.4'84'0973   85-31699
ISBN 0-313-23879-0 (lib. bdg. : alk. paper)

Library of Congress Catalog Card Number: 85-31699
ISBN: 0-313-23879-0

First published in 1987
Greenwood Press, Inc.
88 Post Road West, Westport, Connecticut 06881

Printed in the United States of America

The paper used in this book complies with the
Permanent Paper Standard issued by the National
Information Standards Organization (Z39.48-1984).

10 9 8 7 6 5 4 3 2 1

To the Memory of My Mother

Contents

Introduction

SALLY M. MILLER

The phenomenon of newspapers published in the United States for the benefit of particular immigrant groups appeared in the eighteenth century. However, the ethnic press typically may be termed a late–nineteenth–century institution which is now in many groups marking a centennial. Its peak years occurred between the end of the nineteenth century and the 1930s. While observers then presumed that the demise of the ethnic press was inevitable, since its lifeblood stemmed from open immigration policies then being reversed, such predictions have not proved to be accurate. Rather, war displacement of hundreds of thousands of people and revised federal immigration policies have led to what may be a renaissance of the ethnic media. Groups new to the United States and fresh waves of older groups have demonstrated that the forecasts were parochial and even skewed. They were based essentially on assimilationist expectations concerning the foreign–speaking groups most visible at that time.

The immigrant or ethnic press has received relatively little study. Given its importance in the various communities, especially the non–English–speaking, and the vitality and growth of ethnic studies over the last two decades, the scant attention paid to the press and the limited historiography is remarkable. The only comprehensive work remains the classic by sociologist Robert E. Park, *The Immigrant Press and Its Control*, published in 1922. Useful articles, published, respectively, three and four decades after Park, are "The Role of the Foreign-Language Press in Migrant Integration" by Jerzy Zubrzycki, published in *Population Studies* in 1958, and Joshua A. Fishman, Robert G. Hayden, and Mary E. Warshauer's "The Non-English and the Ethnic Group Press, 1910–1960," in Fishman's *"Language Loyalty in the United States: The Maintenance and Perpetuation of Non-English Mother Tongues by American Ethnic and Religious Groups*, published in 1966. A full-length study appeared at the end of the McCarthy era, but its value was undermined by the xenophobic assumptions of the work: *In Many Voices: Our Fabulous Foreign-Language Press* by Edward Hunter had very limited scholarly value. But the scene is now being set for the type of close scrutiny the ethnic press merits. Various bibliographic works and directories of ethnic newspapers and periodicals have appeared. Archival collections now search out extant newspapers. Scholarly articles and papers are being prepared so that finally a sophisticated historiography appears about to emerge.[1]

The press is the best primary source for an understanding of the world of non–English–speaking groups in the United States, their expectations and concerns, their background and evolution as individual communities.[2] While other printed sources exist, such as occasional publications of cultural associations and parishes, phrasebooks, almanacs, and varieties of pamphlets, no other printed source compares to the press for its ability to provide a multidimensional overview. However narrow, inexperienced, or undercapitalized the various newspapers may have been, they nevertheless each offered a reflection of a group experience. The purpose of this volume is to introduce students of immigration history to the foreign-language press in the United States and, in some instances, in Canada as well. The original essays commissioned for this volume trace the origins of the press in over two dozen groups. They focus on the nature and development of the press, high-lighting personalities, issues, and interests; particular newspapers and editors have been singled out as appropriate; and even the contemporary electronic media are considered in a number of groups. The press is examined in the context of the political, economic, cultural, and social variables in the experience of the different groups and is viewed against the background of relevant country-of-origin events and mainstream American society. In the course of these chapters, readers will be provided with an understanding of the current research in the field in its international dimensions and will also become familiar with the available bibliography.

For purposes of this reference volume, the press is basically defined as newspapers of general circulation rather than special interest publications for the various language groups. To be sure, specialized publications were issued by fraternal, religious, unionist, political, and literary associations, and publications of this kind are mentioned in some chapters. But the overall emphasis is on those newspapers which sought to circulate as widely as possible throughout an ethnic group. The newspapers treated are those by and for individuals of a particular group. Papers which were published by the government of the country of origin and aimed at countrymen abroad, or by the American government or commercial interests seeking the attention of the ethnic communities, are excluded from consideration.

Lubomyr R. Wynar and Anna T. Wynar have argued that the term "immigrant press " is distortive and misleading. The immigrant press served the needs of the immigrant generation, whereas the ethnic press has had a longer life through its appeal to those who continued to live within the context of or to identify with their heritage. Therefore, the term "ethnic press" is the more useful one.[3]

Statistics on the ethnic press are not reliable, and indeed, are much more difficult to accept with confidence than figures for the mass circulation press. The basic newspaper listing, *N. W. Ayer and Son's Directory of Newspapers and Periodicals*, as Park himself noted over sixty years ago, is far from thorough in its compilations of non–English–language newspapers. Moreover, however uncertain circulation figures may be for these newspapers, the readership suggested is at best faulty since issues of such papers were commonly shared as literates read to the nonliterates. The following statistics on non–English–language newspapers in the United States (exclusive of American Indian publications) have been compiled from a number of authors: 794 in 1884; 1,163 in 1900; 1,323 in 1917; 1,037 in 1930; 698 in 1960, and 960 in 1975. These figures should be viewed as in constant flux. Mortality rates were excessive, sometimes a by–product of mergers but often simply due to expiration. Park determined that between 1884 and 1920, while there was a 33 percent total net increase, in actuality 3,444 new papers were started and 3,186 failed. Or, expressed another way, for every 100 papers started, about 93 stopped. That 1917 is the year of the highest number of papers published is not surprising since it fell both in the pre-quota era and during World War I when interest among immigrants in overseas news was greatest. The decrease thereafter is understandable in terms of the shrinking pool of newcomers, until the 1970s, when the lifting of the quota system led to a revived flow into the country and a concomitant increase in the number of non-English newspapers.[4]

Groups which might be covered in this collection number many more than such a volume can accommodate. The *Harvard Encyclopedia of American Ethnic Groups*, edited by Stephan Thernstrom and his associates, covers roughly ninety recognizable immigrant groups with additional clusters as well, based on religion, geography or other variables. The Wynar directory encompasses five dozen groups. Space limitation was a crucial factor here resulting in the inclusion of only twenty-eight groups. Other limiting factors involved accidents of history, i.e., whether specialists existed to undertake the history of particular ethnic presses, whether those specialists were available, and whether they could meet the necessary deadlines. Within those parameters, additional choices had to be made. Some groups were obvious candidates for inclusion. For example, the German and the Jewish presses in the United States both clearly merited coverage, having enjoyed the largest circulation of the foreign-language newspapers. Another likely candidate for inclusion, the Italian press, regrettably could not be covered because no specialist was sufficiently free of constraints to undertake the assignment. However, a work which compensates for its omission here is Pietro Russo's forthcoming *Italian American Periodical Press: 1836–1980*, to be published by the Center for Migration Studies, which will fill that gap in the literature. One group covered herein does not entirely appear to belong in a study of those of immigrant origin: the Mexican Americans or Chicanos. They have been included, however, because they are in part a people who immigrated to the United States and, at the same time, in part a people who became Americans through annexations by the U.S. government of areas in the Southwest. They are thus products of two processes, one of which suggests inclusion. Another group included which might require an explanation is the Irish. While their press was essentially an English-language press, the Irish as an immigrant group required a press of its own and used it in the same manner as foreign-speaking groups. Therefore, the Irish merit inclusion.

Conversely, blacks and Native Americans were excluded on the basis that their presses would not reflect the immigration and adaptation processes. Although both have experienced cultural change, the variables differ. These chapters focus on groups which typically chose to immigrate to the United States and underwent the subsequent adjustment process.

The built-in bias in the coverage of groups here rests in its heavy inclusion of what have been called the "New Immigrant" groups who came from Central and Eastern Europe by the millions at the end of the nineteenth century and the first decades of the twentieth century. These Slavic and other groups have come to be extremely well studied by scholars; specialists were available to scrutinize the history of their presses; and, most important, their presses lasted sufficiently long that it became possible to trace their history. There are other groups who have arrived in the United States over the last two decades who are beginning to establish communities of their own, and are replicating in their numbers those of eighty years ago. Indeed, the numbers of newcomers entering the United States in the 1970s mark that decade as witnessing the greatest influx since the first decade of this century.[5] These Mexicans, Salvedoreans and other Central Americans, Iranians, Koreans, Chinese, Filipinos, Arabs, Cubans and other Caribbean Islanders, Pakistanis, East Indians, and Southeast Asians are developing their institutions and scholars trained to study them. They are changing the face and accents of the United States as did the earlier groups, but at this time it would be premature to include them in a collection of this type.

One final comment on the organization of the work is that the specialists who wrote the various chapters themselves have different backgrounds. They are often, but not always, members of the group about which they have written. Many are academics—historians, sociologists, and members of other disciplines—and some are journalists. Hence, approaches and emphases vary in accord with the perspectives and judgments of the various authors.

Efforts to divide the ethnic press into categories have not been wholly successful. Stanley Zybala has recently traced press categories on the basis of attitude and ideology. After the initial stages of the immigrant press, in which the clergy's role was often crucial, he notes that as the press matured, categorical divisions such as nationalistic, conservative or traditional, and radical have been applied to it. However, he argues that this approach is flawed in that enough diversity and overlapping exist in the treatment of issues to make such divisions useless. Robert Park developed a three-pronged division among the publications which he studied. He described the foreign-language press as "predominantly a commercial press," citing statistics such as the following: in 1920 German publications were 93 percent commercial, Italian ones were 85 percent commercial, and Polish ones were 81 percent commercial. Secondly, publications of organizations promoting "the work of a society or an institution" he termed organs. His third division was that of propaganda papers or journals of opinion which sought circulation and influence among the general public of its group. While Park is correct that the ethnic press was largely commercial, his definition was ambiguous, and his second and third divisions were not the clear-cut separations he suggested. Although he placed religious publications in the "organ" category, they were capable of propagandizing among their group at large, while the propaganda sheets, by which he meant radical political papers, might represent the work of an organization. This ambiguity limits the value of his categories.[6]

In most cases, the earliest press of an immigrant group was founded by the clergy. In this collection, for example, clergy established the first Russian, Romanian, Ukrainian, Portuguese, and Norwegian papers, among others. Such sheets attempted to guard the faith and to defend the church against the host society. The religious press was polemical and frequently acrimonious and often met with success in conserving the immigrants' faith.[7] But it often gave rise to anticlerical newspapers. Nationalistic, temperance, and radical sheets, among others, might then be inspired by discontent with the existing press voices within the group. The proprietary press, however, became the essence of the ethnic newspaper world.

Newspapers appeared where at least the nucleus of a particular community existed, to which a publication might help give form. Population size was a crucial factor in maintaining the minimum necessary circulation. A readership was also required; the level of literacy within a community could be a major variable, automatically limiting possibilities for the success of the press. A persona was often a key factor. An editor or publisher, who might be a local businessman primarily engaged in some other activity, had to be willing to contribute the necessary funds or energy to give life to the operation.[8]

The editors, publishers, and reporters—often the same person who handled a paper alone—were, in the words of one essayist here, of "the thin layer of immigrant intellectuals." They had attained some education in their country of origin, and sometimes journalistic experience as well. They were, therefore, not representative of the immigrant group at large but more often members of its urban elite. If they had in fact been professionals prior to their immigration, the language barrier which they met here might be impassable. The foreign-language press, then, was a logical alternative for these individuals: they could use their general education and perhaps make a living as well. As journalists, such men, and occasionally women, had to write in a language that potential readers could understand, either a particular dialect or vernacular which would be interspersed with words adapted from English and integrating American idioms. At the same time that such concessions were made, numbers of journalists were also providing stable form to languages. Still, it was not unusual for an occasional editor to lament the cultural wasteland in which he found himself.[9]

The press served many functions, and attempts have been made to construct various models of the foreign-language press. As a whole, it was informational, carrying news of the country of origin, of compatriots elsewhere in the United States, and, of course, of the local community. It expressed a group's values, heritage, and changing sense of identity. It also socialized its readers to the United States as it educated them and became itself a tool of adjustment. And it promoted group pride as well as economic and political power. Robert Park suggested that in the various functions the press undertook on behalf of its group's welfare, it ultimately led its people toward participation in American society.[10]

An ebb and flow, related to immigration patterns, shaped the fortunes of the ethnic press. More dependent on population figures than on individual talents or capitalization, the survival rate of individual operations was never encouraging. The numbers of immigrants, the rate of assimilation, and the attraction of the papers for the American-born generations all influenced the fate of an individual operation. Various devices were tried, such as publishing English-language pages or issues (termed by Fishman "mixed" publications), and even converting a newspaper to English entirely. Nevertheless, individual papers continued to collapse even while the ethnic press as an institution remained. Those that have tended to survive longest have not been the commercial papers as Park predicted, but the papers of the fraternal organizations; the organizational membership lists and resources have meant the largest readership (or at least outreach, since these papers automatically entered members' homes) and perhaps the greatest influence.[11]

Different stages characterize the evolution of the foreign-language press. The earliest stage, where the press was inherently an immigrant one, was marked by the greatest impermanence, as fleeting sheets appeared and disappeared. The papers in this trial or pioneering era tended to be one-person operations, and often amateurish. This stage can be considered as essentially lasting until the final decade or so of the nineteenth century. Those immigrant groups which were most visible in the colonial period and through the Civil War and Reconstruction era naturally developed the first immigrant newspapers. Thus, the earliest foreign-language newspapers were those in German, French, the various Scandinavian languages, Dutch, and, in the West, Chinese. The second stage appeared toward the end of the century as different groups began to arrive in increasing numbers, hailing especially from Central and Eastern Europe; at this time newspapers began to publish in Italian, Polish, Yiddish, Bohemian, Russian, Finnish, Slovak, Lithuanian, Serbian, Portuguese, Ukrainian, Armenian, Greek, and Japanese, among others.

Until the last decades of the nineteenth century, these immigrant newspapers tended clearly to lag far behind the American papers in terms of technology, distribution techniques, and variety of features. In content, for the most part they stressed news and editorials of specific interest to their group and reproduced and serialized literary classics of their culture. But, depending on the group experience, some settled into the United States sufficiently so that they became involved very deeply in American politics. The German and the Norwegian papers, as examples, immersed themselves in issues such as slavery, temperance, and electoral politics. One author even argues that some of these older groups published "almost from their inception . . . American newspapers printed in [their own] languages."[12] Conversely, where groups maintained what was known as the sojourner mentality, their papers were less likely to become absorbed in American issues. Toward the beginning of the twentieth century, a notable trend occurred among the more successful papers toward modernization and professionalization. They began to utilize the latest technology, to expand their distribution and advertising networks, to increase their use of so-called American features such as fashions and comics, and in content to move away from sharply defined ethnic-based political commentary toward a tone of journalistic objectivity.

The foreign-language press in general enjoyed its peak years in this era. From 1900 to 1930 it built its greatest circulation at a time when it was in fact in transition—varying by group—from an immigrant press to an ethnic press. In 1917 the number of publications was at its highest, and in 1930 non-English dailies peaked in number. Yet these were the twilight years of the open door policy prior to the National Origins legislation of the 1920s. Reversal of that policy could not help but modify the potential of the press. World War I initially enhanced the vitality of the foreign-language press. The foreign-born and their offspring, too, naturally tended to be caught up in the issues of the war. The newspapers, like their communities, lined up with their countries of origin as European nations took up arms against one another in 1914. Old World loyalties and hostilities were ignited by the events, and the result was a dynamic spurt of growth for existing newspapers and the establishment of new ones to represent specific points of view on the war itself, self-determination, and other issues. In the war era, the German-language press claimed a circulation of 1 million, the Polish and Yiddish press each claimed nearly 1 million, the Italian nearly 700,000, and the Swedish 500,000.[13] But with the preparedness controversy and the intervention of the United States into the war in 1917, any euphoria was dampened. Pressures to assimilate, widespread community tensions, and eventually federal legislation reversed the fortunes of the foreign-language press. While earlier state-level moves had occurred toward regulating non–English–language publications, during the war such efforts crystallized. Federal legislation passed in October 1917 required non–English–language newspapers to file English translations of war news with the authorities, and postal licensing procedures threatened the very existence of the papers. A general pullback occurred: numbers of less well-established newspapers ceased publication under the wartime burdens, while others responded to the chilling effect of the censorship issue by self-regulation. Some papers reduced space given to war news, and others promoted patriotic rallies and Liberty Loan drives. Congressional measures introduced to ban foreign-language publications altogether reinforced such tendencies.

The flowering of the ethnic press appeared to have been brief. But, in fact, the third stage of the press, from the 1930s to the 1980s, featured a decline and then an expansion among ethnic newspapers in this country. As immigration died down under the impact of post–World War I quota legislation, papers folded and circulation decreased among those that survived. The combination of shrinking numbers of newcomers and the aging of the first generation appeared to be a virtually insurmountable barrier for the press. As Fishman reports, non-English dailies declined by 57 percent between 1930 and 1960, and weeklies by 63 percent. Only the monthlies grew, showing a 34 percent increase between 1930 and 1960, but these tended to be special interest periodicals. The mass circulation dailies and weeklies of the previous generation seemed to be succumbing. However, midway in this fifty–year period, new stimuli brought on an impressive revival. Perhaps this might eventually be termed a fourth stage. The numbers of non–English–language newspapers and periodicals grew continually over the last years: in 1960, there were 698; in 1970, 903; and in 1975, 960. Different groups came to dominate this microcosm. Instead of the German, Scandinavian, and Yiddish readers of the past providing a strong basis for the foreign-language press, Spanish and Slavic readers, among others, have taken up the slack. For example, Slavic-language weeklies comprised 11 percent of the non-English dailies in 1910 and 26 percent in 1960, substituting, as it were, for the German share of the market, which fell from 56 percent in 1910 to 15 percent in 1960.[14]

The first factor that explained the revival of the ethnic press was the increase in the numbers of foreign-language speakers since World War II. Displaced persons and political refugees provided a new pool of potential readers. Moreover, many were far better educated than the immigrants of the previous generations. They also tended to be politically conscious, especially those coming from Eastern Bloc nations. Such individuals represented a familiar version of the sojourner mentality. Their eyes were very much on the homeland, and many of their newspapers consequently had their attention riveted to its struggles. When the home society is perceived not to be free, be it Lithuania in 1915, Croatia in 1935, Cuba in 1965, or the Ukraine in 1985, its press focuses on its problems and may serve as a conduit to inform countrymen at home. Indeed, such a press bears an additional role from the press of a group here whose homeland is free. And, as indicated in some of the chapters that follow, responsibilities to countrymen who did not immigrate may take precedence over their press role in the emerging community here. Thus, the state of mind of such a newspaper may remain that of an immigrant press very much caught up in the framework of the homeland and its issues; it may not make the transition into an ethnic press.

Since World War II a division has occurred within many groups between the older immigrants and the newer ones marked by resentment and hostility. Those long settled here, whatever sympathies they might in theory feel for their newly arrived countrymen, often are concerned as to how newcomers might adversely affect the image and status of their group. Negative publicity, the emergence of new social problems, and even specific government policies are concerns of the old–timers. In turn, the newcomers may resent the older generation's seeming affluence and comfort in the United States and the ways in which their group's institutions, for example, the church, may have evolved here. Such a pattern can be observed in the wariness of German and Eastern European Jews toward each other in nineteenth–century America, and in the divisions among old and new Chinese ethnics in the United States over the last two decades. Therefore, the newcomers sometimes have needed a press of their own to represent their distinct point of view.

A third factor was the revival of ethnic consciousness over the past generation following the civil rights movement led by black Americans. A sense of group cohesion, shared identity, and pride stimulated a variety of groups into even their third and fourth generations to grapple with questions of ethnicity. The resultant awareness, which often led to activism on behalf of the group by college students and others, became in itself a catalyst to revive an ethnic press.

A fourth factor in the expansion of the foreign-language press has been the presence of groups new to the United States, either those who earlier had been here in extremely small numbers, for example, Koreans or Sikhs, or those who have come for the very first time. The range of cultures present in the United States have been enormously broadened by the entrance of newcomers from developing nations, especially those from Latin America and Asia. That they need their own media requires no explanation. Just as colonial era and nineteenth-century immigrants needed newspapers to express their views and problems and to provide pertinent information, so have the immigrants of the last decades of the twentieth century.

Over the course of American history, the newspaper world represented by those papers discussed in this volume has been a necessary element in the lives of their respective peoples. Just as schools, churches, fraternal organizations, and community meeting places were essential in the effort to recreate Old World societies in microcosm, the press too was a necessary ingredient in that recreation. Depending on the size of the population, group literacy, the presence of intellectuals and entrepreneurs, and the pattern of settlement, among other variables, inevitably a press arose of larger or of smaller proportions. The press gave its readership information that it wanted and needed. It embodied its public's point of view and values as it did so, and it expressed its essence when it spoke to the outside world. Finally, the press, as it made linguistic, social, and political adjustments to the new environment, led its readers in the same direction.

Much remains to be done before we have a definitive work on the immigrant and ethnic press in the United States. Most unfortunately, the pattern of casual preservation of such papers means that some newspapers are entirely lost to history, while others exist in incomplete runs. Only recently has work in this field developed to the point where efforts are being extended to locate, preserve, and catalogue those newspapers and to develop annotated bibliographies. The Immigration History Center at the University of Minnesota, the Center for the Study of Ethnic Publications at Kent State University, and the Multicultural History Society of Ontario are institutions making important contributions in this area. Small denominational college collections, such as the Swedish-American

materials at Augustana College, have often played a role in salvaging and preserving primary sources which otherwise would have disappeared. The University
of Bremen's project on bibliography and archival preservation of non–English
language North American newspapers in the area of labor is a unique and significant effort. But the important work now being conducted can only be termed
preliminary.

Content analysis is in its early stage. This task must be diligently pursued in
order to understand the histories of various groups as they are revealed in such
documentation. Through the press, scholars can trace historical and sociological
developments, examine social structure, and analyze groups' mores as they are
distinguished from those of mainstream society.[15] Only after such work has been
accomplished can scholars begin to produce the necessary monographs.

The idea for such a volume was first broached by this editor to Dr. James
Sabin, Vice President of Editorial at Greenwood Press, in 1981, and he was
most enthusiastic about the project. The work then proceeded over the next few
years, with the bulk of the chapters being written in 1983 and 1984.

Acknowledgments are always a pleasurable part of the last stages of a work.
A few authors of the essays that follow wish to indicate in these pages sources
of support for or influence on their efforts: Arlow W. Andersen is indebted to
the Norwegian-American Historical Association and to the Luther College Library press collections of Decorah, Iowa. Carlos E. Cortés acknowledges the
research grant assistance he obtained from the Academic Senate of the University
of California, Riverside, and also thanks Jill M. Marks for her diligent and
imaginative work as his research assistant. Joseph D. Dwyer wishes to acknowledge the work of Joseph Velikonja, Ivan Molek, and Jože Bajec, which has
been extremely helpful to him. The editor wishes to try at least to indicate the
number of debts she has accumulated during the four years of gestation of the
project and to express her thanks. First, of course, my greatest debt is to the
various specialists who wrote the individual chapters. Without their talents,
goodwill, and diligence, this volume could not have come to fruition. My col-
league, Dr. Maxine S. Seller of the State University of New York at Buffalo,
provided inspiration for this project through her parallel work in the area of the
ethnic theater in the United States. My editors at Greenwood Press, Marilyn
Brownstein and Cynthia Harris, were supportive and helpful in every way possible. Those who enabled me to locate sources and potential contributors played
a crucial role in the organizational phase of this project. While unfortunately
this list will not be as comprehensive as it might be, the following individuals
have my enthusiastic thanks for their helpfulness: Silvano M. Tomasi, S.J., of
the Center for Migration Studies; Carlton C. Qualey of the Immigration History
Society; Hensley C. Woodbridge of Southern Illinois University; Victor Greene
of the University of Wisconsin-Milwaukee; Betty Ann Burch, formerly editor
of *Spectrum*, published by the Immigration History Research Center; Dorothy
Burton Skårdal of the University of Oslo; Madeline Guiguerè of the University
of Southern Maine; Frederick G. Bohme of the U.S. Bureau of the Census;

Francis M. Rogers, Professor Emeritus, Harvard University; Manoel da Silveira Cardozo, Professor Emeritus, Catholic University of America; Peter A. Munch, Professor Emeritus, Southern Illinois University; Lawrence J. McCaffrey of Loyola University of Chicago; Michael B. Petrovich of the University of Wisconsin-Madison; Joel Halpern of the University of Massachusetts. I also wish to acknowledge the commitment of the late Donn V. Hart of Northern Illinois University who had undertaken the work on the Filipino press.

For general encouragement, help in copyediting, and assistance in the detailed work on footnoting format and bibliographic citations, I extend my warm thanks to Michele M. Ennis of Palo Alto, California.

That this collection is dedicated to the memory of my mother is not pro forma but rather highly appropriate. It is fitting that a book on this subject be dedicated to her because her experiences with the ethnic press reflect a thesis in these chapters. She was born Chaiya Narshen in 1905 in the stetl of Koristashow near Kiev. She grew up as Clara Nixon on the West Side of Chicago, where she observed the adults in the neighborhood reading the *Jewish Daily Forward*. But she, as an adult and until her death in 1984, chose to read Chicago's metropolitan dailies. Her life mirrored some of what follows.

NOTES

1. See the following works: Robert E. Park, *The Immigrant Press and Its Control* (New York: Harper and Brothers Publishers, 1922); Jerzy Zubrzycki, "The Role of the Foreign-Language Press in Migrant Integration," *Population Studies* 12 (1958); 73–82; Joshua A. Fishman, Robert G. Hayden, and Mary E. Warshauer, "The Non-English and the Ethnic Group Press, 1910–1960," Joshua A. Fishman et al., *Language Loyalty in the United States: The Maintenance and Perpetuation of Non-English Mother Tongues by American Ethnic and Religious Groups* (The Hague: Mouton and Co., 1966), pp. 51–74; Edward Hunter, *In Many Voices: Our Fabulous Foreign-Language Press* (Norman Park, Ga.: Norman College, n.d); Lubomyr R. Wynar and Anna T. Wynar *Encyclopedic Directory of Ethnic Newspapers and Periodicals in the United States*, 2nd ed. (Littleton, Colo.: Libraries Unlimited, 1976); Hensley C. Woodbridge, "United States and Canadian National Bibliography: Foreign Languages," *Encyclopedia of Library and Information Science* 36, Supp. 1 (1983); 516–574; "The Ethnic Press: Many Voices," *Spectrum* (Immigration History Research Center) 3 (March 1980): 1–2.

2. See the introduction to the theme issue on the ethnic press of *Polyphony* (Bulletin of the Multicultural History Society of Ontario) 4 (Spring/Summer 1982): 7–9, by editor Robert F. Harney.

3. Wynar and Wynar, *Encyclopedic Directory*, pp. 14–15, 17.

4. Woodbridge, "United States and Canadian National Bibliography," p. 521; Park, *Immigrant Press*, pp. 295–296, 305, 313; Zubrzycki, "Role of the Foreign-Language Press," p. 76; see also Wynar and Wynar, *Encyclopedic Directory*, pp. 17–18, 21 for a summary of a variety of extant statistics.

5. See Raymond A. Mohl, "Cubans in Miami: A Preliminary Bibliography," *The Immigration History Newsletter* 16 (May 1984): 1–2. Immigration statistics show that 8.7 million people entered the United States in the first decade of the twentieth century and 4.5 million in the 1970s.

6. Stanley Zabala, "Problems of Survival for the Ethnic Press in Canada," *Polyphony* (Bulletin of the Multicultural History Society of Ontario) 4 (Spring/Summer 1982): 17–18, 22; Park, *Immigrant Press*, pp. 304–305, 330–332; Julianna Puskás, another specialist, refining Zabala slightly, uses the categories nationalist, socialist, and denominational. Julianna Puskás, "The Differentiation of the Hungarian Newspapers [and] How It Reflects Some Aspects of Acculturation," paper presented at the International Symposium on the Role of the Labor Press in the Acculturation of Working Class Immigrants, 1880s to 1930s in the Atlantic Economies, February 1985, Falkenstein, West Germany.

7. John G. Deedy, Jr. "The Catholic Press: The Why and the Wherefore," in Martin E. Marty, John G. Deedy, Jr., David Wolf Silverman, and Robert Lekachman, *The Religious Press in America* (New York: Holt, Rinehart and Winston, 1963), pp. 67, 69, 72.

8. The author expresses her thanks to Joseph Velikonja of the University of Washington for sharing these ideas from his unpublished 1981 manuscript, "The Periodical Press and Italian Communities."

9. Ulf Beijbom, "The Swedish Press," in Sally M. Miller, ed., *The Ethnic Press in the United States: A Historical Analysis and Handbook* (Westport, Conn.: Greenwood Press, 1986); Park, *Immigrant Press*, pp. 70–72, 79–83; Hunter, *In Many Voices*, p. 20. The readers were often novices, as many immigrants had not been newspaper readers in their countries of origin. See also Milan M. Radovich, "The Serbian Press," in this volume.

10. See, for example, Wynar and Wynar, *Encyclopedic Directory*, pp. 18–19; Marion Tuttle Marzolf, "The Danish Immigrant Newspapers: Old Friend in a New Land," paper presented to the Society for the Advancement of Scandinavian Studies, May 1984, Seattle; Park, *Immigrant Press*, pp. 9, 11, 87–88, 449, 467.

11. Park, *Immigrant Press*, pp. 309, 326, 328; Fishman et al., "Non-English and Ethnic Group Press," pp. 51, 62–65.

12. See tables in Park, *Immigrant Press*, p. 252, and Wynar and Wynar, *Encyclopedic Directory*, pp. 16–17; Zubrzycki, "Role of the Foreign-Language Press" p.77; Arlow W. Andersen, "The Norwegian-American Press," ch. 17 in this volume.

13. Fishman et al. "Non-English and Ethnic Group Press," p. 52; Park, *Immigrant Press*, p. 304. The Fishman article reports a circulation of foreign-language dailies, weeklies, and monthlies in 1930 of about 7 million. There is no way to calculate the number of people who actually read those newspapers.

14. Fishman et al., "Non-English and Ethnic Group Press," pp. 52–55; Wynar and Wynar, *Encyclopedic Directory*, p. 17.

15. Wynar and Wynar, *Encyclopedic Directory*, p. 26.

The Ethnic Press
in the
United States

1

The Arabic–Language Press

ALIXA NAFF

The Arabic-language press was one of the important factors in the remarkably rapid assimilation of the nearly 100,000 Arabic-speaking immigrants to the United States between 1880 and World War I. Inexperienced and bewildered villagers, the majority of whom were illiterate or barely literate peripatetic peddlers, many of them came to depend on information published in their ethnic press. If the reading population was relatively small, those who informed and guided it were nevertheless numerous and eager.

So keen was the penchant for publishing that between 1892 and 1907 (the lifetime of the first Arabic newspaper), twenty-one Arabic dailies, weeklies, and monthlies were published, seventeen of them in New York City and the others scattered in Philadelphia; Lawrence, Massachusetts; and St. Louis, Missouri. In 1907, when the immigrants numbered only about 50,000, there were eleven publications in existence.[1]

Because the migrants originated in the Ottoman province of Syria on the eastern shores of the Mediterranean, which included the autonomous sanjak of Mt. Lebanon—roughly the coastal mountain range north of Beirut, south of Tripoli, and east of the Beqa Plain—they were Syrians. With the exception of a relatively small number of Palestinians, other Arabic-speaking peoples do not appear in the immigration records except sporadically and as transient individuals.

The Syrian immigrants of this period were neither the first nor the last Arabs to come to the United States. They were the first, however, to arrive in any significant numbers as a group. A second major Arab migration, containing a high percentage of skilled and professional, politicized, nationalistic young men and women, began after World War II. The first-wave migrants, although not politicized and nationalistic, left their land with a strong sense of who they were. They came as Syrians, called themselves Syrians, and were known as Syrians. "Arab," to them, was a cultural reference, not a nationalistic one, since at the time of their migration there was no independent Syrian political entity with which to identify. Nor were they identified by the outside world as Arabs, although their language was Arabic and they were fiercely proud of their Arab heritage. The strongest identity factors were more personal. The structure of Ottoman-Muslim society was such that for centuries its members identified themselves by family, religion, sect, and place of origin.

About 90 to 95 percent of the early immigrants were Christian; the rest were Muslims and Druze. About 90 percent of the Christians were from Mt. Lebanon, the major stronghold of Western-oriented Christians. Although the economies of both Mt. Lebanon and Syria proper were not sufficiently depressed to yield despair, neither were they brisk enough to meet rising expectations. Poverty was common, though not abject, and life was difficult. Thus, most of the Syrians were from the land—owners of small disconnected plots who frequently had to supplement their income through crafts and trade.

Syrians were not driven out of their country by economic oppression or by religious or political persecution. Like other immigrant groups, Syrians came to the United States to improve their economic status. The pioneers—those who arrived before and shortly after the turn of the century—came solely to get rich quick and return to their villages to live and raise their children in an environment of economic comfort and security. Syrians who migrated subsequently, for whatever reason—military conscription, or Ottoman oppression during World War I, for example—came to the United States and other parts of the Western Hemisphere because the adventurous "gold-seeking" pioneers had opened the way.

Until 1899 Syrians, in official immigration records, were not distinguished from other subjects of the Ottoman Empire. Lumped together with Turks, Greeks, and Armenians from the empire under the classification "Turkey in Asia," their exact numbers are difficult to determine. The records, however, show that a total of 115,838 Syrians and Palestinians immigrated between 1899 and 1940 to join several thousands who had previously been registered as Turks in Asia. According to census records, there were 206,128 Americans of Syrian and Palestinian origin and descent by 1940, living in every state of the Union and Alaska. This wide distribution was already a fact by 1910, the result of pack peddling, the primary occupation of Syrian immigrants. Women joined the migration from the beginning, and by the peak of Syrian immigration in 1913, wives, mothers, sisters, and daughters constituted about 32 percent of the migrants.[2]

Of the majority listed as illiterate in the official immigration statistics, many may have learned at least the rudiments of Arabic in native and missionary schools. In the homeland, literacy in classical Arabic, the written language, would have served little purpose save to read the Bible or the Quran, and few would have had the time or the motivation to develop their literary skills. In the United States, they may not always have had the time, but they had ample motivation. They were anxious to read and write letters and to read newspapers for information about the homeland as well as the new land. Many taught themselves, or each other, to read and write Arabic in the United States, building on their elementary knowledge. Some brought grammar and children's story books with them or purchased them, usually from newspaper publishers, who not only sold Arabic books published in the United States by the Arabic press but imported a large variety from the major cities of Syria and Egypt.[3]

A fundamental factor in the Syrian experience in the United States was pack peddling. It was not unique to Syrian immigrants; Greeks, Italians, East European Jews, and Armenians had also used it as an expedient initial occupation. Generally, however, these groups preferred the pushcart to the pack and the city to the country. As the Syrians practiced the trade, it initially involved rosaries, crosses, notions, and jewelry, but peddling expanded to include practically everything that a farm wife or housebound pre–World War I town dweller needed or desired. What was unique about the pioneer Syrians was their deep and broad identification with the trade. Despite its demands on their physical and psychological resources, they usually preferred it to the drudgery of the factory and the isolation of American farm life.

Not only did they leave their villages to follow its promise of quick wealth, but they pursued that promise, on foot or by horse and buggy, to every quarter of the American continent. Like the itinerant Jewish merchants of an earlier period, with whom they felt an affinity, the Syrians used peddling as a stepping–stone on the upward path toward personal success and middle–class status. Peddling provided a firsthand, close-up introduction to American life, served as a window to new ideas and values, and raised expectations. Its other basic virtues were that it required no advanced training, capital, or language skills, and was a means of earning money immediately on arrival.

Peddling settlements, made up of relatives and fellow villagers, were incomplete replicas of the village. They were both the peddlers' base and their refuge. It was there that the peripatetic peddler might improve his Arabic literacy, read a newspaper, or have it read to him.

Almost from the beginning the trend was toward permanent residence despite continued vows of old and new immigrants to return to the homeland. As experience washed away the mystery and uncertainty of working and living in the new land, settlements began to mature into communities around ethnic institutions—churches and clubs in particular. Mosques were not built until the mid–1920s. New York was the foremost business, cultural, and intellectual center for Syrians until well after 1948.

Peddling hastened acculturation and in the process contributed to its own obsolesence. Few mourned its passing. Peddlers acquired capital and new values, including the notion of settling permanently in the United States. When Syrians settled down, the majority opened family businesses in cities and towns throughout the country. Dry goods and grocery stores were the most common, but Syrians engaged in businesses of all kinds. Experiences on the road and in settlements were open doors to assimilation; the forces to protect the immigrants against the irresistible pull of American life were too weak within the community. On the one hand, the advantages of acquiring an American veneer were not only economic but social; they enhanced one's prestige in the settlements as well as back home in the village. In addition, nationalistic feelings and ideologies, common deterrents to changing identities, were weak or absent in many Syrians and ambivalent in others. Not to be underestimated was the general satisfaction with what peddling Syrians found in America.

When the immigrants sought explanations for the many aspects of American life which they had witnessed as they roamed from town to town and farmhouse to farmhouse, they turned as much to veteran immigrants as to the Arabic press, which interpreted American life for them as best it could. From its inception in 1892, the press brought elements of American life and values not experienced by Syrians themselves to the attention of the immigrants and provided guidance. While it explained, it also idealized and oversimplified, presenting America, as a rule, in uncritical and glowing terms. In its advocacy of patriotism and good citizenship, it was pedagogical.

In the early years, before experience and self-reform improved their quality, the newspapers provided their relatively small readership, composed mostly of one religious or sectarian community, with ample quantities of social news and gossip, notices from immigrants in search of family or friends, and items on the movement of prominent individuals. Sometimes, too, in these formative years of the Arabic press, paid self-serving laudatory or defamatory paragraphs also appeared. Some of these papers became entangled in the sectarian rivalries of the New York colony while others were used to establish false credit credentials. The practice and the attempt to eradicate it were among the causes of a 1905 riot among Syrians in New York. In the opinion of *The New York Herald*, which reported the event, the trouble seemed to have been that the Syrian press "tried to adapt methods of the society journal and the personal and political editorials of the country newspaper to Oriental conditions."[4]

Usually four to eight pages, these papers also published news and opinion, items on events in the homeland and in the United States, advertisements of products and services of Syrian businessmen, immigrant success stories, and feature aritcles. One such series dealt with the importance of the Arabic press to the Syrian immigrants.[5] Others covered social and economic complexities faced by the immigrants in the New World. The editors, taking a pragmatic approach to the future of Syrians in America, addressed such issues as how to channel the energies of young and adventurous men away from "subversive and immoral" temptations and onto an upward economic path; how to reconcile the widening economic role of women with traditional restraints; how to protect the sanctity of the family; and how to uphold the honor and integrity of Syrians. Because many of these problems were related to the issue of marriage—an issue not only central to the mores and values of Syrian society, but significant to the future of Syrians in America—the Arabic press devoted numerous articles to it.

When an uneasy America, in an attempt to restrict immigration before World War I, classified the peoples of the Eastern Mediterranean as among the excluded Asians, the newspapers rallied the community from 1909 and led a crusade against this discrimination into the courts where the matter was finally resolved in 1915. Typically, the papers covered many aspects of American life, ranging from trivia (such as the number of telephones in the United States and the status of coffee consumption) to support of America's war with Spain, profiles of presidents, and the state of American business. It also kept its readers apprised of the welfare (most of it good), whereabouts, and accomplishments of countrymen in Latin America, which also had received a flood of Syrians, and it published the literary works of Syrians there. Many of its readers were also contributors. Ordinary immigrants asked questions, voiced opinions, and reflected their growing aspirations.

In any retrospective on the Arabic press in America, one cannot fail to detect its cultural ambivalence. While it kept the homeland alive in the minds and emotions of the Syrian immigrants, it also exhorted them to change some of their traditional ways. It published textbooks for learning English, American customs, naturalization procedures, as well as articles on American history and society. It also printed long fullpage lists of Arabic books on a variety of disciplines published in the United States and abroad and made them available to its subscribers. Never before had these predominantly village-centered, unschooled readers learned so much about their own heritage—society, politics, language, history, literature, and the culture of Arabs in general and Syrians in particular—while trying to absorb what American life and culture was about. A satirical item published in 1898 points to this cultural ambivalence. It is an exchange between two fictional immigrants—a traditionalist and an Americanized Syrian—in which the latter, at one point, chides the former by asking him if in America he had not become civilized. "Don't you understand," he stresses, "that we are all intelligent? For when we become Americanized we are able to earn more without working hard and we help each other out by gaining greater prestige." To which the traditionalist replies, "You can be what you want to be. I am going to remain an Easterner. My original ancestor was Adam and it is likely that his language was Arabic. Long live the East . . . !"[6]

Included among the early migrants was a small (counted in the tens rather than the hundreds) but significant group of intellectuals and professionals which was concentrated in the New York colony. Graduates, for the most part, of the religious and secular schools of higher education in the cities of Syria, they provided the impetus for the development of the Arabic press in the United States. It was both coincidental and fortuitous that in New York the publishers, many of whom had little or no prior journalistic training or experience, came together with émigré Arab writers and poets in a symbiotic relationship to form an intelligentsia.

The inner circle of the intelligentsia was the literati, among them Gibran Kahlil Gibran, best known in the United States for his book *The Prophet*. Some had been influenced in the mid-nineteenth century by the Syrian literary revival in Cairo, itself fueled by Syrian exiles to that city. The revival, among other things, was in the process of adapting rigid, centuries-old Arabic poetic forms to the English tonalities of Protestant hymns worked out previously by leading Syrian poets and American missionaries at the American University in Beirut. These innovations, transmitted to America by the émigrés, combined with the influence of free verse in the West to form a revolutionary literary movement which broke with traditional forms. The publishers befriended the intellectuals, and the pages of their newspapers launched, tested, and advanced the early literary output of such luminaries as Gibran, Ameen Rihani, Naseeb Arida, Mikhail Naimi, Iliyya Abu Madey, and Abd al-Masih Haddad. In return, the contributions of these men of letters added to the quality and prestige of the newspapers as well as their publishers.

Before World War I, Arabic publications appeared and disappeared regularly. Between 1892 and 1930 their numbers may have exceeded fifty, only a handful having appeared after the war. The competition for a readership that was limited in number and literacy was keen, made keener by the religious and political biases of the individual newspapers—biases which mirrored those of the Syrian community as a whole in America and in the homeland. Thus, some newspapers vanished almost overnight; others lasted between five and ten years; several lasted two or more decades. *Al-Jami ʿa* (The league; 1906–1913) which, like its publisher, Farah Antoun, was unmatched for its intellectual standards and diversity, lasted only seven years, primarily because it exceeded the literary capacity and interest of its immigrant readership.[7] The most durable newspapers, published for over sixty consecutive years, were *Al Hoda* (The guidance; 1898–1968); *Meraat al-Gharb* (Mirror of the West; 1899–1961), and *Al-Bayan* (The explanation; 1911–1970s). In 1928, despite the decline in the number of Arabic readers, there were six Arabic dailes in New York; a daily and a semiweekly in Detroit; a weekly in Lawrence, Massachusetts; and three monthlies, one in Detroit, and two in New York.[8] What is remarkable is that so many publications at any given time could be supported by so small a population for most of whom newspaper reading was a habit acquired in America. It may be, as some old-timers suggested, that the seeds of the mission schools in Syria bore fruit in America.

The first Arabic newspaper to appear in the United States was *Kawkab Amrika* (Star of America; 1892–1907). It was founded by Najeeb Arbeely, who was assisted by his brother, Ibrahim. Both were sons of Dr. Joseph Arbeely, the learned Damascene medical doctor and educator, who had brought his family to America in 1878. Najeeb, it was said, was accomplished in ten languages when he established the newspaper at the age of thirty. Some of them were acquired at Marysville (Tennessee) College, which he entered in his mid-teens. When the family moved to New York in 1881, he was employed as the Arabic interpreter, assisting his countrymen through the maze of immigration regulations at Ellis Island. In his first term, President Grover Cleveland had appointed him as American consul to Jerusalem in which capacity he traveled to many Arab regions and took a deep interest in Arab social and political affairs. The assignment and travel inspired him to publish a newspaper that would link the Arabic-speaking immigrants with their homeland and inform those left behind about America.[9]

The publishers of *Kawkab Amrika* are credited with introducing the first Arabic characters used in typesetting in the United States, an accomplishment that required a release from the sultan of the Ottoman Empire who had forbidden their export. The successful petitioner was Ibrahim, who had studied medicine in Istanbul at government expense and had won favor at the court.[10] Thus, the door was opened for an Arabic-language press in America.

Kawkab Amrika appeared as a morning paper with three pages of local and homeland news in Arabic, a language whose script reads from right to left, and one in English. From 1901, it began to include a Syrian folklore supplement. It ceased publication on the death of Najeeb in 1907.

Typically, *Kawkab Amrika* took a political stand. It differed from the other Arabic newspapers in that it did not espouse a religious bias. It remained loyal to the Ottoman Empire, perhaps because of the family's Damascene (rather than Lebanese) origin and Eastern Orthodox Christian faith, but more likely because this educated, elite family was among the advocates of the incipient Syrian nationalist philosophy formulated by Syrian intellectuals at the American University in Beirut, where the elder Arbeely had taught for years. It stressed Syrian unity through political and social reforms, respectful coexistence between the numerous rival religious sects, and Syrian patriotism—a patriotism aimed more at the concept of a Syrian people than a Syrian nation—and by implication, loyalty to the Ottoman Empire.[11]

If *Kawkab Amrika* was the first to introduce Arabic characters into the press of America, *Al-Hoda* was the first to use them in a linotype machine, replacing the slower traditional method of setting type by hand.

Before establishing *Al-Hoda*, Naoum Mokarzel experimented with his first journalistic effort in New York in the mid–1880s, calling it *Al-Asr*; the second Arabic newspaper in America, it was short-lived. The third was *Al-Hoda*. Son of a Maronite Catholic priest from Mt. Lebanon, Naoum opposed both the religion of the publishers of *Kawkab Amrika* and their Ottoman allegiance. So, in Philadelphia on February 22, 1898, he founded the paper to serve the cause of a Christian, Maronite-dominated Lebanese nation under French tutelage, independent of the Ottoman Empire. He chose, according to his niece, Mary Mokarzel, Washington's birthday and the city known as the cradle of America's own independence to launch his paper for their symbolic value. At first it was issued as a weekly, but when his younger brother Salloum joined him on the staff, Naoum converted the paper to a daily and moved it to New York in 1903. There he continued to expand its scope and to modernize its presses, its type, and its style at the behest of his brother. At the same time, he pressed the campaign for Lebanese-Maronite political goals. On Naoum's death in 1932, responsibility for the paper was assumed by Salloum, himself a respected essayist and editor-publisher. On Salloum's death in 1952, Mary, his daughter, managed it until 1968, when this influential institution ceased to exist.[12]

Najeeb M. Diab had been the editor of *Kawkab Amrika* and, as such, the first Arab editor in America. He too was Orthodox but was educated in Egypt, including the American University in Cairo. Shortly after he immigrated in the early 1890's, he joined *Kawkab Amrika*. Even as its editor, he disagreed with his employers' politics. As an Arab nationalist, he was highly critical of his employers' politics. As an Arab nationalist, he was highly critical of Ottoman rule. Moreover, as an Orthodox, he opposed the political and religious biases of *Al-Hoda*. He therefore left his position and founded *Meraat al-Gharb* in New York in 1899 to speak for the Syrian Orthodox in America and for Arabism. The paper appeared three times weekly until 1913, when it became a daily. In the mid–1930s, Najeeb's failing health forced it back to a triweekly. After his death in 1936, the paper was managed by his wife, who finally closed it in 1961.

In 1911 the growing Druze and Muslim population, opposed to the Christian emphasis and interpretation of political events, finally had a spokesman of its own in *Al-Bayan*. Its founders were Sulayman Baddur, a Druze, and his partner Abbas Abi Shaqra. Until World War I brought the Ottoman Empire to an end, *Al-Bayan* was staunchly pro-Ottoman. Thereafter, it supported an independent Syrian Arab nation, opposing Western influence and political interference in the homeland. Socially, it mirrored the conservatism of the Druze and Muslim traditions and, to a lesser extent, the cultural ambivalence of the Christian newspapers. Within six months Abi Shaqra left the paper; Baddur managed it until his death in 1941. Thereafter, it passed on to several publishers who moved it from New York to Washington, D.C., and then to Detroit, where it ceased to publish in the 1970s. It began as a weekly, converting to a biweekly in 1915 and a triweekly in 1918.

Several other Arab entrants (hardly a complete list) into the crowded journalistic arena before World War II deserve mention. *Al-Kalimat* appeared as an Arabic bimonthly journal in Brooklyn in 1905 and continues to be published as an English monthly under the title *The Word*. Its founder was the newly ordained Archimandrite Raphael Hawaweeny, the first Syrian Orthodox bishop in the United States, whose primary objective was to bring back members of his flock who had strayed into non-Syrian and non-Orthodox churches, and to guide their spiritual and cultural behavior. In addition to its spiritual messages, it published church news and announcements of marriages, baptisms, deaths, newly built churches, and other social items, thereby providing a link between fellow sectarians and villagers.

As the literary movement in the United States coalesced into an American school of modern Arabic literature, it inspired the formation of Al-Rabita al-Qalamiyya (the Pen League), an influential literary society led by Gibran; as it gained momentum, some of its accomplished participants became publishers focusing on the output of the Pen League.

Al-Fanun (The arts), a literary journal founded by the poet Naseeb Arida in 1913 to publish the works of the Pen League, nurtured the art, the artists, and the literary movement until, lacking popular appeal to an undereducated and, in many cases, barely literate readership, it closed permanently in 1919. Its objectives were assumed by Arida's friend and fellow artist, Abd al-Masih Haddad, whose *Al-Sayeh* (The traveler) had, since 1912, been a biweekly, semiliterary paper. Until the dissolution of the Pen League in 1931, it devoted itself entirely to literature. Iliyya Abu Madey, a giant of the literary movement whose poems and articles had appeared in *Meraat al-Gharb*, published his influential fort-nightly literary magazine, *Al-Sameer* (The entertainer), from 1929 until his death in 1936.

Two publications that testify to the Americanization of the press are *Al-Akhlaq* (The character) and *The Syrian World*. In 1920 Yaqoub Rufail launched an innovation in Arab-American journalism, patterned on some of the most re-spected American magazines of his day. *Al-Akhlaq* (1920–1932), a slick monthly, printed numerous articles of interest to women. Its articles, contributed mainly by members of the intelligentsia and other male and female writers and poets, were topical, literary, and educational, as a sampling of titles, in translation, inicates:

The Syrian Woman and the Press

Between the Old and the New

Are Arabic Schools a Necessity in the United States?

Valuable Treasures in the Tombs of Ottoman Sultans

Freedom of the Man, the Woman, and the Boy

What Is Love?

How Should We Raise Our Children?

Marriage Customs of the Past

Keys to the Doors of Happiness

Her Dual Life—A Play

Our Sons and Daughters

Al-Akhlaq seemed to encourage contributions from talented women. Among the most distinguished was Afifa Karam. In 1912 Mrs. Karam's *Al-Alam an-Nisa'* (Women's world) was among those forays into publishing whose early demise was ordained by their untimeliness. Before the war, the Syrian immigrant community was hardly ready for a women's magazine, let alone a woman pub-lisher. When it came to their status in society and their rights, Syrian women were as conservative as their menfolk. Furthermore, women readers were far fewer than men both in numbers and level of literacy; nor did they have the leisure to read, since a large percentage of them, in addition to their traditional roles as housekeepers and mothers, peddled or worked in the family store or, to a much lesser extent, in factories.

Educated in a religious school in Mt. Lebanon, Afifa Karam emigrated as a bride of thirteen to Louisiana in 1897. She soon recognized her inadequacy in Arabic and ordered Arabic books from *Al-Hoda*. In a few years had mastered the language and began submitting articles to the newspaper.[13] Not only was she among that rare breed of Arab women to break into journalism, she was outspoken in favor of the rights of her sex. In 1909 she wrote, for example, that women were as capable as men. Just as European women worked successfully in scientific and other fields, she believed, Syrian women in America should take advantage of similar opportunities available to them.[14] Mrs. Karam died in 1924 at the age of forty-one, admired and respected by her peers.

The appearance of *The Syrian World* in English in 1926 pointed to the maturation of the Syrian experience—in effect, it signalled the end of an era. The creation of Salloum Mokarzel, it was aimed primarily at the non–Arabic-speaking generation. By the 1920s the Syrian immigrants' apathy toward their cultural heritage was paralleled by apathy toward the Arabic language. With new Arabic speakers and readers from Syria limited to one hundred annually under the Johnson-Reed Immigration Act of 1924, hardly equal to the community's mortality rate, the use of Arabic dwindled. In immigrant homes, where younger children made some knowledge of it imperative, English was increasingly replacing the native language; in the homes of the immigrants' married children, English dominated. The colloquial Arabic which was spoken in many of them was shot through with the corrupted Arabic-English patois developed by their parents. English, the key to becoming American, could not be avoided, not even by Muslims, who were under great pressure to maintain Arabic, so essential to their religion. Attempts of concerned leaders and parents to teach Arabic at home or in churches, mosques, private schools, and clubs were more often than not futile because Arabic had little relevance to the American life and schooling which had primary claim on children's interest and concentration.

Traditionalists, expressing a feeling, suddenly acute, that was spreading throughout the Syrian community, pressed hard for keeping Arabic alive in the United States. They preached and wrote articles, but the hour was late. A Muslim religious leader, in an article published in *Al-Bayan*, entitled "Teach Your Children," feared that the loss of Arabic would render children foreigners and atheists.[15] Naoum Mokarzel, worried by declining subscriptions to *Al-Hoda*, appealed for the maintenance of Arabic and serious attention to its study by the American-born and American-raised generation. The consensus of the Syrian–American readers of *The Syrian World*, where his English-language article appeared, was clear: in America knowledge of Arabic was useless.

The Arabic language crisis was felt most acutely in the publishing community. At its height in 1928, *The Syrian World* reported that "a serious discussion has now developed as to whether the Syrian press has not reached the end of its usefulness." By World War II, at least four New York Arabic dailies and one weekly survived the crisis, albeit considerably reduced in readership and quality.

The content of *The Syrian World* was appropriate to the changed cultural climate. It ws conceived, wrote Salloum Mokarzel, its editor-publisher, "in the spirit of service to the Syrian-American generation" based on the assumption that lack of sufficient knowledge of its "racial traits and historical background renders them somewhat unsympathetic with their parents' attitude." True to the aims of the journal, he invited the use of its pages as a "forum for the discussion of existing problems among Syrians in America in an effort to arrive at their best solutions."[16] His Syrian-American readers responded enthusiastically, revealing a widening generational chasm.

The conflict between the views of the Syrian-Americans and those of their parents was sharpening, and Mokarzel hoped his publication could mediate. He promised to

> give them a broader vision of their racial heritage; and all this to the end that our Syrian-American generation will come to better understand the country of their parents and appreciate more fully their racial endowments which constitute a valuable contribution to the country of their birth.[17]

Accordingly, English-reading Syrians read articles about life in Syria and its political and economic affairs, perhaps for the first time. They learned about the achievements of fellow Syrian-Americans in business as well as in the arts, sciences, and literature. One of its regular features was a variety of interesting and romantic, if not always illuminating, glimpses into Syria's historic and literary past.

Another was the translation of selected items of news and comment from the Arabic-language press. The journal supported or launched movements such as the "Americanization" movement Syrian–Americans organized to "inculcate and impress the doctrine of Americanism upon and make better citizens of Syrian people,"[18] and the protracted one to unify the thinly dispersed and fragmented Syrian community and revitalize interest in its heritage by federating its clubs and societies.

The Syrian World was a singular publication and, while it was relatively well distributed, its readership was limited and elitist because it was, some of its readers complained, "too erudite" and "above their understanding."[19] Although Mokarzel asked for recommendations and installed features to attract a wider audience, its tone and subscribers remained elitist. After announcing in September 1931 its policy to modify its standards, *The Syrian World* ceased publication in 1932 as Mokarzel assumed management of *Al-Hoda* on the death of his brother Naoum. In its time, its influence was, arguably, out of all proportion to the size of its select readership.

Mokarzel, a graduate of St. Joseph's Jesuit University in Beirut, apprenticed in journalism with his brother Naoum at *Al-Hoda*. Dissatisfied with "the menial tasks to which he was assigned"[20] and living in the shadow of his better known and respected brother, he established the Syrian American Press, which published numerous books authored by Syrians in America as well as his monthly journal.

A zealous champion of Americanization and a critic of traditionalism, Mokarzel agreed with the assimilationist goals of Americans of Syrian descent. But he was also dedicated to his cultural heritage. Therefore, he and a cadre of like-minded regular contributors attempted to keep Salloum's pledge to help his readers discover themselves and "to breed in them a consciousness of appre-

ciation for their racial qualities and inheritances so that they may comport themselves with a befitting sense of honor as citizens of this great American nation."[21]
It is important to note that, with respect to those "racial qualities and inheritances," *The Syrian World* could not conceal its political (Lebanese) and religious
(Maronite) biases despite Mokarzel's lofty aims and attempts at impartiality.

Between the wars, the restriction of immigration plus the growing ignorance
of the Arabic language was reflected not only in the declining number of Arabic
publications, but in their quality. Homeland political and social news competed
unsuccessfully with expanding interest in America. To compete for readers'
attention, the Arabic press tried to adjust to the new circumstances. Although
much of what appeared in their publications was, to some degree, pedestrian,
its intellectual content began to yield to local news and social gossip. To compete
with the American press, it adopted the latter's techniques and style and simplified
the Arabic language for readers whose lack of Arabic facility called for an easy,
clear journalistic style—a style which has since influenced journalism in the Arab
world.

Finally, by establishing itself on a sectarian basis, by not addressing itself to
Syrians generally and objectively, the Arabic press, to its own detriment, perpetuated provincial loyalties and exacerbated parochial ones; as a result, individual papers could not generate a broad readership. Nevertheless, the quality
and national status achieved by the Arabic press before World War II have not
since been equalled.

The Arabic press in America played a decisive and responsible role in the
adjustment and assimilation of the immigrant generation and spurred Syrian
villagers toward literacy and self-education. It linked the immigrant colonies
with the homeland and countrymen in the rest of the Western Hemisphere. The
publishers and editors as well as their contributors represented the changing
Syrian society in America. They had enough vision and insight into American
life to recognize that the old ways and values no longer sufficed. Yet, even as
they announced their bold faith in the new land, they retained an almost wor-
shipful praise for the ancestral qualities. If at times they presented an ambiguous
impression about the importance of their cultural heritage, they nevertheless were
determined to sort out confusions and mark a new route for the immigrants in
the New World.

The Arabic press in America reached its nadir in the 1940s. After 1950, Arabic
newspapers and journals multiplied—some weekly, some monthly, some in
English, some in Arabic, some mixed. The emphasis is currently on the politics
and economics of the Arab world, although they do not entirely neglect social
and cultural items. Editorials interpret events in terms of the publisher's ideology
and attitude toward American economic and political involvement in the Middle
East. Although secularism is the dominant publishing principle, when the post–
World War II Arabs talk about unity in the Arab-American community, paro-
chialism and provincialism still get in the way. Old feelings invested in them

seem too powerful to destroy. Competition among papers for a limited audience still results in a high rate of attrition. None of the popular publications, as opposed to academically oriented ones, enjoys the national success or journalistic and literary quality of the earlier Arab publications.

NOTES

1. "The Arabic Language in America," *Al-Hilal* 16 (April 1907: 46–47, in Arabic.

2. Figures compiled from *U.S. Report of the Immigration Commission, 1820–1910* (Washington, D.C., 1911), Table 9, "Immigration to the United States by country of origin and by sex for years ending June 30, 1869–1910," pp. 30–40; Table 10. "Immigration to the United States, by race of people, during period 1899 to 1910," p. 45; Table 27, "Destination of immigrants admitted to the United States, fiscal year 1899 to 1910, inclusive by race of people," pp. 269–292; and working sheets provided to the author by the Department of Immigration and Naturalization, Washington, D.C., undated and pencil noted "OPEC."

3. A variety of religious, historical, and literary books published in the late nineteenth and early twentieth centuries was collected by the author from first–generation immigrants and/or their descendants.

4. "Factional War Is Waged Between Syrians in New York," October 29, 1905, p. 4. See also Henry Melkie, "Arab American Journalism and Its Relation to Arab American Literature" (Ph.D. Dissertation, Georgetown University, 1971), p. 4, in Arabic.

5. *Al-Hoda*, July 1, 1908, p. 4, in Arabic.

6. Ibid., March 22, 1898, p. 16, in Arabic.

7. Melkie, pp. 9, 95–108.

8. Salloum Mokarzel, "Arabic Newspapers in America," *The Syrian World* 2 (May 1928): 36.

9. Biographical data on publishers and their newspapers, unless otherwise noted, are drawn from Melkie.

10. Ibid., p. 28.

11. A. H. Hourani, *Arabic Thought in the Liberal Age, 1798–1939* (London: Oxford University Press, 1962), pp. 101–102.

12. *Al-Hoda, 1898–1968: The Story of Lebanon and Its Emigrants Taken from the Newspaper Al-Hoda* (New York: Al-Hoda Press, 1968), pp. 1–4, 126–128.

13. Yaqoub Rufail, "How Afifa Karam Grew Up and Developed," *Al-Akhlaq* 5 (July 1924): 5, in Arabic.

14. "Women's Talk," *Al-Hoda*, January 9, 1909, p. 4, in Arabic.

15. Kalil Bazzy, "Teach Your Children," *Al-Bayan*, March 28, 1928, p. 6, in Arabic.

16. Salloum Mokarzel, "Forward," *The Syrian World* 1 (July 1926): 2.

17. Ibid.

18. Ibid., 2 (August 1927): 59.

19. "Notes and Comments," ibid. (August 1927): 51–52.

20. Lila Mokarzel Hatab, "Biography of Salloum Mokarzel," in *Al-Hoda, 1898–1968*, p. 127.

21. Salloum Mokarzel, *The Syrian World* 1 (July 1926): 2.

BIBLIOGRAPHY

Hitti, Philip K. *Syrians in America*. New York: George Doran & Co., 1924.

Houghton, Louise Seymour. "Syrians in the United States." *Survey*: Pt. I. "Sources and Settlement" (July 1, 1911); 481–495; Pt. II. "Business Activities" (August 5, 1911); 647–665; Pt. III. "Intellectual and Social Status" (September 2, 1911); 787–803; Pt. IV. "The Syrian as an American Citizen" (October 7, 1911); 957–968.

Katibah, Habib I. *Arabic Speaking Americans*. New York: The Institute of Arab American Affairs, Inc., 1946.

Kayal, Philip M., and Joseph M. Kayal. *The Syrian-Lebanese in America: A Study in Religion and Assimilation*. Boston: Twayne Publishers, 1975.

Melkie, Henry. "Arab American Journalism and Its Relation to Arab American Literature." Ph.D. dissertation, Georgetown University, 1971.

Miller, Lucius Hopkins. *Our Syrian Population: A Study of the Syrian Communities of Greater New York*. N.p., ca. 1904.

2

The Carpatho-Rusyn Press

PAUL R. MAGOCSI

INTRODUCTION

The Carpatho-Rusyn press in the United States is the product of a group of Americans who either immigrated or who are the descendants of immigrants who arrived on these shores for the most part before World War I.[1] As their name suggests, these people came from the Carpathian Mountains in Eastern Europe, more specifically, from a territory that has had several names applied to it in the past—Carpatho-Ruthenia, Ruthenia, Carpatho-Rus', Subcarpathian Rus', Carpatho-Russia, Carpatho-Ukraine, Transcarpathia, the Lemkian Land.[2]

Carpatho-Rusyns never had their own state. Until 1918 they lived within the Austro-Hungarian Empire; the vast majority south of the mountains were within the Hungarian Kingdom, and the Lemkos north of the mountains within the Austrian province of Galicia. After World War I, Hungary's Carpatho-Rusyns joined the new state of Czechoslovakia (with their own semi-autonomous province, Subcarpathian Rus'); the Lemkos of Galicia came to be ruled by the restored state of Poland, although under Polish rule they lacked political autonomy. Since 1945 the Carpatho-Rusyn homeland has been divided between three countries: Rusyns south of the mountains reside within the Soviet Union (in the Transcarpathian Obast of the Ukrainian SSR) and Czechoslovakia (in the Prešov Region of northeastern Slovakia); those north of the mountains— the Lemkos—reside within Poland (generally not, however, in their Carpathian homeland, from which they have been deported).[3]

The Carpatho-Rusyns are Slavs and, for the most part, adherents of eastern Christianity, either Orthodoxy or Greek Catholicism (known in the United States as Byzantine Ruthenian Catholicism). The group speaks several East Slav dialects that are classified by linguists as part of the Ukrainian language. However, language does not necessarily coincide with national or ethnic identity. In the European homeland, the people identified themselves for centuries as Rusyns (*rusyny*) or Rusnaks (*rusnaky*). It was not until after World War II that a Ukrainian identity was adopted by most—although not all—members of the group in Europe. In contrast, the vast majority of Carpatho-Rusyn immigrants and their descendants in the United States have retained a sense of distinct ethnic identity and describe themselves as Rusyns, Rusnaks, Ruthenians, Carpatho-Russians, Lemkos, or sometimes simply as the *po-nashemu* ("our own") people.

Carpatho-Rusyn immigration to the United States was basically a pre–World War I phenomenon. Underdeveloped and backward economic conditions in their rural homeland before 1914 drove as many as 150,000 immigrants to seek a better livelihood in the coal-mining and industrial centers of the Northeast. Pennyslvania, New York, New Jersey, Ohio, and Connecticut had in the early years—and still have—the largest number of Carpatho-Rusyns, who today number approximately 650,000. In those states are also located most of the churches and organizations as well as 95 percent of the newspapers, journals, and almanacs published by the group.

DEVELOPMENT OF THE PRESS

Like other ethnic groups in the United States, the Carpatho-Rusyns brought with them the religious and political differences that existed in the homeland and to which the American experience added even greater diversity. This diversity is best expressed through the Carpatho-Rusyn press, which since its beginnings in the United States has included more than fifty newspapers and journals.[4] For purposes of this discussion, publications may be grouped into four categories: fraternal, religious, political, and cultural.

During the ninety-year history of Carpatho-Rusyn newspapers and journals in the United States, it is the press of the fraternal organizations that has reached the largest numbers of people and therefore has had the greatest influence on the group's development. The oldest, largest, and longest-lasting Carpatho-Rusyn newspaper was the *Amerikansky Russky Viestnik* (American Russian Messenger), the official organ of the Greek Catholic Union (Sojedinenije), which was the first fraternal society set up specifically for Carpatho-Rusyns.[5] The *Amerikansky Russky Viestnik* began to appear in 1892 in Mahonoy City, a coal–mining town in eastern Pennsylvania. Before long it moved to nearby Scranton, then to New York City, and finally, in 1904, went westward to Pittsburgh and then the latter's suburb of Homestead, Pennsylvania, where since 1952 it has been published under the English title *Greek Catholic Union Messenger*.

Initially begun as a weekly, the *Amerikansky Russky Viestnik* appeared twice and then three times a week after World War I, before reverting to a weekly and then to a biweekly after World War II. The language of the *Amerikansky Russky Viestnik* also changed through the years. Initially, it appeared in Carpatho-Rusyn using the Cyrillic alphabet, and for several years before World War I it also had a second edition written in the Latin alphabet and using an East Slovak/ Rusyn transitional dialect (the so-called Sotak dialect). During the 1920s, only a Carpatho-Rusyn edition appeared, but using a Latin alphabet. Finally, in 1952, with the change in name to the *Greek Catholic Union Messenger*, the major language used was English, with a steady decrease in the use of Carpatho-Rusyn, so that today only one column appears in the native language.[6]

It was during the interwar period that the *Amerikansky Russky Viestnik* reached its greatest audience, being sent to the more than 90,000 members of the Greek Catholic Union. Because of its sizeable circulation, its editors, especially Pavel Zsatkovich (1892–1914), Michael Hanchin (1914–1919), Reverend Stephan Varzaly (1929–1937), and Michael Roman (1937–1980), had a profound impact on Rusyn-American public opinion, particularly as it affected relations with churches, politics in the homeland, and the problem of national identity. Basically, the *Amerikansky Russky Viestnik* represented the Greek Catholic Union's self-proclaimed mission to defend and preserve in the United States the religious and national traditions of the Carpatho-Rusyns. To ensure that such efforts had an effect on future generations, the Greek Catholic Union also published a newspaper for teenagers and young adults, the weekly *Amerikansky Russky Sokol* (Homestead, Pennsylvania, 1914–1936), and another for children, *Svit D'itej/ Children's World* (Homestead, 1917–1973).

In a real sense, the subsequent development of other Carpatho-Rusyn press organs came about as a reaction to the Greek Catholic Union and its policies as expressed in the *Amerikansky Russky Viestnik*. The first Carpatho-Rusyn immigrants to split off were the Lemkos, who joined others from Galicia who were discontented with the Greek Catholic and supposedly "non-Russian" orientation of the *Amerikansky Russky Viestnik*.[7] Representing the Orthodox religious and "Russian" national view was the newspaper *Svit* (Wilkes-Barre, Pennsylvania, 1894-), published by the Russian Orthodox Catholic Mutual Aid Society and *Pravda/The Truth* (Olyphant, Pennsylvania; Philadelphia, 1902-), published by the Russian Brotherhood Organization. Although both newspapers still appear today, they have little to do with Carpatho-Rusyns; instead, they represent immigrants and their descendants from all parts of what was formerly eastern Galicia who in the United States claim to be Carpatho-Russians or simply Orthodox Russians.

The next two fraternal newspapers to be published also came into existence after former members of the Greek Catholic Union broke from that organization. In 1915 the *Pravoslavnii russkii viestnik* (Orthodox Russian Messenger; Monessen, Pennsylvania, 1915–17) and later *Russkii viestnik/Russian Messenger/ UROBA Messenger* (Pittsburgh, Pennsylvania, 1917-) were published in order to represent the views of recent Greek Catholic converts to Orthodoxy, who also established their own fraternal society, the United Russian Orthodox Brotherhood in America.[8] Then, in 1918, Greek Catholic Union members in the New York City metropolitan area, dissatisfied with the proportionally larger amounts of accident benefits being paid to miners from Pennsylvania, founded their own fraternal organization, the Greek Catholic Carpatho-Russian Benevolent Association Liberty, with its own newspaper, *Vostok/The East* (Perth Amboy, New Jersey, 1919–1950).[9] Initially representing Byzantine Catholics on the East Coast, by the early 1940s *Vostok* broke with the Byzantine Ruthenian Catholic

Church and supported instead the recently founded American Carpatho-Russian Orthodox Greek Catholic Church.[10]

As for religious and church-related press organs, these also had their beginnings because of dissatisfaction with the Greek Catholic Union's *Amerikansky Russky Viestnik*. Among the first organs to be created was the *Pravoslavnyi amerikanskii viestnik/Russian Orthodox American messenger* (New York, 1896–1970?), which was the official organ of the Russian Orthodox Mission and later Orthodox Metropolia in America, designed especially to serve the needs of those Byzantine/Greek Catholics (mostly Carpatho-Rusyns) who had converted to Orthodoxy. In later years, both the newspaper and its successor, *The Orthodox Church* (Syosset, New York, 1965-) have had little, if any, content directed specifically to Carpatho-Rusyns, but instead have become simply organs of the Russian Orthodox and now "nonethnic" Orthodox Church in America (OCA). More attention is devoted to the specific heritage of OCA members of Carpatho-Rusyn background (especially descendants of the Lemkian Region) in the local monthly newspaper, *The Orthodox Herald* (San Antonio, Texas; Hunlock Creek, Pennsylvania, 1952-).

Among Byzantine/Greek Catholics who did not convert to Orthodoxy, discontent with the *Amerikansky Russky Viestnik* (especially with its criticism of church policy) led to the creation of a new organ, *Rusin* (Philadelphia; Pittsburgh, 1910–1916), published by the Greek Catholic Priests Mission Association under the editorship of cultural activist Reverend Joseph Hanulya. Not long after its establishment, *Rusin* moved to Pittsburgh and became the official organ of the fraternal organization, the United Societies (Sobranije) of Greek Catholic Religion. The United Societies had been founded in 1903 by Greek Catholic Union members who were displeased with its criticism of the church. Thus, both *Rusin* and its successor, *Prosvita/The Enlightenment* (McKeesport, Pennsylvania, 1917-), became for more than two decades the unofficial organs of the Byzantine Ruthenian Catholic Church, which especially during the 1930s, was under almost constant attack from the editors of the Greek Catholic Union's *Amerikansky Russky Viestnik*.[11]

Perhaps because it could count on the services of *Rusin* and *Prosvita*, the Byzantine Ruthenian Catholic Church for a long time did not have its own official press organ. A monthly, *Nebesnaja Carica/Queen of Heaven* (McKeesport, 1927–1955), did serve for close to three decades as the semi-official magazine of the church, and a few attempts were made to publish a diocesan newspaper during the 1940s, but these were short-lived.[12] It was not until 1956 that the *Byzantine Catholic World* (Pittsburgh, 1956-) was begun as the official press organ of the Byzantine Ruthenian Catholic Church. Although English was the predominant language, at least during the first decade many articles appeared in Carpatho-Rusyn, and throughout its history the *Byzantine Catholic World* has carried much information about the Carpatho-Rusyn heritage in both Europe and America. During the 1960s, when the Byzantine Ruthenian Church was raised to the status of a metropolia and two new dioceses were created, separate diocesan newspapers eventually followed as well: *Eastern Catholic Life* (Passaic, New Jersey, 1965-) for the diocese of Passaic, and *Horizons* (Parma, Ohio, 1979-) for the diocese of Parma.

The only other religious press organ of significance is the *Cerkovnyj vistnik/ Church Messenger* (Pemberton, New Jersey, 1944-). This biweekly newspaper is the official organ of the American Carpatho-Russian Orthodox Greek Catholic diocese, based in Johnstown, Pennsylvania, which was founded in 1938 by priests who had broken away from the Byzantine Ruthenian Catholic Church. Because the Johnstown diocese claimed to be preserving traditional Greek Catholic or Byzantine Ruthenian traditions, its publications, such as the *Church Messenger*, still carry at least one page written in Carpatho-Rusyn and are concerned with the specific cultural and religious features of the group. The traditionalist and heritage-oriented approach was also pronounced in three other affiliated publications, the monthly *Holos vostočnoj cerkvi/Voice of the Eastern Church* (Perth Amboy, 1941–1945) and the English-language youth journals, *Carpatho-Russian Youth* (Johnstown, Pennsylvania; Binghamton, New York, 1938–1941) and the *A.C.Y.R. Guardian* (New York; Perth Amboy, 1957–1962).

In contrast to the Carpatho-Rusyn fraternal and religious press, organs unaffiliated with any organization and concerned largely with political and social developments have in general had short life spans. One of the most interesting in this category and the only daily in the history of the Carpatho-Rusyn press in America was the newspaper *Den'* (The Day; New York, 1922–1926). Published and edited by former *Amerikansky Russky Viestnik* editor Michael Hanchin, *Den'* appeared only in Carpatho-Rusyn and carried a wide range of information about the homeland as well as coverage of American and world news of significance to immigrants.[13]

More typical of the Carpatho-Rusyn political press were organs established to fulfill a specific goal. Sometimes that goal concerned the European homeland, such as trying to convince the immigrants to support the idea of unification with Russia during World War I,[14] or to cooperate during World War II with the Czechoslovak government-in-exile, which expected the postwar return of Subcarpathian Rus' (then occupied by Hungary) to a restored Czechoslovakia.[15] As often, the political goal might have been to persuade Rusyn-Americans that they were ethnically and linguistically, and therefore nationally, Russians,[16] or Ukrainians,[17] or that they were a distinct Rusyn nationality whose best hope for survival would be to remain united with a noncommunist Czechoslovakia.[18]

A special category of the Carpatho-Rusyn political press is that published by the Lemkos. In contrast to other Carpatho-Rusyns, the Lemkos came from villages north of the Carpathian Mountains, from the former Austrian province of Galicia. In the United States, the Lemkos have maintained their own organizations and press. Although a Lemko newspaper appeared for a short time in the early 1920s[19] it was not until the publication of the monthly (and later weekly) *Lemko* (New York; Philadelphia; Cleveland, 1928–1939) that this group's press was firmly established. Founded and edited throughout its existence by Dmitry

Vislocky, after 1931 *Lemko* became the official organ of the Lemko Association (Lemko Soiuz). It was succeeded in 1939 by *Karpatska Rus'* (Carpathian Rus'; Yonkers, New York, 1937-), edited for its first two decades by the group's popular writer Simeon Pysh. Until 1980, this newspaper appeared exclusively in Carpatho-Rusyn. The Lemko Association has been concerned with attracting younger members into its ranks and has published several heritage-oriented English publications during the last two decades, but these have all been short-lived.[20] Like other Rusyn Americans, the Lemkos created new press organs because of disagreements with the older *Lemko* and *Karpatska Rus'*, in particular over the latter's generally pro-Soviet stance on political issues and Russophile national orientation regarding ethnic identity. Thus, an anti-Soviet though Russophile faction published a short-lived newspaper during the early 1970's;[21] while anti-Soviet and nationally Ukrainian Lemkos have published two newspapers and a scholarly journal, and most recently have begun a cultural quarterly, *Lemkivshchyna* (The Lemko land; New York, 1979-).[22]

The least successful publications put out by Carpatho-Rusyns in the United States are cultural publications that are not affiliated with either the church or fraternal societies. Nonetheless, from the earliest years to more recent times, several attempts have been made to publish literary, educational, and cultural press organs.

During World War I, and in the wake of the great wave of Carpatho-Rusyn immigration, a large-format literary and religious monthly, *Niva* (The sown field; Yonkers, 1916), appeared. However, this unique experiment in publishing Rusyn-American literature ended after only eleven issues. Somewhat more successful was the monthly publication in Carpatho-Rusyn and English of the Rusin Elite Society, *Vozhd'/The Leader* (Cleveland, 1929–1930). However, after what seemed to be a promising start, it folded when its organizers differed over the controversies then raging within the Byzantine Ruthenian Catholic Church. [23]

It seems that the most successful and longest-lasting cultural organ is the more recently founded English-language quarterly, *Carpatho-Rusyn American* (Fairview, New Jersey, 1978–). Published by the Carpatho-Rusyn Research Center, it is unaffiliated with any church or fraternal organization and strives to fulfill the heritage-seeking needs of third– and fourth–generation Carpatho-Rusyns affected by the American bicentennial celebrations and "*Roots* fever."

THEMATIC CONTENT AND IMPACT OF THE PRESS

With the exception of the few unaffiliated political and cultural organs that tried to represent the interests of the ethnic group as a whole, most publications of the Carpatho-Rusyn press have contained material directed narrowly toward the members of a specfic fraternal organization or religious affiliation. Organizational matters, membership lists, and reports on lodges and individual members have always filled a large portion of the pages in fraternal organs such as the *Amerikansky Russky Viestnik/GCU Messenger*, *Prosvita*, and *Vostok*. At the height of the Carpatho-Rusyn press between 1910 and 1940, these newspapers also carried general international and American news. In particular, they were filled with reports about the homeland, and it was through the substantive reporting in these newspapers that the Carpatho-Rusyn immigrants received the information needed to play a crucial role in the political fate of their homeland in 1918–1919 (unification with the new state of Czechoslovakia), a role that is generally recognized by historians of the period.[24]

The other great issue that filled the pages of the fraternal organs was the so-called celibacy controversy of the 1930s, at which time the Byzantine Ruthenian Catholic Church was obliged to fulfill the Vatican precepts against ordaining any new married priests (a traditional historical rite of the Byzantine or Greek Catholics) in the United States. The *Amerikansky Russky Viestnik* and *Vostok* came down harshly against church authorities, while *Prosvita* used its pages to defend the bishop. During the past two decades, the great political and religious debates are gone from the pages of the fraternal press, each of which is almost exclusively concerned with its own organizational matters and activity.

Similarly, the religious press in earlier years was filled with articles defending and/or propagating the righteousness and rightness of its particular orientation. But during at least the past two decades, the harsh intergroup religious polemics are gone. Instead, each of these religious newspapers is more concerned with the general problems of the larger church with which it is affiliated, whether Catholic or Orthodox.

For many years, political issues also dominated the pages of the Carpatho-Rusyn press. These took two forms: concern with the fate of the European homeland, and debates about the group's national identity. As for the European homeland, criticism of the Hungarian regime before and during World War I turned to (1) heated debates over future political affiliation in 1918–1919; (2) praise and then criticism of Czechoslovak rule or attacks on the Polish regime in the Lemkian Land during the interwar period; and finally (3) general criticism of communism, the Soviet Union, and its satellite states Czechoslovakia and Poland after World War II. The only real exception to this general political pattern is found in the "Carpatho-Russian" Lemko organs *Lemko* and *Karpatska Rus'*, and in the "independent" Orthodox newspaper *Vistnik* (The messenger; McKees Rocks, Pennsylvania, 1936–1955), which for most of their history have expressed favorable views of the Soviet Union and its post–World War II allies Poland and Czechoslovakia.

The other aspect of politics that has filled the pages of the Carpatho-Rusyn press is the question of national identity. As a Slavic minority coming from the Hungarian Kingdom—and at a time during the four decades before World War I when Hungarian authorities were trying to magyarize their national minorities—most Carpatho-Rusyn immigrants came to the United States only with the sense that they were of the Rus' faith (that is, they were eastern Christians), and therefore they described themselves as Rusyns or Rusnaks. But what did this mean in terms of ethnic or national identity? Were they of Rusyn nationality also, or were they Russians, or Ukrainians, or perhaps even Slovaks?[25] All these orientations were debated in the press, and often new organs were founded so that overanxious patriots could express themselves on the question of the "correct" national nomenclature for the group.

Whereas some organs have adopted Russian (*Svit* [The light], *Pravda* [The truth], *Karpato–russkoe slovo* [The Carpatho-Russian word], *Svobodnoe slovo Karpatskoi Rusi* [The free word of Carpathian Rus']) or Ukrainian (*Karpats'ka zoria* [Carpathian dawn], *Lemkivs'ki visti* [Lemko news]) national orientations, the vast majority of the large fraternal and cultural organs (*Amerikansky Russky Viestnik*, *Rusin*, *Prosvita*, *Den'*, *Karpatska Rus'*, *Vozhd'* / *The Leader*, *Carpatho-Rusyn American*) have basically adopted the position that Carpatho-Rusyns (before World War I known as Uhro-Rusins) comprise a distinct Slavic nationality. This is similarly the case with the leading religious organs, *Byzantine Catholic World*, *Eastern Catholic Life*, and *Church Messenger*. This sense of distinctiveness is evident even in those organs which at times have used the term "Carpatho-Russian" instead of Rusyn or Carpatho-Rusyn to define the group. To be sure, use of the term Carpatho-Russian for the first time during the 1930s by leading organs like the *Amerikansky Russky Viestnik*, *Lemko*, and *Vostok* was also accompanied by suggestions that the Rusyns were part of one larger Russian nationality, but by the late 1950s and the 1960s, a sense of distinctiveness from Russians, as well as from Ukrainians and Slovaks, was revived.

Besides the few literary and cultural journals (*Niva* and *Vozhd'*), all of the fraternal organs and some religious and political organs as well have opened their pages to literary works. In fact, while a few separate Rusyn-American collections of poetry, plays, and one novel have been published, it is in the pages of the periodicals that the vast majority of original Carpatho-Rusyn literature produced in America has appeared.[26]

Related to both literary production and the debate over the group's national identity is the problem of language. Until the 1940s, most publications appeared in various Rusyn dialects. Although a few Rusyn-American grammars were published, the norms they set forth were never consistently followed by editors, who for the most part wrote in the language they used (or remembered having heard) in oral communication. Since most of the Carpatho-Rusyn immigrants came from what after 1919 became eastern Slovakia, the language of the press was for the most part in the Prešov Region dialects of Carpatho-Rusyn.[27] There was also an evolution in the use of alphabets, Cyrillic being steadily replaced by Latin (according to Czech orthography) after World War I. The 1940s and 1950s were a bilingual transitional period for most organs; since the 1960s, English has predominated, some form of Carpatho-Rusyn appearing at best in the columns of a dwindling number of older correspondents. The only exceptions to this trend are found in the Lemko press, which has used Lemko dialects (and the Cyrillic alphabet) up to the present (*Karpatska Rus'*), and in the organs begun by post–World War II immigrants which are either in standard Russian (*Svobodnoe slovo*) or standard Ukrainian (*Vistnyk*, *Lemkivs'ki visti*, *Lemkivshchyna*).

CONCLUSION

Since the first Carpatho-Rusyn press organ appeared in the United States in 1892, more than fifty different newspapers and journals have been published by the group's fraternal societies, churches, political organizations, and cultural associations. Very often these organs came into existence to propagate a specific religious, political, or cthnonational orientation. This press not only became a mirror reflecting the wide diversity in Rusyn-American society; in many ways it actually defined what that society was.

This, of course, was because it was through the press that the ideology and justification for the various communities within the group were to be found. As both mirror and creator of Carpatho-Rusyn society in the United States, the press today—with its almost exclusive use of the English language and its concern with American problems—is still a true reflection of the concerns and interests of the group's members.

NOTES

1. On the Carpatho-Rusyns in the United States, see Paul R. Magocsi, "Carpatho-Rusyns," in Stephan Thernstrom, ed., *Harvard Encyclopedia of American Ethnic Groups* (Cambridge, Mass.: Harvard University Press, 1980), pp. 200–210; and Paul R. Magocsi, *Our People: Carpatho-Rusyns and their Descendants in North America* (Toronto: Multicultural History Society of Ontario, 1984).

2. For an introduction to the extensive literature on the Carpatho-Rusyn homeland, see Paul R. Magocsi, "An Historiographical Guide to Subcarpathian Rus'," *Austrian History Yearbook* 9–10 (1973–1974): 201–265; and Marian Jurkowski, "Łemkowszczyzna (materiał do bibliografii)," *Slavia Orientalis* 11 (1962): 525–536, reprinted as J. Kozłowski, "Łemkowszczyzna," *Annals of the World Lemkos' Federation* 2 (1975): 240–254.

3. On Carpatho-Rusyns in the various regions of the European homeland, see, for Transcarpathia: Paul R. Magocsi, *The Shaping of a National Identity: Subcarpathian Rus' 1848–1948* (Cambridge, Mass.: Harvard University Press, 1978); for the Prešov Region: Paul R. Magocsi, *The Rusyn-Ukrainians of Czechoslovakia: An Historical Survey* (Vienna: Wm. Braumüller Universitäts Vlg., 1983); and for the Lemkian Region: I. F. Lemkyn [Ioann Polians'kyi], *Istoriia Lemkovyny* (Yonkers, N.Y. Lemko Soiuz, 1969).

4. A convenient list of most of these is found in Frank Renkiewicz, *The Carpatho-Ruthenian Microfilm Project: A Guide to Newspapers and Periodicals* (St. Paul, Minn.: University of Minnesota Immigrant History Research Center, 1979).

5. Carpatho-Rusyn organizations and publishers used different transliteration systems to render in the Latin alphabet names and titles in their native language. We have reproduced the original forms used by the organizations or individuals. When no such form in the Latin alphabet is available, and for publications mentioned in the notes and bibliography that appeared only in the Cyrillic alphabet, the Library of Congress transliteration system has been used (without final hard signs or diacritics) for Russian or Ukrainian (with the additions, ѣ = î and ы = ŷ for works in Rusyn).

6. A brief early history of the newspaper and an annotated bibliography of its contents before World War I are found in James M. Evans, *Guide to the Amerikansky Russky Viestnik, Vol. 1: 1894–1914* (Fairview N.Y.: Carpatho-Rusyn Research Center, 1979).

7. As they were in the European homeland, Carpatho-Rusyns in the United States are divided into at least three orientations regarding their national or ethnic identity. Perhaps the majority felt and still feel that they form a distinct Slavic nationality called Rusyn (often spelled Rusin), Ruthenian, or, in earlier years, Uhro-Rusyn. Another group, the Russophiles, feel that Carpatho-Rusyns (like Ukrainians and Belorussians) form only a branch of a single, unitary Russian nationality. The third group, the Ukrainophiles, who became active in America only after World War II, believe that Carpatho-Rusyns are the westernmost branch of the Ukrainian nationality and, moreover, that the name Rusyn is simply the historic name for all Ukrainians.

It should be mentioned that even though organizations like the Greek Catholic Union and its newspaper, the *Amerikansky Russky Viestnik*, translated the words *russky, rusky,* and *rusyn* into English as "Russian," for the most part they did not consider themselves similar to the "Great" Russians of Moscow, Leningrad, and so on. Hence the accusation by Russophiles that the Greek Catholic Union was "non-Russian."

8. From its earliest years, the history of the Carpatho-Rusyns in the United States has been marked by defections from the Greek Catholic (Byzantine Ruthenian) Church in favor of some form of Orthodoxy. This movement was particularly pronounced before 1918 and during the 1930s. With each wave of conversions there also followed new Orthodox fraternal societies and newspapers.

9. For the history of this newspaper, see the special issue *Vostok—The East: Twenty Fifth Anniversary, 1918–1943* (Perth Amboy, N.J., 1945).

10. The movement to create this new church began in the early 1930s and reached fruition in 1938. It was sparked by discontent among several Greek Catholic (Byzantine Ruthenian) priests who opposed their own hierarchy's acceptance of the Vatican's determination after 1929 to enforce certain rules governing the practices of Eastern rite Catholic churches in the New World. The most controversial of these was the requirement of celibacy for all new priests, a demand which several Byzantine Catholics felt had violated their centuries-old ecclesiastical right to a married priesthood.

11. The debate between these newspapers originated in the *Amerikansky Russky Viestnik*'s criticism of the Byzantine Ruthenian Catholic Church's first bishop (during the years before World War I) and in its opposition to the hierarchy's position favoring celibacy for new priests (during the 1930s).

For a brief history of *Rusin* and *Prosvita*, see Basil Shereghy, *The United Societies of the U.S.A.: A Historical Album* (McKeesport, Pa.: [United Societies], 1978), pp. 69–72. On the clashes of these newspapers with the *Amerikansky Russky Viestnik*, see Walter C. Warzeski, *Byzantine Rite Rusins in Carpatho-Ruthenia and America* (Pittsburgh: Byzantine Seminary Press, 1971), pp. 194–244 *passim*.

12. These were the biweekly *Eastern Observer* (Homestead; Pittsburgh, 1942–1943) and the monthly *Greek Catholic Sower* (Lisle, Ill., 1949–1950).

13. On the history of *Den'*, see Georgij Sabov, "Jak voznikla perva karpatorusska ježednevna gazeta v Ameriki," in Michael Roman, ed., *1973 Kalendar of the Greek Catholic Union of the U.S.A.* (Homestead, Pa., 1972), pp. 78–82.

14. *Prikarpatskaia Rus'* (Carpatho-Rus'; New York, 1920–1925), published by the Carpatho–Russian National Organization in America, mostly Lemkians and other Russophiles from Galicia; and *Narodna obrana* (National defense; Homestead, Pennsylvania, 1917), published by the American Russian National Defense, mostly recent Greek Catholic converts to Orthodoxy from the Subcarpathian and Prešov Region.

15. *The Carpathian* (Pittsburgh, 1941–1943), published by the American Carpatho-

Russian Council, headed by former Subcarpathian governor Gregory Žatkovich and other Byzantine Catholic Rusyns; *Jedinstvo* (Unity; Gary, Indiana, 1942–1943), published by the Carpatho-Russian Unity, mostly Orthodox Rusyns from the Subcarpathian Region; and *Karpatorusskije Novosti* (Carpathian-Russian news; New York, 1943–1945), published by the Czechoslovak Government-in-Exile Information Service.

16. *Karpato-russkoe slovo* (New York, 1935–1938), published by the Carpatho-Russian National Committee, later the Russian American Union, and edited by a Russophile émigré from Galicia, Viktor Gladik; and *Svobodnoe slovo Karpatskoi Rusi* (Newark, New Jersey; Mount Vernon, New York, 1959-present), published by a post–World War II Russophile from Subcarpathian Rus', Michael Turjanica.

17. *Karpats'ka zoria* (New York, New York; Jersey City, New Jersey, 1951–1952), published by the Carpathian Star Publishing Company; and *Vistnyk Karpats'koho soiuza* (The Messenger of the Carpathian Alliance; New York, 1970–1973), published by the Carpathian Alliance, both organizations composed of post–World War II Ukrainophile immigrants from Subcarpathian Rus' (Transcarpathia).

18. *Rusin/The Ruthenian* (New York, 1952–1960), published by the Council of a Free Sub-Carpatho-Ruthenia (in Exile), comprised of post–World War II Carpatho-Rusyn immigrants associated with the Council of Free Czechoslovakia in Exile.

19. *Lemkovschchyna* (The Lemko land; New York, 1922–1923), published by the Lemko's Committee under the direction of Simeon Pysh.

20. *Lemko Youth Journal* (Yonkers, New York, 1960–1964); *Carpatho-Russian American* (Yonkers, 1968–1969); *Karpaty* (Yonkers, N.Y. 1978–1979). On the early history of *Karpatska Rus'*, see Mykhayl Logoida, "Iak rodylasia 'Karpatska Rus,' " *Lemkivskyi narodnyi kalendar' na 1984 rik* (Yonkers, 1984), pp. 39–40.

21. *Lemkovina* (The Lemko Land; Yonkers, 1971–1981?), published by the former editor of *Karpatska Rus'*, Stefan M. Kitchura.

22. *Lemkivshchyna* is published by the Lemko Research Foundation in New York City, which is an umbrella organization for other Ukrainophile Lemko groups that have had their own organs as well, such as the newspapers *Lemkivs'kyi dzvin* (The Lemko Bell; New York, 1936–1940) and *Lemkivs'ki visti* (Yonkers and Toronto, 1958–) of the Organization for the Defense of the Lemko Land; and the scholarly journal *Annals* (Camillus, New York, 1974–1975) of the World Lemkos Federation.

23. See above, notes 8 and 10.

24. See Victor S. Mamatey, "The Slovaks and Carpatho-Ruthenians," in Joseph P. O'Grady, ed., *The Immigrants' Influence on Wilson's Peace Policies* (Louisville, Ky.: University of Kentucky Press, 1967), pp. 224–249; and Paul R. Magocsi, "The Political Activity of Rusyn-American Immigrants in 1918," *East European Quarterly* 10 (1976): 347–365.

25. Some writers, especially Slovaks, have argued that the term *Rusnak* (used by Carpatho-Rusyn and Slovak immigrants of the Greek/Byzantine Catholic faith who came from what is today northeastern Slovakia) is simply the traditional designator for a Catholic Slovak of the Eastern rite. Therefore, so the argument goes, all Rusnaks (whether ethnically Rusyn or Slovak) should be considered Slovaks. This position is generally expressed by several Slovak publications in the United States and in *Mária* (Toronto, 1961–), the monthly of the Slovak Byzantine Rite Catholic Diocese of Canada.

26. See Paul R. Magocsi, "Rusyn-American Ethnic Literature," in *Ethnic Literatures since 1776: The Many Voices of America* (Lubbock, Tex.: Texas Tech University, 1978), 2:503–520.

27. The language of the Rusyn-American press has attracted the attention of several scholars: Charles E. Bidwell, *The Language of Carpatho-Ruthenian Publications in America* (Pittsburgh: University of Pittsburgh Center for International Studies, 1971); Michal Łesiów, "The Language of Carpatho-Ruthenian Publications," in Richard Renoff and Stephen Reynolds, eds., *Proceedings of the Conference on Carpatho-Ruthenian Immigration* (Cambridge, Mass.: Harvard Ukrainian Research Institute, 1975), pp. 32–40; Paul R. Magocsi, "Carpatho-Ruthenian," in *The World's Written Languages: A Survey of the Degree and Modes of Use, I: The Americas* (Québec: Université Laval, 1978), pp. 553–561; A. D. Dulichenko, *Slavianskie literaturnye mikroiazyki* (Tallin: Valgus, 1981), in which one of the eleven "micro-languages" analyzed by this Soviet sociolinguist is "karpatorusinskii" (amerikanskii).

BIBLIOGRAPHY

Evans, James. M. *Guide to the Amerikansky Russky Viestnik, Vol. 1: 1894–1914*. Fairview, N.J.: Carpatho-Rusyn Research Center, 1979.

Logoida, Mykhayl. "Iak rodylasia 'Karpatska Rus.' " *Lemkivskyi narodnyi kalendar' na 1984 rik*. Yonkers, N.Y.: n.p., 1984.

Magocsi, Paul R. "Carpatho-Rusyns." In Stephan Thernstrom, ed., *Harvard Encyclopedia of American Ethnic Groups*. Cambridge, Mass.: Harvard University Press, 1980.

————. *Our People: Carpatho-Rusyns and Their Descendants in North America*. Toronto: Multicultural History Society of Ontario, 1984.

Renkiewicz, Frank. *The Carpatho-Ruthenian Microfilm Project: A Guide to Newspapers and Periodicals*. St. Paul, Minn.: University of Minnesota Immigrant History Research Center, 1979.

Sabov, Georgij. "Jak voznikla perva karpatorusska ježednevna gazeta v Ameriki." In Michael Roman, ed., *1973 Kalendar of the Greek Catholic Union of the U.S.A.* Homestead, Pa.: n.p., 1972.

Shereghy, Basil. *The United Societies of the U.S.A.: A Historical Album*. McKeesport, Pa. [United Societies], 1978.

Warzeski, Walter C. *Byzantine Rite Rusyns in Carpatho-Ruthenia and America*. Pittsburgh, Pa., Byzantine Seminary Press, 1971.

3

The Chinese–American Press

H. M. LAI

THE PIONEERS

Most students of the subject date the beginning of the modern Chinese press from the introduction of the concepts of Western jounalism first implemented by the publication of Reverend William Milne's *Chinese Monthly Magazine* in Malacca on August 5, 1815.[1] This magazine and most of its immediate successors, many published by missionaries, were not commercial ventures, copies being distributed gratis; they contained basically expository and evangelistic essays along with a few news items. However, their targets were people in all walks of life, and thus, these publications were in conformance with the precepts of modern journalism. The same progenitor also gave birth to the Chinese–American press, which evolved parallel to the Chinese–language press in China and Hong Kong and was closely related to and influenced by the latter. Existence within a small ethnic enclave in a dominant Western society, however, led to development of a number of characteristics which in themselves set it apart.

Three decades after Milne's pioneer journalistic effort, the Gold Rush in California attracted thousands of argonauts from areas all over the globe, including China. The Chinese population in the Golden State increased rapidly from about 800 in 1849 to 25,000 in 1852, and a Chinese community was established in San Francisco, the principal port of entry. The open Western society with flourishing technology and commerce in which the new community found itself provided a favorable environment for the birth of Chinese–American journalism.

San Francisco had expanded from a village to become the largest city in California within a few years during the 1850s. As different groups settled among the growing population, a number of diverse institutions sprang up to fill their needs, including places of worship, clubs and associations, hospitals, newspapers, and so on. These conditions undoubtedly contributed to the motivation to launch the first Chinese–language weekly newspaper, *The Golden Hills' News*, on April 22, 1854.[2]

Howard, the publisher of the journal, noted in one of the initial issues:

We, . . . believing that civil and political knowledge is of infinite importance to the Chinese, both in their individual, social and relative state, have established *The Golden Hills' News* for that special mission. The influence of chapel and press is intended to relieve the pressure of religious ignorance, settle and explain our laws, assist the Chinese to provide [for] their wants and soften, dignify and improve their general character.[3]

The text of *The Golden Hills' News* was handwritten by Chinese brush and ran in vertical columns from right to left. In order to facilitate reading, each page was divided into three rows, apparently an adaptation from the practice of using columns in Western newspapers. Printing was by lithography on a sheet (approximately 48 cm. by 32 cm.) folded along the width to form four tabloid-size pages. This became the accepted format and production method for Chinese–American newspapers until the turn of the century.

This pioneer journal ceased publication soon afterward when Presbyterian missionary Reverend William Speer announced another journalistic enterprise, *The Oriental* or *Tung-Ngai San-Luk*, a weekly which began publishing on January 4, 1855. Aiming to be "an instructive and interesting vehicle of religious and general knowledge, of late news, or whatever may tend to draw the Chinese into the tide of our nation's advancement,"[4] *The Oriental* was also the first of several nineteenth-century newspapers to include an English section aimed at increasing the non-Chinese reading public's understanding of China and the Chinese in America. (Others were the bilingual *Chinese Record*, also known as *The Chinese Recorder*, founded by Professor Augustus Layres in 1876 during the height of the anti-Chinese movement;[5] the *Oriental and Occidental Press*, started by Tong King Chong in 1900 when the Boxers were attacking Westerners in China;[6] and *The Chinese Defender*, published by the Chinese League of Justice in America in 1910 to fight racial discrimination against the Chinese in America.[7] The latter two were in English only.) Reverend Speer was responsible for the English section of *The Oriental*, while the Chinese editor was Lee Kan, a graduate of the Morrison School of Hong Kong.[8] The paper published until the end of 1856, when operations were suspended due to Speer's deteriorating health.

On the eve of the demise of *The Oriental*, Ze Too Yune established *Chinese Daily News* in Sacramento, one of the stepping–off places for the gold mines which had a considerable Chinese population. Apparently the first Chinese–managed newspaper in the United States, it started in December 1856 as a daily. It later became a triweekly and then was issued irregularly, finally suspending publication in 1858.[9]

Scholars have cited Hong Kong's *Chung Ngoi San Po*, published in 1858, as the earliest Chinese daily newspaper;[10] however, *Chinese Daily News* preceded it by more than a year. It should not be surprising that the first Chinese daily was founded in the United States, for this was the first country in the West where the Chinese settled in great numbers and where they had excellent opportunities to observe and learn from the Western press.

During this initial period of Chinese–American journalism, the Chinese population in the United States was small. Illiteracy was high and the readership minuscule, and journals had to rely on financial subsidies and the publisher's zeal. These adverse factors limited the duration of pioneer ventures, but such enterprises did familiarize the Chinese in America with the concept of the press and laid the groundwork for its further development.

By the end of the 1860s, with the completion of the transcontinental railroad spurring California's development, there began a great surge in Chinese immigration to the pacific coast to fill the need for labor to exploit the natural resources of the West. The Chinese population in San Francisco grew to more than 20,000 in the 1870s, and the city became firmly established as the center for economic, political, and cultural activities for the Chinese in America. At that time there were about sixty English– and foreign–language journals in San Francisco, a factor which probably played a role in rekindling interest in Chinese–American journalistic endeavors.

On July 14, 1874, Bocardus and Gordon published the first issue of *San Francisco China News* to begin another phase in the development of the Chinese–American press. Like its predecessors, this publication was tabloid size and lithographed. Besides news item on America and China, the weekly included poems, stories, and essays that catered to more traditional Chinese tastes. It also abandoned the earlier format of dividing the page into horizontal rows. Now each column of characters ran from the top to the bottom of the page, thus making the text somewhat more difficult to follow.

A year later, on September 11, 1875, Chock Wong and Hoffman began another weekly, *The Oriental*, also known as *The Oriental Chinese Newspaper*, published by Wah Kee.[11] This newspaper, which went through several changes in ownership, became one of the longest-lived Chinese journalistic enterprises during the nineteenth century and published for almost three decades, until around 1903.[12] Other San Francisco weeklies were also started within the next few years, including *San Francisco Chinese Newspaper* or *Tong Fan San Bo* (1876–1880),[13] *The Weekly Occidental* (founded 1881; title changed to *The Daily Occidental* in 1900),[14] and the bilingual *American and Chinese Commercial News* (1883–1901),[15] published by Sui Kee. The year 1884 also saw the first attempt in San Francisco to launch a Chinese daily newspaper, *The San Francisco Chinese Evening Daily News*.[16] However, it soon ceased publication as the time was apparently not yet ripe to support such an undertaking successfully.

From the 1850s to the 1880s, San Francisco was the center of Chinese–American journalism. But by the 1880s other clusters of Chinese–American population had developed to the point where similar enterprises could be initiated. In Hawaii, where the Chinese population had reached more than 10,000, *The Hawaiian Chinese News*, a weekly published by Lung Kee, launched its premiere issue in Honolulu on March 16, 1883.[17]. It continued to publish until the end of the first decade of the twentieth century.

Large numbers of Chinese had also been migrating eastward from the Pacific coast since the 1870s and had established communities in big cities in the Midwest and on the eastern seaboard. In 1883 Wong Ching Foo (also spelled Wong Chin Foo) established the weekly *Chinese American* in New York, the eastern city with the largest Chinese population.[18] Journalistic endeavors in other cities followed, for example, *The Chinese Monthly News* in Boston (founded 1891), published by Suey Hoeng and managed by F. Y. Moy.[19] Two Chicago newspapers, also founded by Wong Ching Foo, were the semimonthly *Chinese American* (founded 1893)[20] and the weekly *Chinese News* (founded 1896). [21] However, all these journals were short-lived due to the small Chinese population in the East and Midwest, which offered a very limited market. It was not until the first part of the twentieth century that Chinese–American newspapers were able to establish permanent footholds east of the Mississippi River.

During this stage of development in the nineteenth century, the Chinese–American press, unlike the Chinese press in Hong Kong or China, did not have to deal with restrictions imposed by either a colonial regime or an authoritarian imperial government. On the other hand, the small Chinese population in America—approximately 140,000 in the 1880s—meant low circulations. For example, in 1890 Rowell's *American Newspaper Directory* estimated the circulation of *American and Chinese Commercial News* to be about 1,500 and that of *The Oriental* to be around 750. Low circulation necessarily kept operations on a modest scale. Staffing had to be limited in order to minimize costs. This precluded spending much time on investigative reporting. News articles were most often translations from the English–language press, items submitted by interested outside parties, or reprints and rewrites of articles from Hong Kong or Chinese newspapers. The low budgets and slim profits did not allow accumulation of capital for expansion.

The implementation of the Chinese Exclusion Acts beginning in 1882 drastically restricted Chinese immigration and curbed the growth of the Chinese population. Thus, although the Chinese–American press began at approximately the same time as its counterparts in China and Hong Kong, when the latter began to accelerate their development during the last two decades of the nineteenth century, Chinese–American press enterprises lagged behind in size and scope.

CHINA POLITICS AND PARTY ORGANS

The late nineteenth century and early twentieth century were troubled times for the Chinese in the United States and at home. Consequently, a rise in political awareness occurred that was reflected in increased activity by the press in China and abroad, which also stimulated improvements in journalism standards and production technology.

In the United States, a number of dailies arose. They standardized on use of large sheets (approximately 52 to 58 cm. by 74 to 76 cm.) as in modern U.S. newspapers. The division of a page into rows was once again adopted. Newspapers included more text and advertisements. News reporting was generally categorized and grouped as international, Chinese, national, and local. Frequently there would be an editorial on some current issue. The center pages were usually reserved for a supplementary section which included belles lettres, essays, and other writings. Most of these were reprints from Chinese and Hong Kong publications, although essays and poetry authored by Chinese in America were frequently included.

At the same time, lead type came into use.[22] Although typesetting was laborious, since each type is a representation of only a single character, the resulting copy packed more text onto a page, was much more legible and uniform in appearance, and allowed more copies to be printed at a faster rate than by lithography. However, this technological advance demanded greater capital investment. As long as the circulation of newspapers remained low, there was no incentive for such additional expenditure. However, the increased interest in politics during the early twentieth century assured more support and revenue, in term of investors, advertisers, and subscribers, which made technological improvements possible. With the rise of the new journals, the older apolitical newspapers, which had operated on shoestring budgets and small staffs, found that they were left behind in the competition for readers. Some adjusted by changing to daily publication, but by the end of the first decade of the twentieth century all had either ceased operation or had been absorbed by the more aggressive newcomers.

In 1898 Presbyterian minister Ng Poon Chew established a tabloid weekly, *Wa Mi San Po*, in Los Angeles.[23] Soon he moved to San Francisco and led in the establishment of the daily *Chung Sai Yat Po*.[24] The publication of its first issue on Chinese New Year in 1900 ushered in a new era in Chinese–American journalism. Influenced by American republicanism and Western middle-class ideology, the new daily favored reform in China and in the Chinese–American community. The paper enjoyed wide curculation among Chinese in the western United States and Mexico until its decline in the 1930s and demise at the end of 1950.

Chung Sai Yat Po soon received competition from a number of newspapers established by Chinese political organizations that had arisen in America at the turn of the century. These groups, each advocating its political program for China's salvation, soon turned the overseas Chinese communities into arenas in which they contended. The newspapers they established dominated Chinese–American journalism up to the end of World War II. Nationalistic feelings and China politics became the prevailing themes.

The Reform Party established the first political party newspaper network. In 1899 Kang Youwei fled China and arrived in Victoria, British Columbia, where he founded the Chinese Empire Reform Association (later the Chinese Constitutionalist Party) to further his program to pressure the imperial government to

reform.[25] Recognizing from the outset the importance of influencing public opinion, the Reformers placed emphasis on establishing party news organs in key
overseas Chinese communities. In 1899 San Francisco party adherents gained
control of *Mon Hing Bo*,[26] a weekly which had been publishing since 1892.[27]
The *Mon Hing Bo* changed its English name to *The Chinese World* in 1898 and
went to daily publication around 1901. In 1908 its Chinese name became *Sai
Gai Yat Po*, but the English name *The Chinese World* remained unchanged.[28]
This paper remained a major voice in the San Francisco Chinese community for
more than half a century until it ceased publication in 1969. Reform Party
adherents also established the triweekly *Sun Chung Kwock Bo* or *New China
Press* (1900–1978)[29] in Honolulu, and the semiweekly *Chinese Reform News*
(1904–1937?)[30] in New York City.

An even older political group was the Chee Kung Tong, or Triads, a secret
society originally founded in Southeast China to overthrow the ruling Manchus
and restore Han-Chinese rule in China. This loosely knit, far-flung group had
numerous adherents among the overseas Chinese. Spurred by the Reform Party's
political activism, Chee Kung Tong members established the *Tai Tung Yat Po*
(Chinese free press) in San Francisco under the leadership of Tong King Chong
(1903–1927);[31] a successor organ, *Kung Lun Po* [Morning sun], was published
from 1929–1933.[32] The paper soon aligned itself with the revolutionary movement led by Sun Yat-sen. The Triads also established the *Kai Chee Sun Po*
(1909–1912;[33] the name was changed to *Hon Mun Bo*, 1912–1929)[34] in Honolulu.
After the establishment of the Republic of China, *The Chinese Republic News*
(1913?–1948) was established in New York City.[35]

A third political group, the Revolutionary Party, was first organized in 1895.
Its objective was the overthrow of the reigning dynasty in China. It acquired its
first organ in Honolulu when *The Hawaiian Chinese News* became supportive
of its cause in 1903.[36] Later, supporters founded another Honolulu paper, the
triweekly *Chee Yow Sun Bo* (Liberty news; 1908–1946?), which eventually
became a daily.[37] In the continental United States, the first revolutionary organ,
The Youth, was established as a weekly in San Francisco in 1909.[38] It changed
to the daily *Young China* after Revolutionary Party leader Sun Yat-sen visited
the city the following year[39] and it has continued to publish up to the present.

During the era of civil war in China, successors to the Revolutionary Party,
the Kuomintang (Chinese Nationalist Party), established *Mun Hey Weekly* (1915–
1958; it became a daily in 1927)[40] in New York to facilitate political activities
in the Chinese civil war on behalf of the Kuomintang Guangzhou (Canton)
regime, which was in opposition to the Beijing (Peking) government. In 1927,
after the Kuomintang established hegemony over all of China, party organs of
other groups ceased functioning one by one. By 1940 only *The Chinese World*
of San Francisco and *New China Press* of Honolulu remained. Even then, their
survival depended on financial subsidies from party loyalists.

In the midst of the Kuomintang drive for control of China a split occurred in
the party in 1927 when Chiang Kai-shek established a government in Nanjing

(Nanking) and Wang Jingwei led a rival regime in Hankou (Hankow). Contending factions existed in the Chinese American community. The two principal rivals were the "right," which supported the dominant conservative faction in the Nanjing regime, and the "left," which supported the Wang Jingwei faction consisting of more liberal elements of the party. Each faction attempted to control the party organs and, failing that, to establish rival ones. Rival Kuomintang newspapers arose in San Francisco, Honolulu, and New York. The right faction also founded an organ in Chicago.[41] These organs continued to exist until after World War II.

During the first decades of the twentieth century the Chinese–American press was politically slanted; however, it seldom attracted the attention of U.S. authorities since the Chinese were a small ethnic community and the newspapers were printed in a language that few other Americans knew how to read. Free from the threat of censorship, the Chinese–American press was able to express a greater diversity of viewpoints than its counterparts in the motherland or Hong Kong. It thus played an important role in instilling political awareness and fostering nationalistic feelings among the Chinese of the United States. For example, during the early 1900s the Honolulu Reform Party organ, *Sun Chung Kwock*, urged action against the United States in retaliation for its harsh discriminatory treatment of Chinese immigrants. This led to the 1905 boycott against American goods in China. During the 1920s and 1930s the Chinese–American press was also in the forefront, denouncing Japanese encroachments on Chinese sovereignty, rallying popular support for resistance against aggression, and advocating boycotts of Japanese goods. Such views would have been banned in China during this period.

After World War II and the Nationalist government's later retreat to Taiwan, the circulation of the party newspapers declined, and they closed one by one. By 1980 Kuomintang organs only survived in San Francisco and Honolulu. As for their rivals, *The Chinese World* enjoyed a brief renaissance under Dai Ming Lee during the 1950s as the chief critic in the community against the regime on Taiwan and that on the Chinese mainland. However, financial reverses eventually forced this paper to shut down in 1969. By 1978 its sister publication in Honolulu, *New China Press*, had also ceased publication.[42]

On the opposite end of the political spectrum, the Chinese Marxists were allied with the Kuomintang during the first quarter of the twentieth century, and a separate left-wing press did not exist. However, after the communists were purged from the Kuomintang in 1927, the changed circumstances led Chinese members of the U.S. Communist Party to establish the weekly *Chinese Vanguard* in San Francisco. The paper soon moved to Philadelphia and then to New York City, where it published until the eve of World War II. Edited by Y. Y. Hsu, the weekly supported the militant wing of the U.S. labor movement and the Chinese communist revolution.[43] In 1940 the left finally established its first daily paper, *China Daily News* of New York City.[44]

China Daily News built up a following during the 1940s, but during the anticommunist hysteria of the 1950s and 1960s it was hounded by the federal government, as were other liberal and left institutions. In 1955 Eugene Moy, the publisher, was convicted for violation of the Trading with the Enemy Act during the Korean War.[45] During this era, many fearful readers cancelled their subscriptions, and the paper was forced to semiweekly publication in 1963. It did not resume operation as a daily until January 1977, after relations between the People's Republic of China (PRC) and the United States had improved, and readership for the newspaper again increased in the Chinese–American community.

Earlier, in 1949, Henri Tsoi had established *The China Weekly* in San Francisco, also to voice support for the newly established People's Republic.[46] It became a casualty of the Korean War in 1950 after Chinese troops entered the conflict and *The Chinese Pacific Weekly*, which had handled the paper's typesetting and printing, declined to continue its services. It was not until almost two decades later, when John S. C. Ong and Maurice Chuck led the move to establish the weekly *Chinese Voice* in 1969,[47] that San Francisco once again had such a voice. The *Voice* changed to daily publication in October 1971, but financial problems and an internal split led to suspension of operations in 1972. Before that occurred, Chuck left to start a weekly, *The San Francisco Journal*, in 1972.[48] The paper became a daily in 1983.

In the last few decades changes in the international situation as well as the opening of greater opportunities for Chinese Americans in this country have caused the decline of China politics as the dominant factor in the news. The circulation of party line newspapers has also declined, with their survival often depending on subsidies from supporters. However, although community issues and U.S. national politics are receiving increasing emphasis, China politics still influences newspaper editorial policies, with the focus primarily on the issue of the People's Republic of China versus Taiwan.

NON-PARTY AFFILIATED NEWSPAPERS

Even when China politics dominated, local politics and community issues demanded their share of attention. In addition to the party organs, there arose newspapers which were not officially affiliated with any political group. Although this did not necessarily preclude identification with a particular political viewpoint, many had a pronounced community perspective in their reporting. One of the earliest in this category was the aforementioned *Chung Sai Yat Po* which for the first two decades of its existence was the most influential independent daily.

In 1924, at a time when native-born Chinese Americans were increasing in number, members of the Chinese American Citizens Alliance, an organization of U.S. citizens, founded *Chinese Times*.[49] For many years under the management of Walter U. Lum, this San Francisco paper claimed to speak for American citizens of Chinese extraction. A few years later, *The Chinese Journal of Com-*

merce (1928–1944)[50] was founded in New York City. This paper attacked corrupt practices in the Chinese Benevolent Association and also supported New York's Chinese laundrymen in their fight against the city's discriminatory legislation during the 1930s.[51] Under Thomas P. Chan and Y. K. Chu it was a liberal voice 'n the community until World War II, when it was sold and became a Kuomintang party organ, *The Chinese Journal.*[52]

The emergence of a relatively affluent Chinese–American middle class during the war, plus the influx of capital and the immigration of a number of intellectuals as a result of the post–World War II civil war in China, stimulated further development of the Chinese–American press. During this period several magazines were established, mostly in New York. Most of these publications were targeted at readers who sought only light and entertaining reading matter. One exception was *Chinese–American Weekly* (1942–1970), founded by Wu Chin Foo, who during the war had been ousted from the editorship of New York's *Mun Hey Daily* as a result of a Kuomintang intraparty struggle.[53] Featuring a pictorial section, current events, and articles by Chinese–American writers, *Chinese–American Weekly* became the longest-lived and the most successful Chinese-American news magazine. It was distributed nationally for almost three decades.

A number of daily newspapers were also established, including Wu Chin Foo's widely read *United Journal* (founded 1952).[54] New York City became the leader among all Chinese–American communities in the number of such publications, having eleven dailies, six of them locally owned, in the early 1980s. San Francisco, long the leader in Chinese–American journalism, had eight dailies in the 1980s, but only two were Chinese–American owned. The majority of these newspapers supported the Taiwan regime.

San Francisco became the center for weekly newspapers, beginning with the founding of *The Chinese Pacific Weekly* in 1946.[55] With Gilbert Woo as editor, this tabloid-size paper was noted for its liberal views and its reporting on court trials and immigration, issues of concern to many Chinese Americans. Its success inspired the rise of a number of other weeklies in the city, with eight published at one point during the 1970s. These journals generally emphasized local news. A notable example was Frank Y. S. Wong's *Truth Weekly* (founded 1967), which specialized in sensational news items and was the precursor of several weeklies of similar bent.

The need to inform the English-reading Chinese–American population grew steadily with that segment of the population. By 1920 native-born Chinese had become a majority in Hawaii, and a bilingual weekly, *The Hawaii Chinese News*, was established in 1926 with Ruddy F. Tong as editor and manager. [56] The paper continued until the early 1930s. In the continental United States the first all-English Chinese–American newspaper, *Chinese Digest*, was founded in San Francisco in 1935.[57] This weekly journal, edited by Thomas W. Chinn, reported events of interest to the Americanized population. However, this small and still young group provided a limited market, and *Chinese Digest*'s circulation never exceeded 400, although the circle of readers was much greater.[58] It ceased publication in 1940. In spite of the risks, however, English–language newspapers continued to be started over the years, for example, San Francisco's *California Chinese Press* (1940–1952) with Charles L. Leong and William Hoy as editors; Honolulu's *Hawaii-Chinese Journal* (1937–1957) with William Lee as editor;[59] and New York's *Chinese-American Times* (1955–197?), edited by William Y. Chang.

Various newspapers also tested the market with English supplements. In 1940 a weekly supplement was published in the Kuomintang organ *Kuo Min Yat Po* for twenty-eight weeks before it was dropped.[60] In subsequent years several others were initiated, but most eventually suspended publication after discovering that the gain in circulation, in any, could not justify the expenditure. Only *The Chinese World*, which had financial backing from the Chun Quon family in Honolulu, was able to sustain publication of a daily two-page English section for two decades.[61]

Another successful exception was the bilingual *East/West* weekly of San Francisco, whose founding in 1967 was inspired by the social ferment and rising ethnic awareness of the time. Published by Gordon Lew, the paper aimed to bridge the gap between the Chinese and American cultures in the Chinese–American community. The emphasis of *East/West* was on its English section, which was widely read for its coverage of Asian American community problems and issues. This was one of the first Chinese–American newspapers to adopt offset printing technology. Its Chinese section also set a precedent by using the Chinese typewriter to set copy, thus effecting savings on capital and operating costs. These innovations were soon emulated, first by the weeklies, and then by the dailies. The principal competitor of *East/West* is the English–language *Asian Week*, founded by John Fang in 1979.

The same social factors also stimulated the birth of the Asian American movement in another segment of the community during the late 1960s and led to the launching of a number of movement publications. The best known in this category was the bilingual monthly newspaper *Getting Together*, started in New York in 1970 by I Wor Kuen, a militant Asian American organization. The paper moved its base of operations to San Francisco in 1971 and later became a biweekly. In 1978 it was reorganized as a monthly magazine, *Unity*, and became the organ of the League of Revolutionary Struggle (Marxist-Leninist). Another publication, *Bridge Magazine*, was a bimonthly founded in 1972 by the Basement Workshop, a New York–based liberal Chinese–American group. Published with the intention of building a bridge "between Chinese and Chinese and between Chinese and the larger society," *Bridge* featured articles and reports on Chinese and Chinese–American society. However, by the fourth issue the magazine had adopted an Asian American perspective.

The increase in the Chinese–American population spurred the establishment of newspapers in Chinese communities other than San Francisco and New York. The Los Angeles area, in the 1980s home of the third largest Chinese community in the United States, rapidly became the third center of the Chinese–American press. From a single weekly, the pro-Taiwan *Kwong Tai Press* (founded 1951; reorganized as *New Kwong Tai Press*, 1961),[62] the number of newspapers expanded to three by the mid–1970s and thirteen by the early 1980s, including the first Chinese–American daily in Los Angeles, the short-lived *California Daily News* (founded 1981), which was reorganized as a weekly, *The Tribune*, in 1982. The latter supports the Taiwan regime; however, it is also frequently critical of political repression on the island.

Newspapers also began to appear in cities with smaller Chinese populations. Some were bilingual, with an emphasis on community news. Examples are *Sampan* (founded 1971),[63] published by the Chinese American Civic Association of Boston, and *Southwest Chinese Journal* of Houston (founded 1976), both monthlies, as well as the weekly *Seattle Chinese Post* (founded 1982). There are also Chinese–language newspapers such as Houston's *Chinese Voice Monthly* (founded 1975) and *Voice of Oakland Chinese* (founded 1975),[64] a monthly published by the Oakland Consolidated Chinese Association, as well as the biweekly *Metro Chinese Journal* (founded 1981) in Washington, D.C.

The increasing Taiwanese immigrant population by the late 1970s spurred the launching of other journals, including the *Asia Journal* (1980–1983), the first newspaper to claim to speak for Taiwanese in Taiwan and in the United States. The movement for Taiwan's independence, which gained momentum during the late 1970s, also resulted in the rise of movement organs such as *Formosa Weekly* (founded 1980) of Los Angeles, which claimed to be the succesor to a publication banned in Taiwan in 1979, as well as the semiweekly *Taiwan Tribune* (founded 1981) of New York City.

The arrival of numerous ethnic Chinese among the Indo-Chinese refugees during the latter half of the 1970s and early 1980s led to even greater diversity in the Chinese American press. Because of the common language, the new immigrants have had little problem integrating into the Chinese–American community. But because of their great numbers (some estimates put the figure at 200,000 or higher), as well as their similar experiences in Indo-China and common problems in this country as a group, the Chinese from Indo-China have also established their own institutions. A number of Chinese–language newspapers, most weeklies staffed with former journalists among the refugees, have sprung up to report on community events. The earliest of these is the weekly *Vietnam-Chinese Newspaper* (founded 1981) of Los Angeles. Others have subsequently begun publication or are being planned in San Francisco, New York, and other communities.

NATIONWIDE NEWSPAPERS

Although for years many newspapers had subscribers outside their local areas, especially in small towns where no Chinese newspapers existed, none sought to publish on both the East and West coasts until long after World War II. In 1957 the San Francisco–based *Chinese World* was the first to try a New York edition.[65] However, unable to gain a permanent foothold, the venture failed in 1959. *The China Times*, a pro-Taiwan daily, launched another such attempt in 1963 when it began by publishing concurrent editions in Chicago, San Francisco, and New York. However, it soon contracted its operations to the New York edition only.[66] During the next decade several other New York–based journals also attempted to tap the national market, but without significant success.

Hong Kong and Taiwan newspapers, with their greater capital, were the first to achieve success in national distribution in the United States and Canada. In 1967 the *Sing Tao Jih Pao*, a conservative Hong Kong daily, launched a North American edition through the San Francisco export-import firm Chong Kee Jan. News and feature articles were typeset in Hong Kong and flown to the United States, where news items on the Chinese–American community were added to complete the edition. *Sing Tao* introduced to North American readers a higher standard of reporting and better writing than that previously found in local publications. It also used the smaller type common in Hong Kong newspapers and thus included more text per page than Chinese–American newspapers. Its appearance coincided with a large increase in immigration to the United States, and *Sing Tao* found ready acceptance among the populace. Eventually editions were published in New York as well as in Vancouver and Toronto in Canada. Thus another stage in the development of the Chinese–American press was initiated in which foreign-owned newspapers began competing with the locally owned press. Subsequently, other newspapers from Hong Kong, as well as two papers from the People's Republic of China, have published American editions. In most cases these foreign-owned newspapers merely reprint their home editions, although sometimes local advertisements are added. However, Hong Kong's *Centre Daily News*, which began publishing in New York and San Francisco in 1982, is similar to the *Sing Tao Jih Pao* in format but tends to be closer to the center in its editorial slant on news on Taiwan and the People's Republic of China.

Major Taiwan newspaper publishers entered the American market during the 1970s. In 1976 Taipei's *United Daily News* began publishing *World Journal* in New York and San Francisco.[67] The entry of this well-financed venture into the Chinese–American market led to charges of unfair competition from locally owned journals of conservative bent.[68] *World Journal*'s success also led to the entry of another major Taiwan daily, *China Times*, which began with *Sunday Times Chinese Weekly* in 1977 and then started publishing daily in 1983. Each of these newspapers has connections with powerful central committee members of the Kuomintang on Taiwan. Another newspaper financed by Taiwan export capital is the *International Daily News* (founded 1981).[69]

All three Taiwan-owned papers as well as *Sing Tao Jih Pao* and *Centre Daily News* are major operations with local staffs for news coverage in several North American communities. In 1984 *World Journal* claimed the highest circulation among Chinese–American newspapers.[70]

Not all journals from abroad were successful, however; for example, Hong

Kong's *Wah Kiu Yat Po* failed to find a market for a North American edition launched in New York in 1976. In 1980 *Taiwan Times* established the *Far East Times* in San Francisco, only to close down in 1982.

CONCLUSION

Publishing a Chinese newspaper never was, nor is it now, a lucrative business. Most organs spoke for the interests of specific political groups or factions. In the 1980s the great majority of the newspapers lean to the right of center. Many support the Taiwan regime, reflecting the hold which the Kuomintang still have on important segments of the Chinese–American community. However, in recent years, since the improvement in relations between the United States and the People's Republic of China, a growing number of newspapers have tried to be more even-handed in their reporting on Taiwan and on the PRC. Increasing attention is also being given to Chinese–American issues.

Until recently the reporting style in most Chinese–American newspapers was stereotyped, production methods were archaic, and because of the low circulation, capital was usually unavailable for expansion. A few years ago, with the passing of the older immigrant generation and the declining use of Chinese by the American-born generation, which was rapidly being acculturated into American society, Chinese–language newspapers seemed doomed to extinction. This is illustrated by the example of Hawaii, where the once flourishing Chinese press is moribund. The increased Chinese immigration to the U.S. mainland since the mid–1960s, however, has given the Chinese–American press a new lease on life. The newer newspapers have also brought in a higher, more professional standard of journalism.

During the early 1980s, there were some fifteen dailies (each nationally distributed newspaper is considered to be a single entity regardless of the number of local editions) which included local news items, and seven foreign journals which were reprints of the home editions. There was also an ever changing number of semiweeklies, weeklies, biweeklies, and monthlies, with more than thirty-five at the last count. These phenomena reflect the fact that the Chinese–American community is very complex and consists of a number of diverse components. As a result, it is doubtful whether any other ethnic community of comparable size (about 1 million) in the United States has more varied fare for its reading public.

NOTES

1. Gongzhen, Ge, *Zhongguo Baoye Shi* (History of the Chinese Press) (Beijing: Sanlian Shudian, 1955; reprint of 1935 edition of Commercial Press, Shanghai), p. 64.

2. Karl Lo, "Kin Shan Jit San Luk, the First Chinese Paper Published in America," in *Chinese Historical Society of America Bulletin* 6 (December 1971): n.p.

3. *The Golden Hills' News*, June 10, 1854.

4. *The Oriental*, January 4, 1855.

5. Vol. 1, no. 1 of *Chinese Record* is dated November 13, 1876.

6. Ednah Robinson, "Chinese Journalism in California," in *Outwest* 16 (January 1902): 33–42.

7. *Chinese Defender* 1 (August 1910).

8. E. Kemble and H. Bretner, *A History of California Newspapers 1846–1858* (Los Gatos: The Talisman Press, 1962; reprint of supplement to *Sacramento Union*, December 25, 1858), pp. 119–120.

9. Ibid., p. 117.

10. Ge, *Zhonngo Baoye Shi*, p. 73.

11. Vol. 1, no. 2 of *The Oriental* is dated September 18, 1875.

12. *History of Foreign Journalism in San Francisco* (San Francisco: WPA Project 10008, 1939), 1: 81.

13. Ibid.

14. Vol. 5, no. 228 of *The Weekly Occidental* is dated July 3, 1886; vol. 1, no. 8 of *The Daily Occidental* is dated August 9, 1900.

15. Vo. 1, no. 3 of *American and Chinese Commercial News* is dated March 1, 1883.

16. Vol. 1, no. 28 of *The San Francisco Chinese Evening Daily News* is dated October 12, 1883.

17. Overseas Penman Club, *The Chinese of Hawaii* (Honolulu: Overseas Penman Club, 1929), p. 63, shows a facsimile of the masthead of issue no. 1332, which states that the paper was established on March 16, 1883.

18. Vol. 1, no. 1 of *Chinese American* is dated February 3, 1883.

19. Vol. 2, no. 17 of *The Chinese Monthly News* is dated February 1, 1892.

20. Vol. 1, no. 1 of *The Chinese American* is dated June 23, 1893.

21. Vol. 1, no. 2 of *The Chinese News* is dated November 11, 1896.

22. The exact date when Chinese lead type was first used by the Chinese-American press is uncertain. The earliest seen thus far by the author is the March 24, 1893 issue of *The Oriental Chinese Newspaper*.

23. Vol. 1, no. 7 of *Wa Mi San Po* is dated June 24, 1899.

24. Vol. 1, no. 1 of *Chung Sai Yat Po* is dated February 16, 1900.

25. Kang Weipei, *Nanhai Kang Xiansheng Nianpu Xupian* (Continuation of the chronology of the life of Mr. Kang Youwei of Nanhai) (Taipei: Wenhai Publishing Co., 1972), p. 3.

26. The Chinese World, *Meiguo Sanfanshi "Shijie Ribao" 40-nian Jinian Zhengwen Xiaoqi* (Notice soliciting manuscripts to commemorate the 40th anniversary of *The Chinese World* of San Francisco in the U.S.A.) (San Francisco: The Chinese World, 1930). Pamphlet distributed to the public.

27. The Chinese World, *Meiguo Sanfanshi "Shijie Ribao." The History of Foreign Journalism in San Francisco* gives 1891 as the date of the first issue. An extant issue of the *Mon Hing Yat Bo*, dated January 13, 1904, is vol. 12, no. 337. Since each volume corresponds to a Chinese year, the first issue could have been published on any date from Chinese New Year in 1891 to Chinese New Year in 1892.

28. The Chinese World, *Meiguo Sanfanshi "Shijie Ribao."*

29. Overseas Penman Club, *Chinese of Hawaii*, p. 64.

30. Vol. 1, no. 1 of *Chinese Reform News* is dated March 10, 1904. A facsimile is shown in *The Chinese Community in New York City* (New York: The Chinese Community Research Bureau, Inc., 1950), p. 52.

31. Advertisement in *Chung Sai Yat Po*, March 19, 1903, stating that *Tai Tung Yat Po* will be published soon.

32. Advertisement in *Chung Sai Yat Po*, August 6, 1929, announcing the first issue of *Kung Lun Po* for August 15, 1929.

33. Clarence E. Glick, *Sojourners and Settlers: Chinese Migrants in Hawaii* (Honolulu: University Press of Hawaii, 1980), p. 294.

34. Overseas Penman Club, *Chinese of Hawaii*, p. 64.

35. The initial publication date for this newspaper given by the various sources varies widely: Pei Chi Liu, *Meiguo Huaqiao Shi Xupian* (Continuation of a history of the Chinese in the United States of America) (Taipei: Liming Menhua Shuye Gongsi, 1981), p. 368, gives 1913; *The Chinese Community in New York City*, p. 52, gives 1911; Warner M. Van Norden, *Who's Who of the Chinese in New York* (New York: author, 1981), p. 18, shows a facsimile of the May 26, 1917 issue as vol. 9, no. 20. This would place the first issue in 1909. However, there is no mention of this paper in Feng Ziyou, "Kaiguo qian Hai nei-wai Geming Shu-bao Yilan" (A list of pro-revolutionary publications and newspapers inside China and abroad before the 1911 revolution), in *Geming Yishi* (Reminiscences of the Revolution) (Taipei: Commercial Press, 1965), 3: 139–159.

36. Overseas Penman Club, *Chinese of Hawaii*, pp. 18–21. At the end of 1903 *The Hawaiian Chinese News* published two essays written by Sun Yat-sen attacking the Reform Party and calling for support for the revolution. This marked the beginning of polemics between the Revolutionaries and the Reformers in Hawaii.

37. Overseas Penman Club, *Chinese of Hawaii*, p. 63, cites the beginning date of *Chee Yow Sun Bo* as August 31, 1908.

38. Xiongfei Wen, "Zhongguo Tongmenghui zai Meiguo de Chengli Jingguo" (The founding of the Zhongguo Tongmenghui in the United States) in *Xinhai Geming Huiyilu* (Reminiscences of the 1911 Revolution) (Beijing: Wenshi Ziliao Chubanshe, 1982), 8:335–370. The first issue of *The Youth* is stated to be July 4, 1909.

39. The first issue of the *Young China* daily is dated August 19, 1910. A facsimile is shown in Liu, *Meiguo Huaqiao Shi Xupian* p. 374.

40. Vol. 1, no. 1 of *Mun Hey Weekly* is dated January 23, 1915. A facsimile is shown on p. 52 of the *Chinese Community in New York City*.

41. The organs supporting the right are San Francisco's *Young China*, New York's *Chung Shan Daily News* and Honolulu's *United Chinese News*. Organs of the left faction are San Francisco's *Kuo Min Yat Po* (Chinese Nationalist daily of America), New York's *Mun Hey* (Chinese Nationalist daily) and Honolulu's *Chee Yow Sun Bo* (Liberty news). In 1930 the right faction founded *San Min Morning Post* in Chicago.

42. *Chinese Times* (San Francisco), August 8, 1978.

43. H. Mark Lai, "A Historical Survey of the Chinese Left in America," in Emma Gee, ed., *Counterpoint: Perspectives on Asian America* (Los Angeles: Asian America Studies Center, University of California, 1976), pp. 63–80.

44. Vol. 1, no. 1 of *China Daily News* is dated July 8, 1940.

45. Lai, "Historical Survey." Also see Committee to Support the Chinese Daily News, *The China Daily News Case* (New York: The Chinese Daily News, 1952).

46. Vol. 1, no. 1 of the *China Weekly* is dated May 4, 1949.

47. Vol. 1, no. 1 of *Chinese Voice* is dated September 24, 1969.

48. Vol. 1, no. 1 of the *San Francisco Journal* is dated February 23, 1972.

49. *Chinese Times*, July 15, 1974. The first issue came off the presses on July 15, 1924.

50. Vol. 1 no. 1 of *The Chinese Journal of Commerce* is dated October 28, 1928. A facsimile is shown on p. 53 of *The Chinese Community in New York City*.

51. Leong Gor Yun, *Chinatown Inside Out* (New York: Barrows Mussey, 1936), pp. 26–52, 85–106.

52. Liu, *Meiguo Huaqiao Shi Xupian*, pp. 388–391.

53. Ibid., p. 391.

54. Ibid., pp. 391–392.

55. Interview with Norbert Woo, one of the partners, San Francisco, August 10, 1974.

56. Vol. 1, no. 1 of *The Hawaii Chinese News* is dated April 23, 1926.

57. Vol. 1, no. 1 of *Chinese Digest* is dated November 15, 1935.

58. Interview with Thomas Chinn, San Francisco, November 11, 1983.

59. Vol. 1, no. 1 of *Hawaii–Chinese Journal* is dated November 12, 1937.

60. The first English supplement was published on March 3, 1940.

61. Liu, *Meiguo Huaqiao Shi Xupian*, p. 370.

62. Ibid., p. 394.

63. Vol. 1, no. 1 of *Sampan* is dated October 1972.

64. Vol. 1, no. 1 of *Voice of Oakland Chinese* is dated January 1, 1975.

65. Liu, *Meiguo Huaqiao Shi Xupian*, p. 370.

66. Ibid., p. 392.

67. *The Tribune* (New York), March 28, 1984.

68. *San Francisco Examiner*, March 9, 1976.

69. *The Tribune*, March 28, 1984.

70. *World Journal* claimed 70,000 paid subscriptions in *Editor and Publisher International 1983 Yearbook* (New York). Gibbs C. P. Wang, editor of *World Journal*, San Francisco, in an answer to a December 27, 1983 letter from the writer, stated the circulation to be 40,000. Competitors suspect that these figures are exaggerated.

BIBLIOGRAPHY

Chinese Chamber of Commerce of Hawaii. *Golden Jubilee, Fiftieth Year*. Honolulu: Chinese Chamber of Commerce, 1961.

Chinn, Thomas W., Him Mark Lai and Philip P. Choy. *Syllabus; A History of the Chinese in California*. San Francisco: Chinese Historical Society of America, 1969.

Holder, Charles F. "The Chinese Press in America." *Scientific American* 87 (October 11, 1902): 241.

Ke, Niuyue. "Niuyue de Huawen Baoye" (The Chinese language press of New York). *Nan-beiji Yuekan* (Hong Kong), no.78 (November 16, 1976): 63–67 [in Chinese].

Li, Zijian. "Zeng Shengcun de Niuyue Zhongwen Boazhi" (The New York Chinese language newspapers, struggling for survival). *Bridge* (New York), October 30, 1975, pp. 6–7, 10.

Liu, Houchun. "Niuyue Shi Chuban de Zhongwen Qikan" (Chinese periodicals published in New York City). *The Sinology Monthly* (Taipei), March 1953.

Liu, Pei Chi. "Meiguo Huaqiao Paoye Fazhan Shilue" (A short history of the development of Chinese press in America). *Wenyi Fuxing Yuekan* (Taipei), no. 19. (1971): 49–56.

Lo, Karl. "Kim Shan Jit San Luk, the First Chinese Paper Published in America." *Chinese Historical Society of America Bulletin* 6 (December 1971).

Lo, Karl, and Him Mark Lai. *Chinese Newspapers Published in North America, 1854–1975.* Washington, D.C.: Center for Chinese Research Materials, 1977.

Ow, Yuk. "A Selected List of Published and Unpublished Materials Written by the California Chinese." (Microfilm). Berkeley, Cal.: Bancroft Library.

Pixley, Morrisson. "A Chinese Newspaper in America." *World's Work* 3 (April 1902): 1950–1953.

Robinson, Ednah, "Chinese Journalism in California." *Outwest* 16 (January 1902): 33–42.

Stellman, Louis J. "Yellow Journals." *Sunset* 24 (February 1910): 197–201.

United Chinese Penman Club. *The Chinese of Hawaii Who's Who, 1956–1957.* Honolulu, 1957, pp. 32–33 [in Chinese].

Yang, Wenyu. "Ping Niuyue Huawen Baoye" (A critical look at the Chinese language press in New York City). *Tops*, December 1983 [in Chinese].

Zhengzhi. "Jinri Meiguo Huabu Baoye" (The Chinatown press in America today). *Jingbao Yuekan* (Hong Kong), October 1983, pp. 66–67 [in Chinese].

4

The Croatian Press

GEORGE J. PRPIĆ AND C. MICHAEL McADAMS

The Croatians are one of six South Slavic peoples who have inhabited the western parts of the Balkan peninsula since the seventh century.[1] After the fall of their medieval state, the Croatians lived in personal union with Hungary and then under Habsburg rule until 1918. From 1918 until 1941 Croatia existed within the Serbian-dominated Kingdom of Yugoslavia. Following four years of independence during World War II, Croatia was incorporated into the Socialist Federal Republic of Yugoslavia. Today, every third Croatian lives outside the Croatian homeland.[2] It is estimated that over 1.5 million Croatians, of all generations, live in the United States.

THE EARLY CROATIAN PRESS

In America, Croatian immigrants had the opportunity to found their first free press. The first Croatian newspaper in America was *Slavenska Sloga* (Slavic unity), founded in San Francisco in 1884.[3] In 1892, Vjekoslav Piškulić, a native of Dubrovnik, founded *Dalmatinska Zora* (Dalmatian dawn), also in San Francisco. In nearby Oakland, California, another early publication was *Sloboda* (Liberty), followed by *Trojedna Kraljevina* (The triune kingdom). Most early Croatian immigrants were male Roman Catholics of peasant stock. Since one in three was illiterate, all early Croatian publications were struggling enterprises.[4]

In Hoboken, New Jersey, A. G. Škrivanić founded the first Croatian newspaper on the East Coast, *Napredak* (Progress), on November 21, 1891. In Chicago, where many Croatians settled in the late nineteenth century, *Hrvatska Zora* (Croatian dawn) appeared on August 4, 1892. Owned and edited by political exile Janko Kovačević, this publication lasted only a year.

A former member of the Croatian Sabor (Parliament), Nikola Polić, founded the weekly *Chicago* in that city on October 21, 1892. In July 1893 he issued *Sloboda-Liberty* and later merged the two as *Chicago-Sloboda* in 1896. Ignoring old country politics, he urged his readers to learn the English language and become American citizens. In 1902 Reverend Nikola Gršković, formerly a newspaper editor in Croatia, purchased Polić's newspaper, renamed it *Hrvatska Sloboda* (Croatian liberty), and moved the paper to Cleveland, where it was published until 1904.[5]

THE FRATERNALISTS

A young university student named Zdravko Mužina worked for Polić in Chicago before moving to Pittsburgh in late 1893. At that time some 9,000 Croatians were concentrated in the local steel industry's low-paying, high-risk, unskilled labor pool. Mužina saw the need for a mutual benefit society to insure medical expenses or at least a decent funeral for Croatian workers. In the first issue of his paper *Danica* (The morning star), dated January 4, 1894, he appealed to Croatian workers to establish a strong fraternal society. On January 13, the Croatian Workers' Benefit Society was founded in Pittsburgh, and similar societies were soon established in other cities. On September 2, 1894, fourteen delegates of such organizations formed the Croatian Union in the United States. In 1926 the organization was renamed the Croatian Fraternal Union.

In 1895 Mužina printed the first Croatian almanac in the United States, the *Hrvatsko-amerikanska Danica Kalendar* (Croatian-American morning star calendar). The growth of the Croatian press was aided by the arrival of the first Croatian typographers in America, Josip Marohnić and Kruno Maljevac. Marohnić, known as the father of Croatian publishing in America, arrived in Pittsburgh in 1894. He joined the activists of the Croatian Union and established a printing business and America's first Croatian bookstore. On January 1, 1899, he published the first issue of the monthly *Brico* (The barber).[6]

In September 1896, *Napredak* (Progress) became the official newspaper of the Croatian Union, followed in 1904 by the new monthly (later weekly) *Zajedničar* (The fraternalist). Each member of the National Croatian Society and later the Croatian Fraternal Union received *Zajedničar*. It soon reached more Croatian-Americans than any other publication. The Junior "Nests" of the society began publication of *Pomladak Narodne Hrvatske Zajediče* (The junior order of the National Croatian Society) in 1916, which continues today as the bimonthly *Junior Magazine*. In 1984 the Croatian Fraternal Union, with hundreds of lodges throughout North America and assets in excess of $57 million, celebrated its ninetieth anniversary. *Zajedničar*, in its eightieth year, continues as North America's largest Croatian newspaper.[7]

THE SECOND GENERATION

With a few notable exceptions, most early Croatian newspapers were short-lived. The first Croatian priest in Pennsylvania, Dobroslav Božić, founded *Novi Svijet* (The new world) in Allegheny on December 20, 1897. In March 1898 he founded the first Croatian humor monthly, *Puco* (The shooter), while Reverend

Franjo Glojnarić of Bennet, Pennsylvania, first issued *Glas Istine* (The voice of truth) in 1901. All survived only months or a few years at most.[8]

Narodni List-The National Gazette, a New York weekly established in 1898 by a Dalmatian immigrant named Frank Zotti, survived longer than most. Zotti, "King of the Croatians," was a successful banker, businessman, and owner of steamship agencies. His financial backing allowed *Narodni List* to endure until 1923. Zotti owned and controlled as many as eight newspapers during his prominent career. His publications were newsy, sensational, and patriotic, and advocated an independent Croatia. Organized on a business basis, complete with a large corps of salesmen, *Narodni List* became America's first Croatian daily in 1902 and achieved a peak circulation of over 25,000.[9]

Zotti's fortunes changed in 1906 when he was ousted from the leadership of the National Croatian Society and a talented young journalist named Stjepan Brožović split with Zotti to become the editor of *Hrvatsko-Amerikanske Novine* (Croatian-American newspaper). Zotti's rival, Franc Sakser, published the weekly (later daily) *Hrvastski Svijet-The Croatian World*. It continued, with several name changes, until 1956. The feud between Zotti and the National Croatian Society was reflected in the pages of *Narodni List* and *Zajedničar*, but Zotti's publications survived. The sixteenth anniversary edition of *Narodni List* noted some two dozen Croatian newspapers which had gone out of business.[10]

THE WORKERS' PRESS

Many early publications appealed to the working class. The first was the weekly *Radnik* (The worker), published in Chicago from 1898 until 1905. *Radnička Borba* (Worker's struggle) appeared in Cleveland in 1907. Published by the Yugoslav Socialist Workers' Federation, it continued into the 1970s. In Chicago, America's first socialist Croatian newspaper, the weekly *Radnička Straza* (Worker's sentinel), appeared on Christmas day 1907. Editor Milan Glumac, a skilled typographer from Zagreb, was joined in December 1908 by Todor Cvetkov, a native Bulgarian from Zagreb. Cvetkov became a lawyer and an activist in the socialist antiwar movement during World War I. A rival newspaper, *Hrvatski Radnički Pokret-Croatian Workers' Movement*, appeared in Chicago on December 20, 1911. Edited by Frank Halaus, it claimed to be the "first and only independent Croatian workers' newspaper in America."

In the fall of 1917, Cvetkov's *Radnička Straza* was forced to cease publication because of its socialist and antiwar viewpoint. It reappeared as *Nova Misao* (New thought) and later as *Znanje-The Knowledge*. Despite the Red Scare of 1919–1920, the publication continued in various forms for over twenty years as the official organ of the Workers' Educational Federation. In 1923 Cvetkov and Djuro Kutužović seceded with their socialist group from the South Slavic section of the Communist Party U.S.A. to form the Yugoslav Educational League. *Znanje* became its official paper, joined on August 7, 1923, by the bimonthly *Novi Svijet* (The New World).[11]

PUBLISHERS AND MASTHEADS: THE FLOWERING
OF THE CROATIAN PRESS

While there were the controversial, the manipulative, and the unscrupulous among them, most of the Croatian editors were tireless, idealistic activists attempting to better the lot ot the Croatian people. Between 1890 and 1930 a number of crusading editors became well known to Croatian-Americans. In addition to those already mentioned, such as Mužina and Zotti, others included Gabriel Rački, Majija Šojat, Ivan Mladineo, Ivan Lupis-Vukić, Frano Akačić, Adam Sudetić, Slavoljub Pintar, Vjekoslav Meler, Ivan Krešić, Ivan Stipanović, Milan Petrak, Filip Vukelić, Franjo Tolić, Stanko Borić, Louis Fisher, and Anton Tanasković.[12]

While Pittsburgh, Chicago, Calumet, New York City, San Francisco, and Los Angeles were the centers of Croatian press activity, other publications appeared throughout the country during the first decades of the twentieth century. Steamship companies, engaged in fierce price wars, submitted articles depicting the wonders of America. Fraternal publications concentrated on organizational activities, the economy, and labor unrest. There were papers of every political stamp from extreme left to far right, as well as cultural, religious, and social publications. Special editions, such as those surrounding the conventions of the National Croatian Society in 1897, ran front pages with the Croatian flag and coat of arms in full color. The name *Hrvatska* (Croatia) and the adjective *hrvatski* appeared in the titles of many publications. It was often the practice to title a publication in both Croatian and English, such as A. G. Skrivanic's *Hrvatska-Croatia*, published in Pittsburgh in 1903.

Tracing the history of Croatian publications during this period of rapid growth is difficult. Some early newspapers published only a single issue. Many publications "migrated" with changes in organizational support or, more often, with an editor seeking employment in another city. Finally, titles seemed to be considered in the public domain. Popular names, such as *Hrvatska* (Croatia) and *Američki Hrvat* (The American-Croatian), appeared at different places at different times (and even at the same time), with no relationship to others of the same title. Editors would sometimes adopt the titles of popular Croatian publications from the old country, adding to the confusion.

An illustration of these factors at work begins in Calumet, Michigan, with the introduction of *Rodoljub* (The patriot) in 1902. It was followed in August 1905 by *Hrvatski Radnik* (Croatian worker), voice of the Slovenian-Croatian Union in Calumet. In 1912 the name was changed to *Hrvatska Sloboda* (Croatian librerty), and journalist Marija Sojat, who was also the main representative for the New York daily *Hrvatski Svijet* (Croatian world), joined the staff. In 1915 he bought *Hrvatska Sloboda* and published it as *Hrvatska* until 1928, when it was sold to Vjekoslav Meler, a recent arrival from Zagreb. Meler ended the relationship with the fraternal union and moved the paper to Chicago as thousands of workers moved from Calumet to newer industrial and mining regions. In April 1929 Meler sold *Hrvatska* to Stjepan Vrančić, who renamed it *Jugoslavenski Glasnik* (Yugoslav herald) and later *Hrvatski Američki Glasnik* (Croatian American herald), which survived into the 1950s.[13]

In March 1903 *Hrvat-The Croatian* was published by Dr. Milan Kovačević and the Croatian Christian Political Club of Allegeny, Pennsylvania, and *Velika Hrvatska-Great Croatia* appeared in McKeesport, Pennsylvania, published by the banking firm of George Papa and Company. The humorous monthly *Osa* (The wasp) was published in New York City from 1898 until 1922. A. C. Janković owned and edited *Branik-The Defender* in Chicago from 1898 until 1908, when the name was changed to *Savjetnik* (The advisor). Chicago was also the home of *Vatra i Plamen* (Fire and flame), a magazine issued in 1901. The first of several publications titled *Američki Hrvat* (The American-Croatian) appeared in Cleveland in 1905. Josip Marohnić founded *Hrvatski Glasnik-Croatian Herald* in Pittsburgh in 1908. When Marohnić died in 1921, Ivan Lupis-Vukić moved the paper to Chicago, where it was published until 1932.

A major Croatian newspaper in Chicago from 1902 until 1917 was the weekly *Hrvatska Zastava-Croatian Flag*, edited by Ante Biankini, a popular physician and surgeon. It served as the semi-official publication of the Croatian League of Illinois and during World War I became an advocate of the South Slavic movement, as the daily *Jugoslavenska Zastrava* (Yugoslav flag). The Croatian League of Illinois then undertook its own publication in 1916, *Glasnik Hrvatske Zajedniče Illinois* (The messenger of the Croatian League of Illinois), which was discontinued with the merger of the league into the newly formed Croatian Fraternal Union in 1926.

Ivan Mladineo published the weekly *Hrvatski Narod* (Croatian people) in St. Louis from 1909 through 1915. He moved to New York and established himself as one of the better Croatian writers on the problems of immigration. Another active journalist and organizer was Hinko Sirovatka, who came to America in 1906. In 1907 he published a book in Zagreb about the Croatian-American press.[14]

A number of other short-lived publications appeared during the growth period of the early twentieth century. *Glasnik Družbe Sv. Ćirila i Methoda* (The messenger of Sts. Cyril and Methodius) was published in Kansas City in 1907. In Cleveland, *Sloboda* (Liberty) appeared in 1904, *Nova Domovina* (New homeland) in 1908, and *Svijetlo* (The light) from 1911 to 1914. In nearby Youngstown, *Glas* (The voice) and *Hrvatska Štampa-Croatian Press* appeared and disappeared during World War I. New York was briefly home to *Glas Naroda-The Voice of the People* in 1908, *Volja* (The will) in 1911, and *Illustrovani List* (Illustrated gazette) in 1915.

In Pittsburgh the *American Citizen-Amerikanski Gradjanin* was published between 1913 and 1916; *Iseljenik-The Emigrant* in 1914 and 1915; and *Hrvatske Seljačke Novine-Croatian Peasant Newspaper* in 1915. *Hrvatski Rodol jub-Croa-*

tian Patriot was published as a weekly in Pittsburgh beginning in June 1915 by
B. F. Tolić, who sold the paper to Anton Basetić in 1916. Basetić moved the
publication to Chicago, where it survived until 1919.

In the West, Croatian papers came and went with equal frequency. *Naša Sloga*
(Our unity) was printed in San Francisco until 1906. In 1908 *Jadran-The Adriatic*
appeared weekly and flourished under the guidance of Frano Akačić until 1916.
In 1925 Akačić founded a monthly titled *Narod* (The people) in nearby Oakland
that survived through 1948. The fraternal order Croatian Unity of the Pacific
published the monthly *Sveza-The Unity* in San Francisco from 1910 until 1938,
when that organization merged with the Croatian Fraternal Union.

WORLD WAR I

During World War I, Croatian nationalism increaed dramatically. R. E. Park,
in *The Immigrant Press and Its Control*, counted sixteen Croatian newspapers
in the United States in 1915, fifteen in 1916, and thirteen in 1918, most with
clear political viewpoints. As more and more Croatian publications reached a
national audience, the quality and circulation of the newspapers increased while
the actual number of publications decreased. The decline in numbers did not
mean that no new publications were born during the period. In January 1915
Reverend Ivan Stipanović inaugurated *Rodoljub* (The patriot) in Chicago, which
soon changed its name to *Hrvatski Katolički List* (Croatian Catholic gazette).
Later that year, this weekly merged with *Narodna Obrana* (National defense)
to form *Glasnik Istine-The Herald of Truth*.

In Los Angeles, *Novo Vrijeme* (New time) appeared in 1909, and two publications, *Dalmacija* (Dalmatia) and *Austrijska Zastava* (Austrian flag) appeared
in 1915. The latter reflected a pro-monarchist viewpoint, while *Republika* (The
republic), first published in Los Angeles in 1918, was clearly republican. Pan-
Slavism was reflected in Seattle's *Slobodna Tribuna* (The free tribune), published
by the local Yugoslav Committee from 1914 until 1925.[15]

During the Eleventh Convention of the National Croatian Society at Kansas
City in September 1912, the Hrvatski Savez (Croatian league) was born. Led
by Reverend Niko Gršković, the league called for the destruction of the Austro-
Hungarian Empire and the establishment of a South Slavic (Yugoslav) state.
Gršković's newspaper, *Hrvatski Svijet* (Croatian world), became the voice of
the league, and "Don Niko," as the people called him, a leading activist of the
time. By 1917 *Hrvatski Svijet* had become *Jugoslavenski Svijet-South Slav Her-
aldd* (Yugoslav world-South Slav herald), with a daily circulation of over 12,000.
In 1922 the publication was renamed *Svijet* (The world) and later reverted to
Hrvatski Svijet as the fortunes of Pan-Slavism faded. The famed Slovenian-
American writer Louis Adamic wrote that Gršković's journalism was "a graceful
balance between the Old and New World" and noted that he published "some
of the best editorials in America in any language."[16]

Other editors, Frank Zotti and Martin Krmpotić among them, favored a reformed confederated Habsburg Empire with free Croatian and Slovenian states. A third group advocated complete independence for Croatia. An early leader of this movement was a former priest named Ivan Krešić who came to America in 1906. He worked for Frank Zotti and for Zotti's rival Franc Sakser before publishing his own *Novi Hrvat* (New Croatian) in New York during 1914–1915. In 1921 he founded *Danica Hrvatska* (The Croatian morning star) and in 1923 purchased *Hrvatski List* (Croatian gazette) from S. Brožović, combining them as *Hrvatski List i Danica Hrvatska*, published three times per week.

Another movement of the time was the Sokol (Falcon) gymnastic and athletic organization, made up of dozens of independent units around the nation. Sokol publications included *Sokol-American*, *Sokol Messenger*, *Sokol Republika*, *Sokol Vijesnik*, and *Sokol*.

YUGOSLAVIA AND DICTATORSHIP

The South Slavic nation idealized by Gršković and others became a grim reality in 1918 as a centralized kingdom ruled by Serbia. In January 1929, after the Croatian pacifist leader Stjepan Radić was murdered on the floor of Parliament, King Alexander abolished political parties and most civil rights and declared himself king/dictator.

The Croatian press in America, seldom united on any issue, almost universally denounced the dictatorship.[17] The Chicago weekly *Hrvatski Glasnik-Croatian Herald* published a documentary book titled *Umorstvo u beogradskoi skupštini* (The murder in the Belgrade Parliament) about the assassination of Radić. *Naša Nada* (Our hope), founded in 1921 by the Croatian Catholic Union of Gary, Indiana, and *Zajedičar* of the Croatian Fraternal Union both consistently denounced the new Yugoslav regime. Despite the Great Depression, most papers received funds to be used to support the liberation of Croatia. The Croatian Circle was founded in 1928 as the advocate of Croatian independence in America. Ivan Krešić soon became a leader in the movement and his paper, *Hrvatski List i Danica Hrvatska*, its voice.

Most new publications of the period supported the "Croatian Cause." Chicago's *Američki Hrvat-American Croatian*, the publication of the Croatian parishes in America, and *Hrvatska Republika-The Croatian Republic* of Pittsburgh, both founded in 1922, were harsh critics of the regime. *Narodni List* and others were forced to cease publication as a result of Yugoslav diplomatic pressure, although their mission was continued by *Hrvatski List i Danica Hrvatska*.

The socialist *Radnik* (Worker), later *Radnički Glasnik* (Workers' herald), continued throughout the Depression to champion workers' rights and denounce the Yugoslav dictatorship. Originally published in Chicago by communists Lou Fisher and Steve Loyen, *Radnički Glasnik* moved to Pittsburgh, reappearing as the daily *Narodni Glasnik* (People's herald) during World War II. The Croatian Bureau of the Communist Party, U.S.A., also published the semimonthly *Organizator* in Chicago during the late 1930s.

A handful of publications espoused the Yugoslav government line, and some were openly financed by Yugoslavia. *Novi Rod-New Generation* was one such magazine; it was founded in 1922 by Reverend Brozo Milosević in Chicago. Following the assassinattion of Radić in 1929, the title changed to *Panslavian Review* and Milosević moved to New York, where he continued on a more Pan-Slavic and somewhat less pro-regime course.[18] The monthly *Slavjanski Jug-The Slavonic South*, also of New York, called for strong measures against Croatian "separatism" in Yugoslavia.[19] From 1933 through 1940 the monthly *Jugosloven* (The Yugoslav) was published in Detroit, and during the late 1930s the *Jugoslavenski Glasnik* (Yugoslav messenger) appeared in Chicago. Filip Vukelić, who later became the Croatian–language editor of the Croatian Fraternal Union's *Zajedničar*, briefly published a pro-Yugoslav semimonthly in Chicago.

In response to the dictatorship, Ante Pavelić, the vice-president of the Croatian Bar and Deputy for Zagreb in Parliament, founded the Ustaša (Uprisers or Revolutionaries) movement, which called for the overthrow of the regime and freedom for Croatia. The movement gained support in the United States and in the pages of several new publications, including *Hrvatsko Narodno Pravo-Croatian National Right* published in San Francisco from 1930 to 1935.

America's first Croatian journal, *Croatian Review-Hrvatska Smotra*, appeared in New York in April 1931.[20] In an attempt to reach the American people, the Croatian National Council and the Croatian Circle published a major memorandum on human rights in 1933 which was reprinted by many Croatian and American newspapers and served as a model for future declarations.

In 1933 Hrvatski Domobran (Croatian Home Defenders), the Ustaša organization in America, founded the weekly *Nezavisna Hrvatska Država-The Independent State of Croatia*. The Domobran published the first issue of the English–language monthly *Croatiapress*, an "Information Bulletin of Politics, Economy and Culture," in San Francisco in August 1934. In 1936 it moved to Pittsburgh to join the rest of the Domobran press, which now included a yearly almanac. Pittsburgh was also the home of another nationalist publication, *Hrvatska Riječ-Croatian Word*, from 1935 to 1937.

Each of the major movements, revolutionary, peasant, and communist, sent a steady stream of emissaries to the fertile Croatian colony in North America, fueling controversy and insuring a vigorous press. On the eve of World War II there were at least twenty-three Croatian newspapers active in the United States.[21]

WORLD WAR II

When World War II came to Yugoslavia in April 1941, Belgrade fell in six days. The royal government-in-exile immediately launched a vicious campaign in the British, American, and Serbian-American press blaming the Croatians for the fall of Yugoslavia.[22]

The Croatians established the Independent State of Croatia on April 10, 1941; it was immediately occupied by German and Italian forces. *Nezavisna Hrvatska*

Država-The Independent State of Croatia, published by the Ustaša movement, which now ruled Croatia, welcomed the new state with a special red, white, and blue edition on April 19, 1941. The edition chronicled the history of the Croatian independence movement and ran on the masthead an American flag with the slogan "Long May It Wave." But symbols and patriotic statements did little to ease suspicion concerning the loyalties of Croatian-Americans.

When America entered the war in December of that year, *Nezavisna Hrvatska Država-The Independent State of Croatia* ran the banner headline "Let's Do Our Part." The predominantly English-language issue praised Franklin Roosevelt and called upon Croatians to support America above all. A German-mandated declaration of war by Croatia on the United States the very next week ended all hope for the Croatian liberation movement in America during World War II.

The Croatian Circle took a cautious approach in the pages of *Hrvatski List i Danica Hrvatska*, while still calling for the complete independence of Croatia. In the October 30, 1941 edition, the editors published a front-page editorial noting that the "chains of yesterday were broken only to be replaced by new ones." During 1944 the newspaper ran a series by Mirko Dominis titled "Land of Blood and Tears" which attempted to explain the "Croatian Question" to an American populace preoccupied with the fate of their own nation.[23] The Croatian Circle disbanded in 1948.[24]

As a demonstration of loyalty, some publications attempted to follow the U.S. government line, which was often difficult. The United States maintained a consulate in the Independent State of Croatia during the first few months of the war, then supported the pro-royalist Četniks and finally the communist Partisans by 1944. Pro-communist publications such as *Narodni Glasnik* also attempted to follow unpredictable changes in party line. The popular Croatian Fraternal Union newspaper *Zajedničar* pursued an ambivalent policy of promoting Yugoslav freedom and unity in its English–language section while often advocating Croatian independence in its Croatian section.[25]

THE POST-WAR ERA

When Tito's communists emerged victorious in 1945, hundreds of thousands of Croatians fled to Western Europe, Australia, South America, Canada, and the United States. The dispersal of leaders, parties, and publishers, aided by modern wire services and the advent of dependable and inexpensive air mail, led to a truly international Croatian press during the postwar period. Recent émigrés were as likely to subscribe to Croatian–language periodicals from abroad as any of the traditional Croatian newspapers in the United States.

Many of the smaller Croatian newspapers did not survive the immediate post-war period. The monthly *Križ* (The cross), *Američko Hrvatski Glasnik* (American Croatian herald), and *Hrvatski Svijet-Croatian World* were among the casualties by 1956.[26] Postwar politics also hurt most of the socialist, pro-communist, and pro-Yugoslav publications during the early 1950s. *Narodni Glasnik*, founded in

1907, dropped its pro-Stalinist line and cut open communist ties, but continued as an "independent workers' newspaper." Many others, including *Zajedničar*, were condemned by the House Committee on Un-American Activities as being under "communist influence."[27]

Besides the two fraternal newspapers, *Naša Nada* and *Zajedičar*, the great survivor in postwar America was *Danica*.[28] Ivan Krešić sold the paper to the Croatian Franciscan Fathers of Chicago in 1943. Father Ljubo Čuvalo edited the weekly in 1944 and 1945 and again from 1961 to 1973. Father Castimir Majić (editor 1951–1961 and 1978–), a professional staff of priests and sisters, and a lay technical staff continue to publish *Danica* in its fifty-fifth year (1985), an annual *Hrvatski Kalendar* (Croatian almanac) in its forty-second year, and *Hrvatski Katolički Glasnik* (Croatian Catholic messenger), a religious monthly in its forty-fourth year. The Franciscans have also published a number of books in Croatian and English about Croatia and act as a printing firm for several other Croatian publications.[29]

A number of new postwar publications reflected the anti-communist nature of the new émigrés. During 1952–1953 *Za Boga i Hrvatsku* (For God and Croatia) appeared in Erie, Pennsylvania. *Vitez* (The knight) was published from 1953 to 1956 by the Circle of Croatian Knights in Cleveland, Ohio. *The Truth-Istina* was founded in 1957 by the Central Council of Croatian Associations of U.S.A. and Canada, one of many political blanket organizations.

The American Croatian Historical Review, founded in 1946 by a group of Croatian intellectuals, survived only one year but was the forerunner of a new generation of scholarly journals.[30] *Croatia Press*, first published in Rome in 1947, appeared in Cleveland in 1952, and finally in New York in 1956. Under the leadership of Karlo Mirth, the publication evolved into a semi-annual (technically a quarterly with combined issues) review of the world press by and about Croatians.[31] Now found in all major research libraries, *Croatia Press* is a major resource in Croatian studies.[32] The United American Croatians published a short-lived journal called the *Croatian Review* starting in 1958, only two years prior to the birth of America's premier Croatian-American scholarly journal, *Journal of Croatian Studies*. Published by the Croatian Academy of America, the annual review first appeared in 1960 with over 200 pages of scholarly articles and has been edited since its inception by Jerome Jareb and Karlo Mirth. With the West German–Spanish annual *Hrvatska Revija* and Argentina's *Studia Croatica*,[33] it is one of the foremost Croatian journals.[34]

THE 1960s, THE CROATIAN SPRING, AND BEYOND

As postwar immigrants became older and more settled in America, the Croatian press reflected subtle changes in the Croatian-American community. *Zajedničar* reversed its Croatian– and English–language sections in 1963, facing the reality that many of its 65,000 aging, mostly second– or third–generation subscribers could not read Croatian. It maintained a "neutral" but obviously pro-regime outlook toward Yugoslavia and was openly Democratic and pro-labor in the field of American politics. However, news of the Croatian Fraternal Union bowling tournament would take precedence over both national and international news in many issues. The Croatian Catholic Union's *Naša Nada*, in its sixty-fourth year in 1985, is also a lodge and religious–oriented bulletin using English and Croatian throughout. It reaches almost 4,000 Croatian Catholic Union households in North America each month.[35]

Američki Hrvat-American Croat began as a four-page typewriter-set monthly bulletin in English and Croatian in January 1964. In 1968 it adopted a magazine format primarily in the English language. Publisher Petar Radielović founded the Croatian Information Service in 1974 to publish *American Croat*, now a 130-page English–language annual, and has published over a dozen monographs and books dealing with current Croatian affairs. The Los Angeles–based organization has also entered into radio, television, and wire service news. In 1984 Radielovíc was chosen by the Croatian National Congress, an international blanket organization, to edit and publish *CNC Report*. This English-language monthly was designed to inform and influence opinion in English-speaking countries.[36] The official publication of the Croatian National Congress is *Vjesnik* (Messenger), a Croatian-language monthly sometimes edited in the United States but printed in London.

Another California-based publisher is Adam S. Eterovich, who has published a number of quarterly bulletins, monographs, and books about Croatian, South Slavic, East European, and Balkan ethnicity and genealogy since the early 1960s. Eterovich's firm, Ragusan Press, has become a major name in ethnic research in America.[37]

The relative quiet of the 1960s came to an end with the violent suppression of the so-called Croatian Spring liberalization movement in December 1971. The mass purge created a new generation of exiles, born and educated under a communist system, who were often at odds with the older generation of postwar émigrés. In addition to occupying a great deal of space in the existing Croatian press, the Croatian Spring resulted in a number of new publications.

Hrvatska Borba (Croatian struggle) appeared in Washington, D.C., under the direction of Rudolf Arapović in 1971 as a typewriter-set monthly tabloid. By 1978 it had grown into a thirty–page quarterly. *Hrvatski List* (Croatian gazette) came to the United States from West Germany in April 1979 and merged under that name with *Hrvatska Borba*, which continues under the editorship of Arapović with a monthly circulation of 5,000.[38] *Otpor* (Resistance) also began in West Germany in 1974 as the publication of an outlawed exile organization of the same name. Banned by the West German authorities in 1975, *Otpor* reemerged in New York City in 1975 and finally in Chicago in 1976. Its political message, almost always in Croatian, reaches some 3,000 to 4,000 subscribers worldwide.[39] *Hrvatski Preporod* (Croatian news magazine) took on the name of the outlawed organ of Matica Hrvatska, the ancient Croatian Academy banned in 1972. Its New York office also served *Newyorski Tjednik* (New York weekly), which, despite its name, was an irregular tabloid. Both were published through 1978. *Free Croatia-slobdna hrvatska*, the "Official Bulletin of the Croatian Liberation Army," was one of several short-lived East European "liberation" bulletins to appear in January 1976 in New York. All were published by a group of anti-communists who had little affiliation with the nations they purported to represent.

One of the brightest newspapers of the 1970s was *The Croatian Times*, which published a total of twenty-four monthly issues between January 1977 and December 1978. Edited by Joseph Vrbić in Omaha, Nebraska, the newspaper filled the void between the English–language fraternal publications and the Croatian-language political organs. While clearly anti-Yugoslav, the newspaper maintained a neutral course within the complex world of Croatian politics. Despite a worldwide readership, including an Australian edition, *The Croatian Times* fell victim to lack of funding and boycotts by less moderate publications and organizations.

A more recent Croatian-American publication is *Hrvatska Budućnost* (Croatian future), founded in November 1981 as an unofficial voice of the Croatian Republican Party. Published by Mosor Publishing Company of Los Angeles, the Croatian-language monthly is edited by Tihomil Milas; its current circulation of 3,500 is almost evenly divided among the United States, Australia, and Europe.[40]

The Trumpeter, the official publication of the Croatian Philatelic Society, began as a ten-page mimeographed bulletin in late 1972 and went to a small magazine format in 1975. The quarterly is published in English and Croatian and distributed to the society's 700 members.[41]

CONCLUSION

The year 1984 marked the centennial of the Croatian press in America. While following many of the ebbs and flows affecting the American press as a whole, Croatian publishing in America is still dominated by "old country" politics.[42] Only the fraternal publications such as *Zajedičar* and *Naša Nada*, and some specialized publications can be considered purely American. Most Croatian–language publications, and even the English-language *American Croat* and *CNC Report*, are international publications printed in the United States. The Croatian press is a bridge between the old country and the new. It links Croatians throughout the world and gives notice that the Croatian people have not surrendered their national identity.

NOTES

1. On South Slavic immigrants in America, see George J. Prpić, *South Slavic Immigration in America* (Boston: Twayne, 1978).

2. See George J. Prpić, *The Croatian Immigrants in America* (New York: Philosophical Library, 1971), and Prpić, "The Croats," in Stephan Thernstrom, ed., *Harvard Encyclopedia of American Ethnic Groups* (Cambridge, Mass.: Harvard University Press, 1980), pp. 247–256.

3. For detailed information on the establishment and development of the Croatian press see Prpić, *Croatian Immigrants*, pp. 199–215.

4. George J. Prpić, "The Croatian Newspapers in America before 1918," *Croatia Press* 15 (1961): 7–16; Prpić, "Croatian Papers and Periodicals in the United States 1884–1960," and appendix to Prpić, "Croatian Immigrants in the United States of America," in F. H. Eterovich and C. Spalatin, eds, *Croatia: Land, People, Culture* (Toronto: University of Toronto Press, 1970), 2: 394–478; "Dalmatinska Zora," in *Hrvatska Enciklopedija* (Croatian Bibliographical Institute, Zagreb: 1942). 4: 496.

5. Boniface Soric, *Centennial, 1847–1947* (Pittsburgh: Privately printed, 1947), p. 69; *Danica Koledar 1927* (New York: I. Krešić, 1926), pp. 17–26; *American Almanac for 1950* (McKeesport, Pa.: B. Soric, 1949), pp. 101, 105.

6. Prpić, "Croatian Newspapers," p. 9; Soric, *Centennial*, p. 65.

7. *Zajedničar* and *Junior Magazine* are published by the Croatian Fraternal Union, 100 Delaney Drive, Pittsburgh, Pa. 15235.

8. Prpić, "Croatian Newspapers," p. 9.

9. R. E. Park, *The Immigrant Press and Its Control* (New York: Harper, 1922), pp. 341–352. Also see Nada Kestercanek-Vujica, "Croatian Newspapers and Calendars in the United States," Master's thesis, Marywood College, Scranton, Pa. 1952.

10. Prpić, *Croatian Immigrants*, p. 204; *Nardoni List*, May 26, 1914.

11. *American Almanac for 1950*, pp. 117, 141; Veceslav Holjevac, *Hrvati izvan domovine* (Zagreb: Matica Hrvatska, 1968), pp. 154–174.

12. *American Almanac for 1950*, pp. 117, 141; Holjevac, *Hrvati izvan domovine*, pp. 154–174.

13. Prpić, *Croatian Immigrants*, pp. 166–169, 207–209; *Danica Koledar 1927*, pp. 23–24; *American Almanac for 1950*, p. 133.

14. Hinko Sirovatka, *Kako je u Americi i kome se isplati onamo putovati* (Zagreb: Privately printed), p. 48.

15. *American Almanac for 1950*, p. 137; Prpić, "Croatian Papers," 2: 475–478; Prpić, *Croatian Immigrants*, pp. 209–210.

16. Louis Adamic, *My America* (New York: Harper, 1938), p. 240.

17. Prpić, *Croatian Immigrants*, pp. 207, 214.

18. Ibid., pp. 262–263, 328.

19. Ibid., pp. 257, 286; Prpić, "Croatian Papers," 2: 475–478; *American Almanac for 1950*, p. 129.

20. Joseph Kraja, "The Croatian Circle, 1928–1946," *Journal of Croatian Studies* 5–6 (1965): 153–169.

21. Prpić *Croatian Immigrants*, pp. 274–275; *The Minutes of the Fourth Croatian Fraternal Union Convention in 1935* (Pittsburgh: Croatian Fraternal Union, 1935), pp. 245–249; *American Almanac for 1950*, pp. 149, 153; Ivan Mladineo, *Narodni Adresar* (New York: author, 1937), pp. 33–39; Gerald G. Govorchin, *Americans from Yugoslavia* (Gainesville: University of Florida Press, 1961), pp. 140, 292.

22. Louis Adamic, "The Yugoslav Nightmare Invades America," in *My Native Land* (New York: Harper & Bros., 1943) pp. 399–414.

23. Mirko Dominis, "Land of Blood and Tears," *Hrvatski List and Danica Hrvatska*, February 1–June 3, 1944.

24. Kraja, "Croation Circle," pp. 145–204.

25. Govorchin, *Americans from Yugoslavia*, p. 159.

26. Prpić, *Croatian Immigrants*, pp. 475–478, includes a comprehensive list of Croatian publications in America through 1960.

27. U.S. House of Representatives, Committee on Un-American Activities, *Guide* (Washington: Government Printing Office, 1950), p. 148.

28. *Danica* is published by the Croatian Franciscan Fathers, 4851 S. Drexel Blvd., Chicago, Ill. 60615.

29. Interview with Father Castimir Majić, Chicago, Ill., March 25, 1984.

30. George J. Prpić, *Croatia and the Croatians* (Scottsdale, Ariz.: Associated Book Publishers, 1982), p. 247.

31. George Grlica, "Twenty-fifth Anniversary of Croatia Press," *Journal of Croatian Studies* 17 (1976): 166–178.

32. *Croatia Press*, P.O. Box 1767, Grand Central, New York, N.Y. 10017.

33. *Hrvatska Revi ja*, Postfach 27, D–8–München 1, B.R. Deutschland, or Apartado Correos 14030, Barcelona 17, España, published in Croatian since 1951. *Studia Croatica* is the journal of El Instituto Croata Latinamericano de Cultura, Carlos Pellegrini 743, p. 3/18, Buenos Aires, Argentina, published in Spanish since 1959.

34. *Journal of Croatian Studies* is the annual review of the Croatian Academy of America, P.O. Box 1767, Grand Central, New York, N.Y. 10017.

35. *Naša Nada*, Croatian Catholic monthly, One West Old Ridge Rd., Hobart, Ind. 46342.

36. *American Croat*, an independent magazine, and *CNC Report*, an official publication of the Croatian National Council, are published by the Croatian Information Service, P.O. Box 3025, Arcadia, Calif. 91006.

37. Ragusan Press, 2527 San Carlos Avenue, San Carlos, Calif. 94070.

38. *Hrvatski List*, P.O. Box 4810, Washington, D.C. 20008.

39. *Otpor*, 528 W. Surf St., Chicago, Ill. 60657.

40. *Hrvatska Budućnost*, Post Office Box 338, Canoga Park, Calif. 91305.

41. *The Trumpeter*, publication of the Croatian Philatelic Society, 1512 Lancelot, Borger, Tex. 79007.

42. On European influence on Croatian politics in America, see C. Michael McAdams and Vincent F. Bonelli, "The South Slavs," in Joseph S. Roucek and Bernard Eisenberg, eds., *America's Ethnic Politics* (Westport, Conn.: Greenwood Press, 1982), pp. 345–365.

BIBLIOGRAPHY

Kestercanek-Vujica, Nada. "Croatian Newspapers and Calendars in the United States." Master's thesis, Marywood College, 1952.

Prpić, George J. *The Croatian Immigrants in America*. New York: Philosophical Library, 1971.

———. "The Croatian Newspapers in America before 1918." *Croatia Press* 15 (1961): 7–16.

———. "Croatian Papers and Periodicals in the United States 1884–1960." In F. H. Eterovich and C. Spalatin, eds., *Croatia: Land, People, Culture*. Toronto: University of Toronto Press, 1970.

———. "The Croats." In Stephan Thernstrom, Ed., *Harvard Encyclopedia of American Ethnic Groups*. Cambridge, Mass.: Harvard University Press, 1980.

5

The Danish Press

MARION TUTTLE MARZOLF

The Danes who came to America in the nineteenth century were equally drawn to the rich farmlands of Wisconsin, Minnesota, Iowa, and Nebraska and the industrial cities of the East and Midwest, especially Chicago, Racine, New York City, and Perth Amboy, New Jersey. Although under 400,000 Danes have migrated to America since the 1850s, they managed to establish around 200 weekly and monthly newspapers, magazines, and journals, four of which survive today.

In their earliest efforts in journalism they joined with the Norwegians, with whom they share a language and history, but by the 1870s the Danes were able to begin their own Danish-American newspapers. Their journalism in America passed through four stages: Nordic cooperation, 1840–1869; pioneer, 1870–1899; Danish-American, 1900–1919; and ethnic, 1920 to the present.[1]

The earliest Scandinavian newspaper to have a Danish editor was *Skandinavia* (Scandinavia) which started on January 1, 1847. It was written in Danish and Swedish for all New York City Scandinavians and lasted for eight issues.[2] Similar efforts in Wisconsin and Illinois were started by early settlers. The Reverend Claus Lauritz Clausen, a Danish-born and -educated minister for the Norwegian Lutheran pioneer congregation in Wisconsin, is typical of these early editors.[3] His newspaper, *Emigranten* (The immigrant; 1852–1886), combined church and secular material to provide "safe and sound reading matter for the immigrants."[4] The newspaper took a Democratic stance on political matters but proclaimed its independence from any party. It strongly advocated Americanization of the immigrants. In the first issue an editorial talked about the duty of the new settlers to emancipate themselves from the "degrading bondage of ignorance" and learn American customs and the responsibilities of citizenship.[5]

In small Danish communities in Minnesota and Illinois, other weekly news-papers of the time also promoted the political and religious interests of the Danish settlers. In Chicago, where the Danes formed only a small segment of the Scandinavian community in the 1870s, they were still numerous enough to start their own newspaper in 1868. The staff of *Fremad* (Forward; 1868–1871) was composed of a group of university-educated Copenhageners who were aggressive Democrats.[6] Two years later the newspaper was sold to Republicans. In 1871 the Chicago fire wiped out the fledgling paper. Three years later *Heimdal* (Home valley; 1874–1878) offered a new Danish voice; it was edited by another Copenhagener, Morris Salmonsen.[7] This newspaper was financed by Danish businessmen and politicians in Chicago, and it carried news of the United States and Denmark as well as literary and cultural articles, editorials, and advertisements. Its second owner, an economist and former member of the Danish Parliament, N. C. Fredericksen, attracted an influential body of Scandinavian intellectuals and writers for the sixteen-page publication. Among them were Dr. Christian Fenger, on medicine; Clemens Petersen, on literary criticism; Bishop D. G. Monrad, on the church; and the Danish Socialist Party founders Louis Pio and Paul Geleff on politics. But within four years, *Heimdal*'s subscription list had to be sold to the Norwegian newspaper *Skandinavian*, also in Chicago. Fredericksen later published the magazine *Scandinavian* (1883–1886) in a brief but spirited attempt to provide stimulating articles on Scandinavian politics and culture to the English-reading immigrants and their children.[8]

Pio and Geleff had been forced to leave Denmark in 1877 by the Danish police, and they had hoped to exert a strong influence on journalism in the United States. The two socialists worked on several small Scandinavian publications in Chicago for about eight years. Pio did publish two socialist newspapers in Danish, *Tilskueren* (The spectator; 1878–1882?) and *Den nye Tid* (The new time; 1878?–1884?), along with Marcus Thrane, a Norwegian socialist. He also started socialist communities in Kansas and Florida, both of which quickly failed. Pio eked out his living with a variety of jobs while his wife gave piano lessons. He died in Chicago in 1894. Geleff became a land agent in Colorado and occasionally submitted articles to *Den Danske Pioneer*. In 1920 the Danish Social Democratic Party paid for his passage back to Denmark and financed his retirement there.[9]

The early editors often had college educations and high-minded ideals on religion or politics. Their journalism was based on European styles and intended for the cultured reader. American journalism had already developed a popular newspaper style for ordinary citizens, the penny press. These popular newspapers flourished in the cities, where both immigrants and the American-born found them entertaining and informative.

An adaptation of this popular press gained success among the Danish immigrants in the Midwest, most of whom were farmers, skilled craftsmen, or household workers.[10] Two Danish-born printers successfully established general-interest weekly newspapers for Danes in Nebraska and Minnesota. One of them, Sophus F. Neble (1862–1931), became the best-known Danish editor in the United States, but he originally emigrated in 1883 to seek his fortune in dairy farming. His work on a farm was brief and unsuccessful, and he quickly snapped up an opportunity to set type at the new *Den Danske Pioneer* (The Danish pioneer; 1872) in Omaha, which had started as a political newspaper. Under

Neble it rose to a peak circulation of nearly 40,000 during World War I and a claimed readership of 100,000.[11]

Immigrants, cut off from their homeland except for occasional letters from family and friends, very quickly realized their need for information that would aid them in adjusting to life in the new land. The immigrant newspaper became the one constant element in their changing world. Here was information on the laws and regulations of the new country, news about politics and markets, about customs and society. Here jobs were listed, and experienced farmers wrote in to share advice on crops, weather, and planting. Land, goods, and services were advertised for sale in a language they could understand.[12] The immigrant newspaper was such an important and credible source of information for the newcomers that Sophus K. Winther, in the opening scene of his trilogy *Take All to Nebraska*, described his fictional immigrant family riding along on a sooty American train headed for a prairie town secure in the knowledge that *"The Danish Pioneer* had written that there was a large Danish settlement at this town and new settlers were encouraged to come there."[13]

The immigrant press would garner strength as friend, guide, teacher, and advocate through its decades of service to the new settlers. And although these functions would alter in relative importance as the group assimilated, the immigrant press would always put the immigrants' interests and needs first. In the early years these newspapers blended general-interest news of the United States and the world with news of Denmark and the ethnic American settlements. With Americanization and a decline in new immigrant stock, the papers became Danish-American, and in the final phase, ethnic, keeping alive whatever ethnic identity and spirit was manifested by members of the community.[14]

Sophus Neble's ownership of *The Danish Pioneer* from 1887 until his death in 1931 made it a leader among the Danish-American newspapers. His democratic patriotism burned bright, and his stinging editorials about a repressive conservative government in Denmark in the 1880s got the newspaper banned in Denmark from 1886 until 1898. Banned or not, some issues of the newspaper were smuggled in by printing it on tissue paper and mailing it in envelopes or tucked between sheets of American newspapers.[15]

Neble's praise for the democratic traditions of the United States was as vigorous as his criticism of Denmark in that era. Danish-born American citizens were free and happy to speak their minds, he often pointed out, as he urged them to participate in the free elections and exercise their rights as new citizens. *The Danish Pioneer* followed Danish politics closely in the late nineteenth century, too, so when the Danish workers were locked out of their factory jobs in a strike, Neble's paper collected more than $9,000 to aid the families of the workers.[16] Neble continued to press for changes that would lead to a restoration of civil liberties in Denmark, but his strongest emphasis was on American politics and living conditions among his readers. He raised funds for farmers struck by drought and other disasters. A large part of the newspaper was devoted to news of the several Danish-American settlements from coast to coast. A serialized novel ran in each issue, as was typical of American and European papers in this era. Ads filled only about 18 percent of the space, and these were fairly evenly divided among American, Danish, and Danish-American goods and services.[17]

The editor's opinion was often sought on places to settle and opportunities for work, and Neble delighted in advising the frequently critical Danes to send only their best sons and daughters, those that were willing to work hard, to the United States, where in a few years they would be able to own their own farms. He often had to defend fellow immigrants against the negative stories in the Danish press that characterized immigrants as European castoffs.[18]

As circulation grew steadily through the 1890s, Neble was able to add modern printing equipment and expand the number of pages in his newspaper. Eventually he bought his own building. Literary supplements and almanacs were offered, but he never added other newspapers to his business. His main competitor, Christian Rasmussen (1852–1926), did develop a small chain of Republican newspapers for Minneapolis, St. Paul, Chicago, and Racine in the 1880s and 1890s. Based in Minneapolis, this small "newspaper factory" attained a circulation of 22,500 for its four papers, along with the publication of books and three magazines, and the operation of an advertising agency.[19] *Ugebladet* (The weekly paper; 1881–1959), Rasmussen's original newspaper, was founded in Chicago in 1881 and moved to Minnesota. The others were *Racine Posten* (1905), *Chicago Posten* (1881), and *St. Paul Posten* (1902). They were merged into *Ugebladet* in 1915 and carried localized front and back pages. *Ugebladet*, too, divided its coverage among American, Danish, and Danish-American news. During election campaigns, Rasmussen laced the editorial pages with pictures and profiles of Republican candidates and urged his readers to vote and "vote Republican."[20]

Rasmussen, an affable and good businessman and an ardent Grundtvigian Lutheran, had many reasons for supporting his church's advocacy of retaining the Danish folk heritage, language, and culture in America. Neble, on the other hand, encouraged Americanization, citizenship, and English speaking. Neble, too, could be sentimental about Denmark, but he took the practical view when discussing the future of Danes in America. Rasmussen was one of the few Danes who joined the Norwegian-Danish Press Organization in America. Founded in St. Paul in 1895, primarily as a social club, it sponsored parties and travel excursions for members, and occasionally discussed the problems of running newspapers, especially during wartime. Despite their newspapers' declining circulations, these editors never reached an agreement on ways to combat the situation jointly. Individuality, not cooperativeness, was dominant among them.[21]

All of the Danish-American newspapers that managed to enjoy long lives were founded in the early days when immigration was at its highest. Typical of the urban weekly newspapers that started at this time were *Bien* (The bee; 1882-) of San Francisco, *Nordlyset* (The northern light; 1891–1953) of New York City, and *Revyen* (The review; 1895–1952) of Chicago. They were all local, community newspapers, unlike the Neble and Rasmussen papers, which circulated widely among Danes in Midwestern towns and farmlands.

Bien's editor in 1891, Sophus Hartwick, believed that his paper should be devoted strictly to serving the Danes on the West Coast with necessary information about the motherland, other Danish-American colonies, and the United States and its citizens. He did not intend to compete with the great daily newspapers which he believed covered American and world news adequately.[22] His ethnic-centered philosophy kept *Bien* publishing while other Danish newspapers in the West died. *Bien*'s front page rarely carried general news. It featured a serialized story, letters from readers, and other light items. Inside pages were devoted to news of the Danish communities in California. Not until pages 4 and 5 did readers find news from Denmark, Slesvig, and Norway. It was a formula that would become more typical as other papers in the twentieth century served the more ethnic, less immigrant communities.[23]

Several other Danish publications were started on the West Coast—in Los Angeles, San Francisco, Portland, Tacoma, and Spokane. In New York and Chicago, the urban weeklies served the ethnic neighborhoods but rarely attracted more than 5,000 subscribers. Most circulations hovered around 3,000. *Nordlyset*, in New York City, emphasized culture, drama, music, books, and intellectual discussion of politics and society. Fine-quality white paper instead of newsprint, delicately engraved drawings, and a refined style of writing bespoke its editor's breeding. Editor John Volk made no attempt to seek out readers. The paper would prosper if it was "well written and exhibited leadership qualities," he believed.[24] It attracted only a small portion of the 5,000 to 8,000 Danes in the city, mainly businessmen, lawyers, and professionals.[25]

Close at hand for those Danes who were quick to learn English were the sensational American dailies of Joseph Pulitzer and William Randolph Hearst, with million-a-day circulations that included thousands of immigrant readers. The immigrant city paper was left with the role of serving those who could not yet read English or who preferred to learn more about their fellow immigrants and the old homeland.[26] The rural immigrant newspapers, on the other hand, retained large audiences that needed general news and information as well as Danish-oriented news. The Neble and Rasmussen papers served these general information needs until well into the twentieth century.[27]

In Chicago, the most successful Danish newspaper was *Revyen*, founded by Christian Bøtker (1866–1946), a former teacher and journalist in Denmark. He started his independent socialist paper and brought its circulation to about 5,000 by World War I.[28] He offered political news and socialist arguments, local news and gossip, book reviews, and long letters from correspondents. His paper was not officially aligned with the Socialist Labor Party of America, which for a time did provide a Dano-Norwegian section in its Swedish-language *Skandinavisk Amerikanska Arbetaren* (The Scandinavian-American worker; 1894–1928).[29] In 1896 the Socialist Labor Party attempted a paper for Dano-Norwegians, *Arbej-*

deren (The worker), edited by John Glambeck, a Dane who lived in Chicago and sometimes wrote for *The Pioneer*. This paper lasted four years.[30]

Several specialized magazines were published for Danish-American readers at the turn of the century. They paralleled those available in English and provided features on personalities, travel, literature, homemaking, and humor. The largest were *Spøgefuglen* (The joking bird; 1893–1935) and *Kvinden og Hjemmet* (The woman and the home; 1888–1948?). The former was produced by Axel Kringleback, a jovial Dane who delighted in writing doggerel and political satire.[31]

The women's magazine was published by two sisters—a rarity in Danish-American journalism. The two, Mrs. Ida Hansen and Mina Jensen, were Norwegian-born, but Ida's husband was a Dane.[32] She edited the women's section of a small monthly publication for him, and when that folded after three years, she and Mina began their own magazine. Jensen set the type, while Hansen reported, wrote, and edited. They drove the forms of type by horse and wagon to a print shop in a nearby town until they acquired their own printing plant in Cedar Rapids, Iowa. The magazine grew from eight to fifty-six pages, with literary supplements. It had 80,000 subscribers. An English edition in 1906 lasted only a year, but a Swedish edition had a longer run. The magazine was similar to the popular American *Ladies' Home Journal* and often published translations of fiction from that magazine. It also contained features on people, places, food, clothing, homemaking, crafts, and beauty.

The immigrant church has been an important sustaining force in immigrant cultures, and one of its important activities has been publishing. Danish religious groups published newspapers, magazines, almanacs, hymnals, prayer books, children's magazines, and Christmas books.[33] About a third of the Danish immigrants were church members, most of them Lutheran. But there were large enough groups of Baptists, Seventh Day Adventists, and Mormons to support Danish-language publications for those groups as well as for the more numerous Lutherans.[34]

Because those known as the Grundtvigians celebrated old Danish literature, songs, and history as an important part of their religious life, their interest in retaining Danish language and culture was frequently expressed in church publications. Their newspaper, *Dannevirke* (1880–1951), founded in Iowa, was edited by a succession of pastors and laymen, and took up national as well as religious news and issues.

A split in the American Danish Lutheran Church left the larger Inner Mission group without a newspaper, so they began *Danskeren* (The Dane; 1892–1921) as a counterpart to *Dannevirke*. This newspaper was to be impartial and present news that was more suitable for its readers than a worldly paper like *The Pioneer*. Both Lutheran newspapers carried news and religious material, including sermons, church briefs, and letters, and both were heavily subsidized by their churches, so they carried little advertising.[35]

The early twentieth century brought good times for the stronger Danish immigrant newspapers, but the gradual shift to English speaking was well under way by World War I. The war and anti-immigrant pressure in the 1920s sped up the process. The Inner Mission Danes switched to English in church services in the 1920s, and the Grundtvigians did so in the 1940s.[36]

At the start of the twentieth century, only fifteen of the thirty-four Danish-language papers and twenty-four of the Dano-Norwegian–language papers remained that had been founded during the three previous decades.[37] During the first two decades of the new century, nine new publications appeared, but they soon died. In style, the Danish immigrant newspapers had changed little over the years. They were very gray in overall appearance, the result of long columns filled with small type and few headlines or illustrations. They looked like their older rural American or European ancestors of the mid-nineteenth century. But as rural free delivery service reached more and more of the countryside and as city newspapers and magazines found it easier to reach the farm population, the immigrant newspapers began to modernize. The war news and the shift to English reading at this time encouraged editors to drop the old German-style Gothic type and use the more modern roman type, and larger headlines and photographs became more typical after they had been introduced as a way of emphasizing the war news.

In these years, too, Sophus Neble was actively developing contacts between Denmark and America, serving as an unofficial ambassador on personal visits and discussing this "bridge building" in his newspaper articles. He spent hours advising Danes who asked his opinion on emigration. In 1909 he supported the purchase by Danish-Americans of park land in the Rebild hills near Aalborg, Denmark, where Danes and American Danes could celebrate the American Independence Day. In the 1920s he encouraged the movement by Chicago Danes to establish a Danish worldwide migration archive in Aalborg. And in 1925 Neble was knighted for his services to Denmark.[38]

The Danish-American newspapers frequently carried stories of Danish achievements in America and reviews of new books on such subjects as the immigrants' experiences. The newspapers also paid close attention to the war in Europe. Danes were vigorous critics of the Prussians. Bøtker's socialist newspaper criticized the American Socialist Party's policy on the war, and Bøtker joined in the anti-German criticism. In all the Danish immigrant newspapers Liberty Loan advertisements and patriotic articles explaining American policies and the war effort could be found. The activities of patriotic groups which sprang up at the urging of the government's Committee on Public Information were proudly displayed. The ethnic press played an important role in publishing propaganda and vital information that the government wished to get to its non–English-speaking citizens in a nation at war.[39]

The 1920s brought the end of an era for the Danish-American press. Wartime shortages and inflation were hard on small businesses. Campaigns of fear and distrust, aimed mainly at German-Americans but wounding all immigrant groups to some extent, speeded up Americanization. Speaking English and behaving like an American were considered signs of loyalty, many believed, and nativists pressed this issue forcefully. Some states proposed laws to forbid the use of foreign languages in church, public places, and publications.[40]

The immigrant editor had a difficult task in these years, according to Neble. He had to encourage American patriotism and loyalty, and also explain the situation in Denmark. At the same time he fought to maintain the right to free speech and press against a raging nativism.[41] And he had to take a stand on the new immigration quota proposals that would limit all groups, while aimed at stemming the flow of those from Southern and Eastern Europe.

Neble, ever the realist, expected that the future of the foreign-language press was limited in America, and he anticipated a time not far distant when such papers would no longer be needed. Most Danish immigrants and their children learned English. With quotas that severely cut immigration, the need for a second-language press seemed to be diminishing. His readership was aging, Neble knew, but he saw this as natural and right. As these changes occurred, Neble and other immigrant editors altered the content of their newspapers to emphasize the news from the Danish-American settlements and Denmark and to de-emphasize news of the United States and American politics. Ads became more ethnic, featuring foods, restaurants, and professional services by Danish-trained lawyers and other specialists. By 1930 only eight Danish immigrant newspapers remained, and the 1940s and 1950s brought more closures.[42]

The old editors died—Rasmussen in 1926 and Neble in 1931. *Ugebladet* limped along for a few years under new management, which turned it into an English-language tabloid called *The Midwest Scandinavian*. It ceased publication in 1959; not even the new features and travel ads could save it. *Nordlyset* ceased publication in 1953 after attempting a tabloid style and English summaries plus special columns for women. *Revyen* in Chicago turned into an ethnic paper that celebrated Danishness and nostalgia, and was renamed *Dansk Tidende* (Danish news). It closed in 1952, handing over its circulation list to the venerable *Pioneer*.

The two Lutheran-supported newspapers also ceased publication: *Danskeren* in 1921 and *Dannevirke* in 1951. But the churches continued some of their religious publications in Danish and in English, and when the Grundtvigians lost their church page with the closure of *Dannevirke*, they started a new bilingual church paper, *Kirke og Folk* (Church and life) intended for older church members who still read Danish.[43] In 1983 it took the English name but remained bilingual.

Death and consolidations left *Bien* and *The Danish Pioneer* alone in the secular newspaper field in the 1960s. *Bien* scarcely altered its philosophy over the decades, paying attention to its California Danish communities and remaining in the hands of one publishing family after the original editor retired in 1930. *Bien* was modernized as a tabloid in 1970.[44]

The Danish Pioneer continued its interest in politics and news, running strong editorials throughout World War II. A peaceful postwar period brought increased opportunities for European travel, and *The Danish Pioneer* benefited from this new source of advertising and feature material.[45] The newspaper was saved from extinction in 1958 when a group of Danes in Chicago purchased it from the Neble family and brought it to Chicago, where Hjalmar Bertelsen became editor.

He introduced the tabloid format and completed the shift to a community, ethnic orientation. There would be few editorials thereafter, except on ethnic matters. Most of the sixteen pages of the tabloid were filled with reports from Danish groups and clubs in their communities in California, Chicago, Michigan, Minneapolis, Nebraska, Wisconsin, and New York. Circulation and advertising slowly stabilized and then grew, and some material appeared in English. Bertelsen and the Chicago Danes carried on the paper as a kind of cultural mission, and Bertelsen was knighted by the Danish government in 1960 for his efforts. *The Danish Pioneer* celebrated its centennial in 1972 and, as Bertelsen said, "As long as people want to read about their Danish affairs, the paper will continue."[46]

By the 1980s, *Bien* and *The Danish Pioneer* each registered circulations of around 5,000 and had raised their subscription rates substantially to keep up with rising postal charges. Journalists in Denmark took an interest, and through organizations in both countries it was arranged to send student interns from Denmark's journalist training school to serve as apprentices on the American newspapers, starting in 1978. The newspapers benefited from that fresh editorial talent and began providing more news and features about contemporary Denmark.

Under its new editor, Chris Steffensen, who assumed the position just before Bertelsen died in 1981, *The Danish Pioneer* has taken on a livelier look in the 1980s and runs more current political and cultural news about Denmark, as well as more items in English, although Danish still predominates.[47] A 1983 reader survey indicated that the paper's 12,000 to 15,000 readers want more Danish news and more English items. But the readers are an aging group: 68 percent are fifty or older. Only 4 percent are thirty or under. They are loyal readers, though, because 41 percent have subscribed for more than a decade.[48]

The ethnic revival in America in the 1980s stimulated Danish-Americans to new efforts at cooperation in recapturing their past. An inventory of immigrant sources for research was undertaken, and an immigrant museum is being designed for Elk Horn, Iowa, where the local community had already imported a Danish windmill. The Danes on the West Coast started a national historical organization, the Danish American Heritage Society, which has supported these national ethnic efforts through its journal, *The Bridge*, since 1977. Perhaps because the assimilation of Danes into American life has been relatively easy, the old religious-based frictions have been smoothed out so that their descendants will be able to find ways to share their common heritage in America.[49]

The death of the immigrant press, especially for those groups that came to America in the nineteenth century from Northern and Western Europe, has frequently been predicted. But the papers have not all died. The Danish experience indicates that an ability to change and grow along with the immigrant community makes it possible for the press to live on as long as there is a shred of ethnic distinctiveness to enjoy.[50]

NOTES

1. Marion Tuttle Marzolf, *The Danish-Language Press in America* (New York: Arno Press, Inc., 1979), p. 29.

2. Enok Mortensen, "The Danish-American Press," in Johannes Knudsen, ed., *The Danish-American Immigrant: Phases of His Religion and Culture* (Des Moines: Grand View College, 1950), p. 42.

3. Johannes B. Wist, ed., "Den Norsk-Amerikanske Presse," in *Norsk-Amerika-nernes Festskrift* (Decorah, Iowa: Symra Co., 1914), pp. 9–40.

4. Leola Nelson Bergmann, *Americans from Norway* (Philadelphia: J. B. Lippincott Co., 1950), pp. 171–179.

5. *Emigranten*, January 23, 1852.

6. Morris Salmonsen, *Brogede Minder* (Copenhagen: Gyldendal, 1913), p. 55.

7. Ibid., p. 66.

8. *Scandinavia*, 1883–1886. Copies are available at the Minnesota Historical Society and the Library of Congress.

9. Salmonsen, *Brogede*, p. 71.

10. Marzolf, *Danish-Language Press*, p. 44.

11. *Den Danske Pioneer*, September 19, 1901; N. W. Ayre, *Directory of Newspapers and Periodicals for 1914*.

12. Based on the author's content analysis survey of the major Danish-American newspapers over a hundred-year period. Marzolf, *Danish-Language Press*, chap. 7, 8.

13. Sophus K. Winther, *Take All to Nebraska* (New York: Macmillan, 1936), p. 8.

14. Marion T. Marzolf, "The Danish Immigrant Newspaper: Old Friend in a New Land," paper presented at From Scandinavia to America Conference, September 1983, Copenhagen, Denmark. To be published in Conference Report by the Economic History Department of the University of Copenhagen.

15. *Den Danske Pioneer*, December 23, 1886. For detailed discussion of this case, see Marzolf, *Danish-Language Press*, pp. 59–73.

16. *Den Danske Pioneer*, June 29, 1899.

17. Marzolf, *Danish-Language Press*, chap. 7.

18. *Den Danske Pioneer*, August 23, 1900.

19. C. Rasmussen, "Autobiographical Sketch," *Julegrenen*, December 1906.

20. *Ugebladet*, November 1, 1900.

21. The records of the Norwegian-Danish Press Organization are housed at the Nor-wegian-American Historical Association Archives, Northfield, Minnesota.

22. *Bien*, July 26, 1901.

23. Ibid., September 17, 1896.

24. *Politiken*, May 5, 1904.

25. See U. S. Census of 1890 and 1910, and Marzolf, *Danish-Language Press*, p. 96.

26. Marzolf, *Danish-Language Press*, p. 96.

27. Ibid., p. 98.

28. Circulation figures are from N. W. Ayer & Son, *American Newspaper Annual and Directory*, for appropriate years.

29. Michael Brook, "Radical Literature in Swedish America: A Narrative Survey," *The Swedish Pioneer Quarterly* 20 (July 1969): 113–115.

30. *Arbejderen*, January 26 and February 16, 1899.

31. *Spøgefuglen*, vol. 1, no. 1, November 15, 1893.

32. Wist, *Norsk*, pp. 160–161.

33. Marzolf, *Danish-Language Press*, p. 108.

34. Ibid., pp. 114–116.

35. *Dannevirke*, January 4, 1905. The name *Dannevirke* is that given to the thousand-year-old defense line along the southern border of Danish Slesvig (or Schlesvig in English).

36. *Danskeren*, June 30, 1892. For a complete discussion of the loss of language and Americanization of the Danish Lutherans, see Paul C. Nyholm, *The Americanization of the Danish Lutheran Churches in America* (Copenhagen: Institute for Danish Church History, 1963).

37. Marzolf, *Danish-Language Press*, p. 117.

38. *Den Danske Pioneer*, September 23, 1926.

39. Ibid., February 16, 1922.

40. Marzolf, *Danish-Language Press*, pp. 143–154.

41. *Den Danske Pioneer*, July 26, 1917.

42. Marzolf, *Danish-Language Press*, pp. 154–75.

43. Letter from Reverend Thorvald Hansen, editor of *Kirke og Folk*, dated June 15, 1983, to the author.

44. Marzolf, *Danish-Language Press*, pp. 175–176.

45. Ibid., pp. 176–178.

46. *Berlingske Tidende*, May 9, 1969.

47. Letter from Chris Steffensen, managing editor, *Den Denske Pioneer*, dated June 30, 1983, to the author.

48. *Den Danske Pioneer*, September 6, 1982.

49. The Danish Immigrant Archival Listing at Grand View College's Danish Immigrant Archives, Des Moines, Iowa 50316, has a complete listing of the location of extant collections of Danish-American newspapers as well as records of other groups and individuals. Thorvald Hansen is the archivist. The Danish-American Heritage Society headquarters are at 29672 Dane Lane, Junction City, Oregon 97448.

50. Joshua Fishman, *Language Loyalty in the United States* (The Hague: Mouton & Co., 1966), pp. 52–74.

BIBLIOGRAPHY

Knudsen, Johannes. *The Danish-American Immigrant: Phases of His Religion and Culture*. Des Moines: Grand View College, 1950.

Marzolf, Marion Tuttle. *The Danish-Language Press in America*. New York: Arno Press, Inc., 1979.

Salmonsen, Morris. *Brogede Minder*. Copenhagen: Gyldendal, 1913.

Skaardal, Dorothy Burton. *The Divided Heart: Scandinavian Immigrant Experience through Literary Sources*. Lincoln: University of Nebraska Press, 1974.

Stephenson, George M. "The Mind of the Scandinavian Immigrant." *Norwegian-American Studies* 4. Northfield, Minn., 1929.

6

The Dutch Press

LINDA PEGMAN DOEZEMA

Not unlike the publications of other foreign-language groups in the United States, the life story of the Dutch ethnic press parallels the story of Dutch immigration to the United States and is closely correlated to the acculturation process by which immigrant groups become ethnic groups. As argued by scholars of the ethnic press,[1] the function of these publications varies as the immigrant group works its way through the acculturation and assimilation process and displays decreasing dependence on the publications.

In his study of the immigrant press, Robert E. Park found thirteen Dutch-language publications in existence in 1920.[2] Joshua Fishman, Robert Hayden, and Mary Warshauer note that in 1930 non–English-language publications were still in the majority, but by 1960 English-language publications were in the majority among papers serving Americans of Dutch descent.[3] In 1979, out of sixteen Dutch ethnic publications, only one was published solely in Dutch and three were using Dutch and English.[4]

The Dutch ethnic press has not had a stable existence. Out of approximately 105 publications that came into existence between 1849 and 1979, 87 either died, merged into other Dutch ethnic publications, or became general and non-ethnic periodicals. Of the sixteen remaining publications only five were published prior to World War I: *The Banner, Church Herald* (formerly *The Leader*), *Missionary Monthly* (formerly *De Heidenwereld*), *New Horizons* (originally *Holland Home News*), and *De Wachter* (The watchman). Nine of the sixteen were begun between World Wars I and II. Since the ethnic press was a product of immigration and because its persistence is, to some extent, based upon new arrivals,[5] the instability of the Dutch-American press may be partly attributed to the fact that Dutch immigration has been sporadic, taking place for the most part in several major waves rather than in a continuous flow.

Another destabilizing factor to be considered is the rate at which the immigrants discontinued the use of the Dutch language. These transplants were encouraged both by the preceding emigrants who greeted them in America and by the American economic and political structures to become Americanized. This process included learning English. It was the church that was the key to Dutch language retention. When the Dutch language disappeared in the churches, most of the Dutch-language publications also disappeared.

Despite the instability of their press, it appears that the Hollanders in the United States have supported more of these publications than their numbers would warrant. In 1970, with 110,000 first-generation immigrants and 273,000 of the second generation, the Dutch ranked only eighteenth in size among American immigrant groups. Although small, the group's visibility has been significant primarily because of its "clustering" patterns.[6] Traditionally, Dutch Americans have been known for their clannishness: forming their own settlements or settling in self-contained neighborhoods; adhering primarily to a Dutch Calvinist religious identity sustained by a network of churches, schools, and other associations; maintaining strong family bonds; marrying within their ethnic group; and often employing from within the group. This social and religious structure has allowed for gradual acculturation but has not enhanced assimilation. The group's press perpetuated the use of the Dutch language, maintained contacts between the various Dutch communities, served as a forum for theological issues, brought news from the Netherlands, and introduced the American political scene (which became of great interest, particularly on the local level).

IMMIGRATION HISTORY

Recent scholars of Dutch-American history[7] talk of three phases of emigration: the colonial or commercial phase of the seventeenth century; the great, free, or new immigration of the nineteenth and early twentieth centuries; and the post–World War II or planned migration.

The first major surge of Dutch immigration to North America took place during the Netherlands' seventeenth-century colonial expansion. The formation of the colony of New Netherland was primarily a commercial venture most significantly involving fur-trading activities. New Netherland never became a large colony. The area attracted religious refugees, the unemployed, the poverty-stricken, and adventurers. Most who came hoped for quick profits that would provide them with social prominence when they returned to their homeland.

Although New Netherland fell to the British in 1664, the Dutch continued to be a distinct subculture, maintaining their Dutch Reformed churches and, to some extent, the use of the Dutch language. An elementary school education was available through the churches, with any further formal education reserved for prospective clergymen.

The Dutch Bible, religious manuals, and devotional materials constituted the typical library in the colonial Dutch home. These Dutchmen contributed very little to the literary-cultural scene in colonial America, and very few Dutch books were published in the American colonies. While newspapers had not yet become prominent anywhere, "one of the weaknesses of the Hudson Valley immigration, from the point of view of the spread of Dutch culture, had been that a printing press was never established by it on American soil during the whole of the four decades of occupation."[8] In contrast, the Pennsylvania Germans were supporting two German newspapers by the 1740s.

The second wave of immigrants, who began to arrive in 1846, received considerable assistance from the colonial Dutch Americans, many of whom were successful businessmen and local political leaders, and who to some extent held to the same religious traditions and understood the Dutch language.

This second emigration has been linked to two factors. Pressures of population growth in the Netherlands and a depressed Dutch economy, coinciding with a dissident movement within the Netherlands Reformed Church (the state church) confronted many impoverished people with social and official discrimination. This wave of emigration was a mass movement of neighborhoods, congregations, and kinship groups led by ministers and priests. These groups established farming communities primarily in Michigan; Iowa; the Dakotas; and the fringe areas of Paterson, New Jersey; Chicago; and Milwaukee.

In the twentieth century, the Great Depression and World War II virtually halted Dutch immigration to the United States. The third phase of immigration began immediately after World War II. Due to conditions in the postwar Netherlands, the Dutch government began an active emigration program, encouraging and assisting resettlement abroad. Because of the numerical restrictions of the quota system enacted by the United States Congress in the 1920s, only 3,136 Dutchmen were allowed into the United States annually. Over 40,000 were on the waiting list by 1952. Many Dutch emigrants opted for Canada, Australia, South Africa, New Zealand, and elsewhere. This postwar emigration dwindled after 1953 as conditions in the Netherlands improved.

The postwar immigrants to the United States were primarily Calvinists, with a small influx of Dutch Roman Catholics. The already established Dutch ethnic communities attracted the majority of the Calvinist immigrants, with the Dutch Catholics assimilating into multi-ethnic Catholic parishes.

For the immigrants of all of these phases, the church (the Reformed Church in America and its offshoot, the Christian Reformed Church) was the key to the strong community spirit. Their Calvinist theology went beyond their church life into their homes, communities, workplaces, schools, and politics.

The religious factor also encouraged the retention of the Dutch language. The English takeover of New Netherland in 1664 imposed some language changes for the colonial Dutch. But within their churches they persisted in the use of Dutch for almost a century. In 1794 English became the official language of the Dutch Reformed churches, and by the mid–1800s new arrivals were received by Dutch Americans who knew only a little of their mother tongue.

The immigrants of the second phase established their own congregations using, of course, the Dutch language. English was used early on for business and political activities, but the Dutch language remained prevalent in the churches until World War I, a crucial turning point in Dutch language usage. Not wanting to be confused with Germans or to appear unpatriotic, the Dutch immigrants put aside many of their ethnic ways, including their use of the Dutch language. At that time it all but disappeared in the churches, while it persisted longer in the homes, with the second and third generations corrupting it into a conversational blend called Yankee Dutch.

THE PRESS: FORMAT AND CONTENT

The fragmentary character of Dutch immigration, their clustering settlement patterns, strong kinship and friendship ties, religious traditions and commitments, fervent interest in politics, and the newspaper tradition brought from the Netherlands are all essential to an understanding of the Dutch ethnic press.

The Dutch immigrant publications brought news from the native land and information about friends and relatives who had settled elsewhere in the United States. The press also served as a forum for political and theological discussions, provided local advertising in a language that the immigrants could understand, and announced and reported on marriages, births, deaths, and church activities.

Harry Boonstra provides a comprehensive analysis of the content of the Dutch-American press in Michigan—Dutch-language, mixed-language, and English-language publications.[9] Generally speaking, the characteristics of those publications produced outside of Michigan (the largest concentration of nineteenth-century Dutch immigrants settled in Western Michigan) were essentially the same, since the Dutch communities in Iowa, Chicago, Wisconsin, and elsewhere were similar, though smaller.

Dutch ethnic journalism appeared primarily in two formats, with some overlap between the two. One category was newspapers. Varying in content, depth of coverage, and quality, the newspapers often included items that were concerned with church activities and with moral, religious, or theological issues. The second type included journals and magazines that were predominantly religious, although several of the postwar publications were (and still are) fraternally sponsored and more secular in content. Often included in the religious periodicals were denominational and church news, coverage of church controversies, obituaries, and notices of marriages and other social events. Despite the overlap, each of these categories has within it some distinctive as well as common features.

To generalize, the content of the Dutch-American newspapers included everything from trivial items, local gossip, and poorly written poetry to lengthy articles and editorials on theologically abstract issues and significant national and international political topics.

That local political news was covered in detail is not surprising, since the nineteenth- and twentieth-century Dutch immigrants tended to form their own relatively self-contained communities. Interest and involvement in local politics were undoubtedly self-serving. Particularly between the Civil War and World War I, the Hollanders were numerically strong enough only within their communities to affect the political scene significantly.

National politics received considerable editorial coverage, especially in election years. The coverage of the international scene was, not surprisingly, often limited to the news and politics of the Netherlands, although news from other areas was covered from time to time.

Perhaps the one non-American event that aroused the greatest emotional response in the Dutch ethnic press was the Boer War (1899–1902).[10] The coverage, without exception, sided with the Boers (the Dutch emigrant farmers of South Africa) and condemned the British cause. Not only were the Boers fellow Dutchmen, the English were long-standing rivals of the Dutch. For this three-year period the newspapers published detailed accounts of battles, reported pro-Boer activities being carried on by Dutch Americans, and ran fictional and poetic pieces celebrating the Boer cause.[11]

The other major international event that stirred feelings and produced a sustained journalistic effort was World War I. The Dutch ethnic press in this period documents the progression in the shift from anti-British (left over from the Boer War) and pro-German sentiments to allegiance to the Allied cause. The change in attitude was by no means smooth, and the lack of uniform sentiment is evident in the press.[12] By the time the United States entered the war, the Dutch ethnic press was supporting the Allies. Boonstra speculates that governmental uneasiness and general American distrust of anything foreign at this time was at least partly responsible for this journalistic shift.[13]

Generally speaking, Boonstra found that in some Michigan papers as much as a third of the news was about the Netherlands.[14] Reporters were rarely employed. English-language newspapers, publications from other Dutch-American settlements, and newspapers from the Netherlands were subscribed to by the editors. Selected items about state, national, or international affairs were translated to Dutch when necessary and either reprinted or digested, as were the news items from other Dutch immigrant communities and news from the Netherlands.

News of church and denominational activities and editorials about theological issues occupied a prominent place in Dutch-American newspapers. Contributed poetry was often religious or devotional. The editorials were most often discussions of moral or religious topics. Political issues dominated at election time. It appears that, for these Dutch transplants, controversy was part of their nature and life style. Religion and politics appear to be two areas in which these minimally to moderately educated immigrants schooled themselves and felt obligated to express their opinions. Boonstra notes, "Their journalistic ethics did not exclude a large dose of bickering, namecalling, and rash accusations."[15]

One such controversy, which overlapped the moral, religious, and political spheres, was Prohibition. When Prohibition legislation was being heatedly discussed in many American circles in 1853, the Dutch ethnic press opposed the antiliquor laws with little or no debate.[16] A strictly religious, but temperate people, these Dutchmen felt that this was a social, not a theological, issue, and that Prohibition would not solve the problems of immorality and would prohibit the use of wine for sacramental purposes. The press supported controlled sale and moderate use.[17] But in the early 1900s, Prohibition issues became controversial copy for the Dutch ethnic press. Now the issues were saloons, drinking, and drunkenness. Drunkenness was condemned; frequenting saloons warranted disapproval. But drinking and Prohibition were debatable: personal and Christian liberty versus public decency, evils of drink and brotherly or Christian love.[18] The press chewed on these issues for years, with church and community leaders supplying much of the writing.

Letters submitted by readers covered a wide range of topics. Boonstra found that "the lack of sophistication found in the [reader-contributed] poetry stands in sharp contrast with the theological acumen displayed in the readers' columns."[19]

Within the Dutch ethnic religious press, there were two types of publications: magazines published by the denominations, and theological periodicals. The denominational publications were chiefly devoted to covering church and denominational news, to providing devotional material and inspirational counsel, and to guiding the church members in theological matters.

The theological journals were primarily concerned with doctrinal issues and theological concerns. Doctrinal controversies were for both the denominational and theological periodicals "meaty" substance to present to their readers.

THE NEWSPAPERS

The Dutch-American community was never able to support a daily newspaper; most were weeklies. The first successful weekly paper was the Dutch-language *De Sheboygan Nieuwsbode* (The Sheboygan news messenger), published out of Sheboygan, Wisconsin; its first issue appeared in October 1849. *De Sheboygan Nieuwsbode* notes two other Dutch newspapers introduced at about the same time, neither of which lasted very long: *De Volksvriend* (The friend of the people), published in Grand Rapids, Michigan, which failed after only a few issues (no known extant copies); and *De Nederlander in Noord-Amerika* (The Dutchman in North America), published in New York City by land speculators apparently preying on new Dutch arrivals.[20]

De Sheboygan Nieuwsbode was born out of the determination of Jacob Quintus who, after a couple of unsuccessful publishing attempts, chose the central location of Sheboygan. It was hoped that the paper would serve all Dutch-American immigrants and that the growing Dutch settlements in Iowa, Illinois, Wisconsin, and Michigan would support it through subscriptions. The intent was to provide U. S. and Netherlands news for the Dutch-speaking population. The newspaper did succeed and even acquired subscribers from the Netherlands. The title changed to *De Nieuwsbode* (The news messenger) in 1855, and it merged with the German-language *Sheboygan Zeitung* (Sheboygan newspaper; ceased publication in 1927) in 1860.

Within a year or so of *De Nieuwsbode*'s inception, Dutch newspapers began appearing in the various settlements scattered in the Midwest. In 1850 the Michigan settlement saw the beginning of *De Hollander* (The Dutchman), a product of a two-year effort on the part of Reverend Albertus C. Van Raalte, leader in the founding of the Holland, Michigan, settlement. Initially the newspaper appeared in English and in Dutch. In 1852 the paper changed from a commercial publication by an established firm to an enterprise whose editor and publisher was a member of Van Raalte's congregation. In 1856 the paper began using the Dutch language exclusively. There were difficulties over the years. The editor and Van Raalte had clashed over religious and denominational issues. Since *De Hollander* endorsed the Democratic Party throughout its entire existence, at times the readers were alienated by the editor's political views. The paper lasted until 1895.

In 1852 Giles Van der Wall began publishing *De Nederlander* (The Dutchman) out of Kalamazoo. Since *De Hollander* was Democratic, the intent of this new publication was to provide a newspaper for those Dutchmen who preferred the platform of the Whig Party. This publication appears to have lasted only until the November 1852 election.

In general, prior to the Civil War the Dutch immigrants were strongly Democratic.[21] It was suspected that the Whigs and Republicans had anti-foreigner leanings, and it was believed that the Democratic Party was more sympathetic to local improvements for the frontier settlements.

Jacob Quintus, having sold *De Nieuwsbode*, started the first Dutch newspaper in Grand Rapids, Michigan: *De Stoompost* (*De Amerikaansche Stoompost*; The American steamer). Begun in 1858 or 1859, it suspended publication around 1866. This paper never fared well, probably because of the close proximity of *De Hollander* and *De Grondwet* (The constitution).

One of the most influential and popular of the Dutch ethnic papers, *De Grondwet*, had a large circulation not only in the Michigan settlements but in the Dutch communities throughout the United States. The Dutch paper with the longest continual existence, it was founded in support of the Republican Party and continued this allegiance until its end in 1938. Begun by Jan Roost in 1860, this newspaper became the property of Leendert Mulder (initially its apprentice printer) by 1868 and remained in the Mulder family estate. A weekly published in Holland, Michigan, *De Grondwet* claimed about 1,200 subscribers in 1874 and reportedly had at least 8,000 readers in 1907.[22]

The Republican Party began finding more support among the Dutch immigrants in the late 1850s, and by the end of the Civil War a majority of Dutch immigrants were Republicans. The slavery issue was undoubtedly the cause for the swing in party affiliation, since the Democratic Party tended to be pro-slavery in sentiment.[23] The shift in party loyalty was not unanimous. Many considered slavery to be a sectional issue, and long-standing loyalty to the Democratic Party was not easily relinquished. Thus, opposing opinions supplied copy for *De Hollander* and *De Grondwet* during the late 1850s, with *De Hollander* losing strength after the war.

In 1868 *Vrijheids Banier* (Freedom's banner) first appeared in Grand Rapids; it survived to 1900. The Grand Rapids community also produced a number of short-lived newspapers like *De Nieuwsbode* (The news messenger; 1878), *De Nieuwe Courant* (The newspaper; 1884), and *De Bannier des Volks* (The banner of the people; 1888). The most successful of the Grand Rapids Dutch papers was *De Standaard* (The standard). This paper first appeared in 1875, merged with *The Bulletin* in 1918, and continued as *Standard-Bulletin* until 1943. What little is known about it has been gleaned from secondary sources, since extant files are scant. The paper was founded by J. Van Strien and Dennis Schram and was biweekly for most of its existence. Its political stance varied. In the few surviving issues of *De Standaard* religious items are absent, but in surviving issues of *Standard-Bulletin* church news and religious issues are prominent. *De Standaard* was published in the Dutch language; *Standard-Bulletin* used English and Dutch.

Except for Holland's *De Hollander* and *De Grondwet* and Grand Rapids's *Standard-Bulletin* and its forerunner, very few Dutch journalistic attempts in Michigan were successful. Kalamazoo had two papers, *De Hollandsche Amerikaan* (The Dutch American; 1890–1945) and *De Teekenen der Tijden* (The signs of the times; 1917–1945). Short-lived Dutch newspapers were also produced in Detroit (*De Detroitenaar* [The Detroiter]) and in Muskegon (*De Volksvriend* [The friend of the people]).

In Pella, Iowa, the Dutch community's leader, Reverend H. P. Scholte, entered a partnership with Edwin H. Grant in 1855 and began the weekly known as *The Pella Gazette*. From its inception this paper was Republican in politics and was published in English, with Dutch items appearing on a fairly regular basis. The paper had financial problems for most of its existence, and in 1860 it ceased. During the brief life of *The Pella Gazette*, Scholte made a few attempts to start a Dutch-language paper.

In 1860 Iowa saw the beginnings of its first Dutch-language newspaper. Henry Hospers and Reverend Pieter Oggel, with ten shareholders, purchased *The Pella Gazette*'s equipment and began *Pella's Weekblad* (Pella's weekly). Democratic in politics, the newspaper had a good deal of support from the Iowa Dutch and served Pella and Marion counties until 1942. It is considered to have been among the largest and most successful of the Dutch-language newspapers in the United States, ranking with Michigan's *De Grondwet* and *De Standaard*.

For the Iowa Dutch Republicans, the *Pella Blade* was established in 1865. An English-language paper, it lasted about twenty years. *De Pella Gazette*, Republican and Dutch-language, began in 1867 and died within two years.

Dutch settlements in northwestern Iowa (primarily in Sioux County) were established beginning in 1869. The enterprising Henry Hospers appeared on the scene in 1874, beginning publication of *De Volksvriend* (The friend of the people). Despite financial difficulties (these Dutch settlements were nearly devastated by a grasshopper visitation), Hospers persisted. By the early 1900s, *De Volksvriend* was operating profitably and was serving the newer settlements in Kansas, Nebraska, Minnesota, and the Dakotas. *De Volksvriend* was published in Orange City until 1951. During this time two other newspapers appeared in northwestern Iowa: *De Vrije Hollander* (The free Hollander) and the *Sioux Center Nieuwsblad* (Sioux Center newspaper). Neither enjoyed the wide geographical support or the long continuous existence of *De Volksvriend*.

Although there were as many as 6,000 Dutch living in the Chicago area in 1870, the first attempt at journalism came in the 1880s: *De Nederlander*, a weekly published by J. Esnorff. In 1893 this paper was bought by *De Grondwet* of Holland, Michigan; it ceased to be published under the title *De Nederlander* and was replaced by a Chicago edition of *De Grondwet*.

In the East there were two settlements of Dutch that were compact enough to support newspapers. In the Paterson, New Jersey area *De Telegraaf* (The telegraph) was published from 1882 to 1921, and *Het Oosten* (The East) from 1904 to 1940. The Rochester Dutchmen were served by the *Holland American*, which in its later years included a good share of English-language material.

There were efforts to publish Dutch newspapers in the Dakotas, but with very little success. *De Nederlandsche Dakotiaan* (The Dutch Dakotan), published in Douglas County, South Dakota, served the Dakota Hollanders for approximately two years (1884–1885?). From 1884 to 1887 the *Harrison Globe* published some of its advertisements in Dutch and had a "Hollandsch Gedeelte" (Dutch section) with local and Netherlands news. *De Harrison Bode* (The Harrison messenger) first appeared in 1887, the product of Jan Hospers, son of Iowa Dutch journalist Henry Hospers. This paper was moved from Harrison to Springfield, became *De Springfield Bode* (The Springfield messenger), and ended with Jan Hospers's death in 1900 or 1901. The Dutch population in the Dakotas was never large enough to support a newspaper for any extended period. Also, the three Dutch-language newspapers that tried to serve the area had stiff competition from the successful Orange City *De Volksvriend*.

In Wisconsin, Dutch journalistic efforts were not much more successful than in the Dakotas. *De Sheboygan Nieuwsbode*, the first of the Dutch ethnic presses in the United States, lasted a little over ten years (October 1849-May 1860). In 1859 *De Ware Burger* (The true citizen) appeared in Sheboygan County as a Democratic paper. It moved to Waupun, became Republican, and ceased late in 1859. *De Alto Demokraat* (The Alto Democrat; no extant issues) also had a brief life span.

The Dutch Catholic newspapers had an even more difficult time sustaining themselves. Their audience was smaller than the Dutch Protestant numbers and was more scattered geographically. *De Pere Standaard* (1878), *Onze Standaard* (Our standard; 1896–1907), and *De Volksstem* (1890–1919) were their three publications, all published in De Pere, Wisconsin. *De Volksstem* (The people's voice) merged with *De Gazette van Moline* (The gazette of Moline; Flemish), which later merged with *Gazette van Detroit* (gazette of Detroit; also Flemish). The latter two publications remained Flemish and presumably had little content that would have appealed to the Dutch Catholics.

THE RELIGIOUS PRESS

The religious life of the Dutch Protestants in the United States was (and still is) primarily centered in two major denominations and several smaller ones. The Reformed Church in America dates to 1628 and the colonial Dutch of the New York area. When the second group of Dutch immigrants arrived in the 1840s, the established Reformed Church (still concentrated in the East) welcomed these fellow Calvinists and soon invited the newly formed midwestern churches to affiliate with their denomination. The union became official in 1850. In 1857 four congregations rejected the union and formed what is today the Christian Reformed Church, the second major Dutch Protestant denomination.

Most of the religious publications that are part of the Dutch ethnic press have been sponsored by these two groups. The well-established eastern sector of the Reformed Church began publishing *The Magazine of the Reformed Dutch Protestant Church* in 1826 in New Brunswick, New Jersey. In 1830 this publication became the *Christian Intelligencer* and was published solely in English. It had little appeal for those Reformed churches established by the midwestern immigrants of the 1840s.

To serve these Dutch-speaking churches, Jan Binnekant of Holland, Michigan, began the publication *De Verzamelaar* (The collector) in 1862. In 1865 this weekly changed its name to *De Hope* (The hope) and became the property of Hope College (founded in 1851 by the Reformed churches in the Midwest), whose faculty directed its policies. This Dutch-language church publication served the Reformed Church in the Midwest until 1933.

The Reformed Church in the Midwest did not have an English-language publication until 1906. Published in Grand Rapids, Michigan, *The Leader* merged with the *Christian Intelligencer* in 1934 to form the *Intelligencer-Leader*. In 1944 this publication changed its title to the *Church Herald*, and to this day it serves as the official magazine of the Reformed Church in America.

In 1866 a small group in the East which had seceded from the Reformed Church in 1822 began publishing *The Banner of Truth*. The Christian Reformed Church, which seceded from the Reformed Church in 1857, identified with this group for a short while and eventually assumed responsibility for the publication. In 1903 a group of Grand Rapids businessmen bought the publication, and in 1907 its name was changed to *The Banner*. By 1915 the Christian Reformed Church claimed it as its official English-language magazine, and *The Banner* remains its official organ today.

De Wachter (The watchman) was begun in 1868 to defend the existence of the True Dutch Reformed Church (the earliest name of the Christian Reformed Church). Almost every article and letter in its earliest issues was devoted to a defense of the 1857 split with the Reformed Church or was a response or critique of articles appearing in *De Hope* (the official Reformed Church publication). By 1875 the Christian Reformed Church claimed *De Wachter* as its official publication. (Its English-language sister, *The Banner*, did not become the church's official paper until 1915.) By the 1890s *De Wachter* had laid aside its defensiveness and was devoting itself to church news, theological discussions, and weekly devotional material, in much the same manner as *The Banner*. *De Wachter* continues to be the Christian Reformed Church's Dutch-language magazine, and its content remains similar to that of the turn of the century.

Apart from denominational publications, the Dutch-American religious press also included publications that attempted to combine news and a Reformed theology, theological journals, magazines with mission news, and publications supporting the Christian day school movement.

Perhaps the most influential and significant of these publications was *De Gids* (The guide; 1885–1911), an example of a Dutch immigrant publication which crossed lines between a newspaper and a religious publication. The paper was initially the property of Fas et Jus, an organization promoting a politics with Christian principles. It reported the news while stressing the implications of Christianity in every area of life. Published weekly in Grand Rapids, Michigan, it eventually merged with two other papers and became *De Calvinist* in 1911. In 1918 it was continued by *The Christian Journal* (English-language) and in 1935 became the *Christian Labor Herald* under the sponsorship of the Christian Labor Association. The *Christian Labor Herald* was published until 1980.

RECENT PUBLICATIONS

Today, *De Wachter* is the only Dutch ethnic publication still using the Dutch language exclusively. There are several publications which use both English and Dutch, primarily published by fraternal organizations. Since World War II there has been a marked increase in ethnic consciousness among all Americans, including Dutch Americans. Part of this enhanced interest in ethnic heritage is seen in the membership rolls of the well-established Holland Society of New York (founded in 1855) and those of newer groups such as the Dutch Immigrant Society.[24]

D. I. S. Magazine (founded in 1970) is the organ of the Dutch Immigrant Society. *AVIO* is published by the Dutch Club AVIO of California. Also published in California is *The Holland Reporter*, established in 1965. *Ye Olde Dutch Hill*, begun in 1956, originates in Washington State and is published by the Holland-American Club of the Pacific Northwest.

The Atlantic Observer Knickerbocker International (*The Knickerbocker* from 1938 to 1969) is an English-language magazine published in New York catering primarily to those who trace their Dutch roots back to the colonial days. *De Halve Maen*, established in 1922, chiefly publishes short historical essays, in English, which concentrate on Dutch colonial days. This publication is the responsibility of the Holland Society of New York.

The other publications which continue to cater to Dutch Americans are primarily denominational and are published in English: *The Banner*, published by the Christian Reformed Church; *The Church Herald* of the Reformed Church in America; and *The Standard-Bearer* of the Protestant Reformed Church.

CONCLUSION

The history of the Dutch ethnic press has not been completely unlike that of other ethnic presses. Dutch-language publications continued to be published as long as there were Dutch Americans who could read the language. Until recently, relatively few publications used both English and Dutch.

The early, secular Dutch-language publications served as a primary communications link between the immigrants and their old and new homelands. There were few Dutch ethnic English-language publications that served this news function. As members of the various Dutch settlements learned and used the English language, and as succeeding generations grew further from the Dutch language, there was less need for publications that chiefly stressed news and advertising. These items could be found in the local American newspapers. The successful Dutch newspapers were those published in communities that continued to receive new arrivals. Publications that were religious in content or that carried news from other Dutch communities served the population longer and appear to have had a more stable existence.

In recent years more sophisticated communications and travel have reduced the need for Dutch newspapers among new immigrants. The Dutch ethnic secular magazines that exist today serve to keep traditions and heritage alive but are not the crucial link that was needed in earlier times. The current publications attempt to reach beyond recent immigrants to the second and third (and often further) generations of Dutch Americans.[25]

Religion has been a tremendous force in maintaining a closeknit Dutch subculture in American society. The Dutch learned American ways and the English language relatively quickly, but for the most part maintained their own Protestant churches and a clannishness that is evident even today.

The retention of their ethnic identity through their religious solidarity is evidenced in the number of religious publications which have been born out of this immigrant group. The Dutch ethnic religious press has been continuous and successful, accommodating itself to the inevitable language shift and other changes that come with the acculturation of an immigrant population. The ethnoreligious bonds of the Dutch Americans that have retarded assimilation are the same ties that have kept their ethnic press alive and operative.

NOTES

1. Robert E. Park, *The Immigrant Press and Its Control* (New York: Harper & Brothers, 1922); Edward Hunter, *In Many Voices: Our Fabulous Foreign-Language Press* (Norman Park, Ga.: Norman College, 1960); Joshua A. Fishman, Robert G. Hayden, and Mary E. Warshauer, "The Non-English and the Ethnic Group Press, 1910–1960," in Joshua A. Fishman et al., eds., *Language Loyalty in the United States: The Maintenance*

and Perpetuation of Non-English Mother Tongues by American Ethnic and Religious Groups (The Hague: Mouton & Co., 1966), pp. 51–74; Jerzy Zubrzycki, "The Role of the Foreigh-Language Press in Migrant Integration," *Population Studies* 12 (1958): 73–82.

2. Park, p. 313.

3. Fishman, p. 69.

4. Linda Pegman Doezema, *Dutch Americans: A Guide to Information Sources* (Detroit: Gale Research Company, 1979), pp. 265–266.

5. Park, pp. 313–318.

6. Robert P. Swierenga, "Dutch," in Stephan Thernstrom, ed., *Harvard Encyclopedia of Ethnic Groups* (Cambridge, Mass.: Harvard University Press, 1980), p. 284.

7. Gerald F. DeJong, *The Dutch in America, 1609–1974* (Boston: Twayne Publishers, 1975); Swierenga, pp. 284–295; Herbert J. Brinks, "Recent Dutch Immigration to the United States," in Dennis Laurence Cuddy, ed., *Contemporary American Immigration: Interpretive Essays (European)* (Boston: Twayne Publishers, 1982), pp. 135–154. The two standard works on Dutch Americans are Jacob Van Hinte, *Nederlanders in Amerika: een Studie over Landverhuizers en Volkplanters in de 19e en 20ste eeuw in de Vereenigde Staten van Amerika*, 2 vols. (Groningen, Netherlands: P. Noordhoff, 1928); and Henry Stephen Lucas, *Netherlanders in America: Dutch Immigration to the United States and Canada, 1789–1950* (Ann Arbor: University of Michigan Press, 1955). DeJong's work complements these two major studies with its treatment of the post–World War II period.

8. Arnold Mulder, *Americans from Holland* (Philadelphia: J. B. Lippincott, 1947), p. 215.

9. Harry Boonstra, "Dutch-American Newspapers and Periodicals in Michigan, 1850–1925," Master's thesis, University of Chicago, 1967.

10. Lucas, pp. 565–570.

11. Boonstra, pp. 33–35.

12. Ibid., pp. 36–40.

13. Ibid., p. 39. See also Swierenga, p. 294; DeJong, pp. 205–206.

14. Boonstra, p. 16.

15. Ibid., p. 23.

16. Lucas, p. 544.

17. *De Hollander*, June 15, 1853; December 22, 1853. See Lucas, p. 544.

18. Boonstra, pp. 40–43; Lucas, pp. 575–577.

19. Boonstra, p. 18.

20. *De Sheboygan Nieuwsbode*, December 4, 1849; March 26, 1850; April 2, 1850; August 8, 1850.

21. Lucas, pp. 541–543.

22. Theo DeVeer, "Hollandsche Journalistiek in Amerika," *Elsevier's Geillustreerd Maandschrift* 19 (February 1909): 112.

23. Lucas, pp. 551–562.

24. Swierenga, p. 294.

25. Brinks, p. 151; Swierenga, p. 294.

BIBLIOGRAPHY

Beets, Henry. "Dutch Journalism in Michigan." *Michigan History Magazine* 6 (September 1922): 435–441.

————. "Hollandsche Couranten et Tijdschriften in de Ver Staten" (Dutch newspapers
   and periodicals in the United States). *Gereformeerde Amerikaan* 20 (December
   1916): 514–522.
Boonstra, Harry. "Dutch-American Newspapers and Periodicals in Michigan, 1850–
   1925." Master's thesis, University of Chicago, 1967.
DeVeer, Theo. "Hollandsche Journalistiek in Amerika" (Dutch journalism in America).
   Elsevier's Geillustreerd Maandschrift 19 (February 1909): 107–114.
Lucas, Henry Stephen. *Netherlanders in America: Dutch Immigration to the United States
   and Canada, 1789–1950*. Ann Arbor: University of Michigan Press, 1955.
Mulder, Arnold. *Americans from Holland*. Philadelphia: J. B. Lippincott Co., 1947.
Van Hinte, Jacob. *Nederlanders in Amerika: een Studie over Landverhuizers en Volk-
   planters in de 19e en 20ste eeuw in de Vereenigde Staten van Amerika* (Hollanders
   in America: A study of emigrants and settlers in the nineteenth and twentieth
   centuries in the United States of America). 2 vols. Groningen, Netherlands:
   P. Noordhoff, 1928.

7

The Filipino-American Press

ENYA P. FLORES-MEISER

INTRODUCTION

As noted by Lubomyr and Anna Wynar, the nature and role of the ethnic press in American society are as diverse as the ethnic group it serves. Of relevance to this assertion, however, is the order of reciprocal causality which attends them, perhaps most demonstrably so in a diachronic framework.[1] Both ethnic press and ethnic group reflect one other, providing as they do patterns of continuities and discontinuities of experience within and without the ethnic community. Both periodically gauge, as they are able, the tensions between ethnicity and assimilation.[2] No less integral to this dynamics is the degree of accommodation extended by the host society, yet tempered by the unique experience of the ethnic group itself.

With the above as general premise, the case of the Filipino-American press is herein assessed as its development is juxtaposed to the history of the Filipinos in the United States. Not only a forum for ideas and opinions, the Filipino-American press has been a reservoir of symbols against which the multiple levels of Filipino identities in this country have been articulated. More significantly, the press on the whole has provided the moral force critical to the sense of community in terms of which the intraethnic diversity which has characterized Filipino-Americans is adequately served. As defined here, the ethnic press is restricted to newspapers and periodicals. Publications from Canada, although quite recent, are considered and likewise examined.[3] For clarity, I shall use the terms Filipino-Americans or Filipinos in America to refer to this ethnic group.[4]

Technically, the history of Filipinos in the United States can be dated back to the voyages of the Spanish galleons;[5] it was not until the twentieth century that Filipinos began to immigrate. They arrived in two distinct waves: from the 1920s to the beginning of World War II; and from the period after World War II to the present. Called by Philip B. Whitney a "forgotten minority," the Filipinos in the United States have a history of confusing national identity which was not formally resolved until the 1980 U. S. Population Census.[6] Provided now with the appropriate ethnic category, Filipino-Americans are considered one of the fastest growing minority groups from a single country. Three-quarters of them are found in the western states and Hawaii.[7]

The contrast between the two immigrant waves is stark. The first consisted mainly of unskilled laborers recruited to work in Hawaii plantations, California farms, and Alaska and Washington canneries. Others settled in parts of the American Midwest and East. They were men without families who had little or no education and lived through the high points of institutionalized racism in the United States.[8] Yet many married interracially.[9]

On the other hand, members of the second wave, of whom the majority came after 1965,[10] have considerably more education. Many are trained professionals who have found continuity and growth in their professions in the United States as well as in Canada.[11] Many have been able to immigrate largely because of their profession. They brought with them their families, or portions thereof, and have lived under more socially liberal times. The growing dispersal of Filipino-Americans throughout the country will probably necessitate a study of regional variation soon. But by and large, the internal differentiation brought to bear by such attributes as native language, province of origin, and alma mater is unmistakable in the kinds of voluntary associations that have lately emerged.[12] Thus the present format of typical Filipino-American newspapers necessarily accommodates the interest of the above populations, including a sojourning segment which has resulted for the most part from Ferdinand Marcos's imposition of martial law in 1972.[13]

CHARACTERISTICS OF THE FILIPINO-AMERICAN PRESS

In 1934 Emory Bogardus described the Filipino press in the United States as follows:

The combined newspaper-magazine contains news items, editorials, signed articles, the efforts of columnists, photographs, and advertising. . . . The newspaper-magazine combination is a sound or wise combination, for the clientele is not large enough to justify the publication of a regular newspaper or a magazine. . . .

The Filipino press in the United States is unique in that relatively many publications are printed for a total population that is very limited in numbers. . . .

The fact that there is a large turnover in the Filipino press in the United States and that many publications do not survive more than a year and [a] half or two years is often due to lack of financial resources and backing.[14]

Fifty years later many of the same observations are relevant. The pattern, for instance, of inaugurating and subsequently terminating a newspaper within a short period is still commonplace. In its final issue *Pinoy* explained its inalterable termination as follows: "Financial constraints have forced us to discontinue publication of *Pinoy*. The demands on our staff members' time and effort were enormous."[15]

The circumstances attending *Pinoy*'s fate echo in effect what Bogardus had additionally observed:

The Filipino newspaper-magazine is unique in that it is distinctly a leadership phenomenon. It is usually the result of the individual initiative of one person. . . . It is also the result of the loyalty and activities of a group of followers whom the leader has been able to draw about himself. It reminds one of the early newspaper history of the U. S. where the editor became an independent center of journalistic activities.[16]

Thus the rather informal group made to constitute the staff is often recruited not only from amateurs but from networks of kinsmen and friends. To what degree the newspapers' tenure correlates with the stability of this highly personalistic core of individuals can only be surmised.

In general, Filipino-American newspapers are readily identifiable by the use of such adjectives as Philippine or Filipino in their titles. However, such names as *Cosmopolitan Courier*, *New Quadra Gossip*, *The Informer*, and *Recorder* easily escape detection. More recently, the adoption of names derived from the Philippine national language is evident: *Mabuhay*, *Tambuli*, *Bayanihan*, *Balitaan*, *Kalayaan International*, *Katipunan*. This group of titles conjures up some notions best understood within the framework of the native (or immigrant) culture, presumably intended to awaken sentiments of nationalism in response to Philippine martial law.[17] Or might it also be pertinent that these titles were conceived in the decade when pluralistic orientation was at its peak? The 1970s, after all, saw the celebration of ethnicity in American society not merely as a fashionable trend, but, in fact, as worthy of institutional support.[18] Native titles or not, the rise in the number of Filipino-American newspapers was dramatic between 1970 and 1980. But the current newspaper format has remained relatively unchanged from that described by Donn Hart almost a decade ago:

The Filipino-American press devotes little space to news about the United States or world affairs unless the latter have special significance for Filipinos or the Philippines. Unlike most readers of foreign language newspapers (or television) in their local communities, the typical Filipino-American newspaper gives greatest coverage to group life and interests.

Most of the publications (excluding the anti-Marcos newsletters) devote [themselves to] their local Filipino-American events, e. g. meetings, elections and installations of officers of the hundreds of social clubs, stories of successful Filipino-American businessmen, weddings, baptisms, etc.[19]

In fact, a careful scrutiny of even much earlier newspapers suggests the persistence of this format for a long time. The typical newspaper provides something for everyone: news from various Filipino-American communities in the United States; hometown and provincial news; Manila news as well as that concerning

Filipinos who live elsewhere.[20] A favorite entry often concerns beauty contests. While easily dismissed as frivolous and trivial, the Filipino fascination with beauty queens is quite real.[21]

As the main medium for much ethnic commercial advertising, the typical Filipino-American newspaper is heavily embellished with announcements from travel agencies, insurance companies, Filipino and other Asian grocery stores, and automobile and appliance dealers. On occasion, Filipino-owned financial agencies, dentists, accountants, immigration lawyers, or employment agencies take ads. Few newspapers carry an even proportion between advertisements and content. All publications in the sample were published in English with occasional sections and editorials written in a major Philippine language.[22]

Syndication of by-lines and special features have distinguished the more enduring papers. In at least one case, *The Filipino Reporter*, coverage of international affairs extraneous to the social life of Filipinos here or abroad is more noticeable than in others. Thus while differences among newspapers continue to reflect the geographical region served, as well as the characteristics of the ethnic community addressed, the overall uniformity in format and content suggests one of these factors: (1) close connections among competing newspapers and their staff, or (2) a design intended to appeal not only to a local audience but to a nationwide readership.

Turnover of editors and publishers often results in new formats or titles. Even subscription prices and periodicity may be affected. At present, the bulk of Filipino-American newspapers are published either weekly or fortnightly, but circulation remains modest. In this connection the *Philippine News*, with its subtitle, "The Largest Filipino-American Newspaper," had an estimated circulation of over 89,043 copies in 1982.[23] This constituted about one-tenth of the potential Filipino readership in the country at the time.

Various motives no doubt prompt the creation of a newspaper, not the least of which might be entrepreneurial in character. Given the impermanence of most Filipino-American newspapers, however, few have proved lucrative. Despite this fact, new newspapers and periodicals continue to be inaugurated, giving, to date, an inventory of over 100 titles since 1905. Some appear to have been established to champion a cause, as reflected in the title *Philippine Independence Journal*, or to chronicle an event, as in *Bataan News*. The former newspaper was ephemeral, whereas *Bataan News* kept its name long after the end of World War II; forty years after its inception *Bataan News* became *The Filipino American*.

Beyond the journalistic objective to inform, or the professional ambitions of the individuals involved, the goal of the Filipino-American press understandably appears to focus on two matters: (1) the enhancement of ethnic consciousness, and (2) the "mainstreaming" of the group.

In the struggle to maintain their identity amid a legion of similar publications, ethnic newspapers often adopt subtitles, for example, "An Independent Paper Dedicated to Bringing Filipinos in America Closer Together," "The Largest

Circulated Filipino American Newspaper in Southern California," "The Weekly That Comes in First," "An Impartial and Pro-Community Newspaper," "Your Voice in the Nation's Capital," "A Journal of National Distribution Among Filipinos in America." Regardless of its tenure, the Filipino-American newspaper has sustained a political orientation in the tradition of the Philippine press, once hailed as the freest press in Asia.

The Philippines Mail, with its marked longevity, occupies a very special place in the history of the Filipino-American press. Being the oldest, it has provided a model for its past and current competitors and has fashioned the characteristic format of the ethnic press as it exists today.

THE DEVELOPMENT OF THE FILIPINO-AMERICAN PRESS

The first Filipino periodical on record, the *Filipino Students' Magazine*, was published in 1905 in Berkeley, California, under the editorship of Ponciano Reyes and H. R. Luzuriaga.[24] Directed at a readership of Filipino students (at first known as *pensionados*, and later as "fountain pen" boys, a term used by Lorraine Crouchett), this magazine lasted until 1908. Cross-referenced as *Philippine Review*, it had three publication sites: Berkeley, Boston–New York, and Seattle.

Pensionados were promising Filipino students sent by the U. S. government at its expense to study in American universities. Authorized by Act 854 of the Philippine Commission,[25] the first group of one hundred arrived in the United States in November 1903; hundreds more subsequently followed. The program continued for about three decades contemporaneous with the coming of the first wave of immigrants. Many of these Filipino students, whether in small enclaves or larger ethnic communities, provided the impetus and leadership for early journalistic enterprises. From the start they formed the nuclei in the networks of communication. Carlos Bulosan described this early stage of Filipino-American journalism thus:

The first newspapers were conceived and founded on campuses by . . . young and lonely men. These early publications were amateurish and sometimes dogmatic, but they served as communication lines for the widely scattered students. It is natural, therefore, that most of the columns and news items were devoted to student activities. . . . And because they were all financed by the lean purses of self-supporting students and the meager allowances of others, they existed quietly and briefly, sometimes coming out in one or two issues, and then suspended publication forever.

There is no positive contribution of these early newspapers in the growth of Filipino consciousness in the United States.[26]

On January 22, 1921, the *Philippine Independent News* was published in Salinas, California, becoming the first Filipino newspaper on the mainland.[27] Initiated as the official organ of a fraternity, Caballeros de Dimas-Alang, the

News, under the editorship of Luis Agudo, ran from 1921 to 1926. A trained engineer turned social critic and newspaperman, Agudo was supported by a staff comprised of B. L. Lozares, P. M. Olivete, Gabriel D. Javier, and Philip Barreras. Soon the *News* suffered financial difficulties, leading to changes in its staff and title. Continued at first as *Salinas Valley Mail*, the latter became better known as *The Mail*, which merged briefly with the *Advertiser* to become the *Mail-Advertiser*, and finally *The Philippines Mail*. Its place in Filipino-American journalism is invariably celebrated by anniversary editorials. In one such editorial, staff writer Jose de los Reyes recalled:

The Mail was the training ground of many Filipino newspapermen, some of whom have either gone on to their separate ways as editors and publishers or have become authors of note, not only here but in the Philippines. It had watched over the interests of the Filipino people, fought for their rights, and spared no one when the truth was the difference between life and death.

. . . *The Mail* helped foster causes and movements among Filipinos in this country. In many ways it symbolizes the appearance and growth of the Filipino people on this continent. It was a pioneer in much the same sense as those who came to settle on the land and created wealth for the nation. And though it continued to be the monthly that it is, it is rich in memories, in the history, the struggles and sorrows of the Filipino people in this country.[28]

The example set by *The Mail* was subsequently followed in several California communities and cities outside the state. By 1934 four West Coast newspapers had been started: the *Capital Filipino Press*, *Philippine Star-Press* (a probable merger), *Three Stars*, and *Philippine Triangle*. Controlled by a group of individuals who not only championed the cause of Filipino labor on the West Coast, but also were linked together through multiple editorships for various newspapers, the Filipino press in the United States displayed more unity in cause and style than the many Filipino-American groups it continually sought to integrate. Thus while Luis Agudo was editor of *The Mail*, he also served on the editorial staff of the *Three Stars* of Stockton, which, in fact, he cofounded in 1928 with Villanueva and D. L. Marcuelo. The latter, while editor-in-chief of the *Three Stars*, served in turn as a staff member for another paper. This reciprocal pattern of serving on each other's newspapers solidified a network of individuals who exercised a major role in the integration of Filipino-American communities, particularly in the states of California and Washington.

Numbering among the leaders in these communities, this generation of newspaper editors and publishers was often elected to offices of voluntary associations. Many were university-educated and tried to carve out a respectable life befitting their achieved status, either in the bureaucratic structure of the government or in leadership roles within Filipino-American communities. The results were not always successful. Often they ran into conflict with resident Filipino bureaucrats and diplomats who found little to do abroad. The bureaucrats and diplomats, too, sought leadership legitimization in the same ethnic communities.

The editors were men routinely engaged as key speakers in community affairs. Some actively served as brokers and lobbyists on behalf of their constituency, the Filipinos, vis-a-vis the state and federal governments. Thus, in its first three decades, Filipino-American journalism was involved in a number of issues: the question of Philippine independence from the United States; the problem of Filipino identity in the native as well as the host country; the realities of discrimination and racism in an avowedly democratic society; and the illegality of interracial marriage. These factors were part of the historical background of the state of Filipino ethnicity in this country. In addition, their advocacy of labor reform helped propel the movement that brought Cesar Chavez to prominence.[29] Yet Bulosan was quite critical of the men who wrote on these issues:

Most of them were intellectually inadequate to interpret the socio-economic phase of the depression and therefore greatly lacking of historical perspectives and social responsibility.

And yet, analyzing the whole contribution of this period, it can be said without discrimination that the newspapers had awakened Filipinos to the bitter fact that their presence in the United States presented a new problem. They came to realize, at long last, that there were social and racial discriminations, and economic and political discriminations as well. And even though the editors and writers did not know how these discriminations came about in a country which was founded on the proposition that all men are equal and free, they were able somehow to draw the different tribes of Filipinos closer together for their own mutual protection and interest.[30]

The conception and passage of the Filipino Repatriation Act of 1935[31] engaged the attention of the Filipino-American press for several years. Designed to alleviate the economic problems of the Great Depression years, this legislation provided Filipinos free passage to the islands, prompting the return of many. In May 15, 1933, *The Mail* reported:

Discouraged by the prevailing slack demand for labor, low rates of wages being offered, and slurs such as the law forbidding marriages to Caucasians and [the] Dickstein deportation bill, California Filipinos have started an exodus to their former homes in the Philippine Islands.

A survey made by the *Philippines Mail* which has been confirmed by inquiries of steamship companies reveal[s] that no less than 1600 Filipinos have left the port of San Francisco for the islands within less than three months.[32]

Filipinos elsewhere in the country later followed suit, often for similar reasons. The impending elections for the Philippine Commonwealth government thereafter lured back to the islands some Filipino-American leaders and newspaper editors in the prospect of becoming political candidates themselves or brokers. Among those who left, for various reasons, were editors Luis Agudo, Antonio A. Gonzales, D. L. Marcuelo, and Antonio E. Velasco.

Year	No. of Publications
1900–1910	3
1911–1920	5
1921–1930	21
1931–1940	20
1941–1950	16
1951–1960	12
1961–1970	7
1971–1980	37
1980–1981	1

These departures had little effect on the Filipino population in the United States or on the ethnic press; the number of newspapers only slightly decreased from that of the previous decade. Journalistic issues focused on the following: substandard wages and unemployment; marginal housing conditions and discrimination; and ambiguity of status. Often their self-perceived identity was found inconsistent with that assigned by the host society. In this connection, the press felt it incumbent to safeguard the reputation of the Filipinos on American soil. It routinely ran editorials on the evils of taxi dance halls, gambling, and prostitution. It chided Filipino politicians and bureaucrats for failing to advance the status of Filipinos at home and abroad. And it advised Filipinos to marry among their own kind.[33]

In keeping with tradition, the ethnic press, through the generations, has managed to articulate "Filipino-ness" within the framework of the communities at home and abroad; against the social structure of the host society; or against myriad cultural symbols. It has frequently compared Filipinos and Filipino-Americans to other ethnic groups, especially Asians, presumably to effect a Filipino-American profile. Sometimes the zeal to cast that identity in the "order of things" may be dismissed as short of extreme. Note, for example, such articles as "Filipinos: The Irish of the East," or "Of Puritans and Filipinos."[34] Recognizing the fact that by now the Filipino-American experience represents a wide spectrum in cultural assimilation, the current press, more than before, is keen to mention when appropriate the Filipino ancestry of individuals with marked achievement. On this account, the ethnic constituencies are coached to feel proud and effect solidarity across generations and communities.

The entry of the United States into World War II diverted national attention to the war and accordingly elicited the expected response from the Filipino community and the ethnic press. One newspaper, the *Filipino Forum*, was reissued in 1942; and *Bataan News*, already mentioned, was founded at this time. The subject of Filipino status came into sharper focus in connection with the enlistment policies of the War Department. Neither citizens nor aliens, Filipinos were nationals owing allegiance to the United States. Reactions to the war in

Filipino-American communities in California were dramatic, as reflected in journalistic coverage: withholding labor supply from Japanese farm owners, and
boycotting of other Japanese businesses, including rooming houses; interminable
fund raising through various organizations; and massive military registration.
Filipino collaboration with the United States was total, Filipino identification
unequivocal. Yet Bulosan without explanation characterized the Filipino newspapers during the war period thus: "mostly unpatriotic in tone, nevertheless,
[they] contributed toward the defeat of the enemy."[35]

Filipino participation in the war effort was a basic staple in the ethnic press,
and presumably influenced future government policies toward the ethnic group.
The signing of the Filipino Naturalization Act,[36] obviously prompted by the war,
became a controversial issue. At last, Filipinos were given the choice to apply
for citizenship, an option immediately exercised by thousands, to the dismay of
some.

This new-found status as citizens provided a starting point for the integration
of individuals and families into American society. Involvement in community
affairs, including local politics, followed.[37] Meanwhile, the matters of racial
discrimination and low socioeconomic position vis-à-vis local community structures continued to provoke social and political issues.

With full political autonomy after independence, the Philippines remained
economically enmeshed with and utterly dependent upon the United States. Each
Philippine election was typically climaxed by a presidential trip to Washington
to secure loans and other forms of aid. Each election brought not only internal
cleavage within Filipino-American communities but also within the press corps.
On occasion even the editorial staff of a newspaper was divided against itself.[38]
During this period, until Philippine martial law was declared, Philippine journalism became unsparingly critical of government leaders and politicians—as
did the Filipino press in the United States.

Bridged by a group of active correspondents providing syndicated columns
on both ends of the migration process, the ethnic press maintained interest in
the Philippines. Bulosan aptly described this period:

The Filipino newspapers in California, knowing that the important issues in the Philippines vitally affect the life and security of the Filipinos abroad, shifted their vision
against the political hierarchy and economic corruption in the islands. . . . The Filipino
newspapers in California became critical and vigilant, became, in fact, the revolutionary
factors [at] the expense of bigoted and greedy leaders in the Philippines, and the only
positive weapon with which the Filipinos can now dissect the decaying carcass of island
politics and the anarchy of its economic structure.[39]

On April 7, 1945, the Philippine Press Alliance was organized in Delano,
California, under the guidance of Antonio A. Gonzales, president of the Filipino
Intercommunity Organization of Western States, at a meeting attended by the
editors of six newspapers. The purpose of the alliance was to promote a stan-

dardized format among newspapers, the next logical step being an effort to establish a Filipino national daily.

The ambiguity of Filipino status in the United States continued, and for a brief period after independence it became an important journalistic subject as shown in these headlines:[40] "Filipino-American citizens not for consular jobs," "They may not have thought of us," "Japanese-American evacuees aided, but Filipino internees are not," and "Filipinos abroad pay taxes in the Philippines."

One writer who managed to formulate a wide range of issues and mold them into the Filipino cause during this period was Vincente Villamin. Others like Trinidad Rojo, M. Insigne, Juan B. Sarmiento, D. Cruz, and Antonio A. Velasco also wrote on issues concretely relevant to the Filipino cause.

Concerns about national integration, postwar reconstruction, and chronic economic ills dominated the news about the new republic. On the other hand, the labor struggle (although on the wane), annual celebrations,[41] inaugurals, and the endless visits of Filipino politicians to the ethnic communities filled the pages of many publications. Potpourri columns monitoring innocuous exploits and whereabouts of personalities within and without the local ethnic communities also grew copious. *The Philippines Mail*, for example, during the 1940s and 1950s ran a wide array of very creatively titled columns for such matters.[42]

In the first fifteen years after World War II, the number of ethnic periodicals and newspapers initiated remained basically constant compared to the previous period. This fact suggests, in effect, a fairly steady rate of turnover, termination, and readership. From 1961 to 1970 no more than six new publications were introduced. But by the next decade the number of new titles was more than double that of earlier decades. Some ceased after an issue or two, and others may follow suit.

The unprecedented proliferation of ethnic newspapers and periodicals in the 1970s can be easily attributed to the imposition of Philippine martial law. Bans on the Philippine free press caused an exodus of journalists and political critics to the United States and Canada in numbers sufficient to staff anti-Marcos publications and encourage the financial backing of the dislodged political elites.

In its maiden issue (December 18, 1970) the *Philippine Times*, for example, editorialized thus on the professional status of its staff:

> The men behind the newspaper are professional journalists, who have served in Philippine news organizations and metropolitan newspapers. Our Manila bureau staff writers are outstanding journalists. *The Philippine Times* is a newspaperman's newspaper, devoid of vested interests and prejudices. It is in the hands of people devoted to doing an honest job of information. It is an independent newspaper that will embarrass the powerful and comfort the afflicted, espousing worthy causes for the improvement of society and the community.[43]

Likewise, the *Filipino Reporter* at its debut pointed to the continuation of Philippine journalism on American soil.

Now catering to a wider and more diversified readership than ever before, the ethnic press, besides reporting on politics, covers a growing range of journalistic interests. Editorial subjects vary tremendously, from those about personalities to trivial Philippine customs and slipping traditions.[44] The celebration of the predominantly Roman Catholic rituals in the ethnic communities appears to receive greater attention in the press than was the case decades earlier.[45] Moreover, many guest reviewers and columnists write on their own areas of expertise: nutrition, film-making, medicine, and so on. In its task to instruct, the press has just begun to address bits and pieces of Filipino-American history, perhaps for the benefit of the later immigrants, or the children of the first group, or both.

CONCLUSION

The prospects for the many separate and often redundant Filipino-American publications to become consolidated into a smaller number in the future remain problematic. Already, the Filipino ethnic communities in major United States and Canadian cities are being served by two or three news magazines. If the past is any gauge at all, the existence of many of these publications will prove tentative. A 1981 news release regarding a newly organized Filipino American Press Association gave no indication that such condensation is indeed likely.[46]

On the other hand, the potential for a more coordinated and unified press, viewed in the context of an Asian press, is real. Few publications managed by an all Filipino-American staff have yet taken this direction, and only the *Asian American News*, in bias more Filipino than Asian, has emerged with relative success. Be that as it may, an instructive editorial from the *Filipino Reporter* projects a new crusade and a potential evolution in the ethnic press:

Asian Americans in the United States suffer from what may be called the "under" syndrome. We are underrepresented, underrated, undercounted, undersold and underpaid. In effect, we are the classic underdog in the American scene. . . .

The Asian press, aside from being our first line of defense, is the ideal medium for articulating an Asian viewpoint.

For the Asian press to be able to perform this role, Asian publishers and editors need to get together and agree on a common editorial venture designed to promote the cause of Asian Americanism.

The Asian press must agree to an exchange of materials, and from time to time, print a joint editorial . . . on an issue of far-reaching import to Asian Americans.

The Asian press must organize an information center, staffed by one representative from each newspaper or publication, charged with the function of disseminating, gathering, planning, coordinating and executing activities in accordance with the policies formulated by the center. . . .

The press center [would work] on the premise that Asian American issues or problems are apt to be brought to the attention of the Asian press first because of racial considerations.[47]

In consideration of such a proposal, leadership among the Asian American presses, to say the least, will be crucial.

NOTES

1. Carl H. Knoche, in "The German Immigrant Press in Milwaukee" (Ph. D. dissertation, Ohio State University, 1969), documented in gradual stages the transition of *Germania* from an immigrant press, in the beginning concerned with issues of adaptation to the host community, to its final Americanization; see especially pp. 237–364. The extent to which this process parallels the case of other ethnic groups in itself constitutes a hypothesis. For a more general overview in the development and functions of the ethnic press, see Lubomyr R. Wynar and Anna T. Wynar, *Encyclopedic Directory of Ethnic Newspapers and Periodicals in the United States* (Littleton, Colo.: Libraries Unlimited, 1976), pp. 14–27.

2. No doubt this polarity is not only simplistic but an assumption that is methodologically problematic, for example, does ethnicity suggest resistance to assimilation and vice versa? However, space will not permit the review of exhaustive literature on ethnicity per se and how it stands up to a theory of assimilation.

3. A large repository of Filipino newspapers and periodicals is part of the Southeast Asian Collection, recently renamed the Donn Hart Collection, at Northern Illinois University.

4. The controversy on what is the proper usage, Pilipino or Filipino, to define the former indigenes of the Philippines is a recent one. In the aftermath of Philippine independence, the term Pilipino was employed to identify the national language of the country; the people themselves, however, continue to be called Filipinos (Sp.); but the Philippines, the name for the country, was probably a French transcription. In any case, this confusion has led to differences in terminological reference to this ethnic group.

5. An extensive treatment of this subject is provided by William L. Schurz, *The Manila Galleon* (New York: E. P. Dutton and Co., 1959). For a very abbreviated version, see Lorraine Jacobs Crouchette, *Filipinos in California* (El Cerrito, Calif.: Downey Place Publishing House, 1982), pp. 5–17.

6. Philip B. Whitney, "Forgotten Minority: Filipinos in the United States," *Bulletin of Bibliography* 29 (1972): 73–83. Prior to the 1980 U. S. Population Census, the Filipinos were classified variously with other groups: Pacific islanders; people with Spanish surnames but not Hispanics; or Asians. The history of ambiguity in Filipino status and identity in the United States is a complex one, but for a general background, see H. Brett Melendy, *Asians in America: Filipinos, Koreans, and East Indians* (Boston: Twayne Publishers, 1977), pp. 31–57.

7. Quoting directly from the *Los Angeles Times*, *Bataan News*, July 31-August 6, 1981, noted on its front page: "357,514 Filipinos in California: Largest Asian Group in State." This makes up close to one-half of the 774,640 total Filipino population across the nation. By 1971 the dramatic increase was acknowledged. See also E. Caldwell, "Filipinos: A Fast-Growing Minority," *New York Times*, March 5, 1971, p. 5; "Filipinos Now Number 1 Asian Group in U. S.," *Hawaii Filipino News*, May 16–31, 1981.

8. Emory S. Bogardus, "The Filipino Immigrant Problem," *Sociology and Social Research* 13 (May-June 1929): 474–479; Bogardus, "American Attitudes towards Filipinos," *Sociology and Social Research* 14 (September-October 1929): 50–69; Manuel Buaken, *I Have Lived with the American People* (Caldwell, Idaho: Caxton Printers, 1948).

See also Bruno Lasker, *Filipino Immigration* (Chicago: University of Chicago Press, 1969), 10: 135–142; Trinidad A. Rojo, "Social Maladjustment of Filipinos in the United States," *Sociology and Social Research* 21 (1937): 447–457 (includes extensive bibliographical [journal] references); "Two Seriously Hurt as Escalon Nightriders Eject Twenty-one Filipinos from Their Bunkhouses," *The Philippines Mail*, August 7, 1933, p. 4; "Alfafara Elected Grand Master of CDA," *The Philippines Mail*, February 2, 1943, pp. 1, 3.

9. Barbara M. Posadas, "Cross Boundaries in Interracial Chicago: Pilipino American Families since 1925," *Amerasia* 8 (1981): 31–52; "Marriage Questions," *The Philippines Mail*, March 29, 1944, p. 7; Nellie Foster, "Legal Status of Filipino Intermarriage in California," *Sociology and Social Research* 16 (May-June 1932): 441–454.

10. U. S. Congress, *The Immigration and National Act of 1965*, 30 September, Sec. 203. President L. B. Johnson's signing of this act permitted a massive immigration from Asia when all unused national quotas were pooled together; see Melendy, p. 17.

11. They include accountants, elementary and high school teachers, lawyers, dentists, nurses, and other paramedical professionals. In 1974 there were 7,000 practicing Filipino physicians in the United States (Marina E. Espinas, "Filipinos in New Orleans," in *Proceedings of Louisiana Academy of Sciences* 37 [1974]: 117); see also Patricio R. Mamot, *Filipino Physicians in America* (Indianapolis: Rod's Composing Service, 1981), p. 1.

12. E. B. Almirol, "Filipino Voluntary Associations: Balancing Social Pressures and Ethnic Images," *Ethnic Groups* 2 (1978): 65–92; Jonathan Y. Okamura, "Filipino Hometown Associations in Hawaii," *Ethnology* 22 (October 1983): 341–354.

13. Apart from political refugees and expatriates, a significant number of Filipinos live part of the year in the United States and part in the Philippines. Many of them are parents of immigrants who came annually to validate their immigration cards.

14. Emory S. Bogardus, "The Filipino Press in the United States," *Sociology and Social Research* 18 (July-August 1934): 582–585.

15. *Pinoy*, January 1979, p. 11.

16. Bogardus, "Filipino Press," pp. 582–585.

17. Some editorials have drawn parallels between the Marcos regime and the events that led to the Philippine Revolution in 1896, as well as between it and the Japanese occupation.

18. In 1981 the National Endowment for the Humanities funded an oral history project on Filipinos and Korean Americans under the directorship of Dorothy Cordova. See *Bataan News*, January 30-February 5, 1981, p. 8; the project gave rise to a pictorial book. See Fred Cordova, *Filipinos: Forgotten Asian Americans* (n. p.: Demonstration Project for Asian Americans, 1983).

19. Donn V. Hart, "The Filipino-American Press in the United States: A Neglected Resource," *Journalism Quarterly* 54 (Spring 1977): 135–139.

20. A significant population of Filipinos is found in Canada, England, Germany, and Spain as temporary residents. Others work in Saudi Arabia, Kuwait, and the Emirate States on contract. Occasionally, information about their plight gets into newsprint.

21. Early in its history, *The Philippines Mail* instituted beauty contests which required selling subscriptions on behalf of candidates. For one of the earliest contests, see *The Philippines Mail*, May 29, 1933, p. 3.

22. There are over seventy languages in the Philippines of which five are major: Bicolano, Cebuano, Ilocano, Ilongo, and Tagalog. Ilocano and Tagalog are most often

used in editorials. Presently, a syndicated column, "Kuro-Kuro," by a former Philippine senator, Soc Rodrigo, is carried by a number of the ethnic newspapers.

23. These data were taken from the notes of Donn Hart, who died during work on this project.

24. Hyung-Chan Kim and Cynthia C. Meijia, ed., *The Filipinos in America, 1898–1974: A Chronology and Fact Book* (Dobbs Ferry, N. Y.: Oceana Publications, 1976), p. 2.

25. See Melendy, pp. 31–33; Crouchett, pp. 31–32; Kim and Meijia, p. 1.

26. Carlos Bulosan, "Filipino Newspapers in California," *The Philippines Mail*, October 28, 1948, p. 8. Bulosan was a migrant worker and union activist who wrote on the Filipino struggle from the 1930s until the 1950s; he is regarded as a towering figure in Filipino-American literature. Bulosan's short stories, essays, editorials, letters, poems, and novel are now part of the Filipino-American legacy. See the entire volume of *Amerasia Journal* 6 (1979) for excerpts of his work.

27. Kim and Meijia, p. 2.

28. *The Philippines Mail*, October 1955, p. 2.

29. Crouchett, pp. 40–44; Melendy, pp. 78–81, 101–102.

30. Bulosan, "Filipino Newspapers," p. 8.

31. U. S., Senate Committee on Immigration and Naturalization, *Report* No. 622, Immigration of Filipinos from the United States.

32. *The Philippines Mail*, May 15, 1933, p. 1.

33. "Dance Halls Serious Menace," *The Philippines Mail*, July 24, 1933, p. 2; "Neglects Filipino Status," *The Philippines Mail*, April 9, 1934, p. 2; "Filipinos and Filipinas Should Marry," *The Philippines Mail*, December 30, 1948, p. 2.

34. "Filipinos: Irish of the East," *Asian American News*, May 1–15, 1980, p. 23; "Of Puritans and Pilipinos," *Balitaan*, May 1976, p. 4.

35. For example: "Total Boycott Declared Against Jap," *The Philippines Mail*, January 31, 1942, p. 1; "Filipinos Now Eligible to Enlist," *The Philippines Mail*, January 13, 1942, p. 1; "Stockton Pinoys—Pledge Aid to United States," *The Philippines Mail*, December 22, 1941, p. 1.

36. See Kim and Meijia, p. 45; other related documents include U. S. Congress, Committee on Immigration and Naturalization, *Report* No. 1940, Authorizing the Naturalization of Filipinos.

37. See, for example, "Asura Seeks Board Supervisor Position," *Forum Philippines*, February 16–29, 1976, pp. 1, 12; "Browns for Brown," *Balitaan*, August 1978, p. 1; "Filipinos Win Some, Lose Some in L. A. Elections," *Philippine News*, April 17–23, 1985, pp. 1, 8.

38. Adriano G. Delfino, first editor of the *United Filipino Press* and night editor of *Chicago Northside Newspaper*, resigned over differences with the publisher, Mel A. Vega, a staunch supporter of Quinino; whereas Delfino, a native of Batangas, endorsed Laurel during the 1949 Philippine elections campaign. *The Philippines Mail*, September 16, 1949, p. 3.

39. Bulosan.

40. *The Philippines Mail*, March 1948, p. 1; *The Philippines Mail*, January 1946, p. 2; *The Philippines Mail*, August 1948, p. 4; *The Philippines Mail*, November 16, 1948, p. 1.

41. Among the most important calendrical events observed and editorialized on were Christmas, Rizal Day, July 4th, and Mother's Day.

42. Among them were "Thorns and Roses," *The Philippines Mail*, May 1946, p. 2; "Sari-Sari, Haro-Haro," *The Philippines Mail*, August 1946, p. 6; "Salt and Pepper," *The Philippines Mail*, August 1948, p. 2, "Manila Round-Up," p. 4, and "Filipino Doings," p. 5; "Hash and Rehash," *The Philippines Mail*, February 1949, p. 4.

43. *Philippine Times*, December 18, 1970, p. 6.

44. "Return to Arnis—The Filipino Martial Art," *Bataan News*, September 18–24, 1981, p. 9; "The Kundiman," *Bataan News*, March 10–23, 1978, p. 3.

45. Among them are Lenten observances (*pabasa*); May celebrations (*Santa Cruzan*); and processionals of patron saints. See "Sto. Nino de Cebu Fiesta Draws Devotees," *Bataan News*, January 20-February 4, 1977, p. 3; "Culture-enriching 'Flores de Mayo,' " *Bayanihan Tribune*, May 30, 1978, p. 5.

46. "Fil-Am Press Association Organized," *Bataan News*, December 20, 1981, pp. 1, 15.

47. "Role of Asian Press," *Filipino Reporter*, March 9–15, 1979, pp. 1, 4.

BIBLIOGRAPHY

Bogardus, Emory S. "The Filipino Press in the United States." *Sociology and Social Research* 18 (July-August 1934): 582–585.

Hart, Donn V. "The Filipino Press in the United States: A Neglected Resource." *Journalism Quarterly* 54 (Spring 1977): 135–139.

8

The Finnish Press

A. WILLIAM HOGLUND

Since 1876 American Finns have published almost ninety newspapers in a language that was little used for literary purposes until the start of modern migration from Finland to the United States. Between the sixteenth century and 1809, when Imperial Russia acquired Finland from Sweden, Finnish-language publications numbered only 174, mainly of a religious nature. Only one Finnish newspaper appeared in this period; it lasted less than a year. Even after the Russian takeover of Finland, the Swedish language dominated a society in which it was the mother tongue of about 15 percent of the population. However, by the middle of the nineteenth century the Finnish nationalist movement won more recognition for the majority language, both through the transcribing of the oral epic, *Kalevala*, and through the gradual adoption of Finnish and Swedish as coequal official languages between 1863 and 1883. This bitter fight over language spurred the publication of Finnish newspapers, which outnumbered Swedish ones after 1876. Religious, temperance, and labor movements, too, hastened the growth of newspapers. But this literary activity lagged in the rural areas of Finland that sent immigrants to America. Consequently, Finnish immigrants developed their literary interests more fully in America, where by 1899, according to Akseli Järnefelt (Rauanheimo), they read newspapers more than in their old homeland.

In 1864 the Quincy Mining Company recruited Finnish copper miners from Norway to work in its mines around Hancock and Calumet, Michigan. Upwards of 1,000 Finns arrived via Norway, while almost 3,500 Finns came directly from Finland during the 1860s and 1870s. These pioneers were mainly supporters of Lars Levi Laestadius and his pietistic movement, which was opposed by the hostile Evangelical Lutheran state church of Finland. In 1867 Finnish Laestadians, or Apostolic Lutherans, as they were later known, joined Swedes and Norwegians to establish a congregation in Hancock. Four years later the Finns formed their own congregation. Meanwhile, Finnish Evangelical Lutherans began forming their own churches in the same area. Before these Michigan communities were well established Finns started moving to farms in Minnesota.

In 1876 Anders Johan Muikku pioneered newspaper publishing in Hancock, where local Lutherans invited him to serve their clerical needs. However, the unsuitability of Muikku, a university student, became apparent, and he then established a firm which published the first Finnish-American newspaper called the *Amerikan Suomalainen Lehti* (The American Finnish journal) on April 14, 1876. After publishing at least eleven weekly issues for about 300 subscribers, Muikku ended the paper, but he tried again with a few numbers of the *Lehtinen* (The leaflet) during the same year. Both financial difficulties and Apostolic Lutheran suspicions of a secular paper doomed his efforts.

Two years later Matts Fred inaugurated the next paper, *Swen Tuuwa*, despite financial and other handicaps (for example, his supply of type for printing words with the umlaut "ä" was limited and required the substitution of two "i's" for that letter). Although Fred tried to avoid the local religious controversies, readers pressed for space to wage their disputes. In 1879 he enlarged his paper and renamed it the *Sankarin Maine*, but failed to save his enterprise from collapsing in 1881.

In 1879 August Nylund and his associates established another publishing firm in Calumet because of their dissatisfaction with Fred's paper; they employed Alexander Leinonen to start a newspaper with the same title as Muikku's pioneer publication. The editor of the new *Amerikan Suomalainen Lehti* had worked for railroads in Texas and elsewhere after arriving in America at the age of twenty-three in 1869. He had engaged in religious controversy in the pages of Fred's paper and also had sent glowing reports about America to two newspapers in Finland. His critical remarks about clergymen and officials and about economic opportunities for the poor in his homeland offended Leinonen's overseas editors. After acquiring ownership of the new paper, which was for a time supportive of Apostolic Lutherans, Leinonen sold it to Victor M. Burman, who continued it as the *Amerikan Suomalainen* (The American Finn) in Hancock and later in Chicago, where he suspended it in 1895.

In 1881, after initiating the paper with Leinonen, August Nylund and Fred Karinen (who had been the typesetter for *Swen Tuuwa*) began publishing the *Uusi Kotimaa* (The new homeland), first in Minneapolis and later in New York Mills, Minnesota, and Astoria, Oregon. Eventually Nylund returned the paper to New York Mills. Though sympathetic to the Evangelical Lutherans, he avoided religious partisanship.

The *Uusi Kotimaa* marked the start of two decades of new publishing ventures which produced thirty-two newspapers, usually appearing once a week. New York City had the *New Yorkin Lehti* (The New York journal) and *New Yorkin Suomalainen Lehti* (The New York Finnish journal). Massachusetts's titles consisted of the *Idän Uutiset* (The eastern news) and *Totuus* (Truth), which were both published in Worcester before their transfer to Fitchburg; the *Suomalainen* (The Finn) in Rockport; and the *Finska Amerikanaren* (The Finnish American), which moved from Worcester to Brooklyn, New York, and appeared in the Swedish language for Swedish-speaking Finns. In Ohio, Ashtabula acquired the

Amerikan Sanomat (The American tidings), *Pohjantähti* (The North Star), and *Yhdyswaltain Sanomat* (The United States tidings). Even Rock Springs, Wyoming, had two papers, the *Kansan Ystävä* (The people's friend) and *Lännen Uutiset* (The western news). Astoria, Oregon, had two papers named the *Lännetar* (The westerner), appearing in 1891 and 1897.

But the Midwest had the largest share of new publications. The *Lännetar* of 1891 moved from Astoria to Superior, Wisconsin, where it became the *Siirtolainen* (The emigrant) before its transfer to Brooklyn. Superior was also the place of publication for the *Superiorin ja Duluthin Sanomat* (The Superior and Duluth tidings). In Minnesota, the *Amerikan Suometar* (The American Finn) appeared in New York Mills during the absence of the *Uusi Kotimaa* in 1889, while Minneapolis produced the *Amerikan Uutiset* (The American news), which was relocated in Calumet (formerly Red Jacket), Michigan. Michigan's other titles were the *Kalevan Kaiku* (Kaleva's echo), *Kansan Lehti* (The people's journal), *Päivän Uutiset* (The daily news) (two papers were published under this name), *Suometar* (The Finn), *Uusi Kansan Lehti* (The new people's journal), *Viikon Uutiset* (The weekly news), and *Wäinölä* (The Wäinölä) in Calumet, where a second *Amerikan Suomalainen* (The Finnish American) appeared in 1897; the second *Amerikan Suometar* (The American Finn; 1899) and *Kuparisaaren Sanomat* (The Copper Country tidings) in Hancock; the *Työmies* (The workingman) of 1889 in Ishpeming; and the *Ironwoodin ja Bessemerin Uutiset* (The Ironwood and Bessemer news) and *Kalevala* (The Kalevala) in Ironwood. These titles involved various changes of name, as in the case of the *Kuparisaaren Sanomat*, which became the second *Amerikan Suomalainen* and later the *Suometar*; revivals, such as the *Uusi Kansan Lehti*, which resumed the name *Kansan Lehti*; and mergers, such as the joining of *Uusi Kotimaa* and the *Amerikan Suometar* of 1889 and the creating of the *Amerikan Uutiset* through a union of the *Työmies* and *Yhdyswaltain Sanomat*.

The spread of these publishing ventures beyond Michigan reflected the growth of Finnish communities from Massachusetts to Oregon. Between 1880 and 1893 about 61,000 Finns left Finland, while from 1893 to 1899 another 37,000 secured passports. Their numbers declined in the latter period because of the economic depression of 1893, which reduced opportunities for employment. The men worked in basic industries such as mining, lumbering, and steel mills, and women became domestic servants and textile mill workers. Whatever their initial place of employment, most usually moved, seeking better opportunities in new places, and thousands returned to Finland. By 1900 Finns numbered 62,641, of whom 47 percent lived in Michigan and Minnesota, while over 41 percent lived in Massachusetts, New York, Ohio, California, Washington, Wisconsin, Oregon, Montana, Pennsylvania, Illinois, and New Jersey. Besides providing employment for them, these states became the centers of their organizational and publishing activities.

Newspaper publishers were part of the tiny minority of Finnish entrepreneurs, many of whom had been manual laborers. Their success, like that of local storekeepers, depended on the patronage of fellow countrymen. Matts Fred was a painter who returned to his trade after the collapse of his paper, while Fred Karinen had learned the printing trade with a local English-language journal in Hancock. Other publishers included August Nylund, a watchsmith, and G. A. Grönlund, the proprietor of a steamship ticket agency. When August Edwards arrived in Ashtabula, he was initially engaged as a lay clerical assistant. These publishers organized partnerships and stock companies to raise capital if they lacked money to publish by themselves. Although profit making was their ultimate goal, literary inclinations and ideological commitments also inspired their publishing.

Becoming dissatisfied with these proprietary publishers, temperance and religious groups established their own publishing enterprises. No group could expect consistent support from existing papers because their ownership and editorship changed frequently. Because of the problems of financing and editing publications, however, churches and temperance organizations first published monthlies and yearbooks before starting newspapers. Within a year after its organization in 1888, the Finnish National Temperance Brotherhood subsidized the *Työmies* of Fred Karinen, but withdrew its subsidy when the publisher became hostile to its activities. Another early organizational newspaper was the weekly *Totuus*, begun in Worcester by the Finnish Evangelical Missionary Society in behalf of Congregationalists alienated from the Finnish state church. Two years later pastor Juho K. Nikander joined fellow clergymen and laymen, who had organized the Finnish Evangelical Lutheran Church (or Suomi Synod) in 1890, to publish the *Amerikan Suometar* (The American Finn) in Hancock, dedicated to supporting temperance, preserving Finnish culture, and promoting the organization. Initially the founders established a publishing firm which was transferred to the synod in 1900. Both the *Totuus* and the *Amerikan Suometar* pioneered an approach that undermined the proprietary monopoly on publishing.

In establishing newspapers, these publishers relied on editors to help shape the content of their publications. Even editors with little or no journalistic experience in Finland found employment. Synod Lutherans were fortunate to secure N. J. Ahlman, an experienced journalist, to edit their new paper, while other publishers recruited persons who had developed literary and language skills at lyceums and the University of Helsinki. The lyceum-trained editors included Antero Riippa of the *Siirtolainen* and Kalle Haapakoski of the *Amerikan Uutiset*. Akseli Järnefelt (Rauanheimo) arrived with a graduate degree to work for the *Siirtolainen*, and Victor M. Burman, who became editor and publisher of the *Amerikan Suomalainen Lehti*, had studied law for a few months at the university. Among the most colorful editors was Johan W. Lähde, a young student who went to Ashtabula in 1884 and was ordained after one semester of study at Augustana Seminary in Illinois. In the midst of establishing congregations and losing them because of drunkenness, he became editor of the *Uusi Kotimaa*, which acquired his *Amerikan Suometar* of 1889. Later he edited the *Totuus*, *Idän Uutiset*, and *Finska Amerikanaren*. Though overworked, poorly paid, and lacking adequate assistants, these successful editors became influential personalities.

Whatever the orientation of their papers, the editors and publishers adopted more or less the same format. Most papers began as weeklies, with the exception of Ino (John) Ekman's short-lived daily paper, *Päivän Uutiset* (The daily news) of 1891. The papers devoted much space to old country news items, copied from sources printed in Finland, and translations of news accounts from American newspapers. Other space-consuming material included serialized stories of adventure and romance, often reproduced from old country publications. Also, space was devoted to reports on the activities of immigrant organizations and accounts of visits to Finnish communities. The main source of original writing was often unpaid correspondents who reported on local affairs, industrial accidents, organizational rivalries, and personal matters. Most papers took partisan positions on current issues and disputes, though their stated purpose often was the promotion of harmony as well as morality, enlightenment, and the common good.

All papers had a difficult struggle to survive on their limited capital and talent. They experienced frequent turnover in personnel recruited from the ranks of inexperienced immigrants and their American-educated children. Inadequate financing brought failure to the initial ventures of publishers like Ino Ekman. The economic depression of 1893 hastened the failure of others, like Victor M. Burman, who lost his first paper in Chicago, and G. A. Grönlund, whose initial journalistic venture also collapsed. In contrast, the owners of the *Lännetar* rescued themselves during the depression by reorganizing their paper as the *Siirtolainen* and moving to Wisconsin, later establishing the Finnish American Publishing Company to raise capital for it. Trying to augment income became a perennial responsibility of managers, who solicited advertisements for immigrant businesses, steamship companies, and patent medicines, as well as notices from Finnish organizations. Another source of income was the publishing of scores of small books of adventure and romance for sale by the *Uusi Kotimaa*, *Amerikan Sanomat*, and *Siirtolainen*. In addition, the *Sanomat* retailed gadgets, fountain pens, stationery, and other products. Business managers became vital for economic survival.

Most papers competed for readers in the thirteen states where Finnish settlements had taken root. Often unable to hire full-time agents to solicit subscribers, the papers relied heavily on correspondents, who sometimes collected commissions for their sales. The postal system became the main means of collecting funds and distributing papers, even though it often lost or delayed materials. Consequently, subscribers supported regional papers most commonly if they were compatible with their ideological interests. All these factors limited circulation. In the 1880s the *Amerikan Suomalainen Lehti* had about 800 subscribers, the *Uusi Kotimaa* had about 1,000, and the *Yhdyswaltain Sanomat* led with 2,000. By 1897 the leaders were the *Uusi Kotimaa* with 1,750, the *Amerikan Uutiset* with 4,500, and the *Siirtolainen* with 12,500. In 1898 the representatives of these three papers joined others to control the competition for subscribers. They met and proposed ending the slanderous assaults on each other's character, restoring the good will of readers who thought all papers were antireligious, distributing a blacklist of delinquent subscribers, and requiring a performance bond from the sponsors of new paperes. No follow-up meeting materialized, and the rivalries persisted.

In this atmosphere of disharmony, no newspaper could easily expect to win universal acclaim from readers that did not share its position in religious and other controversies. After the eruption of the initial conflict between Apostolic and Evangelical Lutherans that plagued early publishers, new controversies developed, especially in the late 1880s and 1890s. Clerical opposition to plays and dances split the temperance forces, while in 1890 the proposal of the Evangelical Lutherans to establish a synod precipitated an even greater outburst of anticlericalism. Hostile editors, laymen, and clergymen argued that the synod would introduce such features of the state church as autocratic rule and compulsory taxes. Ino Ekman's *Kansan Lehti* and the *Amerikan Uutiset*, edited by Kalle Haapakoski, led the journalistic attack, which failed to halt the establishment of the Syomi Synod. Dissenting Lutherans formed independent congregations which united as the Finnish Evangelical Lutheran National (meaning "people's") Church in 1898. Other dissenters joined the Congregationalists or remained outside of any church, as did two-thirds of all Finnish immigrants.

Few of these early newspapers survived long enough to compete for readers in the twentieth century. Of the four newspapers established in the 1870s, only the *Amerikan Suomalainen Lehti* lasted until the 1890s. Likewise, the mortality rate was high for the thirty-two new papers started between 1881 and 1899. Over half of them survived for only one to four years, and of the remainder only nine continued into the next century. The latter group included the *Suometar*, *Totuus*, *Lännetar* of 1897, *Amerikan Sanomat*, and *Amerikan Uutiset*, which were all suspended by World War I. The other four included the *Siirtolainen*, *Uusi Kotimaa*, and *Amerikan Suometar*, which disappeared between the late 1930s and the early 1960s, and the *Finska Amerikanaren* (renamed *Norden* [The north]), which is still in existence.

In contrast, newspaper publishers found better opportunities for success between 1900 and 1920, when immigration reached its peak from Finland. During this period almost 237,000 Finns received passports to leave their country, and those who immigrated did so mainly before World War I. By 1920 the number of foreign-born Finns had risen to 150,770 from the 129,669 recorded in 1910, while American-born children of Finnish immigrants almost doubled during the decade, to 130,083. These demographic developments represented the growing resident population that did not return to Finland, established family and institutional ties, and developed stronger political self-consciousness. New and old immigrants were stirred by events in Finland, such as Russification, the general strike of 1905, and the civil war of 1918. Domestically, Finns took an interest in events such as the Minnesota iron strike of 1907 and the Michigan copper strike of 1913–1914 that involved thousands of their countrymen. These events inspired new debates and led to the establishment of more newspapers, thirty-four of which appeared in this period. Sharing and shaping the new ideological enthusiasms of the period, they had a better chance to achieve longevity than the pre–1900 papers.

The most impressive new journalistic undertakings were those of the socialists who headed the emerging labor movement. During the 1890s reformist labor associations such as the Imatra Society of Brooklyn sparked working-class consciousness. Late in 1899 Antero F. Tanner, a doctor converted to socialism shortly before his arrival in America, met with labor activists at the Imatra Society's hall in Brooklyn. The gathering decided to establish the *Amerikan Työmies* (The American worker), which appeared for about six months in 1900 and employed as one of its editors Johan W. Lähde, a former pastor converted by Tanner. However, the paper's failure did not halt the socialist movement, which gained new supporters from Finland and attracted temperance followers and liberal churchmen who had arrived earlier. In 1903 the Imatra Society joined its counterparts to form a league which refused to support the American Socialist party. Dissidents broke away to organize the Finnish Socialist Federation in 1906. Meanwhile, in 1903, Massachusetts socialists acquired a press in Worcester and began publishing the *Amerikan Suomalainen Työmies* (The Finnish American workingman) (later known only as the *Työmies* [The workingman]) under the editorship of Vihtori Kosonen, who had been the business manager of the main socialist newspaper in Helsinki. By 1904 financial and other difficulties led to the establishment of the new publishing company that transferred the paper to Hancock, Michigan, where its subscriptions rose to 13,000 by 1913. In 1911 the company began issuing the paper daily. Between 1907 and 1913 its staff rose from thirteen to sixty-two persons. Supporting the endeavors of the new federation, the *Työmies* also championed the iron and copper mine strikers.

But the socialists were not content with one paper. In 1905 socialists rallied in Fitchburg, Massachusetts, to publish the *Raivaaja* (The pioneer) with an editor, Taavi Tainio, who had been fired by a local Finnish publisher. Subsequently, Frans J. Syrjälä became the paper's longtime editor and defender of parliamentary socialism. Syrjälä was a tailor who had gained socialist editorial experience in Finland. By 1913 the paper had 6,500 subscribers and appeared daily. Two years after its founding, socialists started a third paper, *Toveri* (The comrade) in Astoria, Oregon, which also became a daily. Both papers cooperated with the *Työmies* in publishing and distributing other kinds of literature. The Finnish Socialist Federation supported them by organizing drives to increase circulation and to recruit hundreds of local correspondents and representatives. In 1914, when its membership numbered 15,525 in 274 chapters, the federation faced a bitter struggle over industrial unionism and the Industrial Workers of the World. Three to four thousand members who defected or were expelled started the

Sosialisti, which became the *Teollisuustyöläinen*. In 1917 the industrial unionists replaced it with the *Industrialisti*, winning a circulation of about 10,000 two years later.

Churchmen, too, experienced new enthusiasm for developing their own newspapers. The Synod Lutherans expanded their *Amerikan Suometar* into a triweekly in 1913 when its circulation reached 5,200. At this time the Suomi Synod had 132 congregations with 13,957 adult members. Except for Emil Saastamoinen, who served from 1913 to 1921, the paper's editors were usually short-term appointees, pastors, or faculty members of Suomi College. In contrast, the Finnish Congregationalists were less successful, reviving their defunct *Totuus* as the *Uusi Totuus* for only three years. After undertaking other journalistic ventures in Ironwood, Michigan, the National Lutherans established a weekly, *Auttaja*, in 1906 under the editorship of clergymen such as Pietari Wuori. Reaching 2,900 subscribers by 1909, the paper debated religious issues with Synod Lutherans. Unlike these two groups, the Apostolic Lutherans were slow to publish. Their ranks were divided into factions, and all did not favor newspapers for religious reasons. In 1915 Sanfrid Mustonen and other members of the so-called conservative wing of Apostolic Lutherans established a private company to publish the *Valvoja*, which attracted 7,000 subscribers within four years.

In spite of this growing organizational newspaper competition, private entrepreneurs persisted in starting new papers. Frequently they capitalized on current ideological interests to further their own efforts. In 1904 Alex Heisson briefly employed Taavi Tainio to win socialist readers for his *Pohjan Tähti* (The north star) which he had started in Fitchburg two years previously. Later the Eastern States Temperance League endorsed his paper as its official organ. Another newspaper, the *New Yorkin Uutiset* (The New York news), was initiated in 1906 by a group closely associated with the local Imatra Society in Brooklyn that had become disgruntled with the *Raivaaja*. The group formed a company which soon employed Matti Kurikka, a colorful utopian socialist and an eccentric editor. In addition to these new beginnings, the *Uusi Kotimaa* flourished from the pre–1900 period under the ownership of its founder's sons and the editorship of Lähde, who had rejoined it. Likewise, the *Finska Amerikanaren* survived under the editorship of Edward J. Antell. However, August Edwards's *Amerikan Sanomat ja Suometar* (The American tidings and Finn), which had acquired the *Suometar* of Calumet in 1903 and reached a peak circulation of 11,000 in 1909, collapsed as its subscribers decreased to 5,000 in 1913.

Other developments made Duluth, Minnesota, a major center of newspaper publishing. In 1901 the Päivälehti Publishing Company of Calumet started the *Päivälehti* (The daily journal), which became the first successful Finnish daily newspaper. The new company gained the financial support of local businessmen and professionals like Oscar J. Larson, and it acquired the *Amerikan Uutiset*, which was continued as a weekly. Around 1910 the firm became the property of Jacob (John) E. Saari, a grocer with other business interests. Saari owned the Finnish American Publishing Company, which tried to find a foothold for the

Siirtolainen in Brooklyn, New York, and Kaleva, Michigan, before relocating it in Duluth in 1910. He had also founded a company in Duluth with fellow members of the Knights of Kaleva to revive the *Amerikan Kaiku* (The American echo), which had been established in Brooklyn in 1904 under the editorship of Eero Erkko, who soon returned to Helsinki. The revival effort failed in 1908. Six years later Saari moved the operations of the Päivälehti Publishing Company to Duluth, retaining the daily paper and the weekly *Siirtolainen*, but suspending the *Amerikan Uutiset*. Within a few months the publishers of a temperance weekly, *Raittiuslehti* (The temperance journal), which had been initiated in 1913, acquired the Päivälehti Publishing Company, much to the distress of the Eastern State Temperance League, which feared that its daily would compete with the *Pohjan Tähti*. In 1916 Carl H. Salminen, business manager of the company, took over the operations, with Antero Riippa continuing as his chief editor.

Other newspapers appeared with little success between 1900 and 1920. Among them were the *New Yorkin Sanomat* (New York tidings) in New York; the *Amerikan Kuulumisiä* (The American news), *Kansalainen* (The citizen), and *Niagara* (The Niagara) in Brooklyn; and the *Worcesterin Sanomat* (The Worcester tidings) of Worcester. Hancock, Michigan, produced the *Lännen Sanomat* (The western news), *Lauanti Posti* (The Saturday post), and another paper with a variant spelling, *Lauantaiposti* (The Saturday post). Likewise, Ironwood, Michigan, acquired three: *Ilmoittaja* (The reporter), *Kansan Lehti* (The people's journal), and *Vapaa Sana* (Free speech). Minnesota's share consisted of the *Minnesota Uutiset* (The Minnesota news) and *Pohjalainen* (The northerner) in Virginia and the *Suomalainen* (The Finn) of Ely. While western publishers developed the *Viikko Sanomat* (The weekly tidings) in Aberdeen, Washington, others introduced the *Vapauttaja* (The liberator) in Portland, Oregon, and the *Astorian Sanomat* (The Astoria tidings), *Lännen Kaiku* (The western echo), *Lännen Uutiset* (The western news), and *Tyynenmeren Sanomat* (The Pacific Ocean tidings) in Astoria, Oregon. Except for the *Lännen Uutiset*, which ran for eight years, and the *Astorian Sanomat*, which lasted four years, none lasted more than two years.

In 1913 the major papers had a total circulation of about 77,000. The three socialist dailies, *Raivaaja*, *Toveri*, and *Työmies*, had 25,000 subscribers. While the *Päivälehti* had 7,000, its two weeklies averaged about the same. The *Amerikan Suometar* reported over 5,000, and the *Auttaja*, 1,750. In contrast, the *Uusi Kotimaa* had 9,700; the *Amerikan Sanomat*, *Lännen Uutiset*, and *New Yorkin Uutiset* each had about 5,000; the *Pohjan Tähti*, 2,000; and the *Finska Amerikanaren*, 6,000.

The socialist press aroused the envy and hatred of its rivals. Before the socialist movement was well under way, the *Siirtolainen*, *Päivälehti*, *Amerikan Uutiset*, and *Pohjan Tähti*, among others, flirted with the labor movement, supported social reformism, and even employed socialists. By 1906, however, all this changed as the socialists made inroads into the ranks of the immigrant community. Henceforth the proprietary and church press focused more on the socialist challenge than on religious controversies. The critics denounced socialists as a new threat to religion, property rights, and family relationships.

Although conceding the workers' need for social justice, the *Amerikan Suometar* and other papers dismissed socialists as self-serving leaders who misled the labor movement. Socialist class agitation and encouragement of the iron and copper strikes were blamed for damaging the reputation of Finns as "good" workers. Likewise, Matti Kurikka and other utopians and ex-radicals focused on socialist class warfare as disrupting ancient community bonds. In short, "Finnishness" was endangered, according to the antisocialist press, which came to identify itself more and more as the "true" representative of Finnish nationalism.

The events of World War I further intensified the journalistic rivalry, with socialists upholding the antiwar policy of their party. Nationalist papers were fearful that all Finns would be regarded as disloyal by Americans, expecially after the arrest of the editors of the *Toveri* and *Industrialisti* along with other Finnish radicals, and after the examination of the premises of *Raivaaja* by federal agents. With the support of Carl H. Salminen and other publishers in 1917, the Lincoln Loyalty League denounced radicalism and affirmed patriotism. These nationalists were also outraged by radicals who defended the Russian Revolution of November 1917 and then sided with socialists in the Finnish civil war of 1918. Subsequently, they hailed the civil war as a victory of Finnish bourgeois nationalism. However, all socialists did not remain united after 1918; the *Raivaaja* rejected proletarian internationalism and ultimately moved toward a gradual accommodation with the nationalists. On the other hand, the *Toveri* and *Työmies* challenged the nationalist newspapers, which formed a league with their Canadian counterparts to develop mutual concerns and exploit the wartime hysteria against radicals.

Although few immigrants arrived from Finland after the war, the Finnish press reached the heyday of its circulation during the 1920s. Only one established paper, the *Pohjan Tähti* in Fitchburg, disappeared; however, it was replaced immediately by another *Amerikan Suomalainen* (The Finnish American) in 1926. A new company rescued the financially troubled old-timer, *Finska Amerikanaren*, which lost readers opposing its nationalist stand on the Finnish civil war. Still another veteran, the *Uusi Kotimaa*, was sold in 1920 to a Finnish company supporting the farmers' organization known as the Nonpartisan League; the *Työmies* later gained control of the paper. In contrast, three new newspapers—the *Detroitin Uutiset* (The Detroit news) in Detroit, *Ilmoittaja* (The reporter) in Astoria, and the bilingual *Independent* in Aberdeen, Washington—were short-lived, while the *Kansan Lehti* (The people's journal) of Cleveland lasted into the next decade. Two other new papers were more fortunate, namely, the Synod Lutherans' *Lännen Suometar* (The western Finn), which appeared in Astoria in 1922, and the *Amerikan Sanomat* (The American tidings), established in 1924 at Fairport, Ohio, by a company with rights to Edwards's old publication of the same name. The longest-lived new paper was *Eteenpäin* (Forward). It appeared in New York in 1921 and from there was transferred to Worcester. It challenged the *Raivaaja*, which had been taken over by right-wing members of the American Socialist Party. Both the *Työmies* and *Toveri* remained loyal, however, to the Finnish Socialist Federation, supporting the American Workers' Party. The *Eteenpäin* drew some of its veteran editors, like Knut E. Heikkinen, from the *Työmies*. Likewise, the other newspapers generally had experienced editors.

Undoubtedly, the newspapers maintained circulation partly because of their strong editorial leadership. Also, the press retained its readers' loyalties by cultivating ideological issues in the presentation of current domestic and international developments. By the mid–1920s the labor press (*Eteenpäin*, *Industrialisti*, *Raivaaja*, *Toveri*, and *Työmies*) had 44,000 subscribers. The *Työmies* had the largest circulation of any Finnish paper, at one point reaching over 20,000 readers, and the circulation of *Uusi Kotimaa* increased to 12,000. The four religious papers (*Amerikan Suometar*, *Auttaja*, *Lännen Suometar*, and *Valvoja*) had a total circulation of 17,600, led by the latter, an Apostolic Lutheran publication. The other major papers (*Amerikan Sanomat*, *Finska Amerikanaren*, *New Yorkin Uutiset*, *Päivälehti*, *Pohjan Tähti*, and *Siirtolainen*) attracted 30,811 readers. Total circulation for all Finnish papers was over 104,000.

From the onset of the Great Depression of 1929 to the close of World War II in 1945, the Finnish press lost ground. Between 1920 and 1940 the number of foreign-born Finns declined 27 percent to 117,210, therefore reducing the potential readership. The second generation outnumbered the immigrants, and it increasingly read the English-language press. Editors of the *Amerikan Suometar* and other papers grappled with the possibility of using English; if they had done so extensively, however, Finnish readers might have been alienated. Nevertheless, some second-generation Finnish Americans supported the press and even provided a few replacements for veteran editors. On the other hand, the financial stringencies of the Depression lessened the opportunities for hiring new personnel.

The Depression also reduced the ability of subscribers to support their newspapers and undermined the press operations of both proprietors and organizations. Three leading papers, the *Toveri*, *Uusi Kotimaa*, and *Siirtolainen*, disappeared, while the *Päivälehti* became the property of the *Raivaaja*. Four of the papers (*Amerikan Sanomat*, *Amerikan Suomalainen*, *Independent*, and *Kansan Lehti*) that had been established in the 1920s collapsed during the Depression. Six of the nine new ones appearing during the 1930s failed within their first two years: the *Amerikan Farmari* (The American farmer), Duluth and Floodwood, Minnesota; *Keskilännen Uutiset* (The midwestern news), Chicago; *Pohjois-Amerikan Sanomat* (The North American tidings), Fairport, Ohio; and *Viikkolehti* (The weekly journal), Calumet; and two English-language titles, *Finnish-American Weekly* of Duluth, and *Fin-So-News* of Detroit. The other three included the *Fitchburgin Sanomat* (The Fitchburg tidings), which survived for eight years in Fitchburg; the weekly *Opas* (The guide), established by a private company of liberal Apostolic Lutherans in 1931; and the *Keskilänsi* (The Midwest), started in 1932 by Frans Tuomi in New York Mills, where it was absorbed by the

Minnesotan Uutiset (The Minnesota news), which had been established by Carl
A. Parta and Adolph Lundquist during the same year. Although by the mid–
1930s the existing papers still had a net circulation of slightly over 101,000, the
Depression took its toll and reduced the total to between 70,000 and 80,000 at
the close of World War II. The wartime economic boom gave some relief but
could not reverse the forces of decline. The one new paper, the *Detroitin Sanomat*
(The Detroit tidings), which was established in Detroit during the war period,
did not survive long. In the period from 1930 to 1945 the ideological differences
between the newspapers remained sharp, though all joined in 1938 to commemorate the tricentennial of the coming of Finns to the Delaware Valley.

Since World War II the surviving Finnish newspapers have faced the common
fate of the disappearing institutions of the immigrants whose numbers have
decreased more than 60 percent in three decades, to 45,449 by 1970. During
the following decade the total declined to 29,172. The decreasing numbers of
new immigrants meant lower subscription income in a period of inflationary
costs and provided fewer recruits to serve as correspondents, agents, and editors.
Also, this aging generation was unable to maintain the religious, labor, and other
organizations with strong networks of support for their newspapers. Even organizations such as the Suomi Synod merged with large multi-ethnic associations
that had no need to publish Finnish newspapers. Other organizations simply
disbanded. Labor organizations declined, suffering from the antiradical hysteria
and political repression known as McCarthyism in the late 1940s and 1950s. If
long-established organizations could not survive, most newspapers had little
chance of faring any differently.

However, the newspapers were determined to function as long as possible.
Their publishers raised subscriptions to ten and fifteen dollars or more annually
while reducing the frequency of publication to one issue per week. The publishers
of papers like the *Finska Amerikanaren* sold their equipment and contracted with
other printers to produce their papers using offset techniques of reproduction.
Even proprietary publishers appealed for annual gifts of money, as the labor
press had always done in the past. Another way of saving money was to merge
papers, as in the case of the *Työmies-Eteenpäin* (The workingman-Forward),
which involved two prominent labor papers in 1950. Seven years later the *Opas*
and *Valvoja* united to form the *Pohjolan Sanomat* (The northern tidings), which
suspended publication as the *Amerikan Sanomat* (The American tidings) and
transferred its subscription list to the *Minnesota Uutiset* in 1960. The Minnesota
paper renamed itself the *Amerikan Uutiset* (The American news). Meanwhile,
other papers were abolished. When the *Päivälehti* was suspended by *Raivaaja*
in 1948, a new company tried to replace it with the *Keskilännen Sanomat* (The
Midwest tidings), which appeared in Duluth from 1949 to 1956. Likewise, a
private publisher issued the *Lännen Uutiset* (The western news) in Astoria to
replace the *Lännen Suometar*, ended by Synod Lutherans in 1946. In 1951 the
new paper became the *Columbia Press*, retaining a Finish-language section for
some years. In 1962 the Synod Lutherans also ended their *Amerikan Suometar*,

while the National Lutherans converted their *Auttaja* into a short-lived monthly devotional journal in 1965. In 1975 the *Industrialisti* terminated its activities, leaving five surviving newspapers. Throughout this period circulation declined almost one-half, to about 43,000 at the end of the ten-year period from 1945 to 1955. The total declined to approximately 22,000 in 1965 and to nearly 12,000 by the mid–1970s.

In the early 1980s only five newspapers survived after more than 100 years of publishing by Finns in the United States. The five were the Swedish-language *Norden* and the Finnish *Amerikan Uutiset, New Yorkin Uutiset, Raivaaja,* and *Työmies-Eteenpäin*; total circulation was about 7,500. The *Amerikan Uutiset* had the most subscribers, replacing the *Työmies-Eteenpäin*, which had long been in first place. All clung to a decreasing number of loyal readers and supplemented their declining income from subscriptions with special fund drives and subsidies from the Finland Society of Helsinki. All employed modest staffs which had managed to recruit Finnish-born editors. Whatever their orientation, the papers mirrored the activities of a retired immigrant generation, recalling occasionally the heyday of Finnish publishing, which had once produced not only about 90 newspapers but also over 250 periodicals, including monthlies and yearbooks and even weeklies devoted to women, humor, cooperatives, and literature. In 1983 the editors of the four Finnish-language papers met in Minneapolis, lamenting their common fate and dreaming of new ways to prolong their literary tradition. However, no practical resolutions were forthcoming. It may be that the 1980s will mark the passing of the Finnish-American newspaper.

BIBLIOGRAPHY

Haltrola, David T. "Finnish-Language Newspapers in the United States." In Ralph J. Jalkanen, ed., *The Finns in North America: A Social Symposium.* Hancock, Mich.: Suomi College, 1969, pp. 73–90.

Kero, Reino. "From Soldier of Fortune to Newspaperman: The Story of Alexander Leinonen." *Finnish Americana* 1 (1978): 41–50.

Kolehmainen, John I. "Finnish Newspapers and Periodicals in Michigan." *Michigan History Quarterly* 24 (1940): 119–127.

———. "Finnish Newspapers in Ohio." *The Ohio State Archeological and Historical Quarterly* 47 (1938): 123–128.

———. *The Finns in America: A Bibliographical Guide to Their History.* Hancock, Mich.: Suomi College, 1947, chap. 8: "Newspapers and Periodicals."

———. *Sow the Golden Seed.* Fitchburg, Mass.: Raivaaja Publishing Co., 1955. Reprint. New York: Raivaaja Publishing Co., 1979.

Kostiainen, Auvo. "Features of Finnish-American Publishing." Publications of the Institute of History, General History, University of Turku, Finland, No. 9. Vassa, Finland, 1977, pp. 54–70.

Niemi, Taisto J. "The Book Concern: Six Decades of Service to Suomi Synod and It's [sic] People." In Ralph J. Jalkanen, ed., *The Faith of the Finns: Historical*

    Perspectives on the Finnish Lutheran Church in America. East Lansing, Mich.:
    n. p., 1972, pp. 204–226.
Riipa, Timo. " 'Toimittaja Lähde': The Story of a Finnish Immigrant Newspaperman,
    Temperance Advocate, and Minister." *Finnish Americana* 3 (1980): 30–40.

9

The Franco-American Press

ROBERT B. PERREAULT

Of the nearly 500 French-language newspapers that have appeared in the United States since 1780, over 330 were published between 1868 and the present by and for *Québécois* immigrants and their descendants, the Franco-Americans, in the New England–eastern New York area.[1] For reasons of practicality, the present study will focus primarily on the New England Franco-American press while offering, as an introduction, a brief overview of French-language newspapers published in regions of the United States settled by immigrants from France, Acadia, and Québec.

The birth of the French press in this country occurred with the printing of *La Gazette Française* (The French gazette) aboard the French fleet docked at Newport, Rhode Island, in November-December 1780.[2] From this date until the turn of the nineteenth century, at least ten newspapers, most of them ephemeral, served the French populations of such cities as Boston, New York, Philadelphia, and New Orleans. During the next hundred years Louisiana, peopled heavily by Creoles and Cajuns,[3] became a breeding ground for no less than sixty French newspapers. The most successful among these was *L'Abeille* (The bee), a trilingual (French-English-Spanish) daily, which ran from 1827 to 1916.[4] Elsewhere, New York City, San Francisco, and Los Angeles afforded French journalists a relatively favorable climate. In fact, the two longest-running newspapers in the history of the French-language press in the United States are *Le Courrier des Etats-Unis* (The United States courier), founded in New York in 1828, and *L'Echo du Pacifique* (The Pacific echo) of San Francisco, which dates back to 1852. Both have undergone name changes and are published today as *France-Amérique* (France-America) and *Le Journal Français d'Amérique* (The French journal of America), respectively.[5]

In the vicinity of the Great Lakes, there flourished not a purely French press, but a French-Canadian and Franco-American press. Between 1817 and 1959, Michigan, Illinois, Wisconsin, and Minnesota witnessed the arrival and departure of some forty French-language journals. In terms of longevity, the two most important were *L'Echo de l'Ouest* (The western echo) of Minneapolis (1883–

1929) and *Le Courrier du Michigan* (The Michigan courier) of Lake Linden and later of Detroit (1912–1959) where, during its last thirty years, it remained the Midwest's sole French-language newspaper.[6]

Prior to the establishment of a truly Franco-American press, a breed of short-lived but significant French-Canadian newspapers appeared in New England. The failure of the Insurrection of 1837–1838[7] caused a few rebels or *patriotes* to take refuge in northern Vermont, where they founded newspapers advocating the creation of an independent Canadian republic. The best known of these, *Le Patriote Canadien* (The Canadian patriot) of Burlington, lasted for six months in 1839–1840. Its publisher was Ludger Duvernay, a Montréal journalist and high-ranking *patriote*.[8]

The movement favoring Canadian independence remained alive, as was evidenced by occasional but unsuccessful journalistic ventures. In 1867, the year in which the Canadian Confederation was established, *L'Ordre des Dix*, a New York City–based Canadian independence society, published *Le Public Canadien* (The Canadian public). Two years later, Médéric Lanctôt, a Montréal journalist, politician, and opponent of the Canadian Confederation, founded pro-independence newspapers in Burlington, Vermont and Worcester, Massachusetts; neither lasted more than a few issues.[9]

Financial difficulties aside, these politically oriented newspapers failed largely because they offered little reading material relevant to the daily lives of Québécois immigrants in the United States. The Québécois had come to this country seeking economic relief, and while political events in their native land might have concerned them remotely, they nonetheless had to deal with the realities of their present existence. For most, this meant going from a strongly Catholic, francophone, rural, agrarian society to a largely Protestant, anglophone, urban, industrial milieu that was itself undergoing rapid changes due to technological advances and to an influx of immigrants from many different cultures.[10] Having brought with them their innate sense of ethnic *survivance*, by which they hoped to achieve the American Dream without sacrificing too much of their cultural identity, the Québécois set out to establish, among other institutions, a Franco-American press which aimed at informing and uniting its readers, while aiding them in overcoming their difficulties and realizing their goals.

Prior to the American Civil War, New England had a small, scattered, and transient French-Canadian population. According to U. S. Census figures, there were 49,008 "Canadian-born" individuals in the six-state region in 1850, while in 1860 the level had risen to 70,828.[11] The Civil War left many vacancies in New England's evergrowing textile mills, the livelihood of most Québécois immigrants. During and after the war, mill agents scouted the Québec countryside in search of financially ailing *habitants* whom they seduced with stories of New England's economic opportunities. By 1870 the area's "Canadian-born" population numbered 159,445, an increase of more than 100 percent in ten years.[12]

The development of the New England Franco-American press may be divided into four slightly overlapping stages of evolution: trial period (1868–1890);

golden age (1890–1920); decline (1920–1970); and renaissance (1970 to date). By discussing the various functions of the Franco-American press, it is possible to demonstrate the influential role that newspapers played in the lives of their readers, as well as in the establishment of their institutions.

The first truly New England Franco-American newspaper, *Le Protecteur Canadien* (The Canadian guardian) of St. Albans, Vermont, went to press in 1868.[13] Prior to that year the entire six-state region had only three Franco-American parishes, all in Vermont, and Québécois immigrants elsewhere had two choices: either attend Irish-Catholic churches, where linguistic and cultural differences often led to their alienation, or simply avoid religious services. Fearing the latter and knowing that the Québécois placed much emphasis on the relationship between their mother tongue and their Catholic faith,[14] the Reverend Zéphirin Druon, pastor at St. Albans and vicar-general of the diocese of Burlington, founded *Le Protecteur Canadien* in order to make known the need for French-speaking priests in New England. Though this newspaper went out of existence in 1871 when a fire destroyed its headquarters, it had enjoyed a wide circulation and a strong influence. Between 1868 and 1871 the number of Franco-American parishes in New England rose from three to twenty-two. By the close of the "trial period" in 1890, 148 priests were ministering to a total of 306,453 Franco-Americans in eighty-six homogeneous French-language parishes and in another seventy mixed parishes with a French majority.[15] Out of these parishes grew a large, New England-wide network of schools, hospitals, orphanages, and homes for the poor and the elderly, all administered by religious orders from Québec and France.

The Franco-American press also fulfilled some basic and immediate needs. In addition to providing readers with general news from the local to the international scene in their idiom, French-language journals kept their readers abreast of matters relevant to Franco-American life in their own or other communities. Information of this nature ranged from such minor events as a particular family receiving guests from Québec, to the very major, for example, an attempted ban on the French language in schools. Also included were French news items from elsewhere in the United States, and from Canada and France. All of this helped to create new ties or reinforce existing ones among Franco-Americans, thus giving them a collective and cohesive sense of identity.

Throughout its history, however, the Franco-American press has operated more for the sake of voicing opinions and discussing ideas than for disseminating the news. In collaboration with other Franco-American community leaders, journalists worked toward maintaining, promoting, and protecting the faith, mother tongue, and cultural traditions of their compatriots. They also saw themselves as the champions of civil rights and political advancement for Franco-Americans. And, like their ancestors, the French, Franco-American journalists have always had a passion for polemics.

An early but successful Franco-American newspaper which embodies all of the above characteristics was Ferdinand Gagnon's *Le Travailleur* (The worker).[16]

In 1868, after having pursued a classical course of study in his home town of St-Hyacinthe, Québec, Gagnon migrated to New Hampshire where, in 1869, he founded the state's first French-language newspaper, *La Voix du Peuple* (The people's voice) of Manchester. Following this newspaper's seven-month existence, Gagnon moved to Worcester, Massachusetts, where, in 1874, after several more short-lived attempts, he launched *Le Travailleur*.

As a brilliant writer and orator who eventually became known and respected in francophone circles as far away as the Midwest, Gagnon began his career during an era of uncertainty with regard not only to French-language journalism but also to the future of the Franco-American population as a whole. Although immigrants poured in by the thousands each year, many did so with the intention of remaining in the United States only temporarily, in order to earn money with which to make a new start in Québec. To those readers of *Le Travailleur* who felt alienated or disillusioned in this foreign ambiance, Gagnon, acting as an official repatriation agent for the government of Québec, recommended an immediate return to the homeland. Because not all Franco-American journalists agreed with Gagnon, his views led to one of the first of many fiery polemics by which Franco-American newspapers drew much attention. However, the limited success of the repatriation movement prompted Gagnon to reevaluate and eventually reverse his position. By doing so, he incurred the wrath of the pro-repatriation journalists. The situation intensified to the point where Honoré Beaugrand, an editor from Fall River, Massachusetts, who later repatriated and went on to assume the mayoralty of Montréal, challenged Gagnon to a duel, though the latter declined the invitation.[17]

As small but rapidly developing neighborhoods referred to as *Petits Canadas* (Little Canadas) continued to sprout across New England, it became apparent to Gagnon and others that the Québécois were here to stay. As a result, Gagnon, not wishing to see his compatriots live in and contribute to American society while depriving themselves of the rights and benefits of U. S. citizenship, advocated the formation of naturalization clubs.[18] Many Québécois immigrants experienced some apprehension about forsaking their allegiance to their mother country. Perhaps they longed to return to Québec; perhaps they had grown accustomed to living a sheltered existence within the confines of their Little Canadas; or perhaps they felt threatened or unwanted by the Yankees, many of whom expressed xenophobic sentiments reminiscent of the Know-Nothing era. By 1883 only 425 of 12,000 French Canadians in Lowell, Massachusetts, had registered to vote, while by 1890, of the more than 300,000 "Canadian-born" individuals mentioned earlier, only 28,465 had become naturalized.[19] This stagnation in no way prevented politically ambitious Franco-Americans from achieving office at the municipal and state levels as early as the 1880s.[20] Nor did it discourage newspapermen from going to great lengths to arouse the political awareness of their readers. For example, journalist and political activist Benjamin Lenthier used funds provided by the Democratic Party to create newspapers or to buy existing ones, solely to influence Franco-Americans to back Grover Cleveland in the U. S. presidential campaign of 1892.[21]

With time and with more pressure put upon them by their newspapers and societies, Québécois immigrants became naturalized and began voting to a much greater degree, as evidenced by such accomplishments as those of Aram Pothier, who became mayor of Woonsocket in 1894, lieutenant-governor of Rhode Island in 1897, and governor in 1908.[22]

While the Franco-American press struggled to preserve and promote French life in the United States, journalists also used their newspapers to defend their people's culture. During the early years, because Québec was rapidly losing its population to New England, it became fashionable there to denounce Franco-Americans as traitors to their national birthplace. As rejoinders, Franco-American journalists would publish special editions containing long, well-documented articles clearly demonstrating that within New England's Little Canadas, one could work, be educated, worship, shop, and socialize in French-Catholic surroundings.

One example of the effectiveness of the press in defending Franco-Americans against outside forces was the "Chinese of the Eastern States" incident.[23] Like Chinese-American railroad construction workers in the western states, Québécois immigrants willingly accepted menial jobs, long work days, and meager wages in the textile industry. Consequently, Yankees and others viewed them as an impediment to the potential upgrading of working conditions in the mills, as well as to the passage of a bill by the Massachusetts State Legislature that sought to establish a uniform ten-hour work day. In a report to the legislature, Dr. Carroll D. Wright, chief of the Massachusetts Bureau of Statistics of Labor, referred to the "Canadian French" as the "Chinese of the Eastern States," as a "horde of industrial invaders," as "so sordid and low a people," and an assortment of other such labels.[24] In response to Wright's remarks, Ferdinand Gagnon rallied together has fellow journalists and other influential Franco-American leaders who, through the press and through letters addressed to the legislature, obtained hearings during which they registered their protests. Consequently, Wright reexamined his findings and, in a subsequent report, wrote about the Franco-Americans from a more objective perspective.[25]

In 1886 Ferdinand Gagnon, who would one day be called the "father of the Franco-American press," succumbed to a brief illness at not quite thirty-seven years of age. *Le Travailleur* outlasted its founder by six years. Deprived of the most prestigious journalist and newspaper of the "trial period," Franco-Americans nevertheless inherited the early fruits of Gagnon's dream of creating a solid base and a firm direction for French-language journalism in New England.

During its trial period, the Franco-American press contended with certain factors that hindered its chances for survival. There existed partial or total illiteracy among a segment of the Franco-American population, an indifference, on the part of many, toward reading in general, and a lack of leisure time in which to read. As for newspapers, some simply had too narrow a scope of interest, while others seemed tied to one particular cause, such as Lenthier's political sheets, which spelled death once the cause had disappeared.

In 1886 Ephrem R. Dufresne, editor of *Le Canadien* (The Canadian) of St. Paul, Minnesota, and subsequently founder-editor of *L'Avenir Canadien* (The Canadian future) of Manchester, New Hampshire, declared that the Franco-American press had two enemies: apathy among the people toward anything dealing with "French instruction," and stiff competition from Canadian newspapers, which were readily available wherever a significant francophone population lived in the United States.[26] However, the one striking characteristic of Franco-American newspapers was that they appeared to be competing with one another. In 1890, with a Franco-American population of 16,326, Lowell, Massachusetts, had four French-language journals simultaneously, while in the same year, in Manchester, New Hampshire, five such newspapers vied with one another for sales among 14,063 potential readers. Hence, by 1911, of the more than eighty New England Franco-American newspapers founded between 1868 and 1890, only four remained.[27]

During the "golden age" of the Franco-American press (1890–1920), a few newspapers that had once struggled as weeklies now prospered as dailies. By the turn of the century (or slightly before, in some cases), the cities of Fall River, Lowell, and Worcester, Massachusetts, Manchester, New Hampshire, and Woonsocket, Rhode Island, all had a daily French-language newspaper. Later, New Bedford, Massachusetts, and Lewiston, Maine, were added to this list. In cities and towns with a lesser number of Franco-Americans, such as Biddeford, Maine, Nashua, New Hampshire, Lawrence and Holyoke, Massachusetts, and Pawtucket, Rhode Island, there were long-running weekly or semi-weekly journals.

In the entire history of the Franco-American press, no other period offered better conditions under which to launch a newspaper. The steady flow of immigrants from Québec assured that French life in New England would receive constant nurture and replenishment, thus creating a mood of optimism leading to many more journalistic ventures of various types: religious, temperance, literary, humorous, militant, female-oriented, commercial, historical, fraternal, bilingual, and so on.

Among these, the literary category deserves special attention because the Franco-American press both spawned and fostered Franco-American literature. Journalists encouraged artistic expression by regularly providing space for poetry, fiction, and other forms of creative writing. Although men participated to some degree in these literary activities, much of the credit goes to women who, besides being in charge of female-oriented columns and pages, wrote novels, poems, book reviews, biographical portraits, historical features, and human interest stories. The writings of Anna Duval-Thibault, Corinne Rocheleau-Rouleau, Yvonne Le Maitre, and Hélène Thivierge, among others, filled many pages of *L'Indépendent* (The independent) of Fall River, *L'Opinion Publique* (Public opinion) of Worcester, *L'Etoile* (The star) of Lowell, and *La Justice* (Justice) of Biddeford, respectively. Most novels written in French by Franco-American men and women were serialized in a newspaper before coming out in book form, from 1878, with Honoré Beaugrand's *Jeanne la Fileuse* in *La République* (The republic) of Fall River, to 1936, with Camille Lessard's *Canuck* in *Le Messager* (The messenger) of Lewiston.[28]

By the years immediately preceding the outbreak of World War I, many Franco-American families had lived in New England for two or more generations. At that time, in terms of the bulk of their population, never before had they been and never again would they be as bilingual and as bicultural. Thus, while maintaining strong ties with the Québécois heritage, they gradually began blending into the mainstream of American society. If members of the older generation still read French-language newspapers out of necessity, their offspring continued to do so more by habit or out of a sense of ethnic loyalty, since many could have just as easily read English-language newspapers. Soon, all of this would change.

The decline of the Franco-American press and of the more French aspects of Franco-American life began or at least became more evident after World War I. Several new factors played a role. As is the case with any newspaper, regardless of language, a daily could easily overshadow a weekly, and since most Franco-American newspapers were weeklies, and because nearly every major Franco-American center had its own daily, the weeklies stood little chance of succeeding. Also, larger newspapers, often supported by French-language job printers, offered stiff competition to smaller newspapers, who relied mainly upon advertisements and subscriptions to stay alive.[29] Some working-class Franco-Americans viewed their newspapers as being too elitist, too concerned with matters that touched only the leaders of their ethnic group. At times, these newspapers even took editorial stands that clashed with the basic ideals of the working class, as did *L'Avenir National* (The national future) during a nine-month strike at the Amoskeag Manufacturing Company of Manchester in 1922, by advocating that Franco-American strikers return to work.[30] Journalists themselves blamed the electronic media, radio and cinema newsreels, and later television, for drawing away their readers.

A subtle yet effective force working against the cultural fabric of all ethnic groups, affecting not only their press but also their other institutions, was the steady process of assimilation into the American way of life. While *survivance* had, for perhaps longer than most ethnic groups, allowed Franco-Americans to preserve their mother tongue, they were now well along in their lengthy shift from French monolingualism to English monolingualism, a shift as yet incomplete.[31] There exists a definite correlation between this phenomenon and certain historical events of the 1920s that brought about a bizarre twist in the evolution of the press.

Pro-American and anti-German feelings prevalent during World War I turned into vehement anti-ethnic sentiments in the postwar era, thereby inspiring an

Americanization campaign destined to eradicate all traces of ethnicity in an effort to "unify" the American people under "one flag and one language."[32] The 1920s also saw the climax of decades of conflict between the Irish-American–dominated Roman Catholic Church hierarchy on one side and the Franco-American clergy and laity on the other. In an attempt to give the Church a more American and unified image, its hierarchy adopted policies that sought to accelerate the assimilation of all Catholic ethnic groups, policies that directly clashed with the *survivance* ideology of the Franco-Americans. Of all the confrontations that occurred, none compared to the viciousness and sensationalism that characterized the *Sentinelle* (The sentinel) affair of the 1920s.[33]

In 1924 *Les Croisés* (The crusaders), a secret society based in Woonsocket, R. I., and composed of Franco-American professionals, businessmen, and a few clergymen, founded a journal, *La Sentinelle*, in which they exposed and venomously attacked all whom they viewed as enemies of Franco-American culture. One of *La Sentinelle*'s prime targets was Monsignor William A. Hickey, Bishop of Providence, who led a fund drive for the construction of schools and other institutions. According to the "Sentinellists," in the fruits of this project, financed largely by Franco-Americans, the French language would play a limited or a nonexistent role. When the fiery writings of *La Sentinelle*'s editor, attorney Elphège J. Daignault, and his cohorts surpassed the limits of what more moderate Franco-Americans considered in good taste and respect due a bishop, a faction of "anti-Sentinellists" began retorting in Woonsocket's daily, *La Tribune*. Subsequently, many Franco-American newspapers throughout New England took sides in this issue, which developed into the longest and fiercest polemic in the history of the Franco-American press.

In 1928 Daignault and some sixty of his partisans were excommunicated by the ecclesiastical courts of Rome for having brought a civil suit against Bishop Hickey, and *La Sentinelle* was placed on the Church's *Index* of condemned reading materials. Although the *Sentinelle* affair remained primarily an elitist quarrel, the defeat of the Sentinellists, coupled with the Americanization movement, sped up what would otherwise have been a more gradual assimilation of Franco-Americans at all class levels. Moreover, the Depression of the 1930s ended the continuous transfusion of new ethnic blood from Québec, thereby leaving Franco-Americans to fend for themselves from a linguistic and cultural standpoint. Suddenly, concern over employment, food, and other necessities superseded the will to fight for one's ancestral heritage.

From the 1920s through the 1960s, newspaper after newspaper disappeared, including some of the seemingly invincible dailies, *L'Opinion Publique* of Worcester (1893–1931) and *La Tribune* of Woonsocket (1895–1934). Whereas in 1911 New England had thirty-three Franco-American newspapers, the number dropped to twenty-five by 1935 and to nineteen by 1942.[34] Nonetheless, diehard journalists continued with new ventures that ended in failure, with a few exceptions: *La Justice* of Sanford, Maine (1925–1945); *Le Messager* of New Bedford, Massachusetts (1927–1953); and *Le Journal* (The journal) of Haverhill,

Massachusetts (1927–1956). By far, Wilfrid Beaulieu's *Le Travailleur* of Worcester, founded in 1931 and named in honor of Ferdinand Gagnon's newspaper, outlasted all of its contemporaries. The last of the excommunicated Sentinellists to seek a pardon and be reinstated in the Church, Beaulieu published *Le Travailleur* for forty-eight years, until his death in 1979. During that time, *Le Travailleur*, more a journal of ideas than of news, remained one of New England's staunchest advocates of the French language and attracted readers and correspondents from around the United States, Canada, France, and elsewhere.[35]

In 1937 concerned journalists, including two of New England's best-known twentieth-century newspapermen, Philippe-Armand Lajoie of Fall River and Louis A. Biron of Lowell, formed L'Alliance des Journaux Franco-Américains in order to establish more solidarity among the remaining newspapers. However, as one member of L'Alliance after another passed into history, such as *L'Avenir National* of Manchester (1894–1949), *L'Etoile* of Lowell (1886–1957), and *L'Indépendant* of Fall River (1885–1962)—all powerful dailies—L'Alliance itself followed suit.

In the eyes of any Franco-American journalist, the 1960s must have been one of the darkest moments in the history of that profession. It was an era wherein many Americans preferred the cinema and television to books and newspapers. It appeared that the press in general, not to mention the ethnic press, seemed threatened. In 1963 Adolphe Robert, longtime editor of *Le Canado-Américain* of Manchester, in pointing out that the Franco-American press was far from alone in experiencing difficulties, cited as an example New York's Jewish daily, *Forward*, whose publishers found it expedient to include English-language articles because the Jewish community's younger members could not read Yiddish. He further stated that while the Jewish press remained financially solvent by virtue of an association devoted to this cause, the Franco-American press had nothing comparable.[36]

That same year, Le Comité de Vie Franco-Américaine, a group of New England–wide Franco-American leaders, organized the seventh Franco-American Congress, held in Holyoke, Massachusetts, which had for its theme the fate of the Franco-American press.[37] Among the resolutions passed, most of which were ineffective at this late date, one proclaimed 1964 as the "Year of the Franco-American Press." Ironically, in 1964 *La Justice* of Holyoke went out of print, as did *L'Impartial* of Nashua, New Hampshire, both of which dated back to the turn of the century.

During the final years of the decline of French-language newspapers, the following issues were among those that dominated their editorial pages: the partial or total loss or disuse of French in an ever-growing percentage of Franco-American families, churches, schools, and social organizations; the ignorance or apathy displayed by many Franco-Americans with regard to their ethnic heritage; and, of course, the rapid disappearance of French-language newspapers. In 1967 the recurring question of independence or, specifically, the possible secession of Québec from Canada, occupied its share of space in the Franco-

American press. For his now famous declaration "vive le Québec libre," Charles de Gaulle and Québec's separatists both received the praise of *Le Travailleur* of Worcester and *L'Action* of Manchester, and the condemnation of *Le Messager* of Lewiston, whose editors were in turn criticized by *L'Action* (Action). More recently, the "renaissance" era newspapers, founded by younger, liberal-minded individuals, hailed the election of Parti Québécois leader René Lévesque as Québec's prime minister and supported the *oui* vote in the 1980 referendum on sovereignty-association for Québec.[38]

In 1968, *Le Messager* of Lewiston, the longest-running newspaper, daily or otherwise, in the history of the New England Franco-American press, ceased publication after eighty-eight years.[39] Thus, exactly one century had passed since the birth of the first New England Franco-American newspaper, *Le Protecteur Canadien*. The history of the press had gone full circle, the era for renewal had finally arrived, and the cycle was about to begin again. Undoubtedly, the civil rights movement of the 1960s influenced the possibility for the cultural regeneration of minorities. Among Franco-Americans, there occurred a revival of interest in their ethnic heritage which created a climate conducive to a renaissance of their press.

The 1970s saw the birth of French-language and bilingual newspapers and periodicals whose total numbers, individual circulation, frequency of publication, and influence over Franco-Americans as a whole may never surpass those of their predecessors. However, their very existence, in light of the history of the Franco-Americans and their press, is in itself a small miracle.

Unlike their forerunners, today's Franco-American publications tend to appear quarterly, bimonthly, or monthly. In 1983 the oldest of this new breed, *Le FAROG Forum*, celebrated its tenth anniversary. Published by students at the University of Maine at Orono, its activist tone has attracted readers and correspondents from many walks of life and from well beyond the boundaries of New England. Lowell and Lewiston each have more locally oriented newspapers, *Le Journal de Lowell* (The Lowell journal; 1974) and *L'Unité* (Unity; 1976). Elsewhere, a few English-language newspapers feature weekly or monthly Franco-American columns, such as the *Manchester Union Leader*, the *Portland Press Herald*, and the *Senior Times* of Concord, New Hampshire. In addition, numerous old and new Franco-American societies publish newspapers, magazines, or newsletters whose scope transcends that of the average "house organ," thereby reaching a wider audience. Among these are *Le Canado-Américain* (The Canadian American), *L'Union* (Union), *Le Bulletin de la Fédération Féminine Franco-Américaine* (The Bulletin of the Franco-American Women's Federation), *The Genealogist*, the *AFA Newsletter*, and *InformACTION*.

Outside of New England, this renaissance has manifested itself in Louisiana, where the *Revue de Louisiane/Louisiana Review*, a scholarly periodical, and *Louisiane*, a regional newspaper, have both appeared in Lafayette. Florida's heavy population of francophone retirees, primarily from New England and Québec, has prompted the launching of the *Journal de la Floride* of Hollywood.

It is too early to evaluate fully this renaissance or to predict the future of the Franco-American press. Historical events and the passage of time have transformed what once was a need for French-language newspapers by a majority of Québécois immigrants into what is presently a desire for French-language or bilingual publications by a small but strong minority of Franco-Americans. So long as this minority exists and wishes some form of collective expression, there will always be a Franco-American press. Regardless of what the future holds, the past accomplishments of Franco-American journalists are their legacy to the history of the United States and to one of the nation's ethnic groups. As a whole, Franco-American newspapers form an invaluable archival body, largely unknown and therefore virtually untapped.[40]

NOTES

1. For the most comprehensive list of French-language newspapers in the United States up to 1911, see Alexandre Belisle, *Histoire de la Presse Franco-Américaine* (Worcester, Mass.: Ateliers Typographiques de *L'Opinion Publique*, 1911), pp. 27–38, 216–217, 380–384; for partial updates, see the following: Maximilienne Tétrault, *Le Rôle de la Presse dans l'Evolution du Peuple Franco-Américain de la Nouvelle-Angleterre* (Marseille: Imprimerie Ferran et Cie, 1935), pp. 5–50; Joseph Lussier, "Les Journaux de Langue Francaise aux Etats-Unis depuis 1912," in *Deuxième Congrès de la Langue Francaise au Canada—Mémoires* (Québec: Imprimerie du *Soleil* Limitée, 1938), 1: 367–369; in addition, the following annual publications usually contained a report on the status of all Franco-American newspapers in a given year: *La Vie Franco-Américaine* (Québec: Comité Permanent de la Survivance Francaise en Amérique, 1939–1952) and *Le Bulletin de la Société Historique Franco-Américaine*, new series, 1–19 (1955–1973).

2. Jacque Habert,"Histoire de la Presse Française aux Etats-Unis," *Le Bulletin de la Société Historique Franco-Américaine 1966*, new series 12 (1967): 127–129.

3. The word "Creoles," in this sense, refers to Caucasian descendants of earlier settlers from France living in several American southern states, including present-day Louisiana; Cajuns are descendants of the original deportees from Acadia (1755), the modern-day Canadian provinces of New Brunswick, Nova Scotia, and Prince Edward Island as well as the extreme northeastern part of Maine.

4. Belisle, pp. 380–383.

5. On *Le Courrier des Etats-Unis* see Belisle, pp. 358–368; on *L'Echo du Pacifique* see "Centenaire Francais en Californie," in *La Vie Franco-Américaine 1950*, pp. 316–317; and author's personal interview with Marie Galanti, editor of *Le Journal Francais d'Amérique*, in Québec, April 19, 1983.

6. Belisle, pp. 27–41, 46–47, 52–53, 116–126, 206–207, 216–217; Tétrault, pp. 15–45, 58–59; "*Le Courrier du Michigan—Trentenaire 1912–1942*," in *La Vie Franco-Américaine 1942*, p. 256; "Pierre-Eudore Mayrand" (obituary), *Le Bulletin de la Société Historique Franco-Américaine 1959*, new series 5 (1960): 269.

7. On the Insurrection of 1837–1838, see Mason Wade, *The French Canadians 1760–1967*, rev. ed. (Toronto: The Macmillan Company of Canada, 1975), 1: 152–219; Gérard Filteau, *Histoire des Patriotes*, new ed. (Montréal: L'Aurore/Univers, 1980).

8. Robert Rumilly, *Histoire des Franco-Américains* (Montréal: Robert Rumilly, 1985), pp. 17–25.

9. Belisle, pp. 21–22, 42–47.

10. For a complete, detailed account of the Québécois migration to New England, see Ralph Vicero, "Immigration of French Canadians to New England: A Geographical Analysis," Ph. D. dissertation, University of Wisconsin, 1968.

11. Although these statistics do not, unfortunately, make the distinction between English Canadians and French Canadians, historians have generally agreed that the majority of Canadians migrating to and living in New England at this time were French Canadians. See Yolande Lavoie, *L'Emigration des Québécois aux Etats-Unis de 1840 à 1930* (Québec: Editeur Officiel du Québec, 1979), p. 25.

12. Ibid.

13. Belisle, pp. 61–67; Tétrault, pp. 18, 60; Edouard Hamon, S. J., *Les Canadiens-Francais de la Nouvelle-Angleterre* (Québec: N. S. Hardy, 1891), pp. 169–177.

14. An old proverb still uttered today by certain elderly Franco-Americans states "Qui perd sa langue perd sa foi."

15. Hamon, pp. 179, 231, 311, 349, 365, 399, 421. Hamon obtained his statistics from Franco-American parish records which, in terms of the Franco-American population, were probably more accurate than the figures given by the U. S Bureau of the Census.

16. Belisle, pp. 68–92; Tétrault, pp. 19–21, 61; "Ferdinand Gagnon," in Rosaire Dion-Lévesque, *Silhouettes Franco-Américaines* (Manchester, New Hampshire: Association Canado-Américaine, 1957), pp. 336–340; Benjamin Sulte, ed., *Ferdinand Gagnon: Sa Vie et Ses Oeuvres* (Worcester, Mass.: C.-F. Lawrence et Cie, 1886), pp. 7–24; Josaphat Benoit, ed., *Ferdinand Gagnon: Biographie, Eloge Funèbre, Pages Choisies* (Manchester, N. H.: *L'Avenir National*, 1940), pp. 11–45.

17. Belisle, pp. 93–107, 340–342; Tétrault, pp. 69–74; Jacques Ducharme, *The Shadows of the Trees: The Story of French Canadians in New England* (New York: Harper and Brothers, 1943), pp. 131–134.

18. Tétrault, pp. 75–82.

19. Norman Sepenuk, "A Profile of Franco-American Political Attitudes in New England," in Madeleine Giguère, ed., *A Franco-American Overview* (Cambridge, Mass.: National Assessment and Dissemination Center for Bilingual/Bicultural Education, 1981), 3: 214. With regard to the voter statistics, one must keep in mind that, had women had the vote at this time, the number of registered voters would have been higher.

20. For example, Manchester, New Hampshire, had at least one Franco-American on its city council beginning in 1882, while in 1888 the first Franco-American was elected to the New Hampshire State Legislature where, by the 1890s, the number had risen to ten. See Emile Tardivel, *Le Guide Canadien-Francais de Manchester, N. H. pour 1894–95* (Manchester, N. H.: La Cie de John B. Clarke, 1894), pp. 262–263; Rumilly, p. 160.

21. Belisle, pp. 163–173. Lenthier owned no less than sixteen newspapers simultaneously, including one of that era's rare dailies, *Le National* of Lowell.

22. Ibid., pp. 412–414; Rumilly, pp. 160, 232.

23. Jean-Georges LeBoutillier, "Une Page d'Histoire Franco-Américaine: Un Rapport de M. Carroll D. Wright sur l'Uniformité des Heures de Travail en 1881," *La Revue Franco-Américaine* 2 (April 1909): 423–433; this text was reproduced in Belisle, pp. 321–330. Sr. Florence M. Chevalier, "The Role of French National Societies in the Sociocultural Evolution of the Franco-Americans of New England from 1860 to the Present", Ph. D. dissertation, Catholic University, Washington, D. C., 1972, pp. 91–97; Pierre Anctil, "Un Point Tournant de l'Histoire du Québec: L'Episode des 'Chinese

of the Eastern States' de 1881,'' *Le Canado-Américain*, new quarterly series 7, no. 2 (April-June 1981): 17–19.

24. Massachusetts Department of Labor and Industries, *Twelfth Annual Report of the Bureau of Statistics of Labor* (Boston: Rand Avery and Co., 1881), pp. 469–470.

25. Massachusetts Department of Labor and Industries, *Thirteenth Annual Report of the Bureau of Statistics of Labor* (Boston: Rand Avery and Co., 1882), pp. 3–92.

26. Ephrem R. Dufresne, ''Discours Prononcé par M. E. R. Dufresne, Rédacteur du Journal *Le Canadien* de St. Paul, Minnesota à la Seizième Convention Nationale des Canadiens-Francais des Etats-Unis, Tenue à Rutland, Vt.,'' in Félix Gatineau, ed., *Historique des Conventions Générales des Canadiens-Francais aux Etats-Unis 1867–1901* (Woonsocket, R. I.: L'Union Saint-Jean-Baptiste d'Amérique, 1927), pp. 222–223.

27. Belisle, pp. 31–34, 216 (Newspaper statistics); Hamon, pp. 369, 425, 435 (population statistics).

28. Honoré Beaugrand, *Jeanne la Fileuse: Episode de l'Emigration Franco-Canadienne aux Etats-Unis* (Fall River, Mass.: N. p., 1878); Camille Lessard, *Canuck* (Lewiston, Me.: *Le Messager*, 1936). Little known but nonetheless interesting is the connection between the Franco-American press and two Franco-American novelists who wrote in English. Léo-Alcide Kérouac, a printer and linotype operator, father of Jack Kerouac, worked for *L'Impartial* of Nashua and for *L'Etoile* of Lowell, while Alfred DeRepentigny, a printer, father of Grace DeRepentigny-Metalious, was employed at *L'Avenir National* of Manchester. Both Kerouac and Metalious, better known for their best-sellers *On the Road* (1957) and *Peyton Place* (1956), wrote lesser-known novels that were deeply rooted in their Québécois/Franco-American backgrounds, especially Kerouac's *Doctor Sax* (1959) and *Visions of Gerard* (1963), and Metalious's *The Tight White Collar* (1960) and *No Adam in Eden* (1963).

29. Paul Paré, ''A History of Franco-American Journalism,'' in Renaud S. Albert, ed., *A Franco-American Overview* (Cambridge, Mass.: National Assessment and Dissemination Center for Bilingual/Bicultural Education, 1979), 1: 239.

30. Tamara K. Hareven, *Family Time and Industrial Time: The Relationship between the Family and Work in a New England Industrial Community* (Cambridge, Eng.: Cambridge University Press, 1982), pp. 315–316.

31. For an excellent study on the dynamics of language shifts of entire minority groups due to migration from the mother country to a host country, see Francois Grosjean, *Life with Two Languages: An Introduction to Bilingualism* (Cambridge, Mass.: Harvard University Press, 1982).

32. Rumilly, p. 312.

33. Ibid., pp. 364–503; J. Albert Foisy, *The Sentinellist Agitation in New England 1925–1928* (Providence, R. I.: *Providence Visitor* Press, 1930); Elphège J. Daignault, *Le Vrai Mouvement Sentinelliste en Nouvelle-Angleterre 1923–1929 et l'Affaire du Rhode Island* (Montréal: Les Editions du Zodiaque, 1936); Richard S. Sorrell, ''The *Sentinelle* Affair (1924–1929) and Militant *Survivance*: The Franco-American Experience in Woonsocket, R. I.,'' Ph. D. dissertation, State University of New York at Buffalo, 1976; Robert B. Perreault, *Elphège J. Daignault et le Mouvement Sentinelliste à Manchester, New Hampshire* (Bedford, N. H.: National Materials Development Center for French and Creole, 1981).

34. Belisle, pp. 216–217; Tétrault, pp. 5–14; ''Nos Journaux,'' in *La Vie Franco-Américaine 1942*, pp. 262–263.

35. Oda Beaulieu, ed., *Wilfrid Beaulieu et Son Journal Le Travailleur*, Actes du

Symposium tenu à l'occasion de l'ouverture des Archives Wilfrid Beaulieu—*Le Travailleur* sous les auspices de la Société Historique Franco-Américaine et de la Bibliothèque Publique de Boston le 16 octobre 1982 (Manchester, N. H.: n.p., 1983).

36. Adolphe Robert (under the pseudonym "Le Mohican"), "La Presse . . . Ca Presse," *Le Canado-Américain*, series 3, no. 6 (April-May 1963): 5–6.

37. "Comité de Vie Franco-Américaine," *Le Bulletin de la Société Historique Franco-Américaine 1963*, new series 9 (1964): 75–82.

38. While the Franco-American press, for the most part, has supported the separatist movement in Québec, the Franco-Americans themselves, like the Québécois, are divided over this issue. At the risk of overgeneralizing, one might say that among the Franco-American masses, there tends to be a lack of awareness or concern over the political scene in Québec. Among Franco-American activists and leaders, with some exceptions, the basis for favoring or rejecting separatism appears to be along the lines of generation, with young liberals leaning toward separatism and older conservatives away from it.

39. Barring any unforeseen turn of events, *Le Messager*'s record will be broken within the next few years by the house organs of two fraternal insurance societies, *Le Canado-Américain* of Manchester, founded in 1900 by L'Association Canado-Américaine, and *L'Union* of Woonsocket, founded in 1902 by L'Union Saint-Jean-Baptiste. These are the two longest-running, regularly published Franco-American journals still in existence in New England.

40. The Boston Public Library possesses on microfilm complete or nearly complete collections of over sixty New England Franco-American newspapers, plus a few from New York, Illinois, and Michigan. Other smaller repositories of Franco-American Newspapers, either in their original form or on microfilm, are the libraries of L'Association Canado-Américaine in Manchester, New Hampshire, and of L'Union Saint-Jean–Baptiste in Woonsocket, Rhode Island. In addition, L'Institut Francais, founded in 1979 and based at Assumption College in Worcester, Massachusetts, has begun collecting Franco-American newspapers.

BIBLIOGRAPHY

Albert, Renaud S., ed. *La Presse Chez les Franco-Américains*. Cambridge, Mass.: National Assessment and Dissemination Center for Bilingual/Bicultural Education, 1979.

Beaulieu, Oda, ed. *Wilfrid Beaulieu et Son Journal Le Travailleur*. Actes du Symposium tenu à l'occasion de l'ouverture des Archives Wilfrid Beaulieu—*Le Travailleur* sous les auspices de la Société Historique Franco-Américaine et de la Bibliothèque Publique de Boston le 16 octobre 1982. Manchester, N. H.: n.p., 1983.

Beaulieu, Wilfrid. "La Langue Francaise et sa Conservation par la Presse." In Adolphe Robert, ed., *Les Franco-Américains Peints par Eux-Mêmes*. Montréal: Editions Albert Lévesque, 1936, pp. 129–137.

Belisle, Alexandre. *Histoire de la Presse Franco-Américaine*. Worcester, Mass.: Ateliers Typographiques de *L'Opinion Publique*, 1911.

Benoit, Josaphat. *Ferdinand Gagnon: Biographie, Eloge Funèbre, Pages Choisies*. Manchester, N. H.: *L'Avenir National*, 1940.

"Centenaire Francais en Californie." In *La Vie Franco-Américaine 1950* (Québec: Comité de la Survivance Francaise en Amérique, 1950), pp. 316–317.

Clément, Antoine. "Notre Presse et Nous." *Le Bulletin de la Société Historique Franco-Américaine 1956*, new series 2 (1957): 110–115.

"*Le Courrier du Michigan*—Trentenaire 1912–1942." In *La Vie Franco-Américaine 1942* (Québec: Comité de la Survivance Française en Amérique, 1942), p. 256.

Daignault, Elphège J. *Le Vrai Mouvement Sentinelliste en Nouvelle-Angleterre 1923–1929 et l'Affaire du Rhode Island*. Montréal: Les Editions du Zodiaque, 1936.

Dufresne, Ephrem R. "Discours Prononcé par M. E. R. Dufresne, Rédacteur du Journal *Le Canadien* de St. Paul, Minnesota à la Seizième Convention Nationale des Canadiens-Francais des Etats-Unis, Tenue à Rutland, Vt." In Félix Gatineau, ed., *Historique des Conventions Générales des Canadiens-Francais aux Etats-Unis 1865–1901*. Woonsocket, R. I.: L'Union Saint-Jean-Baptiste d'Amérique, 1927, pp. 216–224.

Filteau, Gérard. *Histoire des Patriotes*. New Ed. Montréal: L'Aurore/Univers, 1980.

Foisy, J. Albert. *The Sentinellist Agitation in New England 1925–1928*. Providence, R. I.: *Providence Visitor* Press, 1930.

Habert, Jacques. "Histoire de la Presse Francaise aux Etats-Unis." *Le Bulletin de la Société Historique Franco-Américaine 1966*, new series 12 (1967): 127–131.

Ham, Edward Billings. "Journalism and the French Survival in New England." *New England Quarterly* 11 (March 1938): 89–107.

Lajoie, Philippe-Armand. "Les Organismes Vitaux: Les Journaux." In Adolphe Robert, ed., *Les Franco-Américains Peints par Eux-Mêmes*. Montréal: Editions Albert Lévesque, 1936, pp. 53–59.

Lussier, Joseph. "Les Journaux de Langue Francaise aux Etats-Unis depuis 1912." In *Deuxième Congrès de la Langue Francaise au Canada—Mémoires*. Québec: Imprimerie du *Soleil* Limitée, 1938, 1: 363–369.

"Nos Journaux." In *La Vie Franco-Américaine 1942* (Québec: Comité de la Survivance Francaise en Amérique, 1942), pp. 262–263.

Paré, Paul. "A History of Franco-American Journalism." In Renaud S. Albert, ed., *A Franco-American Overview*. Cambridge, Mass.: National Assessment and Dissemination Center for Bilingual/Bicultural Education, 1979, 1: 237–260.

Perreault, Robert B. *Elphège J. Daignault et le Mouvement Sentinelliste à Manchester, New Hampshire*. Bedford, N. H.: National Materials Development Center for French and Creole, 1981.

———. *La Presse Franco-Américaine et la Politique: L'Oeuvre de Charles-Roger Daoust*. Bedford, N. H.: National Materials Development Center for French and Creole, 1981.

———. "Survol de la Presse Franco-Américaine." In Claire Quintal, ed., *Le Journalisme de Langue Francaise aux Etats-Unis*. Québec: Conseil de la Vie Francaise en Amérique, 1984, pp. 9–33.

"Pierre-Eudore Mayrand" (obituary). *Le Bulletin de la Société Historique Franco-Américaine 1959*, new series 5 (1960): 269.

Quintal, Claire, ed. *Le Journalisme de Langue Francaise aux Etats-Unis*. Quatrième colloque de l'Institut Francais du Collège de l'Assomption, Worcester, Mass., 11–12 mars 1983. Québec: Conseil de la Vie Francaise en Amérique, 1984.

Robert, Adolphe (under the pseudonym "Le Mohican"). "La Presse . . . Ca Presse." *Le Canado-Américain* 3, no. 6 (April-May 1963): 5–6.

Sorrell, Richard S. "The *Sentinelle* Affair (1924–1929) and Militant *Survivance*: The

Franco-American Experience in Woonsocket, R. I." Ph. D. dissertation, State University of New York at Buffalo, 1976.

Sulte, Benjamin, ed. *Ferdinand Gagnon: Sa Vie et Ses Oeuvres*. Worcester, Mass.: C.-F. Lawrence et Cie, 1886.

Tétrault, Maximilienne. *Le Rôle de la Presse dans l'Evolution du Peuple Franco-Américain de la Nouvelle-Angleterre*. Marseille: Imprimerie Ferran et Cie, 1935.

Wade, Mason. *The French Canadians 1760–1967*. Rev. ed. Toronto: The Macmillan Company of Canada, 1975.

10

The German–American Press

JAMES M. BERGQUIST

In the length of its history and in the prodigious volume and variety of its product, the German-American press represents a phenomenon unlike any of the other ethnic presses in America. From the days of its founding by struggling and resourceful eighteenth-century printers down into the twentieth century, the evolution of the German-American newspaper paralleled the history of American journalism as a whole and was influenced by the same changes in technology, communication, and society. Besides that, of course, German-American journalism was a facet of a very complex and constantly changing immigrant group whose geographical distribution, social structure, and leadership varied with each successive wave of new migration.

Although the precise number will never be known, bibliographers of the German-American press have placed the number of publications issued in German at somewhere around 5,000 during the course of American history.[1] That includes not only newspapers and periodicals of general circulation (which are the primary focus of this essay) but also a bewildering variety of religious and literary journals, trade union publications, organs of mutual benefit and fraternal societies, children's magazines, women's magazines, agricultural journals, and many other special-interest publications. In addition to demonstrating the great variety of the German press, the total output also lends support to the generalization that the German-language press was really an American press published in the German language: its concern was always overwhelmingly with American affairs and the life that the Germans found in the United States, and events and affairs in the old country were usually at the periphery of its interest.[2]

The conditions under which the German press began in eighteenth-century America helped to establish its particularly American character. Probably neither the struggling printers who began the earliest papers nor their readers were very familiar with the standards of journalism in Germany, where newspapers were aimed at a narrow elite of educated and politically conscious people. In any event, such standards were no guide to successful immigrant journalism in America. The risky conditions of the printer's trade, the rudimentary nature of the society, and the state of the potential readership all served to create a new brand of journalism.

The pioneer German printers faced great obstacles. Capital for equipment was not easy to accumulate; the necessary German type was expensive and difficult to acquire. Readers were likely to be spread over a wide area, making distribution difficult. Newsworthy information might be scarce, and much of it was stale; word of events in Europe could easily take four to eight weeks to arrive. Often the whole paper depended upon one man who could combine the printer's skills, German verbal abilities, and enough business sense to keep the paper alive. When such a person died or departed, the paper usually went with him. Given all these problems, it is remarkable that the German press did establish at least a foothold in the 1700s and that some papers endured as long as they did.

Benjamin Franklin is credited with starting America's first known German newspaper, the *Philadelphische Zeitung* (Philadelphia news), in 1732. Franklin later attempted several similar ventures to cultivate the Germans for political and business purposes. He had financial resources, influence, and a printing press. But he lacked German type, standing within the German community, and skillful help with the language. The crudely translated excerpts from his English-language paper were ill suited to German readers. His paper expired after two issues.[3]

More properly regarded as the pioneer of German-American journalism was Christopher Sauer (sometimes spelled Sower; 1695?–1758). After immigrating to Pennsylvania in 1724, he learned the printer's trade in Germantown. He set up his own press in 1738 and a year later produced the first issue of a monthly paper, *Der Hoch-Deutsch Pennsylvanische Geschichts-Schreiber* (High German Pennsylvania annalist). It was later issued more frequently and known as *Pennsylvanische Berichte* (Pennsylvania reports). Sauer saw a religious mission in his journalism; he was a fervent separatist and defender of the pietistic sects agaianst the Lutheran and Reformed German churches. His crusading temper aroused some bitter controversies. One was against Count Nicholas von Zinzendorf, leader of the Moravian sect, who sought to unite Pennsylvania's German churches.[4] In another, Sauer compaigned against Franklin and the Lutheran and Reformed leaders when they conceived in 1754 a plan for charitable schools for the Germans. Sauer denounced it as a plot against the Germans' culture. Heinrich Melchior Muhlenberg, leader of the Lutherans, ruefully admitted that Sauer's paper, which was "universally read by the Germans," had effectively frustrated the whole plan.[5]

Sauer's paper was taken over at his death by his son, Christopher Sauer II, who renamed it *Germantauner Zeitung* (Germantown news). The younger Sauer soon became involved in a political controversy which demonstrated the paper's influence at its zenith. In 1764 Benjamin Franklin and the Quaker Party espoused a plan to petition for a royal government to replace the proprietor. Sauer attacked the idea as endangering the civil liberties of the Germans. In the critical assembly elections of that year, Sauer led the sectarian Germans into the Proprietary Party, and the Quaker Party lost crucial assembly seats.[6]

About the same time, however, Sauer's paper first met with a rival, one which eventually would replace it as the most widely read German newspaper. This was the *Wochentliche Philadelphische Staatsbote* (Weekly Philadelphia public messenger), first published in January 1762 by John Heinrich Miller (1699?–1782). In the troubled years leading to the American Revolution, Miller's paper would develop a following among Germans and influence them toward the patriotic cause. The passage of the Stamp Act by Parliament in 1765 aroused all German editors to protest. While the act levied a tax on all newspapers, it doubled the amount of taxes upon non-English papers.[7] Sauer held to his long-standing pacifist inclinations and did not continue his opposition to the British. Miller, on the other hand, continued to pursue the path toward revolution. His paper became the first to announce (on July 5, 1776) the adoption of the Declaration of Independence. When the British occupied Philadelphia in 1777, Miller had to flee, while Sauer remained and continued his paper in the Loyalist cause. In 1778, however, the Sauers had to leave along with the British, while Miller returned and resumed publication.[8]

The era of the Revolution was one of uncertainty for the struggling German-language press, but the period between the end of the conflict and 1800 was one of rapid expansion. Thirty-eight new German newspapers were started in Pennsylvania during that period, bringing German journalism to many centers of German settlement in areas of the state distant from Philadelphia. Some of these, like the Reading *Adler* (Eagle), proved to be very long-lived journalistic institutions.[9] German journalism began to follow the expansion of German population outward from its Pennsylvania origins, and especially into the back country of Maryland and Virginia. The most active German printer in those regions was Matthias Bartgis (1750–1825) who, having completed an apprenticeship in Philadelphia, set up his printing shop in Frederick, Maryland, in the late 1770s. From that location he published both English and German newspapers. In 1789 he attempted publication of the short-lived *Virginische Zeitung* (Virginia news) at Winchester. By 1793 Bartgis consolidated his activities at Frederick, distributing his *General Staatsbote* (General public messenger) throughout the Maryland and Virginia back country. The first Baltimore German paper to endure for any length of time was *Der Neue Unpartheyische Baltimore Bote und Maryländischer Staats-Register* (New nonpartisan Baltimore messenger and Maryland public register). It was founded in 1795 by Samuel Sower, son of Christopher Sauer II.[10]

With new immigration at an ebb, German-language journalism in the half-century from independence to about 1830 remained tied largely to the population descended from the colonial German migration. This journalism centered in the area that was the heartland of the eighteenth-century settlement, eastern Pennsylvania. In 1808 there were fourteen German papers in Pennsylvania. New papers over the next twenty-five years would appear mostly in regions into which the Pennsylvania German population was expanding—southwestward through Maryland and Virginia, westward through Pennsylvania, and on into adjacent regions of Ohio. Ohio's first German newspaper was the Lancaster *Adler* (Eagle), begun in 1808; it was imitative in style and content of the Pennsylvania German press and reported copiously on events in the Pennsylvania "motherland."[11] While most early nineteenth-century German journalism thus continued to reflect the older Pennsylvania German culture, some older papers like the Reading *Adler* managed to adjust to the interests of the newcomers. More commonly, however, the new immigrants found the Pennsylvania German press too conservative in tone and too archaic in language, and founded their own papers as rivals to the older ones. Only a few of the pre–1830 Pennsylvania German papers survived much beyond the Civil War.[12]

During the decade of the 1830s, a number of developments combined to create what was essentially a new strain of German-American newspapers, serving a new generation of readers, making use of a new leadership, and very often located in new places. The most fundamental of these developments was a rising tide of new German migration to America. From a small trickle in the years after the end of the Napoleonic wars it rose to a steady stream in the 1830s, reaching a rate of about 20,000 newcomers yearly late in that decade. The migrants, most of them from the western parts of Germany, had little connection with the earlier colonial migration; they came for motives that were for the most part economic and that were associated with the pressures of population growth and industrialization. They gravitated toward the larger industrializing cities of the eastern seaboard and the newly opened cities and countrysides of the West. The remnants of the earlier German press were not well located to reach the newcomers and not oriented to suit their interests. The outbreak of unsuccessful revolutions in some German states about 1830 brought an influx of well-educated and articulate refugees to America; this small but influential group was to provide a source of new editorial talent for a reviving German-American press.

The character of this reviving journalism was also influenced by the emergence in the 1830s of a new party politics in the United States. The stimulus to start new newspapers for the German-Americans often received a boost from party organizers and politicians, as rivalry heightened between the Democracy of Andrew Jackson and his various opponents. In general, the economics of publishing in the first half of the nineteenth century made support and patronage from political parties a crucial factor in the existence of any newspaper. German-language newspapers were not immune from this fact of life. There had been some strongly Jeffersonian and strongly Federalist German newspapers in the era of the first American political party system around 1800; by the 1830s, patronage from political benefactors was nearly always necessary to sustain the new German-language press which had developed. This political influence frequently had the effect of producing rival German newspapers of different political persuasions in the major centers of German population.

The surge of German newspaper development in the 1830s produced some very durable newspapers which lasted into the twentieth century. The longest-lasting was the New York *Staats-Zeitung* (Public news), which first appeared on December 24, 1834. Its founding stemmed directly from the needs of the city's German Jacksonian Democrats, who sought a rallying point in the up-coming city election against an administration that they felt to be nativist. The *Staats-Zeitung* quickly won favor with the growing German immigrant com-munity, most of whom were fervent Jacksonians.[13]

A rather small group of journalists played an important role in the expansion of the German press in the 1830s. Not a few were refugees of the abortive uprisings of 1830. Although most arrived without previous journalistic experi-ence, many were educated men with professional backgrounds whose training and political awareness made them good candidates to serve German-American journalism. The close relationships and personal acquaintances among them helped to bind together the new world of German-language journalism. Soon after its inception, the New York *Staats-Zeitung* hired the Bavarian émigré and former civil servant Stephan Molitor (1806–1873) as its editor. His journalistic career took him to the Philadelphia *Alte und Neue Welt* (Old and new world), to the Buffalo *Weltbürger* (World citizen), and finally to the Cincinnati *Volksblatt* (People's page), where he remained until his retirement in 1863. Georg Zahn, who began as business manager of the New York *Staats-Zeitung*, moved to Buffalo to begin the *Weltbürger* in 1837.[14]

By the end of the 1830s, most of the larger centers of the new German immigration had at least one German newspaper. Besides the New York and Buffalo papers, these included the Philadelphia *Alte und Neue Welt* (1834), the Pittsburgh *Freiheitsfreund* (Friend of freedom; begun 1835 in Chambersburg, Pennyslvania), and the Cleveland *Germania* (1837). After several short-lived ventures in the 1830s, Baltimore produced the *Deutsche Correspondent* (German correspondent), founded in 1841 by Friedrich Raine. By the 1840s these and other papers provided a sort of rudimentary information network for German America. Information was shared by the common American journalistic practice of the day of "exchanges"; exchange of free papers by publishers was construed as mutual permission to copy material. Probably the New York *Staats-Zeitung* and the Philadelphia *Alte und Neue Welt* were the papers most frequently copied by others; they were known for their editorial talent, were situated at active German cultural centers, and had the most immediate access to fresh news from Europe.[15]

German migration into the Ohio and Mississippi valleys stimulated a vigorous press there as well. Two papers, the St. Louis *Anzeiger des Westens* (Western informant) and the Cincinnati *Volksblatt*, both well situated to reach German-Americans throughout a wide hinterland, rose quickly to preeminence. The *Anzeiger*, St. Louis's first German paper, was founded in 1835. A number of strong figures served as editors in the pre–Civil War years.[16] The long-lasting *Volksblatt*, born in the election year of 1836, was another product of Jacksonian party politics. When the previously existing German paper was taken over by Whigs to promote William Henry Harrison, German Democratic politicians moved swiftly to finance a new one; the *Volksblatt* thus began a career that would last until World War I.[17] Pioneering papers were founded in other major German centers in the early 1840s. Louisville had a succession of papers beginning with the *Volksbühne* (People's arena) in 1841. Milwaukee's pioneer was the *Wisconsin Banner*, created as a Democratic organ for the campaign of 1844. New Orleans, a gateway to the country's interior for many Germans, had its first German paper, *Der Deutsche* (The German), in 1839–1840; it was followed by *Der Deutsche Courier* (The German courier) from 1842 to 1848, and by the longer-lasting *Tägliche Deutsche Zeitung* (Daily German news) in 1848.[18]

The twelve-year period just before the Civil War witnessed the most dramatic development so far in the history of the German-American press. Rapid growth was in large part a reflection of the rising number of new German immigrants, who provided a new pool of readers. Stimulated by the accelerating problems of industrialization, social instability, agricultural failures, and political unrest, the tide of population movement from Germany to the United States moved upward in the late 1840s, reaching a peak of 215,000 immigrants during the year 1854. By the census of 1860 the total of German-born in the nation was 1,300,000—over a quarter of all the foreign-born in the country and about 4 percent of the entire population. The newcomers were concentrated in the cities of the Northeast and Midwest and in new rural areas just being settled in the upper Mississippi valley. As a highly literate group, the German newcomers offered opportunities both to expand German journalism in areas where it previously existed and to start new journals in the more recently settled areas of German population.

This greatly expanded German press received at the same time a new element of dynamic leaders drawn from the unsuccessful German revolutions of 1848 and 1849. The "forty-eighters," who came as refugees from these upheavals, were but a small proportion of the immigrant wave of the time; but they were talented, well educated, and politically conscious. A few had been journalists in Germany, but more of them had pursued careers in the law or in academe. Upon immigration, the most accessible opportunities for them often lay in the expanding world of German journalism. When it became apparent by the early 1850s that the cause of revolution in Europe was dead, the forty-eighters settled down in the United States and began a new era of German-language journalism. Their presence would dominate the field for several decades.

The number of German-American newspapers rose rapidly. There were approximately seventy of them in 1848; by early 1851, according to a survey of the St. Louis *Anzeiger des Westens*, there were at least eighty-nine. Another tabulation, attempted during the election year of 1856, counted 111 German newspapers. In 1860 the New Ulm (Minnesota) *Pionier* (Pioneer) counted 144 German newspapers. Exact numbers are difficult to determine, but it cannot be denied that it was an age of considerable expansion. Over the same period the number of German newspapers issuing daily editions increased markedly; there were over thirty of these in 1856, and most of the major northern cities had at least one. New York City had three dailies: the *Staats-Zeitung*, the *Staatsdemokrat* (Public democrat), and the *Abendzeitung* (Evening news). Cincinnati had the *Volksblatt*, the *Volksfreund* (People's friend), the *Deutsche Republikaner* (German republican), and the *Wahrheitsfreund* (Friend of the truth). St. Louis had the *Anzeiger des Westens*, the *Tageschronik* (Daily chronicle), and the *Volksblatt* (People's page). The proliferation of daily papers was due in part to the introduction of the telegraph, which, along with more frequent railroad mail connections, gave assurance of a fresh supply of news each day.[19]

Even previously established papers were tranformed by the arrival of newcomers as editors and reporters. For example, a young revolutionary from Austria, Schleswig, and Baden, Oswald Ottendorfer, arrived in New York City in 1850. He took a job in the business office of the *Staats-Zeitung* and quickly gained greater responsibilties. Eventually in 1859 he married Anna Uhl, the widow of a previous proprietor; she had taken charge of the paper and ultimately became the most influential woman in German journalism. The Ottendorfers built the paper into the country's largest German paper and made it a base of great influence in social and political affairs.[20]

In the newly burgeoning German center of Chicago, a succession of forty-eighters transformed the struggling *Illinois Staats-Zeitung* (Illinois public news) into a powerful political force. George Schneider, a former journalist in Germany and a participant in the revolutions in the Rhenish Palatinate, took over in 1851, turned the newspaper into a daily and brought in other skilled and politically astute men to assist him. Such men saw the potential of the press for political influence and frequently showed impatience with the traditional politics of German-America. The *Illinois Staats-Zeitung* helped to lead the revolt of many of Chicago's Germans against Stephen A. Douglas's Democratic organization after the Kansas-Nebraska Act, and Schneider himself was a founder of the Illinois Republican Party in 1856.[21]

The influence of the new, dynamic, and politically oriented leaders could, however, have a disruptive effect. It often produced rival newspapers of different ideological types, with the end result of splintering the world of German journalism. In St. Louis, for example, Heinrich Boernstein, a veteran of the Viennese revolution, took over editorship of the *Anzeiger des Westens* and began to raise antagonisms by his doctrinaire liberal views, his criticism of older German leaders, and his strident anticlericalism. The *Anzeiger* had its political impact in the shifting German alignments of the time, but it also stimulated the creation of new papers in the opposition to it, like the Catholic *Tageschronik* (Daily chronicle) and the Lutheran *Volksblatt* (People's page). In 1858 the *Westliche Post* (Western post), founded by the forty-eighter Carl Daenzer, would emerge to compete for German allegiances in St. Louis; and the two papers would remain rivals for most of the rest of the century.[22]

A similar process of controversy and proliferation was seen in other cities. In

Milwaukee, the Catholic paper *Seebote* (Lake messenger) arose in 1851 to counter the anticlerical sentiments of the forty-eighters then being voiced in the *Wisconsin Banner* and the *Volksfreund* (People's friend).[23] In Louisville, four different papers appeared during the 1850s. Two, the *Beobachter am Ohio* (Observer on the Ohio) and the short-lived *Herold des Westens* (Herald of the West) reflected the view of the forty-eighters. The *Adler* (Eagle), founded in 1852, represented Catholic response. The Protestant *Anzeiger* (Informant), reflecting a moderate position, managed to survive the longest of all, until 1938.[24] Louisville was also the birthplace in 1854 of the *Pionier* of Karl Heinzen, a paper which became the best-known example of the radical political journal. Heinzen, an incorrigibly hot-tempered old revolutionary, left the editorship of the *Herold des Westens* to promulgate his own particular view of nonsocialist radicalism. While still in Louisville he and other radical immigrants drew up the famous "Louisville Platform" (1854), which became a sort of credo of German radical reform. Heinzen continued the *Pionier* for a quarter century, taking it and its uncompromising ideology with him to Cincinnati, New York, and Boston.[25] Other personal radical journals of the time included the Cincinnati *Hochwächter* (Lookout), a vehicle for the radical anticlericalism of the Viennese revolutionary Friedrich Hassaurek; the San Antonio *Zeitung* (News) of Adolf Douai, who introduced the touchy issue of abolitionism into the German community in the slave state of Texas; and a series of papers published by Joseph Weydemeyer, the principal American exponent of Marxism during the period.[26]

The same era of the 1850s saw a new political diversification of German-American journalism. Before 1850 it was automatically assumed that nearly all German papers would support the Democratic Party; the Whig Party seldom managed more than an occasional campaign sheet. But the drastic changes in the political party system during the 1850s, and the struggle that developed for the party allegiance of the Germans, ended this unanimity. After the Kansas-Nebraska Act of 1854, an increasing number of antislavery editors warned immigrants that the Democratic Party had now become an instrument of southern interests which were in no way favorable to the immigrant. Nevertheless, many Germans hesitated to make the change to the new Republican Party, which they feared harbored nativist elements. The continuing struggle for the German vote stimulated both parties to support newspapers of their viewpoint. By the election of 1860, political unanimity in the German press had clearly been shattered and a continuing political debate among German newspapers had become the norm.

A few statistical summaries made by journalists during the decade provide evidence of these new political alignments. In 1851 Heinrich Boernstein of the St. Louis *Anzeiger des Westens* surveyed German journalism and found sixty-seven overtly Democratic papers and only five supporting the Whigs. Another seventeen papers had various radical, religious, or nonpolitical orientations. During the campaign of 1856, when the new Republican Party fielded its first national ticket, a tabulation by the editor of the intellectual magazine *Atlantis*, Christian Esselen, reached an estimate of forty-eight papers supporting the Republican John C. Fremont as against fifty-eight for the Democrat James Buchanan. Many of the Democratic papers were small-town weeklies, however, and among the daily papers eighteen supported Fremont and sixteen were for Buchanan. By the critical election of 1860, the sharp division of German newspapers into different party camps remained. The *Pionier* of New Ulm, Minnesota, estimated during the campaign that of 144 German papers, 73 supported the Republican Abraham Lincoln. Thirty-five supported Stephen A. Douglas, the northern Democrat; fifteen supported John C. Breckenridge, the southern Democrat; ten supported John Bell of the Constitutional Union Party. The remainder were of radical or neutralist persuasions.[27]

The new generation of forty-eighters was especially influential in bringing the German press into a deeper involvement in politics and in building support for the Republican Party. They did not feel the traditional attachments of older German leaders to Jacksonianism, and opposition to slavery seemed the first priority to most. The forty-eighters transformed long-established papers like the St. Louis *Anzeiger des Westens* and the *Illinois Staats-Zeitung* into Republican loyalists. Sometimes new Republican papers were started to challenge existing Democratic ones. There were a few notable exceptions; Oswald Ottendorfer of the New York *Staats-Zeitung* and Gottlieb Theodor Kellner of the Philadelphia *Demokrat* kept their papers within the Democratic Party as they had found them. Editors opposing the Republicans usually pointed to the intolerance, nativism, and temperance fanaticism of some of that party's members.[28]

The German press had now come to play an important role in American politics, but at the cost of considerable conflict within the German group as a whole. When new political alignments clashed with long-established political traditions, emotions could run high. Adolf Douai was forced to leave the San Antonio *Zeitung* and flee to the North after publicly advocating free-soil doctrines. In Baltimore, the forty-eighter Wilhelm Rapp, editor of the *Wecker* (Awakener), insisted on supporting Lincoln's candidacy in 1860 despite the strong pro-southern feelings in that city. Within a week after the firing on Fort Sumter in April 1861, a mob broke into the paper's office and burned it, and Rapp was forced to flee the city.[29]

The general configuration and character of the German-American press as it had formed by the eve of the Civil War would persist during its heyday, which lasted until just before the turn of the twentieth century. No one newspaper dominated the German readership, and the press was geographically spread through many areas of German settlement. German journalism was exceedingly diverse in outlook and viewpoint, reflecting the wide spectrum of ideology and social background of the German immigrant group. Like the American press as a whole at that time, the German-language newspapers survived on the ties they built with political parties and politicians; this protected them from insularity and made them confront the issues of the day. The German press, at the same time that it offered the immigrants the comfort of a familiar language and some tie with the homeland, was nevertheless vigorously involved in American life, debating American issues and playing an important role in politics. The typical German newspaper offered far more than news and discussion of the general events of American life than of European matters.

More than anything else, it was the dynamic growth of the group itself that allowed the German-language press to flourish in the latter decades of the nineteenth century. In the ten years after the end of the Civil War, new German immigrants entered the country at a rate averaging 100,000 to 150,000 each year. After a slump during the depression years of the late 1870s, the annual rate of new German immigrants rose to new highs in the early 1880s, reaching an all-time peak of nearly a quarter of a million in 1882. By the late 1880s immigration from Germany ran about a hundred thousand yearly. But in the wake of the Depression of 1893, the rate of immigration fell off; it hovered around 30,000 yearly from 1895 until World War I, never rising above 50,000 yearly.[30] The German community was thus provided with several fresh waves of newcomers over these decades. The various German states (and the new German Empire after 1871) generally enjoyed a high literacy rate, and thus their emigrants provided the German-language press in America with new readers to enhance its circulation. The development and growth of the German newspaper press in the United States mirrored rather closely the new supply of immigrants, which built up the circulation figures of established newspapers and also helped to create new ones. Newly opened areas of the Great Plains and the Far West spawned German papers; by 1880 there were nine in California, eight in Nebraska, and ten in Texas.[31] The repeated renewal of the supply of new first-generation immigrants throughout most of the nineteenth century was a luxury for German-America that was not enjoyed by most of the other ethnic groups and their presses. This influx provided the German press, like other institutions of the German group, with the feeling that its existence would be perpetual. It also disguised the fact that many of the second generation were turning to English-language newspapers; the confrontation with this reality was postponed until the flow of new immigrants subsided near the turn of the century.

German-American journalism also benefited from the same dynamic developments that were transforming all American journalism. Growing urban populations made possible papers oriented to a mass readership. Rail transportation extended the range of distribution. Cheaper newsprint, high-speed presses, and typesetting machinery reduced the per-copy cost of the newspapers. The telegraph and cooperative news-gathering methods constantly supplied fresh news to hold the readers' interest. The major German-language newspapers could take advantage of the same technological developments, often adopting them as quickly as their English counterparts. By 1896, for example, the Baltimore *Deutsche Correspondent* boasted a full array of new journalistic techniques: a "perfection" rotary press capable of 24,000 copies per hour, linotype machines, stereotype machines, telegraphic dispatches from two news services, and its own Washington news bureau.[32]

That there were few differences between the English-language and the German-language journalistic worlds is demonstrated by the examples of many journalists who, if able to operate in both languages, moved freely between them. The most famous example is Joseph Pulitzer, a young immigrant who began as a reporter with the St. Louis *Westliche Post* in 1868. By the early 1870s, as part owner of the paper, he sought to rebuild circulation by the sensational methods of mass journalism which would later make him famous—local items of human interest, reports of crime, and accounts of spectacular court trials. Eventually Pulitzer would move to the world of English-language journalism, first at the St. Louis *Post-Dispatch* and later at the New York *World*, where he developed to the fullest the mass journalistic techniques that would make him the most famous newspaperman of the era.[33]

As the technology of journalism changed, the economics of publishing changed as well. Advertising, attracted by the large readership, provided an increasing portion of newspaper revenues. Large-scale papers particularly became less dependent on political support and more concerned with maintaining circulation and satisfying advertisers. These factors affected the content of German-language newspapers just as they did the English-language ones. The papers of the 1850s had relied upon extensive political discussion of interest to the party faithful, a column or two of local events, another column of European reports taken from foreign newspapers, and perhaps some commercial or financial data. Surplus space was filled with serialized fiction or abstruse scientific discussion, sometimes even pirated from encyclopedias. The newspapers of the last two decades of the century reflected a much more carefully calculated effort to build circulation by appealing to readers of greatly diverse interests. German newspapers, which by now sensed that they were in competition with the English-language newspapers as much as with each other, introduced human interest features, society columns, fashion sections, more illustrations (including half-tones), puzzles, children's pages, and increasing amounts of sensational coverage.

The German press also followed the lead of the English-language press in the development of the special Sunday edition. Most German dailies before the Civil War had also issued a weekly edition which usually contained the accumulated news columns of the daily papers for one week. Such a weekly edition could be circulated at lower cost to subscribers in the countryside, and also could be sent to European readers interested in what went on in German-America. The Sunday editions which were for the most part introduced in the period 1875–1900 were aimed at the same market reached by the daily paper and consisted of entirely different material from that appearing in the daily edition. The American Sunday newspaper as it is known today was basically the work of Joseph Pulitzer, who perfected the model at the New York *World* in the late 1880s. The German Sunday editions subsequently were patterned largely upon Pulitzer's model and included picture sections, literary and cultural supplements, travel features, and home and fashion news.

The statistics of German-American journalism reflect clearly the combined influences of technology and demography during the last quarter of the century.

The period of most rapid growth lay between the mid–1870s and about 1890; most estimates would seem to agree that the number of general-circulation German newspapers doubled from the mid–1870s to the mid–1880s. In 1876 the Cincinnati scholar H. A. Rattermann counted 74 dailies with a total circulation of 297,037 and 374 weeklies with a total circulation of 1,022,100. In 1880 the decennial federal census included a survey of all newspapers in the United States and found 80 German-language dailies circulating 447,954 copies and 466 weekly German papers circulating 1,326,248. Figures compiled by Carl Wittke from newspaper guides of the time showed that the German press's growth continued to a peak in about 1892–1893; at that point he counted about 800 German general-circulation publications of all sorts, including magazines; the number of German daily newspapers was about 97. Their influence was enhanced by their heavy concentration in certain markets. There were five or more German dailies in such metropolitan centers as New York, Philadelphia, Chicago, Cincinnati, St. Louis, and Milwaukee. In 1880, 28 percent of the daily newspaper circulation in Cincinnati was in the German language; in St. Louis, 21 percent of the daily newspaper circulation was in German. The German big-city newspapers sold for two or three cents each and thus were competitive with the English-language press. Typical subscription costs for weeklies were about two dollars per year.[34]

The country's largest German newspaper during that period was the New York *Staats-Zeitung*. During the 1870s, with its circulation hovering around the 50,000 mark, the *Staats-Zeitung* claimed to be the largest German-language newspaper in the entire world and the sixth largest daily in the United States. The circulation of the paper, along with its companion evening edition, was over 90,000 at the turn of the century. In Chicago, the politically influential *Illinois Staats-Zeitung* published about 23,000 papers daily in the 1890s, but increasingly felt the competition of the more popularly oriented *Abendpost* (Evening post), founded in 1889. The *Abendpost* claimed 47,667 readers in 1910, while the *Staats-Zeitung* claimed 32,500. Pittsburgh had both the *Volksblatt* and the *Freiheitsfreund*, each with a circulation of about 12,000 in the early 1890s. The *Volksblatt* and the *Freie Presse* (Free press) each published about 12,000 daily in Cincinnati. St. Louis had six daily German papers in the early 1890s; the *Anzeiger des Westens* claimed a circulation of 15,000 and the *Westliche Post* about 10,000. In Milwaukee, in about 1900, the *Germania*, founded in 1873, claimed a circulation of over 20,000; the *Herold* had about 15,000 and the Catholic *Seebote* 8,000. In Philadelphia at the turn of the century, the rapidly growing *Gazette* had a circulation of about 40,000, the labor-oriented *Tageblatt* (Daily page) about 41,000, the *Demokrat* 17,000, and the *Abendpost* (Evening post) 5,600. In Cleveland, the venerable *Wächter am Erie*, dating from 1852, merged in 1893 with the *Anzeiger* (Informant). The combined *Wächter und Anzeiger* claimed a circulation of about 19,000. In Baltimore, the *Deutsche Correspondent* had a circulation of about 12,000 in the early 1890s; but by 1900 it was struggling for circulation with the Baltimore *Journal*, a more commercial and less political paper founded in 1882.[35]

From a peak in the early 1890s, the number of German-language newspapers began a slow process of decline. In the decade of the 1890s, when American journalism was undergoing its greatest period of expansion, the German press, although making use of the same tactics of mass appeal, was struggling to maintain its position. From its peak of near 800 in 1893–1894, the total number of general circulation German publications (including monthlies) declined to 613 in 1900 and to 554 in 1910; the number of German dailies dropped from 97 in 1893 to 78 in 1900 and to 70 in 1910.[36] The demographic trends which had stimulated the great expansion of German journalism were now rapidly fading. During the 1880s, the readership of the German papers was provided both by the older generations of immigrants of the middle of the century and by the wave of newcomers. By the mid–1890s the flow of newcomers had slowed drastically and the older generation of immigrants from the pre–Civil War era was being swiftly reduced by mortality. Attempts were made by most German papers to appeal to the support of the second generation, but by all evidences most of these turned instead to the popular and rapidly growing English-language papers. In the mid–1880s in Milwaukee, the German-language dailies circulated twice as many papers (92,000) as the English-language dailies; by 1910 the German-language daily circulation had dropped to 45,000 and the English-language daily circulation was 150,000.[37]

Although there is clearly a picture of general decline in German-American journalism during the two decades before the outbreak of World War I, the fate of individual newspapers varied greatly. Some, beset by dwindling readership, simply gave up, especially those in the smaller towns and cities. Others managed to survive and even grow by picking up the readers of those papers which failed. Still others took part in mergers in order to make the best of a dwindling market. The St. Louis *Westliche Post*, for instance, found its circulation dwindling from about 10,000 to 7,500 during the 1890s. This led to an agreement in 1898 to merge with its long-standing rival, the *Anzeiger des Westens*. The merged newspapers managed to expand their circulation by broadening their area of distribution throughout the Midwest. Yet much of this increase came at the expense of smaller newspapers going out of business in the hinterland.[38] In Cincinnati, the German newspapers managed to increase their circulation by over 24 percent during the decade of the 1890s. Here, as in St. Louis, much of the gain probably represented readers taken over from the journals in the surrounding countryside. Meanwhile, during the 1890s the English-language dailies of Cincinnati nearly tripled their circulation—another evidence that the younger generation of German-Americans was showing its preference for the daily English press.[39]

In many of the major German centers, the pattern was clearly one of lessened competition among the German newspapers and greater effort to stave off the defection of readers to the English-language press. The wave of mergers which began in the 1890s was clear evidence of this. Besides the mergers in St. Louis and Cincinnati, there were those of the *Illinois Staats-Zeitung* and the *Freie Presse* in Chicago (1905); of the *Seebote* and the *Herold* (1898) and of the *Abendpost* and the *Germania* (1897) in Milwaukee; of the *Volksblatt* and the *Freiheitsfreund* in Pittsburgh (1901); of the *Express* and the *Westbote* (Western messenger) in Columbus, Ohio (1903); and of the *Abendpost* (Evening post) and the *California Demokrat* in San Francisco (1903).[40]

The character of the German press was also affected significantly toward the end of the nineteenth century by changes in its leadership. These changes were due in part to the same demographic influences affecting the growth and decline of newspaper circulation—the successive waves of new immigrants, the dwindling of first-generation Germans at the turn of the century, and the different interests of the second generation. The end of the Civil War had found the German press under a leadership heavily influenced by the experiences of the 1848 revolutions and of the intense party politics of the 1850s. Such men perceived themselves as educators and leaders of German-Americans in the whole range of American public affairs. Maintaining a separate world of German-America was not a high priority for them. Thus, for example, Carl Schurz saw a tie to the German press as a necessary and useful adjunct to his political career; in 1867 he accepted a part-ownership and editorship with the St. Louis *Westliche Post*, making it the political base from which he cultivated a Missouri constituency and became a United States Senator and later Secretary of the Interior. Although his active involvement in the paper lasted only a few years, he maintained his co-ownership until his death in 1906.[41] Chicago provided another example. The German politician Anton Hesing, who had acquired political influence with the rise of the Republican Party on the eve of the Civil War, consolidated his power in a potent organization in the postwar years. He purchased the *Illinois Staats-Zeitung* and brought in two experienced journalists of the pre–Civil War generation, Hermann Raster and Wilhelm Rapp, whose influence dominated the *Illinois Staats-Zeitung* into the 1890s. Motivated by a desire to rally the German vote for the Hesing machine, the paper kept its readers at all times attuned to the mainstream of politics.[42]

By the early 1890s the pre–Civil War leaders still active in journalism had been reduced to a relatively small number. Those associated with major papers included Oswald Ottendorfer of the New York *Staats-Zeitung*, Rapp and Raster of the *Illinois Staats-Zeitung*, Gottlieb Kellner of the Philadelphia *Demokrat*, Emil Preetorius of the St. Louis *Westliche Post*, and Carl Daenzer of the St. Louis *Anzeiger des Westens*. But even some of the papers to which these men were tied were softening their political activism in favor of a more conciliatory and neutral posture whereby they could draw readers from all sectors of the German community. Perhaps the traditions of a more activist and ideological journalism were maintained most strongly at this time by the radical German press, which was sustained in the last decades of the century by the growth of an organized labor movement among the urban Germans. The number of socialist-oriented newspapers increased, and there were about twenty-six of them in the early 1890s. The largest was the *Volkszeitung* (People's news) of New York, organ of the Socialist Labor Party, a paper which claimed a circulation of 20,000. The Chicago *Arbeiter Zeitung* (Workers' news) played an active role in the labor radicalism of that city. It became famous at the time of the Haymarket riot of 1886 when it was temporarily suppressed by the police. Its circulation at that point was about 6,000, but by the turn of the century it was circulating about 15,000 copies. The radical press constantly denounced the political and ideological blandness it saw in the rest of the German press. The mainstream press often replied by accusing the radical journals of being unrepresentative of the great majority of German-Americans. They increased their criticism in the wake of the Haymarket riot, as German leaders scrambled to disassociate the German community from the violent radicalism attributed to the rioters. There continued to be active German socialist papers down to the time of World War I in such places as New York, Chicago, Philadelphia, and Milwaukee.

The principal trend of German-American journalism, however, was toward less political activism, and was influenced by a newer generation of leadership gradually replacing that of the forty-eighters. Sometimes the new leaders were second-generation immigrants, sometimes recent newcomers from Germany; but in general they perceived the newspaper more as a business enterprise than as an ideological institution, and were to be found more often in the business office than at the editorial desk. Maintaining circulation and pleasing advertisers were their principal concerns. A variety of circumstances also made such leaders more culturally nationalistic and more defensive of the institutions of German-America. Some of the new generation of journalists brought their nationalistic pride with them from the newly united German Empire, achieved by Otto von Bismarck in 1871. Others envisioned that their newspapers would increasingly rely upon links to the institutional network of German-America, and so made themselves the guardians of that cultural system against outside attacks. The maintenance of a public able to read German was of course crucial to the future of the ethnic newspaper, and so defense of the language became a vital issue for press leaders. When in 1889–1890 states like Wisconsin and Illinois passed laws preventing the use of non-English languages for general school instruction, the German press was unanimous in defense of the language. As the numbers of first-generation immigrants declined and those of the second generation increased, the press mounted a continuing campaign urging language instruction upon the second generation.[43]

The turn-of-the-century journalists did not wholly eschew politics by any means, but they did see the more pressing political issues to be those concered with the defense of the ethnic culture. Some of this is understandable, since it was a period when nativists, prohibitionists, and educational reformers all seemed to be choosing the Germans' way of life as their target. For journalists concerned with keeping the German community together as their clientele, it was an easy course to make much of the issues of cultural defense, on which most Germans would be united, and to avoid other issues of partisan politics, about which Germans might disagree. Indeed, there was a growing inclination in much of the German press to mute controversy within the community and to give a somewhat bland and sugar-coated view of German-America.[44]

The German press continued to be a springboard for active politicians. The most prominent German-American politician at the beginning of the twentieth century was Richard Bartholdt, who began his journalistic career with the New York *Staats-Zeitung* and took charge of the St. Louis *Tribüne* in 1884. Yet Bartholdt, who served in Congress from 1893 to 1915, clearly reflected a politics narrowly based on ethnic cultural defense. As a politician and a newspaperman, he recognized the necessity for minimizing differences within the ethnic community in order to preserve its institutions and promote its defense.[45]

The German press was to find itself ill-prepared for the events in which it would have to play a role after 1914. For twenty years before the outbreak of war in Europe it had been drawing closer to the slowly constricting world of institutional German-America, concerning itself with the defense of those institutions and with German culture. Efforts to rally the German community since the turn of the century had been fostered by the German-American National Alliance, which sought to tie the German press closer to the institutional network. The alliance was an umbrella organization which owed its growth primarily to the support of brewers trying to counter prohibitionism, which was increasingly seen as a threat to German-American culture. In emphasizing the defense of the separate world of German-America, the German press may have built its base upon a narrow segment of the German community, ignoring those German-Americans who had only a marginal interest in the institutions of the ethnic community. The sometimes uncritical defense of German culture by German-American editors gave their readers little guidance in international affairs or the politics of the German Empire, to which the editors gave relatively little attention. Their view of the international rivalries of the day often simply linked the German Empire to their own defense of German culture.[46]

The response of the German-American press to the international crisis developing in 1914 was conditioned by the direction of the press in the preceding years. It seemed natural for the German editors to spring to the defense of the German Empire in response to what they saw as the excessive influence of British propaganda in the English-language press. The British controlled most of the channels for news transmission from Europe, having cut the trans-Atlantic cable from Germany. The German-language papers were eager to offset the British view and refute charges that the Germans were autocratic, militaristic, and brutal as well as responsible for starting the war. They often printed uncritically the official statements of German authorities, who depicted the German forces as righteous and invincible. Most German-American papers thus embarked on a course which contemplated neither the possibility of German defeat nor the possibility of American involvement. These misjudgments made it painfully difficult to adjust to reality later.[47]

The German government made some attempts to assist this defense of their policies. Its most active propagandists were Dr. Heinrich Albert and Dr. Bernhard Dernburg, who organized a German Information Service in New York, which provided news dispatches, speeches, and pamphlets to counter the British-dominated news services. Probably such material had little effect on influencing opinion in the United States outside the German community. But many German-language newspapers accepted and used such material with enthusiasm. Nevertheless, it is hardly correct to picture the German papers as merely the tools of German agents. The press was already emotionally conditioned to leap to the defense of Germany and would probably have done so regardless of the extent of Germany's propaganda activity.[48]

The German press generally underwent a modest revival in the early years of the war. Perhaps some German-Americans who had turned to the English-language press now felt once more the need for support from the German papers in an era when their ancestral culture was under attack. Perhaps the issues being dealt with in the German press now seemed more compelling. Carl Wittke estimated that total German press circulation rose from 782,000 in 1914 to about 950,000 in early 1917. Some German journals saw increases of 25 to 100 percent. The New York *Staats-Zeitung* increased its circulation from 70,000 to 122,000.[49]

In early 1915 the course of events created much more strained relations between Germany and the United States directly. The German government ignored the warnings of President Wilson and adopted a policy of submarine warfare against all Allied ships. In May a submarine sank the British ship *Lusitania*; 124 Americans were among the 1,198 killed. Some German-American newspapers seemed oblivious to the public outrage in the United States, continuing to defend the German position and accusing the British of provoking the incident. More accusations of disloyalty were launched against German editors. There was further embarassment in August when the New York *World* published documents pilfered from the German propagandist Heinrich Albert, revealing his efforts to influence the press.[50]

The election year of 1916 produced a great effort—perhaps the last one—of the German press to wield an influence in presidential politics. Alienated from Wilson, who had now begun to assail ''hyphenism'' in his speeches, the German papers attacked him for having been too much under British influence. In February 1916 the German editors gathered in Chicago to organize a common national press organization, always a difficult objective. In the same conference they joined with other leaders in plans to deny reelection to Wilson.[51] They concentrated on the Republican nomination and were relieved when that party chose Charles Evans Hughes; the alternative, Theodore Roosevelt, had taken to speaking out against the ''hyphenism'' of the Germans. In its support of Hughes, the German press was probably more solidly behind one candidate than in any election since 1852. But this did not translate into a solid voting bloc; many German Democrats adhered to their traditional party loyalties, and the German vote was not as united as the press support. Hughes's narrow defeat by Wilson was a major blow to the ambitions of the German press and other leaders to demonstrate the power of an organized German vote.

Other events of 1916 allowed the German press to continue in its false confidence that a war with Germany was unthinkable and impossible. Fear of war relaxed in May when the German government agreed to suspend its policy of submarine warfare. Many German-American papers continued to herald the eventual victory of German forces over British imperialism. Such attitudes left the German papers very vulnerable when Germany decided in January 1917 to resume submarine warfare. Even as diplomatic relations worsened, German editors pleaded for neutrality and agitated against American intervention. In February the contents of the Zimmermann note, in which the German foreign secretary sought Mexico's assistance against the United States, became public; some German-American journalists denounced it as a British hoax, only to suffer embarrassment when it proved genuine.[52]

The cumulative effect of the attitudes expressed over the previous three years made it a painful and devastating adjustment to reality for the German press when war was declared on April 6, 1917. Some newspapers changed their course rapidly; the *Westliche Post* of St. Louis switched from advocating neutrality to calling for loyalty and the avoidance of any hint of treasonable activity. The German press service reports of the European war suddenly disappeared.[53] But other papers continued to predict German victories and to assail those who had abandoned neutrality. The Milwaukee *Seebote* continued throughout the summer of 1917 to denounce the British as the instigators of the war.[54] In Cincinnati, the *Freie Presse* incongruously placed laudatory dispatches from abroad about Germany's war efforts side by side with stories describing American mobilization efforts.[55] Such confusion reigned for nearly six months in much of the German press. The unpreparedness of the German papers for a declaration of war and their poorly conceived response when it actually came left them open to the rising anti-German hysteria.[56]

The German papers, regardless of their previous stance, found themselves in a difficult position amid that outbreak of superpatriotism. The government's Committee on Public Information (the "Creel Committee") imposed upon the German press the duty of disseminating its propaganda material, which often tended to deride all German culture and to impugn the loyalty of those who clung to German language and culture. In many towns, local vigilance committees campaigned against anything German. The German papers, a highly visible symbol of the despised cultural heritage, became an obvious and vulnerable target.[57] The pervasive mood of suspicion and hostility inevitably had its effect. While some newspapers continued to defend their positions, others receded to a sullen silence on all matters of controversy. Regardless of their position, German newspapers by late 1917 began to see their circulation and revenue falling. Readers could avoid problems and harrassment by simply dropping their subscriptions. Advertisers often decided that the hazards of buying space in the German press far outweighed the benefits.[58]

Government legislation dealt a more direct blow. In early October 1917 President Wilson signed the Trading-with-the-Enemy Act, which included a section requiring foreign-language newspapers to file with the postal authorities translations of all material which concerned government policy or international affairs. Exemptions could be granted to papers which the authorities deemed loyal. The German press, already struggling financially, reeled under the burden. Some went out of business at once; others greatly reduced the space given to political and war news in order to reduce the burden of translating. Many German papers, eager to avoid the expensive requirements, were at great pains to demonstrate their loyalty and obtain the licenses which would exempt them. Seventy-four German papers eventually gained such licenses, but the pressures to demonstrate loyalty proved to be an effective form of indirect censorship.[59] Rigorous enforcement of the law was felt especially by the German socialist press, which had constantly criticized American entry into the war. The Philadelphia *Tageblatt* (Daily page), a socialist paper, lost its mailing privilege, and two of its staff members were convicted of espionage. Editors of other papers were interned as enemy aliens.[60]

In the wake of the harsh experience of the world war, the German press emerged sadly diminished and considerably altered in character. Statistical estimates vary, but it is safe to say that the world of German journalism was reduced to less than half its former scope in a few years. Of about 522 German publications of all sorts in 1917, only 278 remained in 1920. The daily German papers, which had numbered seventy in 1910, stood at only twenty-nine in 1920. What was more, the circulation of all the dailies, which had been over 900,000 in 1910, stood below 250,000 in 1920.[61] The shrinkage of the German press struck especially hard at the smaller and weaker publications—dailies in smaller cities and country weeklies with few resources. The wartime period saw the disappearance of some venerable German papers whose origins predated the Civil War—the Freeport (Illinois) *Deutscher Anzeiger* (German informant), the Buffalo *Demokrat*, and the Detroit *Herold*, to name a few.[62] The case of the Baltimore *Deutsche Correspondent* was perhaps representative of the fate that befell many German papers. While it had amply demonstrated its loyalty during the war and had been among the first papers to gain exemption from filing translations, it still became a target of the general anti-German hysteria. The English-language press assailed it; advertisers shied away, and circulation declined rapidly. The Raine family, which had operated the paper since its founding in 1841, could suffer the loss no longer and bade farewell to their readers on April 28, 1918. Another weekly took over the plant and the name *Correspondent* and continued it as a weekly, but it would never again play the same role in the life of Baltimore.[63]

More significantly, the German press as a force to be reckoned with in American social and political affairs was gone. Chastened by the experience of the war, it made little effort to claim political influence or rally its readers to a cause. It shied away from the postwar international issues; although, like many German-

Americans, they felt betrayed by Wilson and by the peace he produced at Versailles, the German editors for the most part accepted the results without attempting to organize a resistance.[64] The papers needed to persuade German readers to return, but feared to do so by opening up old wounds. Too many old readers now felt that they could get their information from the English-language press, and were perhaps fearful of returning to the much-criticized institutions of German-America. In the aftermath of the attack that had been carried on against the teaching of the German language, it was hard to envision the development of many new readers in the future. The wave of new German immigration predicted by some did not develop. Many German publications, eschewing controversy, turned to the remaining organizations of German-American society and tied themselves even more closely to them in an effort to sustain some support.

By the mid–1920s, some German papers were, however, assuming a more aggressive stance about the promotion and preservation of German culture, and the circulation figures show that some of the old readership returned during that decade. From its very low postwar point of 239,000 readers in 1920, German daily newspaper circulation rose to about 350,000 in 1930. Weekly circulation remained steady. The number of individual publications declined, however, as increasing numbers of localities found that they could no longer support their own German papers. In the process of mergers and discontinuances, the remaining papers managed to survive by picking up some of the readers of the journals that went out of business.

The 1930s, on the other hand, brought a severe downturn. The number of German dailies—twenty-nine in 1920 and twenty-two in 1930—fell to thirteen by 1940.[65] The press was hit simultaneously by the hardships of the Great Depression, the drop in new immigrants, and the accelerating death rate of the generation which had come to the United States in the two decades before 1900. The immediate aftermath of World War I had seen the end of such veterans of German language journalism as the Cincinnati *Volksblatt*, the *Illinois Staats-Zeitung*, the Chicago *Arbeiter-Zeitung*, and the Milwaukee *America*. After the Depression of the 1930s, more fell by the wayside; the Louisville *Anzeiger*, the St. Paul *Volkszeitung* (People's news), and the Kansas City *Presse*, to name a few examples.

The decline and death of the St. Louis *Westliche Post* reflected the trials of the German press in the Depression years. While languishing in the early 1920s, it had raised its circulation figures to about 20,000 in 1924 by absorbing the other remaining St. Louis German daily, *Amerika*. But it hovered on the brink of insolvency and was continued only with the aid of its job-printing business and the outside resources of the owners, the Buder family. When the Depression struck, that support was no longer possible. In 1933 the paper was simply handed over to its employees, but the economic problems of the paper remained intractable. There were great efforts to rally the support of the German social and cultural organizations, but they had their own Depression problems. The paper declined rapidly and filed for bankruptcy in 1938.[66]

Clearly, the future offered little promise for the German press, and survival rather than expansion was the concern of most of the remaining publications. Perhaps the only paper that maintained some semblance of the great daily German papers of the turn of the century was the New York *Staats-Zeitung und Herold*, formed in 1919 from the merger of the old *Staats-Zeitung* with the *Herold*. On the eve of World War II the paper still had a staff of over 200 and a circulation of 80,000. It maintained itself partly by gradually orienting itself to a more national audience as smaller papers disappeared across the country.[67] But the younger generation of the Ridder family, three brothers who took control when their father died in 1915, recognized the need to turn their efforts in new directions. In 1926 they bought the New York *Journal of Commerce* and went on to build a chain of English-language papers across the country. In 1953 they sold the *Staats-Zeitung und Herold*.[68]

Another family followed a different course and attempted to forge declining German papers together into an economically viable chain. Val J. Peter, an immigrant from Bavaria, came to America in 1889 and began a journalistic career with the Rock Island (Illinois) *Volkszeitung* (People's news), which he bought in 1905. In 1907 he moved to Omaha, acquired papers there, and consolidated them as the Omaha *Tribüne*. From this base he went on to make further acquisitions, eventually including journals in Buffalo, Milwaukee, St. Paul, Toledo, Kansas City, and elsewhere. In 1929 the Peter family acquired the weekly Baltimore *Correspondent*, which was on the brink of financial collapse; during the 1930s, they attempted to revive the paper by cultivating the support of German organizations, and even resumed daily publication for a few years in the late 1930s. The Peter formula was to use some common editorial material throughout all the papers and to promote the papers through ties with German institutions in their respective cities. After World War II, the printing of the papers was increasingly consolidated in the Omaha plant.[69] The Peter chain lingered through a long decline; in the late 1960s thirteen papers remained, but the company terminated its business in the early 1980s, merging the remaining papers with the Winona (Minnesota) *America-Herold*, a weekly which previously had absorbed many other dying papers.

Inevitably, the quality of German-American newspapers began to decline as their numbers dwindled. With a few exceptions, the remaining papers had to get by with very small staffs, who had to rely on news service copy, press releases, and "boiler plate" material taken from other newspapers. Local reporting often became a listing of the activities of German organizations. Fear of offending any element of German-America accelerated the trend to the bland, noncontroversial coverage that had begun around the turn of the century. While the German press still provided a basic communications system for institutional German-America, that was a role far less ambitious than it had once seen for itself.

The problem of the German press's position in the face of international developments presented itself once again in the 1930s with the rise of Adolf Hitler to power in Germany. For the most part, the German-language newspapers gave little support to the aims of Nazi Germany; the experience of 1914–1917 was very much alive in the memories of journalists and readers alike. Nazi leaders in Germany who cherished the idea that the spirit of German nationalism among American immigrants would incline them to support Hitler met with disillusionment. In a celebrated incident in mid–1933, Heinz Spanknöbel, a self-appointed leader of the Nazi movement in America, tried to order Victor Ridder, one of the publishers of the New York *Staats-Zeitung und Herold*, to support the Nazi cause; he was summarily thrown out of Ridder's office. Later in the 1930s the German government fostered a more organized campaign of cultural and political propaganda, but it gained neither German-American press cooperation nor the general support of German-Americans.[70] The German-American Bund tried to rally followers with their own papers, such as the *Deutsche Zeitung* (German news) and later the *Deutscher Weckruf und Beobachter* (German morning call and observer); but, like the American Nazi movement itself, their appeal was only to a tiny segment of the recently immigrated German-born and had little effect upon the great majority of German-Americans.[71] The failing of the German press during the 1930s was not so much in giving support to Nazism but rather in being tardy in opposing what was happening within Germany. Some German papers remained noncommittal and attempted neutrality; some pointed to the injustices which they believed had been done to Germany at Versailles and which ultimately brought about the rise of Hitler. German-Jewish organs, like the refugee publication *Aufbau* (Rebuilding), had of course consistently opposed Hitler. In late 1938 outbreaks of anti-Jewish rioting in Germany made the anti-Semitic nature of Hitler's government a matter that the press could hardly avoid recognizing, and stronger criticism from the German press became more common. The influential New York *Staats-Zeitung und Herold* adopted a policy of vigorous condemnation of Hitler, and other papers followed suit. When the United States declared war on Germany in 1941, the German press was not at all in the kind of position it had been in at the outbreak of war in 1917, and could rally German-Americans to the cause of the United States without awkward changes of attitude.[72]

Nor did the experiences during World War II bring the strong reactions against the German-language press that had occurred in 1917–1918. The papers had little record of identification with Nazism; but besides that, the German press simply no longer held a position of great visibility in American life and Americans were unlikely to perceive it as a threat. The pool of readers continued to decline, with little possibility of renewal from new immigration in sight. The number of German dailies declined from thirteen to seven in the decade of the 1940s, but the decline in readers was even more drastic: from an estimated 261,000 to 69,000. Such longstanding papers as the California *Demokrat* and the Pittsburgh *Volksblatt* went out of business during the war. The trickle of new immigrants that came after World War II did not reverse the downward trend. By 1960 there were four daily papers left.[73] By 1983 there was only one, the Chicago *Abendblatt*, which also published a separate edition for Milwaukee. The New York

Staats-Zeitung und Herold became a thrice-weekly paper in the 1970s, and then switched to weekly publication in the 1980s; it published small separate editions for Florida and for Philadelphia.[74]

A few journals would continue to survive, but no one in the early 1980s could talk of any great revival of German journalism in America; it was now apparent how much these once thriving newspapers had been dependent on fresh supplies of first-generation immigrants. The long history of German-American journalism was essentially complete as it passed the landmark of a quarter of a millennium. Not only had it survived longer than any other ethnic press, it had without doubt been more thoroughly involved in American life and history than any other foreign-language press. The vast output of the German press remains not only as a challenge to scholars of immigrant life in America but also as a monument to the millions of German-Americans whom the papers helped to find their way into American life.

NOTES

1. Karl J.R. Arndt and May E. Olson, comps., *German-American Newspapers and Periodicals, 1732–1955: History and Bibliography* (Heidelberg: Quelle and Meyer, 1961). Unless otherwise noted, the details of publication and circulation for different newspapers and publications are based on Arndt and Olson's work.

2. Carl F. Wittke, *The German-Language Press in America* (Lexington: University of Kentucky Press, 1957), uses the theme of the "American" nature of the German press as an integrating idea; see especially p. 6.

3. Wittke, *German-Language Press*, pp. 13–15; John B. Stoudt, "The German Press in Pennsylvania and the American Revolution," *Pennsylvania Magazine of History and Biography* 59 (1938): 79–80; Oswald Seidensticker, *The First Century of German Printing in America, 1728–1830* (Philadelphia: German Pionier-Verein, 1893), pp. 8–9.

4. Seidensticker, *First Century*, pp. 12, 26–27; Felix Reichmann, *Christopher Sower, Sr., 1694–1758: Printer in Germantown* (Philadelphia: Carl Schurz Memorial Foundation, 1943); Donald F. Durnbaugh, "Christopher Sauer: Pennsylvania-German Printer," *Pennsylvania Magazine of History and Biography* 82 (1958): 316–340; Donald F. Durnbaugh, "Was Christopher Sauer a Dunker?" *Pennsylvania Magazine of History and Biography* 93 (1969): 382–391.

5. *Papers of Benjamin Franklin*, ed. Leonard W. Labaree et al. (New Haven: Yale University Press, 1959–), 5: 419.

6. William T. Parsons, *The Pennsylvania Dutch: A Persistent Minority* (Boston: Twayne, 1976), pp. 114–115; Benjamin H. Newcomb, *Franklin and Galloway: A Political Partnership* (New Haven: Yale University Press, 1972), pp. 94–100; James Hutson, *Pennsylvania Politics, 1746–1770: The Movement for Royal Government and Its Consequences* (Princeton: Princeton University Press, 1972), pp. 122–177.

7. *Papers of Benjamin Franklin*, 12: 316, 328–329.

8. Stoudt, "German Press in Pennsylvania," pp. 74–90; Seidensticker, *First Century*, pp. 99–105; Wittke, *German-Language Press*, pp. 20–22.

9. Parsons, *Pennsylvania Dutch*, pp. 115–116; Seidensticker *First Century*, pp. 125–155. The *Adler* suspended publication in 1913; Arndt and Olson, *German-American Newspapers*, p. 587.

10. Dieter Cunz, *The Maryland Germans* (Princeton: Princeton University Press, 1948), pp. 167–174; Klaus G. Wust, "Matthias Bartgis' Newspapers in Virginia," *American German Review* 18, no. 1 (October 1951): 16–18; Klaus Wust, *The Virginia Germans* (Charlottesville: University of Virginia Press, 1969), pp. 152–157.

11. Wittke, *German-Language Press*, pp. 31–32; Seidensticker, *First Century*, pp. 153–155, 169–170; Heinrich A. Rattermann, "Der deutsch-amerikanische Journalismus und seine Verbreitung von 1800 bis zur Einwanderung der sogenannten 'Dreissiger,' " *Deutsch-Amerikanische Geschichtsblätter* 12 (1912): 283–305.

12. Ralph Wood, "Journalism among the Pennsylvania Germans," in Ralph Wood, ed., *The Pennsylvania Germans* (Princeton: Princeton University Press, 1942), pp. 129–164; Wittke, *German-Language Press*, pp. 27–32.

13. Wittke, *German-Language Press*, pp. 44–46; Rattermann, "Der deutsch-amerikanische Journalismus," pp. 304–305; "Das Entstehen der *New Yorker Staatszeitung*," *Deutsche Pionier* 15 (1883–1884): 411–416; Seidensticker, *First Century*, pp. viii, 208.

14. Obituary of Molitor in *Deutsche Pionier* 5 (1873): 191–192; Rattermann, "Der deutsch-amerikanische Journalismus," pp. 304–305; L. A. Wollenweber, "Die Gründung der *New Yorker Staatszeitung*," *Deutsche Pionier* 15 (1884): 454–455.

15. Wittke, *German-Language Press*, pp. 36–44; Rattermann, "Der deutsch-amerikanische Journalismus," pp. 304–305; Wollenweber, "Gründung der *New Yorker Staatszeitung*," pp. 454–455; Cunz, *Maryland Germans*, pp. 257–259; "Das Deutschthum Baltimores," *Deutsche Pionier* 3 (1871): 106–108; Edmund E. Miller, *The Hundred Year History of the German Correspondent, Baltimore, Maryland* (Baltimore: Baltimore Correspondent, 1941), pp. 5–8.

16. Wittke, *German-Language Press*, pp. 54–55; Carl F. Wittke, *Refugees of Revolution: The German Forty-eighters in America* (Philadelphia: University of Pennsylvania Press, 1952), pp. 271–272; Erich F. Hofacker, *German Literature as Reflected in the German-Language Press of St. Louis prior to 1898* (St. Louis: Washington University Press, 1946), pp. 3–5.

17. C. Rünelin, "Geschichte der Gründung des *Volksblatts*," *Deutsche Pionier* 1 (1869): 80–82; A. Ligowsky, "Die ersten deutschen Zeitungen Cincinnatis," *Deutsche Pionier* 1 (1869): 44–46; Wittke, *German-Language Press*, pp. 48–52.

18. Wittke, *German-Language Press*, pp. 52–57; Leonard Koester, "German Newspapers Published in Louisville," *American German Review* 20, no. 5 (June-July 1954): 24; Arndt and Olson, *German-American Newspapers*, p. 177.

19. The estimates of numbers of newspapers are in Friedrich Schnake, "Geschichte der deutsche Bevölkerung und der deutschen Presse von St. Louis und Umgegend," *Deutsche Pionier* 5 (1873): 334–335; *Atlantis* n.s. 5, no. 1 (July 1856); 77–80; Wittke, *German-Language Press*, pp. 75–77; with some additional information from Arndt and Olson, *German-American Newspapers*, passim.

20. Wittke, *Refugees of Revolution*, p. 271; Edwin H. Zeydel, "Anna B. Ottendorfer" and "Oswald Ottendorfer," in *Dictionary of American Biography* ed. Allen Johnson (New York: Scribner, 1928–1937), 14: 106–107; Albert B. Faust, *The German Element in the United States* (Boston: Houghton Mifflin, 1909, 2: 448–450.

21. *Illinois Staats-Zeitung*, April 21, 1898; *Wisconsin Staats-Zeitung* (Wisconsin public news) (Madison), September 23, 1891; Caspar Butz, "Georg Hillgärtner," *Deutsche Pionier* 14 (1883): 468–470; Wittke, *Refugees of Revolution*, pp. 273–274; Alfred E. Zucker, ed., *The Forty-eighters: Political Refugees of the German Revolution of 1848*

(New York: Columbia University Press, 1950), pp. 282, 303, 305, 339–340; Alden L. Powell, "George Schneider," in *Dictionary of American Biography*, 14: 446–447.

22. Heinrich Boernstein, *Fünfundsiebzig Jahre in der Alten und Neuen Welt: Memoiren eines Unbedeutenden* (Leipzig: O. Wigand, 1884), 2: 104–152; Hofacker, *German Literature*, pp. 3–6; Harvey Saalberg, "The *Westliche Post* of St. Louis: A Daily Newspaper for German-Americans, 1857–1938," Ph.D. dissertation, University of Missouri-Columbia, 1967, pp. 32–34; Daniel Hertle, *Die Deutschen in Nordamerika und der Freiheitskampf in Missouri* (Chicago: Illinois Staatszeitung, 1865), pp. 51–53; August Suelflow, "St. Louiser Volksblatt," *Concordia Historical Institute Quarterly* 18 (1946): 108–110. Walter Kamphoefner has pointed out that the refugees of the 1830s exhibited some of the same traits as the later and more numerous forty-eighters; see his "Dreissiger and Forty-eighter: The Political Influence of Two Generations of German Political Exiles," in *Germany and America: Essays on Problems of International Relations and Immigration*, ed. Hans L. Trefousse (New York: Brooklyn College, 1980), pp. 89–99.

23. Bayrd Still, *Milwaukee: The History of a City* (Madison: State Historical Society of Wisconsin, 1948), pp. 67–68, 120, 152; Wittke, *Refugees of Revolution*, pp. 266–269.

24. Koester, "German Newspapers Published in Louisville," p. 24.

25. Carl F. Wittke, *Against the Current: The Life of Karl Heinzen* (Chicago: University of Chicago Press, 1945); Eitel W. Dobert, "The Radicals," in Zucker, *The Forty-eighters*, pp. 170–177.

26. Sally M. Miller, *The Radical Immigrant* (New York: Twayne, 1974), pp. 63–92; Walter L. Wright, Jr., "Friedrich Hassaurek," in *Dictionary of American Biography*, 8: 383–384; Karl Obermann, *Joseph Weydemeyer* (New York: International Publishers, 1947).

27. Schnake, "Geschichte der deutsche Bevölkerung," pp. 334–335; *Atlantis*, n.s. 5, no. 1 (July 1856): 77–80; George M. Stephenson, *A History of American Immigration, 1820–1924*, (Boston: Ginn, 1926), p. 130.

28. Lawrence S. Thompson and Frank X. Braun, "The Forty-eighters in Politics," in Zucker, *The Forty-eighters*, p. 125; C. F. Huch, "Gottlieb Theodore Kellner," *Deutsch-Amerikanische Geschichtsblätter* 9 (1909): 81–85.

29. Wittke, *Refugees of Revolution*, pp. 193–194; "Baltimore 1861: We Want Rapp," trans. Alice H. Finckh, Society for the History of the Germans in Maryland, *Twenty-eighth Report* (1953), pp. 79–82.

30. Mack Walker, *Germany and the Emigration* (Cambridge, Mass.: Harvard University Press, 1964), p. 176 and passim.

31. S.N.D. North, "History and Present Condition of the Newspaper and Periodical Press of the United States," in U.S. Census Office, *Tenth Census of the United States* (Washington, D.C., 1884), 8: 204–210, 285–288, 338–343; T. Herbert Etzler, "German-American Newspapers in Texas with Special Reference to the 'Texas Volksblatt,' 1877–1889," *Southwestern Historical Quarterly* 57 (1954): 423–431.

32. Edmund E. Miller, *Hundred Year History*, pp. 14–15; Wittke, *German-Language Press*, pp. 82–83; Saalberg, "*Westliche Post*," p. 218.

33. Saalberg, "*Westliche Post*," pp. 185–226; W. A. Swanberg, *Pulitzer* (New York: Scribner, 1967), pp. 1–44.

34. H. A. Rattermann, "Der deutsche Presse in den Vereinigten Staaten," *Deutsch Pionier* 8 (1876): 320; North, "History and Present Condition," pp. 127, 183; Wittke,

German-Language Press, pp. 197–209. Many newspaper circulation figures were not audited and probably represent inflated claims.

35. Arndt and Olson, *German-American Newspapers*, passim; Wittke, *German-Language Press*, pp. 213–214; Cunz, *Maryland Germans*, pp. 350–363; Rattermann, "Der Deutsche Presse," pp. 290–318.

36. Wittke, *German-Language Press*, pp. 206–209; Joshua A. Fishman, Robert G. Hayden, and Mary E. Warshauer, "The Non-English and the Ethnic Group Press, 1910–1960," in Joshua A. Fishmann, et al., ed. *Language Loyalty in the United States* (The Hague: Mouton, 1966), pp. 51–74.

37. Still, *Milwaukee*, pp. 264–267; John A. Hawgood, *The Tragedy of German-America* (New York: Putnam, 1940), p. 79; James M. Bergquist, "German-America in the 1890s: Illusions and Realities," in E. Allen McCormick, ed., *Germans in America: Aspects of German-American Relations in the Nineteenth Century* (New York: Brooklyn College Press, 1983), pp. 1–14.

38. Saalberg, *"Westliche Post,"* pp. 275–277, 301–306.

39. Guido A. Dobbert, "The Disintegration of an Immigrant Community: The Cincinnati Germans, 1870–1920," Ph.D. dissertation, University of Chicago, 1965, pp. 99–100.

40. Wittke, *German-Language Press*, pp. 232–234; Arndt and Olson, *German-American Newspapers*, passim.

41. Saalberg, *"Westliche Post,"* pp. 156–196; Hans Trefousse, *Carl Schurz: A Biography* (Knoxville: University of Tennessee Press, 1982), pp. 162–174.

42. Wittke, *German-Language Press*, pp. 92–94; Bessie Louise Pierce, *A History of Chicago* (New York: Knopf, 1937–1957), 3: 349–356; Emil Mannhardt, "Wilhelm Rapp," *Deutsch-Amerikanische Geschichtsblätter* 7 (1907): 58–61; obituary of Raster in *Wisconsin Staats-Zeitung* (Madison), July 29, 1891.

43. Wittke, *German-Language Press*, pp. 221–223; Frederick C. Luebke, *Bonds of Loyalty: German-Americans and World War I* (DeKalb: Northern Illinois University Press, 1974), pp. 45–47; Audrey L. Olson, "St. Louis Germans, 1850–1920: The Nature of an Immigrant Community and Its Relation to the Assimilation Process," Ph.D. dissertation, University of Kansas, 1970, pp. 113–114.

44. Dobbert, "Disintegration of an Immigrant Community," pp. 94–101, 266–271.

45. Hofacker, *German Literture*, p. 7; Richard Bartholdt, *From Steerage to Congress: Reminiscences and Reflections* (Philadelphia: Dorrance, 1930).

46. Wittke, *German-Language Press*, pp. 235–243; Dobbert; pp. 276–278; Luebke, *Bonds of Loyalty*, pp. 86–91; Clifton J. Child, *The German-Americans in Politics, 1914–1917* (Madison: University of Wisconsin Press, 1939), pp. 174–179.

47. Carl F. Wittke, *German-Americans and the World War, with Special Emphasis on Ohio's German-Language Press* (Columbus: Ohio State Archaeological and Historical Society, 1936), pp. 5–21; Child, *German-Americans in Politics*, pp. 1–41; Luebke, *Bonds of Loyalty*, pp. 83–95.

48. Wittke, *German-Americans and the World War*, p. 24; H. C. Peterson, *Propaganda for War: The Campaign against American Neutrality, 1914–1917* (Norman: University of Oklahoma Press, 1939), pp. 134–139; Phyllis Keller, "German-America and the First World War," Ph.D. dissertation, University of Pennsylvania, 1969, p. 113; Luebke, *Bonds of Loyalty*, pp. 127–128; Felice A. Bonadio, "The Failure of German Propaganda in the United States, 1914–1917," *Mid-America* 41 (1959): 40–57.

49. Wittke, *German-Language Press*, pp. 244–261; Wittke, *German-Americans and*

the World War, pp. 37–39; Dobbert, "Disintegration of an Immigrant Community," pp. 264–273; David W. Hirst, "German Propaganda in the United States, 1914–1917," Ph.D. dissertation, Northwestern University, 1962, pp. 41–42.

50. Child, *German-Americans in Politics*, pp. 57, 110; Luebke, *Bonds of Loyalty*, pp. 128–151; Saalberg, "*Westliche Post*," pp. 344–348; Alexander Waldenrath, "The German Language Newspapers in Pennsylvania during World War I," *Pennsylvania History* 42 (1975): 25–37.

51. Wittke, *German-Americans and the World War*, p. 90; Luebke, *Bonds of Loyalty*, p. 162.

52. Luebke, *Bonds of Loyalty*, pp. 157–207; John C. Crighton, *Missouri and the World War, 1914–1917* (Columbia: University of Missouri Press, 1947), pp. 177–181; Wittke, *German-Americans and the World War*, pp. 88, 122; Cunz, *Maryland Germans*, pp. 395–401; Child, *German-Americans in Politics*, pp. 111–152.

53. Saalberg, "*Westliche Post*," pp. 348, 363.

54. Milwaukee, *Seebote*, June-August 1917.

55. Dobbert, "Disintegration of an Immigrant Community," pp. 322–341.

56. Wittke, *German-Language Press*, pp. 261–263; Wittke, *German-Americans and the World War*, pp. 133–135; Cunz, *Maryland Germans*, pp. 398–399; Waldenrath, "German Language Newspapers in Pennsylvania," pp. 37–41; Luebke, *Bonds of Loyalty*, pp. 228–229.

57. Luebke, *Bonds of Loyalty*, pp. 212–216.

58. Wittke, *German-Americans and the World War*, pp. 133–135, 172–175; Saalberg, "*Westliche Post*," pp. 363–371.

59. Luebke, *Bonds of Loyalty*, pp. 241–243; Wittke, *German-Language Press*, pp. 261–266; Waldenrath, "German Language Newspapers in Pennsylvania," pp. 37–41; Wittke, *German-Americans and the World War*, pp. 136–137; Harry N. Scheiber, *The Wilson Administration and Civil Liberties* (Ithaca: Cornell University Press, 1960), pp. 11–27.

60. Wittke, *German-Language Press*, pp. 266–274; Luebke, *Bonds of Loyalty*, pp. 242–243.

61. Luebke, *Bonds of Loyalty*, pp. 271–273; Wittke, *German-Language Press*, pp. 272–274; Fishman et al., "The Non-English and the Ethnic Group Press," pp. 51–74.

62. Wittke, *German-Americans and the World War*, pp. 175–178.

63. Edmund E. Miller, *Hundred Year History*, pp. 16–20; Cunz, *Maryland Germans*, pp. 398–407.

64. Austin J. App, "The Germans," in Joseph P. O'Grady, ed., *The Immigrants' Influence on Wilson's Peace Policies* (Lexington: University of Kentucky Press, 1967), pp. 30–55; John B. Duff, "German-Americans and the Peace, 1918–1920," *American Jewish Historical Quarterly* 59 (1970): 424–444.

65. Fishman et al., "The Non-English and the Ethnic Group Press," pp. 51–74.

66. Saalberg, "*Westliche Post*," pp. 381–404.

67. Wittke, *German-Language Press*, pp. 288–291.

68. *Time*, November 25, 1946; Arndt and Olson, *German-American Newspapers*, p. 399.

69. Edmund E. Miller, *Hundred Year History*, pp. 21–24; Wittke, *German-Language Press*, pp 285–286; Saalberg, "*Westliche Post*," p. 410.

70. Sander A. Diamond, *The Nazi Movement in the United States, 1924–1941* (Ithaca: Cornell University Press, 1974), pp. 121, 193–196, 288–292.

71. Ibid., pp. 142–154.

72. Ibid., pp. 276–278; Wittke, *German-Language Press*, pp. 284–285; Frederick C. Luebke, "The Germans," in John Higham, ed., *Ethnic Leadership in America* (Baltimore: Johns Hopkins University Press, 1978), pp. 84–86.

73. Fishman et al., "The Non-English and the Ethnic Group Press," pp. 51–74.

74. *IMS '83 Ayer Directory of Publications* (Ft. Washington, Pa.: IMS, 1983), pp. 1104–1105; and previous editions of Ayer.

BIBLIOGRAPHY

Arndt, Karl J.R., and May E. Olson, comps. *German-American Newspapers and Periodicals, 1732–1955: History and Bibliography.* Heidelberg: Quelle and Meyer, 1961.

Durnsbaugh, Donald F. "Christopher Sauer, Pennsylvania-German Printer." *Pennsylvania Magazine of History and Biography* 82 (1958): 316–340.

Etzler, T. Herbert, "German-American Newspapers in Texas with Special Reference to the 'Texas Volksblatt,' 1877–1889." *Southwestern Historical Quarterly* 57 (1954): 423–431.

Fishman, Joshua A.; Hayden, Robert G.; and Warshauer, Mary E. "The Non-English and the Ethnic Group Press, 1910–1960," in Joshua A. Fishman et al., *Language Loyalty in the United States* (The Hague: Mouton, 1966), pp. 51–74.

Groen, Henry J. "History of the German-American Newspapers of Cincinnati before 1860." Ph.D. dissertation, Ohio State University, 1944.

Hofacker, Erich F. *German Literature as Reflected in the German-Language Press of St. Louis prior to 1898.* St. Louis: Washington University Press, 1946.

Johnson, Niel M. *George Sylvester Viereck: German-American Propagandist.* Urbana: University of Illinois Press, 1972.

Miller, Edmund E. *The Hundred Year History of the German Correspondent, Baltimore, Maryland.* Baltimore: Baltimore Correspondent, 1941.

Pochman, Henry A., comp., and Arthur R. Schultz, ed. *Bibliography of German Culture in America to 1940.* Madison: University of Wisconsin, 1954.

Rattermann, Heinrich A. "Der deutsch-amerikanische Journalismus und seine Verbreitung von 1800 bis zur Einwanderung der sogenannten 'Dreissiger,' " *Deutsch-Amerikanische Geschichtsblätter* 12 (1912): 283–305.

Reichmann, Felix. *Christopher Sauer, Sr., 1694–1758: Printer in Germantown.* Philadelphia: Carl Schurz Memorial Foundation, 1943.

Saalberg, Harvey. "The *Westliche Post* of St. Louis: A Daily Newspaper for German-Americans, 1857–1938." Ph.D. dissertation, University of Missouri-Columbia, 1967.

Seidensticker, Oswald. *The First Century of German Printing in America, 1728–1830.* Philadelphia: German Pionier-Verein, 1893.

Stoudt, John B. "The German Press in Pennsylvania and the American Revolution." *Pennsylvania Magazine of History and Biography* 59 (1938): 74–90.

Waldenrath, Alexander. "The German Language Newspapers in Pennsylvania during World War I." *Pennsylvania History* 42 (1975): 25–37.

Wittke, Carl F. *German-Americans and the World War, with Special Emphasis on Ohio's*

German-Language Press. Columbus: Ohio State Archaeological and Historical Society, 1936.

————. *The German-Language Press in America*. Lexington: University of Kentucky, 1957.

11

The Greek Press

ANDREW T. KOPAN

Americans are impressed by the fact that of all the emigrants from Europe who have come to the United States, the Greeks preeminently continue to speak their native language (although decreasingly so) and to pass it on to the younger generations.[1] The Italians, Czechs, Poles, and others who arrived in the United States in large numbers during the latter part of the nineteenth century and the early decades of the twentieth forgot their mother tongue after thirty to forty years. It is rare today for their children to speak languages other than English. With the Greeks, however, it seems that precisely the opposite has happened and continues to happen. This is attributed to a number of factors: the strong social and ethnic cohesion of the Greek immigrant family; the presence of an extensive Greek ethnic press; and the influence of the Greek Orthodox Church with its extensive ethnic school system and infrastructure.

While Greek immigrants were primarily an illiterate group when they immigrated to the United States, they were, nonetheless, descendants of one of the most literate societies in the world and were keenly conscious of that heritage. Despite the low level of literacy, there prevailed a strong oral tradition which was reflected in the constant retelling of famous stories from their history, especially from the classical and Byzantine periods. Accordingly, twentieth-century Greek immigrants felt kinship with Homer and Plato as well as with Byzantine culture; nor could they forget that the New Testament and the development of the Christian Church were largely Greek achievements.

The Greek ethnic press developed rapidly in the United States. Greek immigration did not peak until 1907, when 36,404 immigrants arrived.[2] By then, several Greek-language newspapers, including a daily, were already in existence.

One of the principal factors which led to the early establishment of newspapers in the Greek communities of the United States was the Greek immigrants' passion for nationalism and politics. The desire to be informed about political events in the old country and to keep abreast of Greece's wars with Turkey in liberating portions of "unredeemed Greece" made them insatiable devourers of news. This was not unlike the Greek homeland, where readers combed the various newspapers for scraps of information or for arguments to attack or defend government measures; Greeks are among the most avid newspaper readers in the world.[3]

The Greek immigrant who arrived in the United States in the late nineteenth century was not only interested in the politics of his homeland; he was also homesick. Often he continued to live in his memories rather than face urgent problems in the new land. A newspaper from Greece—arriving long after it was published—was about the most welcome gift he could receive. More often than not he was unable to read the much treasured paper when it arrived. But that was not really important; at the cafe or coffee house he would be sure to find some compatriot who knew "enough letters" to read it to him.

GREEK-LANGUAGE NEWSPAPERS

In the 1890s, most of the few thousands of Greek immigrants settled in the larger American cities where economic opportunities were greatest. It was only natural that the first ethnic Greek newspapers would appear there. The first to try to fill this need was a professional journalist, Constantine Phasoularides, a graduate of the Great Greek National School of Constantinople.

Phasoularides had arrived in America in 1889 and during his early years in the United States attended the Massachusetts Institute of Technology. His original plan had been to return after a while to Constantinople, where he had worked as a school teacher and on a newspaper, the *Neologos*, published by Stavros Voutyras. In 1892, however, he settled in New York and decided to start a newspaper which would serve as a link between the Greek immigrants in the United States and the old country. He soon had an improvised printing shop, and in September 1892 he produced the first Greek-language newspaper to be printed in America, the *Neos Kosmos* (New World).[4]

This paper circulated at irregular intervals, although "circulated" is just a figure of speech. The Greeks in New York at that time numbered no more than 600, and they were difficult to contact. Widely scattered, they chiefly worked as railway track laborers, shoeshiners, dishwashers in restaurants, and so on, with few links between them. Distribution of the paper was a very real problem. In the hope of attracting readers, Phasoularides would leave copies in coffee shops either owned or frequented by Greeks so that those interested could buy them from the proprietor. This system, of course, was not the most suitable, and *Neos Kosmos* ceased publication after a few months.

It had, however, planted the seed that was to produce scores of Greek-language newspapers in the United States. Some of them survived for many years, while others quickly disappeared owing to lack of financial backing. In spite of this, so many newspapers were published that an informed observer of the early immigrant community maintained that the Greeks published more newspapers proportionate to their numbers than any other nationality in the country.[5] Since the appearance of *Neos Kosmos*, it has been estimated that well over a hundred

Greek newspapers have been published in the United States at one time or another.[6]

Apart from *Neos Kosmos*, of which unfortunately no copy is known to exist, the *Atlantis*, which appeared on March 1, 1894, in New York must be assumed to have been the first successful attempt to found a Greek-language newspaper. The director and publisher was Solon J. Vlasto, who had arrived in the United States in 1873 at the age of twenty from the island of Syros in Greece.[7]

Unlike Phasoularides, Vlasto was not a professional journalist and knew little about the technical side of the work. On the other hand, he was intelligent and ardently devoted to his native country, and had as his basic aim the moral support of his compatriots and the raising of the cultural standards of the small and poor Greek community.

Before embarking on his newspaper venture, Vlasto ran a thriving import-export business—one of the few successful Greek enterprises in the United States at that time. While still managing his business he began to write a kind of Greek bulletin which he posted ouside his offices. This bulletin included information of use to Greek immigrants in solving problems in the new land. Numerous Greek workers acquired the habit of visiting Vlasto's offices to learn the latest news from the old country and to obtain advice regarding their new life. The interest in the bulletin displayed by these immigrants convinced the astute and ambitious Greek of his compatriots' need for an organized newspaper which could be their guardian and moral supporter. The outcome was the appearance of *Atlantis*.

The *Atlantis* first appeared as a weekly paper, then biweekly, and later every other day. By 1905 it was published daily, the first of its kind in the Greek community of America. Still later, in keeping with his avowed aim, Vlasto began using his presses to publish a variety of self-help books and guides for the use of Greek immigrants. Through the years, the *Atlantis* not only became the largest Greek newspaper in America, with a circulation of 30,100 in 1914 (higher than any Athenian daily in Greece at the time), but also the most influential.[8] Conservative in politics (usually supporting the Royalist faction in Greece), it appealed to the Royalist sentiments of most Greek immigrants. Its patrons also found useful the increasing variety of guidebooks (such as Greek-English dictionaries and almanacs) published by the newspaper.

Unfortunately, in 1972, due to back taxes owed and disputes with the typesetters' union, Solon G. Vlasto, nephew of the newspaper's founder, who became publisher in 1945, was forced to close the paper; its assets were sold at a public auction by the Internal Revenue Service.[9] Thus, after seventy-nine years of continuous publication, the oldest extant Greek newspaper in America came to an end, taking with it the only Greek family newspaper dynasty to evolve in the United States.

The third Greek-language newspaper to be established was *Thermopylae*, published on a weekly basis in 1900 by John Booras in New York. Five years later, Constantine Phasoularides (who had established the first Greek newspaper in 1892), began publishing *Semaia* (The flag), also in New York. The following year, 1906, Booras and Phasoularides joined forces and published *Thermopylae-Semaia*, a daily, in New York, as a competitor to the *Atlantis*, but it lasted only until 1907.

At about the same time, Socrates A. Xanthaky, editor-in-chief of *Atlantis* from 1897, resigned his position after a series of disputes with Vlasto. Seeking to compete with the *Atlantis*, Xanthaky gathered sufficient funds to start publication of *Panhellenios* (The Pan Hellenic), in 1908 as a tri-weekly. By 1910 this newspaper served as the mouthpiece for the Pan Hellenic Union, the first national organization seeking to coordinate Greek interests in America. However, after an ongoing editorial dispute between the two newspapers, and following a financial scandal during the 1912–1913 Balkan Wars in which the Pan Hellenic Union was implicated, Xanthaky lost his battle, and the *Panhellenios* stopped its presses in 1913.[10]

The only Greek-language newspaper to compete seriously with *Atlantis* was the *Ethnikos Keryx* (National herald), which first appeared on April 2, 1915, to fill the void left by the defunct *Panhellenios*. It was founded by Petros Tatanis, a successful merchant who, after raising $100,000, launched *Ethnikos Keryx* to do battle with *Atlantis*. Provided with such adequate capital, *Ethnikos Keryx* became the first Greek newspaper begun as a daily. It also made it possible for the paper to employ one of the top Greek journalists in the country, Demetrios Callimachos, who served as editor for twenty-seven years, until 1942. Although trained as a Greek Orthodox priest, he spent most of his life in journalism in the three cultural centers of Hellenism—Constantinople, Smyrna, and Athens— before coming to the United States in 1914. He became involved with the moribund Pan Hellenic Union and preached to Greek immigrants the "Great Idea" of a resuscitated Greek (Byzantine) empire to be built upon the ruins of the collapsing Ottoman Empire with which Greece was embroiled in the Balkan Wars. As the vigorous editor-in-chief of the newly founded *Ethnikos Keryx*, he was to have a great influence on the Greek-American reading public and on community politics.[11]

Polarization of the two Greek dailies developed over the Royalist-Venizelist feud wherein *Atlantis* remained loyal to the conservative cause and supported King Constantine of Greece in his opposition to entry into World War I, while *Ethnikos Keryx* supported Greece's Liberal Prime Minister Eleutherios Venizelos in joining the war on the side of the Allies in pursuit of the "Great Idea." This was to have a profound impact on the Greek community in America, hopelessly dividing it for almost two decades. The battle of words and the impassioned editorials written caused Greek immigrants to subscribe to the newspapers supporting their political views. As a result, circulation figures increased considerably for both papers and by 1920 stood at 35,000 for *Atlantis* and 30,133 for *Ethnikos Keryx*. By 1926 Callimachos's paper edged ahead of *Atlantis*, with the two newspapers sharing approximately 70,000 readers.[12]

With the restoration of the monarchy in Greece in 1935 and the proclamation of the Metaxas dictatorship in 1936, the influence of Greek politics began to diminish in both papers as well as in other Greek-language newspapers in the country. The onset of the Great Depression, the erosion of Hellenic sentiment brought about by the assimilative forces of the American environment, and the fact that a new generation of American-born Greeks was growing up who were indifferent to political events in Greece removed Greek politics from the front pages of the ethnic press. Instead, the newspapers began to reflect more on Greek-American concerns that affected the Greek immigrants and their offspring. With reference to American politics, the two dailies took opposite points of view, *Ethnikos Keryx* supporting Franklin D. Roosevelt and New Deal legislation, and *Atlantis*, now labeling itself an independent newspaper, consistently supporting Republican interests and critizing Roosevelt's programs.[13]

In this respect, the two newspapers continued to maintain distinct identities. Despite the growing Americanization of Greek immigrants, *Atlantis* still continued to be supported by the monarchist-conservatives, while *Ethnikos Keryx* continued to appeal to the republican-liberals. But editorials became less heated as political moderation returned to Greece. While these leading dailies did not entirely cease to report political events in Greece, the distant disputes now had less attraction for Greek immigrants and their children.

Petros Tatanis directed the affairs of *Ethnikos Keryx* until 1939 (though he had sold the newspaper to Euripides Kehagias a few years previously). In 1939, however, the paper was acquired by Paul Demos, a Chicago attorney. He in turn sold it in 1940 to Basil I. Vlavianos, who had come to the United States in 1939 after completing university studies in France and Germany. In 1947 the paper was sold again, to Bobby Marketos, who had pursued a journalistic career since his arrival from Greece in 1937. He introduced an improved English Sunday supplement to the paper in order to attract the growing American-born generation. Thirty years later, in 1977, Marketos sold the newspaper to Brooklyn-born Eugene T. Rossides, who had served as assistant secretary to the United States Treasury Department in 1969–1973. An attorney by profession, with considerable publishing experience in the trade industry, he nevertheless resold *Ethnikos Keryx* within two months, preferring apparently to devote his time to his position as chairman of the American Hellenic Institute, a Greek-American trade-lobbying group in Washington, D.C.[14] The present owners of *Ethnikos Keryx*, George Leonardos and Anthony H. Diamantaris, continue to publish the newspaper in Long Island City, New York, but with a drastically reduced circulation of around 20,000.

With the demise of *Atlantis* in 1973, *Ethnikos Keryx* became the only Greek-language daily in the United States. Its solitary position was challenged, however, in 1977, when another Greek-language daily, *Proini* (Morning news), made its appearance in New York City. Published by Fannie Petallides, the paper conducted an aggressive campaign to enroll subscribers who were part of the post–World War II wave of Greek immigrants to the United States. In 1983, in order to appeal to English-speaking Greek Americans, a companion paper, the *Proini*

Weekly Review, was launched in tabloid form, completely in English, with Greek American novelist Athena Damis-Dallas as editor. Whether *Proini* will be able to develop a national readership like that of *Ethnikos Keryx* remains to be seen.

Since the first appearance of the ill-fated *Neos Kosmos* in 1892, some one hundred Greek language newspapers and periodicals of every description have seen the light of day in the United States. Of these, one of the most important was the *Hellenikos Astir* (Greek star) of Chicago, which was first published in 1904. Chicago was an important center of Greek immigration, and for a long while its Greek population even exceeded that of New York City.[15] It was only natural that a Greek-language newspaper would be established there in the early years of Greek immigration. Indeed, the *Hellenikos Astir* was preceded in 1902 by *Hellas* (Greece), a weekly published by Michael Soteropoulos, Basil Koutsogiannis, and Demetrios Antonopoulos, but it ceased publication in 1912, after a life span of only ten years.

A contributing cause to the decline of *Hellas* was no doubt the appearance of the *Greek Star* (as the *Hellenikos Astir* became commonly known). Founded by the colorful Peter S. Lambros in conjunction with Demetrios Evtaxias and Demetrios Manousopoulos, leaders in the early Chicago Greek community, it soon emerged as the leading Greek-language newspaper, eclipsing all other such papers subsequently published in Chicago. Under the leadership of Lambros, who served intermittently for forty-one years as publisher and editor (other editors during this period were Evtaxias, 1904–1905 and 1922–1931; Nicholas Lambropoulos, 1917–1918; and Nicholas Tsilimbaris, 1919–1922), the Chicago weekly achieved national recognition, though it never achieved the national circulation of the two New York dailies.

In 1944 the *Star* was acquired by Andrew Fasseas, a Chicago businessman and Republican Party leader who served as the Illinois State Director of Revenue and was a past supreme president of the American Hellenic Educational and Progressive Association (AHEPA), the largest Greek fraternal organization in the nation. George Founteas was appointed editor to succeed Lambros, serving until his retirement in 1954, when the current editor, Nicholas Philippidis, was appointed. In 1984, the *Greek Star* was acquired by the United Hellenic American Congress, a national umbrella organization of Greek Americans under the leadership of Chicago industrialist Andrew A. Athens, headquartered in Chicago. In an editorial in its first edition under the new publisher—UHAC Communications, Inc.—the new owner pledged that "the *Greek Star* will continue to be an independent newspaper primarily for and about the Greek community—its people, its life, its concerns, its interests."[16] It should be noted that during the 1960s the *Greek Star* made the transition from an all Greek-language paper to a bilingual and finally to an almost exclusively English-language newspaper. This pattern was followed by practically all Greek-language newspapers that survived beyond World War II and was reflective of the acculturation taking place in the Greek-American community.

The *Greek Star* is now the oldest continuously published Greek ethnic newspaper in the country, spanning almost the entire history of Greek journalism in the United States. Its durability can in part be attributed to the fact that until its acquisition by UHAC, it had only two owners and three major editors.

The other permanent paper in Chicago is the *Hellenikos Typos* (Greek press), founded in 1929 by Greek-trained journalist Paul Javaras and Elias Georgopoulos as a weekly. It merged in 1934 with the *Thessaloniki*, another Chicago weekly established in 1913 by Constantine Damaskos in cooperation with the Salopoulos brothers, Constantine, a pharmacist, and Nicholas, a physician who also served as Greek Consul General in Chicago. It was ably edited by Javaras from 1934 until his death in 1956, when it was sold to a consortium and edited by Major Constantine Chapralis, a retired Greek army officer. On November 23, 1962, the *Hellenikos Typos* changed hands again, and Aris Angelopoulos, an Athenian newspaper correspondent and graduate of Northwestern University's Medill School of Journalism, assumed the editorship. He still holds this post and has since acquired ownership of the paper.

Like the *Greek Star*, the *Hellenikos Typos* began as an exclusively Greek-language paper, but by the 1960s it too had succumbed to the acculturative influence of the milieu, becoming primarily an English-language paper, though it has consistently maintained a Greek-language section to accommodate the postwar Greek immigrants. Probably due to the editor's official contacts with Greek newspapers abroad, the *Hellenikos Typos* prints more news about political events in Greece and the activities of Greeks abroad than does the *Greek Star*, which generally restricts itself to Greek-American news. The two papers have become competitors over the years and have different political orientations—the *Hellenikos Typos* traditionally favoring the Democratic Party, the *Star*, at least until its acquisition by UHAC, the Republican Party. In 1982 the *Chicago Tribune* reported the circulation of the *Star* at 14,600 and that of the *Hellenikos Typos* at 14,800, a decline from previous years for both papers.[17]

OTHER NEWSPAPERS

Though the two big dailies, *Atlantis* and *Ethnikos Keryx*, dominated the Greek-language press in New York, numerous other newspapers appeared there, many of them short-lived, but representing a variety of types and orientations—hometown association, fraternal, ecclesiastical and religious, trade and occupational, satirical, and political. Among those established in New York were the following:[18] *Phrouros* (Sentinel), 1909–1910; *Nomotagis* (Loyalist), 1918–1924; *Phoni tou Ergatou* (Voice of the worker), 1918–1923; *Embros* (Forward), 1923–1939, organ of the Greek Division of the Communist party in the United States; *Neon Vima* (New tribune), daily, 1933–1934; *Eleutheria* (Liberty), daily, 1939–1941; *Ergatis Thalassis* (Sea worker), organ of the Greek Sea Workers Union, 1942–1946; and *Eleutheros Typos* (Free press), 1943–1947. Two of the most enduring papers in New York were the satirical and literary Greek-language papers, *Satyros* (Satyr), and *Kambana* (Bell), both of which were continuously published for over thirty years, enjoying wide popularity because of their humorous and sometimes irreverent attacks on established Greek institutions. They were published and edited by Kostas Zambounis and Leonidas Stellakis, respectively.

Several monthly Greek-language newspapers also made their appearance intermittently. Several of them, while headquartered in New York, were actually printed in Greece. Among them were *E Nea Yorki* (New York) and *Geneki Ethniki Epitheoris* (General national review).

Chicago, as the second great center of Hellenism in the United States, spawned several Greek language newspapers in addition to the *Greek Star* and *Hellenikos Typos*. Indeed, from 1921 to 1926 the Greek community was able to support three dailies—*Kathemerini* (The daily), *Tachydromos* (Express), and *Embros* (Forward). The latter, similar to its New York namesake but noncommunist in orientation, was the official organ of the Greek Workers' Union of America, headquartered in Chicago.[19] But the high costs of publishing as well as reduced subscriptions, caused in part by the turmoil and partisanship engendered by the Royalist-Venizelist feud, which had repercussions in Chicago as well, forced them to become weeklies and eventually to cease publication. Other newspapers established were *Athena*, 1905–1911; *Mikroula* (The small one), 1905–1906; *O Loxias* (The blade), 1907–1919; *Anexartitos* (Independent), 1914–1919; as well as several others of shorter duration.

In addition, several newspapers, similar to trade journals, were published which catered to restaurant owners and confectioners, the two largest business endeavors in which Greek immigrants were engaged. Chicago has its own satirical papers—*Sanida* (Sounding board), 1905, and *Spitha* (Spark), 1934—which, like their New York counterparts, received popular support, appealing perhaps to the individualistic and iconoclastic nature of Greeks.

Chicago was also the center of several intellectual newspapers or journals. One of the most impressive was *Nea Zoe* (New era), a semimonthly published from 1920 to 1924 which concerned itself with the problem of Greek immigrant adjustment in the New World. Another, *Synchroni Skepsi* (Contemporary thought), published between 1927 and 1929, was perhaps the only Greek philological or literary publication in America, and had great appeal for the intelligentsia. Another newspaper, the *Scholikon Pneuma* (School spirit), probably was the only educational newspaper in the Greek community; it was published monthly, beginning in 1926, by the students of Chicago's oldest Greek educational institution, Socrates School.

In other centers of Greek population, Greek-language newspapers were also to be found from the early days of Greek settlement. Among those that were published in Boston were the following: *Ethniki* (National), *Demokratia* (Democracy), *Anorthosis* (Restoration), *Athinai* (Athens), and *Ethnos* (Nation), all of them weeklies. San Francisco, an important terminus for Greek immigrants in the Far West, had its first Greek newspaper in 1907, when the *California* was founded by Anastasios Mountanos. The paper is still being published by the founder's descendants after being revived twice. Another important paper there was the *Eirenikos* (Pacific), established in 1906 and later renamed *Prometheus*; it continued publication until 1942. The weekly *Telegraphos* (Telegraph) was published in San Francisco from 1922 to 1927.

Detroit also had its share of Greek-language papers. Two of the most important newspapers published there were *To Vima* (The tribune), starting in 1927, and *Athinai* (Athens), from 1931. Pittsburgh, Pennsylvania, had an especially active Greek community with at least four weeklies: *Elegchos* (The auditor), established in 1905; *Helios* (The sun), 1908; *Enosis* (Union), 1908; and *Neos Kosmos* (New World), 1922–1931. Several weeklies were published in the historic Greek community of Lowell, Massachusetts, of which the most important were *Metanastis* (The immigrant), in 1905; *Patris* (Fatherland), also established in 1905 and continuing publication until 1926; and *Greek American*, established in 1941. The nation's capital has the *Kosmos* (World), first published in 1922 for a short time. A different *Kosmos* was published in the growing Greek community of Los Angeles from 1931 on, along with *The Echo*, which ceased publication in 1944.

Because Greek immigrants settled in population centers throughout the nation, Greek-language newspapers are to be found in all parts of the United States. New York, with its large concentration of Greeks, has witnessed the emergence of over forty such newspapers since 1892. Chicago ranks next with over twenty-five different titles, followed by Boston (eight), San Francisco (six), Lowell, Massachusetts (five), Pittsburgh (four), Detroit (three), Salt Lake City (three), Los Angeles (three), Atlanta (three), Youngstown, Ohio (three), Manchester, New Hampshire (three), Lynn, Massachusetts (two), and Washington, D.C. (two). Cities which have had at least one publication include Haverhill, Peabody, Worcester, Holyoke, and Springfield, Massachusetts; Nashua, New Hampshire; Canton and Cleveland, Ohio; St. Louis and Kansas City, Missouri; Milwaukee; Minneapolis; and Seattle.[20]

PERIODICALS AND JOURNALS

A natural development in the history of any ethnic press is the emergence of ethnic periodicals and journals. The Greek community had its share of them, covering every spectrum of interest; most were published monthly. The most impressive of these periodicals were those published by the two New York dailies—*Atlantis* and *Ethnikos Keryx* (or *National Herald*). Profusely illustrated (sometimes with colored photographs) and printed on semigloss paper, each edition containing from thirty-five to fifty pages and covering every conceivable topic from international affairs to history, travel, and ethnic concerns, they were greatly sought after and became ubiquitous household items in many Greek homes throughout America. Both journals had a long and consistent period of publication. The *Monthly Illustrated Atlantis* was first published in 1910 and ran until the mid 1930s; after World War II it was replaced by smaller bilingual editions on glossy paper. The *Monthly Illustrated National Herald* was first issued in 1915; in 1979, after a period of suspended publication, it was replaced by a glossy bimonthly journal completely in English.

Despite the almost total domination of these two giants in Greek-language publication during the early years, other periodicals appeared. Most of them did not compare in longevity to those put out by *Atlantis* or the *Ethnikos Keryx*, but they did provide alternative reading. Among them, in New York City, were the following: *E Niki* (Victory), a political journal; *Olympia*; *Ethniki Annagenisis* (National regeneration), edited by Demetrios Callimachos, the able editor of the *Ethnikos Keryx* in cooperation with two professors from Harvard University, the poet Aritides Phoutrides and the philosopher Raphael Demos; *Deltion* (The bulletin), the organ of the Federation of Liberal Societies in the United States; *Ekklesiastikos Keryx* (Ecclesiastical herald), a religious journal; and the *Estiator* (The restaurateur), official organ of the Greek Restaurateurs of New York.

In 1934 the Greek Orthodox Archdiocese of North and South America established its official ecclesiastical journal, *Orthodoxos Paratiritis* (Orthodox observer). The publication was initially conceived by Archbishop Athenagoras Spyrou, who had been dispatched by the Ecumenical Patriarch of Constantinople in 1930 as head of the Greek Orthodox Church in America, in order to heal the schism caused by the Royalist-Venizelist controversy within the church community. It was believed that a neutral publication providing impartial religious and patriotic information of a spiritual nature would gradually close the wounds that greatly impaired the unity of the Church. Published in impeccable Greek on a biweekly, later monthly, basis with Bishop Germanos Polyzoides as its first editor, it eventually became a familiar national publication, mailed to the homes of church members. It continued publication until 1971, when it was replaced by a bilingual tabloid newspaper.

Chicago also had its share of periodicals. Some were trade journals, but several catered to the literary tastes, such as the *Proodos* (Progress), *Hestia* (Hearth), and *Panorama*; there were also a number of religous and inspirational journals.

Perhaps the most prolific sources of ethnic Greek periodicals were the numerous fraternal organizations, mutual benefit societies, hometown associations, cultural/religious clubs, and youth groups that sprang up throughout the nation. The Greek immigrant community was one of the most highly structured in the nation, with extensive voluntary associations from the cradle to the grave.[21] Most of them produced house organs. One of the largest was *The Ahepan* (American Hellenic Educational and Progressive Association news), official organ of the largest Greek fraternity in the nation, founded in Atlanta in 1922. Because of its avowed objective to assist the Greek immigrant in his adjustment to American life, it was culturally assimilative and early advocated Americanization. To this end, in 1927 it began to publish its monthly journal completely in English. The magazine continues to be published, having peaked at a circulation of 55,000 copies.

A rival organization, the Greek American Progressive Association (GAPA), was established in Pittsburgh shortly after AHEPA was founded; it promoted a contrary goal—the cultural maintenance of Greek identity, including its language—and accused its rival group of betraying this Greek heritage. This culturally conservative group published its own journal, the *Vima tis Gapa* (The tribune of GAPA), in 1924, completely in Greek. Similarly, many of the hometown associations banded together into national associations, issued their own organizational journals in Greek, and joined GAPA in support of preserving Hellenic identity. Among the most notable were the publications of the Pan Arcadian Federation, the Pan Cretan Association, the Pan Messenian Federation, and, to a lesser extent, the Pan Epirotan Brotherhood.

In the 1930s several youth organizations were established, many by the hometown associations, to promote identity with the ancestral homeland. Those organized by AHEPA and GAPA promoted the goals of their fraternity. It was not until 1951 that a national youth organization was established; it was born at a conference in Chicago under the aegis of the Greek Orthodox Church. Known as the Greek Orthodox Youth of America, its objectives were primarily religious, and to this end it established an English-language journal, *The GOYAN* (The Greek Orthodox youth of America news) in 1954. Edited in Chicago, it continued quarterly publication until 1966 and appeared sporadically thereafter, reaching a national circulation among its membership of 35,000.

Chicago's *Athene* magazine (1941–1967) was the most successful Greek periodical published in English to appeal to non-Greeks and second-generation Greek Americans whose language was English. Other cultural journals made their appearance in the 1950s and 1960s. Among the most important were the *Argonautes* (The Argonaut), published in Greek by journalist Elias Ziogas in New York between 1959 and 1967, and *The Charioteer*, published in English semiannually since 1960 by a New York cultural group. Also in the late 1960s and into the 1970s, three magazines with formats resembling that of the now defunct *Athene* attempted to fill the void left by that magazine: *Hellenism*, published by the *Greek Press* of Chicago; the *Greek World*, in New York; and *Pilgrimage*, in Wheaton, Illinois. Although printed in English, all three enjoyed only a brief existence.

Among the more scholarly journals with academic credentials whose readership extends beyond the Greek community are *The Greek Orthodox Theological Review*, published quarterly since 1954 by the Holy Cross Orthodox Press for the Holy Cross Greek Orthodox School of Theology at Hellenic College in Brookline, Massachusetts; *The Journal of the Hellenic Diaspora*, published quarterly since 1973 by Pella Publishing Company in New York; and the new *Journal of Modern Greek Studies*, first published in 1893 by the Johns Hopkins University Press as the official semiannual organ of the Modern Greek Studies Association. All three journals are published in English and have excellent reputations; because of the specialized nature of their content they have a limited readership.

ENGLISH-LANGUAGE NEWSPAPERS

While it is true that the Greek-language press, since World War II, has received new impetus, it is also true that the English-language press in the Greek community has also made enormous strides. The former reflects the dramatic increase of Greek immigration to the United States in the postwar period as a result of the Displaced Persons Act of 1948 and the Immigration Reform Act of 1965, which eased quota restrictions and brought in over 235,000 new arrivals during the 1951–1980 period.[22] It was only natural that the influx of this large number of Greeks would enlarge considerably Greek readership, thus contributing to the founding of new Greek-language papers such as the daily *Proini*, which appeared in 1977.

But it was equally true that during the postwar years Greek language usage was rapidly declining among the American-born offspring of the first Greek immigrants. This and other assimilative processes brought about the erosion of Hellenic sentiment following the Depression and World War II, generating a demand for greater English usage in the Greek community, with the parallel demand for an English-language Greek ethnic press.

The English-language branch of Greek-American journalism was initiated by the publication in 1923 of *The Democrat*. Billing itself as "The First Greek Newspaper Published in English," it came out monthly from 1925 until it closed in 1931. Nothing more is known about it.[23]

Perhaps the finest Greek newspaper in the English language was the *American-Hellenic World*, founded in Chicago on March 28, 1925, by the poet and writer Demetrios Michalaros, who in 1923 had also launched *The Greek Review* as an English-language periodical; he was assisted by William J. Russis, a former professor of French at the University of Minnesota. It became the most ambitious and polished newspaper of its kind. While ostensibly favoring assimilation, it editorialized, nevertheless, that "those people descended from Greece and other Hellenic lands, constituted one of the most virile, progressive and law-abiding elements in our otherwise heterogenous and polyglot immigrant population."[24] Similarly, it denied emphatically that "the so-called Mediterranean races were in any way inferior to the Northern races or unsusceptible to conversion to the ideals which primarily are the prerequisites of the Anglo-Saxon mentality."[25] A newspaper of superior quality, the *American-Hellenic World* maintained a large staff and published on a weekly basis. But its inability to develop a large Greek or American readership and the consequent financial strain forced it to become a monthly in 1928 and finally to disappear several years later.

Despite these early failures, other papers printed in English continued to appear in the hope of capturing the readership of second- and third-generation Greek Americans. Most have been short-lived. One that has survived to this day is the *Chicago Pnyx*, founded in 1939 by Peter N. Mantzoros. Published semimonthly and catering to fraternal, business, and professional news, it has the distinction of being the oldest English-language newspaper operating in the Greek community.

The only English-language newspaper that has rivaled the *American-Hellenic World* of Chicago, perhaps surpassed it, is the *Hellenic Chronicle* of Boston. Founded in 1950 by newsman Peter Agris, and ably edited for the past thirty-three years by James Anagnostos, it has become the most professional newspaper in Greek-American journalism. With a nationwide circulation of 40,000, it is the largest newspaper of its kind. Carrying international and national Greek news and regional news of Greek communities in the United States, this weekly paper "dedicated to American, Hellenic and Orthodox ideals," has become the model emulated by other Greek-American newspapers.

On October 20, 1971, the Greek Orthodox Archdiocese in New York City made its entry into the newspaper field by launching the biweekly and bilingual *Orthodox Observer*. Replacing the monthly periodical *Orthodoxos Paratiritis* (Orthodox observer), which it had published since 1934, the *Orthodox Observer*, in tabloid format, became the new official organ of the Greek Orthodox Archdiocese Press for the Church in the United States. Under the competent editorship of P. J. Gazouleas (who had served as one of the last editors of the *Atlantis* from 1960 to 1971), it has reached a circulation of 135,000, making it the largest Greek newspaper, not only in the United States but in the entire world. The *Orthodox Observer* is not a regular newspaper, being an organ of a religious corporation; as such it is committed to publishing religious information and reports on the activities of the Church. But because in the Greek Orthodox Church the distinction between religion and ethnicity is blurred, since in many instances secular and sectarian activities are intermingled, the *Orthodox Observer* can indeed be classified as an ethnic newspaper. Because it is mailed to all church members, it has become the most widely circulated Greek ethnic newspaper in the nation with a bilingual readership.

In recent years, due in part to the rise of the New Ethnicity,[26] a number of other English-language newspapers have appeared. Perhaps the best known are the *Hellenic Times* of New York, published weekly since 1973, and the *Hellenic Journal* of San Francisco, appearing biweekly since 1975. Others are *Greek Sunday News* (English and Greek), in Boston; *Hellenic Voice*, published in the large Greek community of Astoria, New York; *National Greek Tribune* (Greek and English) in Detroit; *The Hellenic Voice* (English and Greek), in Cleveland; and the *National Tribune* (English and Greek), also in New York City.

These papers, along with the older established ones, are once again addressing themselves to overseas issues and concerns. This has no doubt been occasioned by the rise of the New Ethnicity, but has been especially accelerated by the course of recent international events—the invasion of Cyprus by Turkey in 1974, the restrictions on Turkish citizens of Greek descent residing in Istanbul, and the ongoing harassment of the Ecumenical Patriarchate, world center of the Greek Orthodox Church in Istanbul.

The invasion and partial occupation of Cyprus by Turkey aroused and united the Greek-American community in a way that no previous issue has. This event, along with Turkey's insistence on sharing control of the Aegean Sea and some of the Greek islands between the two nations, led to the establishment of a new national Greek-American organization, the United Hellenic American Congress. In concert with other Hellenic organizations, it created an effective Greek-American lobby which succeeded in persuading Congress to impose an arms embargo on Turkey and to provide financial and military aid to Greece.[27]

In this respect, the Greek-American press, unlike in the days of the Royalist-Venizelist fued, has been unanimous in defense of Greece and Cyprus. In essence then, the Greek ethnic press has come full circle and is once again publishing news on overseas concerns, albeit to an American-born readership.

The Greek ethnic press, whether printed in Greek or English, has been a conspicuous and influential part of Greek community life in America. Despite its shortcomings and its partisanship, it reflected the vitality of Greek immigrants as they sought to adjust to their new lives and to preserve their religio-cultural legacy. Despite its high mortality rate and its ongoing factionalism, the Greek ethnic press contributed to the social cohesion of the community, fostered language maintenance, cultivated ethnic pride, and nourished a sense of identity and survival in an alien environment. But at the same time, despite its role as a carrier of ethnicity, the Greek ethnic press has also been a means of assimilation.[28] And herein lies the present dilemma of the Greek language press. While the decline of Greek language usage has been temporarily arrested with the arrival of a large number of immigrants from Greece, the process of assimilation continues to take its toll as these new immigrants become Americanized. This will in turn contribute to the demise of the Greek-language press as in the past, unless there is a new wave of immigrants from Greece. It may be that only the English-language Greek press will survive, given the resurgence of ethnicity and the rise of the concept of cultural pluralism which has replaced the melting-pot doctrine. But this too is open to conjecture. Only time will tell.

NOTES

1. No less an authority than the *Encyclopedia Britannica* stated in 1955 that Greek immigrants were "pre-eminently successful" in transmitting their language to their children. See *Encyclopedia Britannica*, 1955 ed., s.v. "Orthodox Eastern Church," by Matthew Spinka.

2. Department of Commerce, Bureau of the Census, *Statistical Abstract of the United States, 1972* (Washington D.C.: Government Printing Office, 1972) p. 92.

3. Theodore Saloutos, *The Greeks in the United States* (Cambridge, Mass.: Harvard University Press, 1964), p. 19.

4. Practically all writers on Greek immigrants in America state that the *Neos Kosmos* was published in Boston. But there is some evidence that it may have been published in New York. See Costas Politis, "The Greek Press of America," *Eikones*, no. 26 (March 1958): 26–27.

5. Harry Pratt Fairchild, *Greek Immigration to the United States* (New Haven: Yale University Press, 1911), p. 209.

6. S. Victor Papacosma, "The Greek Press in America," *Journal of the Hellenic Diaspora* 5 (Winter 1979): 46. In addition to Papacosma's excellent article on the Greek-American press, see also Bobby (Charalambos) Malafouris, *Hellenes is Amerikis 1528–1948* (Greeks in America 1528–1948) (New York: privately printed, 1948), pp. 227–248; and S. G. Canoutas, *O Hellenismo en Ameriki* (Hellenism in America) (New York: Cosmos, 1948), pp. 227–241.

7. Malafouris, p. 232.

8. *Ayer's American Newspaper Annual, 1914* (as cited in Papacosma, p. 49).

9. *New York Times*, October 27, 1973.

10. Malafouris, p. 232; Canoutas, p. 174.

11. *Hellenikos Astir* (Greek star), January 10, 1908. For this turbulent period in Greek-American history see Saloutos, pp. 138–209.

12. *Ayer's American Newspaper Annual* provides these statistics (as cited in Papacosma, pp. 53–54).

13. Papacosma, p. 54.

14. Eugene T. Rossides, ed., *American Hellenic Who's Who in Business and the Professions* (Washington, D.C.: American Hellenic Institute Inc., 1979), pp. 159–160.

15. Andrew T. Kopan, "Greek Survival in Chicago: The Role of Ethnic Education, 1890–1980," in Peter d'A. Jones and Melvin G. Holli, eds., *Ethnic Chicago* (Grand Rapids, Mich.: William B. Eerdmans Publishing Co., 1980), p. 84.

16. *Greek Star*, December 6, 1984. As far as it can be determined, this is the first time that an important Greek ethnic newspaper was acquired by a major Greek ethnic organization.

17. *Chicago Tribune*, January 26, 1982.

18. For a complete listing of these newspapers, see Malafouris, pp. 227–241.

19. *Forty Years of Greek Life in Chicago, 1897–1937* (Chicago: Aristotle Damianos, 1937), p. 118. A complete listing of the Greek newspapers and periodicals published in Chicago during this period is to be found on pp. 117–119. In Greek.

20. Malafouris, pp. 239–241.

21. Andrew T. Kopan, "Education and Greek Immigrants in Chicago, 1892–1973: A Study in Ethnic Survival," Ph.D. dissertation, University of Chicago, 1974, pp. 102–111.

22. Charles C. Moskos, Jr., *Greek Americans: Struggle and Success* (Englewood Cliffs, N.J.: Prentice-Hall, Inc., 1980), p. 11, Table 1–1.

23. Papacosma, p. 58.

24. *American-Hellenic World* (Chicago), March 28, 1925.

25. Ibid.

26. For a thorough discussion of this phenomenon, see Michael Novak, *The Rise of the Unmeltable Ethnics* (New York: Macmillan Company, 1971); for a contrasting view, see Mark Krug, *The Melting of the Ethnics* (Bloomington, Ind.: Phi Delta Kappa, 1976)

27. For a succinct overview of the resurgence of Greek-American concern for the interests of Greece and in procuring justice for Cyprus vis-a-vis United States foreign policy relating to Turkey and Greece, see Christopher Madison, "Effective Lobbying, Ethnic Politics, Preserve U.S. Military Aid for Greece," *National Journal*, May 4, 1985, pp. 961–964.

28. Robert E. Park, *The Immigrant Press and Its Control* (New York: Harper & Bros., 1922), p. 79.

BIBLIOGRAPHY

Papacosma, S. Victor. "The Greek Press in America." *Journal of the Hellenic Diaspora*
     5 (Winter 1979): 46.
Politis, Costas. "The Greek Press of America." *Eikones*, no. 26 (March 1958): 26–27.

12

The Irish–American Press

EILEEN McMAHON

The Irish-American press helped guide many Irish from rural Catholic Ireland into urban, industrial, Protestant America. It filled various needs of the Irish community, the most important being the providing of practical information on the United States. Irish Catholic clergymen often spoke through this medium to instruct their displaced flock in a confusing new world. By 1830 the Irish had assumed command of the urban American Catholic Church and had made its diocesan newspapers vehicles for an Irish point of view. Irish nationalists also saw in the press the opportunity to generate interest in a movement to liberate Ireland from the shackles of British colonialism.

Irish Catholics began their exodus to America in significant numbers in the 1820s. By 1922 as many as 7 million Irish had found refuge and a new home in North America.[1] Although the majority of Irish immigrants were peasants, their primitive farming skills, their poverty, the communal nature of Catholicism, and their desire to live together made the industrial cities of the North and East a more fitting place to settle than the vast and lonely farms of the Midwest. As an urban proletariat they helped generate America's industrial and transportation revolutions. While cities offered the Irish unskilled jobs, urban life and poverty forced many into crime, alcoholism, mental illness, and slum living.[2]

Anglo-American Protestants were unprepared for and alarmed at this unprecedented influx of aliens into their country and the social problems they seemed to create. Although the Irish culture, with its crude manners, social misconduct, and disease-ridden slums, irritated Anglo-Americans, Irish Catholicism seemed even more threatening to American institutions and values. To Anglo-Americans, it contradicted the liberal, democratic principles of the American Enlightenment expressed in the Declaration of Independence and the Constitution. Catholicism represented Old World despotism, idolatry, ignorance, and superstition. Many Americans doubted the ability of Catholics to be loyal to the United States when their faith demanded allegiance to the pope, who was both a spiritual and temporal ruler infamous for meddling in the affairs of states.[3] Some thought this Irish Catholic invasion involved a popish plot designed to destroy American freedom.

In cities such as Boston, New York, and Philadelphia conflicting Irish and Anglo life styles and values often resulted in violent clashes.

Anglo-American prejudice toward Irish Catholics made them feel unappreciated and inferior. Irish-Americans then retreated into their own neighborhoods, which polarized the immigrant and American communities. The Irish-American press played an important part in working out misunderstandings and easing fears. It instructed the Irish about the United States and also emphasized to American newspapers that Catholicism and Irishness were not threats to the liberty and independence of the United States and that they could exist harmoniously with American institutions.[4]

Within the Irish-American press were two distinct types of papers. Some addressed their readers as a national group in the United States having their own unique political, economic, and social interests connected with both America and Ireland. Others dealt chiefly with religious issues and with the Irish as Catholics, although many of these were also sympathetic with other Irish concerns. Since the Irish dominated the Catholic Church and were the first large group of Catholics in the United States, a study of the Irish-American press must include the Catholic as well as the nationalist press.

From the 1820s to the mid–1840s Irish newspapers of any kind had difficulty surviving. The Irish-American population had not achieved sufficient numbers to sustain a distinct ethnic press. During this period Catholic publications enjoyed more success than did nationalist ones. Nationalist opinion had not yet been fully formed and articulated, but Catholicism was very much a part of Irish identity. The most successful and enduring Irish Catholic newspapers were the Boston *Pilot* and the New York *Freeman's Journal*.[5]

The Catholic press began with the intention of helping immigrants to retain and strengthen their faith and to foster a sense of community among the Irish in the strange and sometimes hostile environment of the United States.[6] Editors believed that their religion could aid in the adjustment process, serving as a guide for responsible and upright living.[7] They spotlighted models of sobriety and discipline for their readers to follow, but their suggestions often went unheeded as many Irish continued to indulge in alcohol and crime. While they admonished the Irish for their antisocial behavior, editors felt troubled about Catholicism being identified with this conduct. They were afraid that nativists would seize upon these examples to prove Catholicism's negative impact on America. Catholic editors defensively argued that the Irish who committed crimes had been subjected to public education and Protestant influences or had given up the practice of Catholicism. Irish social problems were also considered the product of miserable living conditions rather than of defects in character or religion. Blaming American institutions and Protestants for Irish Catholic problems further outraged native Americans. Editors of American papers reacted to these accusations with diatribes against the Irish and their religion. Catholic editors responded in kind.[8]

In addition to sustaining the faith of their people and defending their reputation,

Catholic newspapers found themselves continually trying to dispel inaccurate ideas held by Protestant Americans about their religion. These efforts were ineffective. The theological and consequent social chasm was too wide and too deep to be bridged. But what troubled native Americans most was the institutional growth of the Catholic Church in the 1840s and 1850s. The Catholic press boasted of Protestant conversions to the Roman Church and the growth of Catholic churches, schools, and orphanages.[9] The Boston *Pilot* arrogantly proclaimed that "Catholicism will obtain an ascendancy over all the minds of the land."[10] The Catholic press also encouraged Irish-Americans to form their own societies to foster Irish and Catholic identities. Catholic editors made these suggestions to protect their readers from negative Protestant influences, but native American editors interpreted these boastings as a rejection of their country and way of life, further deepening their suspicion of perceived anti-American activity by Catholics and their pope.[11]

As part of its desire to create a sense of unity and identity, the Catholic press cultivated the Irishness of its readers. The *Pilot* and the *Freeman's Journal* had taken their names from newspapers in Ireland and often expressed sympathy and support for Daniel O'Connell and his Repeal movement. Irish Catholic editors frequently used the word "patriotism" when describing their feelings toward Ireland and openly discussed the possibility of involving the United States in a war to liberate Ireland from British rule. They expected the American public to sympathize with Ireland's fight for independence because the United States was the product of an anticolonial war against Britain and because Irish nationalism represented those same liberal, democratic principles. Instead, the nationalistic concerns of the Irish antagonized nativist feelings because they seemed un-American.[12]

Despite nativist anxiety, the Catholic press continued to make demands on its host society. For example, Catholics and liberal non-Catholics demanded an indemnity award from the Commonwealth of Massachusetts for the Ursuline Sisters, whose Charlestown convent was burned by nativist rioters in 1834. The *Pilot* was at the forefront of this crusade and criticized or praised legislators for the way they voted on the measure. When the Democrats refused to act on a petition for indemnification, the *Pilot* became the spokesman for an independent political organization designed to win restitution from the state. In the excitement the paper began dreaming of controlling the destiny of the state by urging its people to vote for candidates sympathetic to their cause in the 1843 elections. But the sisters never received money, and the *Pilot* was bombarded with criticism by native-born Americans for bringing religious interests into politics. In defending its position, the *Pilot* said that the clergy was not involved in electioneering and had the right to represent the views of its readers.[13] Undeterred by Anglo-Protestant criticism, the newspaper boldly stated in November 1843 that "Catholics are accused of seeking political influence but they have not half enough of it."[14]

Although some papers such as the *Pilot* believed that it was their duty to involve themselves in politics to protect the interests of Irish Catholics, the Catholic press in general stayed out of the political arena. But when Catholic newspapers did express sympathy for a political party, it was for the Democrats. Their Jacksonian egalitarianism attracted the Irish, who had been subjugated by the Anglo-Irish Protestant ascendancy in Ireland. The Democratic Party was also less nativistic, encouraged quick naturalization, and promised jobs for votes. By supporting a single political party, Irish Catholics appeared to be an imposing voting bloc and confirmed nativist fears of alien influences in American life and the pope's plans to conquer the United States. Irish Catholic involvement in politics undoubtedly influenced a certain number of nativists to support anti-Catholic and anti-immigrant policies.[15]

Gradually, Irish Catholics realized the potential of the press in arguing and defending their own interests to the host society. In the early 1840s the *Freeman's Journal* was organized to promote the Catholic cause in the New York school controversy. Public education had been a major controversial issue between nativists and Irish. In these schools Catholic children were required to read the Protestant Bible for religious instruction, and textbooks often made disparaging remarks about Catholicism. In order to protect their children from insults and Protestant proselytism, Catholic parents tried to gain influence over the Protestant-controlled school board. But to Protestant Americans, Catholic resistance to the study of the scriptures proved to them that Catholics feared that the holy book would expose the errors of popery. The *Freeman's Journal* defended Catholic parents and Archbishop John Hughes of New York and supported the Maclay Law of 1842, which broke up the Protestant monopoly over education and forbade state aid to religious schools. Like the Boston *Pilot*, the *Journal* encouraged Catholics to vote for supporters of their cause. Aggressiveness of this sort further inflamed nativist fears and hatred of the Catholic presence in America.[16]

By the mid–1840s the Catholic press learned that strident demands upon the host society were not the best strategy for achieving its goals. It avoided the threatening crusades of the early 1840s, seeking to defend its position rather than to alter the status quo. Newspapers toned down their aggressive style and advised readers to forgive their enemies and avoid provoking further conflict. The *Pilot*, which had become the most widely read Irish Catholic paper in the United States, stopped making demands on Americans and encouraged self-improvement for the Irish. It argued that they must learn to rely on themselves alone and stop antagonizing native-born Americans.[17]

Catholic press moderation deserves some credit for reducing nativism. But other factors might have been more important, such as the 1848 revolutions in Europe, the contribution of naturalized Irish-Americans to war efforts, the suffering of the Irish Famine, and the early liberalism of Pius IX. Perhaps the Catholic press's biggest contribution toward alleviating nativism was the encouragement of immigrants to move west. Catholic journalists thought that Irish peasants would be spiritually and economically better off in rural America.

Although most Irish remained in the urban centers of the North and East, their leaders' advice eased nativist anxieties of a unified Catholic conspiracy against the United States.[18]

The late 1840s and early 1850s marked a distinctive change in the nature of the Irish press. The Great Famine of 1846–1849 cast at least a million poor, sick, starving, and embittered Irish men and women onto the American shore. These destitute people needed practical information to help them cope with their new surroundings. Irish and Catholic newspapers answered their need. Famine refugees, along with immigrants who followed in later years, formed a massive readership that sustained a vital and diverse Irish-American press. The abortive Young Ireland revolt of 1848 forced many talented and articulate nationalists to flee Ireland. Many came to the United States, where they sought to continue their political activity and formed newspapers to express their views. They succeeded in creating a distinctively "nationalist" Irish-American press that grew rapidly in the next decade. While most publications were located in New York or Boston, they had countrywide circulation.[19]

Newspaper editors became very important in the Irish-American community. Immigrants depended upon them not only for information but also for perspectives and interpretations of the New World. They felt the need to identify with someone who could articulate their fears and champion them to the American community. Editors were powerfully positioned to focus their readers' attention on issues they considered important and to promote their own causes and shape opinion. For the most part, they were responsible individuals who helped the Irish learn about and assimilate into American society.[20]

Some immediate help that editors could offer their readers was information of ship sailings and arrivals and much desired news of home. They provided "Information Wanted" columns so that friends and relatives could advertise to find one another and also offered news of employment opportunities. Lessons on the folkways, symbols, and values of American culture were standard fare.[21]

Irish-American editors believed and often repeated that America was a refuge for the Irish rather than a temporary place to make money and go back to Ireland. They encouraged newcomers to make America their permanent home, and Reverend John Roddan, an editor of the *Pilot*, advocated quick naturalization, stating that "every man owed love and duty to the country which is his by birth or willing choice."[22] Editors enthusiastically encouraged their followers to assimilate quickly into American life, and they had complete faith in their readers' ability to shed old customs and acquire American ways.[23] Sometimes discrimination in the workplace and in social situations made it difficult for the Irish to understand the desirability of conforming to Anglo-American practices, but many Irish heeded assimilationist editorial advice.[24]

Editors made many specific suggestions to the Irish on how to adjust to American mores. For instance, in 1849 the Boston *Pilot* warned against the old Irish custom of waking the dead, which seemed alien and peculiar to native Americans. Editors also encouraged the Irish to behave responsibly and not indulge in activities like drinking and brawling, which cast the Irish community in a bad light. As keys to success, they stressed thrift, knowledge, industry, and enterprise, qualities usually associated with the Protestant work ethic.[25]

Irish-American editors were generally optimistic about the United States and its desirability as a new home. But occasionally anxiety and ambivalence about America and its opportunities surfaced. From time to time their newspapers revealed feelings of alienation and disillusionment with American society. Its materialism and individualism seemed repugnant to them, and at times the future of the Irish seemed bleak when faced with nativism and discrimination. But discouragement and cynicism were fleeting. Generally, editors nurtured American patriotic sentiment in their readers and encouraged them to display dedication to American political traditions and institutions to dispel nativist animosity. Editors demonstrated patriotism themselves when they converted from their original sympathetic leanings toward the South to strong support for the Union after the outbreak of the Civil War. During the war, articles and series such as "Records of Irish-American Patriotism" appeared in the *Pilot*. As Irish-American casualties were reported, the American press and nativists withdrew charges of Catholic disloyalty to the United States. Thus Irish-American editors proved to be shrewd leaders.[26]

Beside their concern for the Irish community's adjustment to and acceptance in America, Irish-American journalists, like many of their readers, never forgot the troubles of old Ireland. Its continued subservience to Britain concerned many Irish-Americans. Some famine refugees believed that their forced exile was the result of British genocidal policies. Anglo-American Protestant persecution and scorn seemed to repeat the degrading experiences of the Irish under British rule. Feelings of anger, resentment, and inferiority haunted the Irish. They responded by creating a vigorous and aggressive Irish-American nationalism. Many Irish felt that they would gain the respect of Anglo-Americans and ease tensions if their homeland was a free nation. The Irish-American press assumed the responsibility of supporting and even shaping nationalist activities.[27]

Irish-American editors believed that keeping the Irish aware of their heritage was the first step in building a movement for Irish independence. They did this by not only publishing political and economic news of Ireland, but also by listing notices of births, deaths, marriages, and court proceedings there. Irish short stories were reprinted in the Irish-American press along with messages from Irish prelates. Editors also implied that no honorable immigrant could ignore his responsibilities to the land of his origin. Their motivation was to generate enough interest in Ireland and things Irish to unite, organize, raise money, and develop measures to fight for an independent Irish republic.[28]

While the goal of Irish-American nationalism had unanimous support among editors, the means of accomplishing it inspired sharp exchanges and prolonged controversy between those Irish editors who emphasized nationalism and those who emphasized Catholicism. Conflicts stemmed from different interpretations of Irish history by the Catholic press and the Irish-American nationalist press.

Catholic editors thought of Irish history as the working out of a religious drama. The Irish were martyred Christians assigned to spread God's word, and the Irish immigrant in America was His instrument to bring Catholicism to the New World. Nationalist editors viewed Irish history in more worldly terms and rejected Catholic fatalism. England was simply oppressing the Irish, and the famine was its way of exterminating a troublesome people.[29] John Mitchell of *The Irish Citizen* believed that England was "engaged in systematically lashing herself into one of her periodical passions for Irish blood."[30]

Many nationalist editors supported revolutionary means to achieve independence for Ireland. They considered British rule illegitimate and felt that physical force was the only way of liberating Ireland before the British did more harm to the country and people. The Irish Republican Brotherhood, popularly known as the Fenians, was formed as a secret revolutionary organization in Ireland and the United States for this purpose. However, Catholic bishops in Ireland disapproved of the violence and secretive oath taking of the Fenians, and in 1870 the Church condemned secret organizations and excommunicated many Fenians. This had a tendency to discredit revolutionary nationalism. Many nationalist editors and Fenians resented the Church's intrusion into politics and attacked it for preventing the Irish from improving their lot.[31]

While Catholic and nationalist editors attacked each other's position on nationalist strategies, both sides knew that they could not easily dismiss the power each had over Irish America. The Catholic Church commanded the love and allegiance of most Irish immigrants, but nationalism also enlisted a good number. Although sympathetic to the Fenians, the *Pilot* straddled the conflict, hoping to mollify the two sides.[32] But a solution was not reached until after 1866. The Fenian invasion of Canada in that year was a fiasco and started a decline in its influence and membership. In the 1870s constitutional nationalism in the form of Home Rule began to provide an alternative that was acceptable to most Catholic and nationalist editors. A reconciliation was worked out in the pages of the Irish-American press, and the unity of Irish-American nationalism made possible the success of the Irish Parliamentary Party in Britain.[33] Still, independence was long in coming and not complete.

Perhaps the most important reason for the success and vitality of the Irish-American press, besides its large readership, was the talent and strong character of its editors. They had a tremendous influence on shaping Irish nationalist opinion and helping the Irish transform themselves from foreigners and immigrants to American citizens. Their adventurous lives and colorful personalities drew many followers.[34]

Patrick Donahoe published the Boston *Pilot* for more than sixty years. He saw it become the most influential Irish-American newspaper. Two of Donahoe's editors shaped a distinct Irish-American perspective. John Roddan, a controversial and conservative cleric, committed the *Pilot* to a stern, uncompromising Catholicism as editor from 1849 to 1857.[35] Poet and patriot John Boyle O'Reilly edited the *Pilot* from 1870 to 1890. Under his direction the paper reached its highest circulation, and he helped shape moderate Irish nationalism and Catholicism into a respectable creed of how Irish-Americans could achieve status and power. Although he had been a Fenian and always sympathized with the Brotherhood, he reevaluated his opinion of revolutionary nationalism after the Canadian invasion. His moderation won him the honor of the Irish Catholic community and the esteem of his contemporaries from other religious and national backgrounds. O'Reilly did more than any other man of his generation to help bridge the gulf between Catholics and Protestants of New England.[36] In 1876 the *Pilot* became the official organ of the Archdiocese of Boston.[37]

From 1848 to 1885, James A. McMaster edited the New York *Freeman's Journal and Catholic Register*. He was a convert from Episcopalianism and became spokesman for the Catholic interests of the Irish immigrants.[38]

Thomas D'Arcy McGee was the first Irish nationalist exile of 1848 to set up an Irish-American nationalist newspaper. McGee escaped British suppression of the Young Irelanders, disguised, oddly enough, as a priest. Within six weeks of his departure from Belfast he had published the first issue of his paper, *The Nation*, in New York. While catering to Irish-American needs and tastes, McGee was primarily devoted to Ireland's liberation. When Archbishop John Hughes of New York criticized Young Ireland's militancy, McGee struck back by accusing the Irish clergy of being responsible for the collapse of the Irish revolution. Hughes responded by describing *The Nation* as dangerous to faith and morals. *The Nation* lost circulation as a result of Hughes's criticisms, and the paper folded within two years. The conflict, though, reveals the extreme nationalist feelings and ambitions of McGee and others of his generation as well as the strong Catholic identity of Irish immigrants and the power of the clergy. McGee grew to appreciate the role Catholicism played in the lives of immigrants, rejected revolutionary nationalism, and claimed to be a devout Catholic. He relocated in Boston and started *The American Celt*, which reflected his growing conservatism and acceptance of more moderate and Catholic opinion. This switch lost him the support of revolutionaries, yet he was never able to dispel the suspicion of the moderate Catholic community. In 1857 McGee left the United States for Canada, where he became a member of the Canadian cabinet and was later assassinated by a Fenian.[39]

John Mitchell, an Ulster Protestant and Young Irelander, wrote for the Irish *Nation*. During the Great Famine he became convinced that constitutional agitation was useless in advancing Irish causes. He then founded the *United Irishman* to inspire others toward revolutionary nationalism. His advocacy of rebellion in 1848 got him convicted and transported to Van Dieman's Land. In 1853 he escaped, making his way to the United States, where he founded *The Citizen*. Like the early McGee, he was primarily interested in an independent, republican Ireland and quarreled with the Catholic clergy and editors over nationalist issues. But his extreme form of nationalism and his denunciations of the Catholic clergy even brought down the wrath of the now moderate McGee, who accused him of carrying out a No-Popery campaign. Mitchell lost many friends and readers for his support of the southern states during the Civil War. His defense of white racism and elitism tainted his nationalism. In 1867 Mitchell started *The Irish Citizen*, editing it in a more tempered style. In 1874 he returned to Ireland.[40]

Patrick Lynch, an old Repealer and newspaperman in Ireland, came to the United States in 1847. He worked for several American newspapers, including the *New York Herald*. In the summer of 1848 he edited the *Pilot*. Lynch sympathized with the Young Irelanders and argued that the clergy through its interference and opposition was responsible for their failed revolt. Like other supporters of revolutionary nationalism, his views antagonized Catholic clergymen and editors. In 1849 Lynch edited the *Irish-American*, attempting to reconcile nationalism with Catholicism. However, his efforts were premature since tensions from the failed 1848 rebellion were still strong between revolutionary and Catholic nationalists. Lynch died in 1857, but not before he made the *Irish-American* the highest circulating Irish nationalist newspaper of the decade.[41]

As editor of the *Irish World* between 1870 and 1913, Patrick Ford became one of the most controversial and prominent Irish journalists in the United States. An immigrant from Galway, Ford surpassed other Irish-American editors in the effort to instruct and direct the Irish in their new country. Ford suggested that the immigrant who was truly loyal to Ireland support constitutional measures and individual advancement through education and hard work. His newspaper became the voice of the politically conscious Irish-American working class. He endorsed trade unions until 1886, defending violent labor activity as an understandable response to the exploitations of capitalism and monopolies. He also supported socialist doctrine and, additionally, urged Irish urban dwellers to move west.[42]

Ford opposed slavish devotion to the Democratic party. He felt that the identification of the Irish with one party impaired their assimilation into mainstream America and made it difficult for them to use their votes to force American politicians to address the Irish Question. In 1886 Ford worried that the association of the Irish with the Haymarket Square riot and other violent labor activity would arouse nativist hostilities. For the sake of the Irish community's acceptance in America, Ford renounced his more radical beliefs and called for understanding and reconciliation between labor and management.[43] Through the *Irish World* Ford tried to bridge the gap between the Irish-American community and the American reform tradition.[44]

John Devoy, an ex-Fenian and political refugee from the United Kingdom, has been described as the "ideologue" of Irish-American nationalism. Under his direction the Clan-ne-Gael became the dominant revolutionary nationalist organization in Irish America. Although a physical-force nationalist, Devoy had a more realistic outlook on Ireland's political situation than the Fenians. In his papers the *Irish Nation* (1881–1885) and the *Gaelic American*, founded in 1903, he single-mindedly pursued his objective of an Irish party in the United States which would have the interests of Ireland as its sole object. Since Devoy's papers never addressed the more pressing concerns of Irish-Americans, they never met with great success. But his *Irish Nation* did represent an important group of revolutionaries.[45]

During his years in the United States, James Connolly, the leading Marxist socialist and labor leader in Ireland, edited the monthly publication of the Irish Socialist Federation, the *Harp*, from 1908 to 1910. As one of the founders and organizers of the Industrial Workers of the World (IWW), he was an important figure in the labor and socialist movements in America. Connolly's main interest, however, was the advancement of socialism, particularly in Ireland.[46]

The mid-nineteenth century marked the height of Irish-American journalism. By the 1880s the Irish-American press had finished much of its work of helping the Irish adjust to American life. From that time on, Irish ethnic newspapers began reflecting class interests rather than immigrants' concerns.[47] Gradually, Irish-American assimilation into mainstream American society reduced the need for ethnic newspapers. However, since the mid–1960s the general revival in ethnic pride has spawned a growing interest in Irish and Irish-American history. Several scholarly journals have emerged to cater to this interest, among them *Eire-Ireland, The James Joyce Quarterly*, and *The Irish Literary Supplement*. The American Committee for Irish Studies was founded in 1960 to provide a forum for those interested in the subject. Today it boasts a membership of 700 scholars and supporting public.

In addition to these scholarly publications, there has been an increase in the number and circulation of Irish-American newspapers, especially since the troubles began in Northern Ireland in the late 1960s. *The Irish Echo* is published in New York and is the most popular Irish-American newspaper. It supports Irish Republican Army (IRA) activities. *Callahan's Irish Quarterly*, published in San Francisco, is a more sophisticated magazine than the *Echo* but is primarily interested in political events in Ireland and has IRA leanings. The *Irish American*, published in Chicago, is neutral on the IRA but does cover its activities. It is primarily interested in sports, culture, and Irish and Irish-American events. These publications are mainly supported by recent Irish immigrants.

The Irish-American press served its constituents in many ways, from helping them understand, adjust to, and eventually assimilate into American society to arousing and formulating Irish nationalist opinion. It must be pointed out, however, that Irish-Americans were not as dependent upon ethnic newspapers as other immigrant groups. They spoke English and were to an extent culturally Anglicized. Familiarity with Anglo-Protestant political institutions and values made it possible for the Irish to accommodate themselves to the United States fairly rapidly. The general American press was often sufficient for their needs. A significant number of Irish-Americans also worked for important American newspapers, particularly the *New York Herald*, but Irish contributions to American journalism have not been studied. The only extensive investigation of Irish influence on the general press is by Charles Fanning.[48] His study of the Irish-American columnist Finley Peter Dunne, creator of the fictional Mr. Dooley, an Irish-American bartender-philosopher, has shown Dunne to be a pioneer literary realist and a social historian. Dunne created the first artistically realized urban ethnic neighborhood in the pages of the American press.

As a historical source, the Irish-American press holds the keys to understanding the character, hopes, aspirations, disillusionments, and achievements of America's first large immigrant group. While there are several excellent studies of this topic, the field is rich enough to warrant further investigation.

NOTES

1. Kerby A. Miller, "Emigrants and Exiles: Irish Cultures and Irish Emigration to North America, 1790–1922," *Irish Historical Studies* 22 (September 1980): 97.

2. Lawrence J. McCaffrey, *The Irish Diaspora in America* (Bloomington: Indiana University Press, 1976), pp. 63–69.

3. Ibid., pp. 85–106.

4. William Leonard Joyce, *Editors and Ethnicity: A History of the Irish-American Press 1848–1883* (New York: Arno Press, 1976), pp. 3–13.

5. Robert Francis Hueston, *The Catholic Press and Nativism 1840–1869* (New York: Arno Press, 1976) p. 14.

6. Ibid.

7. Joyce, pp. 102–103.

8. Hueston, pp. 33–38.

9. Ibid.

10. Ibid., p. 38.

11. Ibid., pp. 33–41.

12. Ibid, pp. 14–30; and Oscar Handlin, *Boston's Immigrants, 1790–1880: A Study in Acculturation*, 2nd ed. (Cambridge, Mass.: Belknap Press of Harvard University, 1959), p. 173.

13. Paul J. Foik, C.S.C., *Pioneer Catholic Journalism*, Monograph Series XI (New York: United States Catholic Historical Society, 1930), p. 170.

14. Hueston, p. 47.

15. Ibid., pp. 42–43.

16. Vincent P. Lannie, *Public Money and Parochial Education: Bishop Hughes, Governor Seward and the New York School Controversy* (Cleveland: The Press of Case Western Reserve University, 1968), pp. 214, 229. Also see Richard Shaw, *Dagger John: The Unquiet Times of Archbishop John Hughes of New York* (New York: Paulist Press, 1977).

17. *Pilot*, August 31, 1844, p. 278.

18. Hueston, pp. 110–28.

19. Joyce, p. 54.

20. Ibid., pp. 3–10.

21. Ibid., p. 12.

22. Ibid., p. 130.

23. Ibid., p. 136.

24. Ibid., pp. 141–143.

25. Ibid., p. 131.

26. Hueston, pp. 133–134, 141–143.

27. Ibid., pp. 74–93.

28. Ibid., pp. 74–75.

29. Handlin, p. 138.

30. Joyce, p. 77.

31. Hueston, pp. 85–90.

32. Joyce, p. 86.

33. Hueston, p. 155.

34. Ibid., p. 5.

35. Ibid.

36. Francis G. McManamin, *The American Years of John Boyle O'Reilly, 1870–1890* (New York: Arno Press, 1976), Introduction.

37. Eric Foner, *Politics and Ideology in the Age of the Civil War* (New York: Oxford University Press, 1980), pp. 162–163.

38. Joyce, p. 6.

39. Ibid., pp. 6, 82–83; Foik, pp. 170–171.

40. Joyce, pp. 6–7, 79–81.

41. Ibid., p. 7.

42. James Paul Rodechko, *Patrick Ford and His Search for America: A Case Study of Irish American Journalism 1870–1913* (New York: Arno Press, 1976), pp. iii-v, 271.

43. Ibid., pp. 91–94.

44. Foner, p. 161.

45. Joyce, pp. 164–166.

46. Carl Reeve and Ann Barton Reeve, *James Connolly and the United States: The Road to the 1916 Irish Rebellion* (Atlantic Highlands, N.J.: Humanities Press, Inc., 1978), pp. ix-xiii.

47. Joyce, p. 9.

48. Charles Fanning, *Finley Peter Dunne and Mr. Dooley: The Chicago Years* (Lexington: University of Kentucky Press, 1978).

BIBLIOGRAPHY

Fanning, Charles. *Finley Peter Dunne and Mr. Dooley: The Chicago Years*. Lexington: University of Kentucky Press, 1978.

Foik, Paul J., C.S.C. *Pioneer Catholic Journalism*. Monograph Series XI. New York: United States Catholic Historical Society, 1930.

Foner, Eric. *Politics and Ideology in the Age of the Civil War*. New York: Oxford University Press, 1980.

Handlin, Oscar. *Boston's Immigrants, 1790–1880: A Study in Acculturation*. 2nd ed. Cambridge, Mass.: Belknap Press of Harvard University, 1959.

Hueston, Robert Francis. *The Catholic Press and Nativism 1840–1869*. New York: Arno Press, 1976.

Joyce, William Leonard. *Editors and Ethnicity: A History of the Irish-American Press 1848–1883*. New York: Arno Press, 1976.

Lannie, Vincent P. *Public Money and Parochial Education: Bishop Hughes, Governor Seward and the School Controversy of New York*. Cleveland: The Press of Case Western Reserve University, 1968.

McCaffrey, Lawrence J. *The Irish Diaspora in America*. Bloomington: Indiana University Press, 1976.

McManamin, Francis G. *The American Years of John Boyle O'Reilly, 1870–1890*. New York: Arno Press, 1976.

Miller, Kerby A. "Emigrants and Exiles: Irish Culture and Irish Emigration to North America, 1790–1922." *Irish Historical Studies* 22 (September 1980).

Reeve, Carl, and Ann Barton Reeve. *James Connolly and the United States: The Road to the 1916 Irish Rebellion*. Atlantic Highlands, N.J.: Humanities Press, Inc., 1978.

Rodechko, James Paul. *Patrick Ford and His Search for America: A Case Study of Irish American Journalism 1870–1913*. New York: Arno Press, 1976.

Shaw, Richard. *Dagger John: The Unquiet Times of Archbishop John Hughes of New York*. New York: Paulist Press, 1977.

13

The Japanese-American Press

HARRY H.L. KITANO

The early part of the twentieth century saw a significant immigration from Japan to the United States and with it a need for Japanese-language newspapers. The immigrant group was a largely literate one, and news was especially important since both local and international events were directly relevant to their lives. For example, the hostility of the dominant group, especially in California, was reflected in a variety of laws, rules, and regulations which created problems for the Japanese immigrant. The larger issue of U.S.-Japan relations brought forth a number of other questions and problems, especially concerning conflicting loyalties, so that the mixture of language, issues, and problems provided a fertile background for ethnic newspapers.

Therefore, if in 1900 questions were asked concerning the need, the format, and the future of Japanese-American newspapers, the answers would no doubt have been: "Yes, there is a need for newspapers printed in Japanese"; "no, there is little need for an English-language section now, but probably in the future when an American born and educated generation comes of age"; and "yes, the future of the Japanese-language press looks strong because there is a steady stream of new immigrants and there is a constant flow of news that directly affects their lives."

Issues, needs, and the nature of the population have changed over time so that in the 1980s there are mixed messages concerning the ethnic press. For example, in 1983 Hiro Hishiki, publisher of the *Kashu Mainichi* (California daily), one of the two Los Angeles–based Japanese-American dailies, said, "You're looking at a broken newspaperman."[1] Kenneth Toguchi, the editor of a Hawaiian-based English-language publication, concurs with this gloomy assessment and writes that "the future of Japanese language publications is dismal".[2] The reasons given are that "the number of Issei [first-generation immigrants] is rapidly decreasing and the number of new Japanese immigrants is minimal. Acculturation of the younger generations . . . has sealed the fate of the Japanese language presses."

But the Japanese press has survived any number of gloomy predictions. For example, Henry Mori remembers the many discussions in the 1930s concerning the viability of Japanese-American newspapers.[3] Most of the papers were operating in extremely precarious economic circumstances and employees were often paid in food, goods, and forms of reimbursement other than cash.

The World War II evacuation was another period of crisis for Japanese-American newspapers. The entire Japanese population along the West Coast was placed in concentration camps, and the ethnic press, with the bulk of its publishing centered in California, came to a halt. There was an attempt by government authorities to relocate and scatter the Japanese Americans to the Midwest and to the eastern seaboard; therefore, it would have been reasonable at the end of World War II to predict the demise of the Japanese-American press.

But in spite of the evacuation and the period of resettlement to other parts of the country, the majority of the Japanese Americans eventually returned to California and the West Coast. With their return came the reestablishment of the ethnic press. The *Encyclopedic Directory of Ethnic Newspapers* in 1972 listed twelve Japanese and Japanese-English publications, and four Japanese publications in the English language.[4] There were two dailies in Los Angeles, the *Rafu Shimpo* (Los Angeles daily news), established in 1903 and having a 1972 circulation of 19,699; and the *Kashu Mainichi* (California daily), established in 1931 and having a circulation of 5,610. San Francisco also published two dailies in 1972, the *Hokubei Mainichi* (North American daily), reestablished in 1948, with a 1972 circulation of 7,000; and *The Nichi-bei Times* (Japanese-American daily news), reestablished in 1946 with a circulation of 6,990. Hawaii also published two dailies in 1972, *The Hawaii Hochi* (Hawaii times), circulation of 12,125; and the *Hawaii Times*, circulation 12,475. Other newspapers were in Chicago (*The Chicago Shimpo* [The Chicago news], circulation 3,020 on a semiweekly basis); Seattle (*Hokubei Hochi* [Hokubei times], circulation 2,050); Washington, D.C. (*Japanese American Society Bulletin*, circulation 1,100 on a monthly basis); New York (*The New York Nichi-bei* [The New York Japanese-American], circulation 1,066 on a weekly basis), and in the Rocky Mountain area (*Rocky Mountain Jiho* [Rocky Mountain news], circulation 1,030 weekly; *The Utah Nippo* [The Utah daily news], circulation 910, three times per week). Therefore, in 1972 there was an active ethnic press, centered primarily in California and Hawaii.

In 1984 all of the above-named newspapers on the mainland were still in existence, and several were planning to modernize their equipment and expand their publications.[5] The future of the Japanese-American press is uncertain, however, and those who are closely involved with it have mixed responses, ranging from pessimism to plans for expansion.

Surprisingly, Hawaii, an area with a very high concentration of Japanese and one where the ethnic press would appear to be very popular, has seen a decline in its ethnic newspapers. In 1984 *The Hawaii Hochi* was the sole surviving daily, with a circulation of approximately 10,000. The *Hawaii Times*, its major competitor, has been reduced to a weekly, with a circulation of 2,000.[6]

Why are there these differences between Hawaii and the mainland? Will the disappearance of the aging Issei spell the end of Japanese-language newspapers? Will the American-born generations support an ethnic press? In order to address these questions we will analyze some demographic factors and acculturation, then present examples of all-English and Japanese-language newspapers.

DEMOGRAPHIC FACTORS

Demographic factors affecting the Japanese-American press include size and distribution of the population and generation. The total Japanese-American population is small, 700,974 as reported in the 1980 census, so that the economics of supporting a specialized ethnic press has always been a problem. As might be expected, the Japanese-American newspapers are published in the states with the most Japanese. In 1980 the five most populous states for the ethnic group were California (261,817), Hawaii (239,618), Washington (26,369), New York (24,254), and Illinois (18,550). Cities with high concentrations of Japanese included Los Angeles (49,335) and San Francisco (12,046).

The Japanese are further stratified by age-generation, with the current majority composed of English-language Nisei (American-born second generation) and Sansei (American-born third generation). The original Issei, who immigrated to the United States between 1890 and 1924 and who in the past provided the bulk of readership for the Japanese-language press, are a rapidly disappearing generation (many seventy-five years old or more). The Issei remain the group most interested in the Japanese-language newspapers, especially in the obituary columns and community notices.

Some loss in readership has been made up by new immigrants, businessmen, students, tourists, and visitors from Japan, somewhat offsetting the declining number of Issei. However, it is interesting to note that many of the Japanese characters (kanji) used by the vernacular press are of a past era, whereas the newcomers are used to the newer kanji. The cost of modernizing old-fashioned equipment, including the kanji, is a major problem. Clearly, the declining number of those who read Japanese threatens the economic survival of the ethnic press. It is in fact surprising that such a relatively large number of newspapers serves such a small population. The pie appears to be divided into very small pieces; as one editor said, "You'll never get rich running a Japanese American newspaper."[7]

ACCULTURATION AND ALTERNATIVES

The acculuration of the population, especially the Nisei and Sansei, has had a telling effect on the ethnic press. Acculturation has provided a wide number of options for the English readership and has been linked to the demise of the ethnic press. For example, the younger generations can turn to the metropolitan press, television, radio, and magazines for their news. There are also church bulletins, throwaways, and local newsletters which carry ethnic news and notices; ethnic clubs and organizations provide other information sources, so that an ethnic newspaper carrying ethnic news for an English-speaking and -reading audience has many competitors.

One other competitive source for the English-language readership has been the broadening coverage of papers such as *East-West* and *Asian Week*. Both of these San Francisco–based weeklies were aimed initially at a Chinese readership, but they have become increasingly Pan-Asian, with articles to interest all Asian Americans. The English sections of the Japanese-American newspapers have also reflected this trend.

PROJECTED MODEL

The projected model envisioned by the pioneers of the Japanese-American press was as follows: an initial period during which an all Japanese newspaper would serve the Japanese immigrant, to which in time a small but ever expanding English section would be added to serve the needs of American-born generations. Such a model could conceivably see the phasing out of the sections printed in Japanese as the immigrant generation dies out. What began as newspapers printed primarily in Japanese would eventually become papers written for an English-reading ethnic population. Such a model would follow the acculturation of the Japanese in America and reflect the changing demographic nature of the population, which is now primarily Nisei and Sansei.

But that model has not yet worked out in the predicted fashion. The newspapers still devote the major portion of their space to a Japanese-reading audience, with a minor section in English.

ENGLISH-LANGUAGE PUBLICATIONS

There have been attempts by Japanese Americans to publish papers in English, but with the exception of *The Pacific Citizen*, a weekly publication of the Japanese American Citizen's League (JACL), they have been short-lived.

For example, *The Crossroads*, an all-English weekly established in 1949, struggled through many lean years before folding in 1971. The editor, owner, and publisher finally walked away from the publication because he saw no future in the venture. Problems included lack of advertising, small circulation (2,450 in 1972), and limited outlook for future growth. Therefore, in the 1970s, the need for an all English newspaper for a Japanese-American audience in Los Angeles was yet to be established.[8]

THE PACIFIC CITIZEN

The most successful newspaper for the acculturated Japanese American is the national weekly, *The Pacific Citizen*. William Hosokawa writes of its origin in

1929 as a monthly under the name *Nikkei Shimin* (Japanese-American citizen) which in 1932 became *The Pacific Citizen* and the official publication of the Japanese American Citizens' League (JACL).[9] The paper saw its purpose as a connecting link between the Issei and Nisei, and one of its major goals was to emphasize the duties and responsibilities of American citizenship.

Prior to World War II, its contents often consisted of items from the various JACL chapters, a social calendar, and news items garnered from the English sections of the Japanese dailies in California. The paper was generally considered to be pro-American and pro-integration, and its appeal was to acculturated Nisei who made up the primary membership of the JACL.

World War II placed additional responsibilities on the publication as it became a weekly. It was forced to move from San Francisco to Salt Lake City and served as the only national journal for the group, most of whom were behind barbed wire. Under the editorship of Larry Tajiri it became a first-class publication and kept its readership apprised of "life outside the camps," as well as of legislative and political issues which would have an effect on their lives. The weekly was especially alert in covering cases of discrimination and unfair treatment of Japanese Americans, and generally advocated a "keep faith in the United States" position.

After World War II, the newspaper moved to Los Angeles. In 1952 Harry Honda, the current editor, was appointed. *The Pacific Citizen* remains the only national journal for Japanese Americans and features local, national, and international events of interest to the group. The JACL now has chapters in Hawaii and Japan so that news from its membership covers areas outside of the mainland. *The Pacific Citizen* also carries a number of regular columnists; it is one of the most professional publications in the Asian-American community.

The periodical conducted a marketing survey in 1983 which showed that its readers were relatively affluent Nisei.[10] For exmaple, the great majority of its subscribers were Nisei, over forty-five years of age, with household incomes of over $30,000 per year. There were over 23,000 subscribers and an estimated reading audience of 75,000, making it the most popular and most widely read publication for Japanese Americans. The newspaper is primarily for a Nisei audience, and if there ever comes a time for a more frequent English-language publication than a weekly, *The Pacific Citizen* could probably fulfill that need.

THE HAWAII HERALD

Looking ahead to the eventual demise of Japanese-language publications, *The Hawaii Hochi* began publishing the *Hawaii Herald*, an all English journal directed at Hawaii's Japanese Americans. It originally started as a weekly in 1969, but the paper lacked focus and support, and publication was suspended in 1973. The current *Herald* was started in 1980; its paid circulation a few years later was about 5,000. The *Herald* is one of the most interesting and relevant periodicals for younger Japanese Americans. Recent issues have included articles on drugs; alcohol; identity; the Japanese-language schools; a Sansei growing up in Japan; children of mixed marriages; and influential ethnics. However, a recent survey by the paper indicated that over 88 percent of its readership was over forty years of age, so that the problem of reaching a younger generation remains unsolved.[11]

A short-lived attempt to reach a younger generation of Asian Americans was *Gidra*, initially published with the support of the Asian-American Research Center at UCLA. A group of young Asian American students felt the need to address issues from an activist, antiestablishment, youthful viewpoint in the 1960s. The publication never had a solid subscription base and disbanded after several years.

ENGLISH-LANGUAGE SECTIONS

Most of the Japanese-American dailies continue to publish English sections of varying length and quality. Honda is of the opinion that the "golden age" of the English-language sections in terms of interest, writing, and content was during the 1930s when there were a host of critical issues and a large number of interested and talented young Nisei who had few outlets for their opinions and concerns.[12] It was an era of vicious anti-Japanese feelings during which myriad issues and problems confronted an American-born generation with "Japanese faces." The Carnegie Foundation funded a research project during the period to study the Japanese Americans, culminating in a book by Edward Strong titled *The Second Generation Japanese Problem*.[13]

The Nisei organized their own athletic leagues, social organizations, debate groups, political organizations, and religious conferences, creating a wide audience for ethnic news. Talented writers who could not find opportunities in the larger society made local contributions; the issues of acculturation, loyalty, the future of the Nisei in America, conflicts with parents, educational and economic concerns, discrimination, and prejudice provided ample material for writers. Being part of the Japanese-American community in the pre–World War II era was similar to being a resident of a small town, and the English section of the daily was an important community link. The ethnic network was further reinforced by the delivery system; often a friend or neighbor delivered the newspaper to each household, giving a family access to an extra source of community news. But the small subscription base and the limited incomes of the Nisei restricted the growth of the English-language sections.

A special feature of the English section (and of the Japanese-language section) is the special New Year's editions. Essays, poems, short stories, debates, all-star ethnic athletic teams, and year-end summaries are published in a style which contrasts sharply to the general thinness of the papers throughout the rest of the year. The New Year's edition also carries a large number of year-end greetings from individuals and businesses, which lets the community know that one is still alive and well, and which provides much-needed revenue for the publishers.

The content of much of the current English-language sections has not changed over time. The *Rafu Shimpo*, a Los Angeles-based publication, is the largest daily, with 22,000 subscriptions. Its publisher, Akira Komai,[14] early emphasized the sports section as a means of getting Japanese Americans involved in athletics, and the same emphasis continues to this day. There are still many Japanese-American athletic organizations, and there are readers interested in team standings, individual exploits, and the like. Otherwise, the English section serves as minor supplementary reading to the metropolitan newspaper, radio, and television. There are occasional columnists, notices of meetings, a social calendar, and the obituary column.

The most interesting Japanese-American columnist writes regularly for the *Kashu Mainichi*, a Los Angeles–based daily. George Yoshinaga, in a column titled "The Horse's Mouth," voices opinions and takes stands which are often controversial.[15] For example, in a recent column he questioned the continued existence of Japanese athletic leagues, which were originally established because of physical size limitations and the need for social interaction. Most observers felt that these leagues would eventually disappear but, to his consternation, Yoshinaga found that the teams are a major part of Japanese-American social life and that now there are more leagues, more players, and more tournaments than twenty years ago. The columnist also does not hesitate to question the wisdom and actions of prominent Japanese Americans.

Generally, the English sections of the dailies remain adjuncts to the Japanese-language sections. There is little original, creative reporting, and the problems of readership and finances appear as formidable barriers to longevity.

Japanese Americans interested in journalism as a career find better opportunities in the metropolitan press; better known journalists such as Bill Hosokawa (*Denver Post*) contribute to *The Pacific Citizen* but have established their careers essentially outside of the ethnic press.

JAPANESE-LANGUAGE PUBLICATIONS

Newspapers often reflect the tastes and views of their publishers, so that when the papers begin to rely primarily on "cutting and pasting," they begin to exhibit homogeneity. One of the more common complaints about current ethnic newspapers is their relative sameness, especially when dealing with national and international events, since most rely on similar sources.

Newspapers were associated with the beginning of Japanese immigration. Yasuo Sakata reports that in the late 1880s a publication was issued by student-laborers in San Francisco espousing liberal points of view unpopular with the Meiji government in Japan.[16] The primary audience for the publication was the Japanese in Japan.

The emphasis of the early Japanese-language press was on news of Japan. The majority of the immigrants were young males who had envisaged a temporary work stay (dekasegi),[17] so that questions of a permanent life in America were not of paramount importance. However, Abiko, founder of the *Nichi-bei Times*, was one leader who sought to encourage the sojourners to stay permanently. He encouraged a broad world view rather than a narrow focus on Japan, and stressed the desirability of making a good impression in this country through good character and behavior.[18]

An interesting insight into Japanese attitudes toward confronting the reality of American racism in the nineteenth and early twentieth centuries was offered by intellectuals such as Yukichi Furuzawa.[19] Japanese were well aware of the vicious anti-Chinese sentiments in California, but believed that the problem was caused by the Chinese peasant laborers' lack of education. Therefore, there was a naive belief that with modernization and Westernization, the Japanese would be treated as equals and would not be the target of racial discrimination.

THE HAWAII HOCHI

The history of ethnic newspapers is often that of strong and dedicated personalities, often willing to take financial risks for their papers, which they viewed as an essential community service. *The Hawaii Hochi* provides an example of a paper founded by a strong man, willing to take chances for what he believed was right. One of the most interesting ethnic newspapers, *The Hawaii Hochi* was founded by Fred Makino. Makino's life has been touched upon by Beekman,[20] Jacobs and Landau,[21] Kitano,[22] and Kotani.[23] Makino was born in Japan in 1877, the son of an English silk merchant father and a Japanese mother. He immigrated to Hawaii and founded the *Hochi* on December 12, 1912. Prior to that time, there were several other Japanese newspapers in Hawaii; the October 16, 1905, issue of the *Yamato* wrote of the need for the Japanese-language press:

There are sixty or seventy thousand Japanese in Hawaii. . . . We believe it to be for the best interests of this large population that they be furnished with newspapers, published in the Japanese vernacular, couched in simple language, suited to their comprehension, giving them the latest news and changes so rapidly going on in their motherland . . . also . . . comment[ing] on any laws or administrative regulations of the territory affecting the rights or interests of our countrymen domiciled here.[24]

There were many relevant issues affecting the Japanese American in Hawaii. They had been brought to the islands as contract laborers, and life on the plantations was often primitive and brutal.

Makino founded his paper on the principles of nonpartisanship and independence. He did not want to become the mouthpiece of special interest groups, monied groups, or Japanese organizations. As such, his paper often took stands that were unpopular, and Makino even went to jail for his convictions.

Makino believed that the plantation owners were exploiting the Japanese, but rather than fatalistically accepting the status quo, his strategy was to organize and strike back. He helped the Japanese to found their own unions; when he found that a large number of non-Christian picture brides were being married in Christian ceremonies conducted by Christian ministers upon debarkation in Honolulu, he was able to provide a Buddhist alternative. He worked actively against the Foreign Language Press Law which would have forced all foreign-language newspapers to be translated into English and filed with the attorney general. The costs of such a procedure would have been enormous and would have resulted in the demise of the ethnic press.

In 1919 the Hawaii legislature introduced two bills to control the 180 Japanese-language schools with their 44,000 students. Makino successfully opposed these measures; other similar laws were also tested, and the *Hochi*-sponsored language school law test eventually went to the Supreme Court in 1927. The Court declared the Hawaii law to control foreign-language schools unconstitutional.

But Beekman indicates that Makino's paper paid dearly for its activism.[25] It lost most of its advertising, and when interviewed in 1927, Makino said that his circulation was only 12,000. But he predicted that in ten years he would have 30,000 subscribers, a dream which did not materialize.

The "golden age" of the Japanese-language sections was in the 1920s, according to Yugi Ichioka.[26] Just as in the English sections, the combination of young, talented individuals, burning issues, and the lack of other outlets combined to make the Japanese-language sections original, creative, and interesting.

The period preceding World War II was a difficult one for the *Hochi*, as for all Japanese-language newspapers. The differences between the Japanese-language sections and the English sections became pronounced; for example, the Japanese-language sections received most of their news from Domei (Japan) and referred to the Japanese army as "our army," whereas the English sections wrote of "the Japanese army."[27] However, it is difficult to generalize about the newspapers as a whole; there was, no doubt, a degree of nationalism and ethnic pride among the Issei readership in the initial victories of their mother country. Since the Issei were aliens, ineligible for United States citizenship under the laws at that time, there was a strong tendency to identify with Japan, but there was also the recognition that, for the majority, the future was in the United States. This was especially true of families with American-born children; the issue for the newspapers was partially solved with the Japanese attack on Pearl Harbor, as a result of which the military suspended the publication of all Japanese newspapers. They were later permitted to publish, but under strict military censorship.

Makino died in 1953, and in 1962 the *Hochi* was sold to the *Shizuoka Shimbun* (Shizuoka newspaper) of Japan. There was some trepidation on the part of the new owners that the local Hawaiian residents might resent this "foreign" intrusion, but the takeover has improved the newspaper. The new owners brought in modern equipment and have also used the facilities for outside printing orders, which has helped to subsidize the publication of the Japanese daily.

Currently the *Hochi* relies for most of its news on *Kyodo* (Japan) news, and on translations from the Associated Press (AP) and United Press International (UPI). Like most Japanese sections of ethnic dailies, it carries two serials, one

from the samurai era, and one "modern" drama. The obituaries and local ethnic
news for the specialized community remain important. But the dynamism and
the crusading character of its early founder appear to be missing. Perhaps there
are not as many burning issues facing Japanese Americans now.

One other point concerning Japanese newspapers deserves comment. There
has been a lack of a lively "letters to the editor" column; even so-called controversial issues evoke little response in the form of letters. Partial explanations
for this lack include a hesitance to challenge authority and to voice opinions in
public and also a desire to avoid overt conflict; no matter what the reason, the
paucity of letters to the editor continues to the present day.

HAWAII

Major problems facing the ethnic press in Hawaii are competitive news sources
and the lack of leadership among the younger age groups. Radio and television
stations as well as the metropolitan newspapers in Hawaii are much more Japanese
news oriented than their counterparts on the mainland; therefore, a person of
Japanese ancestry does not have to rely solely on the ethnic newspapers for
ethnic news. For the Japanese-language reader, there is also the option of sub-
scribing to newspapers from Japan.

Therefore, although there is a large Japanese population in Hawaii, pessimism
exists concerning the future of the ethnic press. The paucity of younger readers,
especially for the English-language sections, the lack of charismatic, dedicated
leadership, and financial problems appear to warrant such an outlook. Nevertheless, over 600,000 tourists from Japan visit Hawaii annually, and many Japanese businesses now have island locations. There remains a limited potential
for an ethnic press.

THE MAINLAND

The mainland outlook appears more promising. Several publishers have invested in new equipment, and the competition from other news sources for ethnic
content is limited. Scattered mainland communities may underscore the need for
diversity; what is of interest to the Seattle reader (for example, obituaries, or
the social calendar) will not necessarily be of interest to the Los Angeles resident.

Problems appear to be similar in both settings: a dying Issei population; the
general lack of interest in the ethnic press among the younger generations;
competition from metropolitan dailies, radio, and television; outmoded equipment; economic problems; a dependence on similar news sources; emphasis on
cut-and-paste journalism; and an inability to train, hire, and retain talented
journalists.

In summary, the Japanese-American press, which began publishing in the
latter part of the nineteenth century, has performed a necessary service in the
ethnic community. The newspapers' most successful periods have corresponded

to the existence of serious issues, such as discriminatory legislation and unfair treatment of Japanese Americans. In this context the predictions of its demise may be taken as an optimistic view of the relationship between the ethnic group and the dominant community.

The future of the Japanese-language section is intimately related to new immigration, which is low at the present, and to the number of Japanese businessmen and visitors (which is growing). The Issei survivors, in the past the backbone of the press, will not be here much longer.

The future of the English-language section appears to depend on its competitive potential. A lively, informative, first-class newspaper focusing on issues relevant to the ethnic group should have a promising future, given the changing demographic picture of the population. The changing demographics may suggest Pan-Asian publications. The Issei developed and supported Japanese-language newspapers; the Nisei have selectively supported English sections of the vernacular press and *The Pacific Citizen*; the question is, What will the newer generations do?

NOTES

1. Gary Critser, "Readers Shy Away from Japanese American Press," *Christian Science Monitor*, April 27, 1983, p. 2.

2. Kenneth Toguchi, personal letter, October 26, 1982.

3. Group interview with former employees of English-language sections of Japanese-America newspapers, October 25, 1982. In attendance were Kats Kunitsugu, Henry Mori, Vince Tajiri, Bob Okazaki, Mas Imon, and Harry Honda. The group mentioned that any move toward unionization would probably kill the ethnic newspaper. There was also the recognition that many of the surviving papers were family operations. Nisei (second-generation) publishers often followed in the steps of their parents; it may be that the third generation (Sansei) will not carry on newspaper publishing in a similar fashion.

4. Lubomyr R. Wynar and Anna T. Wynar, eds., *Encylcopedic Directory of Ethnic Newspapers and Periodicals in the United States* (Littleton, Colo.: Libraries Unlimited, 1972), pp. 97–98.

5. Interview with Harry Honda, editor of *The Pacific Citizen*, January 11, 1984. All of the newspapers were still publishing with the possible exception of the *Japanese American Society Bulletin*, Washington, D.C., for which there was no information.

6. Toguchi, 10/26/82 letter.

7. Honda, 1/11/84 interview.

8. Discussion with William Hiroto, former editor and publisher of *The Crossroads* on October 28, 1982 at a congressional reception, Los Angeles, California.

9. William Hosokawa, *Quest of Justice* (New York: William Morrow, 1982).

10. Unpublished document provided by Harry Honda, editor of *The Pacific Citizen*.

11. Toguchi, 10/26/82 letter.

12. Honda, 1/11/84 interview.

13. Edward Strong, Jr., *The Second Generation Japanese Problem* (Stanford, Calif.: Stanford University Press, 1934).

14. The Issei publisher of *Rafu Shimpo* died in 1983. Family members have since taken over the paper.

15. George Yoshinaga, "The Horse's Mouth," *Kashu Mainichi*, January 1, 1984, p. 1.

16. Interview with Yasuo Sakata, March 28, 1984. A follow-up unpublished paper was made available on March 29. Sakata and Yuji Ichioka are part of a research team which will publish a collection of studies based on Japanese-language newspapers in Hawaii, Canada, and the United States.

17. Sakata 3/28/84 interview.

18. Ibid.

19. Ibid.

20. Alan Beekman, "Japanese Language Press of Hawaii, What Now?" *Pacific Citizen*, December 23–30, 1983, p. B–1.

21. Paul Jacobs and Saul Landau, *To Serve the Devil*, 2 vols. (New York: Random House, 1971).

22. Harry H.L. Kitano, *Japanese Americans* (Englewood Cliffs, N.J.: Prentice-Hall, 1976).

23. Roland Kotani, "Unrelenting Search for the Truth," *The Hawaii Herald*. September 17, 1982, p. 4.

24. Beekman, "Japanese Language Press."

25. Ibid.

26. Interview with Yuji Ichioka, research historian at UCLA, October 28, 1982.

27. Beekman, "Japanese Language Press."

BIBLIOGRAPHY

Beekman, Alan. "Japanese Language Press of Hawaii, What Now?" *Pacific Citizen*, December 23–30, 1983, p. B–1.

Critser, Gary. "Readers Slip Away from Japanese American Press." *Christian Science Monitor*, April 27, 1983, p. 2.

Hosokawa, William. *Quest of Justice*. New York: William Morrow, 1982.

Jacobs, Paul, and Saul Landau. *To Serve the Devil*. 2 vols. New York: Random House, 1971.

Kitano, Harry H.L. *Japanese Americans*. Englewood Cliffs, N.J.: Prentice-Hall, 1976.

Kotani, Roland. "Hawaii Hochi . . . Future Directions." *The Hawaii Herald*, October 1, 1982, p. 6.

———. "Unrelenting Search for the Truth." *The Hawaii Herald*, September 17, 1982, p. 4.

Strong, Edward, Jr. *The Second Generation Japanese Problem*. Stanford, Calif.: Stanford University Press, 1934.

Wynar, Lubomyr R., and Anna T. Wynar, eds., *Encyclopedic Directory of Ethnic Newspapers and Periodicals in the United States*. Littleton, Colo.: Libraries Unlimited, 1972.

Yoshinaga, George. "The Horse's Mouth," *Kashu Mainichi*, January 1, 1984, p. 1.

14

The Jewish Press

ARTHUR A. GOREN

The Jewish press in America, beginning in 1843 with the appearance of the first successful periodical, the monthly *Occident and American Jewish Advocate*, reflected the presence of both an acculturated Jewish community and a continual flow of Jewish immigration. The foreign languages in which the periodicals appeared—German, Yiddish, and, to a lesser degree, Hebrew and Ladino—demonstrated the diversity of cultures Jewish immigrants brought with them in the nineteenth and early twentieth centuries. From the 1930s to the 1980s, following the decline or demise of the older foreign-language press, new periodicals in German, and then in Yiddish, Hebrew, and Russian, responded to the needs of the most recent immigrants. However, the first journals published for any length of time were English language—Anglo-Jewish—papers which multiplied and changed as the Americanized segment of the community grew in size and complexity. Thus, from the beginning of the Jewish press, English-language periodicals nurtured an ethnic culture in English. In this respect, the Jews differed from most other ethnic groups, where the demand for information about the new country in the immigrant's native tongue and the hunger for news from the Old World provided the impetus for establishing foreign-language newspapers, and language loss coincided with the passing of the immigrant press. When language loss occurred to the Jews, most notably during the past four decades, highly acculturated second-, third-, and fourth-generation Jews produced a remarkably multifaceted ethnic press in English that had a venerable tradition.[1]

Significantly, even during the middle third of the nineteenth century, when a substantial Jewish immigration from German-speaking countries changed the complexion of American Jewry (in 1880 two-thirds of the 250,000 Jews in the United States were of German origin), Anglo-Jewish periodicals outnumbered those in German and survived longer. The first German-language periodical of any longevity, the monthly *Die Deborah*, was founded in Cincinnati in 1855 by Isaac Mayer Wise, the leading Reform rabbi of the time, as a women's supplement to his English-language *Israelite*. The following year another Reform rabbi, David Einhorn of Baltimore, began publishing *Sinai*. Twenty-five years later, in addition to *Die Deborah*, only the *Zeitgeist* (Spirit of the age), published in Milwaukee, was appearing solely in German, while two Anglo-Jewish weeklies carried German-language sections. In the early 1900s, the last periodical in German ceased publication. Altogether, during the life span of the German-Jewish immigrant generation, sixteen periodicals publishing wholly or partly in German had appeared. In contrast, in 1855 five Anglo-Jewish weeklies or monthlies were being published. Within two years, two more appeared. Between 1880 and 1903 the number rose from seven, published in five cities, to thirty-two, published in twenty-two cities.[2]

Important as the German-Jewish press was as guide and voice for German-speaking Jews, its frailty is also noteworthy. This characteristic was, of course, endemic to the immigrant press in general. However, there were peculiarly Jewish factors which require explanation. In the lands of their birth, the Jewish immigrants had only recently come under the influence of the Enlightenment. They were in the process of adapting their communal life and religious practices to the secular and cultural ideals which promised a new social order, liberal and humane and open to Jews. Political emancipation and social integration appeared to them to be imminent. Bitterly disappointed when neither occurred, German-Jewish immigrants arrived in the New World predisposed to America's democratic ethos of individualism and accommodation. They were also proud of their German cultural heritage, under the influence of which they had prepared themselves for an equal place in society. During the first few decades of their settlement, the immigrants used German in their homes, synagogues, and clubs, listened to sermons in German, and taught the language in their private schools. Thus they bore a dual ethnicity, German and Jewish, the former cultural and affectional, and the latter increasingly defined in universal religious terms, yet retaining the sense of kinship with Jews everywhere. Immigrants whose ethnic identity was more German than Jewish were drawn into the German social and cultural milieu and in their reading habits preferred the thriving daily and weekly press serving German Americans, rather than the smaller, more circumscribed German-language Jewish press. Hence, the commitment to Americanization on the part of the German-Jewish immigrants, their rapid acculturation, and the option of entry into German-American life, accounted for the ascendency of English.[3]

Paradoxically, the mass emigration from Eastern Europe, which began in 1881, contributed to the growth and quality of the Anglo-Jewish press. The presence of a highly visible Yiddish-speaking population heightened the self-consciousness of the established Jews, now mostly middle-class and well integrated into American life. The flood of Eastern European Jewish immigrants presented a threat to their status. However, a host of new problems involving the integration of new immigrants into society required public discussion and communal solutions. Both factors intensified and extended Jewish organizational life and stimulated the expansion of the Anglo-Jewish press.

During the forty years of mass migration, 2.3 million Jews from Russia,

Poland, Galicia, and Romania settled in the United States. The Eastern European Jews brought with them a highly developed communal tradition, a strong collective identity, and a richly textured Yiddish culture. For generations, government repression from without and an exacting religious culture from within produced and then sustained the self-contained Jewish settlements of Eastern Europe. Treatment by the secular authorities as a corporate group enabled the Jews to maintain more readily a communal polity sanctioned and prescribed by their own religious law and custom. Language reinforced Jewish separatism. Hebrew, the language of prayer, was studied by all male children. It linked the generations in a lineal continuum to the people's biblical beginnings, and, laterally, as lingua franca of the Jewish diaspora, enabled distant communities possessing different vernacular languages to maintain ties. Yiddish, the spoken language of Jews who originated in German-speaking countries, moved eastward with the migration of Ashkenazi (German) Jews to Poland beginning in the fifteenth century. Derived from Middle-High German with a considerable mixture of Hebrew as well as some Polish and Russian, and written in Hebrew characters, it became the exclusive language of Eastern European Jews.[4]

Contemporaneous with the mass exodus to America, secular ideologies spawned by the Haskalah, the Jewish Enlightenment, and abetted by economic change and dislocation, shook the social, religious, cultural, and communal structure of traditional society. Socialism, Zionism, and assimilationism, in numerous variations, developed into well-organized movements by the beginning of the twentieth century. A secular modern Hebrew literature flowered. Jews also wrote in Polish and Russian for an acculturated Jewish public. Most dramatically, a fledgling literature in Yiddish, closely tied to efforts to radicalize the impoverished masses, matured into a modern literary medium coequal with Hebrew. The best authors of the period and its leading polemicists published in the spirited and influential Hebrew and Yiddish press which in the repressive political conditions of the Russian Empire occupied a crucial place in the intellectual and cultural life of the people.[5]

The immigrants transplanted this flourishing, sometimes frenetic group life to the densely populated settlements they formed in New York, Philadelphia, Chicago, and other large eastern and midwestern cities. The first periodicals they began to publish, in both Hebrew and Yiddish, appeared in the 1870s. However, the most important index of the intensity and creativity of the burgeoning settlements of Yiddish-speaking immigrants was the rise of a powerful Yiddish daily press. These newspapers represented the full range of political opinion and defined and defended a variety of versions of Jewish life. In addition to the functions performed by the immigrant press in general, the Yiddish dailies published belles lettres, literary criticism, and essays of broad cultural content, providing Yiddish writers, essayists, and propagandists with an influential forum.[6]

The first successful Yiddish daily, the *Yiddishe Tageblat* (Jewish daily news), appeared in 1885. Significantly, it was religiously and politically conservative, an indication that the radical and secular elements among the immigrants were comparably small in number and lacked the resources or will to launch a daily. In 1916, the peak year for the Yiddish press, eleven dailies with a circulation of 650,000 were published, five of these in New York City. The majority held radical or secular views. The pacesetter among them was the socialist *Forverts* (Forward). An estimated 2 million people read the Yiddish daily press. Immigration restriction and the gradual passing of the immigrant generation took its toll, but the process was gradual at first. In 1940 eight dailies, of which four appeared in New York, had a circulation of 400,000. Then came a precipitous decline to three in 1960, all published in New York. The last remaining Yiddish daily, the *Forverts*, became a weekly in 1983.[7]

The steady rise in the numbers of refugees from Germany, Poland, and other east central European countries beginning in the mid–1930s slowed somewhat the decline of the Yiddish daily press and led to the establishment of periodicals in other foreign languages. Between 1934 and 1941, as Hitler's anti-Jewish measures became more brutal, 150,000 Jewish émigrés reached the shores of America. Most of them were German-speaking. A presidential directive in 1945 and special legislation in 1948 and 1950 enabled 137,000 Jews who survived the Holocaust to enter the United States. Finally, under the liberal immigration policy inaugurated in the 1960s, about 400,000 Jews settled in the United States, increasing the number and diversity of the foreign-born Jewish population. They came from Poland, Hungary, Latin America, Israel, the Soviet Union, and Iran, victims of anti-Semitism, political upheaval, and economic insecurity.[8]

The journals these immigrants founded registered not only their linguistic needs but a range of group experiences and cultural backgrounds unknown to earlier waves of Jewish immigrants. To illustrate: the German-language *Aufbau* (Reconstruction), which began appearing as a weekly in 1938, quickly achieved a reputation for literary excellence reflecting the intellectual attainments of Germany's Jews on the eve of Hitler's rise to power; *Algemeine Journal* (The general journal), a Yiddish weekly, was founded in 1972 by the Lubavitcher Hassidim, an ultra-Orthodox sect determined to shelter its followers from secular influences, including that of the existing Yiddish press; immigrants from Israel established the Hebrew-language *Yisrael shelanu* (Our Israel) in 1979, finding the older Hebrew-language weeklies, edited by Jews who had acquired Hebrew as a second language in the United States, of little interest. Significantly, Jewish immigrants from the Soviet Union failed to publish their own periodical. But they did constitute an overwhelming percentage of the editorial staff and readers of the daily non-Jewish *Novoye Russkoye Slovo* (The new Russian word) and the weeklies *Novi Amerikanitz* (New American) and *Novoya Gazetten* (New gazette), an indication of the absence of a strong Soviet-Jewish collective identity. In 1984 only seventeen foreign-language periodicals appeared, the majority in Yiddish.[9]

Anglo-Jewish weeklies and monthlies dominated the Jewish press in the postwar decades. In ways strikingly parallel to the situation at the turn of the century, a highly acculturated American Jewry expanded its communal organization to aid brethren in other parts of the world, and reinforced a sense of Jewish self-consciousness. Second- and third-generation Jews joined synagogues and Jewish civic bodies, supported Jewish social agencies, and took part in Jewish educational and cultural endeavors, creating an impressive communal structure. The Anglo-Jewish press assumed a crucial role as it linked a dispersed, highly suburbanized population to the local network of Jewish associational life. It fostered, moreover, a feeling of unity and consensus notwithstanding institutional rivalries, clashing views, and tensions endemic to American Judaism's denominationalism.[10]

The Anglo-Jewish press has served these ends by simultaneously extending its scope and sharpening its focus. Community newspapers, published privately or owned or subsidized by the local federation of Jewish philanthropies, provide their readers with coverage of international, national, and local news of Jewish interest. These periodicals reach a majority of the Jewishly identified households in the community. On another level, national Jewish organizations have expanded their house organs to include topical and cultural material; these magazines have the largest single circulation of any category of the Anglo-Jewish press. Journals of opinion, religious or secular, have multiplied in response to the urbane tastes of an increasing number of well-educated Jews. Meanwhile, the professionalization of Jewish communal life has stimulated the growth of specialized journals. Finally dissenting voices in the community—students, women, and those dissatisfied with consensus communal policy—have produced a significant number of journals. Taken together, the 195 periodicals published in 1984—excluding annuals, directories, and children's magazines—faithfully mirror the many-sidedness of American Jewish life.[11]

THE RISE OF THE COMMUNITY NEWSPAPER

The brief existence of the first Jewish periodical to appear in the United States suggests the preconditions that were necessary for the establishment of a stable press. *The Jew*, published monthly in New York, lasted from March 1823 to March 1825. At the time, less than 1,000 Jews lived in the city, and 3,000 more were scattered in a half-dozen other eastern cities and in smaller rural settlements, a number insufficient to support a periodical for long. *The Jew*, moreover, devoted itself to a single issue: combatting Christian missionary endeavors to convert Jews. The monthly disregarded events within the Jewish community, an indication not only of the publisher's single-minded purpose but of the absence of any demand for a communal news medium. Each of the urban Jewish settlements maintained a single congregation which served as the religious and social center for the small homogeneous Jewish populace. Two decades later, when *The Occident* began to appear in Philadelphia, the Jewish population had increased fifteenfold and spread to the Midwest and South. During its twenty-six years of existence, *The Occident* recorded the quadrupling of the number of Jews and the establishment of an organized Jewish life in 160 places across the continent. Congregations multiplied from 8 in 1820 to 77 in 1850 to nearly 200 in 1870. The journal also noted with alarm the fragmentation and secularization of communal life. Philanthropic institutions, benevolent societies, fraternal orders, cultural associations, and social clubs proliferated in the large urban centers where most Jews settled. Cultural differences brought from Europe intensified functional segmentation and eroded a sense of community. At the same time, *The Occident* chronicled the legal, social, and religious manifestations of anti-Jewish feelings and the lack of any effective response.[12]

These developments, already in evidence in the early 1840s, moved Isaac Leeser, the German-born and trained rabbi of Philadelphia's prestigious Mikveh Israel Congregation and the leading spokesman of traditional Judaism, to launch *The Occident*. Leeser was also encouraged by the rise of Jewish periodicals in Germany, England, and France, and the role they played as spokesmen, advocates, educators, and promoters of Jewish group life. Where geography separated American Jews and organizational allegiances divided them, *The Occident* intended to reach Jews everywhere and foster Jewish solidarity. During its first eighteen years of existence, *The Occident* listed subscribers in thirty-three states and territories. It disseminated information on Jewish affairs, served as a forum for the exchange of ideas, and energetically defended Jewish interests. Accounts of synagogue life, Jewish schools, and philanthropic institutions appeared regularly. *The Occident* diligently monitored the general American and religious press on issues affecting American Jewry, especially Sunday laws, the vestiges of political restrictions, religion in the public schools, public expression of anti-Jewish sentiments, and missionary activities. It gave close coverage to such sensitive issues as the 1850 United States treaty with Switzerland, which discriminated against American Jews. The monthly also kept its readers well informed of Jewish events abroad. In 1859, when a Jewish child in Bologna, Italy, was secretly baptized and then forcibly abducted by the Catholic Church, *The Occident* supplied its readers with long accounts of the protest actions of English and French Jewry, answered the defenders of the Church, and approved the public meetings which called on the president to intercede. Leeser was elected a member of the delegation that met with President James Buchanan. However, Leeser's view of American Jewry as a religious community made "the diffusion of knowledge of Jewish literature and religion" the central purpose of his journal. Sermons, didactic articles, often translated from European periodicals, and polemical editorials attacking the rising movement of Reform Judaism gave *The Occident* the tone of an American religious monthly. Leeser's principal communal goal was the establishment of a national union of Jewish congregations with the authority and means to improve the quality of Jewish religious life. In this respect, *The Occident* echoed the calls for unity which so preoccupied the Protestant religious press.[13]

Although the secular and nonsectarian dimensions of Jewish life received greater weight in the periodicals that began to appear in the 1850s and later (see below), Leeser's pioneering journal proved to be a prototype in important ways.

Other rabbis followed him in establishing periodicals which served as extensions of their pulpits and vehicles for winning a national following. Their rabbinical calling to uphold and defend Judaism, the educational attainments and literary skills required of their office, and their station as communal leaders predisposed them to publishing. Isaac Mayer Wise is the outstanding example of the preacher-publisher. Wise founded the weekly *Israelite* (later *The American Israelite*) in 1854, only months after accepting the pulpit of Cincinnati's B'nai Jeshurun synagogue. Vigorously advocating the cause of Reform Judaism, Wise stressed Reform's compatibility with the American democratic ethos, its belief in human progress, and its rejection of "antiquated" and "fanatic" Orthodoxy. Eager to win readers, *The Israelite* struck a more popular stance than *The Occident*. Wise balanced didactic and polemical articles with stories and serialized novels. The weekly appearance of *The Israelite* gave Wise's lively coverage of political affairs a timeliness which was especially welcome. More than any other Anglo-Jewish weekly during the nineteenth century, *The Israelite* achieved a national circulation. Wise's journalistic skill and his position as the dominant figure in the expanding Reform movement with which his weekly was so intimately identified explains much of the success of *The Israelite*. Wise edited the paper for nearly half a century, until his death in 1900. Still published, *The American Israelite* is the nation's oldest Jewish journal.[14]

Among Wise's rabbi-editor colleagues were Samuel Myer Isaac, who founded the conservative *Jewish Messenger* in New York in 1857; Julius Eckman, whose *The Weekly Gleaner* began appearing in San Francisco in 1858; Moritz Spitz, who began publishing the *Jewish Voice* in St. Louis in 1884; and Chicago's Emil Hirsch, who founded *The Reform Advocate* in 1891. Influential rabbis, they never achieved the national prominence of Wise, nor did their journals compete successfully with *The Israelite*. Like *The Israelite*, their periodicals combined a personal, partisan journalism when dealing with religious questions with political analysis, literary and historical essays—often translations of the work of outstanding European scholars and publicists—and brief reports of American and European Jewish life.[15]

Beginning in the 1870s and gaining momentum in the 1880s, community-conscious laymen in the major Jewish population centers entered the field of Jewish journalism. Some of the community papers were owned by single proprietors who had gained journalistic experience before immigrating to the United States; others were businessmen who saw the commercial possibilities in a Jewish newspaper. In this category were Robert Lyon's *Asmonean*, which appeared weekly in New York from 1849 to 1859 and was the forerunner of the community newspaper, New York's *Jewish Times*, published by Moritz Ellinger from 1869 to 1879; Rochester's *Jewish Tidings*, founded by Samuel Brickner and Louis Wiley in 1887; and the *Hebrew Observer*, established in Cleveland in 1889 by Hiram Strauss and Samuel Oppenheimer. In other cases, the newspapers were founded as stock companies attracting investors from among communal leaders and young professionals. New York's *American Hebrew*, which began appearing in 1879, and Philadelphia's *Jewish Exponent*, established in 1887, are notable examples.[16]

Seeking a broad, local following, the community weeklies reported the full range of Jewish opinion with commendable fairness. They adopted moderate positions on social, political, and religious issues, and supported noncontroversial, ameliorative measures for improving the quality of Jewish communal life. In a statement which well expressed the consensual thrust of the local papers, Baltimore's *Jewish Comment* announced in its first issue that it "is to stand for this community" and for "the Jew and Judaism in their truest and broadest sense—without any modifying adjectives." The paper would try, furthermore, "to interest all sections and classes of the Jewish community."[17]

In practice, the Anglo-Jewish press of the time served only one section and class, the established, Americanized stratum of the Jewish population. To succeed commercially, the community weeklies recognized that their readers, as the *Jewish Comment* remarked, "most want to know what their neighbors are doing." (The Baltimore paper also announced that it would "furnish this community with both what it wants and what it needs.") Thus, in addition to the standard fare of national and foreign news, fiction, and articles on Jewish history and religion, the papers devoted much space to the affairs of the established synagogues, philanthropies, and clubs, and to the betrothals, marriages, deaths, and gossip of the social elite. Theater news, fashions, stock quotations, and sports were regular features. Women's interests received considerable coverage, proof that middle-class women were avid readers with special concerns. Columns were devoted to "the new woman," "raising children," and "household hints." The advertisements reflected the affluent, middle-class consumer society that the papers appealed to (household furnishings, piano lessons, medicines, and beauty salons), and the commercial occupations of its wage-earners (banks, law offices, insurance companies, shipping agents, and hotels).[18]

Increasingly, the situation of Eastern European Jewry occupied the attention of American Jews. The Anglo-Jewish press responded by broadening its news coverage of conditions and events in Eastern Europe and by detailed reports of Western Jewry's efforts to cope with the increasing flow of emigration. Understandably, the arrival of large numbers of immigrants to a community received close attention, and their integration became a subject of discussion in the local paper. Occasionally, expressions of antipathy and fear of the immigrant Jews appeared in the Jewish press. Such articles focused on the immigrants' Orthodoxy or radicalism, or on compact settlements, which were seen as obstacles in the way of Americanization. More often, the established community's paper glossed over the gulf that separated the two groups and emphasized communal responsibility for the immigrants' uplift. On a national level, the problems of integration, immigration restriction, and social dislocation agitated Jewish public opinion. The Anglo-Jewish press served as the sounding board for the rising demand for better organized, centralized endeavors. In the early 1900s, when the established community mobilized its resources in a concerted effort to integrate the Eastern

European immigrants, the community newspapers reached the crest of their influence. The Anglo-Jewish press now described the political, social, and cultural interests of a heterogeneous ethnic group in contrast to three decades earlier, when it had perceived American Jewry as a unified religious community well rooted in America.[19]

THE ERA OF THE YIDDISH PRESS

The flowering of the Yiddish press, which began about 1905 and lasted for nearly half a century, was preceded by a long period of gestation. In 1870 the first Yiddish periodical to appear in the United States, the *Yidishe Tseitung* (The Jewish journal), began an irregular existence with long interruptions until its demise in 1877. (The *Tseitung*'s subtitle is noteworthy: "A Weekly Paper of Politics, Religion, History, Science and Art." This all-encompassing educational purpose, typical of the Haskalah approach, became a hallmark of Yiddish journalism in America.) Of the nine Yiddish journals launched during the 1870s, only one, the *Yidishe Gazeten* (Jewish gazette), founded by Kasriel Zevi Sarasohn in 1874, survived. In 1885, when Sarasohn established his daily, the *Yidishes Tageblat*, the *Gazeten* became the *Tageblat*'s weekly magazine.[20]

A number of reasons account for the early failure of the Yiddish press. The Yiddish-speaking population was relatively small. In New York, it rose from about 15,000 in 1870 to about 35,000 ten years later. (This approximation is based on an estimated 40,000 Eastern European Jews migrating to the United States during the 1870s, half of whom settled outside of New York.) A considerable portion of the newcomers, furthermore, were unaccustomed to newspapers. They came from small towns, were Orthodox in religious outlook, and until their migration were insulated from the secular influences of which the press was so conspicuous a product. In fact, the first Jewish journal of any longevity appeared in Eastern Europe only in 1857. Its language was Hebrew, and it was edited by Haskalah writers who addressed the educated elite. Five years later a Yiddish periodical appeared as a supplement to a new Hebrew-language journal. Although the 1860s and 1870s witnessed a significant growth in the Eastern European Jewish press, which now included Russian-language periodicals, it made little impression on the social types who composed the early wave of immigrants. Ezekiel Sarasohn, son and partner of the publisher of the *Gazeten* and *Tageblat*, described the attitude toward the existing Yiddish press of the small-town Polish and Lithuanian Jewish immigrants who settled in New York in the 1880s.

The older ones among them did not have the slightest need for a newspaper and its functions," Sarasohn observed. "They loved to hear the news, that is, from one who read aloud. To read for themselves, and every day at that, did not even enter their imagination. How can a Jew sit down to read a newspaper on an ordinary workday? The younger ones, those that had some education, read German newspapers. The *Maskilim* [devotees of the Hebrew Enlightenment movement] were satisfied with *Ha'maggid* [the leading Hebrew journal in Eastern Europe]. The very young were ashamed of a newspaper with Hebrew characters.[21]

But the early publishers and editors were themselves *maskilim*, and their cultural biases also impeded the growth of the Yiddish press. Zevi Hirsh Berenstein, who began publishing the short-lived *Post* in 1871, founded soon after *Ha'tzofe be'erets ha'hadasha* (The observer in the new land), the first Hebrew-language periodical on American soil. *Ha'tzofe* appeared intermittently for five years. Kasriel Sarasohn, the first successful Yiddish publisher, also tried his hand editing a Hebrew journal, and several of the Yiddish periodicals of the 1870s carried columns in Hebrew. Clearly, these pioneer publishers and the small coterie of writers who gathered about them brought to the United States an ideological and sentimental commitment to Hebrew. They belonged to the mid-nineteenth-century generation which saw Hebrew as the medium for modernizing East European Jewry and as the language of national revival. In America they found few followers and discovered a completely different reality than in Europe. Yiddish became a compromise. They turned to it as the one means of reaching the common people who required guidance in adjusting to the New World and, no less important, cultural nourishment to maintain their Jewishness.[22]

However, Yiddish, as a language, presented problems for these early journalist-intellectuals. A strong element of condescension marked their attitude toward it. They considered it the jargon of the uneducated masses and deprecated it as inadequate for literary expression. Consequently, publishers, editors, and contributors endeavored to raise the standards of the common person's language, which they reluctantly used, by employing a heavily Germanized Yiddish style and vocabulary. Samuel Niger, the noted critic of Yiddish literature, summarized the result: "Unaccustomed to reading even their mother tongue, they [the immigrants] could hardly be expected to read a heavy Germanized language."[23] Neither a sizeable populace nor a popular journalistic idiom existed as yet. In the twenty years between 1885 and 1905 both deficiencies were satisfied, transforming the immigrant community and its press.

The pogroms of 1881 and 1882 that engulfed over 200 Jewish communities in tsarist Russia, followed by a draconian policy of economic pauperization, expulsions, and administrative oppression, jarred the limits of Jewish sufferance. Flight was one response, and 200,000 Jews immigrated to the United States in the 1880s, 500,000 in the 1890s, and another 1.5 million from 1900 to 1914. An ideological realignment among Jewish intellectuals was another response. Reformists and revolutionaries, disillusioned by the passivity of Russia's liberals and socialists to Jewish persecution, now channeled their energies into Jewish affairs. At the same time, the literary intelligentsia, through the medium of the Hebrew and the Russian-language Jewish press, became more assertive in supporting and influencing the array of Jewish socialist and nationalist parties which began to emerge during these years. By the mid–1880s the initial effects of these developments in Russia were visible in Jewish immigrant quarters, especially on New York's Lower East Side.

Abraham Cahan, the future editor of the *Forverts*, is a telling illustration of this process. Born into a pious family but exposed in his youth to Russifying influences and Western culture, Cahan joined an underground socialist-revolutionary cell in Vilna. In 1882, after eluding the Russian police, he arrived in New York, where he quickly assumed a dominant place in Jewish radical circles.[24] Cahan soon realized that as a socialist preacher his natural constituency was Yiddish-speaking workingmen. In addressing his audiences, he adopted a homely, idiomatic Yiddish rather than the Russian of the Jewish radical elite or the Germanized Yiddish or Hebrew of the *maskilim*. In the mid–1880s and early 1890s, when Cahan collaborated in launching the first radical journals in Yiddish, he adapted the popular idiom of the lecture platform to the printed page. "We used the simplest Yiddish imaginable," Cahan recalled years later when he described the *Neie Zeit* (New era), the pioneer radical periodical, which he founded in 1886. Another innovation, which Cahan and his emulators would use very effectively in the *Forverts*, was the artlessness with which a complex subject like socialism was presented. When the first issue of *Neie Zeit* appeared on Shevuot, the holiday celebrating the giving of the Torah to Moses, Cahan, the secularist, linked the two events metaphorically, tapping the religious sentiments of many of his readers. "I told the Jewish workers," he wrote in his memoirs, "that the socialist thought which we will expound must become their Torah."[25]

A number of Russian-speaking stalwarts among the Jewish intelligentsia attempted, in fact, to establish a Russian-language socialist press. In 1889 Louis Miller, who fled Russia because of his revolutionary activities, founded *Znamya* (The banner), the first such weekly. Miller soon turned to Yiddish journalism. He participated with Cahan and Morris Hillquit (see below) in launching the weekly *Arbeiter Zeitung* (Workers' news) in 1890, collaborated with Cahan in the founding of the *Forverts* in 1897, and eight years later published his own daily, *Warheit* (Truth). Others among the Russian-Jewish intelligentsia, like Jacob Gordin, Isaac Hourwich, and George M. Price, tried their hand at publishing Russian-language journals during the 1890s before becoming writers for the Yiddish press. Altogether, six such journals appeared fitfully during the decade.[26]

At the other end of the Jewish immigrants' language spectrum, Hebrew continued to engage the interest of a devoted group of *maskilim* who struggled to maintain a Hebrew press. Between 1882 and 1914, twenty-three Hebrew-language periodicals appeared; the great majority existed for less than a year. *Ha-Ivri* (The Hebrew), founded in 1892, maintained itself, with interruptions, until 1898 under the editorship of Gerson Rosenzweig and the financial support of Kasriel Sarasohn. Zev Wolf Schur, a writer of some distinction, published *Ha-Pisgah* (The summit) intermittently from 1889 to 1899, moving from city to city in pursuit of a livelihood and support for his journal. In 1909 a Hebrew daily, *Ha-Yom* (The day), appeared briefly. Further attempts were made during the following decade. Only two journals survived for any length of time, *Ha'toren* (The mast), 1913–1925 (with interruptions), and *Ha'ivri* (The Hebrew), 1916 to 1926. Feeble as the Hebrew press was, it provided an outlet for Hebrew authors in America and published some of the important European writers. Zionist and sympathetic to traditional Judaism, the Hebrew press remained the province of a small group of dedicated Hebraists. *Ha'doar* (The post), founded in 1921 as a daily but reorganized nine months later as a weekly, continues to appear to this day.[27]

Clearly, language was laden with political meaning. In Eastern Europe, the rise of Zionism inspired a new growth in the Hebrew-language press, which in turn became the vehicle for an outpouring of literary and publicistic writing. An opposing ideology crystallized in the 1890s and early 1900s. The newly founded Bund, the General Jewish Workers' Union, in its dispute with Russian socialists over the right to function as an autonomous Jewish socialist party, defended the legitimacy of its Jewish national and cultural program. Yiddish, the Bundists asserted, represented the folk genius of the ascendant Jewish proletariat and the authentic expression of its nationality. Jewish socialists and Zionists engaged in a language war which resonated in the Yiddish press in the United States. The Yiddishists rejected the notion of a rejuvenated Hebrew culture as elitist, reactionary, and utopian. For the Zionists, Yiddish was a passing phenomenon, the product of a particular time and place in the history of the Exile. National redemption—the return to Zion—was linked to the renaissance of Hebrew culture.[28]

The main debate in the United States, however, revolved around the status of the Yiddish language itself and was conducted almost exclusively within radical circles. Was Yiddish a transitory phenomenon, as the cosmopolitan Jewish intelligentsia claimed, a convenient means of communicating with Jewish workers until their Americanization and, it was hoped, their conversion to socialism? Hillquit exemplified this older cosmopolitan view. Arriving in New York in 1886 from Riga, Latvia, where German was his native tongue, he learned Yiddish in order to organize the Jewish immigrants in the garment industry. He played key roles in forming the United Hebrew Trades in 1888 and in placing the Yiddish radical press on a more stable basis. Hillquit soon entered American socialist politics. He was one of the founders of the Socialist Party in 1901, ran for political office on the Socialist ticket, and rose to national leadership. The most influential ideologue of Yiddishism, Chaim Zhitlowsky, settled in New York in 1908, although his writings appeared in Yiddish periodicals in the United States well before then. On his arrival, he began publishing the monthly *Dos Naye Lebn* (The new life), which appeared until 1914. He defined Yiddish culture as socialist and Jewish, and its literature as one that was bound up with the struggle of an oppressed people. Surveying Jewish immigrant life at the end of the first decade of the twentieth century, Zhitlovsky was convinced that nowhere else were Jews building a Yiddish cultural nationality with such success and permanence.[29]

And indeed, by the end of the nineteenth century one could speak of a Yiddish national literature. In the novels and stories of Mendele Mocher Sforim, I. L. Peretz, and Sholom Aleichem, the folk-life of East European Jews acquired a dignity, authenticity, and moral passion which reflected the reality of a culturally creative people. The Yiddish press in the United States brought this literature, together with the growing literature of immigrant writers in America, to masses of Yiddish readers. Thus literature assumed an important place in the Yiddish press, filling the multiple roles of social commentary, literary art, and Yiddishist, cultural self-consciousness.[30]

For the Yiddish press, the 1890s proved to be a transition period. The *Tageblat*'s hegemony as sole Yiddish daily was broken in 1894 when the socialist *Abend-blatt* (Evening paper) and the *Teglicher Herald* (Daily herald) were founded. The first Yiddish daily outside of New York, the Chicago *Yiddisher Kurier* (Jewish courier), made its appearance. Toward the end of the decade, socialist factionalism and differences over journalistic policy led to a split in the *Abend-blatt* and the founding of the *Forverts*. The Yiddish dailies also assumed some of the features of the American popular press—sensationalism, partisan news reporting, and highlighting of crime and vice. Alongside the best in Yiddish fiction and poetry, the Yiddish dailies serialized titillating romantic novels. Among the journals founded during the 1890s, two are especially worthy of note: the *Freie Arbeiter Stimme* (Free voice of the workingman), an anarchist weekly, and *Die Zukunft* (The future), a social-democratic monthly. During the following decade both journals achieved stability and won reputations for literary excellence and breadth of interests.[31]

The remarkable growth of the Yiddish press took place during the ten years prior to the outbreak of World War I. The new wave of immigrants that came in the wake of the Kishinev pogrom of 1903 and the collapse of the 1905 revolution brought large numbers of Jews who had been exposed to a quarter of a century of social and cultural change and political agitation. Among the immigrants were scores of writers, journalists, and publicists. Nachman Syrkin, the leading theorist of Socialist-Zionism, settled in New York in 1907. Baruch Charney Vladeck, who had been imprisoned for propagandizing for the Bund, immigrated in 1908, the year Zhitlovski arrived. By 1914 such leading literary figures as Abraham Reissen, Sholom Asch, Peretz Hirschbein, and Sholom Aleichem were residing in New York. Together with the earlier arrivals—editors Cahan, Miller, and Peter Wiernik, poets like Morris Winchevsky, Morris Rosenfeld, and Yehoash (Solomon Bloomgarden), and dramatists Jacob Gordin and David Pinski—they formed an illustrious Yiddish literati. They staffed the daily newspapers and founded and edited an array of literary and political journals. Among the latter were the *Yiddisher Kemfer* (The Jewish fighter), a Socialist-Zionist weekly, still published; the *Yiddishes Folk* (The Jewish people), founded in 1909 by the Federation of American Zionists; and the *Groyser Kundes* (Big stick), a satirical weekly.[32]

A ready public, undergoing the throes of social and economic adjustment, provided ardent readers for the mass-circulation dailies that came of age during this period. Circulation rose from 66,000 in 1900, to 120,000 in 1904, to 500,000 in 1914. For the immigrants, the paper of their persuasion was the most accessible and authoritative source of information, guidance, and news. It introduced its readers to American history, civics, manners, and customs. Instruction took such forms as serialized histories of the American people, exposés of corrupt government, paeans to the value of public school education, and analyses of the causes of Jewish criminality. The *Morgen Zhurnal* (The morning journal), an Orthodox paper founded in 1901, published, for example, articles on the constitutional issue of separation of church and state to support its call for boycotting Christmas ceremonies in the New York public schools. A *Warheit* editorial appealed to parents to enroll their children in the Boy Scouts. (The editorial began with the injunction: "Our Jewish sages declared that every father ought to teach his son three things—horseback riding, swimming and shooting.") Irving Howe, in his discussion of the Yiddish press, succinctly describes the "sociological imagination" which informed the *Forverts* accounts of immigrant life: "Were Jewish children starting to take piano lessons? Were East Siders finding new occupations ranging from real estate to gangsterdom? Were lonely immigrant girls succumbing to the lure of suicide? Were *yentes* (busybodies) moving to West End Avenue and becoming 'fancy ladies'? The *Forward* bustled to look into all these matters." Interpreting America to the immigrants and reporting their responses formed the substance of the Americanization role of the Yiddish press. No less important in the Americanization process was the zeal the papers displayed in dealing with American politics. Their political ardor and partisanship called out for commitment and engagement.[33]

The Yiddish-reading public allied itself with one or another of the Yiddish dailies. One can, in fact, speak of "communities of readers." Each paper appealed to a different constituency marked off by political tendency, Jewish outlook, social class, and institutional ties. Orthodox Jews (in practice or in sentiment), usually lower middle class, would normally read the *Morgen Zhurnal* or the *Tageblat*. (The *Tageblat* began to decline with the appearance of the *Morgen Zhurnal* and merged with it in 1928.) Standing for "Orthodox Judaism and patriotic Americanism," the *Morgen Zhurnal* denounced its rivals for not devoting enough attention to American institutions. The paper was aggressively Republican, conservative on social issues, and provided extensive coverage of religious affairs. It rallied support for Orthodox philanthropic institutions and denounced both Reform Judaism and socialism as blasphemous. In decrying the decline in religious observance, the desecration of the Sabbath, and the poor state of Jewish education, the paper also placed the blame on "materialistic America" and misguided Americanization. At the other end of the spectrum, the *Forverts*, which during the peak year of 1916 had 37 percent of the Yiddish newspaper circulation while the *Morgen Zhurnal* accounted for 20 percent, was the paper of the Jewish labor movement, giving it coherence and a sense of direction. Leaders of the Jewish trade unions, the Socialist Party, and the Workmen's Circle Order were key figures in the Forward Association, which controlled the paper. The *Forverts* carried notices of union meetings, reported extensively on industrial disputes, and at strike time published appeals for contributions to the strike funds. Under Cahan's direction, the paper also established a rapport with its readers which other papers sought to emulate with mixed success. Through the "Bintl Brief" (Bundle of letters) column, in which readers turned to the editor for advice, through contests which the paper ran, and by eliminating much of the socialist disputatiousness and the antireligious rhetoric of his predecessors, Cahan broadened the appeal of the paper. The *Warheit*, founded by Louis Miller as a socialist competitor of the *Forverts*, gave more attention to Jewish issues than its opponent. It opened its columns to Socialist-Zionists and Yiddishist nationalists. Politically, the paper moved toward the Democratic Party and supported Tammany Hall candidates. When the *Tog* (The day) appeared in 1914 as a liberal, pro-Zionist paper, restrained in tone and addressing a better educated public, the *Warheit*'s circulation fell until it was taken over by the *Tog* in 1918. In 1922 Jewish left-wing socialists and communists established the *Freiheit* (Freedom). For a time, in addition to a hard core of Yiddish-speaking communists, it attracted some of the younger left-wing intellectuals, but the paper's complete subservience to Communist Party positions alienated all but the most zealous believers. Outside of New York, Yiddish dailies existed for extended periods of time in Cleveland and Philadelphia, two appearing in Chicago.[34]

The social and economic integration of the immigrant generation, well advanced by 1930, found expression in the Yiddish press in the trend toward a more consensual position than had been the case during the prior period. Beginning in the mid–1920s, but especially following the 1929 riots in Palestine, the previously anti-Zionist *Forverts* showed increasing sympathy for Zionist settlement in Palestine. In 1936 it endorsed Franklin D. Roosevelt for president, breaking its historic support of the Socialist Party. The *Morgen Zhurnal* abandoned its anti-Zionist stand earlier than the *Forverts* and tempered its political and religious conservatism. The *Tog* maintained its centrist position but adopted some of the more popular journalistic features of its competitors. The 1930s and 1940s were also years when important new novelists, essayists, and poets began appearing in the Yiddish dailies. Among them were Jacob Glatstein, Shmuel Niger, Isaac Bashevis Singer (a Nobel Prize Laureate), and Aaron Zeitlin. Jewish issues now preoccupied the Yiddish dailies. The fate of European Jewry following the rise of Hitler, the rescue efforts and the Holocaust of World War II, the struggle to establish a Jewish state during the immediate postwar years, and the concern for the new state's security removed all vestiges of ideological differences. The dwindling number of readers—often bilingual—read the Yiddish press for the maximum coverage it gave to Jewish matters. Americanizer, window to the outside world, and interpreter of Jewish immigrant life from its beginnings into the 1920s, the Yiddish daily press became increasingly the ethnic press of the older generation. Nevertheless, it retained its place as forum and focus of Jewish cultural creativity. With the decline and eventual death of the Yiddish dailies in the years 1953 to 1983, the task of filling these functions fell upon the Anglo-Jewish periodicals.[35]

THE ANGLO-JEWISH PRESS, 1900–1985

During the half century that Yiddish journalism guided and spoke for the immigrant generation, the Anglo-Jewish press lost its position as the collective voice of the Americanized community. Two reasons stand out. First, the weeklies, the largest component of the Anglo-Jewish press, failed to keep pace with the expanding Jewish population. While the number of weeklies rose from seventeen in 1900 to forty-four in 1950, the Jewish population increased from 1 million to over 5 million; English became the preferred, or the only language, read by four out of every five Jews. The total circulation of the weeklies lagged far behind the growth of the English-speaking Jewish public as well.[36] Second, the papers changed little during the intervening years and continued to address the older, settled community. In representative papers like the *American Hebrew*, the *American Israelite*, and the *Jewish Exponent*, departments such as "Milestones: Events Along Life's Highway," or "Social and Personal" received more space than political affairs or cultural matters. Edited in most instances by a single individual with little or no staff, the papers counted on sermons, reports from organizations, and information supplied by the established synagogues, philanthropies, and clubs for their copy. For national and international news of Jewish interest, the papers increasingly depended upon the Jewish Telegraphic Agency, a news service established in 1917. The reporting was dull and shallow. For many, particularly among second-generation Jews—the offspring of the East European immigrants—the Jewish weekly press appeared staid, distant, and intellectually vacuous. Stephen S. Wise, the prominent rabbi, Zionist, and communal leader, summed up this view by referring to the Jewish weeklies as "Weaklies," alluding, as well, to their policy of avoiding controversy.[37]

The emergence of national magazines, usually monthlies, hardly filled the cultural void. Sponsored by national organizations, they combined the functions of house organs and journals of Jewish affairs. As early as 1886, B'nai B'rith, the first nationwide Jewish secular organization, began publishing *Menorah*, which changed its name to the *B'nai B'rith News*, then to the *National Jewish Monthly*, and, currently, to the *International Jewish Monthly*. The parent journal was described in an 1893 survey of the Jewish press as containing, besides "official matter and what appertains to subordinate lodges, editorials and contributions of a literary and scientific character on Jewish affairs and subjects which are readable and instructive."[38] In 1901 the newly founded Federation of

American Zionists launched the *Maccabaean*. Broad in scope in its early years, it nevertheless fell short of its goal of reaching a general readership. The Intercollegiate Menorah Association, a Jewish campus organization, began publishing the *Menorah Journal* (discussed below) in 1915. Appearing as a quarterly and then as a monthly until 1930, it was published irregularly thereafter, closing down in 1961. During the interwar years, the number of new journals increased. Among those of some moment were the weekly *New Palestine*, which replaced the *Maccabaean* in 1921 and is currently published as a quarterly under the name *American Zionist*; *Liberal Judaism*, first published in 1935 by the Reform movement and now appearing as *American Judaism*; the *Jewish Frontier*, founded by the Labor Zionists in 1934 and still published; and the *Reconstructionist*, begun as a bimonthly in 1935 by the Reconstructionist Foundation (a Jewish religious movement) and now published monthly. Both the *Jewish Frontier* and the *Reconstructionist* are highly respected journals of opinion.[39]

Of the attempts to establish journals of intellectual stature, the *Menorah Journal* warrants attention on two counts. At its peak, during the 1920s, the journal was considered one of the better literary quarterlies in the country. However, literary excellence was also linked to "advancing Jewish culture and ideals." The purpose of the *Menorah Journal* was to demonstrate to those who were ambivalent about their Jewishness that "fostering the Jewish 'humanities' was a spur to human service."[40] For the founders and supporters of the journal, the estrangement of college-educated Jewish men and women from their Jewish past loomed as a major threat to group survival. The convergence of the intellectual challenge, the community's endorsement, the exclusion of Jews from some fields of university teaching, and skillful editing enabled the journal to tap a rich array of talent. It attracted a group of eminent Jewish writers, thinkers, and public figures that included Louis D. Brandeis, Ludwig Lewisohn, and Mordecai M. Kaplan. Among its non-Jewish contributors were John Dewey, Lewis Mumford, and Mark Van Doren.[41] A number of young writers and poets—including Babbette Deutsch, Lionel Trilling, Clifton Fadiman, and Herbert Solow—were drawn to the journal by its young editor from 1925 to 1930, Elliot Cohen. In the course of time, some of the younger writers lost all ties with Jewish life and moved to the radical left or assimilated into the academic and literary world. Others continued to affirm the centrality of their Jewishness, writing for or editing Jewish periodicals. And there were those who moved easily between the two worlds. The tensions were similar to those the Yiddish-speaking intellectuals had experienced—of identifying with universal humanistic values or believing that Jewish culture and ideals furthered those values. For the American-born, however, language gave them the choice their forebears hardly had.[42]

Before considering the recent history of the Anglo-Jewish press, note should be taken of the Judeo-Spanish (Ladino) language newspapers which served the Sephardic Jews (or Sephardim). These Jews, whose ancestors were expelled from Spain in the fifteenth century, immigrated to the United States from Turkey and the Balkan states. Speaking and reading a medieval form of Spanish mixed with some Hebrew and written in Hebrew script, the Sephardic immigrants settled mainly in New York. Language, custom, and certain religious rites divided them from the Yiddish-speaking immigrants. The Sephardim established their own network ᴼᶠ communal institutions, and in 1910 Moise Gadol, a public-spirited immigr⸱⸱⸱ ⸱ ⸱rom Bulgaria, began publishing a weekly, *La America*. The paper offered advice, exhorted its readers to create a united Sephardic community, and published accounts of outlying Sephardic settlements in the South and Far West. In 1925, *La America* succumbed to the rival *La Vara* (The baton), a more popularly written paper, which published until 1948. An influx of Sephardic Jews in the post–World War II era prompted efforts to foster Sephardic culture, but the community was too diverse and the second and third generations too acculturated to support either a Ladino or English periodical.[43]

During the years following the end of World War II, the Anglo-Jewish press mirrored the heightened self-awareness of a Jewish public composed in the main of second- and third-generation Jews. National service organizations like the B'nai B'rith and Hadassah, the women's Zionist organization, expanded the range of their interests, grew in membership, and came to view educational and cultural programs both as important in themselves and as a means of motivating members to fulfill their philanthropic and public service responsibilities. To achieve these ends, B'nai B'rith and Hadassah transformed their newsletters and house organs into mass-circulation, family-type magazines. Professional journalists produced popularly written, attractively laid out journals whose contents ranged widely and briefly over political and cultural topics of Jewish interest and institutional matters of importance to the organization. A member's dues included a subscription to the organization's journal, giving the *Hadassah Magazine* an impressive circulation of nearly 400,000, and B'nai B'rith's *Jewish Monthly* close to 200,000. These circulation figures attracted advertisers and helped to underwrite production costs.[44]

Although the mass-circulation journals sponsored by the national organizations varied, an issue of the *Hadassah Magazine*, by way of example, suggests their character. The August-September 1983 issue featured a symposium on the effect of assimilation on American Jews, a biographical essay on David Ben Gurion, the first prime minister of Israel, and a short story.[45] Columnists posted in Jerusalem and Washington reported on Middle East developments. A freelance writer offered a human-interest story about life in Israel, and a travelogue described historic sites of interest to Jewish tourists visiting Prague. Departments included the president's column, which dealt with the organization; a Hebrew column; a book review section; an art column; and a summary of the month's important events. Except for the president's column, all of the articles were authored by established writers, journalists, and scholars. Nevertheless, the facile style and the brevity of the articles hardly allowed for reflective thought or in-depth analysis.

The Jewish religious press, perhaps the least developed of all areas of Jewish journalism, underwent a similar transformation. The establishment of new synagogues and the expansion of synagogue membership that accompanied the suburbanization of American Jewry invigorated the central directing bodies of the religious wings of Judaism. They were called upon to train and supply rabbinical leadership for the expanding movements, to advise on Jewish education and youth activities, and to raise funds to support the movement's theological seminaries and national institutions. Once again mass circulation magazines became indispensable, providing a sense of denominational identity and loyalty and informing lay members about current religious issues. *Reform Judaism*, the Conservative movement's *United Synagogue Review* and its *Women's League Outlook*, and the Orthodox *Jewish Life*, representing American Judaism's three denominational movements, together reach about 800,000 homes.[46] Yet despite their utility, their content has been criticized for not matching their technical and journalistic standards. Writing in 1963, David Silverman, a Conservative rabbi and educator, depicted the mass-circulation Jewish religious press in these terms:

Editorial focus is so wide as to be meaningless. Many of the articles are of the "how to" variety—how to run a synagogue membership campaign, how to incrase attendance at worship services or how to listen to the rabbi's sermon. There is also the constant note of group self-congratulation. . . . There is no extended treatment or critical analysis of how Judaism can and should affect civil society.[47]

The number of local weeklies has hardly increased since 1950, but they have grown in size, news coverage, and circulation. As the social and cultural barriers dissolved between the older stratum of the community and the much larger element of Americanized and native-born children of the East European migration, the Anglo-Jewish weeklies adapted themselves to a highly organized community committed to group survival at home and financial and political aid for Israel and for Jewish communities under stress abroad. These developments have gone hand in hand with the growth of local federations of Jewish philanthropies. Public relations experts and press officers funnel news releases and other information about the agencies they represent to the community papers. Syndicated columnists and Jewish press associations supply news, commentary, and political analysis. At the same time, traditional features of the community newspapers of the past—announcements of the rites of passage, calendars of community events, and honors—still bulk large in the allocation of space. Background stories on religious holidays, a commentary by a rabbi on the biblical portion of the week, reviews of Jewish books, and departments discussing Jewish art, music, sports, and travel appear with some regularity in most papers.[48]

One consequence of these trends has been a uniformity of tone and an avoidance of controversy. With small, if any, reportorial staffs, the weeklies have been completely dependent on the stock press releases and publicity handouts provided by the major Jewish institutions. National and international affairs tend to be covered in a prosaic fashion since the Jewish news services, mainly the

Jewish Telegraphic Agency, are in part financed by the central communal funds. Finally, critics point to the trend toward community ownership of the weeklies. Of the forty-eight weeklies published in 1985, eight are owned outright by the local federation of philanthropies and others receive financial aid in one form or another from the federation. Community support militates against disinterested criticism, some claim; papers tend to be mouthpieces of the establishment.[49]

Despite these constraints, talented and forceful editors have succeeded in improving the quality of their papers. Those in Baltimore, Philadelphia, Detroit, and Boston are such instances. The Baltimore *Jewish Times*, which claims to be the largest Jewish weekly publication in the nation, for example, is privately owned. Its weekly issues average 175 pages, much of which is advertising. In addition to carrying syndicated columnists, its editors undertake investigatory reporting on local issues. Moreover, the weeklies reach a majority of the Jewish homes in all but the very largest communities. In New York City, a recent sample of the Jewish population indicated that three households in ten received at least one Anglo-Jewish paper. With all their flaws, the weeklies bring their readers news of the Jewish world unavailable elsewhere, and a record of local institutional and social life which fosters communal sensibilities.[50]

However, the mass-circulation press has failed to satisfy the growing segment of the Jewish populace that is college educated, informed on Jewish matters or eager to be, and influential in the community. Nor can the popular Jewish press meet the needs of religious professionals—rabbis, educators, and scholars. To fill this void, a number of serious journals of Jewish thought and letters were established in the postwar years and particularly between 1945 and 1960. Each denominational association of rabbis launched its own quarterly: *Conservative Judaism* in 1945, the *Journal of Reform Judaism* in 1953 (known as the *Journal of the Central Conference of American Rabbis* prior to 1978), and the Orthodox *Tradition* in 1958. The American Jewish Congress, a civic defense agency concerned with protecting Jewish and human rights, began publishing a quarterly, *Judaism*, in 1952, dealing with Jewish religion, philosophy, and ethics. (The organization's more conventional and popular magazine, *Congress Monthly*, was established in 1933.) What is surely the most influential of the intellectual journals, *Commentary*, began appearing monthly in 1945.[51]

Subsidized by the American Jewish Committee but retaining editorial independence, *Commentary* had as its announced aim to be "a journal of significant thought and opinion on Jewish affairs and contemporary issues." Its first editor, Elliot Cohen, brought much of the intellectual zest and originality that marked his years as editor of the *Menorah Journal* in the 1920s to the new magazine. He and his successor, Norman Podhoretz, have kept *Commentary* close to the center of the American intellectual scene, while at the same time addressing Jewish issues of intellectual moment and Jewish communal problems.

In the sense that its editors addressed the American Jewish intellectual more American than Jewish in his knowledge—who was to be shown the intellectual richness of Jewish cultural life—*Commentary* continued the direction of the *Menorah Journal.*[52]

The magazine has discussed the central issues of American society and has contributed to clarifying the Jewish position in provocative essays. By publishing the fiction of Saul Bellow, Elie Wiesel, and Bernard Malamud, the literary criticism of Lionel Trilling and Alfred Kazin, and the writings of scholars like Gershon Scholem and Jacob Katz it has established itself as a notable journal of letters and opinion.[53]

Commentary has also been the object of harsh criticism from its beginning. Among other charges hurled at it, it has been said that it has not treated American Jewish life with sympathetic understanding, that it has overlooked writers identified with Jewish institutional life, and that it increasingly has drawn back from coverage of topics of Jewish interest. Most recently, it has been faulted for its neoconservatism.[54]

One of its most important contributions has been the role it has played as gadfly and stimulant. Other journals of Jewish thought have been founded in part to challenge *Commentary*'s intellectual preeminence among Jewish journals. *Midstream*, established in 1954 under the auspices of the American Zionist movement, focused on Jewish issues, Zionism, diaspora-Israel relations, and contemporary Israeli society. It played an important role in bringing notable Israeli writers to the attention of the English-reading public. *Moment*, an independent monthly, began appearing in 1975 and clearly sought to balance *Commentary*'s detached criticism of Jewish life and its increasingly conservative stance.[55]

During the late 1960s a plethora of "little magazines" appeared, constituting what is known as the Jewish Student Press movement. Influenced by the protest movements of the 1960s and the radical student press, these Jewish student papers carried criticism of the hierarchical, philanthropic character of the Jewish community, the "ossification" of establishment thinking, and the poverty of Jewish spiritual life. Surely the longevity of the editors at the helm of the major journals of Jewish opinion also induced young intellectuals to strike out on their own. A number of periodicals survived the peak of the outburst of protest and dissatisfaction. *Response*, established in 1967, is one such journal. Its issues on the Jewish woman, the *Havura* movement calling for changes in the organization of Jewish synagogue life, and the Yom Kippur War are instances of this genre of magazine at its best.[56]

Taken as a whole, the Anglo-Jewish press of the last four decades reflects the broad social and cultural consensus of an affluent, well-educated, middle-class community both integrated into American life and committed to Jewish group survival. This affluence and intellectual sophistication leads, from time to time, to self-examination, soul-searching, and, for some, disenchantment with the style and content of Jewish life in America. Thus, alongside the mainline press— the weeklies and organizational monthlies that reinforce the sense of community—there exist the journals of opinion, the scholarly periodicals, and the "little magazines" which demonstrate the vitality of Jewish religious and secular life.

NOTES

The author wishes to thank Professor Deborah Dash Moore of Vassar College for her valuable comments on this chapter.

1. Robert Singerman, "The American Jewish Press, 1823–1983: A Bibliographic Survey of Research and Studies," *American Jewish History* 73 (June 1984): 422–444; Joshua A. Fishman, Robert G. Hayden, and Mary E. Warshauer, "The Non-English and the Ethnic Group Press, 1910–1960," in *Language Loyalty in the United States*, ed. Joshua A. Fishman (The Hague: Mouton and Co., 1966), pp. 65–68, 71–73; David Wolf Silverman, "The Jewish Press: A Quadrilingual Phenomenon," in *The Religious Press in America*, ed. Martin E. Marty et al. (New York: Holt, Rinehart and Winston, 1963), pp. 125–126. In his insightful study, which analyzes the Jewish press from the perspective of the religious press, Silverman ignores the nineteenth-century Anglo-Jewish periodicals which most resemble the American religious press.

2. *The Jewish Encyclopedia* (New York: Funk and Wagnals, 1905), 9: 616–640; Albert M. Friedenberg, "Main Currents of American Jewish Journalism: Journals Printed in the German Language," *The Reform Advocate*, May 27, 1916, pp. 516–523; Isaac M. Wise, "Bibliography of the Jewish Periodical Press: German Journals," *The American Israelite*, June 15, 1893, pp. 4–5; *Jewish Newspapers and Periodicals on Microfilm* (Cincinnati: American Jewish Periodicals Center of Hebrew Union College, Jewish Institute of Religion, 1984).

3. Rudolf Glanz, *Studies in Judaica Americana* (New York: KTAV, 1970), pp. 203–247; Naomi W. Cohen, *Encounter with Emancipation: The German Jews in the United States, 1830–1914* (Philadelphia: Jewish Publication Society, 1984), pp. 3–17, 58–63.

4. Arthur A. Goren, *The American Jews* (Cambridge, Mass.: Harvard University Press, 1982), pp. 4–11.

5. Moses Rischin, *The Promised City: New York's Jews, 1870–1914* (Cambridge, Mass.: Harvard University Press, 1962), pp. 38–47.

6. Meyer Waxman, *A History of Jewish Literature* (New York: Yoseoff, 1960), 4: 1283–1289; J. Chaikin, *Yiddishe Bleter in America* (New York: Privately printed, 1946), pp. 112–114, 127–136, 175–178, 231–240.

7. N. Goldberg, "Di yidishe prese in di fareiynikte shtetn, 1900–1940," *YIVO Bleter* 18 (November-December 1941): 100–138; *American Jewish Year Book* 21 (1919–1920): 587–593; 61 (1960); 398–401; 82 (1982): 353–361; *New York Times*, January 5, 1983, part II, p. 4.

8. Mark Wischnitzer, *To Dwell in Safety: The Story of Jewish Migration since 1800* (Philadelphia: Jewish Publication Society, 1948), p. 289; Leonard Dinnerstein, *America and the Survivors of the Holocaust* (New York: Columbia University Press, 1982), p. 287; Chaim I. Waxman, *America's Jews in Transition* (Philadelphia: Temple University Press, 1983), pp. 189–202.

9. Robert E. Cazden, *German Exile Literature in America* (Chicago: American Library Association, 1970), pp. 61–65; C. Waxman, *America's Jews*, pp. 193–196, 197–202; *American Jewish Year Book* 84 (1984): 135, 320–328.

10. Daniel J. Elazar, *Community and Polity: The Organizational Dynamics of Amer-*

ican Jewry (Philadelphia: Jewish Publication Society, 1976), pp. 281–285; Goren, *American Jews*, pp. 100–114.

11. *American Jewish Year Book* 84 (1984): 320–328.

12. George L. Berlin, "Solomon Jackson's *The Jew*: An Early American Jewish Response to Missionaries," *American Jewish History* 71 (September 1981): 10–28; Bertram W. Korn, *Eventful Years and Experiences: Studies in Nineteenth Century American Jewish History* (Cincinnati: American Jewish Archives, 1954), pp. 27–55; Cohen, *Encounter*, pp. 39–55.

13. Maxwell Whiteman, "Isaac Leeser and the Jews of Philadelphia," *Publications of the American Jewish Historical Society* 48 (June 1959): 214–220; Lee M. Friedman, *Pilgrims in a New Land* (New York: Jewish Publication Society, 1948), pp. 163–174; Naomi W. Cohen, "Pioneers of American Jewish Defense," *American Jewish Archives* 29 (November 1977): 119–133; Rudolf Glanz, "Where the Jewish Press Was Distributed in Pre-Civil War America," *Western States Jewish Historical Quarterly* 5 (1972–1973): 4–6.

14. Bertram W. Korn, *American Jewry and the Civil War* (Philadelphia: Jewish Publication Society, 1951), pp. 8–9; James G. Heller, *Isaac Mayer Wise: His Life, Work and Thought* (New York: Union of American Hebrew Congregations, 1965), pp. 267–273; Cohen, "Pioneers," pp. 140–149; Glanz, "Jewish Press," pp. 7–10.

15. Cohen, *Encounter*, p. 165; Hyman B. Grinstein, *The Rise of the Jewish Community of New York 1654–1860* (Philadelphia: Jewish Publication Society, 1947), pp. 88–89, 216–218; *Reform Advocate*, February 20, 1891, p. 1; Robert E. Levinson, "Julius Eckman and the *Weekly Gleaner*: The Jewish Press in the Pioneer American West," in *A Bicentennial Festschrift for Jacob Roder Marcus*, ed. Bertram W. Korn (Waltham, Mass.: KTAV, 1976), pp. 329–336; Isaac Markens, *The Hebrews in America* (New York: Privately printed, 1885), pp. 272–274.

16. Grinstein, *Rise*, pp. 215–217; Lloyd P. Gartner, *History of the Jews of Cleveland* (Cleveland: Western Reserve Historical Society, 1978), pp. 212–213: Stuart Rosenberg, *The Jews of Rochester, 1843–1925* (New York: Columbia University Press, 1954), pp. 99–100; Philip Cowen, *Memories of an American Jew* (New York: Privately printed, 1932), pp. 40–41, 43–84; *Jewish Exponent*, April 15, 1887, p. 1; April 22, 1887, p. 6.

17. *Jewish Comment*, April 26, 1895, p. 4.

18. *Jewish Exponent*, April 22, 1887, pp. 7, 8, 10; May 6, 1887, p. 11; *Jewish Comment*, April 26, 1895, pp. 4–8; May 3, 1895, pp. 5–6; July 19, 1895, pp. 5–8.

19. *Jewish Messenger*, March 29, 1889; September 25, 1891; *Jewish Comment*, April 26, 1895, pp. 1–4, 6–8; *Jewish Exponent*, April 15, 1887, pp. 6–10; May 27, 1887, pp. 3, 5.

20. Samuel Niger, "Yiddish Culture," *The Jewish People, Past and Present* 4 (1955): 271–273; Moshe Shtarkman, "Vichstikste momentn in der geshichte fun der yidisher prese in Amerika," in *75 yor idishe prese in Amerika*, Yaacov Glatshtein et al., eds. (New York: n.p., 1945), pp. 9–25.

21. Louis Greenberg, *The Jews in Russia* (New Haven: Yale University Press, 1944), pp. 101–145; Moses Rischin, *Promised City*, pp. 20, 115–119; Niger, "Yiddish Culture," p. 274.

22. Moshe Davis, *Beyt Yisrael b'Amerika* (Jerusalem: Magnes Press, 1970) pp. 31–66; Shtarkman, "Vichstikste momentn," pp. 15–19.

23. Niger, "Yiddish Culture," p. 273; Chaikin, pp. 46–62.

24. Jonathan Frankel, *Prophecy and Political Socialism, Nationalism and the Russian*

Jews, 1862–1917 (Cambridge, Eng.: Cambridge University Press, 1981), pp. 54–90; Ronald Sanders, *The Downtown Jews: Portrait of an Immigrant Generation* (New York: Harper and Row, 1969), pp. 28–39, 56–75; Irving Howe, *World of Our Fathers* (New York: Harcourt, Brace and Jovanovich, 1976), pp. 101–115.

25. Sanders, *Downtown Jews*, pp. 98–99, 106–113; Abraham Cahan, *Bleiter fun mein Leben* (New York: Forward Assn., 1926), 2: 240–243.

26. Rischin, *Promised City*, pp. 129–130; Sanders, *Downtown Jews*, pp. 100–103, 372–378; Ezra Mendelsohn, "The Russian Roots of the American Jewish Labor Movement," *YIVO* 16 (1976): 168–170.

27. J. K. Miklisanski, "Hebrew Literature in the United States," *The Jewish People, Past and Present* 4 (1955): 308–309; Rischin, *Promised City*, pp. 127–128; M. Waxman, *History* 4: 1297–1303; Michael Gary Brown, "All, All Alone: The Hebrew Press in America from 1914 to 1924," *American Jewish Historical Quarterly* 59 (1969–1970): 139–163.

28. Frankel, *Prophecy*, pp. 171–227; Howe, *World*, pp. 291–295.

29. Howe, *World*, pp. 240, 500–507; Arthur A. Gorenstein [Goren], "A Portrait of Ethnic Politics," *Publications of the American Jewish Historical Society* 50 (March 1961): 202–226.

30. Sanders, *Downtown Jews*, pp. 128–131; Chaikin, *Yiddishe Bleter*, pp. 104–112.

31. Shtarkman, "Vichstikste momentn," pp. 40–41; Chaikin, *Yiddishe Bleter*, pp. 104–112.

32. Chaikin, *Yiddishe Bleter*, pp. 195–214; Niger, "Yiddish Culture," pp. 294–300; Howe, *World*, pp. 503–507.

33. Mordecai Soltes, *The Yiddish Press* (New York: n.p., 1925), pp. 137–138, 155–157, 178–180, 189, 212–214; Howe, *World*, p. 531; *Morgen Zhurnal*, December 7, 1906, p. 1; December 10, 1906, p. 4; December 23, 1906, p. 1; December 24, 1906, pp. 1–5.

34. Chaikin, *Yiddishe Bleter*, pp. 175–195; Howe, *World*, pp. 533–543; Arthur Aryeh Goren, "Orthodox Politics, Republican Jews: Jacob Sapherstein and the *Morgen Zhurnal*," Eighth World Congress of Jewish Studies, Panel Session, Jewish History, *Proceedings* (Jerusalem, 1984), pp. 65–71.

35. Howe, *World*, pp. 451–459, 542–545.

36. *American Jewish Year Book*, 1900, pp. 636–637; ibid. 52 (1951); ibid. 53 (1952), p. 235; Goren, *American Jews*, p. 2; Fishman, *Language Loyalty*, pp. 35–44; Goldberg, *YIVO Bleter* 18: 140, 155–157.

37. *The American Israelite*, September 17, 1936, pp. 2, 4–7; November 5, 1931, pp. 2–7; *Jewish Exponent*, January 24, 1936, pp. 7–8; January 17, 1936, pp. 1–3, 5–8; *American Hebrew*, November 1, 1929, pp. 757–759, 768; May 24, 1929, pp. 44–47; April 8, 1938, pp. 22–26; Gary Rosenblatt, "The Jewish de-Press," *Moment*, November 1977, p. 46.

38. Wise, *The American Israelite*, June 15, 1893, pp. 4–5.

39. Naomi W. Cohen, "The *Maccabaean*'s Message: A Study in American Zionism until World War I," *Jewish Social Studies* 18 (July 1956): 163–166; *American Jewish Year Book* 38 (1936): 537–543; ibid. 23 (1921): 272–276; ibid. 32 (1930): 208–212; ibid. 53 (1952): 506–511.

40. *The Menorah Journal* 1 (January 1915): 1.

41. Ibid., pp. 13–19; Mordecai Kaplan, "Toward a Reconstruction of Judaism," ibid. 13 (April 1927): 113–130; Ludwig Lewisohn, "Midchannel," ibid. 15 (September 1928):

231–254; John Dewey, "The Principle of Nationality," ibid. 3 (October 1917): 203–208.

42. Mark L. Krupnick, *"The Menorah Journal* Group and the Origins of Modern Jewish Radicalism," in Ralph M. Aderman, ed., *The Quest for Social Justice* (Madison: University of Wisconsin Press, 1983), pp. 235–251; Alan Wald, "The *Menorah* Group Moves Left," *Jewish Social Studies* (Summer-Fall 1976): 289–320; Robert Alter, "Epitaph for a Jewish Magazine: Notes on the *Menorah Journal*," *Commentary* (May 1965): 51–55; Alan Wald, "Herbert Solow: Portrait of a New York Intellectual," *Prospects*, no. 3 (1977): 423–436; Elinor Grumet, "Elliot Cohen: The Vocation of a Jewish Literary Mentor," *Studies in the American Jewish Experience* 1 (1981): 8–25.

43. Marc D. Angel, *La America: The Sephardic Experience in the United States* (Philadelphia: Jewish Publication Society, 1982), pp. 11–16, 107–128.

44. Deborah Dash Moore, *B'nai B'rith and the Challenge of Ethnic Leadership* (Albany: State University of New York Press, 1981), pp. 195–249.

45. The symposium included the following participants: Arthur Hertzberg, Blu Greenberg, Milton Himmelfarb, and Robert Gordis.

46. Silverman, "The Jewish Press," pp. 150–151, 153–158.

47. Ibid., p. 152.

48. Bernard Postal, "The English-Jewish Press," *Dimensions in American Judaism* 4 (Fall 1969): 31–34; *American Jewish Year Book* 85 (1985): 392–399.

49. Rosenblatt, "The Jewish de-Press," pp. 46–48; Silverman, "The Jewish Religious Press," pp. 161–166; Donald Altschiller, "The Problems and Prospects of Jewish Journalism," in *The Sociology of American Jews*, ed. Jack Nusan Porter (Washington, D.C.: University Press of America, 1978), pp. 155–162.

50. *Jewish Times* (Baltimore), September 6, 1985; Rosenblatt, "The Jewish de-Press," pp. 44–48.

51. Robert Gordis, "The Genesis of *Judaism*: A Chapter of Jewish Cultural History," *Judaism* 30 (1981): 390–395; Silverman, "The Jewish Press," pp. 149–150.

52. William Novak, *"Commentary* and the Jewish Community: The Record since 1960," *Response* 19 (Fall 1973): 49–56; Bernard Avishai, "Breaking Faith, *Commentary* and the American Jew," *Dissent* 28 (1981): 237–241.

53. Symposia such as "Jewishness and the Younger Intellectuals," *Commentary* (April 1961): 306–359, and "The State of Jewish Belief," ibid. (August 1966): 71–100, became benchmarks in measuring the intellectual profile of American Jews. By their selection of participants, *Commentary* editors were accused by critics of skewing the results.

54. Novak, "Commentary," pp. 57–66; Avishai, "Breaking Faith," pp. 242–256.

55. *Midstream* 1 (Autumn 1955); ibid. (April 1969); *Moment* (January 1976): 13–17; ibid. (October 1978): 11–16.

56. David De Nola, "The Jewish Student Press—Pulsebeat of the Movement," *Jewish Book Annual* 32 (1975–76): 33–36; *Response* 4 (Winter 1970–1971); 5–7, 17–19; ibid. 7 (Summer 1973): 2–187; ibid. 7 (Winter 1973–1974): 5–155.

BIBLIOGRAPHY

Altschiller, Donald. "The Problems and Prospects of Jewish Journalism." In *The Sociology of American Jews*, ed. Jack Nusan Porter. Washington, D.C.: University Press of America, 1978.

Brown, Michael Gary. "All, All Alone: The Hebrew Press in America from 1914 to 1924." *American Jewish Historical Quarterly* 59 (1969–1970): 139–163.

Cazden, Robert E. *German Exile Literature in America*. Chicago: American Library Association, 1970.

Chaikin, J. *Yiddishe Bleter in America*. New York: Privately printed, 1946.

Friedenberg, Albert M. "Main Currents of American Jewish Journalism: Journals Printed in the German Language." *The Reform Advocate*, May 27, 1916, pp. 516–523.

Glanz, Rudolf. "Where the Jewish Press Was Distributed in Pre-Civil War America." *Western States Jewish Historical Quarterly* 5 (1972–1973): 4–6.

Goldberg, N. "Di yidishe prese in di fareiynikte shtetn, 1900–1940." *YIVO Bleter* 18 (November-December 1941): 100–138.

Jewish Newspapers and Periodicals on Microfilm. Cincinnati: American Jewish Periodicals Center of Hebrew Union College, Jewish Institute of Religion, 1984.

Levinson, Robert E. "Julius Eckman and the *Weekly Gleaner*: The Jewish Press in the Pioneer American West." In *A Bicentennial Festschrift for Jacob Roder Marcus*, ed. Bertram W. Korn. Waltham, Mass.: KTAV, 1976.

Miklisanski, J. K. "Hebrew Literature in the United States." *The Jewish People, Past and Present* 4 (1955): 308–309.

Niger, Samuel. "Yiddish Culture." *The Jewish People, Past and Present* 4 (1955): 271–273.

Rosenblatt, Gary. "The Jewish de-Press." *Moment* (November 1977).

Shtarkman, Moshe. "Vichstikste momentn in der geshichte fun der yidisher prese in Amerika." In *75 yor idishe prese in Amerika*, ed. Yaacov Glatshtein et al. New York: N.p., 1945.

Silverman, David Wolf. "The Jewish Press: A Quadrilingual Phenomenon." In *The Religious Press in America*, ed. Martin E. Marty et al. New York: Holt, Rinehart and Winston, 1963.

Singerman, Robert. "The American Jewish Press, 1823–1983: A Biobibliographic Survey of Research and Studies." *American Jewish History* 73 (June 1984): 422–444.

Soltes, Mordecai. *The Yiddish Press*. New York: N.p., 1925.

Wise, Isaac M. "Bibliography of the Jewish Periodical Press: German Journals." *The American Israelite*, June 15, 1893, pp. 4–5.

15

The Latvian and Lithuanian Press

EDGAR ANDERSON AND M. G. SLAVENAS

The Latvians and Lithuanians hail from the Baltic countries, which form a distinct geographic group on the eastern shores of the Baltic Sea and comprise the modern republics of Lithuania, Latvia, and Estonia. While, in some respects, they also have a common history, they are ethnically and linguistically diverse. The Lithuanian and Latvian languages belong to the ancient Baltic branch of the Indo-European linguistic family, forming a link between the Slavic and Teutonic branches. The Estonian language belongs to an equally ancient Finno-Ugric family of languages. Within this linguistic diversity, the Estonians and Latvians are united by a common Lutheran faith, similar history, and parallel cultural trends. The eastern Latvians, called Latgallians, serve as a link with the Lithuanians, sharing a common Roman Catholic Church, similar cultural developments, and centuries-old historical ties. During the second half of the sixteenth century all Lithuania and Latvia had been united politically, but the union did not last long enough to have a permanent influence.

LATVIAN ETHNIC PRESS

The first Latvians arrived in North America during the seventeenth century along with the Swedes; Latvians also came from their own West Indian settlements in Tobago. Sporadic Latvian emigration continued during the latter part of the eighteenth century and the first half of the nineteenth century. The most distinguished immigrant from Latvia was Georg Heinrich Loskiel (1740–1814), bishop of the Moravian Church, famed Latvian poet, and successful missionary among the Indians. For some time the Latvians were too few in number to consider bringing out publications in their own language. The 1850 census, which grouped Latvians and Lithuanians together because they spoke related languages, counted 3,160 Latvians and Lithuanians in the United States; in 1870 the number had reached 4,644.

The situation changed radically, though, during the latter part of the nineteenth century when thousands of Latvians arrived in the United States to escape persecution by their German and Russian overlords, to find better employment in the New World, and to enjoy greater secular religious freedom. The 1900 census showed a total of 4,309 Latvians residing in the United States, but this figure did not include a number of stowaway Latvian sailors or the many Latvians registered by U.S. immigration officials as Russians, Germans, or Scandinavians. Their recognized leader was Jacob Sieberg (Zībergs, 1863–1963), who founded the first Latvian Evangelical Lutheran Church and the first Latvian Benefit Society in the United States; he also published seven books and established the first Latvian newspaper in the United States, the *Amerikas Vēstnesis* (American herald), which appeared twice monthly from June 1, 1896, to December 15, 1919. From 1916 to 1918 it also contained a monthly supplement, the *Baznīca un Skola* (Church and school). The tone of the newspaper was strongly nationalistic and religious. It also stressed loyalty to the United States, and from 1917 to 1919 advocated independence for Latvia.

The late nineteenth century, which saw the arrival of deeply religious Latvian nationalists, also witnessed the advent of the first Latvian socialists and anarchists, who not only hated the Russian tsarist regime but also dreamed about an international socialist brotherhood. With the exception of their common language and similar difficulties in adjusting to new conditions in their chosen haven, they found nothing in common with Latvians who did not share their Marxist and atheistic convictions. Their oldest publication was a weekly newspaper, the *Amerikas Latviešu Avīze* (American Latvian newspaper), which made its brief appearance from October 21, 1896, to March 3, 1897. It was followed by a "scientific and literary socialist" monthly, the *Auseklis* (Morning star), from April 1898, to August 1901. Its most distinguished editor was Dāvīds Bundža (1873–1901). All three periodicals were published in Boston.

From November 1901 to December 1905 a religious and literary Latvian Baptist monthly, the *Amerikas Latvietis* (American Latvian), made its appearance in Philadelphia. More Latvian Baptist publications followed. In content a very distinctive Latvian Lutheran weekly newspaper, the *Dieva Sveiksme* (Praise to the Lord) made its brief appearance in Boston from January 1 to March 23, 1906. It was published by the colorful and poetic pastor Jānis Steiks (1855–1932).

From April 1902 to October 9, 1917, an official monthly of the Latvian Social-Democratic Society (later the American Latvian Social Democratic Workers Federation), the *Proletārietis* (The proletarian), was published, at first in Boston, then from July 1903 to June 1904 in Zurich (Switzerland), then again in Boston, and from August 1912 in New York. Its most distinguished editors were Dr. Miķelis Valters (1874–1968), Ernests Rolavs (1874–1907), and Jūlijs Vecozols (1884–1945). As early as 1903 the paper demanded the separation of Latvia from Russia. From 1913 to 1914 its circulation reached 10,000 copies. The paper was not radical enough for some American Latvian socialists, who briefly continued the traditions of the *Amerikas Latviešu Avīzes* by publishing their own monthly, later bimonthly, the *Amerikānietis* (The American), from January 1904 to December 15, 1905. This, too, was published in Boston.

In the meantime, a bloody Latvian revolution, led by socialists against the Russian tsarist regime, had run its course from January 1905 to the end of 1906. Thousands of Latvian revolutionaries who survived the confrontation with the tsarist armed forces made their way to Western Europe and North and South America. Unlike the earlier emigrants, they were well educated and considered themselves as missionaries of the socialist gospel even in their new countries of refuge. Although they left their country of origin as fighters for a good cause, in the United States they were generally viewed as dangerous radicals. They needed new periodicals to express their ideas and viewpoints. Thus the official monthly (later weekly) of the Latvian Organization of the American Socialist Party (after 1919 the American Communist Party), the *Strādnieks* (Worker), was published from January 1, 1906, to December 30, 1919. Its most important editors were Jānis Kļava (1882–1922), Dr. Jānis Ozols (1878–1968), and Fricis Roziņš (1870–1919). It was published in Boston and had monthly supplements, *Māksla un Zinība* (Arts and science, 1907–1908) and *Strādnieka Literārais Pielikums* (Worker's literary supplement, 1907–1908). From July 1907 to June 1908 a socialist political, scholarly, and literary journal, the *Brīvā Tribūna* (Free tribune), appeared in New York. The year 1907 also witnessed the birth of an arts journal, the *Zvans* (The bell), in Philadelphia.

The Latvian anarchists made their appearance in New York with their official paper, the *Brīvība* (Liberty), from December 1908 to 1913. From June 1909 to the fall of 1910 it was published in Paris, France. A splinter group of Latvian anarchists published its own periodical, the *Melnais Karogs* (The black flag) from 1911 to 1914, at first in Paris, but from August 1912 to July 1914 in New York. In 1909 another official socialist paper of the Organization for the Liberation of the Proletariat, the *Internacionāle* (The international), was published underground somewhere in the United States.

Other kinds of Latvian publications also made their appearance in this period. A religious newspaper, the *Laiks un Mūžība* (Time and eternity), was published by poet Fricis Freidenfelds (1886–1959) in Boston in 1908. A political, humorous, and satirical arts magazine, the *Pērkons* (The thunder), was published by Kristaps Rāviņs (born 1886) and Jānis Līdumnieks (Lejenietis) in Philadelphia from September 1909 to July 1911. The latter writer also edited a political, scholarly, and literary journal, the *Gaisma* (The light), in New York in May 1912. Its offshoot was the *Dekadentu Gaisma* (Light of decadents). A religious group in New York published the short-lived *Ļauzu Kancelis* (People's pulpit) in 1912.

Several other short-lived Latvian publications appeared during World War I. From September 1913 to September 1917 the *Jaunā Tēvija* (The new homeland) appeared in Philadelphia. There was the *Apskats* (Review) in Chicago, a monthly, which was started in January 1914 and ran for at least sixteen issues. A solid literary and artistic monthly, the *Prometējs* (The Prometheus), was published regularly in San Francisco from July 1915 to October 1917 by Jānis Ozoliņs (Burtnieks, 1894–1959). Finally, the *Drauga Balss* (Voice of a friend), an illustrated, progressive Latvian Baptist journal, was published in New York from December 1917 to December 15, 1919.

An ambitious Latvian nationalist newspaper, the *Amerikas Atbalss* (American echo), replaced the oldest Latvian newspaper, *Amerikas Vēstnesis*, in 1920. It was published in New York and had as editors Christopher Roos (Rūsis, 1887–1963) and Kristaps Rāviņš. It also had an English supplement. The newspaper survived, however, only until 1922. The expected assistance from the new government of independent Latvia was not forthcoming. This government had been helped by the *Latvija Amerikā* (Latvia in America), the bulletin of the Central Committee of the American National Lettish League, in 1919. The Latvian nationalist press in America disintegrated because periodicals were readily available from Latvia.

Little is known about some American-Latvian communist publications, among them the *Komunists* (The communist; 1917 [?]), the *Jaunais Prometējs* (The new Prometheus), the *Liesma* (The flame), and the *Āzis* (Billy-Goat), all most likely published in 1919 and having no more than a few issues each. In 1920 there also appeared a *Biļetens* (Bulletin) of the "Worker" subgroup of the Philadelphia Latvian Social-Democrats.

In the struggle for domination in Latvia, the radicalized socialists, communists, and anarchists had lost to the overwhelming majority of nationalists. Most radical socialists and communists went to the Soviet Union or remained in the United States, where they felt the need for publications of their own to unite them and sharpen their ideological sense. Boston again became the site of the Latvian communist publications. From January 29, 1920, to December 30, 1922, the communist weekly newspaper the *Rīts* (Morning) was published by the Latvian section of the American Communist Party. Renamed *Strādnieku Rīts* (Workers' morning), it continued to appear from January 6, 1923, to December 29, 1934. In 1934 it was merged with the *Amerikas Cīņa* (Struggle of America), the Latvian organ of the American Labor (Communist) Party and of the American Latvian Workers' Association, which was published in the quarters of the *Daily Worker* in Chicago (later in New York and Boston) from March 16, 1926, to 1934. After the merger both of these newspapers appeared as the *Strādnieku Cīņa* (Workers' struggle) from January 5, 1935, to 1939 in Boston as a weekly. *Strādnieku Cīņa* was replaced by the *Amerikas Latvietis* (The American Latvian), which was published in Boston from 1940 to 1976, with heavy subsidies from American and Soviet communist sources. After the "old guard" of the Latvian communists had gone to their graves, the newspaper ceased publication because it lacked sufficient readers. In 1945 it had become the mouthpiece of the Latvian communist government created by the Soviet Union after its military takeover of Latvia. The editors and publishers of this newspaper were Eduards Mauriņš

(1889–1982), Jānis Liepiņš (Richard Hansen, 1879–1951), and Kārlis (Charles) Dirba (1887–1969).

During the interwar period a few feeble attempts were also made to revive the American Latvian nationalist press. In 1926, in New York, Gustavs Dancis (1877–1953) launched a moderate nationalist newspaper, *Amerikas Latviešu Ziņas* (American Latvian news), but it closed the same year because of financial problems. A longer run was enjoyed by the Latvian journal *Auseklitis* (The little morning star), which was published in Boston from 1926 to 1933.

During World War II moderately nationalistic and fervently religious American Latvian Baptists became very active. From April 1941 to October 1944 the cultural and religious monthly (later quarterly) *Ausma* (The dawn) was published in Boston by Dr. John Daugman (1903–1952); and from February 15, 1942, to March 1947 another Baptist monthly, *Drauga Vēsts* (A message from a friend), was published in New York by Dr. Kārlis Purgailis (1909–). These publications defended the rights of Latvia to regain its independence from the yoke of Nazi Germany and Soviet Russia. They also supported Latvian refugees and displaced persons who had become homeless and those who did not want to live in their homeland, which was now occupied by Soviet armies and security forces which had engaged, since 1941, in genocide and wholesale deportation of the Baltic peoples.

Tens of thousands of Latvian displaced persons, refugees, and sailors reached the shores of the United States. Most of the newcomers were highly educated and imbued with a spirit of Latvian nationalism. They were mainly interested in restoration of independent Latvia and had little in common with the "Old Latvians" of America. They created their own press, newspapers, and journals, for a variety of purposes. Because of their education, experience, and, in many cases, previous knowledge of English, it was not difficult for most of them to adapt themselves at least outwardly to the American way of life. Unlike the Latvian communists, the newcomers wholeheartedly supported the U.S. government and the American democratic system. In time they established roots in American society, still remaining faithful to their Latvian nationality and culture and their perceived mission to help regain independence for their homeland.

The first of the new breed of the Latvian publications was the monthly *Tālos Krastos* (At the distant shores), an illustrated newspaper published in Philadelphia by Edgars Brūveris (1920–1977) and Dr. Edgar Anderson (1920–) from June 23, 1948, to January 25, 1950. It soon gave way to the most important American Latvian newspaper to date, the *Laiks* (The time), in Brooklyn, New York, which has been published twice weekly without interruption since November 8, 1949, by a highly successful veteran publisher, Helmārs Rudzītis (1903–). Its circulation has been constantly maintained at 12,000 to 13,000, and it has subscribers all over the world. From January 1955 to December 1963 it also contained a literary monthly supplement, *Laika Mēnešraksts* (Time monthly). The newspaper has employed a number of distinguished professional editors, Kārlis Rabācs

(1902–1983), Arvīds Klāvsons (1900–1964), Ēriks Raisters (1905–1967), Ēvalds Freivalds (1913–1969), Arturs Strautmanis (1910–), Jānis Vītols (1911–), and Dr. Ilgvars Spilners (1925–). Veteran newsman Olgerts Liepiņš (1906–1983) published his own newspaper, *Amerikas Vēstnesis* (Messenger of America), from October 11, 1955, to October 25, 1967, continued as *Vēstnesis* since December 1973, with the help of Osvalds Akmentiņš (1914–) in Boston. It often attacks the "seamy side" of the Latvian society here and its presumed lack of patriotism. Highly nationalistic in content is the Canadian Latvian weekly newspaper *Latvija Amerikā* (Latvia in America), which has been published in Toronto since October 6, 1951, and enjoys considerable readership in the United States. Its principal editors have been Dr. Hugo Vītols (1900–1976), Ingrida Vīksna (1920–), and Aleksandrs Kundrats (1915–), and its editor in the United States is Viktors Irbe (1922–).

According to the U.S. Census, in 1930 only 38,091 persons declared themselves as Latvian, but the census of 1970 counted 86,413 Latvian Americans residing in the United States. Actually there were more than 100,000 Latvians, but many of them no longer labeled themselves Latvians. Practically all of them were bilingual, and some were trilingual. Many still maintained professional interests in various enterprises in Latvia or functioned within their fields from a Latvian point of view. These factors help to account for the highly diversified Latvian magazine literature in the United States. There was high enough circulation to maintain publication, and the publishers and editors donated their time and labor. For political and cultural reasons some of these publications also appeared in English.

The beautifully illustrated magazine the *Tilts* (The bridge) appeared quite regularly in Minneapolis from December 1949 to 1976. Its sole publisher and editor was Hugo Skrastiņš (1914–). Another important magazine, the *Treji Vārti* (Three gates), has been published in Michigan since January 1967. Its principal publishers and editors have been Alberts Birnbaums (1903–), Roberts Krūklītis (1906–), Dr. Nikodem Bojars (1925–) and Dr. Edgar Anderson (1920–). Of shorter duration were the *Atstari* (Reflectors), published in Grand Rapids, Michigan, from November 1951, to December 1959; the *Laikmets* (The era), published in Minneapolis from June 1953 to 1968 by Arvīds Eglītis (1921–); and the *Latvju Žurnāls* (Latvian journal), published in New York by Vilis Stāls (1908–) from November 1951 to June 1956.

Five major religious magazines have been published in the United States recently: the *Ceļa Biedrs* (Travel companion), a Lutheran monthly in Minneapolis since January 1956; the *Dzimtenes Balss* (The voice of the native country), a Catholic monthly in Chicago since January 1969; the *Jaunais Laikmets* (The new era), a journal of the Latvian New Church in New Jersey since the fall of 1952; the *Kristīgā Balss* (Christian voice), a Baptist monthly published in the United States and Canada since July 1950; and the *Labietis*, a journal devoted to the protection of ancient Latvian religious beliefs and traditions, published every third month since January 1955.

Latvian children and youth have their own magazines. The most popular is the *Mazputniņš* (Little birdie), edited by Dr. Laimonis Streips (1931–) and Līga Streips (1936–) since January 1959. There is also a Lutheran periodical for little children, the *Bitīte* (The little bee), published since January 1948; others include the religious periodical *Jaunatnes Ceļš* (The road of the youth), published since 1969; the illustrated youth magazine *Mēs* (We), which appeared in the United States and Canada from July 1961 to the spring of 1969; and the *Mūsu Ceļš* (Our road), which made a brief appearance from September 1956 to March 1960.

There are also several military magazines: the *Daugavas Vanagi* (later *Daugavas Vanagu Mēnešraksts*; the Monthly for the hawks of the Dauagava), in existence since January 1954; the *Kadets* (The cadet), since 1967; the *Kaŗa Invalids* (The war invalid), since 1957; the *Lāčplēsis* (The bear slayer), from January 1946 to 1978; and the *Strēlnieks* (The rifleman), a magazine of the veterans of World War I, published since January 1957, at first in New York, and later in Chicago.

There are also many specialized magazines and journals. Those which appear in Europe and have only some American-Latvian editors are excluded from this account. A number of magazines are published mainly in the United States, however. Deserving mention are the *Dzelzceļnieks Trimdā* (The railroader in exile; 1953–83), as well as a number of magazines for Latvian philatelists, numismatists, and collectors in general: the *Latviešu Filatēlists* (1956–1966), *Kolekcionārs* (1959–1965), *Krājējs* (Collector; since 1966), and the *Latvian Collector* (since 1968). Latvian chess players have produced *Latvian Gambit* (since 1968). Latvian lawyers published *Laviešu Juristu Raksti* (Annals of the Latvian jurists; 1959–1968). Even Latvian newsmen had their own publications, including a yearbook from 1952 to 1953; and young Latvian writers have published *Lara's Lapa* (Sheet of LARA) since 1974. Track and field athletes put out *Latvju Vieglatlētika* from 1963 to 1967. Theater enthusiasts issued *Skatuve un Dzīve* (The stage and life) from September 1959 to January 1962. Foresters published *Meža Vēstis* (The news from the forest) from June 1948 to the fall of 1981 and since then *Meža Šalkas* (Rustle of the forest). Agriculturists have produced *Zeme un Tauta* (The land and people) since 1955. The *Latvju Mūzika* (Latvian music) has been regularly published in Michigan since July 1968, and the more recent *Latvju Māksla* (Latvian arts) has been published in Michigan since May 1975. There are also several academic journals: the *Akadēmiskā Dzīve* (Academic life; since 1958), the *Latviešu Humanitāro Zinātņu Asociācijas Rakstu Krājumi* (The annals of the Latvian Humanities and Social Science Association; since 1957, with summaries in English), the *Baltic Students News* (1964–1970), the *Universitas* (since 1954; circulation 6,000), and the *Vārti* (The gates; 1952–1953).

Political journals have been published mostly in English, such as the *Baltic Appeal to the United Nations* (May 1967-March 1968), *Baltic Review* (1953–1970), *Latvian Bulletin* (1951–1953), *Latvian Information Bulletin* (since 1940 in Washington, D.C.), *La Revue Baltique* (1959–1960, in French), *Revista Bál-*

tica (in New York and Buenos Aires, in Spanish, 1957–1967), and *Latvijas Brīvībai* (For freedom to Latvia; 1952–1969). The American Latvian Association also issues a number of regular publications for various purposes. Last but not least, one should also mention a plethora of circulars and bulletins of more or less local importance in a number of dense Latvian settlements and societies.

There are no signs to indicate that the Latvian national press will disappear in the United States in the foreseeable future. Latvian Americans have taken the opportunities offered by the United States for shelter and work. Although a small group, they have every reason to be proud of their contributions to their adopted homeland, particularly in various fields of science and its practical applications. At the same time, they have political reasons to maintain their national consciousness and their national press in order to bolster the spirit of their suppressed fellow Latvians in the homeland.

BIBLIOGRAPHY

Anderson, Edgar. "Latvians." In *Harvard Encyclopedia of American Ethnic Groups,* ed. Stephan Thernstrom. Cambridge, Mass.: Harvard University Press, 1980, pp. 638–642.
————. "Latvians Abroad." In *Cross-Road Country Latvia*, ed. Edgar Anderson. Waverly, Ia.: Latvju Grāmata, 1953, pp. 342–357.
Bibliography of Latvian Publications Published Outside Latvia 1940–1960, comp. Benjaminš Jēgers. 2 vols. Stockholm: Daugava, 1968–1972.
Bibliography of Latvian Publications Published Outside Latvia 1961–1970, comp. Benjaminš Jegers. Stockholm: Daugava, 1977.
Latviešu periodika. Vol. 1. 1768–1919. 2d ed. Comp. K. Egle, V. Lūkina, Ā. Brempele, and V. Jaugietis. Riga: Latvijas PSR Zinātņu akadēmija, Fundamentālā bibliotēka, 1977.
Latviesu periodika. Vol. 2. 1920–1940. Revolucionārā un padomju periodika. Comp. Ā. Brempele, E. Flīgere, and V. Lūkina. Riga: Latvijas PSR Zinātņu akadēmija, Fundamentālā bibliotēka, 1976.

LITHUANIAN ETHNIC PRESS

A noteworthy achievement of the Lithuanian-American community is its extensive press, which was created at the end of the nineteenth century during the first massive wave of Lithuanian immigration and is sustained in the 1980s by post–World War II émigrés.[1] Its development in the first phase of its history is closely linked with the rise of Lithuanian national consciousness, which was imported to this country in the 1880s and 1890s by a handful of young intellectuals; they had been influenced by the ideas of the Lithuanian national revival formulated in the pages of *Aušra* (Dawn), published from 1883 to 1886 in East Prussia.[2] Their attempts to rouse the community and their disputes in defining community membership resulted in the proliferation of short-lived periodicals (many of them published and edited by the same persons or groups) which is characteristic of this phase.

The first massive waves of Lithuanian immigration began after the abortive Polish-Lithuanian uprising of 1863 and continued until about 1914, at which time about 200,000 people had entered the United States. Unlike the participants of the 1863 insurrection, who belonged to the Polish-educated intelligentsia, the vast majority of immigrants in the 1860s and 1870s were unskilled single young men from Lithuanian villages who had very vague notions about their national identity. Because Lithuania was under Russian rule and heavy Polish influence, they were classified as Russians or Poles by the U.S. immigration authorities, who did not establish a separate entry for Lithuanians until 1899; the federal census did not distinguish Lithuanians from other groups until 1910.

While precise figures are not available, it is estimated that by the end of the century about 50,000 Lithuanians had already settled in the coal mining towns of eastern Pennsylvania and the large industrial cities of New York, Boston, Baltimore, Cleveland, and Chicago. They settled close to established Polish communities and joined Polish congregations, but as their numbers grew in the 1870s and 1880s, so grew the number of those who wanted church services and organizations in their own language.

The first Lithuanian newspaper, *Lietuwiszka Gazieta* (Lithuanian gazette), appeared in New York in 1879, about four years before *Aušra*. It was published by Mikas Tvarauskas, a survivor of the 1863 uprising, who also compiled and printed the first English-Lithuanian dictionary. Like many after him, Tvarauskas served as publisher, editor, and typesetter, found subscribers, and collected payments. His paper, which had 139 paid subscribers, died the following year. Nevertheless, Tvarauskas tried again in 1884, this time in cooperation with twenty-three-year-old Jonas Šliūpas, a new arrival, who before emigrating had lived in East Prussia; an *Aušra* editor, he was sought by Russian and German authorities for his political activities. Tvarauskas decided to call the new paper *Unija* (Unity), a reminder of the historical union between the two nations. Šliūpas, as did others associated with *Aušra*, rejected this heritage and promoted Lithuania's cultural, historical, and linguistic distinctiveness. Collaboration proved impossible and the two men separated. In 1885 *Unija* died, and Šliūpas started his own paper, *Lietuwiszkasis Balsas* (Lithuanian voice), with about 500 subscribers, which lasted until 1889. He also founded and listed as publisher Lietuvos Mylėtoju Draugija (Lithuanian Patriots' Association.)

Dr. Jonas Šliūpas remains a singular figure in the history of Lithuanian America, which he helped to shape as author, publisher, editor, public speaker, founder of numerous societies, and spokesman for the left wing. He introduced socialism and freethinking to his countrymen, and he was especially consistent in his attempts to raise the level of their education and to heighten their ethnic awareness independent of the church. Šliūpas's entry into the publishing field is significant because it affirmed the special link of the young press with *Aušra* and the commitment to maintain the written culture which was prohibited at home. As a former *Aušra* editor, Šliūpas created a network of contributors from Lithuania, among them Juozas Andziulaitis, Juozas Adomaitis-Šernas, and his future wife, Eglė Malinauskaitė. Like Tvarauskas before him, Šliūpas was acutely aware of the dual role of his periodical.[3] Unlike the typical ethnic newspaper, whose main function is to cushion the shock of uprooting by providing the newcomer with moral and practical support during the difficult period of adjustment, the Lithuanian-American press from its very beginning addressed not only the immigrant community but also readers in the homeland who received it clandestinely via the "book carriers." Thus a precedent was set to be followed by all Lithuanian-American publications until the revocation of the press ban in 1904 and to a lesser degree until the restoration of Lithuania's independence in 1918. The growth of Lithuanian America as a publishing center surpassing East Prussia was demonstrated by the Lithuanian ethnographic exhibit during the Paris World Fair in 1900.[4]

Although *Lietuwiszkasis Balsas* was received with enthusiasm in Lithuania, it had little mass appeal in the New World. Nevertheless, it was perceived as a threat by the large pro-Polish segment of the community, which threw its support behind a new periodical published in Plymouth, Pennsylvania, in 1886, by J. Paukzstis, a young local businessman who soon became a book publisher as well. *Wienibė Lietuwninkų* (Unity of Lithuanians), its name eventually changed to *Vienybė*, is today the oldest Lithuanian-American periodical and celebrated its centennial in 1986. Although it was founded to preserve the status quo under the tutelage of the clergy, its editorial position kept changing with its editors, even within the first decade of its existence, and by 1895 it had already established its independence from church control.[5] In general, *Vienybė* tried to follow a nonaligned middle position. Its many changes reflect the changes which the community underwent.

Under its first editor, D. T. Bačkauskas, *Vienybė* promoted the "Catholic life" and good Polish-Lithuanian relations, while Reverend A. Varnagiris and Reverend M. Juodyszius used its pages to anathematize Šliūpas and prohibit the reading of his paper.[6] *Vienybė*'s more attractive appearance, larger print, advertisements, and easy reading matter in the familiar Polonized vernacular made it popular with the rank and file, which was conservative, undereducated, and devoutly Catholic. Many of its original readers followed Bačkauskas when he left in 1888 to establish his own paper, *Saulė* (Sun), in Mahanoy City, Pennsylvania. An unpretentious miners' paper, in 1908 it had a circulation of 8,000.[7] It existed until 1959.

Vienybė's first significant change was the abandonment of its initial pro-Polish position. In 1889 Plymouth became the home for the first all-Lithuanian parish, with the newly arrived Reverend A. Burba (Šliūpas's onetime friend) serving as its pastor and *Vienybė*'s spiritual advisor. Under Burba's influence, *Vienybė* raised the level and quality of its publishing, improved its language, encouraged contributions from abroad, and established the practice of serializing longer works which could later be reprinted in book form. More important, it made a decisive turn in the direction of the new patriotism, albeit within the framework of the Roman Catholic Church. Burba belonged to the new generation of young patriot-priests who began arriving in this country in the late 1880s and early 1890s and inaugurated the peculiar blend of nationalism and Catholicism which has remained a characteristic trait of Lithuanians to this day. This was also the time of the final split with Šliūpas and the secular nationalists who demanded separation of religion and nationality. Arguments over the role of religion in defining Lithuanianism led to the well-known newspaper war that raged over a quarter of a century, forcing the community to take sides.

By 1892 Šliūpas had already started a new periodical, *Apszwieta* (Enlightenment), published in Baltimore by his newly founded Lietuvių Mokslo Draugyståe Amerikoje (Lithuanian American Science Society) and printed by Martynas Jankus in East Prussia. This was the first serious Lithuanian literary and scientific magazine, a monthly in book format with a total of fifteen issues published. From 1894 to 1896, in Scranton, Pennsylvania, Šliūpas edited the socialist-oriented *Nauja Gadynė* (New era), and from 1910 to 1915 the freethinking *Laisvoji Mintis* (Free thought). By that time there was already a significant increase in socialist periodicals due to an influx of political émigrés following the Russian revolution of 1905. One of the 1905 émigrés was Stasius Michelsonas who, in 1908, took over the initially Catholic South Boston *Keleivis* (Traveler) and turned it into a socialist weekly; its circulation eventually reached 23,000. Another was Pijus Grigaitis, who in 1913 became the editor of *Pirmyn* (Forward) in Baltimore and in 1914 of *Naujienos* (News) in Chicago.[8] Two early socialist periodicals which turned communist were *Kova* (Battle) and *Vilnis* (Wave). *Kova* (1905–1918) was the organ of the newly founded Lithuanian-American Socialist Party; its first editor was J. O. Širvydas. *Vilnis* started in South Boston in 1911 and since the decisive split between the socialists and the communists has been the official organ of the Lithuanian-American Communist Party, with Rokas Mizara and Antanas Bimba as its long-term editors.[9]

On the Catholic side, in 1893–1894 Reverend Burba launched *Valtis devyniolikto Amžiaus* (Boat of the nineteenth century) in Plymouth. At about the same time, Reverend J. Žebris, another new arrival, assumed the editorship of the nearly bankrupt *Bostono Lietuviszkas Laikrasztis* (Boston's Lithuanian newspaper) and soon thereafter, having bought its press and equipment, inaugurated the weekly *Rytas* (Morning) in Waterbury, Connecticut, with a circulation of about 1,000.[10] In 1896, in Mount Carmel, Pennsylvania, Reverend J. Žilius-Žilinskas (Jr. Jonas) assumed the editorship of *Tevynė* (Motherland), organ of the newly founded Lithuanian-American Alliance (SLA), which still exists. An outstanding figure among the editor-priests of the time was Reverend Antanas Milukas, Šliūpas's foremost antagonist, author of innumerable publications, including important source books on Lithuanian-American immigration history. Milukas's entire life was dedicated to publishing. Upon his arrival in 1892, at the age of twenty-one, he assumed the editorship of *Vienybė*, and from 1894 that of the bankrupt *Garsas* (Voice), which he purchased, changing the title to

Garsas Amerikos Lietuvių (Voice of Lithuanian Americans). Milukas deserves special mention for the quality quarterly *Dirva* (Field), later *Dirva-Žinyčia* (1896– 1906), a literary and scientific magazine in book format, many issues of which were the equivalent of monographs. From 1903 until his death in 1943 his name was associated with *Žvaigždė* (Star), which through 1909 also served as organ of the new Roman Catholic Lithuanian-American Alliance (RKSLA). After Milukas's death, his valuable library in Philadelphia was inadvertently destroyed,[11] a grim footnote on ethnic publishing.

A weekly which still exists is the Catholic *Darbininkas* (Worker), founded in Boston in 1915 by Reverend F. Kemėšis to combat Michelsonas's *Keleivis*. In 1959 *Darbininkas* was taken over by the Franciscan Brothers and moved to Brooklyn, where it was consolidated with two other weak papers, *Amerika* and *Lietuvių Žinios* (Lithuanian news). The editor-in-chief from 1950 to 1966 was Simas Sužiedėlis. It is presently edited by Reverend K. Bučmys.

The newspaper war which started in the East soon moved to Chicago. The most distinguished newspaper during the first twenty years of the twentieth century was *Lietuva* (Lithuania), which marked the true beginning of Chicago's Lithuanian press.[12] *Lietuva* was bought in 1893 by its publisher, A. Olšauskas (Olszewsi), who was a prominent Chicago banker, book publisher, and, in 1910, first president of the Lithuanian-American Press Association. The paper had modern printing facilities and a long-term professional editor, the tolerant J. Adomaitis-Šernas. Its circulation was around 6,000.[13] The liberal *Lietuva* engaged in bitter polemics with *Katalikas* (Catholic), which appeared from 1899 to 1914 as the right arm of Reverend M. Kriaučiūnas (Krawczunas), powerful pastor of the first Lithuanian parish in Chicago.[14]

Just before the outbreak of World War I, Chicago, which to this day remains the cultural and publishing center of Lithuanian America, became the home of two powerful and popular dailies which still exist: the Catholic *Draugas* (Friend) and the socialist *Naujienos* (News). *Draugas*, the current subtitle of which is *The Lithuanian Worldwide News*, was started in Wilkes-Barres, Pennsylvania, by the Lithuanian Roman Catholic Priests Association of America; it moved to Chicago in 1913 with its editor, Reverend A. Kaupas. It became a daily in 1916, and since the 1920s has been published by the Marian Brothers. Its circulation as of 1976 was 21,000.[15] Its long-term editor-in-chief was L. Simutis. Now edited by Reverend P. Garšva, *Draugas* still offers a quality literary supplement.

Naujienos, with the English subtitle *The Lithuanian Daily News*, was started in 1914 by the Chicago chapter of the Lithuanian-American Socialist Alliance and was from then until his death in 1969 edited by Dr. Pijus Grigaitis, who consistently maintained the democratic socialist point of view. In 1976 its circulation was 22,600,[16] but it has declined since then appreciably more than that of *Draugas*. Its present editor is M. Gudelis. A newspaper widely read at the present time in this country is the Canadian-based *Tėviškės Ziburiai* (Lights of the homeland), edited by Reverend P. Gaida.

Two periodicals often classified as "nationalist"[17] which started at about the same time and still exist are *Dirva* (Field) and *Sandara* (League). *Dirva* began in Cleveland in 1915. Its first editor was V. K. Jokubynas, and from 1918 to 1948 it was edited by K. S. Karpius. It is now the organ of the Lithuanian National Association and is edited by V. Gedgaudas. *Sandara* is the organ of the Lithuanian-American National League, begun in 1914 with Šliūpas as one of its founders. In 1918 the league bought the Boston-based *Ateitis* (Future), changed its name to *Sandara*, and transferred it to Chicago; its long-term editor (1929–1976) was M. Vaidyla. Another long-lasting paper was *Amerikos Lietuvis* (American Lithuanian), 1914–1955, in Worcester, Massachusetts, edited by M. Paltanavičius. Also still in existence are the Catholic *Vytis* (Knight), published since 1915 by the Knights of Lithuania to fill the needs of young people, and *Garsas* (Sound), organ of the Lithuanian-American Catholic Alliance, which was started in 1917 in Brooklyn with J. Kaupas as editor. Both papers have sections in English.

Women's periodicals deserve special mention. The first was *Lietuvaitė* (Lithuanian woman), several issues of which appeared in McKees Rock, Pennsylvania in 1910.[18] In 1916 the Lithuanian Women's Progressive Alliance in Philadelphia began *Moterų Balsas* (Women's voice) with 2,500 readers; its name changed to *Darbininkių Balsas* (Voice of working women) after it turned communist in 1919.[19] The Catholic counterpart was *Moterų Dirva* (Women's field), published in 1916 by the Lithuanian-American Roman Catholic Women's Alliance in Worcester, Massachusetts; it still exists. Its counterpart in Canada is the monthly *Moteris* (Woman), edited by Nora Kulpavičienė-Kulpa.

The formative first period of the Lithuanian-American press ended with the outbreak of World War I, which also marked the beginning of restrictions on the flow of new immigrants. The second phase, spanning the period between the two world wars, coincided with the period of Lithuania's independence, which was supported by the press, with the exception of the communist wing. The emergence of Lithuania as a new independent state with its own government and a clearly defined territorial base helped the community to clarify its ethnic identity and offered reinforcement through travel and cultural exchange. On the other hand, Lithuanian-Americans, who had been slow in joining the mainstream, were now participating in American public and political life in growing numbers. One of the pressing concerns of the papers was to keep in touch with this new and quickly assimilating generation by introducing the use of English. From 1917 to 1942 fourteen Lithuanian periodicals were published in English or in both languages in Chicago alone.[20] English was also used, as it is now, to inform the American public about the community and its concerns.

World War II and the implementation of the 1939 German-Soviet Pact resulted in Lithuania's occupation by the Soviet Union and its eventual incorporation as a Soviet Socialist Republic. It also resulted in a new exodus, some 30,000 political refugees entering the United States after the passage of the 1948 Displaced Persons Act. This much smaller but well-educated and active wave of new immigrants in many instances revitalized the aging press, but it also created its own newspapers; most of the periodicals listed by Lubomir and Anna Wynar and J. Balys were produced by this group.[21] With their self-images well defined after two decades of independence, these people view themselves as exiles and continue to denounce Lithuania's loss of independence. Once again the ethnic press finds itself imbued with a sense of mission and obligation to the homeland. At the present time it is particularly responsive to the needs of Soviet Lithuanian dissidents, providing a forum for the underground "samizdat" publications and publicizing human rights violations. There are also several English-language newsletters published solely for this purpose.[22]

Lithuanian-American Protestants, always a minority, are represented by *Mūsų Sparnai* (Our wings), organ of the Lithuanian Evangelical Reformed Church in Exile, and *Svečias* (Guest), organ of the Lithuanian Evangelical Church. There are several publications for young adults: *Ateitis* (Future) for Catholics, *Mūsų Vytis* (Our knight) for academic-oriented scouts, *Skautų Aidas* for younger scouts, and a children's monthly, *Eglutė* (Little evergreen), published in Putnam, Connecticut, by the Sisters of the Immaculate Conception. Also available are several ideological-political journals representing parties which existed in independent Lithuania and were transplanted to this country in the 1950s.[23] With circulation figures ranging from about 500 to 1,000, many of these magazines exist because of the dedication of—and sometimes financial subsidies by—their publishers and editors, who are often the same people who started them some thirty years ago. The press is aging, but it is still vigorous and able to stir controversy within the community. Moreover, it provokes responses in Soviet Lithuania, where it is followed closely.[24] An important and long neglected matter is the need for archives to ensure that extant periodicals do not become bibliographical rarities.[25]

NOTES

1. Frank Lavinskas lists a total of 170 periodicals published during the period from 1879 to 1955. See Lavinskas, *Amerikos lietuvių laikraščiai: 1879–1955* (Long Island City, N.Y.: Privately printed, 1956). According to Lubomyr R. and Anna T. Wynar, Lithuanians, when compared with forty-three other ethnic groups, rank eleventh in number of publications, with forty-two periodicals having a circulation of 139,239. See Wynar and Wynar, *Encyclopedic Directory of Ethnic Newspapers and Periodicals in the United States*, 2nd ed. (Littleton, Colo.: Libraries Unlimited, 1976), pp. 142–150. John P. Balys, supplementing Wynar, lists twelve newspapers and forty-two journals. See Balys, "The American Lithuanian Press," *Lituanus* 22 (Spring 1976): 42–53. For a comprehensive overview see Vaclovas Biržiška, "The American Lithuanian Publications, 1875–1910," *Journal of Central European Affairs* 18 (Winter 1959): 396–408. Also see Dana J. Tautvilas, "The Lithuanian Press in America," Master's Thesis, Catholic University of America, 1961. Information from Tautvilas is reprinted in Leo J. Alilunas, ed., *Lithuanians in the United States: Selected Studies* (San Francisco, Calif.: R&E Research Associates, 1978). John P. Balys has also prepared a union list, *Lithuanian Periodicals in American Libraries* (Washington, D.C.: Library of Congress, European Division, 1982).

2. Following the final partition of the Polish-Lithuanian Commonwealth in 1775,

Lithuania was under Russian rule. After the abortive uprising of 1863, Lithuanian-language publications in the Latin alphabet were prohibited by the tsarist government. The ban ushered in an era of illegal printing and book smuggling from abroad, especially from East Prussia, a Lithuanian-inhabited area within the Prussian Empire where Lithuanian publications were permitted, although subject to censorship. *Aušra*, edited by Dr. J. Basanavičius and his followers, was the first of several periodicals now associated with the Lithuanian renascence which in 1918 led to the proclamation of independence.

3. Excerpts from *Lietuwiszka Gazieta* were reprinted by Šliūpas in the 1885 issues of *Aušra* and in *Laisvoji Mintis*, Nos. 1–4. See Vytautas Sirvydas, ed., *Juozas O. Širvydas: 1875–1935* (Cleveland, Ohio: Dirva, 1941), p. 169.

4. Juozas Kriaučiunas, "Lithuanians at the Paris World Fair," *Lituanus* 28 (Winter 1982): 26–39. See also Antanas Kučas, *Lithunians in America* (Boston, Mass.: Encyclopedia Lituanica Press, 1975), pp. 82–87.

5. Širvydas, *Juozas O. Sirydas*, p. 182. Širvydas edited *Vienybě* from 1903 to 1905 and from 1907 to 1912, giving it a socialist slant. Under his editorship circulation reached 5,000. See V. Širvydas, "Vienybě," in *Encyclopedia Lituanica* (Boston, Mass., 1976), 5: 114–117. Since 1940 *Vienybě* has been associated with the Juozas Tysliava family.

6. Stasys Michelsonas, *Lietuvių išeivija Amerikoje, 1865–1961* (South Boston, Mass.: Keleivis, 1961), p. 188.

7. Balys, "American Lithuanian Press," p. 45.

8. Michelsonas, p. 195. Upon his retirement, Michelsonas donated his newspaper to the Lithuanian-American Socialist Party. The paper was discontinued in 1979, with Jackus Sonda as editor, marking the end of the Lithuanian-American socialist press. The editorial position of *Naujienos* changed after the death of Dr. P. Grigaitis.

9. Ibid., p. 194.

10. After Žebris's tragic death, the paper was continued by Reverend P. Saurusaitis as *Tarnas bažnycios* (Servant of the Church). See Jonas Puzinas, "Ankstyvoji Amerikos lietuvių išeivija ir jų spauda," *Karys* No. 6/1423 (June 1966): 178. Also see William Wolkovich-Valkavičius, "The Impact of a Catholic Newspaper on an Ethnic Community: The Lithuanian Weekly *Rytas*, 1896–98, Waterbury, Conn.," *Lituanus* 24 (Fall 1978): 42–53. Also see, by the same author, *Lithuanian Pioneer Priest of New England* (Brooklyn, N.Y.: Franciscan Press, 1980).

11. Vladas Mingėla, *Kunigas Antanas Milukas: jo gyvenimas ir darbai* (Detroit, Mich.: Monografijai leisti komitetas, 1962), p. 241.

12. David Fainhauz, *Lithuanians in Multi-Ethnic Chicago until World War II* (Chicago, Ill.: Lithuanian Library Press, 1977), p. 167.

13. Balys, "American Lithuanian Press," p. 46.

14. The power struggle between the two newspapers and the men behind them is related in detail by Victor Greene as an illustration of the religionist-secularist controversy. See Greene, *For God and Country: The Rise of Polish and Lithuanian Ethnic Consciousness in America, 1850–1910* (Madison, Wis.: State Historical Society of Wisconsin, 1975), pp. 145–161.

15. Balys, "American Lithuanian Press," p. 47.

16. Ibid.

17. Cf. Kučas, *Lithuanians in America*, pp. 189–199.

18. Lavinskas, p. 55.

19. Michelsonas, p. 201. Also see Širvydas, *Juozas O. Širvydas*, pp. 265–267; and Aleksas Ambrose, *Čicagos Lietuvių Istorija: 1869–1959* (The history of Lithuanians in

Chicago: 1869–1959) (Chicago, Ill.: Amerikos lietuvių istorijos draugija, 1967), pp. 196–201.

20. Fainhauz, p. 167.

21. Cf. Wynar and Wynar, *Encyclopedic Directory*, and Balys, *Lithuanian Periodicals*. Also see Enata Skrupskelis, "The Lithuanian Immigrant Press in the U.S. after World War II," Master's thesis, University of Chicago, 1961.

22. Cf. *Violations of Human Rights in Soviet Occupied Lithuania* (Lithuanian-American Community, Inc.), *The Chronicle of the Roman Catholic Church in Lithuania* (Lithuanian Roman Catholic Priests League in America), the newsletters *Bridges* (Lithuanian-American Community), *Baltic Bulletin* (Baltic American Freedom League), and *ELTA Information Bulletin* (Lithuanian National Foundation). For an analysis of the Lithuanian ethnic press and its coverage of developments in the Soviet Baltic area, see David M. Crowe, "The Contemporary Baltic Press in the Non-Soviet World," *Lituanus* 24 (Spring 1978): 57–71. Scholarly articles in English appear in *Lituanus* and *Journal of Baltic Studies*.

23. *Naujoji Viltis* (New hope) by the National Lithuanian Society of America, *Sėja* (Sowing) by the National Democrats, *Tėvynes Sargas* (Motherland's guardian) by the Christian Democrats, *Varpas* (Bell), by the Social Democrats, *Į Laisvę* (To freedom) by the Liberal Christian Democratic Front. The Lithuanian Historical Society publishes *Tautos Praeitis: Lithuanian Historical Review*.

24. Especially closely followed by Soviet intellectuals and officials and commented upon in the Soviet Lithuanian press are *Metmenys* (Outlines), a cultural and literary journal edited by Vytautas Kavolis (the liberal counterpart of the Catholic *Aidai*) and the Chicago-based journal of opinion *Akiračiai* (Horizons). See Tomas Venclova, "Ar galima kultūros kuryba išeivijoje," *Pasaulio Lietuvis* 1/23 (January 1980): 3.

25. The Balys union list *Lithuanian Periodicals in American Libraries* reveals many incomplete collections.

BIBLIOGRAPHY

Bagdanavičius, Vytautas, et al., eds. *Kovos metai del savosios spaudos* (Lithuania's fight for a free press). Chicago: Lietuvių Bendruomenės Chicago Apyg. Leidinys, 1957.

Balys, John P. "The American Lithuanian Press." *Lituanus* 22 (Spring 1976): 42–53.

————. *Lithuanian Periodicals in American Libraries*. Washington, D.C.: Library of Congress, European Division, 1982.

Biržiška, Vaclovas. "The American Lithuanian Publications, 1875–1910." *Journal of Central European Affairs* 18 (Winter 1959): 396–408.

Crowe, David M. "The Contemporary Baltic Press in the Non-Soviet World." *Lituanus* 24 (Spring 1978): 57–71.

Encyclopedia Lituanica. 5 vols. Boston: Encyclopedia Lituanica Press, 1970, 1972, 1973, 1976, 1978.

Fainhauz, David. *Lithuanians in Multi-Ethnic Chicago until World War II*. Chicago: Lithuanian Library Press, 1977.

Gaida, Pranas, et al., eds. *Lithuanians in Canada*. Toronto: Canada Ethnica, 1967.

Jakštas, Juozas. *Dr. Jonas Šliūpas*. Chicago: Akademinės Skautijos Leidykla, 1979.

Kantautas, Adam, and Filomena Kantautas. *A Lithuanian Bibliography: A Checklist of Books and Articles Held by the Major Libraries of Canada and the United States*. Edmonton: University of Alberta Press, 1975. *Supplement*, 1979.

Kučas, Antanas. *Lithuanians in America*. Boston: Encyclopedia Lituanica Press, 1975.

Lavinskas, Frank. *Amerikos lietuvių laikraščiai: 1879–1955* (The Lithuanian Press in the U.S.A.: 1879–1955). Long Island City, N.Y.: Privately printed, 1956.

Michelsonas, Stasys. *Lietuvių išeivija Amerikoje: 1865–1961* (Lithuanians in America: 1865–1961). South Boston, Mass.: Keleivis, 1961.

Puzinas, Jonas. "Ankstyvoji Amerikos lietuvių išeivija ir jų spauda." *Karys* No. 5(1422) (May 1966), pp. 131–138; No. 6(1423) (June 1966), pp. 176–179.

Širvydas, Vytautas, ed. *Juozas O. Širvydas: 1875–1935*. Cleveland: Dirva, 1941.

Skrupskelis, Enata. "The Lithuanian Immigrant Press in the U.S. after World War II." Master's thesis, University of Chicago, 1961.

Tautvilas, Dana J. "The Lithuanian Press in America." Master's thesis, Catholic University of America, 1961.

Wolkovich-Valkavičius, William. "The Impact of a Catholic Newspaper on an Ethnic Community: The Lithuanian Weekly *Rytas*, 1896–1898, Waterbury, Conn." *Lituanus* 24 (Fall 1978): 42–53.

———. "Toward a Historiography of Lithuanian Immigrants to the United States." *Immigration History Newsletter* 15 (November 1983): 7–10.

Wynar, Lubomyr R., and Anna T. Wynar. *Encyclopedic Directory of Ethnic Newspapers and Periodicals in the United States*. 2d ed. Littleton, Colo.: Libraries Unlimited, 1976.

16

The Mexican–American Press

CARLOS E. CORTÉS

In 1926 Ignacio Lozano, a Mexican immigrant publisher who had escaped from the turmoil of the Mexican Revolution, established a weekly newspaper entitled *La Opinión* in Los Angeles. As of 1984, *La Opinión* was still in operation under the direction of his son, Ignacio Lozano, Jr. As the nation's oldest current Mexican-American newspaper, *La Opinión* stands as a notable success story in the perilous history of the Mexican-American press, rooted in the larger historical process of the Mexican-American people.[1]

The Mexican-American press can only partially be considered an immigrant press, because Mexican Americans (Chicanos) are only partially an immigrant-origin people. Chicanos became part of the United States through two processes—annexation and immigration. Mexican Americans first entered U.S. history via annexation. In 1822 Anglo-Americans from the United States began to settle in the northeastern corner of Mexico, which had just won its independence from Spain. In 1835, supported by some native Mexicans who opposed the central government, Anglo settlers revolted and, in 1836, established the independent Lone Star Republic. When, in 1845, the Republic joined the United States as the state of Texas, the 5,000 Mexicans in Texas became the first large group of Mexican Americans.

Closely following the Texas annexation came the 1846–1848 U.S.-Mexican War, during which U.S. forces occupied Mexico's northern provinces of New Mexico and California and captured Mexico City, the nation's capital. The subsequent 1848 Treaty of Guadalupe Hidalgo recognized U.S. possession of northern Mexico (about one-third of Mexico's territory—one-half counting Texas) and specified the rights of the some 75,000 Mexicans living in the annexed territory. Finally, in 1854, via the Gadsden Treaty, Mexico sold to the United States a 30,000-square-mile strip of land (on which some 5,000 Mexicans were living) in today's southern New Mexico and Arizona. As historian David Weber has described it, Mexicans in these three territorial transfers had truly become "foreigners in their native land."[2]

THE NINETEENTH CENTURY

The press history of that part of northern Mexico that would ultimately become part of the United States began during Mexico's 1810–1821 struggle for independence from Spain. In the 1810s Spanish-language newspapers such as *La Gaceta* and *El Mexicano* were published in that area of Spain's Viceroyalty of New Spain (later Mexico) that would become the state of Texas.[3] Following the 1821 independence of Mexico, three, or possibly four, newspapers operated for brief periods in New Mexico prior to the 1846–1848 U.S.-Mexican War, beginning in 1834 with *El Crepúsculo de la Libertad*.[4] While no newspapers existed in Mexican California, the 1834 arrival in Monterey of a printing press led to the issuance of a variety of publications.[5] In Texas, too, the press continued to produce publications.[6] These pre-U.S. press developments in northern Mexico established a tradition for what would become the Mexican-American press after 1848.

Following the U.S. conquest and annexation of northern Mexico, Spanish-language journalism continued. It is impossible to measure definitively the extent of the Mexican-American press. The ephemeral existence of so many Chicano newspapers, the common failure of libraries to collect and preserve these publications, and the general lack of scholarly interest in Chicano journalism prior to the last two decades are major obstacles in efforts to reconstruct the history of the Chicano press. However, in the early 1970s a giant step was taken with the publication of the valuable pioneering bibliographical work on the Mexican-American press by Herminio Rios and Guadalupe Castillo.[7] Restricting themselves to the five southwestern states of Arizona, California, Colorado, New Mexico, and Texas, Rios and Castillo identified 372 Mexican-American newspapers that were established prior to 1940. While their work is limited regionally, and while the authors indicate that their efforts are preliminary, an analysis of their two published bibliographies suggests the general contours of Chicano press history and illustrates the problems of moving beyond those contours.

Rios and Castillo list 136 Chicano newspapers established during the nineteenth century. Yet, because of the difficulty of locating complete sets of newspapers or even full records of their publication dates, the authors succeeded in identifying termination dates for only 20 of the 136 papers. Of the twenty newspapers whose beginning and ending dates could be specified, eight ceased publication in the nineteenth century and twelve continued into the twentieth century. Of the remaining 116 whose final publication dates could not be specified, 11 were known to have entered the twentieth century (for a total of twenty-three known survivors of the nineteenth century). However, for 105 of the 136 nineteenth-century newspapers, the trail of evidence ran out during the nineteenth century, making it impossible to specify how long they lasted or how many managed to enter the twentieth century. Despite the fuzziness of this data, the number of journalistic efforts and, in some cases, the newspapers' longevity indicate a determination on the part of Mexican Americans to operate newspapers, to keep their communities informed, to report about Mexican-American affairs, and to provide an outlet for Chicano expression.

According to Rios and Castillo, New Mexico, with the largest nineteenth-century Mexican-American population, also had the largest number of newspapers, with fifty-two; it was followed by Texas, with thirty-eight; California, with thirty-four; Arizona, with eleven; and Colorado, with one. Of newspapers whose publication frequency was given, nearly 80 percent were weeklies. Six daily newspapers were found: *Correo del Río Grande* (Brownsville); *El Eco del Pacífico* (San Francisco); *El Eco Mexicano* (Los Angeles); *El Hispano Americano* (El Paso); *El Tecolote* (San Francisco); and *La Voz del Pueblo* (Las Vegas, New Mexico).

The founding dates of the newspapers suggest a rising tide of nineteenth-century Chicano journalism. Beginning with the newspapers founded during the 1850s, the number of new publications virtually doubled each decade through the 1880s. They rose from six new papers during the 1850s to twelve new ones in the 1860s, twenty-two in the 1870s, and forty-two in the 1880s. In the 1890s alone, fifty new Chicano newspapers were founded. Paradoxically, New Mexico, with the largest Mexican-American population at the time of annexation, did not have its first new Mexican-American paper until the 1860s, after both California and Texas. However, by the end of the century, Chicano journalism appears to have flourished in New Mexico, as nearly half of the Mexican-American newspapers established in the 1890s were in that state. In addition, New Mexico's Spanish-language periodicals united as La Prensa Asociada Hispano-Americana (the Spanish American Associated Press), the first Mexican-American press association.[8] Texas also showed a steady increase, but Arizona leveled off in the rate of newly established newspapers, while California witnessed a decline from nine new papers in the 1880s to five in the 1890s.[9]

Content, philosophy, and political orientation varied from newspaper to newspaper and from place to place. Newspapers often took strong editorial positions, ranging from criticism of societal discrimination to appeals for action and changes of behavior or attitudes among Mexican Americans. Current news stories varied from the local scene to national and international events, particularly from Latin America. Newspapers ran a wide variety of feature stories and sometimes didactic articles, including moral instruction. For example, in his study of nineteenth-century child rearing among Mexican Americans, historian Richard Griswold del Castillo uncovered numerous examples of articles aimed at teaching children, particularly little girls, how to act, and lecturing parents, particularly mothers, on parental responsibilities. Likewise, newspaper writers commonly used the press to champion such beliefs as the sanctity of marriage.[10] Poetry, too, regularly graced the pages of nineteenth-century newspapers. Love poems, for example, proved to be a particularly popular form of Chicano expression, and newspapers provided a convenient public outlet for emotion and the love of lyrical language.

Chicanos also developed their own ''musical press'' as an alternative means of recording and transmitting news of events. This occurred through the use of the *corrido*, a type of song with guitar accompaniment, which often told the story of important historical events or celebrated Chicano heroes. Seldom written down, but transmitted from singer to singer, these musical records have come down to us over the decades. In recent years scholars, led by the pioneering Chicano folklorist Américo Paredes, have begun to tape record and even in some cases to publish these songs in printed form.[11]

THE TWENTIETH CENTURY

The twentieth century has brought major changes in the history of Mexican Americans, and these in turn have affected the Mexican-American press. Probably the most significant and most continuing of these changes has been the dramatic increase in Mexican immigration. During the second half of the nineteenth century, immigration was relatively modest. However, the trickle of immigration turned into a flood during the 1910 Mexican Revolution, as thousands of Mexicans fled north for sanctuary in the United States during that turbulent decade.

While conditions pushed, opportunities in the United States pulled. The United States had jobs—in industry, in mines, on railroads, and in agriculture—at wage levels far higher than in Mexico. In the 1920s the pace of Mexican emigration increased as nearly 500,000 Mexicans entered the economically expanding United States on permanent visas, accounting for some 11 percent of that decade's total U.S. immigration. Thousands more entered informally without documents, many unaware of the required legal processes, others to avoid fees and bureaucratic border delays. While most Mexicans settled in the Southwest, by the end of the decade about 10 percent resided outside of the Southwest, particularly in the Midwest and the Pacific Northwest.

Mexican immigrants expanded the size of traditional Mexican-American *barrios* (neighborhoods) and established new barrios and *colonias* (communities). Mexican-American political, cultural, patriotic, and mutual aid organizations developed, while the very growth of barrios and colonias fostered the expansion of Chicano small businesses, particularly restaurants, retail stores, services, and construction firms. Of course, barrio expansion provided fertile soil for the further growth of the Mexican-American press.

During the first three decades of the twentieth century, according to the Rios-Castillo bibliographies, 203 Mexican-American newspapers were established in the Southwest. Moreover, these statistics do not reflect the emergence of the Mexican-American press outside of the Southwest, most notably in Chicago.[12] As in the nineteenth century, the bulk (more than two-thirds) were weeklies. However, more than 10 percent were dailies, a sharp jump from the nineteenth-century pattern.

From 1900 to 1909, forty-seven newspapers came into existence, led by New Mexico with twenty-five and Texas with eighteen. California continued its journalistic decline, with only two new papers. In the 1910s the number of newspaper inaugurations more than doubled, to ninety-nine, as Texas took the lead with forty-four new publications, followed by New Mexico with twenty-eight. California, along with Texas a major recipient of the increased Mexican immigration, gained sixteen new papers.[13] Arizona's number also rose, from two to ten, while Colorado launched its first twentieth-century Mexican-American newspaper.[14] According to the Rios-Castillo bibliographies, the 1910s marked the high point of new Chicano journalistic endeavors, probably spurred by the tremendous debate within the Mexican-American community concerning the issues and events of the Mexican Revolution.[15]

During the 1920s the number of new publications dropped to fifty-seven. California, with its rapidly growing Mexican immigrant population, was the only state to record an increase in new endeavors, from sixteen to twenty. Quite likely, this decline in new papers reflected the fact that so many Chicano communities now had newspapers rather than any decline in journalistic entrepreneurship.

The Great Depression of 1929 and the drastically reduced U.S. job market sharply curtailed Mexican immigration. In cooperation with the Mexican government, which rued the loss of so many able workers, U.S. federal, state, county, and local officials instituted the Repatriation Program, through which 500,000 persons, including naturalized citizens and U.S.-born spouses and children of departing Mexicans, were shuttled to Mexico. Repatriation shattered families, decimated barrios and colonias, forced small businesses to close, and removed potential citizens (and therefore potential voters and newspapers readers).

The impact of the Depression and the Repatriation Program was felt in the Mexican-American press. New journalistic endeavors fell by 50 percent from the level of the 1920s, with California suffering the sharpest decline (from twenty to three). Texas, with fourteen, continued to lead in newspaper inaugurations, as it had since the beginning of the century.[16]

The end of the Depression and the coming of World War II brought another migration reversal. The wartime expansion of the U.S. armed forces and war industries created a new labor shortage; Mexican workers were once again welcome. Large-scale immigration continued after the war. Immigration of Mexicans with permanent visas exceeded 30,000 in every year from 1960 to the late 1970s, while other Mexican immigrants, referred to as undocumented or illegal immigrants, have come primarily to fill less attractive agricultural, industrial, service, and domestic positions. In addition, the Bracero Program (1942–1947, 1951–1964) provided for Mexican *braceros* (those who work with their arms—laborers) to come as short-term contract workers.

The World War II era is often viewed as a watershed in Chicano history, renewing hope where the Depression had brought despair. Some 350,000 Mexican Americans served in the armed forces and won seventeen medals of honor. Following the war, the G.I. Bill of Rights provided veterans with new opportunities through such benefits as educational subsidies and loans for business and housing. Moreover, returning Chicano servicemen led challenges against traditional discriminatory practices. Renewed immigration brought new growth to Chicano communities, a resurgence reflected in the growing importance and social activism of such newspapers as Ignacio Lopez's outspoken *El Espectador* in Pomona, California.

THE CHICANO MOVEMENT

Then, in the 1960s, came the Chicano movement, one of the dynamic forces for societal change that arose during that decade. The movement has given rise to action in many areas of American life—politics, economics, education, and religion—and in society in general. One of its major reflections has been the increased growth and dynamism of the Chicano press. However, this growth has been more than merely quantitative; it has also been qualitative, as the Chicano press has moved into new types of publication endeavors. Along with the traditional types of newspapers—commercial and organizational—a boom occurred in university and high school student newspapers, some of which have already been published for well over a decade. Chicano newspapers are born every year. A few prosper; some simply survive; others die.

There have also been a number of efforts to create economically viable Chicano magazines. Some of these began as newspapers and grew into magazines, such as Los Angeles's *La Raza* (1967–1975). In addition, Chicanos have been in the forefront of efforts to build Latino magazines, covering the many U.S. Hispanic groups. As in the case of newspapers, these efforts have had mixed success.

While it may be many years before any definitive decision can be rendered, it now appears that the more localized, focused Chicano magazines have achieved a higher degree of stability than the more ambitious, national Latino magazines. Current examples of such success, if not large-scale prosperity, are *Caminos*, published monthly in San Bernardino, California, since 1979, and *Low Rider*, a monthly magazine aimed at a younger audience, particularly those interested in remodeling old cars into sleek, often dazzlingly artistic automobiles.

Major national Latino magazines have had to struggle for existence. Numerous initiatives have failed to get off the ground or have perished almost immediately. The first national effort to gain an extended foothold was *La Luz*, established in 1971 by Daniel Valdez and published in Denver, Colorado, until 1981. While it covered the U.S. Latino community and even Latin America in general, it devoted most of its attention to Mexican-American life. More ambitious has been the slicker *Nuestro*, published first in New York and later in Washington, D.C. It was launched with great fanfare in 1974 and has continued into 1984 despite editorial and economic problems. Withdrawing from the list of national Latino magazines, at least temporarily, was *Agenda* (1970–1981), a bimonthly publication of the National Council of La Raza in Washington, D.C. Less popular in orientation than *La Luz* and *Nuestro, Agenda* focused on a more serious discussion of major Latino issues and often published theme issues on such topics as immigration, politics, civil rights, and the media. As of 1984, Latinos were also publishing at least two national magazines dedicated to the business community, *Hispanic Business* and *Hispanic Review of Business*, the latter an initiative of *Nuestro*.

Statistics on the number of Latino, including Mexican-American, newspapers and magazines are imprecise. For example, according to one estimate, from 1980 to 1983 an average of sixteen Hispanic newspapers and magazines were launched each month. However, only 20 percent of these newspapers and 5 percent of these magazines lasted more than two years.[17]

In addition to magazines, the Chicano movement has given birth to a number of scholarly journals. University campuses have provided homes for some of these journals, such as *Aztlán, International Journal of Chicano Studies Research* and the *Hispanic Journal of Behavioral Sciences*, both published at the University of California at Los Angeles, as well as *Crítica: A Journal of Critical Essays*, at the University of California, San Diego. More broadly Latino are such university-based scholarly journals as the *Bilingual Review* (presently at the State University of New York, Binghamton), the *Revista Chicano-Riquena* (currently at the University of Houston), and *Chiricu* (Indiana University).

There have also been a number of private efforts to create scholarly, literary, or hybrid Chicano journals. Probably the most renowned was *El Grito. A Journal of Contemporary Mexican American Thought*. The demise of its publisher, Quinto Sol, ended that journal, but one of Quinto Sol's publishers, Octavio Romano, then established Tonatiuh International. The latter has published *Grito del Sol*, which is more strictly literary in orientation than was its predecessor, which carried a broad range of entries from scholarly articles to poetry.

Finally, there have been Chicano book publishers and distributors. Such small but aggressive publishers as Tonatiuh International, Editorial Justa, and Perspectiva Publications have provided an outlet for books by or about Chicanos, books often rejected by mainstream presses because of their supposed lack of potential audiences. Moreover, a number of Chicano distributors, such as Relámpago, have provided purchasers with convenient access to Chicano subject matter books, a critical need considering the ephemeral nature of so much Chicano material and the small staffing of so many Chicano presses.

PROBLEMS FACED BY THE MEXICAN-AMERICAN PRESS

Throughout its century and a quarter history, the Mexican-American press has faced a number of problems. The three foremost among these have been financial instability, limited readership, and language.

Insufficiency of money has forced the Mexican-American press to be heavily dependent on outside sources, such as Anglo advertisers and government agencies. This financial dependence on non-Chicanos, who have the ability to sever the monetary arteries, has tended historically to moderate editorial policy, mute the critical voice, and restrict the militance and social activism of many Mexican-

American newspapers. The problem of undercapitalization continues to haunt most of the Mexican-American press today, as reflected in the demise of newspapers and magazines.

One way of overcoming the problem of undercapitalization and the resulting undue influence of governments and advertisers is through large readership—by making the Mexican-American press such a good outlet that businesses will advertise whether or not they approve of the editorial policy. Unfortunately, limited readership has also historically plagued the Mexican-American press. Low levels of literacy have long been a major Mexican-American problem. In turn, the traditional low literacy rate has meant that the potential Mexican-American readership does not nearly measure up to the total Mexican-American population.

The literacy problem is compounded by the two-language nature of the Mexican-American population. Not all Spanish-speaking Chicanos read Spanish, nor do they all read English. Part of the Mexican-American population reads Spanish, part reads English, part reads both, part reads neither. These linguistic realities force elements of the Mexican-American press to make critical decisions on the language or languages in which to publish, further dividing an already limited market.

ROLES OF THE MEXICAN-AMERICAN PRESS

The struggle for survival has been the central problem in the history of the Mexican-American press. But the dilemmas facing the Mexican-American press transcend questions of money, readership, and language. They go to the heart of just what role, or roles, the Mexican-American press has played and should play.

In a seminal article in a 1977 issue of *Journalism History*, Felix Gutiérrez hypothesized that Chicano newspapers (his generalizations can also be applied to Chicano magazines) have played three major roles—as instruments of social control, as instruments of social activism, and as reflections of Chicano life.[18] As instruments of social control, they have spread official government information about how Americans are supposed to act and have socialized Chicanos into the "American way of thinking."[19] As instruments of social activism, they have protested against discrimination, pointed out the lack of public services for Mexican Americans, raised Chicano social consciousness, and exhorted Mexican Americans to take action.[20] As reflections of Chicano life, they have printed poetry, essays, letters, and other forms of Mexican-American expression.

I would like to expand this framework by adding three more roles that the Chicano newspapers have played throughout history: they have been preservers and transmitters of Chicano history and culture, maintainers and reinforcers of language, and strengtheners of Chicano pride. While informing their readers of current events, Chicano community activities, employment opportunities, local services, and important social issues, they have also, albeit unconsciously, served as preservers and transmitters of Chicano history and culture for future generations who would find in them a record of their heritage. As maintainers and reinforcers of language, they have preserved the Spanish language in print, reinforced its use, and provided the opportunity for Chicanos to experiment with bilingual expression and develop their own unique vocabulary and means of communication. As strengtheners of Chicano pride, they have provided a sense of identity and spirit that comes from knowing that Mexican Americans have their own vigorous press tradition.

Some newspapers have taken the more conservative tacks of U.S. socialization and Chicano cultural, historical, and linguistic preservation. Others have adopted a more militant, social change orientation. All have provided the sense of symbolic pride that comes from their very existence. In general, conservatism has proved more palatable for advertisers and government and, as a result, most of the "successful" Mexican-American newspapers in terms of longevity and financial stability have been of the more conservative variety.

The Mexican-American press has developed in different linguistic packages involving Spanish and English, reflecting the diversity of the Chicano reading community and the fact that non-Chicanos are part of the readership. Some publications are completely in Spanish or English; some carry full texts of all articles in both Spanish and English; some carry different articles in Spanish and English; and some carry full articles in one language and brief synopses of articles in the other language. Even in those publications that use some Spanish, there are differences in approach. Some use only traditional Spanish; others champion the use of variations of Chicano Spanish, or even bilingual writing that integrates Spanish and English words, sometimes within the same sentence and particularly in poetry. English-language Chicano publications have sometimes functioned as instruments of social activism, cultural reflection, and historical preservation, yet they obviously have contributed little to Spanish linguistic maintenance. Conversely, while the Spanish-language press has helped to maintain Spanish language usage in the United States, much of that medium has contributed little in the area of constructive social change or community awareness.

COMPARISON WITH THE CHICANO ELECTRONIC MEDIA

In the past two decades, the history of the Mexican-American printed press has been paralleled by the development of the Chicano electronic press. Spanish-language television and radio stations now operate throughout the country. In television, as of late 1981, the national Spanish International Network (SIN) numbered 10 full-power television stations and 112 affiliates, including cable systems and translators (low-power repeater stations). Thirty-nine were in Texas, fifteen in New Mexico, fourteen in Arizona, ten in Connecticut, seven in California, five in Florida, four in Oregon, three each in Colorado and New York, two each in Illinois, Kentucky, and Pennsylvania, and one each in Arkansas, the District of Columbia, Idaho, Massachusetts, Missouri, and Washington.[21] By early 1984 SIN had nearly doubled in size to include 11 conventional stations, 11 low-power stations, and 219 cable television stations. In addition, as of 1982, there were two independent Spanish-language television stations, while the Spanish-language cable service, GalaVision, had 92,000 subscribers in 102 cities spread throughout fifteen states and Puerto Rico. In the same year Chicano-owned and -operated Buena Vista Cable Television of Los Angeles took its place in the ranks of the growing Chicano electronic media.

For radio, there is now the National Association of Spanish Broadcasters (NASB)—stations which broadcast exclusively or largely in the Spanish language—and the Southwest Spanish Broadcasters Association, composed of stations with Hispanic ownership.[22] As of 1979, some 159 stations belonged to NASB. However, as with the Latino print media, statistics on the Spanish-language electronic media vary greatly. According to one 1983 listing, more than 100 stations broadcast full-time in Spanish, while some 60 more provided ten or more hours of Spanish-language broadcasting.[23] In contrast, one 1982 publication listed 581 Spanish-language radio stations and 105 Spanish-language television stations in the United States.[24] Yet all of these statistics imply more progress than they truly signify.

First, language does not signify control. For the most part, Spanish-language radio and television stations are owned and controlled by non-Hispanics. While some of these stations may follow socially constructive policies toward the Mexican-American community, this still does not mean that Chicanos are determining their own media destiny. As of 1981, minorities owned only 164, or 1.8 percent, of the nation's commercial radio and television stations and only 32, or 2.3 percent, of the noncommercial stations. Nationally, only twenty-five Latinos owned commercial stations and only nine owned noncommercial stations.[25]

Moreover, as in the case of the print media, language and content are distinct matters. Broadcasting in Spanish has helped to maintain and reinforce Spanish-language usage. However, not all Spanish-language stations have taken the lead in community action or have served as instruments of constructive social change.

Spanish International Network television programming consists largely of sports, movies, musical shows, and soap operas (*novelas*), with a heavy reliance on imported programs. Sports telecasting, in any language, may be a nice placebo, but it hardly increases Chicano community awareness and knowledge. *Novelas*, which comprise one-third of SIN's air time, may entertain viewers, but *El derecho de nacer*, *El milagro de vivir*, and other Spanish-language equivalents of *As the World Turns* and *Father Knows Best* hardly exemplify Chicano power. And while *Disco Fiebre* and *Lucha Libre* may be pleasantly diverting, they cannot be considered indices of Chicano progress. By the same token, Spanish-language music stations and music shows with Spanish-speaking disc jockeys do not usually receive high marks for social change.

However, content aside, the Chicano electronic media have certainly surpassed their print siblings in terms of both survival and prosperity. While the Chicano print media have struggled to survive, Spanish-language television and radio have expanded impressively. Relatively few members of the Chicano print media have gained some economic prosperity, while the profit sheets of Spanish-language electronic media have shown impressive gains.

There are several reasons for this differential. The first is the issue of literacy. Unlike the print media, television and radio do not demand literacy, so their comparative success, particularly with the less literate Mexican immigrants, should come as no surprise. Second, there is the issue of media habits. According to various studies, Chicanos have a far greater penchant for listening, watching, and obtaining their information from the electronic media than from the print media (a penchant increasingly paralleled by the U.S. population in general),[26] generating, as a result, greater economic support for the electronic media in the form of advertising.[27] Third, most advertisers feel that advertising campaigns in mainstream print media already reach English-reading Hispanics, so they spend most of their "Hispanic" budget on the Spanish electronic media in order to reach Spanish-speaking Latinos, including many who do not read English.[28] So as Mexican-American newspapers and magazines still struggle to interest advertisers, the latter are increasingly using Spanish-language television and radio to spread their messages.

THE FUTURE OF THE MEXICAN-AMERICAN PRESS

While the current outlook for the Mexican-American press does not seem as bright as that of Spanish-language radio and television, it certainly is not bleak. The single most dramatic indication of this brighter future comes from population statistics. The survival and growth of the print media depend on readership, particularly Chicano readership, and that population is growing rapidly.

According to a comparison of the 1970 and 1980 censuses, while the U.S. national population grew by 11.6 percent during the decade of the 1970s, the Hispanic population (which is about 60 percent Mexican American) grew by 61 percent. Moreover, Hispanics are eight years younger on the average than Americans in general, meaning that Chicanos will form an increasing number and percentage of those entering the newspaper-reading and magazine-consuming age. Finally, Chicano literacy rates are improving, meaning an even greater expansion of the potential reading public. The Population Institute in Washington, D.C., predicts that Hispanics could comprise one-third of the nation's population by the year 2030.

As mainstream advertisers discover the Hispanic market, Mexican-American newspapers and magazines could well benefit if it is demonstrated through circulation figures that they reach a sizeable special market that can not be reached as effectively by other means. Unprecedented growth of the Mexican-American media, both print and electronic could result.

Another factor auguring well for the future of the Mexican-American press is the growth of Hispanic media organizations. In December 1982 the National Association of Hispanic Publications was formed during the First National Chicano Media Conference in San Diego. The association held its first annual conference in Los Angeles in September 1984. The association has as one of its goals the promotion of Hispanic publications as an advertising outlet, as well as an effective medium for other communications.[29] This was followed by the establishment of the National Association of Hispanic Journalists at the Second National Hispanic Media Conference in Washington, D.C., in April 1984.[30]

As of early 1984, according to one estimate, there were more than 200 daily or weekly Hispanic newspapers in the United States, with another 200 being published less frequently, along with over 100 Hispanic magazines and journals. These had a reported circulation of more than 4 million. Spanish-language or bilingual newspapers were being published in forty-seven states.[31]

Clearly this is a dynamic era for Hispanic journalism in general and for Mexican-American journalism in particular. What is impossible to predict is whether this dynamism will mean a major growth in Mexican-American print press, or whether the major beneficiaries will be the Spanish-language electronic media and those Chicano journalists whose goals are integration into mainstream media, not participation in the Mexican-American press.[32]

NOTES

1. Among the studies of *La Opinión* are Francine Medeiros, "*La Opinión*, a Mexican Exile Newspaper: A Content Analysis of Its First Years, 1926–1929," *Aztlán, International Journal of Chicano Studies Research* 11 (Spring 1980): 65–87; and Ricardo Chavira, "A Case Study: Reporting of Mexican Emigration and Deportation," *Journalism History* 4 (Summer 1977): 42–47.

2. David Weber, *Foreigners in Their Native Land: Historical Roots of the Mexican Americans* (Albuquerque: University of New Mexico Press, 1973).

3. *El Misisipí* of New Orleans (1808–1810), the first periodical in the United States to use the Spanish language, was started by an Anglo firm, William H. Johnson and Company. Most of its news came from Spanish-speaking nations, with little coverage of local events. See Félix Gutiérrez, "Spanish Language Media in the U.S.," *Caminos* 5 (January 1984): 10–12.

4. Two other newspapers were *La Verdad* and *El Payó de Nuevo Méjico*, while another *El Crepúsculo* is reported to have been published, although no copies are known to be extant and the newspaper's very existence is a matter of debate. Felix Gutiérrez, "Spanish-Language Media in America: Background, Resources, History," *Journalism History* 4 (Summer 1977): 37–38.

5. Edward C. Kemble and Helen Bretnor, *A History of California Newspapers, 1846–1858* (Los Gatos, Calif.: Talisman Press, 1962), pp. 14–15, 52–53.

6. For example, David Weber, ed., *Troubles in Texas, 1832: A Tejano Viewpoint from San Antonio* (Dallas: DeGolyer Library, Southern Methodist University, 1983).

7. Herminio Rios and Guadalupe Castillo, "Toward a True Chicano Bibliography: Mexican-American Newspapers: 1848–1942," *El Grito. A Journal of Contemporary Mexican-American Thought* 3 (Summer 1970): 17–24; Herminio Rios C., "Toward a

True Chicano Bibliography—Part II," *El Grito. A Journal of Contemporary Mexican-American Thought* 5 (Summer 1972): 40–47. (Hereafter cited as *Rios-Castillo Bibliographies.*)

8. Gutiérrez, "Spanish-Language Media," p. 65. For a case study, see Annabelle M. Oczon, "Bilingual and Spanish-Language Newspapers in Territorial New Mexico," *New Mexico Historical Review* 44 (January 1979): 45–52.

9. Computed from *Rios-Castillo Bibliographies*.

10. Richard Griswold del Castillo, *La Familia: Chicano Families in the Urban Southwest, 1848 to the Present* (Notre Dame, Ind.: University of Notre Dame Press), pp. 81–83, 85.

11. Américo Paredes, *A Texas-Mexican Cancionero: Folksongs of the Lower Border* (Urbana: University of Illinois Press, 1975).

12. In his classic study of Mexican labor in the United States, economist Paul Taylor drew heavily from Chicago's Mexican-American press. See Paul Taylor, *Mexican Labor in the United States*, 3 vols. (Berkeley: University of California Press, 1928–1934).

13. For a case study of three Mexican-American newspapers founded in Los Angeles during this decade, see Ramón D. Chacón, "The Chicano Immigrant Press in Los Angeles: The Case of 'El Heraldo de Mexico,' 1916–1920," *Journalism History* 4 (Summer 1977): 48–50, 62–63.

14. Computed from *Rios-Castillo Bibliographies*.

15. For an interesting study of this debate see Richard Griswold del Castillo, "The Mexican Revolution and the Spanish-Language Press in the Borderlands," *Journalism History* 4 (Summer 1977): 42–47.

16. Computed from *Rios-Castillo Bibliographies*.

17. Kirk Whisler, "The Growth of Hispanic Print Media," *Caminos* 5 (January 1984): 13. One preliminary and self-admittedly incomplete listing of Hispanic (not just Spanish-language) publications can be found in Joshua A. Fishman, ed., *Language Resources in the United States*, Vol. 1: *Non-English-Language Print Media* (Rosslyn, Va.: National Clearinghouse for Bilingual Education, 1981), pp. 26–30.

18. Gutiérrez, "Spanish-Language Media," pp. 38–41, 65–66.

19. For a discussion of this phenomenon in nineteenth-century New Mexico, see Porter A. Stratton, *The Territorial Press of New Mexico, 1834–1912* (Albuquerque: University of New Mexico Press, 1969), p. 12.

20. For example, see the chapter on Francisco Ramírez and his Los Angeles newspaper, *El Clamor Público* (1855–1859), in Leonard Pitt, *The Decline of the Californios: A Social History of Spanish-Speaking Californians, 1848–1890* (Berkeley: University of California Press, 1966), pp. 181–194.

21. National Spanish International Network Station List (1981).

22. "Minority Organizations: Looking for Strength in Numbers," *Broadcasting*, October 15, 1979, pp. 45–47.

23. "Spanish Language Radio: A Directory," in *Caminos' 1983 National Hispanic Conventioneer* (San Bernardino, Calif.: Caminos Corporation, 1983).

24. Joshua A. Fishman, Esther G. Lowy, William G. Milan, and Michael H. Gertner, eds., *Language Resources in the United States*, Vol. 2: *Non-English-Language Broadcasting* (Rosslyn, Va.: National Clearinghouse for Bilingual Education, 1982), pp. 35–60, 63–67.

25. Lee Marguilies, "Inside TV," *Los Angeles Times*, February 16, 1982, Part 6, p. 9. Minorities are here defined as blacks, Hispanics, and Asian and Indian Americans.

26. For example, see the 1980 study of Chicano media habits in seven southwestern cities, reported in Bradley S. Greenberg, Michael Burgoon, Judee K. Burgoon, and Felipe Korzenny, *Mexican Americans and the Mass Media* (Norwood, N.J.: ABLEX Publishing Corporation, 1983), pp. 81, 97–98.

27. For an examination of the advertising potential of the Hispanic media, see Antonio Guernica and Irene Kasperuk, *Reaching the Hispanic Market Effectively: The Media, the Market, the Methods* (New York: McGraw-Hill, 1982).

28. Jorge G. Castro, "The Challenge Ahead for Hispanic Print," *Caminos* 5 (January 1984): 9.

29. *Caminos' 1983 National Hispanic Conventioneer*, p. 49.

30. Juan González, "On the Road to Equality: Latino Journalists Organize," *Nuestro* 8 (June-July 1984): 35.

31. Whisler, "Growth," p. 13.

32. For an optimistic view of the future of the Hispanic press, see Tom Díaz, "The Blossoming of the Hispanic Press," *Nuestro*, October 1984, pp. 22–27.

BIBLIOGRAPHY

Del Olmo, Frank. "Chicano Journalism: New Medium for a New Consciousness." In Michael C. Emery and Ted Curtis Smythe, eds., *Readings in Mass Communication*. 2nd ed. Dubuque, Iowa: William G. Brown, 1974.

Fishman, Joshua A., ed. *Language Resources in the United States*. Vol. 1: *Non-English-Language Print Media*. Rosslyn, Va.: National Clearinghouse for Bilingual Education, 1981.

Greenberg, Bradley S., Michael Burgoon, Judee K. Burgoon, and Felipe Korzenny. *Mexican Americans and the Mass Media*. Norwood, N.J.: ABLEX Publishing Corporation, 1983.

Guernica, Antonio, and Irene Kasperuk. *Reaching the Hispanic Market Effectively: The Media, the Market, the Methods*. New York: McGraw-Hill, 1982.

Gutiérrez, Félix. "Reporting for La Raza: The History of Latino Journalism in America." *Agenda* 8 (July-August 1978): 29–35.

Rios, Herminio, and Guadalupe Castillo. "Toward a True Chicano Bibliography: Mexican-American Newspapers: 1848–1942." *El Grito. A Journal of Contemporary Mexican-American Thought* 3 (Summer 1970): 17–24.

Rios C., Herminio. "Toward a True Chicano Bibliography—Part II." *El Grito. A Journal of Contemporary Mexican-American Thought* 5 (Summer 1972): 40–47.

Shearer, James F. "Periódicos Espanoles en los Estados Unidos." *Revista Hispánica Moderna* 20 (1954): 45–57.

"Spanish-Language Media Issue." *Journalism History* 4 (Summer 1977).

Stratton, Porter A. *The Territorial Press of New Mexico, 1834–1912*. Albuquerque: University of New Mexico Press, 1969.

Wagner, Henry R. "New Mexico Spanish Press." *New Mexico Historical Review* 12 (1937): 1–40.

17

The Norwegian-American Press

ARLOW W. ANDERSEN

Journalists are at times subjects of admiration and trust. At other times they may carry the onus of suspicion and disdain. Since they deal mainly with affairs of the moment—the news, as it is called—they become identified with practical and immediate concerns. Many newspaper folk, gifted with literary talent and with more than adequate technical equipment, have succeeded in presenting the news with keen perception and effectiveness. Others have garbled the human record, whether by design or ignorance, and have pursued their special interests too aggressively. Søren Kierkegaard, the Danish philosopher of the nineteenth century, scorned this kind of news reporting and editorializing when he relegated journalism to "the lowest depth to which people can sink before God." On the other hand, he respected an honest historical approach. To repeat his sagacious words, "Life must be lived forwards, but it can only be understood backwards."[1]

Norwegian immigrants found America to be a land of newspapers. They were aware that Norway had already introduced freedom of the press, but the sheer magnitude of the American institution impressed them and inspired them to establish their own weekly journals, published in their own language. Having imbibed of the democratic spirit in the home country, they cherished the opportunity for expression in the new land. The resulting Norwegian-American press supplied a political medium as well as a cultural tie for the 800,000 who eventually emigrated from Norway. Politics and other public affairs came to be reflected in the news reports. Suggestions for reform commonly appeared with other commentary in the editorial columns. Hopes for the success of the great democratic experiment in the New World never faded, but the road to glory was rough. In compensation, Norwegian editors and their immigrant readers usually found comfort in the knowledge that, in the long run, their own future as well as that of America would be brighter.

Norwegian-American newspaper publishers and editors, many of them graduates of the University of Christiania (now Oslo) and of Norway's technical schools, generally enjoyed the respect and trust of their readers. They were well educated in the Western tradition. Some of them established long-lasting weekly newspapers of large circulation among their Nordic countrymen, including a clientele not only Norwegian but also Danish and Swedish. For the most part, they rose above the trivial in their vision, in their understanding of American events and political procedures, and in their proposed solutions to problems. When it is taken into consideration that most had also received thorough religious instruction in their childhood, it is not strange that they demonstrated social and moral responsiveness of a high order in their adopted country. Of course, there were those who rebelled against their Lutheran heritage, yet even they in their politics practiced, in effect, a form of religion, inasmuch as politics compelled devotion and gave meaning to life.

Scandinavian scholars make the point that, while northern Europeans of today are avid readers, such was hardly the case in the nineteenth century. Before the politically turbulent 1880s, the press in Norway directed itself mainly toward the social and intellectual elite. Therefore, the near avalanche of newspapers printed in America in the Norwegian language came as a surprise to the pressmen of Christiania, Bergen, and Trondhjem (now Trondheim). The contrast between the Old World and the new is striking. Servants, cotters, and laborers in nine-teenth-century Norway found newspapers too expensive and not necessary to their simple way of life. In America, on the other hand, the status of the immigrant improved to the point where he or she subscribed to at least one of the many weekly journals carrying welcome news from the homeland and from the Nor-wegian settlements concentrated in the upper Middle West. The newspaper, which at worst helped to seal out the winter cold on the rustic cabin wall, aided immeasurably in the transition to an understanding of American customs and institutions. As time went on, more and more announcements, reports, and editorials appeared in English, a further boon to adjustment in the new society.

In the case of the Norwegian ethnic press, several hundred titles came and went in the century following 1847, the year in which the first strictly Norwegian newspaper, *Nordlyset* (The northern light), was founded in Norway, Wisconsin. The average life span of these magazines and newspapers, mostly secular but including some church periodicals, was ten years. About one-third survived a year or less. In 1946 only forty were still in circulation.

Over a span of a century some 113 papers were published in Minneapolis. Next in order were Chicago with 76; Decorah, Iowa, with 40; Fargo, North Dakota, with 23; New York City with 17; Madison and La Crosse in Wisconsin, each with 17; Brooklyn with 13; and Eau Claire, Wisconsin, with 8. Of the 500 or more newspapers and other periodicals, some of them primarily religious organs, 216 were published in Minnesota, 85 in Illinois, 82 in Wisconsin, 62 in North Dakota, 57 in Iowa, 42 in Washington State, and 30 in New York State. Apparently the peak of publication came between 1877 and 1906. In the decade 1877–1886 about 100 papers were founded; in 1887–1896 about 142; in 1897–1906 about 104. Since then the establishment of new journals has declined sharply, from 68 in 1907–1916 to only 10 in 1937–1946.[2]

In the 1980s only three Norwegian-language papers were being published, with much of their material in English. These were *Nordisk Tidende* (Northern times) of Brooklyn (founded in 1891), *Western Viking* of Seattle (1931), and *Vinland* of Chicago (revived in 1976). *Minnesota Posten* of Minneapolis (1957) ceased publication in 1980. Some formerly well-established journals succumbed earlier: *Minneapolis Tidende* (Minneapolis times) in 1935, *Skandinaven* (The Scandinavian) of Chicago in 1941, *Reform* of Eau Claire, Wisconsin, in 1941, and *Decorah-Posten* (Decorah post) of Iowa in 1972, two years short of its centennial.

Foreign-born newsmen wrestled seriously with public issues before and after the War between the States. The third quarter of the nineteenth century brought many trials as well as challenging opportunities to Americans of European birth. The Norwegian press reflected that era, one so full of greatness and meanness alike in politics, foreign affairs, the slavery debate, bloody warfare between "rebels" and "damned Yankees," and finally Radical Republican domination of the South as well as the North. Social and economic problems called for solution. Should the parents, the community, or the state determine the kind and quality of education available to young Hans and Sigrid? Should drunkenness be condoned, as a demonstration of the exercise of personal freedom? Should white women trail black men in the struggle for the right to vote? Should public lands in the undeveloped West be made more readily available to genuine settlers rather than to speculators? What ought to be done for the unskilled and exploited immigrant laborers in the rapidly growing industrial centers?[3]

How did the pioneer Norwegian-American press respond to these questions? Perhaps the experience and the editorial policy of Knud Langeland in *Nordlyset* and in *Skandinaven*, after 1866, reflect many of the attitudes of his journalistic colleagues in America. This articulate and sensitive man rose from humble beginnings in his native country to become the Nestor of his countrymen in America. As a boy in his rural homeland, near Bergen, he was taught by an itinerant teacher whose religious fanaticism was accentuated by his crippled body. Only the Bible and religious tracts should be read by the people of the servant class, he insisted. An uncle came to Knud's rescue, loaning him books of wider scope and offering to read his papers on various themes. Not so with the parish pastor, who despised secular literature and, to make matters worse, scolded the boy for not bringing a gift in advance of the day of confirmation. Knud was the tenth child in the family. His mother had had enough of giving. Yet the persistent minister openly requested the gift in front of the congregation on confirmation Sunday. Knud would never forget this embarrassing incident.[4]

Langeland's public career in America, after his immigration in 1843, began with his election to the Wisconsin state assembly in 1859. His success marked a breakthrough for Norwegian Americans in politics, an advance from the local to the state level. As a Republican he favored the platform which, among other objectives, called for limitations on the extension of Negro slavery with an eye toward its eventual elimination. He approved of public education as an instrument of Americanization. At the same time he defended his Norwegian constituents against nativist charges of lack of patriotism. Readers of *Nordlyset* and its successor *Democraten* (The democrat) were frequently exposed to translations of government documents, among them the federal and state constitutions.

The supreme test of loyalty to a united America came in the presidential campaign of 1860 and in the ensuing war of North against South. Whatever doubts *Emigranten* may have had concerning the qualifications of Abraham Lincoln, the Republican candidate for the White House, they were soon dissipated in the universal clamor for a military victory. Most Norwegians cast their ballots for Lincoln. Not long after the Confederate firing on Fort Sumter, editor Carl Fredrik Solberg declared, "God is with the American soldier." For both sides the war became a crusade.[5]

Colonel Hans Christian Heg and his Fifteenth Wisconsin Infantry regiment of volunteers proved to be the chief rallying point for Americans of Norwegian birth. The nearly all-Norwegian unit suffered heavy casualties, through disease and combat, and won distinction on the field of battle. Heg's death after being wounded at Chickamanga stunned his countrymen. Possibly they had lost a man whose stature would have some day brought him to Congress. By way of compensation, survivors of the war would come forth as honored members of the Grand Army of the Republic to be favored in future political contests. Meanwhile, *Faedrelandet* (The fatherland) of La Crosse, Wisconsin, reaffirmed the Norwegian position. In its words, the American republic was "a glorious institution." Reflections on Lincoln's assassination served to enhance that shining image of America. *Emigranten* called him the second father of his country. Others likened him to Moses, who had led his people to within sight of the promised land.[6]

In matters of reform, Langeland's appreciation of the democratizing function of the public school has been mentioned. But sectional turmoil in the 1850s may have prevented a serious look at the educational process by other newsmen. Yet Chicago's *Skandinaven*, carrying on in the spirit of Langeland, resumed the agitation for educational advancement. Temperance, women's rights, and free government land also became objects of its special concern. However, Norwegian writers produced no national leaders in these efforts from 1850 to 1875. This is not to say that they were indifferent but, until later in the century, they published, for example, no temperance journals, although they were familiar with the problem of alcoholism from the homeland. They put their trust, for the time being, in education and moral restraint rather than in legislation.[7]

For a direct attempt to dethrone King Alcohol one must look to *Reform*, published in Eau Claire after 1889. Despite its seeming one-sidedness, this newspaper ranks culturally as one of the most outstanding. Its editors, Ole Broder Olson to 1903 and Waldemar Ager thereafter, supported total abstinence, yet they shied away from the political pressure tactics of the Anti-Saloon League, which drew heavy financial support from major Protestant denominations. Both men were much in demand as lecturers. Ager became known for his ethnic awareness and for his interesting and meaningful novels, one of which was entitled *Paa Drikkeondets Konto* (To the account of the liquor evil). Both also ran, unsuccessfully, as Prohibition candidates, Olson for Congress and for lieutenant-governor of Wisconsin, and Ager for state treasurer. Ager's wide literary tastes induced him to publish in *Reform*, in the Norwegian language, such classical works as *Quo Vadis* and *Oliver Twist*. Olson and Ager were not narrow-minded. Their interests ranged through the entire spectrum of reform.

The women's rights movement gained impetus, in part, from the emancipation of the slaves. Here also the Norwegian-American press lagged in supporting the cause, as did the national press as a whole. Yet some observant men and women saw in the struggle a correlation between temperance and the rights of women. Nevertheless, many owners and editors recognized the value of running a regular women's column in their journals. *Skandinaven* went further when it authorized the monthly publication of *Husbibliothek* (Home library) in 1873. Under the guidance of Ingeborg Rasmussen, who served on *Skandinaven*'s editorial staff for many years, this publication dispensed information and inspired women to apply their talents outside the home as well as in it. Inevitably, some were drawn into politics and social reform. In 1888 Ida Hansen and Mina Jensen began publication of *Kvinden og Hjemmet* (The woman and the home) in Cedar Rapids, Iowa. The circulation of this monthly reached a healthy 75,000. Hans A. Foss was for many years editor of *Kvindens Magasin* (The lady's magazine), a Minneapolis periodical, beginning in 1905.

As momentum increased for passage of a woman suffrage amendment, Norwegian spokesmen were generally sympathetic. The movement also had its detractors, however, as when Peer Strømme, who served briefly as editor of several papers, and Senator Knute Nelson of Minnesota complained of the bizarre behavior of the more militant "skirts-persons." Aside from a newly won respect for women, resulting from their war work in 1917–1918, the example of Norwegian women abroad may have had its effect. Many immigrants belonged to the generation following Norway's women's rights leaders—Camilla Collett, Gina Krog, and Aasta Hansteen. Hansteen was well acquainted with feminist leaders in the United States, having spent several years in New England. In keeping with the progressive spirit, most Norwegian pressmen in the United States hailed the Nineteenth Amendment when it was adopted in 1920.

A small minority of immigrant newspapers espoused the cause of materialistic socialism at mid-century. In Norway Marcus Thrane, hardly Marxist in his aims, organized workingmen's associations and headed the drive for an eight-hour day in industry. For his efforts he was imprisoned. Upon his release he came to Chicago, where he published successively two short-lived newspapers, *Marcus Thranes norske amerikaner* (Marcus Thrane's Norwegian American) in 1866 and *Dagslyset* (The dawn) from 1869 to 1876.

In his monarchical homeland Thrane had advocated a republican form of government and better opportunities for advanced education for the lower classes. He also fulminated against the "money power" and the Lutheran "priestly caste," both in Norway and in America. At one time his ideas were considered dangerous to the functioning of Norwegian institutions, but his star gradually ascended in working-class Norway, especially following his death and simple burial in Eau Claire, Wisconsin, in 1890. In 1949 the Labor (Social Democratic) government arranged to have his remains transported and interred with appropriate ceremonies in Oslo, in Vor Frelsers Gravlund (Our Savior's Cemetery), a national shrine.

The Haymarket riot of 1886 and the Pullman strike of 1894, both centered in Chicago, were interpreted by the nation as a whole as indicative that socialism was not the solution for the workingman. However, its zealous proponents later published *Social-Demokraten* in Chicago from 1911 to 1921. Under the masthead "Liberty, Equality, Fraternity," this metropolitan weekly shifted entirely to English in 1921 and changed its name to *Voice of Labor*, which survived only two years. *Gaa Paa* (Go forward), more radical in its socialism than was Thrane, was published in Minneapolis in 1903, to be followed by *Folkets Røst* (The voice of the people), 1919–1925.

Among the newspapers of the half-century from 1875 to 1925, Chicago's *Skandinaven* ranks as the most influential politically. Intended mainly for Norwegians, despite its more pretentious title, it extended its readershp far beyond the metropolitan area. *Skandinaven* presented itself as an independent Republican paper. Johannes Wist of *Decorah-Posten* credited it with being "the political paper par excellence."

Without the rocklike personality and wide experience of John Anderson, *Skandinaven* would not have been launched. Of humble origin, he immigrated as a lad to Chicago in 1845. Anderson worked at many things, including typesetting for Chicago newspapers. In 1866 he persuaded Victor F. Lawson to join him in establishing *Skandinaven*. Lawson (originally Lassen and then Larsen) was to leave two years later to found the *Chicago Daily News*. Anderson made every effort to reach the Norwegian community. He instructed his newsboys to meet the incoming immigrant trains and to give free copies of the paper to passengers who could not afford to buy them. Before his death in 1910, Anderson, generous in humanitarian causes, became known as one of Chicago's civic leaders. *Skandinaven's Boghandel* (book trade) was in itself impressive. Over 500 titles were printed before the paper ceased publication in 1941.

Skandinaven reached its peak as a political force during the editorship of Nicolay Grevstad, from 1892 to 1911. As a former student leader at the University of Christiania, he joined the staff of *Dagbladet* (The daily paper) in that city in 1880. He was dismissed in 1883. The management of this otherwise liberal journal did not appreciate his enthusiasm for Johan Sverdrup, who was then in the forefront of the fight for parliamentary government. After a few years in Chicago, Grevstad bought the *Minneapolis Times*, an English-language publication. As editor of *Skandinaven*, he often printed his editorials in English in order to reach the general public.

With over 300 papers making their debut in the last quarter of the nineteenth century, it is difficult to select with fairness a few representative titles. In general, those which satisfied most readers and which survived more than a few years are discussed here. In the Republican category were *Nordvesten* (The Northwest) of Minneapolis-St. Paul, from 1881 to 1907, and *Amerika* published in Chicago from 1884 to 1896 and in Madison, Wisconsin, thereafter until 1922. Political opponents claimed, with dubious evidence, that James J. Hill of the Great Northern Railway really controlled *Nordvesten*. This paper was absorbed by the *Minneapolis Tidende* in 1907.

Amerika survived a turbulent history of thirty-eight years. An earlier editor, Peer Strømme, consistently espoused the philosophy of the Democratic Party. Had it not been for his genial personality, quiet wit, and good humor, this Mark Twain among the Norwegians would have been less acceptable to Republican readers. In Madison, *Amerika* became identified with Rasmus B. Anderson, formerly a professor of Scandinavian languages and literature at the University of Wisconsin (1885–1889). President Grover Cleveland named him, then a young Democrat, as minister to Denmark, but Anderson turned staunchly Republican in the 1890s. Johannes Wist characterized the mercurial Anderson as being "in strife with both churchly and worldly powers." On two issues, neither of them political, Anderson was unbending. As his biographer states, he felt that Norwegian-American cultural life was threatened by naturalistic literature and that newspapers should not carry "unclean" advertisements, particularly those making misleading claims for patent medicines of high alcoholic content or featuring sexual material. Contemporary authors in Norway, like Knut Hamsun, Arne Garborg, and Henrik Ibsen, should be disavowed in America, and readers should be warned of spurious claims of patent medicine manufacturers.[8]

Minneapolis Tidende (1887–1935) traced its lineage back to *Emigranten*. Thorvald Guldbrandsen published this prominent journal of the upper Middle West. During Sigvart Sørensen's editorship, from 1891 to 1923, *Tidende* increased its circulation substantially, thanks to continued Norwegian immigration. Although personally leaning toward the Democrats, Sørensen dealt more with nonpolitical matters. Carl G. O. Hansen, an independent Republican, succeeded him.

Some newspapers were reluctant to support either of the two major parties; among them were *Normanden* of Grand Forks and Fargo, North Dakota (1887–1954); *Fremad* (Forward) of Sioux Falls, South Dakota (1894–1935); and *Fram* (Forward) of Fargo-Moorhead (1898–1917). All were temperance-minded. *Normanden*, managed by P. O. Thorson from 1893 to 1924, saw many editors come and go. More than any other, this "reform" journal could pride itself on securing adoption of a prohibition clause in the North Dakota state constitution of 1889. In 1925 the paper was moved from Grand Forks to Fargo. *Fremad*, under its sturdy founder and editor Johan F. Strass from 1896 to 1924, paralleled *Normanden* in some ways. *Fram*, like *Normanden* and *Fremad* moved toward support of Robert M. La Follette, Theodore Roosevelt, and progressivism. It was absorbed by *Normanden* in 1917.

At the turn of the century the charismatic figure of Theodore Roosevelt dominated the news. Before he burst upon the political scene as governor of New York, some Norwegian-American commentators were complaining about the weak enforcement of the Interstate Commerce Act of 1887 and the Sherman Anti-Trust Act of 1890. To Norwegian consumers, the hideous "trust-troll" who guarded the economic bridge over which they must pass threatened them as surely as he had the Billy Goats Gruff. President Roosevelt's distinction between good and bad trusts failed to allay suspicion of the moguls of finance and business.

The foreign policy of the master of the Big Stick drew varied responses. During the conflict with Spain over Cuba and the Philippine Islands, Roosevelt made it clear, as assistant secretary of the navy, that action was his forte. The yellow press of New York's William Randolph Hearst and Joseph Pulitzer reveled in his successes. Norwegian journalists generally fell into the professed humanitarian and prowar line, but the question of intervention in the Philippines, after Spain's defeat, later divided them. Senator Knute Nelson and editor Nicolay Grevstad of *Skandinaven* stood by President William McKinley in his desire for annexation of this Far Eastern outpost, but Rasmus B. Anderson and Hans A. Foss balked at interfering with Emilio Aguinaldo's independence movement.[9]

A different problem in foreign relations, with its origin in the nineteenth century, engaged the attention of Norwegian Americans. The union of Sweden and Norway in 1814, as a part of the Vienna settlement after the Napoleonic wars, proved acceptable to Norwegians when the king of Sweden recognized their liberal constitution. However, throughout the following century national and democratic feelings intensified. In 1905 the Norwegian parliament voted for separation. Norwegians then decided by plebiscite to continue the monarchical institution and invited a Danish prince to take the new throne. He chose the name Haakon VII, thus continuing the line which had been broken by several centuries of direct Danish rule. The Norwegian-American press followed the events of 1905 closely.

Norwegian spokesmen in America were in full agreement on complete independence but not on the form of government to be adopted. Some favored monarchy, others a republic. Monarchy, it was said, might be more acceptable in most European capitals and would better insure recognition for Norway. A republic, on the other hand, would please France and the United States. *Amerika* and Brooklyn's *Nordisk Tidende* seemed to gloat over the break with Sweden. Both favored a republic but resigned themselves to a different outcome. At any rate, wrote Emil Nielsen of *Nordisk Tidende*, Haakon VII became king not by the grace of God but by the will of the people. Newspapermen serving Swedish subscribers in Illinois and the Dakotas proceeded more cautiously. Grevstad of *Skandinaven* gave full reports on the crisis in the spring of 1905 but carefully avoided offending Swedish readers. A. A. Trovaten, longtime manager of Fargo's *Fram*, made it clear that no wall should stand between Swedes and Norwegians in America.[10]

As World War I began in the summer of 1914, no papers, perhaps, expressed the immigrant reaction more fully than *Skandinaven* and Eau Claire's *Reform*. Satisfied with Taft's administration earlier, and still tantalized by the exuberant personality and progressivism of Theodore Roosevelt, not to mention La Follette's more vigorous reformism, they now had to adjust to Woodrow Wilson's style after the three-way presidential contest between William Howard Taft, Roosevelt, and Wilson in 1912. John Benson, now editor of *Skandinaven*, and Ager of *Reform*, neither associated with Wilson's Democratic party, endorsed his neutrality stand in 1914–1917. Ager qualified his support, warning that "running England's errands" was not exactly neutral behavior. He believed that German reports on the war were more reliable than British ones. In 1916 he preferred Charles Evans Hughes, the son of an immigrant Welshman, over Wilson but conceded that Wilson was more given to nonintervention. *Skandinaven* also preferred Hughes, the Republican candidate. Seldom were Norwegian Americans so divided. Anderson of *Amerika* contended that Wilson should be reelected. *Pacific Skandinaven* of Portland, Oregon, went for Hughes. *Decorah-Posten* simply wrote off the two party platforms as being similar, leaving no meaningful choice.[11]

A sizeable number of editors joined with Senator La Follette of Wisconsin and Congressman Asle J. Grønna of North Dakota in taking a noninterventionist stand. The Mormon *Bikuben* (The bee hive) of Salt Lake City, while propagating its religious views for Scandinavian proselytes in Utah, commented regularly on national affairs. Its message was military preparedness, with the brakes on. "Let peace flow out of Zion" was its prayer. *Fram* and *Fremad* of the Dakotas advised against American involvement. *Pacific Skandinaven* and *Reform* agreed with them. The smaller socialist journals, *Gaa Paa* and *Social-Demokraten*, remained pacifist, as did the Socialist Party of America, but not its counterparts in the belligerent countries of Europe. The absence of the larger metropolitan papers in the antiwar category may have significance. Generally, Norwegian immigrants and their sons and daughters residing in smaller communities, and somewhat removed from the wartime excitement on the eastern seaboard, were more likely to turn their backs on the fighting in Europe.[12]

When war was declared against Germany in April 1917, the Norwegian element was measured by the yardstick of 100 percent Americanism. Freedom of speech became an important issue. In Iowa the governor attempted to prevent foreign-speaking citizens from using their mother tongue in public places, even in telephone conversations. For so doing he was roughly handled in the immigrant press. One of the most effective protests against charges of un-Americanism was Ager's novel, *Paa Veien til Smeltepotten* (On the way to the melting pot), which ran serially in *Reform* and was later published in book form. He eloquently defended the so-called hyphenates, who had been denounced by Roosevelt and Wilson. All foreign-language periodicals were required by law to submit translations of their articles and editorials before publication. But Norwegian Americans, like other ethnic groups, demonstrated their loyalty to the war effort in military service, by purchasing Liberty Bonds, and for the time being by supporting their idealistic and humanitarian president in his war aims.[13]

In 1919, while the Senate debated whether to make formal peace with Germany and to incorporate in the treaty the covenant of the League of Nations, as Wilson was insisting, public interest in world affairs waned. *Amerika* and *Skandinaven* reflected skepticism, but several journals continued to defend the idea of American membership in the League. *Decorah-Posten* called the League a good beginning on the road to peace. *Minneapolis Tidende* observed that Norway would be a member and agreed with its venerable statesman and Arctic explorer Fridtjof Nansen that an organization of this kind was necessary. In keeping with the isolationist, back-to-normalcy, and business trend in American thinking, the Norwegian-American press generally supported the Republican presidential candidates, Warren G. Harding and Calvin Coolidge, in the elections of 1920 and 1924, respectively. Democratic candidates scarcely received a nod.[14]

Norwegian-American identity consciousness intensified in 1925. The centennial of the arrival of the Sloopers in New York harbor called for a special celebration. The various *bygdelag*, composed of folk from particular valleys and regions of Norway, contributed heavily toward the success of the June meeting in Minneapolis-St. Paul. Various *bygdelag* newsletters covered the story. The Sons of Norway, organized in 1895, did their part through their own publication, the monthly *Viking*, begun soon after 1900. President Coolidge accepted an invitation to speak. The historian of the *bygdelag* movement calls attention to Ager's view that the festival was "a major argument for a pluralistic society." In Ager's opinion, the melting-pot concept would result only in "vulgarization" of American culture.[15]

If Ager envisioned a Norwegian-American community that would continue to use the Norwegian language indefinitely, his hopes fell considerably short of realization. Immigration from Norway declined to a mere trickle in the late 1920s and the 1930s. Use of the mother tongue suffered with the passing of each generation. In the newspaper field, by 1925, a number of prominent personalities had ascended to the journalistic heaven which Kierkegaard would have denied them. Among them were Johannes Wist of *Decorah-Posten*, P. O. Thorson of *Normanden*, Johan Strass of *Fremad*, and Peer Strømme, who had served on the staffs of several journals. Kristian Prestgard guided *Decorah-Posten* from 1923 to 1946, and Einar Lund from 1946 to 1962. Nicolay Grevstad returned to *Skandinaven* from 1930 to 1941, only to preside over its demise. *Minneapolis Tidende* survived under Carl G. O. Hansen until 1935. Brooklyn's *Nordisk Tidende* enjoyed strong leadership after Andreas N. Rygg with Hans Olav Tønnesen and Carl Søyland taking over until its present editor, Sigurd Daasvand, took the helm. In Seattle Henning C. Boe still carries on successfully with the *Western Viking*.

Economic and cultural developments of the 1920s adversely affected the foreign-language press. The rapidly expanding automobile, radio, and movie industries played a significant part as homogenizing agents in American society. Together they promoted standardization in speech and style of living. These factors, coupled with the superpatriotic postwar discouragement of the use of foreign languages in church, school, conversation, and in the print media, meant that the Norwegian-American press could never be the same. To its credit, however, the press seldom had fought the English language. It encouraged bilingualism and, at the same time, the preservation of personal and group identity. It stimulated the Norwegian community to influence public affairs and to appreciate the rocks and rills and templed hills, as they continued to enjoy, in retrospect, the mountain streams and the fjords of their forebears.

NOTES

1. Søren Kierkegaard, quoted in "The New Concerns about the Press," *Fortune Magazine* 91 (April 1975): 121.

2. Olaf Morgan Norlie, "Norwegian-Americana Papers, 1847–1946" (Northfield, Minn.: mimeographed, 1946), pp. 30, 33. Norlie lists some 570 titles, including a number of church periodicals.

3. Arlow W. Andersen, *The Immigrant Takes His Stand: The Norwegian-American Press and Public Affairs, 1847–1872* (Northfield, Minn.: Norwegian-American Historical Association, 1953), see especially chapters 4, 5, and 6.

4. Knud Langeland, *Nordmaendene i Amerika* (The Norwegians in America) (Chicago: John Anderson Publishing Company, 1888), pp. 126–135.

5. *Emigranten*, April 23, 1861. This journal was founded in Inmansville, Wisconsin, (1852–1857), and was later moved to Madison (1857–1868).

6. *Faedrelandet*, January 14, 1864; *Emigranten*, April 17 and 24, 1865.

7. *Skandinaven og Amerika*, June 26, 1873; *Skandinaven*, January 29 and April 30, 1874, January 5 and March 2 and 30, 1875. When Langeland resigned from *Skandinaven* in 1872, he and John A. Johnson and Victor F. Lawson published *Amerika*. On January 1, 1873, the two papers were merged. A year later the name reverted to *Skandinaven* alone. See Jean Skagerboe Hansen, "*Skandinaven* and the John Anderson Publishing Company," *Norwegian-American Studies* 28 (1979): 35–68.

8. Peer Strømme also edited, at one time or another, *Norden* (The north) of Chicago; *Superior Posten* of Wisconsin; *Kvartalskrift* (Quarterly writings) of Decorah, Iowa; and *Normanden* (The Norwegian) of Grand Forks, North Dakota. His *Erindringer* (Reminiscences) was published posthumously in 1923. On Rasmus B. Anderson's opposition to "the corrupt press," see Lloyd Hustvedt, *Rasmus Bjørn Anderson: Pioneer Scholar* (Northfield, Minn.: Norwegian-American Historical Association, 1966), chapter 10.

9. *Skandinaven*, January 25, April 19, June 28, September 22, and October 25, 1899; *Amerika og Norden*, January 25, February 22, and April 5, 1899; *Nye Normanden*, September 11 and October 16, 1900; Knute Nelson in U.S., *Congressional Record*, 55th Congress, 3rd sess., January 20, 1899, pp. 831–838.

10. *Minneapolis Tidende*, August 29 and November 24, 1905; *Fremad*, July 13, 1905; *Normanden*, July 5, 1905; *Amerika*, June 16 and July 14, 1905; *Nordisk Tidende*, March 23 and 30, October 5, and December 7, 1905; *Fram*, June 23, 1905, See also Terje Leiren, "American Press Opinion and Norwegian Independence," *Norwegian-American Studies* 27 (1977): 224–242; Barry Hogan, "Two Fatherlands: North Dakota's Norwegians in 1905," *North Dakota Quarterly* 49 (Autumn 1981): 52–64.

11. *Skandinaven*, October 9, 1914, and October 7, 1916; *Reform*, January 26 and November 15, 1915, June 13 and October 31, 1916; *Amerika*, October 27, 1916; *Pacific Skandinaven*, November 10, 1916; *Decorah-Posten*, June 23, 1916.

12. *Bikuben*, November 11, 1915; *Fram*, July 6 and August 3, 1916, November 8, 1917; *Fremad*, November 11, 1917; *Pacific Skandinaven*, July 30, 1915, and March 9, 1917; *Reform*, October 19, 1915, and October 31, 1916; *Gaa Paa*, July 28, 1917; *Social-Demokraten*, October 6, 1916.

13. *Skandinaven*, October 31, 1918; *Minneapolis Tidende*, February 8, 1917; *Decorah-Posten*, June 29, 1917. In his review of Ager's novel, Gunnar Lund of *Washington-Posten* described it as "the year's greatest book for Norwegian Americans. Ager swings the whip of satire masterfully." It was a source book on Norwegian psychology, Lund wrote.

14. *Amerika*, March 14, 1919; *Skandinaven*, February 19, 1919; *Decorah-Posten*, May 2, 1919; *Minneapolis Tidende*, April 3, 1919.

15. Odd Sverre Lovoll, *A Folk Epic: The Bygdelag in America* (Boston: Twayne, 1975), p. 169. The official history of the Sons of Norway is C. Sverre Norborg, *An American Saga* (Minneapolis: Sons of Norway, 1970).

BIBLIOGRAPHY

Andersen, Arlow W. *The Immigrant Takes His Stand: The Norwegian-American Press and Public Affairs, 1847–1872*. Northfield, Minn.: Norwegian-American Historical Association [hereafter N.A.H.A.], 1953.

———. *The Norwegian-Americans*. New York: Twayne, 1975. See especially chapters 5, 6, and 7.

Anderson, Rasmus B. *Life Story of Rasmus B. Anderson*. Madison, Wis.: 1915.

Hansen, Carl G. O. *My Minneapolis*. Minneapolis: Standard Press, 1956.

———. "Pressen til borgerkrigens slutning" (The press to the close of the Civil War). In *Norsk-Amerikanernes Festskrift 1914*. Decorah, Iowa: Symra, 1914. Pp. 9–40.

Hansen, Jean Skagerboe. "*Skandinaven* and the John Anderson Publishing Company." *Norwegian-American Studies* 28 (1979): 35–68.

Hustvedt, Lloyd. *Rasmus Bjørn Anderson: Pioneer Scholar*. Northfield, Minn.: N.A.H.A., 1966. See especially chapter 10.

Langeland, Knud. *Nordmaendene i Amerika* (The Norwegians in America). Chicago: John Anderson Publishing Company, 1888. Pp. 126–135.

Lovoll, Odd Sverre. "Decorah-Posten: The Story of an Immigrant Newspaper." *Norwegian-American Studies* 27 (1977): 77–100.

———. *A Folk Epic: The Bygdelag in America*. New York: Twayne, 1975. Excellent on bygdelag publications.

———. "The Norwegian Press in North Dakota." *Norwegian-American Studies* 24 (1970): 78–101.

———. ed. *Cultural Pluralism versus Assimilation: The Views of Waldemar Ager*. Northfield, Minn.: N.A.H.A., 1977.

Naeseth, Henriette C. K. "Kristian Prestgard: An Appreciation." *Norwegian-American Studies and Records* 15 (1949): 131–139.

Norlie, Olaf Morgan. "Norwegian-Americana Papers, 1847–1946." Northfield, Minn.: mimeographed, 1946.

Qualey, Carlton C. *Norwegian Settlement in the United States.* Northfield, Minn.: N.A.H.A., 1938. Extensive use of newspapers, periodicals, and bygdelag publications, all listed in the bibliography, pp. 260–264.

Roedder, Karsten. *Av En Utvandreravis' Saga: Nordisk Tidende gjennom 75 År* (From an emigrant newspaper's saga: Nordisk Tidende through seventy-five yers). Brooklyn, N.Y.: Northway Printers, 1966.

Solberg, Carl Frederick. "Reminiscences of a Pioneer Editor." *Norwegian-American Studies and Records* 1 (1926): 134–146.

Søyland, Carl. *Skrift i Sand* (Writing in the sand). Oslo: Gyldendal Norsk Forlag, 1954. Reminiscences of one who edited *Nordisk Tidende* from 1940 to 1963.

Strømme Peer. *Erindringer* (Memoirs). Minneapolis: Augsburg Publishing House, 1923.

Wefald, Jon. *A Voice of Protest: Norwegians in American Politics, 1890–1917.* Northfield, Minn.: N.A.H.A., 1971.

Wist, Johannes B. "Pressen efter borgerkrigen" (The press after the Civil War). In *Norsk-Amerikanernes Festskrift 1914.* Decorah, Iowa: Symra, 1914. Pp. 41–203.

18

The Polish–American Press

A. J. KUZNIEWSKI

The Polish-American press has always been a particularly clear window through which to view the self-understanding and assimilation of the sons and daughters of Poland in the United States. It was obvious even to the first generation of Polish-Americans that their journalistic enterprise was connected with their adjustment to the New World. When, for instance, a turn-of-the-century historian attempted to explain the prominence of the press in the Polonian immigrant community, he cited the example of the Americans, for whom "the newspaper is as necessary as a piece of bread or a glass of water." This national passion for news and journalism, he argued, had a "decided influence" on the growth of the Polish-American press.[1] Although many of the newcomers had been familiar with newspapers in partitioned Poland,[2] American freedom and prosperity attracted ambitious young writers and publicists who brought journalistic vitality and popularity to countrymen in America. Their journalism addressed the needs of a group which, by the very act of immigration, had constituted itself as no longer purely Polish. The result was a press whose strengths, peculiarities, changes, and disagreements have represented an evolving community with remarkable and sometimes dramatic accuracy.

Because Polish immigrants were frequently recorded in the United States as nationals of one of the three countries that had partitioned their homeland in the eighteenth century, statistics on the number of immigrants are only estimates. Most scholars agree, however, that about 2 million Poles settled permanently in the United States between 1850 and 1924. Beginning with agricultural settlements in Texas and Wisconsin before the Civil War, the first wave of Polish immigrants came mostly from Germany before 1890. Thereafter, Galician Poles from the Habsburg Empire and then Russian Poles rounded out the figure. Most of the newcomers found employment in the expanding industrial cities of the Northeast and in mining centers in Pennsylvania. By 1920 Chicago counted 400,000 Polish-Americans. New York and Pittsburgh followed with about 200,000 each; Buffalo, Milwaukee, and Detroit numbered 100,000; and Philadelphia and Cleveland had at least 50,000. Descendants of the original immigrants and a new influx

of Poles after World War II swelled the size of the Polish-American community
to at least 6 million by 1980; but the assimilation process accounted for a decline
in the number able to speak and read Polish after about 1930, when there were
over 3.3 million first- and second-generation Polish-Americans.[3]

The role of the ethnic press was directly related to the stages by which these
newcomers assimilated to life in the United States. The emerging consensus
among historians and sociologists is that the pioneer generation of Polish-American life extended from the beginning of the economic migration until about
1900. It was a time when Polish life in America was organized around Catholic
parishes and larger organizations like the Polish Roman Catholic Union and the
Polish National Alliance. Rising ethnic consciousness spurred Polish-American
leaders to educate immigrants simultaneously about the implications of their
Polish and American identities. The second stage, which peaked about the time
of World War I, featured strident assertions of national and ethnic claims. It
was a time of preoccupation with the role American Poles, as the "Fourth
Partition," could play in the reestablishment of Poland. Simultaneously, community leaders stressed the legitimacy of the Polish language and customs in
America, emphasizing Polish culture as worthy of assimilation in a pluralistic
society. These years witnessed the crusade for "equality" within the Roman
Catholic Church, the stable development of the Scranton-based Polish National
Catholic Church, and angry debates between "nationalists" and "clericalists"
over the primacy of faith and fatherland. After the reestablishment of Poland,
the Polish community in America entered a new phase, one characterized by
absorption in internal processes. This change resulted from the realization that,
by declining to re-emigrate to an independent homeland, immigrants were com-
mitting themselves to the United States, where a new, more "Americanized"
generation was coming into its own. Furthermore, Polish politics in the interwar
period alienated many Polish-Americans. This third stage has been more open-
ended than were the first two, yielding gradually to a period in which the
descendants of Polish immigrants continue to claim their ethnic heritage in a
variety of ways, but always as Americans of Polish descent.[4]

Throughout these stages, the fundamental purpose of the Polish-American
press was to carry news of the new and old countries, to educate readers about
the ethnic community and the circumstances of life in America, and to serve the
needs of the sponsors—whether ideological, fraternal, or connected with a local
conflict.[5] These tasks have been broken down further by sociologist Eugene
Obidinski, who described six distinct functions. First, the Polish-American press
served as a "super-territorial instrument for communication" among the various
Polish-American communities to build up and reinforce ethnic identity. Second,
it was "a common expression of Polish and Polish-American culture [to] transmit
symbols, values, and interests" of the ethnic subculture. Third, the press tied
readers to community institutions, to political issues of particular interest to the
community, and to their evolving ethnic heritage. Fourth, the press facilitated
status competition, publicizing Polish-American activities in ways that "con-

fer[red] . . . prestige or honorific status upon particular individuals and upon the community generally.'' Fifth, the press served to advance individual power by influencing group opinion. And finally, the press socialized immigrants to the larger community through the transmission of information which explained what was expected of them in unfamiliar circumstances. The first five of these functions, according to Obidinski, have remained valid for the Polish-American press throughout its history. The sixth has seen increasingly limited applicability as the number of living immigrants has diminished.[6]

The long line of Polish immigrant newspapers in America began in 1863 with the appearance of *Echo z Polski* (Echo from Poland) in New York City. Published by a mysterious printer who used the pseudonym Schriftgiesser (German for ''type-molder''), and edited by Romuald Jaworowski, of whom almost nothing is known today, the paper agitated on behalf of the Polish Insurrection of 1863 and expired along with its cause in 1865. The first paper concerned with Polish-American life, *Orzeł Polski* (The Polish eagle), originated among the Polish settlements of Franklin County, Missouri, in 1870. It was probably published by an ex-priest, Szczepankiewicz, who used the pen name Dr. Sacconi. He secured the editorial help of Ignacy Wendziński, a teacher and Polish activist who fled to the United States after participating in the 1863 insurrection. Directed at working-class immigrants, the paper reached a circulation of nearly 300 as a biweekly and, at times, a weekly. By the time the paper folded in 1872, it had inspired two local immigrant pastors, Jan Barzyński and a Jesuit, Alexander Matauszak, to bring out a rival, *Pielgrzym* (The pilgrim). Barzyński moved the paper to Detroit in 1873 and sold it the following year to new publishers who transferred the operation to Chicago. Renamed *Gazeta Katolicka* (The Catholic gazette), the paper achieved a circulation of 6,000 within twenty years. If nothing else, these experiments showed that a lively press, complete with local news, news from Poland, and letters to the editor, could find a market in the United States, but only in areas of heavy Polish settlement.[7]

During the 1870s, a number of small newspapers were founded in Chicago, New York, and Milwaukee. They were often of poor quality, usually limited to four pages, and tended to be moved from place to place as their publishers sought support. One of the most successful was the literary monthly *Przyjaciel Ludu* (The friend of the people), organized in Chicago in 1876 by Ignacy Wendziński. In time, he changed it to a weekly and adopted a more popular format. By 1879, facing active competition in Chicago, he moved the paper to Milwaukee where, after a year, he became involved in a squabble with his chief investor and publishing partner, J. Rudnicki. Eventually, Rudnicki gained control and moved the paper back to Chicago, where it failed in 1884.[8] The most successful paper of the 1870s, *Gazeta Polska* (The Polish gazette), was founded in Chicago in 1873 by Władysław Dyniewicz, who had been a machinist before immigrating in 1866. Active in Polish affairs in Chicago, he became convinced of the need for popular education and put his entire family to work in a print shop which published a variety of books, pamphlets, textbooks, and handbooks for Polish immigrants as well as the paper, which by 1892 had achieved a circulation of 9,000.[9]

In the 1880s, the Polish-American press increased in numbers and stability. One reason for these gains was the sponsorship of journals by two competing fraternal societies: the Polish National Alliance's *Zgoda* (Harmony; 1881-) and the Polish Roman Catholic Union's *Wiara i Ojczyzna* (Faith and fatherland; 1887–1898), supplanted by *Naród Polski* (The Polish nation; 1897-), were generally connected with their respective organizations' Chicago headquarters. Other successful papers were connected with the growth of the immigrant communities, permitting the accumulation of sufficient money, talent, and experience to make stable newspapers and even dailies a possibility. The first successful daily was Milwaukee's *Kuryer Polski* (The Polish courier), founded in 1888 by Michael Kruszka, an ambitious young man whose family in German Poland was ardently pro-nationalist. Kruszka left Europe at age twenty when he ran afoul of the law for campaigning on behalf of Polish candidates for the Reichstag.[10] By 1890, *Dziennik Chicagoski* (The Chicago daily news) had been founded by the Ressurectionist congregation of Catholic priests in an effort to present a pro-clerical line to a readership which swelled to 7,800 in the space of five years. Buffalo was the third city to receive a daily with the emergence of *Polak w Ameryce* (The Pole in America), founded in 1895 by Jan Pitass, the pastor of a large Catholic parish.

All together, over 110 newspapers were initiated in Polish-American communities in the 1880s and 1890s. Some were associated with sponsors powerful enough to guarantee financial backing from nonjournalistic sources; and some were published by unusually competent and resourceful publicists like Milwaukee's Kruszka and Toledo's Antoni A. Paryski, who in 1889 founded the weekly *Ameryka*, which achieved a circulation of 8,500 by 1895. Other pioneer era newspapers thrived on specialization. The family-owned Worzałła Publishing Company of Stevens Point, Wisconsin, for instance, achieved success with *Rolnik* (The farmer) after 1891, while religious specialization was carried forward by *Straż* (The guard), founded in 1897 in Scranton as the organ of the Polish National Catholic Church. These papers and other religious, political, sports, and music journals provided recognition and employment to an emerging group of publishers and writers.[11]

In the first two decades of the twentieth century, the arrival of multitudes of Polish immigrants guaranteed the prosperity and expansion of the press. Over 170 new journals were launched between 1900 and 1920, including important new metropolitan Polish dailies: Detroit's *Dziennik Polski* (The Polish daily news; 1904), Buffalo's *Dziennik Dla Wszystkich* (Everybody's daily; 1907), Chicago's *Dziennik Związkowy Zgoda* (The Polish daily Zgoda; 1908), Cleveland's *Wiadomości Codzienne* (The daily news; 1910), New York's *Nowy Świat* (The new world; 1919), and Pittsburgh's *Pittsburczanin* (The Pittsburgher; 1920). Periodicals sponsored by Polish Roman Catholic religious orders also expanded during this period, as did journals sponsored by specialized organizations like the Polish Women's Alliance, which initiated *Głos Polek* (The voice of Polish women) in Chicago in 1910.[12]

With this growth came the exacerbation of the clericalist nationalist split whose roots stretched back at least to the 1880s. Ostensibly, the disagreement centered on whether religious or national issues should have priority in Polish-American life. The clerical faction tended to insist that common life be centered around the social, religious, and educational life of the parishes on the grounds that only good Catholics could be good Poles; nationalists stressed commitment to the restoration of Poland and a structuring of "hyphenated" life in America without religious exclusivity. Practically speaking, the dispute often furnished an ideological justification for opposing parties who were contending for leadership at the local and national level. Usually, but not always, priests and their relatively conservative allies were clericalist, while the remaining laymen and a few outspoken priests were nationalist. Several groups of disaffected Catholics broke with their church in the mid–1890s over issues of lay trusteeism and the allegedly anti-Polish policies of the Catholic hierarchy in the United States. Eventually, they united as the Polish National Catholic Church. Finally, socialists and other radicals attracted smaller followings, but maintained active opposition to the other factions within the ethnic community.[13]

After 1880 the various groups fought extended, bitter, and sometimes violent newspaper wars in an effort to turn the tide of opinion over the meaning of Polish-Americanism. Most significant among the nationalist journals were Paryski's newspaper, which merged with Buffalo's *Echo* in 1904, and Kruszka's *Kuryer Polski*, which spearheaded a campaign that threatened clerical control of Roman Catholic parishes and schools by urging laymen to withhold contributions and to organize themselves as an opposition movement within their church. Kruszka's newspapers were eventually banned by Wisconsin's Catholic bishops in 1912, and his Federation of American Catholic Laymen was forbidden, but the popularity of his papers remained high. Not even the three successive efforts to found pro-clerical opposition papers in Milwaukee, culminating in *Nowiny Polskie* (The Polish news; 1906), seriously harmed his publishing enterprise: the *Kuryer* eventually reached a daily circulation of 20,000.[14] Other cities, especially Chicago and Buffalo, experienced similar newspaper warfare early in the twentieth century when, in the words of one historian, the atmosphere was marked by "bitter invective, mud-slinging, court-battling, and street-fighting."[15]

The journalistic invective was interrupted by the outbreak of World War I and efforts to publicize the twin causes of Polish war relief and Polish independence. Division reasserted itself in the midst of the war, however, as two organizations started to contend for public suport of the war effort. The older was the Committee for the National Defense (KON), organized before the war with broadly based support to prepare for the expected upheaval to liberate Poland. After 1914 the KON was linked with the pro-Austrian, anti-Russian policies of Marshal Pilsudski, who hoped to establish democratic socialism in a reconstructed Poland. When socialists and other leftists became prominent in the KON, conservative elements withdrew to form the National Committee (RN), which enjoyed the support of Ignace Paderewski, Henryk Sienkiewicz, and many of the American clergy; it hoped for the defeat of the Central Powers and was linked with the European leadership of Roman Dmowski. The divisions were carried into the Polish-American press, which divided basically along the lines of the previous nationalist–clericalist split. Nevertheless, there was in the wartime controversy a fundamental agreement about the necessity of material relief and about political activity on behalf of Poland. The course of events favored the RN, particularly because of Paderewski's influence in the Wilson administration and his success at selling the goals of his organization to American audiences through a series of concert-lectures. After the United States entered the war, official suppression of pro-German sentiment helped to stifle the KON further. But Wilson's strong endorsement of Polish independence neutralized some of the resentment of KON supporters and persuaded RN members that Paderewski's success with the White House constituted ample justification for their particular approach to Polish matters. In 1917 and 1918, therefore, a great majority of the Polish-American community wholeheartedly supported the war effort, and the press generally endorsed the sentiment.[16]

After the war, the restoration of Poland helped to transform the identity of the Polish ethnic community and, with it, the press. Having chosen to remain in the United States, the immigrants and their descendants became preoccupied with their own, American concerns. Moreover, the economic and political development of Poland was controversial. The issues became particularly clear after Pilsudski's coup of 1926, when the Polish-American press divided in its reaction. Pro-government papers included Chicago's *Daily Zgoda*, Detroit's *Dziennik Polski*, Cleveland's *Wiadomości Codzienne*, New York's *Nowy Świat*, Milwaukee's *Kuryer Polski*, Pittsburgh's *Kuryer Codzienny* (Daily courier), and Buffalo's *Dziennik Dla Wszystkich*. Antigovernment papers were Chicago's *Dziennik Zjednoczenia* (The union daily news), Detroit's *Rekord Codzienny* (The daily record), Cleveland's *Monitor* and Pittsburgh's *Pittsburczanin*. Neutral were Chicago's *Dziennik Chicagoski*, Milwaukee's *Nowiny Polskie*, and Toledo's *Ameryka-Echo*.[17]

In lieu of any consensus over the course of events in the old country, the papers concentrated on the growth and development of the local and national ethnic communities. Local social events, athletic events, parish news items, meetings of fraternal and veterans' groups, and even American comic strips began to fill the pages. Formats were altered to resemble the English-language dailies with attractive mastheads and news items on the front page. Instead of copying news items from the American dailies, the larger Polish papers now began to subscribe to press services, particularly United Press International (UPI). Most papers included serialized versions of novels on a regular basis; often they were popular historical novels designed to cement solidarity between the homeland and the immigrants by reminding them of their common historical foes and their common Christian faith. In 1925 the combined circulation of the twenty daily papers was about 410,000, while that of the more than sixty weeklies was 800,000. Circulation figures for the dailies indicated the sources of support within the publishing community: fourteen general news dailies printed 300,000 copies; three socialist dailies had a combined circulation of 56,000; two dailies published under religious auspices totaled 50,000; and the lone communist daily sold several thousand copies. Although circulation and advertising (including holiday notices from business and community leaders and a declining but still significant number of patent medicine ads) peaked in the 1920s, the number of new publications began to fall; only sixty-nine publications were intiated during the 1920s.[18]

The early 1930s were the turning point for Polish-American journalism. Although those years did not coincide with a new phase in the evolution of the Polish-American community, the economic consequences of the Great Depression, the effects of immigration restriction, the passing of a great number of immigrants into middle and old age, and the gradual loss of competent editors and publishers through death and retirement meant the beginning of the end of the Polish–language press as it had appeared during the heyday of immigration. In 1930 there were still 129 newspapers in existence, and the total readership was about 1 million. But the number of European-born Poles was declining rapidly in the United States.[19] As a result, the Polish papers, which had begun to experiment with English-language supplements as early as 1910, now began to use English in earnest. Some introduced English sections into the paper, among them Milwaukee's *Nowiny Polskie*, Chicago's *Dziennik Zjednoczenia* and *Dziennik Związkowy*, and Detroit's *Rekord Codzienny*; but others experimented with a weekly edition, as did Milwaukee's *Kuryer Polski* with *The American Courier* in 1939. Despite these efforts to come to terms with the assimilation of the Polish-Americans, advertising revenue and readership continued to shrink in the 1930s. By 1938 only fifty-three weekly and ten daily newspapers were still publishing.[20]

The passing of the immigrant generation did not spell the end of the Polish press in America. Rather, as one scholar has observed, the publishers have achieved "survival through adaptation"[21] from a base still largely located in the older Polish areas of New York, Pennsylvania, Illinois, and Michigan. True enough, the total number of Polish-American newspapers shrank to about forty in the early 1960s and to about half that number by the early 1980s, and most of them were weeklies and monthlies.[22] But there were signs of life that showed that the Polish press in America was continuing to serve the needs of a community which still identified with Polish roots in some sense. Two metropolitan dailies survived into 1984. Chicago's *Dziennik Związkowy*, using minimal English for sports, youth features, and an occasional editorial translated for the benefit of politicians, maintained a circulation of 14,800 and enjoyed the backing of the Polish National Alliance. In New York, *Nowy Dziennik* (The new daily news), begun as a replacement of *Nowy Świat* by recent immigrants in 1971, continued to appear five days a week with a circulation of 12,000. Presumably, it catered more to displaced persons and later immigrants of the postwar period than to the more assimilated Polsih-Americans who traced roots to the great migration which ended in 1924.[23] Weeklies like Detroit's *Dziennik Polski* (12,000 circulation in 1983) and the Stevens Point paper *Gwiazda Polarna* (The north star; 25,400) remained successful. The journals of religious groups and fraternal organizations, now generally appearing in bilingual editions, rounded out the picture. The most important among them included the Polish National Alliance's *Zgoda* (98,000), the Polish Roman Catholic Union's *Naród Polski* (35,000), and the Polish National Catholic Church's *Rola Boża/God's Field* (7,300).[24]

The most creative form of adaptation has undoubtedly been the publication of exclusively English Polish-American papers, beginning in 1948 with Scranton's *Polish American Journal* (now *Pol-Am Journal*), after about thirty-seven years as a Polish–language paper. Such publications addressed English-speaking readers who were somewhat assimilated but still drew an important part of their self-understanding from a Polish-American (as opposed to a purely Polish) heritage. One of the most important, the *Pol-Am Journal*, with a 1983 circulation of over 34,000, achieved economy of scale by printing five separate editions, including national and Chicago editions, and three separate editions for different fraternal societies. Other English-only papers included Buffalo's *Am-Pol Eagle* and a weekly English edition of New York's *Nowy Dziennik*. [25] Some of the latter-day characteristics of the Polish-American press were clearly evident in Buffalo's *Polish-American Voice* an issue-oriented journal which first appeared in February 1983.[26] The paper was run as an offshoot of a computer typesetting business, and its editors pledged themselves to honor the accomplishments of the past, to attract young people to become involved in the ethnic community, and to promote community development through maintenance of a journalistic forum of opinion and support of cultural activities like polka radio programs. The inaugural edition featured local news and a four-page "Polka Supplement," but nothing on Poland itself.

The same thematic pattern was evident in a content analysis of six contemporary Polish-American newspapers undertaken by Eugene Obidinski. His results indicated that well over half of the content concerned Polish-American culture, the group's image, and its institutional life. Only about 14 percent of the material was given over to Poland and news of the old country. Yet, Obidinski asserted, the press was still performing a service consistent with the traditions of the past:

The largest proportion of articles related to vested interests of Polonian associations and individuals. Political activities, programs and objectives of fraternal organizations, and organized forms of ethnic activism received more space . . . than did items related to family and religious activities or scholarly-intellectual achievements. . . . the persistent coverage of achievements of Polonian community members and celebrities not only reaffirms the argument that "names make news," but also the fact that the news articles are a means for public recognition and a source of honorific status within the communities.[27]

Clearly then, the community-oriented direction of the post–World War I Polish ethnic press, reinforced as the years go by, has continued to provide a limited basis for success. Since most readers of Polish-American newspapers no longer look to them for news of the world, community news and items of individual recognition fill the pages of papers which, for all their liveliness, are far from being the giants they were in the past.

A final form of adaptation of the Polish-American press, broadly speaking, has been specialization through the appearance of professional, religious, and special interest journals which reflect the development of particular segments of the ethnic group. Professional journals like *The Polish Review* (sponsored by the Polish Institute of Arts and Sciences in America and devoted to the history and culture of Poland and east central Europe) and *Polish American Studies* (journal of the Polish American Historical Association) are examples of scholarly publications sustained by a largely Polish-American membership. Newsletters like the *Bulletin* of the Pilsudski Institute of America and the Kościuszko Foundation *Newsletter* publicize the work and research sponsored by the charitable efforts of the Polish-American community. The Orchard Lake schools in Michigan publish *Pan z Wami* (The Lord be with you), a Polish-language brochure with texts for the Polish Mass.[28]

Cooperation among Polish-American journalists and publishers has been difficult to achieve, partly because ideological differences and economic rivalry initially tended to raise the level of suspicion. The first call to organize a formal guild of journalists came from the Polish National Alliance (PNA) at its convention of 1891. The resultant group, unable to flourish in the atmosphere of heated competition between the PNA and the Polish Roman Catholic Union, quickly disbanded. A second effort to unite Polish-American journalists originated in Buffalo in 1894 when journalist Henryk Nagiel arranged a meeting of newspapermen of various editorial stances. It, too, failed, as did a third effort, headed by Milwaukee publisher Michael Kruszka in 1909, and a fourth, in Chicago the following year. At last, the fifth effort, which occurred in 1911 at the behest of Stefania Laudyn-Chrzanowska, led to the founding of the Society of Journalists and Writers, which adopted a charter including a mutual commitment to promote the Polish nationality among the younger generation, to support the improvement of Polish schools in the United States, to foster unions among Polish workers, and to highlight the role of women in the future of the Polish-American community. The group held annual meetings for three years and reached a membership of forty-seven, representing thirty-two publications. The journalistic divisions of World War I, however, led the members to disband the organization in 1914.[29]

The sixth and only successful effort to organize Polish-American journalists was the handiwork of Joseph Przydatek, editor-in-chief of *Dziennik Chicagoski*, who in 1928 invited twenty-nine editors representing eighteen publications to work out a code of laws and call a convention. The result of their efforts was the Association of Polish Journalists in America, which met for the first time in Detroit in April 1929. The organization, designed to be professional and non-politica vas unified around six aims, which included the inculcation of professional aid responsible journalism among the members and the protection of "the good name of Poles and Poland." In 1934 the group considered joining the American Newspaper Guild but was unable to comply with the guild's regulations concerning affiliation with organized labor. By the late 1930s the association came to be dominated by journalists from newspapers that had failed during the depression. As a result, the active members, about fifty strong, reorganized themselves as the Association of Polish Journalists and Publishers. The decline of Polish-language journalism in America after World War II led to the gradual demise of the association.[30]

The problems that impeded the quest for a professional organization emphasize the impression that a very difficult set of circumstances beset Polish-American journalists, particularly in the first generations. In his 1924 study of the Polish-American community, the Polish vice–consul in New York depicted the situation clearly:

The status of the Polish journalist in America is hard and difficult. Above all, the abnormal situation of the publishers forces the journalist to a position as journeyman, who, often, must use his pen to a task not in conformity with his own opinions, so that he may not lose his means of livelihood. His professional job, situated under scarcely hygienic conditions, and including night work, is very fatiguing and, in many establishments, includes 12 hours work daily.[31]

In general, these journalists worked in enterprises organized like the American press, with boards of directors, business managers, and departments for advertising, circulation, editorial policies, and maintenance. The editor-in-chief on larger papers was assisted by a city editor and a subeditor for news of Poland. Editors of fraternal journals were generally chosen at annual conventions, thereby introducing organizational politics into personnel decisions. For their services, editors of the 1880s earned about $6 per week, a figure which grew to about $20 per week by 1900 and $75 per week by 1920, when the supporting staff earned monthly wages of between $80 and $200. Despite the resolution of the journalists' meeting of 1911, the Polish-American press remained a predominantly male bastion: in 1940, a careful survey of the field disclosed only about ten active women journalists.[32]

Given the difficulty of their task, the personalities and insights of the publishers and editors were crucial. Particularly in the period of ideological conflict, national commitment, and personal journalism before 1920, the founders of the Polish-American press stand out in clear relief as dedicated but very human servants of the evolving community. By turns passionate, committed, vindictive, and petty, they were a powerful influence on the adjustment process of their fellow countrymen. Biographical accounts of Polish-American journalists disclose few common threads. Some received gymnasium and even university education in Poland and America; others were self-educated and entered the newspaper field through apprenticeship. A few left teaching and other pursuits to write, but most were newspapermen through their entire adult lives. Some of the pioneer publicists, like Chicago's Resurrectionist founding father, Vincent Barzyński, and Buffalo's Polish parish builder, Jan Pitass, established newspapers while pastoring tens of thousands of souls. Others, like Milwaukee's Michael Kruszka and Winona's Hieronim Derdowski, built, with very little money, nationally known enterprises by dint of hard work, faith in the future, knowledge of their people, and passion for controversy. Kruszka took up newspaper work in America; but Derdowski was a professional journalist and talented editor whose writing had helped to foster national sentiments among the Kashubian people of Poland's Baltic coast before he emigrated in 1884. Henryk Nagiel, dubbed by one critic "the most capable writer of his times," tried in the 1880s and 1890s to write for papers in Buffalo, New York, and Chicago, but found that he was "unable to reconcile himself with American circumstances." Abandoning the struggle in 1896, he returned to Poland, where he edited a newspaper in Lwów until his death.[33]

Perhaps the best known Polish-American journalist was Antoni A. Paryski (Panek) of Toledo. The son of a Polish farmer, he had been educated in a gymnasium and was working in Warsaw's main post office when his anti-czarist activities forced him to leave the country in 1883 at age eighteen. In America he worked for a while as a farm hand as he studied English. An effort to obtain a medical education failed when he ran out of money. Feeling drawn to the immigrant press, he worked for a while for Polish newspapers in Detroit, Chicago, and Winona, and for an English newspaper in Chicago. Next, Michael Kruszka recruited him to write for *Krytyka* (The critique), a pro-labor paper in Milwaukee. Soon Paryski joined the Knights of Labor and became involved as an organizer; but a personal meeting with Terence Powderly convinced him that Powderly was corrupt, so he returned to newspaper journalism for English and Polish papers in Philadelphia, Cleveland, and Buffalo. By 1886 he was in Toledo, working on *Gwiazda* (The star). After three years, he broke with the editor and began to issue his own journal, *Ameryka*. He was successful enough by 1902 to purchase Buffalo's *Echo*, which he merged with his first paper to form *Ameryka-Echo*; it achieved a circulation above 100,000 by 1920. Attacked by clericalists, he followed a course independent of the Catholic Church, stating his belief in the power of the community to judge the good from the bad. Paryski's success stemmed in part from his ability to introduce yellow press techniques into the Polish community. Moreover, he trained agents to criss-cross the country to promote his newspapers and books, to sell products from the glove factory he established, and to offer banking services through his savings company. By the time he died in 1935, he had acquired the reputation of being the "Polish

Hearst." He sold Polish bonds, supported Polish-American institutions, and published 2,000 different titles including the novels of Henryk Sienkiewicz and Boleslaw Prus, school books, devotional literature, and anticlerical tomes—over 8 million copies in all.[34]

Over the years, critics have faulted Polish-American journalists for their instability, their irresponsibility, and their bastardization of the Polish language through the use of words like "sztor" (store) and "sajdwok" (sidewalk).[35] Yet the record shows that they have done reasonably well in balancing educational and civic goals with the necessity of reflecting a group which has been rather consistently in flux. It is appropriate, therefore, that a recent historian has characterized the development of the Polish-American press as thoroughly American, in the broad and pluralistic sense of the term.[36] He was not far from the mark. After all, the journals were the product of an American context which forced journalists to work at the painful and thrilling point of intersection between the traditional and the new. The tensions that resulted brought into the open the best and the worst of Polish-American life, but they also clarified the issues and answers that pertained to the process of adjustment. In retrospect it seems almost inevitable that, in reading and responding to their press, the immigrants and their descendants learned to act—and think—like Americans.

NOTES

1. Wacław Kruszka, *Historya Polska w Ameryce* (Milwaukee: Drukiem Spółki Wydawniczej Kuryera, 1905–1908), 4:85.

2. William Thomas and Florian Znaniecki, *The Polish Peasant in Europe and America* (repr.; New York: Octagon Books, 1974), 2: 1367–1396; Piotr S. Wandycz, *The Lands of Paritioned Poland* (Seattle: University of Washington Press, 1974), pp. 371–372.

3. Victor Greene, "Poles", in *Harvard Encyclopedia of American Ethnic Groups*, ed. Stephan Thernstrom (Cambridge, Mass: Harvard University Press, 1980), pp. 791–793, 800; Andrzej Brożek, *Polonia Amerykańska, 1854–1939* (Warsaw: Wydawnictwo Interpress, 1977), pp. 35–36, 223.

4. For interpretations of the stages of assimilation for Polish-Americans, consult the following sources: Brożek, *Polonia*, pp. 59–94, 170–192; Daniel Buczek, "Three Generations of the Polish Immigrant Church: Changing Styles of Pastoral Leadership," in Stanislaus A. Blejwas and Mieczyslaw B. Biskupski, eds., *Pastor of the Poles* (New Britain: Central Connecticut State College Polish Studies Program Monographs, 1982), pp. 21–29; Greene, "Poles," pp. 801–802; Victor Greene, *For God and Country: The Rise of Polish and Lithuanian Ethnic Consciousness in the United States, 1860–1910* (Madison: State Historical Society of Wisconsin, 1975), pp. 66–99, 174–176; Helena Lopata, *Polish Americans: Status Competition in an Ethnic Community* (Englewood Cliffs, N.J.: Prentice-Hall, Inc., 1976), pp. 143–148; Helena Lopata, "Intergenerational Relations in Polonia," in Frank Renkiewicz, ed., *The Polish Presence in Canada and America* (Toronto: Multicultural History Society of Ontario, 1982), pp. 271–284; and Stanislaus Blejwas, "Old and New Polonias: Tensions within an Ethnic Community," *Polish American Studies* 38 (Autumn 1981); 59–62.

5. Kruszka, 4: 84. See also Edmund G. Olszyk, *The Polish Press in America*

(Milwaukee: Marquette University Press, 1940), pp. 14–19; and Karol Wachtl, *Polonja w Ameryce* (Philadelphia: Polish Star Publishing Co., 1944), pp. 200–217.

6. Eugene Obidinski, "The Polish American Press: Survival through Adaptation," *Polish American Studies* 34 (Autumn 1977): 42–46.

7. Henryk Nagiel, *Dziennikarstwo Polskie w Ameryce* (Chicago: Drukiem Spółki Nakładowie Wydawnictwo Polskiego w Ameryce, 1894), pp. 8–9, was one of the first to describe *Echo z Polski*. On *Echo* and *Orzeł Polski* and *Pielgrzym*, see also Kruszka, 4: 97–108; Wachtl, p. 227; and, especially, Bernard Pacyniak, "An Historical Outline of the Polish Press in America," in *Poles in America: Bicentennial Essays*, ed. Frank Mocha (Stevens Point, Wisc.: Worzalla Publishing Co., 1978), pp. 510–513. Kruszka argues that Schrifgiesser was actually a Polish Jew who emigrated for political reasons. Circulation figures are in N. W. Ayer and Son's *American Newspaper Annual*, published in Philadelphia.

8. Kruszka, 4: 117–122; Wachtl, p. 218.

9. Three sources on the early history of the Polish-American press are Kruszka 4: 83–123, and 5: 3–84; Jan Kowalik, *The Polish Press in America* (San Francisco: R & E Research Associates, Inc., 1978), pp. 2–7; and Pacyniak, pp. 510–522. Kruszka is idiosyncratic in his descriptions and sometimes inaccurate, but has the advantage of personal knowledge of many of the journalists and papers. Kowalik sometimes follows Kruszka too closely, but his and Pacyniak's accounts are modern, synthetic, reasonably scholarly, and disappointingly brief.

10. Stefan Rachocki, "Michał Kruszka," in Kruszka, 5: 34–51.

11. Olszyk, pp. 50–62; Brożek, pp. 153–156; Nagiel, pp. 11–15; Kowalik, pp. 4–5. *Rolnik* was founded in 1891 by Zygmunt Hutter, an educated immigrant of the upper class, and Teofil Krutza, a tailor who helped fund the enterprise, which attracted 300 subscribers in the first year. In 1903 they sold out to Steven and Joseph Worzałła. Steven worked as a printer for Hutter before buying the newspaper and printery. *Rolnik*, November 1, 1958.

12. Olszyk, p. 76; Kowalik, pp. 6–8.

13. Good accounts of the nationalist–clericalist controversy include Greene, *God and Country*; Anthony J. Kuzniewski, *Faith and Fatherland: The Polish Church War in Wisconsin, 1896–1918* (Notre Dame, Ind.: University of Notre Dame Press, 1980); Lawerence D. Orton, *Polish Detroit and the Kolasinski Affair* (Detroit: Wayne State University Press, 1981); and Joseph John Parot, *Polish Catholics in Chicago, 1850–1920.* (Dekalb: Northern Illinois University Press, 1981). On the Polish National Catholic Church, see Hiernim Kubiak, *The Polish National Catholic Church in the United States of America from 1897 to 1980: Its Social Conditioning and Social Function* (Krakow: Nakładem Uniwersytetu Jagiellońskiego, 1982).

14. *Dziennik Milwaucki* (The Milwaukee daily news) mounted an unsuccessful effort to oppose the *Kuryer* from 1899 to 1905. Apparently, its circulation remained below 1,800, compared with the *Kuryer*'s claimed circulation of 9,000 in 1903. When *Dziennik* folded, it had debts of $8,900 and assets of only $4,400. Anthony J. Kuzniewski, "Faith and Fatherland," Ph.D dissertation, Harvard University, 1973, pp. 197–199, 256–261. See also Pacyniak, p. 515.

15. Olszyk, p. 19.

16. Louis L. Gerson, *Woodrow Wilson and the Rebirth of Poland, 1914–1920* (New Haven: Yale University Press, 1953), pp. 46–54, 67–93; Louis L. Gerson, *The Hyphenate in Recent American Politics and Democracy* (Lawrence: University of Kansas Press,

1964), pp. 70–72, 77–78; Olszyk, pp. 20–24. Gerson is a professional scholar and a Polish immigrant. Olszyk's account of the controversy relies heavily on the work of Stanisław Osada, *Prasa i Publicystyka Polska w Ameryce* (Pittsburgh: Nakładem i Drukiem "Pittsburczanina," 1930). Osada had been active in Polish-American affairs for years when he wrote the account. See also Brożek, pp. 133–144; and Pacyniak, pp. 521–522.

17. Olszyk, pp. 20–21.

18. Ibid., pp. 36–39, 76; Oskar Stanisław Czarnik, "Wybory beletrystyczne 'Dziennika Chicagoskiego' w latach 1921–26 i 1938–39," in *Kultura skupisk polonijnych* (Warsaw: Biblioteka Narodowa, 1981), pp. 168, 170–171; Wachtl, p. 220. Frank Renkiewicz, personal correspondence, June 6, 1894; Pacyniak, pp. 519–520.

19. Olszyk, pp. 63–68.

20. Ibid., pp. 64–69; Kowalik, pp. 7, 24–28.

21. The phrase was coined by Eugene Obidinski in an article written for *Polish Amercian Studies* in 1977. Above, n. 6.

22. Kowalik, pp. 12–28.

23. Like other ehnic groups, Polish-Americans have experienced tensions and misunderstanding between older immigrants and their descendants and the immigrants who arrived after World War II. The latter, generally more political and literary than the former, are critical of the Americanized culture and attitudes of assimilated Polish-Americans. Blejwas, "Old and New Polonias," pp. 72–83.

24. Kowalik, *Polish Press*, pp. 11–12; John Krawiec (editor of *Nowy Dziennik*) telephone interview, January 11, 1984. Circulation figures are from the 1983 *Ayer Directory of Publications*, now issued by the IMS Press in Fort Washington, Pennsylvania.

25. Obidinski, pp. 53–55; Pacyniak, p. 525; Krawiec interview; Henry J. Dende (editor and publisher of *Pol-Am Journal*), telephone interview, June 7, 1984. My understanding of the adaptation process has been helped greatly by the Renkiewicz correspondence.

26. Buffalo was unusual in being the locus of two English-language Polish-American newspapers in 1984—*The Pol-Am Eagle*, founded in 1958, and *The Polish American Voice*. In the estimation of one analyst, the *Eagle* deals more with "facts and events," while the *Voice* "deals with issues and has a more sensational appeal." Sr. Ellen Marie Kuznicki, personal correspondence, January 11, 1984.

27. Obidinski, pp. 48–54.

28. Ibid., pp. 47–48; Kowalik, pp. 9, 16–17.

29. Osada, p. 87; Olszyk, pp. 18, 33–35.

30. Olszyk, pp. 33–35; Krawiec interview.

31. Mieczyslaw Szawleski, *Wychodztwo Polskie w Stanach Zjednoczonych Ameryki* (Lwow: Wydawnictwo Zakladu Narodowego Imienia Ossolinskich, 1924), p. 164, quoted and translated in Olszyk, pp. 30–31. A brief description of Szawleski's life and work may be found in Brożek, p. 195.

32. Olszyk, pp. 28–31.

33. The estimation of Nagiel is in Osada, pp. 53–54. For accounts of other early Polish-American journalists, see Nagiel, pp. 76, 96–98; Kruszka, vols. 4 and 5; Wachtl, pp. 218–231, 240–243; and Parot, p. 85.

34. Wiktor Rosinski, *Antoni A. Paryski: Życie, Prace i Czyny, 1865–1935* (Toledo: Ameryka-Echo Press, 1945); Kowalik, p. 4; Pacyniak, pp. 517–518; Wachtl, p. 227.

35. Olszyk, pp. 43–49.
36. Kowalik, pp. 43–44.

BIBLIOGRAPHY

Books

Brożek, Andrzej. *Polonia Amerykańska, 1854–1939* [American Polonia, 1854–1930]. Warsaw: Wydawnictwo Interpress, 1977.

Kowalik, Jan. *The Polish Press in America*. San Francisco: R & E Research Associates, Inc., 1978.

Kruszka, Wacław. *Historya Polska w Ameryce* [Polish history in America]. 13 vols. Milwaukee: Drukiem Spółki Wydawniczej Kuryera, 1905–1908.

Kuzniewski, Anthony J. *Faith and Fatherland: The Polish Church War in Wisconsin, 1896–1918*. Notre Dame, Ind.: University of Notre Dame Press, 1980.

Nagiel, Henryk. *Dziennikarstwo Polskie w Amreyce* [Polish journalism in America]. Chicago: Drukiem Spółki Nakładowie Wydawnictwo Polskiego w Ameryce, 1894.

Olszyk, Edmund G. *The Polish Press in America*. Milwaukee: Marquette University Press, 1940.

Osada, Stanisław. *Prasa i Publicystyka Polska w Ameryce* [The Polish press and journalists in America]. Pittsburgh: Nakładem i Drukiem "Pittsburczanina," 1930.

Renkiewicz, Frank. *The Poles in America, 1608–1972: A Chronology and Fact Book*. Dobbs Ferry, N.Y.: Oceana Publications, Inc., 1973.

[Rośinski, Wiktor]. *Antoni A. Paryski: Życie, Prace i Czyny, 1865–1935* [Anthony A. Paryski: Life, work, and accomplishments, 1865–1935]. Toledo: Ameryka-Echo Press, [1945].

Wachtl, Karol. *Polonja w Ameryce* [Polonia in America]. Philadelphia: Polish Star Printing Co., 1944.

Waldo, Artur L. *Zarys Historii Literatu Polskiej w Ameryce* [An outline of the history of Polish literature in America]. Chicago: Nakładem "Dziennika Zjednoczenia," 1938.

Wepsiec, Jan. *Polish American Serial Publications, 1842–1966: An Annotated Bibliography*. Chicago: Privately printed, 1968.

Articles

Czarnik, Oskar Stanisław. "Wybory Beletrystyczne 'Dziennika Chicagoskiego' w latach 1921–26 i 1938–39" [Fictional selections of the *Dziennik Chicagoski* in 1921–26 and 1938–39.]. In *Kultura skupisk polonijnych*, Warsaw: Biblioteka Narodowa, 1981, Pp. 166–189.

Greene, Victor. "Poles." In *Harvard Encyclopedia of American Ethnic Groups*. Ed. Stephan Thernstrom. Cambridge, Mass.: Harvard University Press, 1980. Pp. 787–803.

Obidinski, Eugene. "The Polish American Press: Survival through Adaptation." *Polish American Studies* 34 (Autumn 1977): 38–55.

Pacyniak, Bernard. "An Historical Outline of the Polish Press in America." In *Poles in America: Bicentennial Essays*. Ed Frank Mocha. Stevens Point, Wis.: Worzalla Publishing Co., 1978. Pp. 509–529.

Unpublished Sources

Flisinski, Wacław Stefan. "Prasa Polonijna w Ameryce w Latach 1842–1972" [The Polonian press in America in the years 1842–1972]. 2 vols., 1973. Typed MS in archives of the Polish Roman Catholic Union of America, Chicago.
Wolanin, Alphons S. "The Polish American Press." Paper written at Graduate Library School, University of Chicago, December 1952. Copy in archives of the Polish Roman Catholic Union of America, Chicago.

19

The Portuguese Press

LEO PAP

For the purposes of this survey of the historical development and the present status of the Portuguese press in the United States, "Portuguese ethnic press" is here defined as those newspapers and other periodicals produced essentially by and for immigrants from Portugal. This is not quite the same as the Portuguese-language press: on the one hand, there are or have been a few Portuguese-language periodicals published in this country for the primary purpose of commerce or cultural relations with the Portuguese-speaking half of South America, viz., Brazil, rather than to serve immigrants from Portugal.[1] These are excluded. On the other hand, we can marginally include a few periodical publications written in English but aimed largely at Portuguese ethnics—in this case at the American-born or American-educated children of immigrants from Portugal.[2]

The term "Portugal," in this context, covers more territory than the average American reader tends to associate with it: not only the westernmost part of continental Europe bordering on Spain, but also, out in the Atlantic, the Azores, and Madeira Islands, and, in a more limited sense, the Cape Verde Islands off the northwestern part of Africa. Politically, the Azores and Madeira are and always have been an integral part of the Portuguese state, even though in recent years these islands have attained a measure of regional autonomy. The Cape Verde Islands were a Portuguese colony from their intitial settlement until 1975, when they became an independent country. The large majority of Portuguese nationals who have immigrated to the United States over the past one hundred years or so have come from these insular parts of Portugal, chiefly the Azores, rather than from continental Portugal.

Portugal, even if we include the islands just mentioned, is a small country. Its total current population is about 10 million, with less than 1 million living in the three archipelagos. But its rate of emigration has been and continues to be one of the highest in Europe. Historically, Brazil, a Portuguese colony from the early sixteenth century into the nineteenth century, has been the main focus of Portuguese overseas emigration; but the United States (including Hawaii) has been the second major overseas destination for over a century. Canada has become a third major focus since World War II.

A few basic facts about Portuguese settlement in the United States are needed for an understanding of the Portuguese ethnic press. Prior to the mid-nineteenth century, the presence of Portuguese speakers in what is now the United States was no more than sporadic, although dating back to the Age of Exploration. Groups of Portuguese Jews settled in New Amsterdam (New York) and nearby British colonies starting about 1640, retaining use of the Portuguese language for special occasions. Contacts of the whaling industry between New England and the Azores brought the first appreciable numbers of Azorean settlers to American shores, about the middle of the nineteenth century. Real mass migration from insular (and later from continental) Portugal to New England and adjoining areas started about 1880 and continued into the 1920s, attracted largely by the labor needs of textile mills in New Bedford, Fall River, and other cities, with a spillover into New York and its environs. Beginning with the Gold Rush in about 1850, the Portuguese also began directing their attention to California. Large numbers of them, again chiefly Azoreans, settled in the areas around San Francisco and then farther south, concentrating on farming (dairy cattle and truck gardening) rather than on factory work. In spots along the California coast, as well as in New England, the Portuguese have also played an important role in the fisheries. Madeirans and Azoreans were drawn to the Hawaiian Islands in substantial numbers between about 1880 and 1900 as contract laborers to work on the sugar plantations. From the plantations many of them soon drifted into urban and agricultural jobs.

Between 1870 and the early 1920s, after which heavy restrictions based on nationality quotas reduced immigration into the United States from a stream to a trickle, some 250,000 Portuguese immigrants settled in this country. About one–fourth of this total sooner or later returned to their native land. As of 1920, when the United States census inquired about the ethnic composition of the poupulation by mother tongue, about 105,000 foreign-born white persons living in the continental United States reported Portuguese as their mother tongue. (This figure excluded Hawaii, any nonwhite Capeverdeans, and any American-born.) By 1940 the corresponding total of foreign-born speakers of Portuguese had dropped to 84,000 (because the throttling of immigration was now reducing the proportion of Portuguese-born to American–born). In that same year, 1940, some 120,000 white persons born in the United States but with at least one foreign-born parent reported that Portuguese was their mother tongue; this would mean a total, as of 1940, of over 200,000 persons then living in the continental United States (not counting residents of Hawaii and some Capeverdeans elsewhere) who claimed they had learned Portuguese as their first language in the home.

New American legislation in the late 1950s and especially in the early 1960s relaxed immigration restrictions considerably, first for Azorean earthquake vic-tims and then generally. The Portuguese, encouraged by the special admission of Azorean refugees, took more advantage, proportionately, of this partial re-opening of the gates of immigration than did many other nationalities: by 1967 Portugal had become one of the four leading sources of new immigration to the United States (after the United Kingdom, Italy, and Taiwan). Between 1960 and 1982, some 160,000 persons emigrated from Portugal to this country. This new and relatively heavy wave of Portuguese (chiefly Azorean) immigration—leading to a revitalization of the Portuguese ethnic press—has been directed in the main toward the traditional Portuguese settlement centers in southeastern New England and also to some localities around metropolitan New York (such as Newark, N.J.) and in California. Let us assume that between one–fourth and one–third of the 200,000 United States residents who in 1940 reported Portuguese as their mother tongue are still alive and residing in this country. With the new immigration since the late 1950s (and allowing for some retromigration to Portugal), we may then estimate that close to a quarter of a million persons living in the United States in the mid–1980s claim Portuguese as their mother tongue and are thus potential readers of Portuguese immigrant newspapers.

Reading newspapers presupposes literacy. What about the literacy rate among Portuguese immigrants? United States immigration statistics indicate that almost 70 percent of all Portuguese immigrants fourteen years of age or over admitted between 1899 and 1910 could neither read nor write. That fact placed the Portuguese at the bottom of the scale among all immigrant nationalities, and it accurately reflected the literacy rate in Portugal as a whole, lowest among all European countries at that time—and probably even now. Between 1911 and 1917, that is, after the fall of the Portuguese monarchy, when a rising proportion of immigrants came from continental rather than insular Portugal, the figure dropped to about 50 percent. After the introduction of the literacy test in 1917 to bar further immigration of illiterates (other than close relatives of earlier settlers), the average educational level of new Portuguese arrivals naturally improved. In 1929 the Portuguese government itself prohibited the emigration of most illiterates. The new Portuguese mass immigration that began around 1960 has brought in a majority of people who have had at least some elementary schooling, and many with urban backgrounds. By contrast, the vast majority of Azoreans and other Portuguese who came to the United States up to the end of World War I, and even many who came during the period of quota restrictions, had emerged from a relatively closed and isolated peasant environment, where the cultural horizon was for the most part limited to the native village or district, and news travelled mostly by word of mouth.

The growth and survival of an ethnic press—which in the American context means a press exclusively or largely written in language other than English—depend not only on the literacy level, size, and settlement pattern (degree of compactness, etc.) of the corresponding immigrant (or pre-Anglo) population. They also depend on prevailing attitudes toward the use of English—what extent and in what context a given ethnic group is interested in continued use of the traditional non-English tongue. The overall trend in this country, of course, has been to adopt English for most or all purposes at the expense of the non-English ethnic tongue, chiefly because fluency in English is perceived as a prerequisite for socioeconomic advancement. There are significant variations by ethnic group and by time period, but the central question is to what extent the second generation, born and reared in the United States, is interested in reading non-English newspapers. The children of Portuguese immigrants have shown relatively little interest.

The issue involves not only usage of a non-English ethnic tongue—in this case Portuguese—versus English, but also the degree and type of intrusion of English elements—chiefly vocabulary, and to a lesser extent grammatical patterns—into Portuguese speech, and from there into newspaper style. Additionally, there is the difference between standard language and regional or social dialects: most of the earlier immigrants from the Portuguese islands, who had little or no formal education, spoke a dialect somewhat removed from standard literary Portuguese, with Capeverdean Creole as the extreme case (really being a separate language). Should Portuguese immigrant newspapers attempt to adhere to the style of standard written Portuguese as much as newspapers in Portugal, or should they veer closer to casual immigrant speech by adopting Anglicisms and regional slang—or should they even give some space to outright English text (for example, for sports reports or advertisements) in order to attract second-generation readers? All Portuguese immigrant newspapers have made and are making some stylistic concessions of the first sort;[3] a few have also tried the second and more radical kind of accommodation at one time or another.[4]

The first Portuguese-language newspaper founded by immigrants in the United States was the weekly *Journal de Notícias*, published at Erie, Pennsylvania, from 1877 to 1884 by João M. Vicente, a native of the Azores who first settled in Boston after a whaling cruise, and by his brother (or older son?) Antonio. Antonio Vicente moved on to San Francisco in 1884, to found the weekly *Progresso Californiense* which was short-lived. Three years later, with a partner, he established the weekly *União Portuguesa*, which was to remain in publication at Oakland until 1942.

Portuguese-language journalism in California had actually begun in 1880, a few years prior to Vicente's arrival, when a Brazilian started a weekly called *Voz Portuguesa*; it expired after six years. The anti-Catholic feeling of the 1880s prompted the appearance in 1888 of *O Amigo dos Católicos* (The friend of the Catholics), under the direction of Father Fernandes, born Manuel Francisco Fernandes in the Azores. Fernandes had been employed in sheepraising and in mining in California until, in 1877, he decided to return to the Azores to study for the priesthood. Upon resettling in California, he was ordained at Santa Barbara, then attempted some missionary work in Hawaii and in Macau (Portugal's colony off the China coast), ending up in 1892 as pastor of the new Portuguese church in Oakland. His newspaper changed hands to become *O Arauto* in 1896, then was renamed *O Jornal de Noticias* in 1917.

By that time there were other competing papers catering to the California Portuguese: not only the above-mentioned *União Portuguesa*, founded in 1887, but also *O Reporter*, dating from 1897 (discontinued during World War I); *A Liberdade*, founded as a weekly at Sacramento in 1900, published as a daily in Oakland from 1920 to 1926, then reverting to weekly status until its extinction in 1936; the weekly *O Imparcial*, also at Sacramento, 1903–1932; *O Labrador Português* (The Portuguese farmer), a San Joaquin Valley weekly reflecting in its name the interests of the Portuguese farming communities there, 1912–1932; and a few more publications of short duration.

A *Liberdade* (Liberty) was guided throughout its lifetime by Guilherme Silveira da Gloria, who, like Fernandes, had studied for the priesthood in the Azores. He was ordained in California and became a pastor in Oakland (as of 1896); however, a few years later Gloria abandoned the priesthood to marry a native of California and to become a "liberal" fulltime journalist. He also authored many poems, published in two volumes in 1935 and 1940. In the 1930s and 1940s, the leading (and soon the only) Portuguese-language paper in California was the weekly *Jornal Português*.

Retracing our steps to the beginnings of Portuguese immigrant journalism, in the Hawaiian Islands Portuguese-language weeklies made their appearance within a few years after the arrival there of several thousand (largely illiterate) plantation laborers from Madeira and the Azores: *O Luso Hawaiiano* opened shop in 1885, another paper called *A Liberdade* perhaps even a year or two earlier. These and several others published in the 1890s were short-lived; but *O Luso* lasted from 1896 until the 1920s (Portuguese immigration to Hawaii came to an end shortly before World War I).

In New England, the major Portuguese settlement area in the United States, the Portuguese immigrant press had its beginning in the early 1880s, about the same time as in California and Hawaii. According to one source, a weekly called *Luso-Americano* was published in Boston and New Bedford from 1881 to 1889. According to another source, a paper by the name of *A Civilizacão* appeared in Boston in 1883 or shortly before. More directly documented is the fact that in 1884 Manuel Garcia Monteiro tried to float a newspaper in New Bedford upon his arrival there from the Azores.

Monteiro was a young intellectual of upper-class background; in some letters to a friend subsequently published, he lamented the difficulty of making a living out of a paper dependent on a readership of "ignorant hippopotamuses" (i.e., semiliterate factory workers). He soon quit journalism, ultimately becoming a Boston physician.[5] Monteiro's experience was placed in focus, half a century later, by a veteran Portuguese newspaperman in New Bedford who reminisced that, prior to the arrival of more literate immigrants during and after World War I, Portuguese weeklies were usually produced on presses made for the printing of receipts, tickets, and pamphlets; only if this kind of printing prospered did the newspaper flourish too—even if it had hardly any subscribers.[6]

Yet, even if they provided only a meager living, Portuguese-language newspapers kept cropping up in the ethnic communities of New England. Three of those appearing in the 1890s were the short-lived (*O Novo Mundo*, *O Colombo*,

O Português). Two other papers established at about that time were of longer duration and marked the beginnings of political journalism: the weekly *Correio Português* espoused the cause of republicanism (in Portugal), while a publication called *Portugal* endorsed the Portuguese monarchy. (This was the major issue in Portuguese politics at the time. The monarchy finally fell in 1910.) The *Independente*, founded in 1897 in New Bedford, managed to survive until after World War II. So did the *Novidades*; founded in Fall River in 1907, it had a strong Catholic emphasis, and later supported the Salazar dictatorship in Portugal, which replaced the republic in the 1920s. Another paper called *O Popular* seems to have been the first to be published in different local editions or sections (Boston, Fall River, Lowell, Providence, etc.).

By the close of World War I, the Portuguese communities in the East (that is, southeastern New England plus, increasingly, metropolitan New York–New Jersey) even had a daily Portuguese-language paper, as did those in California: the weekly *Alvorada*, founded in New Bedford about 1900, became a daily in 1917; it soon changed its masthead to *Diario de Noticias* (Daily news), under which name it was to survive until 1974.

As of about 1910, there were seven Portuguese-language weeklies of small circulation in New England (two each in Boston, Fall River, and New Bedford, and one in Lowell), three in California, and several in the Territory of Hawaii.[7] By the early 1920s, in all three areas together, there were about two dozen such periodicals (mostly weeklies, two dailies, two monthly magazines).[8] This number was cut in half by the mid–1930s. Between about 1880 and the late 1940s Portuguese immigrants founded some ninety different newspapers and magazines, mostly in Massachusetts and California; many of these little enterprises lasted only a few years or even a few months, with up to two dozen appearing at the same time when Portuguese immigration was at its height shortly before and after World War I, and about ten in publication at the end of World War II.[9] Their number waned in the 1950s and 1960s, but by the mid–1980s had rebounded to about a dozen.

Before outlining the current status of the Portuguese ethnic press, a brief content analysis of a few old newspaper issues, somewhat randomly selected, follows, along with some biographical data later about one Portuguese-American whose journalistic career has spanned the last sixty years.

1. *A Voz Portuguesa*, San Francisco, August 5, 1880 (first issue): Lead article exhorting the California Portuguese to organize for greater political strength, to vote against the Republicans and for the exclusion of Chinese immigrants. Article on Camões (Portugal's poet laureate), reprinted from a Brazilian newspaper. First installment of a serial on the history of Portugal. Miscellaneous local and international news. Advertisement from Portuguese immigrant hostelries in San Francisco and Boston, from quack physicans, etc.

2. *O Arauto*, Hayward, June 27, 1896: Front page obituary for Father Fernandes. Six columns of brief news items, mostly about Portuguese individuals and fraternal lodges

in California, accidents, theft in Chinatown, court actions, visitors, etc. Nine columns of foreign news, including five from the Azores, one from Lisbon. Appeal for unity of the Portuguese settlers; bits on their history. Forecast of McKinley election. Serial installments: one page from a book on Portugal's past and present; one page translated from a French novel; one page translated from an English book on Madeira. A visitor's praise of Hayward. Business section (three pages): produce prices on San Francisco market, ads, list of Portuguese books for sale, etc.

3. *O Luso*, Honolulu, December 31, 1910 (first three pages only): Front page: photo of Christmas tree outside Honolulu's Executive Mansion; dynamite attack on a foundry in Los Angeles; wedding of a Japanese with a white woman (deemed a shocking event); literacy classes for naturalization started by Portuguese club; episodes in Portugal's history; hunger epidemic in China; lynching attempt in West Virginia; revolts in Mexico and the Caroline Islands; train robbery in Peru. Page 2: suicide of Portugal's mint director; a religious parable and poem; elections in Portugal; commercial ads. Page 3: ads; reprint article from Lisbon paper on proposed change of Portuguese flag.

4. *O Popular*, New Bedford, January 9, 1919: Long article (reprinted from a Lisbon paper) on assassination of Portuguese prime minister. Editorial on question of independence of Azores. Summary of a speech by President Wilson. Departure of commander of United States naval base in Azores. Commercial ads and notices. Local community news: reports of club meetings and of a talk on naturalization requirements; personals; ads of forthcoming entertainments, etc. Serial installments (a Portuguese novel; translation of a French novel). Death of ex-President Roosevelt. List of Portuguese books for sale. News items from Azores, island by island.

Random issues over the next half century and more demonstrate similar coverage and emphases.

The *Luso-Americano*, drawing on the support of thousands of new Portuguese immigrants who have settled around Newark, as well as in nearby Greater New York over the past ten years or so, is currently the most substantial and prosperous Portuguese-American newspaper. Its weekly issues, in tabloid format, run from forty-eight to sixty pages and are similar in layout and design to major English-language tabloids. Although this paper carries on its masthead the description "Portuguese-American *bilingual* newsweekly," it is written almost entirely in Portuguese, except for two pages containing "News and Notes" appealing to the young and a small part of the advertising.

In contrast to Newark's *Luso-Americano*, born half a century ago, several other current weeklies were founded in recent years, in response to the heavy new wave of Portuguese immigration, and partly to fill the void left by the demise of the daily *Diario de Noticias* in 1974. Second and third place may currently be assigned, respectively, to the *Portuguese American*, published in Bristol, R. I., and to the *Portuguese Times* in New Bedford, Massachusetts. The former, located in a town whose population has come to be more heavily ethnic Portuguese (over 50 percent) than any other community in the United States, started out as *The Azorean Times* in 1975, then gradually changed its banner to *Comunidade*, and as of 1984 switched to its current name, designed for its broader appeal to Americanized readers. In addition to its "national edition," it is now also published in three apparently separate editions for Fall River, New Bedford, and Greater Boston. It is published in a slightly larger format than the *Luso-Americano* but has only half as many pages, about twenty-four to thirty-two.

The *Portuguese Times* (New Bedford), written entirely in Portuguese despite its English name, was founded in 1972; it is very similar to the *Portuguese American*; but since each paper has its own set of local correspondents, each tends to complement the other. The weekly *Jornal* (Fall River), founded as *Jornal de Fall River* in 1975, has stopped the fight for subscribers by offering free distribution, apparently depending entirely on advertising revenue. A weekly tabloid averaging about two dozen pages, it offers less specifically Portuguese material than the other papers, depending partly on translations from various Anglo sources and often featuring a bilingual front page editorial.

The dean of Portuguese-American journalists at the time of his death (at age eighty-three) in October 1983 was Vasco Jardim, a native of the Portuguese island of Madeira. Jardim had come to the United States in 1920 and while working in a hat factory in Fall River had become a contributor to the *Diario de Noticias* in nearby New Bedford. Within a year, he started his own weekly newspaper, *Esperança* (Hope), which lasted a few months. A job in a Brooklyn bar owned by a compatriot was next. By 1923 Jardim was back in Fall River to work for the *Fall River Globe* at $9 per week, reporting on the local Portuguese community. He also attended night school, studying English and graphic arts. Before long he tried again to bring out his own newspaper, *O Vigilante*, but failed once more. In 1928 he moved to Newark, N.J. which was then becoming a new center of Portuguese immigration, and took a job in a print shop. Over the next few years several new Portuguese-language newspapers made their appearance in Newark, each failing within a few months. By 1932, when the local Portuguese community was sufficiently organized to plan for a clubhouse and church of its own, Jardim was called in to make another journalistic effort, and the weekly *Luso-Americano* was born. It continues to appear without interruption, despite Jardim's death, and is under the control of his heirs.

In California, the weekly *Jornal Português* of San Pablo can look back on half a century's existence under its present name; it claims to have been founded in 1888, as it "descends" from the *Amigo dos Catolicos* via the *Arauto* and the *Jornal de Noticias*. It had its heyday in the 1930s and 1940s, and for a time thereafter dwindled to little more than a propaganda organ of Portugal's Salazar regime and Catholicism. Slimmed to twelve pages, it purveys some news from Portugal and the California Portuguese communities and also continues the old tradition of carrying some serialized fiction in each issue. The *Voz de Portugal* (Hayward, California) started as a weekly in 1960 and is now an eight-page monthly of little substance. The *Portuguese Tribune* (San Jose) was founded as a tabloid weekly in 1979, comparable in size and general appearance to the *Portuguese Times* of New Bedford (but, of course, with emphasis on the West Coast rather than the East), sometimes including a page of fiction and/or a feature in English. (Repeated queries about this paper's current status have remained unanswered; perhaps it is going out of business.)

But the Portuguese ethnic communities still produce individuals eager to put together a newspaper of their own. In October 1983 a new publication (presumably a weekly) called *Novidade* is reported to have made its debut in Tulare, California. Similarly, in Newark, N.J. a free-distribution biweekly by the name of *Portuguese News* started appearing recently; and in the same city two more weeklies, *Imagem* and *Corta e Cola*, have been announced as forthcoming.

Judging from the perusal of several thousand Portuguese immigrant newspaper issues representing dozens of small journalistic enterprises collectively spanning about a century, it appears that in the aggregate these papers have performed (and keep performing) their task rather well, channeling ethnic community news and opinion, maintaining some contacts with the old country, and furthering integration into American society while delaying the fading-away of Portuguese speech and traditions. Some of these papers have taken a more marked ideological or political position than others on such questions as insular regionalism versus development of a national Portuguese consciousness; monarchy versus republic; the role of the Catholic Church; the fascistic Salazar regime that ruled Portugal from the 1920s through the 1960s; and speed or methods of Americanization. The overarching concerns, most of the time, have been to try to secure a measure of recognition within the new multiethnic American environment for the lowly Portuguese (largely Azorean) immigrant, to fight perceived discrimination, to foster greater unity within the ethnic community in the face of such divisions as Azorean versus Continental (from mainland Portugal), foreign-born versus American-born, and so on.

To conclude this survey, brief mention should be made of some other mass media related to the Portuguese ethnic newspapers. Several efforts at publishing Portuguese-language magazines were made between about 1900 and 1930: a weekly journal called *Açores-America* probably was the first, in 1903; published at Cambridge, Massachusetts, it lasted half a year. In 1917 an illustrated magazine called *A Luzitania* appeared in Boston; it lasted for one year. More successful was the monthly *Revista Portuguesa*, in Hayward, California, devoted to "agricultural, commercial, and literary" matters, according to its subtitle; it appeared from about 1914 to 1925. In 1920, presumably as a reflection of the women's emancipation movement following World War I, there was a short-lived *Jornal das Damas* (Ladies journal) in New Bedford. The literary and leftist-liberal *Cosmopolitano*, illustrated, with occasional columns in English (such as a women's page), appeared every one to three months from 1922 to about 1925 at Fairhaven, Massachusetts. The quarterly *Varões Assinalados* (Outstanding men), with a focus on leftist-liberal personalities, made a one-year showing in New Bedford in 1924. From 1926 to 1929 an illustrated monthly magazine called *Portugal-America* appeared in Cambridge, Massachusetts. There seem to have been no further undertakings of this kind in Portuguese until very recently: a bimonthly by the name of *Novos Rumos* (New directions) has entered the scene in Newark; and a semiannual journal called *Gavea-Brown*, devoted to literary output by recent immigrants from Portugal, is now in its third year (edited at Brown University, Providence, R.I.).[10]

Generally speaking, newspapers do not have as much importance as media of communication today as they once had, because of the rise of radio and television. To some extent, this also applies to the Portuguese ethnic communities in the United States. English-language radio and television programs may hold only limited attraction for foreign-born residents who know little English; but they are better than nothing (especially in their musical and pictorial contents) for the functionally illiterate who cannot even read newspapers in their native tongue. (The illiteracy rate among Portuguese ethnics is of course much lower now than a half a century ago, due to the higher educational level of recent immigrants and the large proportion of American-born or American-educated descendants of immigrants.) Portuguese-language broadcasts started supplementing the Portuguese-language newspapers, and the English-language media, in the 1920s: the first such program was heard in 1922 over a New Bedford station, and California followed suit a few years later. These radio programs experienced a much fuller development in California than in the East or in Hawaii, including the formation of radio clubs. Several of the California programs became daily ones; most of those in New England were limited to weekends, until very recently. Airing of Portuguese-language community news and commericals along with entertainment continues today in both areas several times a week, including a few programs carried by local television stations (currently led by TV Channel 20 in the New Bedford area, which presents several hours of Portuguese material every day). Thus, the Portuguese-American public has both an electronic and a print media from which to select.

NOTES

1. Still published are *Seleçoes do Reader's Digest* (Portuguese edition of *Reader's Digest*, monthly, Pleasantville, N.Y.) and *As Americas* (Portuguese edition, complementing English and Spanish editions, of a Pan-American Union monthly, Washington, D.C.). The following titles no longer appear: *A Fazenda* (New York), *Em Guarda* (Washington), *O Novo Mundo* (New York).

2. *The Lusitanian* (monthly, published from about 1932 unitl some years after World War II at Oakland); *St. Anthony's Visitor* and *Fatima Magazine* (Catholic propaganda quarterlies, 1940s to 1960s, published at St. Anthony's [Portuguese] Mission, Bronx, N.Y.); *The Continental Magazine* (monthly, published by the Portuguese Continental Union of the United States, a mutual aid society at Plymouth, Mass., 1938–1939); *U.P.E.C. Life* (quarterly bulletin of the *União Portuguesa do Estado da California*, a mutual aid and insurance society at San Leandro, Calif., founded in 1888; now largely in English); *Cape Verdean* (1971- , monthly or irregular, published at Lynn, Mass., to serve ethnics from the [former] Portuguese colony of the Cape Verde Islands).

3. As often as not, this is not a conscious concession but the natural writing style of contributors with no special literary training.

4. For fuller details on language conditions among the Portuguese ethnics, see Leo

Pap, *Portuguese-American Speech* (New York: King's Crown Press [Columbia University], 1949); see also my general account of Portuguese immigration and immigrant institutions, *The Portuguese-Americans* (Boston: Twayne, 1981).

5. Henrique das Neves, *Individualidades* (Lisbon: Pereira, 1910), pp. 57–81.

6. *Diario de Noticias* (New Bedford), May 3, 1944, p. 9.

7. Information for New England and California is based largely on Portuguese consular reports. For Hawaii, cf. Edgar C. Knowlton, Jr., "The Portuguese Language Press in Hawaii," *Social Process in Hawaii* 24 (1960): 89–99. Also useful for the history of Portuguese newspapers in California is August Mark Vaz, *The Portuguese in California* (Oakland: 1965), pp. 142–149. I have not seen the Master's thesis by Geoffrey L. Gomes entitled "The Portuguese Language Press in California, 1880–1928" (History Department, California State University, Hayward, 1983).

8. According to Robert E. Park, *The Immigrant Press and Its Control* (New York: Harper, 1922), p. 318, the number of Portuguese-language publications in the United States (presumably excluding Hawaii) rose from three in 1892 to six in 1904, ten in 1911, and eighteen in 1920. Maurice R. Davie, *World Immigration* (New York: Macmillan, 1936), p. 486, counted twenty papers in 1920, but this number fell to eleven by 1934. *The Handbook-Bibliography on Foreign-Language Groups in the United States and Canada* (New York: Council for Home Missions and Missionary Education Movement, 1925), p. 24, lists twenty-three such periodicals for 1923. For New England alone, as of 1922–1923, Eduardo de Carvalho (then the Portuguese consul in Boston) counted one daily and four weeklies, plus two illustrated monthly magazines published in New Bedford; three weeklies in Fall River; and one (Protestant religious) monthly in Boston; in addition, at least two new weeklies and two monthlies began appearing in Fall River, Lowell, and Cambridge, while two other weeklies in New Bedford gave up the ghost after a few months. Cf. Eduardo de Carvalho, *Os Portugueses na Nova Inglaterra* (Rio de Janeiro: Colonial Reading: 1931), chap. 4.

9. See Pap, *Portuguese-American Speech* (1949), pp. 29–31, 154. Considering the small readership base, the total number seems excessive, reflecting a high degree of individualism and little journalistic business sense. The same situation had prevailed in Portugal: in the Azores alone, 312 different newspapers and magazines were born and died between 1830 and 1886, half of these on the single island of São Miguel, most of them having had a life span of a few months to two years. (Archivo dos Açores 8: 485–556.) On the other hand, the Portuguese are not the only ethnic group in the United States exhibiting such a picture of splintered and ephemeral journalistic enterprise: among the French Canadians in New England, 200 to 300 different French-language newspapers had seen the light of day up to 1943, with about 20 still in publication at that time. (Jacques Ducharme, *Shadows of the Trees* [New York: Harper, 1943], p. 127.)

10. For the benefit of future historians who may wish to inspect back files of Portuguese ethnic publications, here is a list of those available and their specific locations, as far as known:

O Arauto (Hayward and Oakland): incomplete file at Harvard College Library, and on microfilm for 1896–1916 at General Library of University of California, Berkeley.

Aurora Hawaiian (Honolulu): complete file for 1889-1891 held by Hawaiian Historical Society, Honolulu.

Colonial (a weekly published at Fairhaven Mass., 1925-c. 1950): complete file for 1931–1945 at New York Public Library, and scattered issues at Library of Congress.

Colonia Portuguesa (Oakland): incomplete file for 1924–1930 on microfilm at General Library of University of California, Berkeley.

Continental Magazine (Plymouth, Mass.): complete file for March 1938-February 1940 at New York Public Library and at Library of Congress.

Diario de Noticias (New Bedford): a complete back file of this important daily newspaper, spanning about fifty years (late 1920s–1974), is reported to be deposited at Southern Massachusetts University, North Dartmouth, Mass., in the care of Gregory Rocha. Incomplete file also at Library of Congress and at Harvard College Library.

Jornal Português (Oakland): complete file for 1932–1955 at Midwest Inter-Library Center, Chicago; 1934–1940, on microfilm, at General Library of University of California, Berkeley; 1940, incomplete, at Library of Congress.

O Luso (Honolulu): incomplete file for 1896–1897 and 1910–1923 held by Hawaiian Historical Society, Honolulu.

Luso Hawaiiano (Honolulu): incomplete file for 1885-1886 and 1889-1890 held by Hawaiian Historical Society.

Luta (a Catholic propaganda paper published weekly or monthly by a Portuguese priest in New York City, 193?–1970): incomplete file at Library of Congress.

O Popular (New Bedford): incomplete file for 1917–1924 at Midwest Inter-Library Center, Chicago, and at Harvard College Library.

Popular (Honolulu): Complete file for 1911–1912 held by Hawaiian Historical Society, Honolulu.

Revista Portuguesa (Hayward): complete file, c. 1914–1925, at New York Public Library.

União Lusitana Hawaiiana (Honolulu): complete file for 1892–1896 held by Hawaiian Historical Society, Honolulu.

União Portuguesa (Oakland): complete file for 1917-1942 at Midwest Inter-Library Center, Chicago.

Voz Portuguesa (San Francisco): some early issues, 1880 +, at Library of Congress.

BIBLIOGRAPHY

Gomes, Geoffrey L. "The Portuguese Language Press in California, 1880–1928." Master's thesis, California State University, Hayward, 1983.

Pap, Leo. *The Portuguese Americans*. Boston: Twayne, 1981.

Vaz, August Mark. *The Portuguese in California*. Oakland: Brotherhood of the Divine Holy Ghost (I.D.E.S.), 1965.

20

The Puerto Rican Press

JOSEPH P. FITZPATRICK

It is very difficult to define the limits of the Puerto Rican ethnic press in the United States. The increasingly varied character of Spanish-speaking communities, especially the community in the New York metropolitan area, has led to a situation in which newspapers and magazines are directed to a general Spanish reading market rather than to a specific Hispanic group. The Puerto Ricans in recent years have not had an ethnic press comparable to, for example, the Jewish press or the Polish press, reflecting an ethnic identity and a common set of ethnic interests.[1] As with so many other aspects of their migration, the Puerto Rican experience is unique. The problem of identity that the group has wrestled with; the lack of attention on the part of the larger community to its particular values, contributions, and problems; the absence of leadership at critical moments—all of these can be seen in the role of the press in Puerto Rican life. In this sense the analysis of the role of the press throws added light on the Puerto Rican experience. This may give to non–Puerto Ricans and Puerto Ricans alike a clearer insight into their experience and enable them to respond to it creatively. This chapter will seek to describe the role of the press in three phases of its history: (1) in the early years, namely, the late nineteenth and early twentieth centuries; (2) the middle years between World War I and World War II; and (3) the contemporary period since World War II, the era of the great migration and the rapid increase of Puerto Ricans in the continental United States.

THE EARLY YEARS

The Puerto Rican press played a long and significant role in the early period of Hispanic journalism in the United States. New York was the center for most of the revolutionary movements of the Caribbean colonies against Spain that developed during the latter part of the last century. It was the base for organizations dedicated to freedom and independence, the center where they met, and the place where they spread the gospel of independence through a variety of small but significant newspapers.

New York witnessed a gathering of remarkable men and women, many of whom distinguished themselves by their achievements. Prominent among them were Ramon E. Betances (1827–1898), an early and vigorous leader in the movement for Puerto Rican independence who came to New York in 1867. Eugenio Maria de Hostos (1839–1903) was another. Lola Rodriguez de Tio frequently spent time in the city. She was the author of "La Borinqueña," the national hymn of Puerto Rico, which she recited for the first time in 1868. Francisco Gonzalo (Pachin) Marin (1863–1897), who had founded his revolutionary paper, *El Postillon*, in Puerto Rico, came to New York in 1891, where he continued to publish the paper after it had been twice suppressed as subversive on the Island. Sotero Figueroa, Santiago Iglesias (1872–1939), founder of the Socialist Party in Puerto Rico, and Luis Muñoz Rivera (1859–1916), father of Luis Muñoz Marin, also spent time in New York. It was a group of colorful, militant, and zealous men and women.[2]

From this background emerged the early Puerto Rican papers, which had one clear purpose: to achieve the independence of Puerto Rico and the Caribbean nations from Spain. In 1865 a group of political militants in New York City formed the Republican Society of Cuba and Puerto Rico. They founded a newspaper called *La Voz de America* (The voice of America). Outstanding among the founders of *La Voz* were a Cuban revolutionary, Juan Manuel Macia, and a Puerto Rican, José J. Bassora. The paper had branches in Philadelphia and New Orleans.

Ramon Emeterio Betances established contact with this group when he was organizing his revolutionary effort at Lares, Puerto Rico. After the failure of the Lares rebellion, "El Grito de Lares," in 1868, a large number of Puerto Ricans came to New York as exiles. They later formed the Club Borinquen in 1892 under the leadership of Sotero Figueroa as president and Antonio Velez Alvarado as vice-president. They were joined by D. Enrique Trujillo, who brought his paper, *El Porvenir*, with him and continued to publish it in New York. *Borinquen*, a bimonthly newspaper of the Puerto Rican section of the Cuban Revolutionary Party, was established in 1898 under the editorship of Robert H. Todd.

This represents a significant period of Puerto Rican journalism, featuring a strong and persistent effort of some of the most able men and women of Puerto Rico to use the press as an important element in the struggle for independence. They were a sadly discouraged and disappointed group when the United States took possession of the Island in 1898 and failed to grant independence to Puerto Rico. Luis Muñoz Rivera had founded a paper, *La Democracia*, in Puerto Rico, demanding autonomy from Spain, a goal which he largely achieved. He saw this terminated by the United States. Realizing that the struggle had shifted to Washington, he came to New York in 1901 and founded a weekly, *The Puerto Rico Herald*, published in English and Spanish. This was an important voice of Puerto Rican protest during the early years of discussion and controversy in the U.S. Congress about the status of Puerto Rico. Muñoz Rivera published a blistering criticism of the Foraker Act, which marked the imposition of a governing system by the United States on Pureto Rico in 1898. He called it "a Tyranny such as is known only on the Steppes of Russia, the Dominions of the Ottoman Porte, or among the despotic Mandarins of the Celestial Empire."[3] Muñoz Rivera publicized his views and those of his colleagues in their efforts to achieve autonomy for Puerto Rico. This effort would leave them with a sense of self-respect while retaining a favorable relationship with the United States. The press had a brief but influential history in the struggle for a political status acceptable to the Puerto Ricans.

With the unilateral granting of citizenship to the Puerto Ricans by the U.S. Congress through the Jones Act in 1917, a great period terminated for the Puerto Rican press. It had kept alive the hope of independence among the Puerto Rican people; it failed to convince Congress to agree to it. It was a period marked by an admirable spirit of nobility and dedication. Nothing since has taken its place.

THE MIDDLE YEARS

After 1898 another Puerto Rican movement to New York began, this time of poor Puerto Ricans seeking economic opoortunity on the continent. In 1910 the U.S. census counted 1,500 Puerto Ricans in the United States, 554 of them in New York City. By 1930 the number had increased to 52,774, the great majority of them in New York City. They gathered in small clusters that are well described in a recent publication by Virginia E. Sanchez Korrol.[4] She calls them *colonias*, small neighborhood concentrations which had a vitality and character that served as a small enclave of Puerto Rican life in New York City. They were populated mostly by unskilled and semiskilled workers who had come to New York seeking available jobs. The neighborhoods tended to cluster around the sources of employment. Storekeepers, businessmen, and professional persons became the heart of these well-organized neighborhoods along with the local parish or political club.

After World War II the great migration began.[5] In 1950 the census reported 301,375 Puerto Ricans on the mainland; 245,880, over 80 percent, were in New York City. The 1980 census reported 2,013,945 Puerto Ricans on the mainland, with 860,552 in New York City. This is a large and important population. In fact, one-third of all Puerto Ricans live on the mainland. It would seem that out of this large number of people enjoying the rights of citizens, with none of the complications an alien must face, a strong and influential press would have emerged. Such has not been the case.

La Prensa was established in New York City in 1913 to serve a small population of immigrants from Spain who settled in Manhattan in the area of 14th Street and 8th Avenue. The restaurants and shops on 14th Street, between 7th and 8th Avenues, are still characteristic of this small Spanish group, as is the church, Our Lady of Guadalupe, which was founded in 1902 to serve that community. *La Prensa* was founded and edited by José Campubrí, and directed its attention mainly to the interests of the immigrant community from Spain. It paid little attention to the growing numbers of Puerto Ricans in the city or to their interests. However, for many years it was the only Spanish–language press in the city. If Puerto Ricans were to have a periodical in Spanish to read, it would have to be *La Prensa*. The paper ran a daily column, "Informaciones de Puerto Rico," which consisted mainly of political news about the island. Its news coverage was international, and a review of issues during the 1930s reveals few news items about the Puerto Ricans in New York City. However, it did provide the services of a community paper. These are mentioned by Lawrence Chenault[6] and are described in detail by Sanchez Korrol.[7] Included were items on social events and community celebrations as well as want ads and local announcements appealing to neighborhood residents. It served as a source of community information and assisted community groups in fund raising. From this point of view it was the link that bound the many small and varied Hispanic communities together.

La Prensa tended to be sympathetic to insurgent movements generally. It supported the Nationalist Movement in Puerto Rico, a movement which it saw as linking the interests of the Puerto Ricans around an ideal cause.[8] It was sympathetic to the rebellion of Sandino in Nicaragua against the presence of U.S. Marines supporting the traditional autocratic government of the Somozas. The paper became politically involved during the upheavals in Spain during the 1930s. It supported the Loyalist cause during the Spanish Civil War (1936–1939) and actively recruited the Abraham Lincoln Brigade, a group of Americans who fought with the Loyalists in Spain. The political involvement of *La Prensa* made it controversial. It lost considerable prestige among some segments of the Hispanic community, but it continued to publish. Having no other Spanish press was a handicap for the Puerto Ricans. They had difficulty enough coping with their adjustment to life on the mainland, but when they needed a strong advocate in the press, the only general interest newspaper available in Spanish was directing its attention to events in Spain.

Sanchez Korrol describes in detail two other short-lived papers which did serve as advocates for the Puerto Rican community during the 1930s.[9] *Grafico*, a weekly published from 1926 to 1931 by some of the skilled workers in the cigar industry, was an outspoken critic of the bias, discrimination, and exploitation suffered by Hispanics (mainly Puerto Ricans). And *Revista de Artes y Letras*, published from 1933 to 1945 by some highly educated Puerto Rican women in the community, was dedicated to promoting Puerto Rican culture and the arts. It also became a source of important information for the community and a strong advocate for Puerto Rican interests in the field of education.

THE CONTEMPORARY PERIOD: POST–WORLD WAR II, 1946–1960

The rapid increase of the Puerto Rican population after 1946 and subsequent developments prompted changes in *La Prensa*. (*El Diario de Nueva York*, for example, had been founded in 1948 and was a competitor.) In 1958 Francisco Cardona, formerly press secretary of Puerto Rico's Governor Luis Muñoz Marin, was appointed editor of *La Prensa*, the first Puerto Rican to hold that position. He changed the format of the paper to a tabloid and directed its attention to the interests of the Puerto Rican community in the city. In 1960 *La Prensa* was purchased by Fortune Pope, a prominent Italian who was the owner and publisher of *Il Progreso*, the best–known Italian paper in the city. Pope also founded a radio station, WHOM-FM and AM, which began broadcasting in Spanish during the 1950s. In order to strengthen the Puerto Rican staff of *La Prensa*, Pope also hired away from *El Diario* José Lumén Román, a popular political and newspaper figure in the Puerto Rican community. Lumén Román created the Spanish American News Agency, SANA, to provide news to the press about the Hispanic community. Thus, in the early 1960s, *La Prensa* became, to a much greater extent than before, a paper related to the Puerto Rican community and serving Puerto Rican interests.

In 1962, however, *La Prensa* was sold by Fortune Pope to O. Roy Chalk, who was also owner of *El Diario de Nueva York*. The two papers merged and became known as *El Diario de Nueva York/La Prensa* and remain so until the present.

The newspaper most closely related to the Puerto Rican community in New York has been *El Diario de Nueva York*. However, it is only by broad definition that it can be said to constitute a Puerto Rican press. It has never been owned by a Puerto Rican, and during much of its life span its editor was not Puerto Rican. However, if one asked the question, What is the Puerto Rican paper in New York?, the answer would be *El Diario*. It has always addressed itself to the Puerto Rican community, and proclaimed itself from the beginning "The Champion of the Puerto Ricans and Hispanics."

El Diario was founded in 1948 by Porfirio Domenici, a Dominican who had previously been the ambassador of Santo Domingo to Switzerland. He was married to a woman from Venezuela, and some of his financial backing came from Venezuelans. He appointed as editor a well–known Puerto Rican, Vicente Gegel Polanco, who had become involved in political controversy in Puerto Rico and had relocated to New York. Gegel Polanco was replaced in 1952 by José Davila Ricci, an experienced journalist from Puerto Rico and a close associate of Luis Muñoz Marin, then governor of Puerto Rico. The potential of *El Diario* as a political influence was becoming recognized. But Davila Ricci's editorship ended shortly when he was accused of involvement in questionable legal activities.

In 1954 Stanley Ross was appointed editor and was to remain in that position for the next eight years. He had considerable experience as a newspaper correspondent in Latin America. Ross was a significant name during some of the most difficult years of the Puerto Rican experience. The Puerto Rican population was rapidly increasing, and the exploitation of Puerto Ricans in housing and employment was widespread. The rise in crime was blamed on them, and they became the scapegoats for the increasing ills of New York City.[10] They had few advocates in the city. In terms of the press, *El Diario* sought to fulfill its slogan, "The Champion of the Puerto Ricans." José Lumén Román, for example, was interested in investigatory journalism; he did an exposé of the problems in the camps of Puerto Rican migrant farm workers in 1953.[11] Since the Migrant Farm Worker Program was run by the government of Puerto Rico, the exposé did not sit well with Governor Muñoz Marin or the officials at the Office of the Commonwealth of Puerto Rico, who were responsible for monitoring the program.[12] Lumén Román also undertook a nationally significant exposé of the formation of phantom labor unions among Puerto Ricans in the New York area. Labor racketeering at its worst was involved, and thousands of Puerto Ricans were being exploited in the process. Lumén Román, together with a group of students from Fordham College and the Association of Catholic Trade Unionists, exposed the situation in hearings before a congressional committee, and bona fide unions began to move in and take over.

El Diario developed other important links to the Puerto Rican community. It inaugurated an interesting public grievance procedure at its Orientation Center. Ordinary citizens with popular grievances would simply appear at a small office at the newspaper and air their grievances about consumer fraud, exploitation in housing, employment, union activities, and other matters. The staff members at *El Diario* would act as advocates to assist them, often using the columns of the press to publicize grievances. Puerto Rican leaders insist that this was the inspiration for the establishment of a consumer fraud unit in the city government.

The Orientation Center led to other developments in the form of legal aid. It became the place where interested and dedicated young lawyers would gather to assist the poor in cases that required legal assistance. This informal volunteer process of community action legal services became a model for government agencies that later developed.

El Diario as well as *La Prensa* had the usual features of a community newspaper for Puerto Ricans and Hispanics: columns on social and cultural activities; extensive coverage of sports events in Puerto Rico and those involving Puerto Ricans on the mainland; want ads of all kinds, with a focus on the interests of Puerto Ricans and Hispanics; letters to the editor; and feature columns by Puerto Rican writers about Puerto Rican life in New York. Editorially, both papers were favorable to Muñoz Marin in Puerto Rico and promoted Puerto Rican interests in New York City. Both were very critical of Fidel Castro and his communist government in Cuba; both spoke critically of Rafael Leonidos Trujillo as an oppressive dictator in Santo Domingo, especially on the occasion of his assassination in 1961.

During this period the best-known figure in Puerto Rican journalism was Luisa Quintero, generally recognized as the grande dame of the Puerto Rican press in New York City. Completely dedicated to the interests of the Puerto Rican people, and thoroughly familiar with all their problems, sufferings, and grievances, she was their advocate par excellence. Her column, "Marginalia," appeared regularly in *La Prensa* and later in *El Diario/La Prensa*, and her reports on the activities and experiences of the Puerto Rican community were a source of reliable information about the situation of her people. Politically, she was an enthusiastic supporter of Muñoz Marin and the Partido Popular (the Popular Democratic Party of Puerto Rico) and of the Democratic Party on the mainland. She was sensitive to the culture of the Puerto Ricans and sought to keep alive their cultural activities. She was concerned about their values and their religious life: she covered religious activities, particularly Catholic activities, with great care. Her presence kept the larger community aware of the interests of the Puerto Ricans, and kept Puerto Ricans aware that someone was speaking for them. For a generation Luisa Quintero's influence was outstanding. No one has emerged to take her place.

She played an important role in a celebrated case, protesting the sentencing to death of Salvador Agron, who would have been the youngest person ever to die in the electric chair in New York State. The vigourous protest of the Puerto Rican community won a decision from Governor Nelson Rockefeller to commute the sentence to life imprisonmnent with the possibility of parole. This was one of the first major political victories won by Puerto Ricans at the state level.

THE CONTEMPORARY PERIOD: 1960–1984

The 1960s began a period of increasing confusion and uncertainty for the Puerto Ricans and for the Puerto Rican press. New waves of other Hispanics began to crowd into the New York area: Cuban refugees from Castro's Cuba; large numbers of Dominicans, many of them without documents, the so-called illegal immigrants; and an increasing number of immigrants and refugees from Central and South America. By 1970, Puerto Ricans were no longer the dominant Hispanic community in New York that they had been during the 1950s. In 1975, for example, almost half the Hispanic marriages in New York City involved non–Puerto Ricans.[13] The 1980 census reported 1,406,024 Hispanics in New York City, probably an undercount; 860,552 of this number, or 61 percent, were Puerto Ricans. Dominicans now represent the second largest Hispanic group in the city, followed by large numbers of Cubans and Central and South Americans. By 1980 neither the census nor the Board of Education was reporting data on Puerto Ricans alone; all the Spanish-speaking groups were reported under one category as "Hispanics."

Similar complications affected the Hispanic press. As indicated above, the turmoil of buying, selling, and reorganization did not result in a strong Puerto Rican or Hispanic press. Nevertheless, publisher O. Roy Chalk appointed Puerto Rican editors and sought to make *El Diario de Nueva York/La Prensa* responsive to the interests of the Puerto Rican community and the increasing numbers of other Hispanics coming into the city. Discriminatory practices were publicized and attacked; the interests of Puerto Ricans in the schools, particularly the demand for bilingual/bicultural programs, were supported; Lyndon Johnson's Great Society program and War Against Poverty were supported as programs which would benefit the Hispanics of the city; strong opposition was expressed to the U.S. involvement in Vietnam. The growing concern of the Hispanic community about deliquency, thievery in the neighborhoods, and drug addiction was frequently publicized. This was largely the tone of the paper into the 1970s. Meanwhile, links between the Latin nations and New York became closer through air travel. The newspapers from Colombia, Ecuador, Santo Domingo, and Puerto Rico reach newsstands in New York on the same day that they are published. These papers preserve a sense of identity with the country of origin for many Hispanic New Yorkers. But they do not fulfill the role of an ethnic press for people seeking to establish a place in the United States.

In 1981 the Reverend Sun Myung Moon and the Unification Church established a Spanish–language newspaper in New York City. Realizing the usefulness of the press in disseminating his ideas, Sun Myung Moon established News World Communications, which now publishes four newspapers: *The Washington Times*; *The Tribune* (New York); *The Harlem Weekly*, directed toward black residents in New York City; and *Noticias del Mundo*, directed toward the Spanish-speaking of the New York area. José Cardinale, an Argentinian, is the editor of the latter. Also in 1981, the Gannett newspaper chain bought *El Diario/La Prensa,* naming a prominent Puerto Rican, Mañuel Bustelo, as editor. Thus, in the 1980s, the rapidly expanding Hispanic population of the New York area has a national news chain and an international religious group from Korea competing for the Spanish newspaper market.[14] *El Diario* continues to support policies generally associated with the poor and the Democratic Party. *Noticias del Mundo* is much more conservative and reflects the attitudes of the Reagan administration.

The Gannett Corporation owns a chain of ninety papers. It is interested in the Hispanic market. It first bought the *Tucson Citizen* and appointed as editor a Chicano journalist, Gerald Garcia. *El Diario* was its second such move, and the appointment of Bustelo exemplifies its policy of appointing promising young Hispanics to take responsibility for the papers. Bustelo insists that he is an independent editor on political and social issues. Aware of the troubled history of *El Diario*, he wants to be seen as an editor who is beholden to none. He speaks of the appointment of Anthony Alvarado as chancellor of the New York City school system as an example of the kind of influence he would like to exert. The paper consistently supported the candidacy of Alvarado, and was one of the strong Puerto Rican voices raised in his support.[15]

A number of factors are involved in the current orientation of *El Diario/La Prensa*. In view of diversification of the Hispanic population, the paper addresses itself to the interests of all the Hispanic groups. This limits the attention given to predominantly Puerto Rican issues. Secondly, Bustelo is committed to a policy of linking *El Diario* to a nationwide network of the Hispanic press. He shares the conviction of many that only through the creation of a strong, unified, nationwide Hispanic front will the Hispanics of the nation be able to exercise their potential power and achieve their objectives. For example, he was very influential in the development of the First National Conference on Spanish Language Media, held in California in 1982. Bustelo was the principal speaker at the first plenary session of the conference, reflecting his own influence among his peers as well as the importance of *El Diario* as one of the major Hispanic dailies in the United States. The objective of the conference was to bring together Hispanic journalists, public relations representatives, and professionals in the media in order to exchange information, ideas, and experiences so that they might serve the Hispanic community nationwide more effectively. If *El Diario* becomes national, its attention to Puerto Rican issues and interests will decline. In the meantime, its circulation has declined in New York while *Noticias del Mundo* is threatening to capture a larger segment of the Hispanic market.[16]

It is not realistic to speak of the Puerto Rican press. It is widely remarked that the paper read by most Puerto Ricans is the *New York Daily News*, which has the largest circulation of any paper in New York City. It is well edited for the rank and file reader. Tabloid in form, easy to read, available on almost every street corner, it covers the events that catch the interest of working people. As a popular newspaper, the *Daily News* outdistances all Hispanic newspapers. An increasing number of Puerto Ricans and other Hispanics read English; many are more at home in English than Spanish. They are more likely to buy the paper that attracts them most, whether in English or Spanish.

All the media, including television, radio, newspapers, and periodicals, look to a broad, diversified, and increasingly scattered Hispanic audience. *Hispanic Business* is published in California but circulates in New York as the national Hispanic business magazine. *Temas*, a popular monthly begun in 1950 and edited by a Cuban, José de la Vega, circulates among all Hispanic groups in New York and elsewhere. A recently founded magazine, *U.S. Hispanic Affairs*, is published by a Cuban, Daniel Ramos, for a general Hispanic audience. *Nuestro*, a monthly general interest magazine, published in English in New York, aims at a national market of Hispanics who prefer English to Spanish but still have definitely Hispanic interests.

Consequently, the development of Hispanic Link, a national news service from Washington, D.C., reflects the growing network of the Hispanic press and the effort to get accurate news about Hispanics to the general English–language press. Hispanic Link was established by the Hispanic Media Association of Washington, D.C. Its president, Charles Erickson, is director of Hispanic Link. He has long been an advocate for accurate news about the Hispanic community and seeks to correct the tendency to caricature Hispanics in biased news stories and editorial comments. Erickson is probably the best informed person about the Hispanic press in the United States, and about Hispanic journalists who are employed by the non-Hispanic press.

New York has the largest Puerto Rican population of any city in the continental United States. For this reason, the present chapter has centered its attention there. However, Puerto Ricans have dispersed into small cities and towns in New York State, Massachusetts, and Connecticut. There are large concentrations in northeastern New Jersey and in the Camden–Philadelphia area, as well as in Florida,

Illinois, and California. In most of these areas there is no specific Puerto Rican press. The communities in the Miami area have a press dominated by Cubans; in California, by the Mexican Americans. The role of the press in the Puerto Rican experience reflects the problems which beset the Puerto Rican community in general. Without a press of their own, Puerto Ricans have largely depended on others to represent their cause. Some non–Puerto Rican advocates have been dedicated friends and supporters. But, in fostering a sense of identity there is no substitute for a press that can be called one's own. Since the early part of the century, the Puerto Ricans have never had a press which both fostered and reflected the identity of the Puerto Rican community.

Assimilation into the mainstream of American life is a process that is defined and evaluated differently depending on the perspective a person has on the meaning of migration. However, whatever the larger interpretation of the migration, or the hopes for a continuity of culture, a process of adjustment is inevitable, and in that process a strong sense of identity and the solidarity of a strong community are critical; they give newcomers a sense of support and self-assurance as they cope with their adjustment to a new and strange land. Puerto Ricans have had to adjust to a new life without many of the supports that earlier immigrants enjoyed. It has been more difficult for them to establish strong neighborhood communities. Sanchez Korrol describes their early existence; but apart from the Barrio in East Harlem these were not able to develop into strong and enduring migrant communities.[17] During the 1970s many Puerto Rican neighborhoods were burned out, and the residents scattered to other parts of the city and elsewhere. Furthermore, Puerto Ricans were the first Catholics to arrive in large numbers without their own clergy. They had to depend on priests of European background to learn Spanish and minister to them; they were received into existing Irish or German or Italian parishes, but were not able to establish parishes of their own as had older ethnic groups, whose parishes played a central role in the stability of early immigrant communities. Their involvement in elections has been mysteriously and unfortunately slow in contrast to the intensity of political involvement in Puerto Rico. As a result they are not adequately represented by elected Puerto Rican officials. Until recently Puerto Ricans were taught almost entirely by non–Puerto Rican teachers. They have had to struggle with many handicaps that earlier newcomers did not face. The lack of a strong Puerto Rican press is only one of them.

Collaboration with other Hispanics on a national level may be the pragmatic response of Puerto Ricans to this problem. They are creating their own national groups, as examples, the National Association of Puerto Rican Women and the National Puerto Rican Coalition. Thus, with a sense of their own identity and solidarity, they move toward collaboration with others. They are very active in the National Association of Latino Elected or Appointed Officials (NALEO), and the Hispanic Caucus in Congress. They are also members of the National Hispanic Council on Aging. The present trend toward national publications directed toward common Hispanic interests may be a reflection of this trend; it could be a step into the future. In this context, a close relationship with a national press would very likely be a substantial advantage.

NOTES

1. The role of the ethnic press is discussed in detail by Joshua A. Fishman, *Language Loyalty in the United States* (The Hague: Mouton, 1966), Chap. 3, "The Non-English and Ethnic Press." Also in J. Zubrzycki, "The Role of the Foreign Language Press in Immigrant Assimilation," *Population Studies* 12 (1958): 73–82. For a general discussion of the problems of Puerto Ricans in their adjustment to the mainland, see Joseph P. Fitzpatrick, *Puerto Rican Americans: The Meaning of Migration to the Mainland* (Englewood Cliffs, N.J.: Prentice–Hall, 1971).

2. This is a neglected period of Puerto Rican history in New York. There has been little scholarly inquiry into or publication about it. A popular presentation of the people involved can be found in Federico Rives Tovar, *Encyclopedia Puertoriqueña* (New York: Plus Ultra Educational Publishers, 1970).

3. See "Letter of Muñoz Rivera to President William McKinley," in the first issue of the *Puerto Rico Herald*, 1901. The remarkable statement of Muñoz Rivera before the United States House of Representatives on May 5, 1916, reveals his dedication and his yearning for democracy in Puerto Rico. His indictment of U.S. policy toward Puerto Rico is one of the most severe criticisms ever leveled at the United States. It is found in U.S. *Congressional Record*, 64th Congress, 1st Sess., 1916, 53, pages 7470–7473. It is reprinted in Kal Wagenheim and Inez Jimenez de Wagenheim, *The Puerto Ricans: A Documentary History* (New York: Praeger, 1973), pp. 126–135.

4. Virginia E. Sanchez Korrol, *From Colonia to Community: The History of Puerto Ricans in New York City, 1917–1948* (Westport, Conn.: Greenwood Press, 1983). Before this excellent publication appeared, the best source of information about the Puerto Rican community during the middle years was Lawrence R. Chenault, *The Puerto Rican Migrant in New York* (New York: Columbia University Press, 1938).

5. See Joseph P. Fitzpatrick, "Puerto Ricans," in *The Harvard Encyclopedia of American Ethnic Groups* (Cambridge, Mass.: Harvard University Press, 1981), for details on the migration.

6. Chenault. p. 129.

7. Sanchez Korrol, pp. 70–71.

8. See the editorial, 6/29/32, on the new Nationalist Movement in Puerto Rico.

9. Sanchez Korrol, pp. 72–76.

10. See Joseph P. Fitzpatrick, "Crime and the Immigrant," in Gus Tyler, ed., *Organized Crime in America* (Ann Arbor, Mich.: University of Michigan Press, 1962), pp. 415–421.

11. This was a program in which Puerto Ricans came as visiting farm workers under a contract arranged and monitored by the Department of Labor in Puerto Rico.

12. This office was established in New York in 1948 by the governor of Puerto Rico to be of service to the Puerto Ricans migrating to New York. The newspaper *Grafico* had always demanded either a person or an office to serve as an advocate for Puerto Ricans in New York. Foreigners had their consulates to intervene for them, but, as American citizens, Puerto Ricans had no one. The Office of the Commonwealth was Muñoz Marin's effort to fulfill this function.

13. Joseph P. Fitzpatrick and Douglas Gurak, *Hispanic Inter-marriage in New York*

City: 1975 (New York: Hispanic Research Center, Fordham University, 1979), p. 14, Table 2.

14. See Mark D. Uehling, "Extra! Extra! Extra! Rivalry in New York: A Profile of Two Newspapers," *Nuestro*, September 1983, pp. 20–21.

15. Alvarado faced embarrassing public questioning about his personal finances. Pressures developed for his resignation. *El Diario* continued to support him and gave wide publicity to the resentment of Puerto Ricans who insisted that Alvarado was a scapegoat in a corrupt educational system in which "no one but Alvarado is being investigated." Later in the year, Alvarado left office.

16. As of this writing, Bustelo has been replaced as editor of *El Diario/La Prensa*. Its circulation has been dropping, while that of *Noticias del Mundo* has been increasing. With a new editor, *El Diario/La Prensa* may enter a new phase.

17. See Fitzpatrick, *Puerto Rican Americans*, chapter 1.

BIBLIOGRAPHY

Ayer, N. W. & Sons. *Annual Directory of Newspapers and Periodicals*. Philadelphia N. W. Ayer & Sons.

Fishman, Joshua A., *Language Loyalty in the United States*. The Hague: Mouton, 1966. (Chap. 3, "The Non-English and Ethnic Press.")

Fitzpatrick, Joseph P., *Puerto Rican Americans: The Meaning of Migration to the Mainland*. Englewood Cliffs, N.J.: Prentice–Hall, 1971.

———. "Puerto Ricans." In *The Harvard Encyclopedia of American Ethnic Groups*. Cambridge, Mass.: Harvard University Press, 1981.

Guernica, Antonio, and Irene Kasperuk. *Reaching the Hispanic Market Effectively: The Media, the Market, the Methods*. New York: McGraw Hill, 1982. (Chap. 2, "Print.")

Rives Tovar, Federico. *Encyclopedia Puertoriqueña*. 3 vols. New York: Plus Ultra Educational Publishers, 1970.

Zubrzycki, J. "The Role of the Foreign Language Press in Immigrant Assimilation." *Population Studies* 12 (1958): 73–82.

21

The Romanian Press

GERALD J. BOBANGO

Making the very best of imperfect statistics, one may estimate that some 85,000 Romanians, most of them from Transylvania, had come to the United States by 1920, while another 5,400 native-born Americans were of Romanian parentage. The vast majority of those arriving in the peak period between 1895 and 1920 were single men between the ages of eighteen and forty-five, 97 percent of them unskilled laborers, who settled in the industrial heartland of the mid-Atlantic and Great Lakes states. New York, Chicago, Detroit, Cleveland, Pittsburgh, Youngstown, Gary, Akron, Canton, Erie, and Johnston all had active and substantial Romanian colonies by the end of World War I.

Despite the increasingly rapid passing of the pioneer generation of Romanian immigrants, Romanian-language and Romanian-English publications devoted to the concerns and interests of the second– and third–generation ethnic community continue to appear in the United States and Canada today. In the summer of 1983, well-known Cleveland journalist Theodore Andrica counted twenty-eight in the United States and seven in Canada.[1] A majority of these seem to appear with fair regularity, others only sporadically. The tradition established for Romanian-American journalism by the pioneer priest Father Moise Balea, who placed on the masthead of the premier number of his newspaper *America* in 1906, ''published when I have time, money, and disposition,'' has not been lost.

A complete catalogue of the Romanian press in America has yet to be compiled. The researcher encounters what as early as the 1920s appears to be a bewildering proliferation of regional and local newspapers, little magazines, ''journals,'' bulletins, official and semi-official organs of this or that Romanian group, church, or beneficial society, many of which appeared only for one or two issues, then ceased to exist or reorganized and appeared again under a different name. It is likely that dozens of local or even wider-ranging publications remain unknown to us today, so long as the records of numerous Romanian societies and parishes during the early years of the century continue to molder in dozens of crumbling parish halls and society basements, or in the attics and closets of descendants of club secretaries. Thus, even a total number expressing the volume of the Romanian-American press remains at best an educated estimate. The most expert student on the subject, Gretchen Buehler, noted in January 1980 that at least 150 Romanian periodicals had appeared since 1900.[2]

From the beginning, editors and writers of the Romanian-American press borrowed both titles and formats of publications in Romania for their new ventures by way of stressing their continuity with the homeland journalistic tradition and at the same time attracting a wide readership among the homesick immigrant population, eager for anything which put them in touch *"cu țara"* (with the country). Thus, the first paper to appear in Romanian, the *Curierul Româno-American* (The Romanian-American courier), published in New York City in April 1900, evoked the historic *Curierul Românesc* published by the famous Ion Heliade Radulescu after 1829, and even the very first Romanian gazette, the 1790 publication in Jassy, *La Courrier de Moldavie*. *Vremea Nouă* (The new time) was the second sheet to appear, in October 1900, also in New York, and after this there was no looking back. "Newspapers grow like mushrooms," exclaimed one contemporary journalist about the years that followed.[3]

The year 1906 brought the first number of what was to be the longest-lived Romanian newspaper in the New World, Moise Balea's *America*, subtitled "The Organ of the Romanians in the United States, and especially [those] of the Greco-Eastern Churches"; it saw the light of day in Cleveland on September 1. Almost simultaneously, however, the Romanian Catholic (Uniate) priest, Father Epaminonda Lucaciu, had produced the first number of *Românul* (The Romanian), also in Cleveland, as a rallying point for the numerous Transylvanian Catholic immigrants—and, to be sure, as an agent of conversion for the even larger Orthodox population. *America* and *Românul* thus carried on a struggle for souls and subscriptions of the transplanted faithful. In the end, the fact that Catholic emigration from Romania never came close to the numbers of Orthodox who settled in America decided the issue between the rival publications. With the merger of the two major Romanian beneficial organizations—the Union of Romanian Societies in America and the League of Assistance—to form the Union and League of Romanian Societies in America as of 1928, Father Balea's *America* became the official organ of the Union and League, and remains so today.

Besides such publications so closely connected with the emerging church and lay society organizations in the early years, other papers appeared under the same mastheads or as so-called continuations of identical publications in Romania. *Adausul literar al ziarului "Libertatea"* (Literary additions to the newspaper "Liberty") in Cleveland in 1917 presented itself as the continuation of the Orastie-Bucharest offering *Foaia interesanta pentru petrecere și învățătura* (Interesting pages for pastimes and learning), while by 1920 one could find in Bucharest *Progresul literar și teatral* (Literary and theatrical progress), which four years earlier had appeared in Detroit under the title *Progresul, cea mai mare gazeta săptăminala româneasca în America* (Progress, the largest weekly Romanian gazette in America).[4]

Gretchen Buehler has described well the tone and content of such early Romanian papers, emphasizing their role not only in preserving traditional Romanian culture among the transplanted brothers, but in eliciting and forging a significant body of original Romanian-American literature and folklore among the immigrant working class:

The editors, understanding the role and the task of a press organ for its ordinary readers, some of them modest, many without schooling, tried to interest them in the promotion of culture, publishing . . . texts written and collected by them. They even launched campaigns for original texts, or organized poetry competitions with various prizes.[5]

The cumulative effect of such efforts over the next twenty years (the period 1919–1939 particularly), as church calendars, society publications, poetry, novels, sketches, and dramatic pieces began to emerge from the Romanian-American population, was to produce a literary record of the immigrant experience, a sometimes humorous, sometimes tragic, but always insightful record of the physical and spiritual drama undergone by thousands of men and women who found themselves uprooted from all that was familiar and forced to adapt to what was often less than a friendly new environment.

Along with the numerous weekly, biweekly, or monthly newspapers came a fair number of widely circulated books aimed at the immigrant community, most of them published by the same presses churning out the copious news sheets written by those responsible for the daily or weekly press. While some works were traditional literature and even original Romanian-American writing, the most popular books were self-help manuals for a semilettered Romanian audience, especially those for learning English on one's own, or containing legal advice. Books on becoming an American citizen were also numerous, although given the slow pace at which members of the pioneer generation sought U.S. citizenship, one suspects that such works were purchased more often than read. Publications which did get much handling, though, were music and song books, collections of theatrical pieces for church and society groups, and even joke books such as *Glume româneşti americane* (Romanian-American jokes), which appeared in Cleveland in 1914.[6]

Undoubtedly *America* remained the Romanian newspaper with the single largest readership among the organized immigrant community throughout the 1920s and early 1930s, with perhaps *Steaua Noastră* (Our star), begun in 1912 and published entirely in Romanian until its final issue in 1931, running a close second as a popular paper not ostensibly aligned with any particular lay or religious organization.[7] Appearing each Wednesday, *Steaua Noastră* bore the names of Philip Axelrad as publisher and S. Janovici as editor, but beyond their names, no information has come to light about this pair, whose paper carried the subtitle *Gazeta Tuturor Românilor* (The gazette of all Romanians) and was priced at a mere two dollars per year to be affordable to its working–class readership. Based at 72 Greenwich Street in New York, *Steaua Noastră* was only one product of what Axelrad called his *Biblioteca Romậna* (Romanian library), which also sold popular and inexpensive works for immigrants, such as Axelrad's own *Dictionar Complet Romận-Englez* (Complete Romanian-English dictionary), which appeared first in 1917 and in an expanded edition the following year.

By the 1930s, however, Romanian life in America was on its way to being institutionalized, and one of its most important publications resulted from the establishment of the first and ultimately largest Romanian church organization, the Romanian Orthodox Episcopate of America, with its foundation at a Detroit church congress in the spring of 1929.

Even before a bishop was chosen for America, an interim committee of priests and laymen which acted as a temporary executive body arranged for the Reverend Ştefan Opreanu to devote a page of his Chicago newspaper *Tribuna Romậna* (The Romanian tribune) to episcopal affairs, thereby assuming a semi-official status as the organ of the emerging episcopate. At the 1932 congress, Opreanu proposed to publish a full-scale diocesan paper, *Glasul Vremii* (Voice of the times), based in Cleveland, for a two dollar annual subscription rate. *Glasul Vermii* would not only carry advertising, but special contributions earmarked for it from various parish functions, and would even offer insurance policies at a modest one dollar per annum—an obvious effort to woo parishioners from their devotion to the Union and League and its organ *America*, even though plans called for *Glasul* to be printed by the *America* printing shop. The ambitious project came to naught, for the Romanian Ministry of Cults was unprepared to subsidize any church at all in America, much less a church paper, at this time, and *Glasul Vremii* was suspended after the fifth issue for lack of funds.[8] Except for two calendars called *Viata Nouă* (The new life) published by Opreanu in 1934 and 1935, the new episcopate remained without any official news organ until the appearance of *Solia* (The herald) in February 1936. Even then, its beginning years were less than auspicious.

Solia, a weekly paper of four pages, was based in Youngstown, Ohio, where Father Ioan Stanila, pastor of Holy Trinity parish and a former editor of *America*, served as its director. At the Youngstown Printing Company, the journalist-printer Ioan G. Gaspar was an outstanding lay activist of the fledgling episcopate. The inaugural issue of *Solia* contained the usual potpourri to be found in the ethnic press of the day, combining new bishop Policarp Morusca's inaugural invocation for the guidance of the Holy Spirit and the strengthening of Romanian souls with a curious juxtaposition of proverbs from Turkish folklore and Benjamin Franklin. News from the parishes and comments on the springlike weather in Romania were set beside "Why Lincoln Grew a Beard." *Solia* was off, if not running.

The first editorial expressed the hope that the gazette of the Church would "beat on the door of the hearts of its readers," developing their Christian and Romanian lives. *Solia* indeed did much beating on Romanians' doors in the years ahead, trying to get its readers to pay for their overdue subscriptions. By

September 1936 the paper was moved to Detroit, where Father Opreanu now took charge of it in his reorganized *Solia Nouă* office. The first episcopate calendar, or annual almanac, also named *Solia*, had already been printed there, and was destined eventually to become the single most widely circulated of the traditional Romanian religious calendars, matching the annual *Calendarul America* published by the Union and League.

The church newspaper, however, did not fare better in Detroit, despite a new administration and the earnest efforts of Opreanu and Father Gheorge Lupu. In September 1938 *Solia* was suspended and did not appear for nearly a year. Bishop Policarp attributed the problem not to lack of money, but to apathy, and told the church congress that year:

Out of some 4,973 members of our parishes only 1440 are subscribers to the paper, and of these only 467 are paid up. Many are in arrears . . . since the very beginning of the paper's appearance. There are delegates at this Congress itself who do not subscribe . . .

What can be the cause? It seems to me it is not lack of money . . . but basically disinterest toward printed material. Old people don't read, because many don't know how. Or they are interested only in polemical or critical writing. Young people read only what pleases them . . . funny papers.[9]

Those who enjoyed polemics had much to please them in *Solia* (and in the Romanian-American press in general) during the next fifteen years, as the Romanian Episcopate experienced a severe internal schism and divided into two camps of priests, one of which controlled the official news organ and used it to lambast the other. This situation, combined with the postwar events in Romania itself, produced by 1950 a division of the Romanian Orthodox Church in America into two separate episcopates, one remaining canonically and administratively united with the Romanian Patriarchate in Bucharest, and the other—containing a large majority of the faithful and their parishes—becoming an autonomous American diocese refusing any connection with communist Romania. Both groups claimed to be the legitimate successor of the prewar episcopate, as the autonomous church elected Viorel D. Trifa, then editor of *Solia*, as its bishop in 1951, while the group tied to Bucharest had already chosen an Akron priest, Andrei Moldovan, as its bishop some months earlier. Moldovan now began to publish both a newspaper and annual calendar named *Credinţa* (The faith), and for the next five years *Solia* and *Credinţa* slashed, insinuated, and sought to discredit each other.

Under the tutelage of the preposterous Nicolae Neamtu-Martin appeared a yellow sheet called *Episcopia* which, along with its successor, *Tribuna*, for more than two years churned out pages of slanderous assaults against Bishop Trifa. Only those used to the extremities of a divided ethnic press could appreciate such material in context. Finally in 1960, when the autonomous Romanian Episcopate was firmly established and the Moldovan camp had lost its suit in the U.S. Supreme Court to win control of the financial assets of the episcopate did Martin's voice, and indeed, the great Romanian-American Schism itself, begin to fade. Yet the imbroglio surfaced in a new guise in the mid–1970s, as Martin's anti-Trifa diatribes were dragged out once more in an effort to have the bishop deported.

Not all Romanian-Americans, of course, were Orthodox in their confession. While relatively minuscule in numbers, Romanian Baptists began to publish *Luminătorul* (The enlightenment) in 1925, which continues today as a Detroit monthly, written half in English and half in Romanian.[10] Approximately 2,000 Romanian Catholics (Uniates, Byzantine Rite Catholics) might peruse *Unirea* (Union), published monthly since 1950, first in Dearborn, then in Cleveland.

Certainly one of the most popular secular journals of Romanian affairs during World War II was *The New Pioneer*, published from 1942 to 1948 in Cleveland, entirely in English. Its goal of maintaining Romanian consciousness and tradition among an immigrant community whose second generation was rapidly losing its ethnic identity was well received, more so when it was revived in 1977 as the *American-Romanian Review*, which continues today under its original editor and publisher, Theodore Andrica. The *Review* now appears under the aegis of the American-Romanian Heritage Foundation and has perhaps 1,000 subscribers.

With the exception of *The New Pioneer* and perhaps one or two scattered cultural publications, however, the balance of the Romanian-American press, especially after 1945, offered a potpourri of polemics covering the entire range of the political spectrum from left to right, although the majority clearly belong on the right, with a variety of papers differing from each other only in the rabidity with which they condemned the Romanian communist regime.

The *Biblioteca Andreiu Şaguna* (The Andrei Şaguna library) began in 1950 and was moderate in tone, unlike *Porunca Vremii* (Master of the times) and *Fiii Daciei* (Sons of Dacia). *Porunca* first appeared in 1946 and was revived in 1968 as a fiercely anticommunist monthly in New York, while *Fiii Daciei* continues today as a quarterly. *Romania*, bimonthly organ of the Romanian National Committee in New York, appeared as early as 1946 and has a circulation of about 2,000, with many readers among Romanian exiles in Latin America and Europe. The two decades after the war saw thousands of Romanian refugees spread throughout the United States and Canada, many of them former members of radical right movements such as the nationalist-messianic Legionaries, whose antiforeigner and anticommunist philosophy placed them in the forefront of opposition to the post–1945 Romanian regime. New Press organs came into being to continue their political-ideological struggle from exile. The Legionary diaspora, especially concentrated in New York, Michigan, Illinois, California, and Ontario, is a mainstay of the Romanian-language press in America today, along with those contributors and readers representing the thought of the prewar Romanian National Liberal Party, and those who hold sacred the memory of Peasant Party leader Iuliu Maniu. Romanian exile opposition via a vocal (and often vehement) press in America thus has a forty–year tradition behind it.

Romania's forerunner was *Lumina* in 1945, which came into being to expose communist infiltration into the Union and League at a time when that body's leadership went through a decidedly leftist phase.

Offsetting these publications to some extent were *Deşteptarea* (The awakening) and its successors. Strongly antifascist in tone, from 1914 to 1939 *Deşteptarea* gave American readers perhaps the best coverage of news from Romania, which *America* before 1947 did not sufficiently offer. In 1939 *Deşteptarea* became *Românul-American* (The Romanian-American), which continued to be published in Detroit until 1968, almost as an American counterpoint to the official Bucharest press *Scînteia*. With the opening of the Romanian Library in New York City during the late 1960s as a Romanian semi-official "cultural relations" office, the *Romanian Bulletin* superseded *Românul-American* in extolling the Ceauşescu regime, although its moderate tone signaled the era of Romanian-American friendly cooperation which the Nixon visit of 1970 opened. For a time the *Bulletin*, distributed widely and freely each month, especially in the academic community, evolved into a well-received news magazine of Romanian culture, with increasing emphasis on Romanian-American affairs and scholarship. The end of the decade, however, saw the replacement of the skillful directorship of Emilia Gheorghe and Ion Monafu with that of more hard-line Bucharest bureaucrats, and the *Bulletin* dwindled to inconsequence by 1980.

The year 1984 found the Romanian-American press alive and thriving, characterized by a sizeable number of publications spreading from New York to Pittsburgh, from Toronto to California. The great majority are scholarly-cultural in format and tone, and stress analysis of Romanian affairs as opposed to Romanian-American happenings—a change of emphasis from the period 1906–1950. The newspapers of the two episcopates, along with *America*, remain the major sources of Romanian-American news, along with the *American-Romanian Review*.

Of limited circulation are *Orizont Românesc* (The Romanian horizon), published in Los Angeles, and the twenty-four-page *Micro-Magazin* (Little magazine), now in its twelfth year, published in Astoria, New York, combining anticommunist political analysis with historical-literary selections. *Dreptatea* (Justice) appeared in 1973, calling itself "The Independent Information Organ of Romanians in America" and, under the editorship of Dean Milhovan, a former Romanian lawyer, strives to be convincingly anticommunist and anti-legionary alike. More purely cultural is the twelve-page *New York Spectator*, the voice of Serban C. Andronescu and his American Institute for Writing Research. Worthy of note for students and Romanian specialists are the literary quarterly *Drum* (The path), and *Romanian Sources*, a semiannual journal now in its tenth year. Both are the work of Ion Halmaghi of the University of Pittsburgh and stress traditional Romanian prewar scholarship, anticommunism, and historic irredentist claims to Transylvania, Bessarabia, and Bukovina. The foregoing, indeed, may be said to represent the general *modus vivendi* which by the 1980s much of the Romanian-American press had arrived at with the Romanian regime: a combination of criticism, ranging from moderate to harsh, allied with concerted efforts to preserve and promote awareness of traditional Romanian culture among the descendants of the American immigrant community by making a sharp distinction between the present government and the unspoiled "Romanian people." As opposed to the 1950s, when boycotting of Romania and Romanian contacts seemed appropriate, today's emphasis is on travel and contact with the motherland and the promotion of cultural relations, so long as these are seen as divorced from any endorsement of the regime.

Yet the voice of the Romanian right and the exile community remains strong. *Curierul* (The courier; note the linkage with the historic nineteenth–century Romanian liberal press name) is issued in Santa Clara, California, as the "Organ of the National Romanian-American Congress," whose address is in Chicago. One of its stated purposes, according to editor Gabriel Balanescu and Congress President Alexander E. Ronnett, is "to assist the Romanian exile[s] in their struggle for the liberation of the motherland from communist tyranny."[11] The appearance of this quarterly of some twenty pages in 1980 makes it the newest major Romanian publication on the American scene, although its circulation remains extremely limited.

The year 1976 produced the first issue of what is commonly called "the largest Romanian newspaper in the Free World," *Cuvântul Românesc*, (The Romanian voice [although The Romanian word would be more accurate]), published monthly in Hamilton, Ontario, under the directorship of George Balaşu. Featured are assaults on the Romanian communist regime, personal attacks on Nicolae Ceauşescu—often viciously satirical—combined with news from the exile community and the Romanian diaspora, church news, literary and historical analysis of a high quality, omnipresent arguments over Romanian rights in Bessarabia, and one or two pages devoted to Romanian-American news. *Cuvântul* thus contains elements of both the polemical anticommunist and the purely cultural Romanian press. The section under the rubric "Mica Publiciate" (Little ads) is reminiscent of a 1910 immigrant newspaper, with its offers of marriage desired by Romanian widows ("with university studies, 1,63m tall, pretty, a good cook") to any likely reader in America; requests for sponsors to allow advertisers to emigrate and find work in Canada; or advertisements seeking relatives or friends who left Romania in 1948 and were thought to have settled "around Chicago." With a circulation in 1984 between 4,500 and 5,000, *Cuvântul* remains indispensable to the educated Romanian of the West. Its counterpart in Toronto, *Ecouri Româneşti* (Romanian echoes), is much smaller in scope.

Finally, the most recent Romanian publishing venture is that of the newly founded (1978) Romanian-American Heritage Center, in Grass Lake, Michigan, rapidly emerging as the major repository of materials on Romanian immigration and ethnicity in the United States and Canada. Having already published two major books since 1979 on Romanian church history and language maintenance in America, the center began a quarterly newsletter entitled *Information Bulletin* in September 1983.

Thus, after three-quarters of a century, the Romanian press in America continues to have as at least one of its main motivations that noted by Fathe Ioan Podea in 1912: the dissemination and strengthening of Romanianism among the "faraway brethren." It remains in many ways as it began—often polemical, sometimes anticlerical, much of it working-class oriented, some of it esoterically written, it would seem for the interwar Romanian intellectual now in exile in the West. It is, given the relatively small size of the Romanian population in America compared to other ethnic groups, a vital part of the North American ethnic press, a voice almost unwaveringly against communism, if not always for democracy. It is, as Victor Greene so aptly phrased it, a voice to Romanians speaking for God and country.

NOTES

1. Theodore Andrica, "Romanian Publications in America," *American Romanian Review* 7 (May-June 1983): 18–19.

2. Gretchen Buehler, "Literature în Primele Periodice Românești din America," *România Literară* 13 (17 ianuarie 1980): 21.

3. Ibid., p. 20.

4. Ibid.

5. For insight on literacy in the Romanian-American community and the choice of reading materials, see Josephine Gratiaa, "Roumanians in the United States and Their Relations to Public Libraries," *Library Journal* 47 (May 1, 1922): 401; and Gerald J. Bobango, "The Union and League of Romanian Societies: An 'Assimilating Force' Reviewed," *East European Quarterly* 12 (1978): 85–92. Another entire category of Romanian "literature" in America is the collected body of Romanian Societies' and Union and League Minutes, record books, annual reports, and convention programs spanning the years from 1906 to the present. C. R. Pascu (in 1931) and Șofron Feckett (in 1956) published twenty-five and fifty year histories of the Union and League, respectively.

6. Buehler, "Literature," p. 20. A complete study of the Romanian press during the first decade in America also must include Reverend Ioan Podea's listing in his *Românii Din America* (Sibiu: Tipografia Arhidiecezană, 1912) pp. 77–82.

7. The importance of *Steaua Noastră* in Romanian-American publishing history is evidenced by the fact that it alone, of the nonchurch, nonsociety publications, is preserved on microfilm at the Immigration History Research Archives of the University of Minnesota.

8. On this period and the entire subsequent history of the Romanian Church and its publications in America, see Gerald J. Bobango, *The Romanian Orthodox Episcopate of America: The First Half-Century, 1929–1979* (Jackson, Mich.: Romanian-American Heritage Center, 1979).

9. Ibid., p. 108.

10. The case of the Romanian Baptist press is a typical example of the proliferation of publications brought about by schisms or dissension within congregations or societies. Although *Luminătorul* enjoyed a circulation of perhaps only 1,500, in 1971 some Romanian Baptist congregations broke away from the main body and began publishing their own independent paper in Chicago, *Semănătorul* (The sower), so that the tiniest Romanian

religious group in the country, the Baptists, thus has two newspapers, equal in number to those serving the many thousands of Orthodox faithful.

11. *Curierul* 3 (Ianuarie-Martie 1983): 20.

BIBLIOGRAPHY

Andrica, Theodore. *Romanian Americans and Their Communities of Cleveland*. Cleveland, Ohio: The Cleveland Press, 1977.

Bobango, Gerald J. *Romanian Orthodoxy in Youngstown, 1906–1981*. Youngstown, Ohio: Holy Trinity Romanian Orthodox Parish, 1981.

————. "Romanians." In Stephan Thernstrom, ed., *Harvard Encyclopedia of American Ethnic Groups*. Cambridge, Mass.: Harvard University Press, 1980.

Druţu, Şerban, and Andrei Popovici. *Românil în America*. Bucureşti: "Cartea Românească," 1926.

Galitzi, Christine Avghi. *A Study of Assimilation among the Romanians in the United States*. New York: Columbia University Press, 1929.

Popovici, Andrei. "Americanii de Origine Română." *Sociologie Românească* 2 (1937): 1–32.

Schiopul, Ion Iosif. *Românii din America*. Sibiu: W. Krafft, 1913.

Trifa, Valerian D. *Solia: Istoria vieţii unei gazete româneşti în America*. Detroit: Romanian Orthodox Episcopate of America, 1961.

Wertsman, Vladimir, ed. *The Romanians in America, 1748–1974*. Dobbs Ferry, N.Y.: Oceana Publications, 1975.

22

The Russian Press

HALYNA MYRONIUK

The Russian-language press in the United States had its beginning over a century ago, as early as 1868. It appeared in the West with the first settlements of Russians in Alaska and along the Pacific coast. These settlements were a "part of the steady eastward expansion of the Russian Empire through the steppes and tundra of Siberia to the Pacific Coast, led by fur traders and seal hunters interested in finding pelts and skins for their Russian and European markets."[1] However, this venture proved to be unprofitable, and in 1867 Alaska was sold to the United States. About half of the Russians returned home; many of the others moved to California.[2]

It is only when Russians began to arrive in larger numbers in the 1880s on the East Coast that we begin to see the serious appearance of the Russian-language press. With New York as the center and lifeline of the Russian community around the turn of the century, the Russian-language press began its long and checkered history.

The first Russian newspaper in America was the bilingual *Svoboda-The Alaska Herald* (San Francisco, 1868–1873), published by a Ukrainian priest, Agapius Honcharenko. Its Russian articles attempted to inspire sympathy among the larger public for the anti-tsarist movement in Russia.[3]

The Alaska Herald was subsidized by the United States government in an effort to Americanize Alaska's Russian immigrant populace quickly. Its first four issues, appearing in March and April 1868, "satisfied the requirements of Honcharenko's subsidy: the first two issues contained translations into Russian of the United States Constitution."[4] However, Honcharenko's relations with the United States government became strained due to his criticism of it. As a result the government stopped subsidizing *The Alaska Herald* and Honcharenko was forced to seek financial aid elsewhere. Nevertheless, Honcharenko managed to publish *The Alaska Herald* until 1873.

During the 1890s a number of short-lived socialist and radical Russian newspapers appeared, such as *Znamia* (The banner; New York, 1889–1892) and *Progress* (New York and Chicago, 1893–1894), which called for revolutionary changes in the capitalist economic system and often carried articles by leading Russian socialist thinkers.[5] Their readership was generally limited to left-wing intellectuals, especially among Jews from Russia.[6]

The early generation of Russian immigrants who settled on the East Coast were mainly peasants and laborers. Many had never learned to read in their homeland; those who could read tended to have great difficulty in understanding articles written by "editors who brought to this country the European concept of a press addressed exclusively to the highly educated, deliberately formal and abstruse."[7] Many thought a newspaper was some new-fangled American store, and that everything advertised belonged to the newspaper and was on sale on its premises.[8] News, editorials, and advertising were all one to them.[9] The role of a newspaper in a democracy was one of the most difficult concepts for them to grasp.[10] The foreign-language papers had to begin to teach them how democracy worked in practice. And so, when editors wrote articles that were above the heads of their readers, it was understandable that some newspapers ran a deficit. One such newspaper was the socialist *Novyi Mir* (New World) of New York (1911–1920). Its business editor pleaded with the editors to write more simply, "but none . . . were obliging enough to write so that they could be understood."[11]

The editor of *Novoye Russkoe Slovo* (New Russian word), Mark Weinbaum, gave other examples of a similar problem his newspaper encountered in the early days. Readers had to be recruited and introduced to the newspaper from among the immigrant masses, nearly all peasants, for whom the printed word was a wonder.[12]

Among the most successful and influential Russian socialist papers was *Novyi Mir*. It was one of the largest dailies, having 8,000 subscribers before it was closed down in 1920 by the American government because of its affiliation with the Communist Party in America.

Novyi Mir was founded in 1911 by the Russian Socialist Publishing Association and represented the Social Democrats, or Mensheviks. Until the fall of 1915 there were no Bolshevik papers in the United States.[13] Gradually "the Russian Bolshevik sympathizers decided to secure control of the paper *Novyi Mir*."[14] They were able to persuade the revolutionary Nikolai Bukharin to come to Sweden in 1916 to take a position as an editorial staff member. Later the next year, with the arrival of Leon Trotsky in New York, the Boshevik wing managed to oust the Mensheviks from the editorial board and made Trotsky editor of *Novyi Mir*. Trotsky served on the staff from January 15, 1917, to March 27, 1917, and thereafter returned to Russia to help overthrow the Kerensky government.

The problems that *Novyi Mir* encountered and that later led to its closing began when it resolved in 1916 to refuse war loan advertisements. In October 1917 its second–class mailing privileges were withdrawn by the post office.[15] Its newspaper office was raided by agents of the Lusk committee, a New York State

Senate Committee investigating seditious activity, and its printing presses were damaged.[16] *Novyi Mir*, as such, ceased to exist.

Nonpolitical newspapers for workers first appeared among Russian immigrants from Galicia.[17] Of these, the two most important were fraternal publications, received by all members of their respective organizations. The first was the weekly *Svit* (The light), published in Wilkes-Barre, Pennsylvania, of the Russian Orthodox Catholic Mutual Aid Society. It was founded in 1895 and was edited for many years by the Reverend Peter Kohanik (1880–1969). Its major circulation was among Carpatho-Ruthenians, and it had little influence in the Russian colony. The second newspaper, the semiweekly *Pravda* (The truth), was founded in 1900 in Philadelphia by the Society of Russian Brotherhoods. This paper also attained little influence within the Russian colony.

Of the four Russian dailies established in the United States prior to 1920, *Russkoe Slovo* (Russian word), founded in New York in 1910, is still the most important and widely circulated. Renamed *Novoye Russkoe Slovo* (New Russian word) in 1920, it currently has a circulation of 26,000. It is the oldest and largest Russian-language daily outside Russia. Although in Russian, it puts its prime emphasis on American news, on what is happening in the United States and locally in New York and other metropolitan areas where people of Russian background congregate.[18] It provides international news as well. Special features include articles on Russian literature and the publication of underground material received from the Soviet Union.[19]

Its first editor was Ivan K. Okuntsov, the educated son of a Siberian Cossack. An ardent atheist and a school teacher he eventually became a revolutionary. He understood the masses of the people and knew how to speak to them in their own language. Okuntsov provided the majority of articles and news in *Novoye Russkoe Slovo*. During World War I he was forced to leave his job as editor due to family problems and his criticism of government military spending. The job of editor then went to L. M. Paslovsky, the son of the publisher. Although he was educated, Paslovsky lacked the know-how of a newspaper man. After Paslovsky's departure in 1920 the newspaper came into the hands of V. I. Shimkin, and the editor's post was taken up by the well-known journalist A. I. Iakovlev.

During its first twenty years *Novoye Russkoe Slovo* endured many hardships. At times it seemed that the newspaper would fold because of declining circulation and threats from the communist faction of the Russian community. The revolutionary events in Russia and later the depression years 1929–1933 also left their mark. The communist wave spread among the Russian immigrants, and soon *Novoye Russkoe Slovo*, which maintained a democratic position, began to lose its readership. At this crucial time Iakovlev decided that it was possible to save the newspaper if it took the line of least resistance and adopted a pro-Soviet tone.[20]

After Iakovlev's departure from the newspaper in 1921, a rapid turnover of editors occurred. Among these were Mikhail E. Vilchur, D. Z. Krynkin, and

I. L. Durmashkin-Verushchyi. In 1922 Mark E. Weinbaum joined the *Novoye Russkoe Slovo* editorial staff. It was during the following year that the Americanization issue was fiercely debated among the Russian community, especially between the two dailies, *Novoye Russkoe Slovo* and *Russky Golos* (1917-). *Novoye Russkoe Slovo*'s editorial policy was to bring controversial issues out into the open. It was instrumental in helping Russians become American citizens. Weinbaum "advised his readers to recognize that their future and the future of their children lay in this country, and urged them to become its citizens without delay."[21] His references to Russia as "a land of sad and sometimes heart-breaking memories" aroused the ire of a writer for *Russky Golos*, who expressed his emotions in a glowing tribute to the motherland and with contemptuous references to those "who would turn coldly away from the land of their birth in its hour of trial and suffering."[22] This response in turn flooded the newspapers with many letters.

A more serious problem faced by *Novoye Russkoe Slovo* was its confrontation with the communists. Dissatisfied with earlier commitments made by the paper's editors, Shimkin and Weinbaum decided to return the newspaper to a firm democratic, anticommunist position. At first they met with heavy opposition. The communists destroyed a large number of newspapers sold in kiosks, threatened to boycott the paper, broke up anticommunist meetings, and beat individual anticommunists.[23] *Novoye Russkoe Slovo* was also threatened with destruction by a crowd of communists when the newspaper became the first in the United States to publicize the horrible famine in the Soviet Union during the early 1930s. *Novoye Russkoe Slovo*, in its struggle with the communists, was aided by the Union of Russian Workers and individual mutual aid societies which later united into the Russian Consolidated Aid Society (ROOVA).

Earlier, in 1923, with the arrival in New York of a new group of Russian immigrants, the so-called white or Constantinople emigration, *Novoye Russkoe Slovo* had been enriched by new contributors to its pages as well as by a new readership. Among the new contributors whose articles raised the quality of the newspaper were S. V. Zhivotovsky, L. M. Kamyshnikov, M. A. Stern, and many others.

Later *Novoye Russkoe Slovo* began to receive articles from Russian émigrés in Paris, such as Andrei Sedych, who eventually immigrated to the United States and became a member of the editorial staff; he is presently the editor. Other arrivals included M. K. Zheleznov-Argus, who became an outstanding columnist for *Novoye Russkoe Slovo* and the foreign-language press in general. His real name was Macy Eisenstadt, but he wrote under the pseudonym that he had adopted as a youthful newspaperman in Riga before the Russian Revolution. Argus came to the United States in 1923. At the height of the Great Depression, he began his work with *Novoye Russkoe Slovo*. He was a gifted writer and was exceptionally popular with many readers who appreciated his simplicity of style, logic, honesty of convictions, and personal courage.[24] Argus came under attack many times for his anticommunist views by the Checkist papers in Moscow and

New York. His many *feuilletons*, on the other hand, found a willing audience among the readers of *Novoye Russkoe Slovo*.[25]

At the end of World War II, many Russians finding themselves to be displaced persons in Europe (especially in Germany), feared that they were in danger of being forcibly returned to the Soviet Union. The Russian–American newspapers came to their aid. At first, there were no newspapers circulating in the camps. *Novoye Russkoe Slovo* reached the camps at the end of 1947 and found many eager readers who wanted to know what life was like in America.

Novoye Russkoe Slovo helped many of these individuals to come to the United States. It explained to the new arrivals the American way of life. Later it ran articles on naturalization, Social Security, insurance, and other topics, serving "not only as an outlet for political thought and literary information but as a defender of the rights and interests of its readers, for which those articles were written."[26]

The longevity of *Novoye Russkoe Slovo* was best explained by former editor Mark E. Weinbaum as due to the "continuous influx of literate immigrants and accumulation of cultural strength, talented writers and journalists, who enriched the newspaper with their articles, essays, and their works of art."[27] Its survival, despite all the problems it encountered, is "an indication of the value and importance the Russian community has placed on the newspaper."[28]

Other daily papers that appeared along with *Novoye Russkoe Slovo* were *Russky Golos* (Russian voice; New York, 1917-) and *Russkaia Zhizn'* (Russian Life; San Francisco, 1921-). The 1920s were the "high point for the Russian-American press."[29] It "had a circulation of 75,000 copies, which included a substantial proportion of Russian-speaking Jews."[30] In 1921 *Ayer's American Annual* gave the circulation for *Novoye Russkoe Slovo* as 32,256 and that of *Russky Golos* as 35,143. Forty years later, according to a survey conducted by the American Council for Nationalities Service in 1961, circulation for *Novoye Russkoe Slovo* was 24,995 and that of *Russky Golos* was 5,324, a marked drop for the latter. Recent studies on the ethnic press in America by Wynar and Wynar show *Novoye Russkoe Slovo* to have increased its circulation by nearly 1,000, while that of *Russky Golos* has decreased sharply, to 2,584.

Once a daily with an impressive circulation that at times surpassed that of *Novoye Russkoe Slovo*, *Russky Golos* now appears as a weekly. It was founded in 1917 under the editorship of Ivan K. Okuntsov, also the first editor of *Russkoe Slovo*. At that time it was considered a "radical newspaper, and came to support the Bolshevik side."[31] At the present time *Russky Golos* "provides general, international, national, and local news coverage, plus coverage of Russian life in the United States."[32]

The daily *Russkaia Zhizn'* (Russian life) was founded in 1925 in San Francisco. It is published by Russian Life, Inc., and did not become incorporated until 1950. Among its longtime editors have been I. N. Obukhovich and currently Ariadna Delianich. This publication serves the American-Russian community and Russian nationals abroad, with the aim of preserving Russian language, culture, and literature.[33] It was described by Okuntsov as unique among Russian American papers as "the only independent democratic newspaper."[34] It gives worldwide news of politics, literature, history, science, and social events, plus news of émigré organizations, Orthodox churches, and accomplishments of members of the Russian émigré community. Its current circulation is nearly 2,500, as opposed to 2,312 in 1961.[35] A local paper, it is much the same today as when it began publication, and tends to cater to the "social and cultural life of the large Russian-speaking community in California."[36]

In 1928 yet another daily began publication, *Novaia Zoria* (New dawn), also published in San Francisco. In 1946 it had a circulation of 7,012. Currently, it has a slightly larger circulation, at 2,818, than does its neighbor *Russkaia Zhizn'*. *Novaia Zoria* provides general news coverage.

One of the last dailies to appear in the United States was *Rossiia* (Russia). Founded in 1933 in New York as a right-wing publication, it had a circulation in 1946 of 12,000. In 1961, according to the survey conducted by the American Council for Nationalities Service, *Rossiia*'s circulation was down to 2,122. The explanation for this decline given by Edward Hunter (who in 1960 estimated the circulation to be 2,000) was that "this figure seems to be declining with the death rate [rising] among old White Russian emigres, who differ strikingly from the World War II Russian exodus."[37] He further suggested that *Rossiia* "could have picked up circulation from among the World War II refugees from the Soviet Union."[38] But monarchial appeal was not taken seriously by these post–World War II expatriates. At present its circulation has declined to 1,650. It has become a semiweekly and provides general news coverage.

Chicago also played its role in the development of the Russian-American press. Its Russian community put out thirty-four Russian-language periodicals. Many of them were short-lived, while others had longer life spans. The first Russian-language publication in Chicago was *Progress* (1893–1894), a socialist and radical newspaper. Others with longer runs included *Golos Truzhenika* (Voice of the toiler; 1917–1927), the organ of the Russian anarchist group, *Svobodnaia Rossia* (Free Russia; 1917–1923), a weekly organ of the Independent Orthodox Church; and *Rassviet* (Dawn; 1926–1934). The latter was first published in New York, as a daily, and was moved to Chicago in 1926. As a daily, it had been the organ of the Russian Progressive Unions and Cultural-Enlightened Organizations. However, in 1934 it became the organ of the Orthodox Church with the participation of Bishop Leontii Turkevich and other priests. As a result its editors, the anarchists Morovskii and Rubezhanin-Gaiduk, lost their ideological influence in the midwestern states.

Numerous other weeklies and monthlies also appeared in Chicago. Among these were the progressive weekly *Staroe v Novom* (The old in the new; 1911–1912); the weekly *Russkii v Amerike* (Russian in America; 1913–1918); the national-patriotic *Utro* (Morning; 1914–1915), of which only six numbers appeared; a medical weekly, *Domashnii Vrach* (Home doctor; 1916–1918), which failed because of the high cost of printing; and the illustrated journal *Russkoe Obozrenie* (Russian review), published in Russian with a few pages in English.

Among the events affecting the entire Russian-American community was recognition of the Soviet government by the United States. The topic was widely disputed in many newspapers and journals. In some cases petitions were published requesting Russian-American readers to "vote" for or against recognition of the USSR by the United States. One journal, *Russkoe Obozrenie*, concluded from its survey that the majority of the Russian-American community was indeed in favor of the Soviet Union's recognition. What was interesting about the outcome of these surveys was that many people who favored recognition were not sympathetic to the Bolsheviks.[39] Opponents of recognition were relatively few.[40]

The circulation of Russian-language newspapers and journals dropped dramatically during World War II. But publications rose in number from nineteen in 1942 to forty in 1960.[41] Many of these were "quarterlies, monthlies, and bimonthlies which were produced by every sort of nostalgic organization, from the Association of Russian Imperial Naval Officers in America, Inc., and the Gallipoli Society in the U.S.A. to the Union of Russian Jurists Abroad, and what is simply called Group of Kuban Officers in the United States."[42]

Such organizations were not ideological splinter groups, but rather focal points of people who had assimilated into American society but remained sentimentally attached to small groups as their only reminder of the past.[43] Many of them read English-language papers and also subscribed to *Novoye Russkoe Slovo* and other Russian-language newspapers.[44]

The 1940s saw a new group of Russians settling in the United States. These were the Russian émigrés from Paris. When Paris fell to the Germans in 1940, New York temporarily replaced it as the center of Russian émigré intellectual life.[45] A number of Russian writers came to New York, among them Mark Aldanov, Vladimir Nabokov, and Vassily Janovsky, and critics Gleb P. Struve and Mikhail O. Zetlin.[46] Some of these individuals were instrumental in establishing literary journals that are still in existence today, for example, *Novyi Zhurnal* (New review).

Novyi Zhurnal was founded in 1942, in New York, by Zetlin and Aldanov. It is the most influential journal in the Russian-American community today, with a current circulation of 1,400. It was modeled after the so-called "thick journals of nineteenth–century Russia, with issues numbering 300 to 400 pages and containing contributions of literary, scholarly, and journalistic content."[47] Since 1942, *Novyi Zhurnal* has published some seventy separate works.[48]

Another influential journal that was established along with *Novyi Zhurnal* but lasted only eight years was *Novosel'e* (New home). It was founded in New York in 1942 and was edited by the poet Sophia Pregel'. At present, the major forums for Russian émigré literature are still the *Novyi Zhurnal* and the daily newspaper *Novoye Russkoe Slovo*.[49]

The Russian Orthodox Church in its drive to establish itself in the New World also made its contribution to and greatly influenced the Russian-American press in America. Despite its early internal problems, the ramifications of the Russian Revolution, and the political involvements of the post–1920 immigrants,[50] it has managed to maintain its influence on the Russian community until today. Although these problems led to the eventual split and creation of three separate churches in the United States, the Russian religious press grew.

The earliest Russian Orthodox Church publication to appear was the *Russko-Amerikanskii Pravoslavnyi Viestnik* (Russian-American Orthodox messenger; New York, 1896). It was the official paper for the Russian Orthodox mission and was published in English and Russian.

There were a number of other church publications which were religious in content. These tended to deal with the overall life of the Orthodox Church. The foremost, the *Amerikanskii Pravoslavnyi Viestnik*, had an English supplement, *Pravda* (The truth), which began publication on March 26, 1902. There were about thirty such religious publications, many of which folded within one year of their establishment, while others underwent name changes and managed to survive longer. Today there are at least eleven such publications, six published in the Russian language and five in English.

The Russian Orthodox Church was the first sector of the Russian-American press to use the English language in its publications for the Orthodox faithful in America. It was joined in this effort by the Federated Russian Orthodox Clubs, whose English-language publication, *The Russian Orthodox Journal*, founded in Wilkes-Barre, Pennsylvania, in 1928, is still published. *The Orthodox Herald*, founded in 1952 in San Antonio, Texas, has the largest circulation of the five English-language publications, 5,020. Second in circulation is *The Russian Orthodox Journal* with 3,300. *One Church*, founded in 1947 in Youngstown, Ohio, has a circulation of 2,500. Next in size is the St. Vladimir Theological Quarterly. Founded in 1952 and published in Crestwood, New York, it has a circulation of 1,300. Its present editor is the Reverend John Myendorf. *Orthodox Life*, founded in 1950 in Jordanville, New York, by the Holy Trinity Monastery, is fifth, with a circulation of 1,250.

The oldest church publication still being issued in the Russian language is *Pravoslavnaya Rus* (Orthodox Russia). It was founded in 1928 in Jordanville, New York, and has a circulation of 1,600. Published by the Holy Trinity Monastery, it "features articles and news on Eastern orthodoxy from the view of the Russian Orthodox Church outside Russia."[51] Another journal still in existence today is *Pravoslavnaya Zhizn'* (Orthodox life). It has served the newer arrivals in America and "features lives of Saints and information about the Eastern Orthodox Christianity of the Russian Orthodox Church outside Russia."[52] The newest arrival, the *Ezhegodnik Pravoslavnoi Tserkvi v Amerike* (Annual of the Orthodox Church in America), began in 1975, sponsored by the Orthodox Church in America. It has a circulation of 1,000 and features religious news and guidance for Russian-speaking clergy and laity of the church.[53] It reports events, activities, appointments, and transfers of clergy from Orthodox churches all over the world.[54] It also includes doctrinal instruction, biographies of religious figures, and messages from members of the clergy.[55]

In its early efforts to gain members and converts, especially among the immigrant workers, the Russian Orthodox Church met with fervent opposition from the Russian Social Democratic Workers Party (RSDWP). This group's "primary objective was to foster a revolution in Russia and to influence the American worker on behalf of this cause."[56] They were, however, unsuccessful in their efforts to win the immigrant Russian worker over to their side. The RSDWP's "first newspaper was the *Russko-amerikanskii Rabochii* (Russian American worker), published from 1908, with its headquarters under D. Dubinow's management."[57] From the beginning the newspaper attacked religion and the church.[58] This position caused many immigrants to become suspicious of the RSDWP and react negatively to it. The Russian worker, "coming out of an agricultural background where the church had considerable influence, viewed the Russian Church in America as the only institution that was of his heritage, spoke his language, and represented his ethnic tradition."[59]

Russkii Emigrant, a secular paper with a Russian Orthodox perspective, was widely read among the Russian immigrant community. It sought to strengthen the Russian patriotism of its readers in America, and it included news of Russia.

The Russian–American press was instrumental in influencing, shaping, and educating the Russian immigrants. It taught them how to read, think, and formulate their political outlook. Some newspapers nurtured their relations with God and the Russian Orthodox Church, while others attacked religion and the Russian Orthodox Church.

An alternative Russian-language press appeared that managed to function successfully alongside these two opposing groups: the secular and nonideological press, especially *Novoye Russkoe Slovo*. It not only helped to educate the Russian immigrant and maintain a balance within the Russian community, but played a major part in the Americanization process, which prepared Russians to become citizens.

The Russian–American press today is conservative. Its circulation is about 49,000, in comparison to 75,000 in the 1920s. This decline is directly related to assimilation and to ignorance of the language among more recent generations.[60] However, the recent emigration from the Soviet Union could lead to a revival of the language, although the number of recent émigrés to have settled in the United States is not large enough to substantially influence the direction the Russian–American press may take. But this group is not idle and is making itself heard. Among the new titles to appear within the last several years are the weekly *Novyi Amerikanets'* (New American; New York, 1980-) and most recently *Strelets* (Sagittarius; New Jersey, January 1, 1984-) The future of the Russian–American press looks promising, but it is unlikely that it will ever regain the circulation level that it enjoyed in previous decades.

NOTES

1. Paul Robert Magocsi, "Russians," in *Harvard Encyclopedia of American Ethnic Groups*, ed. Stephan Thernstrom (Cambridge, Mass.: Harvard University Press, 1980), p. 886.

2. Ibid.

3. Ibid., p. 890.

4. Theodore Luciw, *Father Agapius Honcharenko: First Priest in America* (New York: Ukrainian Congress Committee of America, 1970), p. 60.

5. Magosci, p. 890.

6. Ibid.

7. Robert Ezra Park, *The Immigrant Press and Its Control* (1922; repr. Westport, Conn.: Greenwood Press, 1970), p. 68.

8. Edward Hunter, *In Many Voices; Our Fabulous Foreign-Language Press* (Norman Park, Ga.: Norman College, [1960]), p. 128.

9. Ibid.

10. Ibid.

11. Park, p. 68.

12. Mark E. Weinbaum, "Piat'desiat let'," *Novoye Russkoe Slovo* 50 (April 1960): 17203:9.

13. Park, p. 241.

14. Jerome Davis, *The Russian Immigrant* (New York: The Macmillan Company, 1922), p. 124.

15. Ibid., p. 125.

16. Ibid.

17. Magocsi, p. 890.

18. Hunter, p. 124.

19. Lubomyr R. Wynar and Anna T. Wynar, *Encyclopedic Directory of Ethnic Newspapers and Periodicals in the United States,* 2nd ed. (Littleton, Colo.: Libraries Unlimited, Inc., 1976), p. 166.

20. Weinbaum, 17203:9.

21. Ibid.

22. Ibid.

23. Ibid.

24. Mikhail Eisenstadt-Jeleznov Papers, Immigration History Research Center Collection, University of Minnesota.

25. Aside from his duties on the staff, Argus managed to attend New York University and to write several books, in both Russian and English. Among his most familiar works are *Moscow on the Hudson* and *A Rogue with Ease* (both in English) and *The Eastern Hero* (in Russian). Ibid.

26. M. L. de Branzburg, "Chitatel' i zakon," *Novoye Russkoe Slovo* 50 (April 1960): 17203:23-24.

27. Weinbaum, 17203:9.

28. Ibid.

29. Magocsi, p. 891.

30. Ibid.

31. Ivan K. Okuntsov, *Russkaia emigratsiia v Severnoi i IUzhnoi Amerike* (Buenos Aires: Izd. Seiatel', 1967), p. 334.

32. Wynar and Wynar, p. 168.
33. Ibid.
34. Okuntsov, p. 336.
35. Wynar and Wynar, p. 168.
36. Hunter, p. 122.
37. Ibid., p. 121.
38. Ibid.
39. This was reflected in comments such as : "Bolshevism was for bolsheviks, but Russia is our motherland and she is hurting from that, because she is ill, and not from bolshevism or other parties." "My," *Russkoe Obozrenie* 3 (June 1929): 6.
40. Opponents argued that "the Soviet government is wrecking and destroying morals, feelings of patriotism" and that "it is not national and not for the people, but only for its Communistic Party." Ibid.
41. Hunter, p. 123.
42. Ibid.
43. Ibid.
44. Ibid.
45. Magocsi, p. 891.
46. Ibid.
47. Ibid.
48. It was the first to publish, in 1955, in Russian, an excerpt from the novel *Doctor Zhivago* by Boris Pasternak, and later published manuscripts of Soviet writers who had fled the Soviet Union, such as Anatolii Kuznetsov, IUrii Krotkov, and Arkadii Belinkov.
49. Magocsi, p. 891.
50. Ibid., p. 889.
51. Wynar and Wynar, p. 167.
52. Ibid.
53. Ibid., p. 166.
54. Ibid.
55. Ibid.
56. Gennady Klimenko, "Russians," in *The New Jersey Ethnic Experience*, ed. Barbara Cunningham (Union City, N.J.: William H. Wise and Co., [1977]), p. 379.
57. Ibid.
58. Ibid.
59. Ibid.
60. Magocsi, p. 891.

BIBLIOGRAPHY

Davis, Jerome. *The Russian Immigrant*. New York: The Macmillan Company, 1922.
Eisenstadt-Jeleznov, Mikhail, Papers. Immigration History Research Center, University of Minnesota.
Hunter, Edward. *In Many Voices: Our Fabulous Foreign-Language Press*. Norman Park, Ga.: Norman College, [1960].
Klimenko, Gennady. "Russians." In *The New Jersey Ethnic Experience*, Ed. Barbara Cunningham, Union City, N.J.: William H. Wise and Co., [1977].
Luciw, Theodore. *Father Agapius Honcharenko: First Priest in America*. New York: Ukrainian Congress Committee of America, 1970.

Magocsi, Paul Robert. "Russians." In *Harvard Encyclopedia of American Ethnic Groups*, ed. Stephan Thernstrom. Cambridge, Mass.: Harvard University Press, 1980.

Okunstov, Ivan K. *Russkaia emigratsiia v Severnoi i IUzhnoi Amerike*. Buenos Aires: Izd. Seiatel', 1967.

Park, Robert Ezra. *The Immigrant Press and Its Control*. Repr. Westport, Conn.: Greenwood Press, 1970.

Weinbaum, Mark E. "Piat'desita let'." *Novoye Russkoe Slovo* 50 (April 1960): 17203:9.

Wynar, Lubomyr R., and Anna T. Wynar. *Encyclopedic Directory of Ethnic Newspapers and Periodicals in the United States*, 2d ed. Littleton, Colo.: Libraries Unlimited, Inc., 1976.

23

The Serbian Press

MILAN M. RADOVICH

The largest South Slavic nation populating present-day Yugoslavia, with about 9 million (43 percent) of its inhabitants, is represented in the United States ethnic mosaic by an estimated 300,000 American Serbs of the first and second generations. It is one of the smallest ethnic groups in the United States.[1]

Linguistically, Serbs belong to the large Slavic family of nations that includes Russians, Ukrainians, Poles, Czechs, Slovaks, Bulgarians, Croats, Slovenes, and Macedonians. The latter four belong to the inner circle of South Slavic nations. Serbs speak Serbian, or Serbo-Croatian, and in writing they use two alphabets: Cyrillic and Roman.

The great majority of Serbs belong to the Eastern Orthodox Christian rite. The official name for their church is the Serbian Orthodox Church. There are Serbs of Moslem as well as of many other religious confessions.

The first significant arrival in the United States of Serbian immigrants, mainly from rural areas of the Austro-Hungarian Empire, took place during the industrial revolution at the beginning of the twentieth century. The second largest wave followed World War II, when many thousands of displaced persons arrived. The most recent immigration from Yugoslavia has brought to these shores mostly well-trained people seeking improvement in their economic condition.

Beginning with George Fisher (Dorde Sagić), the first well-known Serbian immigrant, who landed on the shores of Louisiana in 1815, Serbs looked toward America not only as a country of great opportunity, but above all as a land of unsurpassed freedom and justice. The great Serbian poet, Prince-Bishop Peter Petrović-Njegoš (1813–1851), in spite of his love for "mother Russia," found America to be the only country to which he would go if he could have chosen his destiny. The Serbs who could choose did just that.

The history of Serbian journalism in America began with the establishment of the first Serbian communities at the end of the nineteenth century. Among these first arrivals, the need to communicate and to exchange ideas, opinions, and news was extremely important. Peasants from Lika, shepherds from Hercegovina, lumbermen from Bosnia, and fishermen from Dalmatia and Montenegro—Serbs and Croats alike, despite their geographical diversity—had one unifying characteristic: their mother tongue.

In the new country, with its totally strange culture, this factor played an important role. Religious, regional, national, and sociopolitical differences were set aside, at least for the moment, because of the many shared problems that daily faced the newcomers. The immigrants realized that to improve their social condition they had to unite and organize so that their voices would be stronger.

In the United States, where a free press was a long-established tradition and freedom of association a respected constitutional right, the Serbs from all the South Slavic lands found a haven, as had ethnic groups that had arrived earlier. For the first time, Serbian cultural, political, social, and religious organizations flourished with no fear of persecution, censorship, or government control or interference. Under such conditions Serbian newspapers were able to function as a real voice of their people. The Serbian press connected widespread Serbian settlements in the New World and also served as a sentimental tie with the Old World. Newspapers became an indispensable part of the immigrants' life, their cultural and informational bread and butter.

The first Serbian-Montenegrin journal to be issued in the United States was called *Slavenska Čitaonica* (Slavic readingroom); it was started in San Francisco in 1869. Its publishers were Montenegrins and Dalmations, who had organized a literary and library society, the first such institution among South Slavs on this continent.[2] While most immigrant periodicals responded to large ethnic communities with traditions of long-standing and abiding cultural ties to their respective mother-countries, the Serbs from Montenegro, Dalmatia, and Hercegovina were newcomers scattered in quite small settlements surrounding the bay area of San Francisco. They centered their immigrant community not around a religious or political organization but around a cultural institution, a library. The Slavonian Literary and Library Society and its publication, written in Serbo-Croatian, became a significant social institution.

The second Serbian newspaper, also in San Francisco, was called the *Greek-Russian Slavonian* (or Eastern Orthodox Slavonian); it made its appearance in 1870. Other papers, with their founding dates, were the following: *Srbin Amerikanac* (The Serbian American), 1893; *Draškova Sloga* (Draško's concord), later called *Slavianska Sloga* (Slavic concord), 1893; *Sloboda* (Liberty), 1893; *Silni Dušan* (Dusan the mighty), 1897; *Slavensko Jedinstvo* (Slavic unity), 1897; and *Nezavisnost* (Independence), 1900. All were based in San Francisco. It would not be inappropriate, considering the exclusive concentration of early Serbian journalistic activity in that city, to call this late nineteenth-century stage the "San Francisco Period."

On examining the issues found in these first immigrant papers, one can see that the politics of the home country was one of the dominant concerns from the beginning. The research of Adam Eterovich shows that the San Francisco Library Society and its journal supported the cause of "Slavonian" nationalism among Montenegrins, Dalmations, and Hercegovinians during the 1875 uprising against the Turks in the homeland.[3] A comparison with later Serbian American newspapers shows that the Serbian immigrants' involvement in the politics of the home country was no less intense in 1875 than it was in 1914, 1941, or today.

A second stage in the development of the Serbian American press corresponds to the Iron and Steel Age of American history, especially from 1900 to 1930. It might well be named the "Pittsburgh Period." During these years Serbian immigrants flocked to the newly industrialized areas ranging from New York to East Chicago. Serbian political, social, religious, and fraternal organizations and their organs sprang up and flourished all over the region. During the first half of this period, between 1900 and 1914, no fewer than fifty Serbian periodicals were founded.

Jovan Skerlić (1877–1914), the famous Serbian scholar and literary critic, submitted a paper entitled "Historical Review of Serbian Newspapers 1791–1911" to the Tenth Congress of Slavic Newspapermen held in Belgrade in early 1911 in which he reported that by the end of 1910 fifteen Serbian newspapers were being published in the United States and Canada,[4] only one of which was Canadian—*Otadžbina* (Fatherland), of British Columbia.

The World War I period saw another twenty-four Serbian-language newspapers come into existence in the United States. The period between the war and the onset of the Great Depression in 1929 witnessed yet another sixteen Serbian-language newspapers. From this "Pittsburgh Period" date some of the most important and best-edited Serbian newspapers such as *Srpska Straža* (Serbian guard); *Sloboda* (Freedom); *Srpski Dnevnik* (Serbian daily); *Srbobran* (Serb defender); *The American Srbobran*; *Kanadski Glasnik* (Canadian herald); *Radnička Borba* (Workers' struggle); and *Ujedinjeno Srpstvo* (United Serbdom). Altogether there must have been about 100 Serbian-language periodicals during this period, three of which were dailies.

The third, and most recent, phase, the "Chicago Period," derives its name from the Serbian-American organizations and their respective publications that began to settle in the greater Chicago area. Historically the period can be divided into two parts: the first covering the Depression and war years, from 1930 to 1945, when twenty-four distinctly Serbian periodicals were founded; and the second, the post-war era, when another forty or so periodicals were added. The main reason for this substantial increase is seen in the considerable influx of new Serbian immigrants, consisting mainly of World War II political refugees, and displaced persons and their families. This led to a rejuvenation of the ethnic community and added vigor to the older immigrant generation, whose political interest in the mother country was thus restored. In addition, more than thirty church bulletins or other types of religious periodical literature came to be published regularly by the Serbian Orthodox churches and parishes all over the continent.

In total, over the past century there have been some 200 Serbian newspapers or journals, varying in scope and character. They have ranged from dailies to annual calendar-almanacs, and from the radical left to the radical right. Only two of the oldtimers, *The American Srbobran* and *The Voice of Canadian Serbs*, survived almost unchanged through the years. All other pre–World War II Serbian immigrant publications ceased to exist. The last Serbian socialist newspaper, *Radnička Borba*, ended its career in 1966. Statistically, their average birth rate of two per annum was matched by an equally high death rate. The increased mobility of the immigrants caused in part by shifting patterns of industrialization, brought about the dispersal of many settlements, and as they melted away, so, too, did their periodicals and newspapers. Economic depressions and strong competition created by automation and unionization also combined to drive many ethnic presses as well as native publishing companies out of business.

CURRENT SERBIAN-AMERICAN PERIODICALS

As of 1984, twenty-nine Serbian journals and newspapers were being published in the United States and Canada. Sixteen are published in the Serbo-Croatian language and in the Cyrillic alphabet. Six are bilingual, and seven are published in English. They vary in publication frequency from weekly (one) to annual. There are no longer any Serbian dailies or semiweekly periodicals published in North America.

These publications fall into the following categories: political; religious; cultural; fraternal; veteran (Chetnik); and scholarly and academic publications.

Bratstvo (Fraternity) is a well-edited Serbian monthly published since 1945 in Toronto by Alija S. Konjhodžić, a professional newspaperman. As a Muslim Serb, he is a supporter of the idea that the destiny of Bosnia lies in union with Serbia. As a political immigrant from Communist Yugoslavia after World War II, he also expresses strong anticommunist feelings through his paper. Its circulation is 1,400. *Srpska Zora* (Serbian aurora) is a bimonthly from Chicago published since 1975 by Branislav M. Stanišić, a former officer in the Royal Yugoslav Army. Pan-Serbian in outlook, anticommunist in essence, this paper is the voice of Chicago's "Serbian People's University."

Four newspapers and one journal are organs of various Serbian political organizations. *Glas Kanadskih Srba* (The Voice of Canadian Serbs) is the oldest Serbian monthly in Canada. It has been published since 1944 in Windsor, Ontario, by the Serbian Shield Society of Canada. It continues *Glas Kanade* (The voice of Canada), which started in 1934. It is presently a sixteen-page paper, four of which are in English. A substantial portion of it is devoted to advertising. In the past, well-known émigré Serbs associated with Serbian cultural life and a democratic political orientation published and edited this newspaper, including Boža Marković, Pero Bulat, Adam Pribićević, Radmilo Grdjić, Professor Jovan Jovetić, Fedor Rajić, and Professor Radoje L. Knežević. Relative to Serbian émigré political opinion, it may be said that the views of this newspaper are generally well balanced. Its editorial policy supports the idea of a democratic Yugoslavia in which all would share basic rights. *Sloboda* (Liberty) of Chicago is the organ of the right-wing Serbian National Defense of America. It has been published bimonthly since 1952. Its chief editor is Vukale Vukotić. Dragiša Kašiković, who became associate editor in 1964, was mysteriously killed in his Chicago office in June 1977. Past editors of *Sloboda* have included such prominent figures as Dr. Božidar Purić, former prime minister of the Yugoslav government-in-exile; Colonel Uglješa Mihailović; and others. This newspaper is a voice of post–World War II anticommunist refugees from Yugoslavia and of various groups of displaced persons. It features mostly news from Yugoslavia. *Kanadski Srbobran* (The Canadian Srbobran) is a biweekly of the Serbian League of Canada and has been published since 1951. Its present editor-in-chief is Lazar Stojšić. *Serbian Democratic Forum*, which appears irregularly, has been published in English since 1972 by the Chicago-based Serbian National Committee. The St. Sava Serbian Literary Association, yet another Chicago-based organization, began publishing *Srpska Borba* (Serbian struggle), a conservative pan-Serbian biweekly, in 1946, under the editorship of Dr. Slobodan Drašković. After his death in 1982, this newspaper became a monthly. It is now published in Flushing, New York, and edited by Budimir Srećković.

Religious Publications

Three religious periodicals are published by the Serbian Orthodox Church of America and Canada, and an additional three by the Free Serbian Orthodox Church, not including individual parish publications. *The Path of Orthodoxy* is an official monthly bilingual publication of the Serbian Orthodox Church of America and Canada. Its circulation is 3,000 copies. Religious news from the national and international scene as well as other religious matters appears in its sixteen pages.

The *Annual Almanac* is published by the Clergy Association of the Serbian Orthodox Church of America and Canada, edited by the Very Reverend Djordje Lazić. This bilingual almanac includes an up-to-date list of all the priests and parishes under the jurisdiction of the church. *The Serbian Missionary* is the voice of Serbian students at Holy Trinity Monastery (Russian Orthodox) in Jordanville, New York, published occasionally and devoted to spiritual matters.

Since 1965 the Free Serbian Orthodox Church has published in English the *Diocesan Observer* in Libertyville, Illinois, under the editorship of a professional journalist, Milan Karlo; it is the official weekly organ of a dissenting group. The Clergy Brotherhood of the same group has issued, since 1964, its own *St. Sava Calendar-Almanac* with listings of its clergy and parishes. The bilingual *Diocesan Herald* has been published irregularly since 1964 by the same diocese.

Cultural Publications

Five journals are primarily devoted to literary and historico-political writings. One of the best of this group, and certainly the oldest, is the semiannual *Glasnik*

(Herald), published in Chicago by the Serbian Historical and Cultural Association "Njegoš" since 1958. Its first editor, Jovan Kontić, and his successor, Dušan Petković, were both highly educated. The journal regularly publishes historical documentation on Yugoslav politics between the two world wars as well as book reviews on the subject. *Književni Vesnik* (Literary messenger) has been published since 1964, semiannually, in Cleveland, Ohio, by the Free-Yugoslav Writers' Association. Its editor is Borivoje Karapandžić, a Serbian émigré writer. It is primarily involved in cultivating Serbian literature by political émigrés. The Serbian Writers' Association has published irregularly, since 1974, its *Srpski Dogovor* (Serbian accord), the main sponsor and literary contributor to which is its president, Petar Martinović-Bajica of California, a poet and former Yugoslav army officer.

The newest cultural organization among the Serbs in the Greater Chicago area, the Serbian Academic Club, has published its *Glasnik* (Herald) since 1972. This is the only nonpolitical Serbian cultural publication. At present the editor is Branko Obradović.

Serb World-USA is a bimonthly publication whose purpose is to maintain the history and culture of the Serbs in America and to report on interesting Serbian activities worldwide. It began as *Serb World* in Milwaukee, Wisconsin, in 1979 under the editorship of Dan Sokolovich. In 1984 it moved to Tucson, Arizona. Presently, its editor is Mary Nicklanovich Hart and its publisher is Sophie Grubisich Chuk.

Fraternal Publications

The oldest and largest Serbian fraternal organization in the United States and Canada, the Serb National Federation, has published continuously, since 1906, its weekly bilingual *The American Srbobran*. This newspaper has played a significant role in the history of the Serbs in the United States. Distinguished men in Serbian cultural, political, social, and religious life have been regular contributors: M. Pupin, N. Tesla, P. Radosavljevich, J. Dučić, T. Djonović, Bishop Nikolaj Velimirović, B. Purić, K. Fotić, M. Gavrilović, and many others. The editors have been highly qualified journalists, professors, and diplomats. As a fraternal newspaper, its prime aim is to bring important organizational news to the membership (20,000) of the Serb National Federation. Serbian sections also feature news and political commentaries as well as book reviews on subjects of interest to readers.

The American Srbobran, whose political significance on the Serbian ethnic scene in America is discussed below, is the largest and most widely read Serbian newspaper in the world outside the homeland. It is also the second oldest Serbian newspaper still being published anywhere, predated only by Belgrade's *Politika* (Politics), which began in 1905. Two professional editors, Jovan Bratić and Ann Tumbas, run this newspaper today. For second- and third-generation Americans of Serbian descent, its English section is the only weekly connection with their heritage.

Veterans' (Chetnik) Publications

This group of periodicals was founded after World War II by veteran organizations of the Chetnik guerrillas, supporters of the late General Draža Mihailović. When the war ended, as fierce opponents of the communist regime in Yugoslavia, the Chetniks were forced to flee abroad. Seven publications by Chetnik veterans' organizations have appeared. Some of them are organs of regional military units organized in the homeland during World War II. They include the following periodicals: *Vidovdan* (St. Vitus Day), edited by Božidar Sokolović; *Četničke Novine* (Chetnik newspaper), edited by D. Marić, and *Ravnogorska Misao* (Ravnagora idea), edited by M. Radosavljević, both published in Milwaukee, Wisconsin; *Chetnik* (in English), edited by D. Dokmanović; *Srpske Novine* (Serbian news), edited by V. Vukotić, and *Ravnogorski Borac* (Ravnagora fighter), both in the Greater Chicago area; and *Konjički Glasnik* (Herald of the Royal Cavalry), edited by V. Djelević and published in Rochester, Michigan. *Srbija* (Serbia) is published in Canada under the editorship of Momcilo Djujć, well-known Chetnik leader and resident of the United States. In addition to being the official organs of their respective organizations and thus printing news of special interest to their members, they are regularly involved in active anticommunist agitation and other political activities.

Scholarly and Academic Publications

Serbian Studies is a semiannual journal published by the North American Society for Serbian Studies (NASSS) and connected with the University of Illinois at Chicago. Its editor since it began publication in 1980 has been Professor Nicholas Moravčevich. *Serbian Studies* publishes scholarly articles on all aspects of the Serbian cultural heritage as well as materials related to the Serbian immigration to North America. *The Tesla Journal*, an international annual review of the sciences and humanities, has been published by Tesla Memorial Society, Inc., of the United States and Canada since 1981. Its editors, Professors G. V. Tomashevich and H. J. Birx, are notable scholars.

PROBLEMS FACING THE SERBIAN-AMERICAN PRESS

The number of Serbian-American newspapers, past and present, noted here is fairly impressive. Many of the editors have been highly regarded members of the Serbian-American community. The continued arrival of new Serbian immigrants has constantly enhanced that community. Still, the question of how long the ethnic Serbian-American press will survive must be given serious consideration.

Serbian newspaper publishing in America was initiated largely by individuals who, through personal effort and sacrifice, wished to help their own people. Often, a successful local businessman would initiate and fully support such a publication. For example, *Sloboda* (Liberty), founded in 1893 in San Francisco, was financed by a businessman from Fresno, California. In 1901 Dmitar Šaban purchased from his own savings the press used to print *Srbin* (Serb).[5] Occasionally travel agents started Serbian-American papers. Many newspapers sprang up, but few survived, for success required perseverance and the ability to adapt to constant change. The situation today is no easier for Serbian-American publishers.

Aging is a problem facing all of the ethnic presses in this country. The average age of Serbian-American newspaper editors, sixty, and of their readers, fifty-five, is a factor that works against the immigrant Serbian press in America. The old traditional ethnic neighborhoods, where the concentration of a given group made the distribution of newspapers easy and inexpensive, no longer exist. The lack of qualified bilingual printers, editors, and correspondents and the inadequacy of advertising revenues are also serious problems, but most serious of all is the lack of new readership and supporters. Newspapers that belong to organized groups such as church, political, or fraternal organizations face the same problems, despite institutional backing. Furthermore, the rising cost of publishing and mailing suggests the necessity for some form of cooperation among several organizations or financially secure institutions.

The problems are generational, political, and "ethnic." Editors, publishers, contributors, and those with decision-making powers belong to earlier generations. There are many subjects that they choose not to cover, while they focus essentially on politics and history. News concerning Serbian communities throughout the United States is frequently ignored. The news that in 1976 Pittsburgh witnessed the consecration of a new multimillion dollar Serbian Orthodox cathedral which earned the first prize of the American National Society of Architects was hardly mentioned in some lay Serbian-American newspapers. In some instances, politically biased and often extremely righteous editors of Serbian-American newspapers do not allow voices of dissent to be heard, even when they emanate from their own rank and file. Printing opposing viewpoints is not common in the Serbian-American political press. Traditional critical exchanges of letters with the editors are hardly known. While the readership of the press is often well educated—80 percent of all immigrants to the United States since 1970 are highly trained professional people, compared with 20.3 percent of those who came to this country before 1910[6]—the Serbian immigrant press has not advanced much beyond the editorial level it had achieved by 1910.

Most typical of "pure" ethnic newspaper writing geared especially to American-born Serbs is the English edition of the *American Srbobran*. According to Lubomyr and Anna Wynar, with second-, third-, and even fourth-generation

Americans the "immigrant" press of their forebears turns "ethnic" mainly by disassociation from the politics of the mother country.[7] While this may be the case with some ethnic groups, it does not apply to the Serbian-American community. Among secular publications, with the exception of the English edition of the *American Srbobran* not a single Serbian-American newspaper has turned "ethnic" in this sense. They have remained "immigrant" in nature from their inception. The second and third generations of Serbian Americans have not produced their own ethnic newspapers. The post–World War II political immigrants are involved in the politics of the mother country just as the first immigrants from Bosnia, Hercegovina, Lika, Dalmatia, Montenegro, and Serbia were. The newcomers are not interested in being assimilated. They consider this stage in their lives as temporary, just as the first Serbian immigrants did. The dream of "return" is so strong that it blocks out the reality of "no return." The English edition of the *American Srbobran* still unites a number of second- and third-generation Americans of Serbian descent through fraternal, sports, and other activities, attempting to keep them from forgetting their ancestral traditions, culture, language, and religion. In a word, the Serbian-American press attempts to Serbianize in a positive way rather than to Americanize.

Good ethnic intracommunity relations depend in large measure on a good press. Even more, according to Wynar and Wynar, "the survival of ethnic communities and ethnic life in the United States is largely a result of the continued existence of the ethnic press."[8] The better the immigrant press, the slower will be the process of assimilation and the longer the life of ethnicity.

"STRIFE AND PUBLISHING"

In his pioneer book *Srbi u Americi* (The Serbs in America), published in 1917 in Geneva, Switzerland, Pero Slijepčević named the chapter dealing with publications in the United States and Canada "Strife and Publishing,"[9] a very appropriate title for a discussion of the significant characteristics of the Serbian immigrant press in America.

Serbian publishing in the United States has been inseparably connected with disputes, hot arguments and, occasionally, long and expensive court battles. Without these conflicts there would almost certainly have been at least 100 fewer Serbian American newspapers. Political disagreements caused deep rifts in the community, resulting in a proliferation of organizations as well as newspapers sponsored by them. Eventually, the "embattled public" would abandon the newspapers thus created, and the publishers would cease operations. Traditional Serbian *inat* (spite) found a great opportunity in American freedom of the press that was not always properly utilized. Of the three periods of Serbian-American journalism mentioned earlier, only the San Francisco period was a peaceful one; the Pittsburgh and Chicago periods may well be best remembered for their fierce journalistic warfare. The difference can be explained by the nature of the earliest Serbian settlers, their small numbers, and the social conditions in earlier times.

The first Serbian weekly, *Sloboda* (Liberty), established in 1893 by the Serbian Library of San Francisco, was indeed a cultural journal reflecting its editors' tastes (Veljko Radojević and Lazar Radulović) until 1906, when the press and its entire inventory burned to the ground. Its successors, *Srpska Nezavisnost* (Serbian independence) of Oakland, and San Francisco's *Glasnik* (Herald), long the leading Serbian newspapers in the West, kept a generally restrained tone over the confrontations between the Pittsburgh and New York Serbian organizations. Chicago's *Ujedinjeno Srpstvo* (United Serbians), owned by the well-known publisher and businessman John Palandech, withdrew from the dispute, being unwilling to risk becoming involved in the struggle between the various fraternal organizations.

The two leading journalistic opponents in the decade after 1908 were Pittsburgh's *American Srbobran*, organ of the Serbian Orthodox Federation Srbobran, and the *Srbobran* of New York City, serving the fraternal organization *Sloga* (Concord), led by Columbia University Professor Michael I. Pupin. The anti-intellectual trend of the Pittsburgh leadership, particularly that of *American Srbobran* editor Budimir Grahovac, played an important part in this protracted feud. Leaders of both factions exchanged unjust accusations. Several newly formed publications soon joined in the fray. *Srpski Dnevnik* (Serbian daily), which supported the "Pupin party," was edited by Boža Ranković, perhaps the best writer among Serbian immigrants of his day. This group was opposed by *Dnevni Glasnik* (Daily herald) and *Bič* (The whip), whose editors were Djordje Stejić and Dušan Silaški, respectively. Very often these newspapers preferred publishing accusations and counteraccusations against prominent fellow Serbs to denouncing the Austro-Hungarian invaders of the mother country, Serbia, for their atrocities.

Among the South Slavs in the United States, just as in their homeland, the Serbs from Montenegro had primacy in establishing printing institutions. The editors of all the early Serbian newspapers in the San Francisco Bay area were from Montenegro. At the time there were some 20,000 Montenegrins in America to support their newspapers and organizations.[10]

The first of many Montenegrin fraternal organization newspapers, *Rodoljub* (Patriot), was published in New York City, beginning in 1901. Montenegrin newspapers did not actively participate in the fraternal struggle between the Srbobran and Sloga federations. However, they did not escape the strife during the 1918 crisis over Montenegro's unification with Serbia, when some groups sided with the former monarch, King Nicholas after his dismissal by the Montenegrin Parliament in Podgorica. The perceived importance of newspapers in this conflict was demonstrated when Prime Minister Nikola Pašić of Serbia sent to the United States four capable Montenegrins with funds to organize supporters of unification.[11] Jovan Djonović became the editor of *Narodna Misao* (National idea), based in Butte, Montana; Todor Božović inaugurated *Oslobodjenje* (Liberation) in Chicago; Stevo Bogdanović reorganized the *Slobodna Tribuna* (Free tribune) in Seattle, Washington; and Mićun Pavićević became the publisher and editor of *Kanadski Glasnik* (Canadian herald) in Welland, Ontario.

Most other Serbian-American newspapers joined in this unification struggle by attacking the supporters of the Montenegrin separatist movement. Detroit's *Crnogorski Glasnik* (Montenegrin herald) was a leading supporter of King Nicholas, however, and bitterly opposed unification. Finally, officials of the Kingdom of Serbia's diplomatic mission in Washington, D. C., had to intervene. By the end of 1918 some normalization of relations was achieved in Serbian communities throughout the United States. By this time the war was over and the Montenegrin Serbs were united with the other Serbs.

The Serbian and Montenegrin governments were not the only ones deeply involved in Serbian immigrant journalism in America. The Austro-Hungarian Ministry of the Interior accused the *American Srbobran* of being a culprit in the Banja Luka trial in Bosnia and banished the newspaper from the entire empire.[12] Later Boža Ranković, editor of *Srpski Dnevnik*, was accused of conspiracy in the unsuccessful assassination attempt against Governor Slavko Cuvaj of Croatia in 1912. Neither charge was true. Vienna found it useful, however, to find good excuses to prevent distribution of Serbian-American newspapers among the Serbian subjects of the Austro-Hungarian monarchy. During the Balkan Wars and later, throughout World War I, the Serbian-American press did much through its patriotic writing to help raise volunteers for the Serbian army as well as financial and medical aid. Austro-Hungarian intelligence tried in many ways to use certain ethnic publications to weaken the Allied war effort. Also, relations between Serbs and Croats in the United States were occasionally disturbed by Austro-Hungarian agents during World War I as part of their psychological warfare.

The two decades between the world wars saw an increase in Serbian-American journalism with the addition of a number of Serbian newspapers having a Yugoslav orientation. This could also be said for some Croatian and Slovenian periodicals. Such newspapers included *Jugoslovenski Glasnik* (Yugoslav herald), 1921; *Jugoslovenski Forum* (Yugoslav forum), 1926; *Jugoslaven* (The Yugoslav), 1927; *Jugoslovenski-Americki Glasnik* (Yugoslav-American herald), 1935; *American-Yugoslav Reflector*, 1939; *Jugoslovenske Novosti* (Yugoslav news), 1940; and others. Most of them, as well as the older Serbian and Croatian newspapers, were also deeply involved in the mother country's politics and quarrels. They actually took sides in the bitter daily confrontations of Serbian and Croatian deputies in the Yugoslav Parliament, over causes that often had no meaningful relation to life in the United States. This politically oriented press seldom carried articles on American history, working conditions, or employment possibilities in the United States. Editors followed the mass hysteria, in some cases, of their readership, on whose support they counted, instead of challenging its validity.

During World War II and the Axis Powers' occupation of Yugoslavia, the

Serbian press in the United States and Canada represented not only free Serbs but also the Yugoslav government-in-exile, at least its Serbian component. Thus the *American Srbobran* became, in fact, a semi-official organ of the Royal Yugoslav Government. When the news of the Ustashi (Croatian Fascist) atrocities first reached the United States, the *American Srbobran*, in its issue of November 4, 1941, published a long report entitled "The Slaughter of the Serbs in 'Independent' Croatia." This shocking news stirred all Serbs as well as the entire free world. The Croatian separatist press in the United States, which was in some cases controlled by the Ustashi, proceeded with counteraccusations, defending and even justifying such brutalities. New intraethnic press warfare erupted and became so heated that the United States Department of State had to intervene.[13]

The second important stand of the Serbian-American press during World War II was its total support for the resistance movement in Yugoslavia led by Draža Mihailović. This also included the communist organ *Slobodna Reč* (Free world) until the end of 1942. After that date *Slobodna Reč* began to follow Moscow's directive in giving its full support to the communist-led guerrillas under Tito's leadership. As the struggle between these two resistance movements in Yugoslavia grew, so too did the feud between Serbian nationalist and communist newspapers in the United States. Postwar Chetnik-American newspapers, some of which were discussed above, have continued their political warfare against the oppressive communist regime of Yugoslavia to the present.

The most recent great controversy to stir up Serbian-American communities has been the schism within the Serbian Orthodox Church in the United States and Canada since 1963. This split has affected not only religious institutions but Serbian-American organizations, communities, and even individual families. Mutual public recriminations and malicious charges and insults have surpassed all previous quarrels, in duration as well as in consequences. Yet a positive aspect of this altercation has been a certain revitalization of social life. New churches, halls, and publications have appeared on all sides. Of particular interest for the history of the schism are *The Official News Digest* of the "Mother Church" group and the *Diocesan Observer* of the dissenters.

The four major controversies in the life of Serbian immigrants, as seen through their newspapers, have had many negative consequences, not so much because of the issues at stake as for the rancor and verbal abuse they have generated. The personal attacks have been bitter beyond measure, to the point of losing sight of the main issues. But there have been some positive results as well. The feud of the fraternal organizations between 1908 and 1918 ended with the unification of the contending brotherhoods. The quarrel over Montenegrin unification with Serbia during and just after 1917 ended with the creation of Yugoslavia. Serbian and Croatian relations in the United States between the two world wars slowly normalized but reflected the crises and confrontations in the mother country. The conflicts of the World War II period continued well into the Cold War era with its anticommunist flavor. The last of these fights, the Serbian

Orthodox Church schism, has created a deep cleavage in the Serbian-American immigrant and ethnic community since 1963 that will take some time to heal.

The only newspaper to have passed through all these struggles, playing a significant role in each of them, is the *American Srbobran*. Its editors for the past seventy-five years have been quite successful in voicing the opinion of the largest group and thus creating the impression at least, in the view of its relatively large circulation, that the *American Srbobran* is the voice of the majority. But responsible editors would have attempted to defuse controversies. Had there been a greater insistence on objectivity and tolerance in the press, public opinion might have been encouraged to strive for a constructive resolution of disagreements.

YUGOSLAV AND SERBIAN SOCIALIST PERIODICALS

The first South Slav (Yugoslav) socialist organization in the United States was organized in the summer of 1907 when a group of Pittsburgh workers formed the Yugoslav Political Club. The labor movement in America as well as in the mother country was then in the midst of a campaign to organize and to fight for the improvement of miserable working conditions. Accordingly, the Yugoslav Political Club began to publish a weekly newspaper, *Radnička Straža* (Workers' guard).

The first editor of *Radnička Straža*, and at the same time an early political organizer of Yugoslav workers in the United States, was a Serb from Vojvodina, Milan Glumac. A professional newspaperman and longtime editor of socialist newspapers, Glumac was a member of the Social Democratic Party in the homeland. Expelled by the authorities, Glumac went to Pittsburgh and, from there, to Chicago, where he became the editor of *Narodni Glas* (Voice of the people), the organ of the Yugoslav Socialist Federation, a section of Eugene Debs's American Socialist Party from 1911. As an editor, Glumac regularly used materials from South Slavic socialist newspapers in his American newspapers and complained at times that he had come to an environment that was intellectually on a lower level than his own and that there was nobody around to help him in his task.[14] This problem of intellectual communication faced all other editors of the Serbian immigrant press. Later, Serbian socialists Blagoje Savić, Spasoje Marković, and Vladimir Bornemisa, and the Bulgarian Todor Tsvetkov were to edit *Narodni Glas*. Its peak circulation reached 4,000 copies a week by 1912.

The Yugoslav section of the American Labor Party published a weekly, *Radnička Borba* (Workers' struggle), which started in Cleveland, Ohio, in 1908. Its editors were Lazar Petrović, Danilo Kozomara (who later became a Serbian Orthodox priest), and Milan Jevtić, a newsman. The American Labor Party and its Yugoslav section belonged to a utopian rather than revolutionary wing of the American socialist movement.

When, in 1919, the Communist Party of the United States was organized, some Yugoslavs who had left the American socialist movement formed their own section of the American Communist Party. Their first official organ was a small, clandestine bulletin. The former socialist journal, *Znanje* (Knowledge), published in Chicago and edited by the party's only two intellectuals, Djuka Kutuzović and Todor Tsvetkov, became the first Yugoslav communist newspaper in the United States. After their expulsion from the party, the two former editors began to publish, in Chicago, a dissident communist cultural journal, *Novi Svijet* (The new world), attached to the Yugoslav Educational Alliance. In 1925 the dominant left wing of the party changed the name *Znanje* to *Radnik* (The worker) and started its daily publication, which lasted until 1932.

During the economic crisis of the 1930s, various workers' organizations were formed whose principal aim was to provide funds for the regular publication of their newspapers and political pamphlets. In 1934, when the Communist party of Yugoslavia began its own internal structural changes along nationality lines, the Yugoslav communists in the United States and Canada were likewise required to reorganize on the same pattern. As a consequence of this political transformation, the weekly *Slobodna Reč* (free world) of Pittsburgh was born. The Slovenian communists had a journal, *Naprej* (Forward), while the Croatian leftists retained *Radnik*, which in 1935 changed its name to *Glas Radnika* (The workers' voice) and, in 1936, to *Radnički Glasnik* (Workers' herald).

For quite some time the chief editorial writer for both the Serbian and Croatian communist newspapers was Nikola Kovačević, a former organizational secretary of the party in Yugoslavia, who used the pseudonym Jankin Starčević for the articles he wrote for *Glas Radnika*. He was replaced by another organizer of the Communist Party of Yugoslavia, Srdja Prica. In 1939 Dr. Mirko Marković bought, with party funds, a building and a printing press in Pittsburgh where he established his headquarters, from which all Yugoslav communist activities in the United States were directed until 1946. All three Yugoslav communist newspapers then published in America were printed in Pittsburgh.[15] There are at present no communist-supported or communist-oriented Serbian newspapers in the United States.

Since their first appearance in Pittsburgh some seventy years ago, Serbian American socialist and communist immigrant newspapers, like their nonsocialist and noncommunist counterparts, were primarily interested in the politics of the mother country and in Old World movements. After World War II, all of the Serbian communist activists in the United States returned to Yugoslavia.

The history of Serbian journalism is at the same time the history of Serbian immigration. For better or worse, they cannot be divided. John Rothman, editor of the *New York Times*, in his introduction to the *New York Times Index* (1967) wrote: "The newspaper is one of the most valuable sources in the study of history, and is the only source that gives a day to day account of events and trends from a truly contemporary point of view. *The file of old newspapers is a storehouse of history.*" The storehouse of immigrant history, "the insight into the spirit of the Serbian age in America," depend entirely on those files.[16]

NOTES

Parts of this account are from a chapter to be included in M. B. Petrovich's *History of Serbs in the USA* (in preparation).

1. Michael B. Petrovich and Joel Halpern, "Serbs," in Stephan Thernstrom, ed., *Harvard Encyclopedia of American Ethnic Groups* (Cambridge, Mass.: Harvard University Press, 1980), pp. 916–926.

2. Adam S. Eterovich, *A Guide and Bibliography to Research on Yugoslavs in the United States and Canada* (San Francisco: R and E Research Associates, 1975), p. 50.

3. Ibid., p. 47.

4. Jovan Skerlić, *Istorijski pregled srpske štampe 1791–1911* (Belgrade: Prosveta, 1966), p. 93.

5. *Spomenica Srpskog narodnog saveza* (Pittsburgh, Pa.: Srpski narodni Savez, 1951).

6. "Immigrants and the American Labor Market," Manpower Research Monograph No. 31 (Washington, D. C., 1974), p. 69.

7. Lubomyr R. Wynar and Anna T. Wynar, *Encyclopedic Directory of Ethnic Newspapers and Periodicals in the United States*, 2d ed. (Littleton, Colo.: Libraries Unlimited, 1976), p. 14.

8. Ibid.

9. Pero Slijepčević, *Srbi u Americi* (Geneva, Switzerland: Ujedinjenje, 1917), p. 50.

10. Djordjije-Djoko D. Pejović, *Iseljavanje Crnogoraca u XIX vijeku* (Titograd: Istorijski Institut Narodne Republike Crne Gore, 1962).

11. Dimitrije Dimo Vujović, *Ujedinjenje Crne Gore i Srbije* (Titograd: Istorijski Institut Narodne Republike Crne Gore, 1962), p. 249.

12. *Govori branitelja u kaznenoj parnici protiv Adama Pribićevića i 52 drugova radi zločinstva veleizdaje* (Zagreb: Naklada Branitelja, 1909), p. 84.

13. Constantin Fotitch, *The War We Lost* (New York: Viking, 1948), pp. 130–135.

14. Stojan Kesić, *Radnički pokret u jugoslovenskim zemljama do 1914. Godine* (Belgrade: Narodna Knjiga, 1976), p. 167.

15. Luka Marković, *Borba u iseljeništvu za novu Jugoslaviju* (Belgrade: Komunist, 1975), p. 73.

16. John Rothman, ed., "Introduction" in *The New York Times Index: 1851–1862*, vol. 1 (New York: Bowker, 1967).

BIBLIOGRAPHY

Čizmić, Ivan. *Jugoslavenski iseljenički pokret u SAD i stvaranje jugoslavenske države 1918*. Zagreb: Sveučilište-Institut za hrvatsku povijest, 1974.

Gakovich, Robert P., and Milan M. Radovich. *Serbs in the United States and Canada: A Comprehensive Bibliography*. St. Paul, Minn.: University of Minnesota, 1976.

Jugoslovenski napredni pokret u SAD i kanadi 1935–1945. Toronto: Nordam, 1983.

Lojen, Stjepan. *Uspamene jednog iseljenika*. Zagreb: Znanje, 1963.

Purić, Božidar. *Biografija Bože Rankovića: Doprinos istoriji srpskog iseljeništva u Severnoj Americi*. Munchen: Iskra, 1963.

24

The Slovak-American Press

M. MARK STOLARIK

While the Slovaks are one of the smaller ethnic groups in the United States (approximately 500,000 came from the Kingdom of Hungary before World War I, and today they number between 1 and 2 million), they have published at least 220 different newspapers, ranging from dailies to quarterlies, since 1885.[1] More than half these newspapers were established and edited by about thirty individuals or organizations, and these produced eleven kinds of publications that reflected four distinct political orientations: Slovak nationalist, Magyarone, Czechoslovak, and socialist or communist. The newspapers appeared in the principal areas of Slovak settlement in the United States (Pennsylvania, Illinois, Ohio, New York, and New Jersey), and they mirrored the religious composition of the Slovak people (Roman Catholic, Lutheran, Calvinist, and Greek Catholic). The Slovak press in America, therefore, was as complex as that of any other group in this country.

The independent, commercial, general news press appeared first among American Slovaks, and it would eventually produce eighty-seven titles, or 40 percent of the overall total.[2] Its first title was a weekly *Bulletin* of American and world news printed on a mimeograph machine by Ján Slovenský, an information officer at the Austro-Hungarian Consulate in Pittsburgh in 1885. In 1886 he teamed up with his cousin Július Wolf (a saloonkeeper), and together they launched the more ambitious *Amerikanszko-Szlovenszke Noviny* (American-Slovak news). It was written in the Spiš dialect of eastern Slovakia, utilized Magyar orthography, and affirmed loyalty to the King of Hungary, who was also Emperor of Austria.[3]

The linguistic and political orientation of the first Slovak newspaper in the United States both pleased and offended a small group of intellectuals who had accompanied their overwhelmingly peasant and worker countrymen to the United States. The Roman Catholic priest Jozef Kossalko praised the paper while the ex-seminarian Peter V. Rovnianek condemned the linguistic and political policies of *Amerikanszko-Szlovenszke Noviny*, and Rovnianek eventually won. By 1889 he had persuaded the founders to make him editor, to allow him to publish in the central Slovak (literary) dialect, and to foster the cause of Slovak nationalism.

He then changed the spelling of the title to *Amerikánsko-Slovenské noviny*, and most other Slovak newspapers, whether independents or not, adopted the nationalist philosophy (69 percent) and the use of literary Slovak (90 percent).[4]

A small group of dissidents, largely Roman Catholic priests, tried to counteract the growing nationalism of American Slovaks by publishing their own newspapers. Jozef Kossalko led the way with his independent weekly *Zástava* (Flag; Plymouth, Pennsylvania, 1889), and later with *Naša Zástava* (Our flag; Bridgeport, Connecticut, 1906–1907). He and his colleagues, among them the Reverends Ján E. Chudatsik of Chicago, Béla Kazinczy of Braddock, Pennsylvania, and Imre Haitinger of New York City, published a total of twenty-two "Magyarone" (pro-Hungarian) newspapers (nineteen independent, two religious, one socialist) in various eastern Slovak dialects before World War II, but they never succeeded in winning a large following, and their newspapers were very short-lived.[5] For example, while the average duration of all 220 Slovak newspapers in the United States was 13.6 years, Magyarone publications survived, on the average, only four years.

Meanwhile, Rovnianek's *Amerikánsko-Slovenské noviny* was a huge success. By 1889 it had 2,700 subscribers, which made it the largest Slovak newspaper in the world. In the Kingdom of Hungary, due to political and economic oppression, no Slovak newspaper had more than 1,000 subscribers at that time. By 1910 Rovnianek's weekly had an estimated 40,000 subscribers (the largest ever achieved by a Slovak-American newspaper); had the publisher not been ruined by stock speculation, his paper might have survived to this day. Instead, Rovnianek fled west to escape his creditors, and his newspaper folded in 1922. Besides having founded, in 1890, the National Slovak Society, the first nationwide fraternal society of American Slovaks, Rovnianek also published and/or edited six other periodicals, including literary, humor, regional, and English-language titles. He also served as the second president of the Slovak League of America, the cover organization of all Slovak-American fraternal groups. Rovnianek left a deep imprint on both newspaper and fraternal life in the United States and can rightly be considered the "father" of the nonsectarian Slovak-American community.[6]

The most successful competitor of *Amerikánsko-Slovenské noviny*, and the longest-lasting Slovak newspaper in America, was *Slovák v Amerike* (The Slovak in America). This "worker's weekly" was founded in 1889, by former Knights of Labor organizer and later fraternal leader Anton Š. Ambrose in Plymouth, Pennsylvania. It then changed hands and by 1891 was purchased by the typesetter Ján Spevák of New York City. He hired as editor the political émigré and superb writer Gustáv Maršall-Petrovský, and the newspaper instantly competed successfully with Rovnianek's weekly for the hearts, minds, and pocketbooks of American Slovaks. During World War I it even became a daily; now a monthly, it is the only surviving exclusively Slovak-language newspaper in the United States.[7]

Among the publishers and editors of independent Slovak newspapers in the

United States in the early years, four other individuals deserve mention: Ján Pankuch, Ján A. Ferienčík, Jozef Hušek, and Milan Getting. Pankuch had come to America as a young man and had learned the typesetting trade in Cleveland in various Czech printeries in the 1880s. He eventually went into business for himself and founded five newspapers, the most famous of which were the weekly *Hlas* (Voice; 1907–1947) and *Denný hlas* (Daily voice; 1915–1925), both published in Cleveland.[8] Ján A. Ferienčík, meanwhile, had given up teaching in Hungary and moved to the United States in the early 1890s where he subsequently edited half a dozen major Slovak newspapers, including Pankuch's *Denný hlas*. Ferienčík is remembered for his Slovak nationalism and fine writing style.[9] Jozef Hušek was the son of a Czech immigrant to Slovakia. Young Jozef had chafed under Hungarian rule and left for the United States as an uncompromising Slovak nationalist at the turn of the century. He helped found and edit in Cleveland the semimonthly *Kritika* (Criticism; 1914–1915), which later turned into the weekly *Obrana* (Defense; 1915–1972), one of the most popular of Slovak-American newspapers, especially among the first two generations, who liked to reminisce in letters to the editor about the "good old days."[10] Milan Getting was an early and dedicated champion of "Czechoslovakism" in America. He worked to create a unitary Czechoslovakia, composed of Czechs and Slovaks, with the Czechs eventually assimilating the Slovaks on the ruins of Austria-Hungary; he preached this philosophy in *New Yorský deník* (New York daily; 1913–1975). He and his cohorts succeeded in their aims during World War I, and his newspaper continued to champion this cause until it folded.[11]

While the independent commercial press arose first and produced the largest number of titles among Slovak-Americans, it was not the most successful or the longest-lasting. Very early in their history Slovak-Americans also founded religious and fraternal presses which would show greater resilience and stability than any of their competitors.

Four years after the first independent papers arose among American Slovaks a religious weekly also appeared. It was established by the first Slovak Roman Catholic priest to have come to America, the Reverend Ignác Jaškovič of Hazleton, Pennsylvania. He called his newspaper *Katolícke noviny* (Catholic news; 1889–1891), and it was the earliest of thirty-three religious periodicals that would be published between 1889 and 1984. Since Jaškovič was a tyrannical publisher who fired editors at will, his paper survived only two years. However, all Slovak religious denominations eventually established their own newspapers; such papers lasted an average of 16.2 years. This compared very favorably with the independents, which lasted an average of only 7.4 years. Among the other important religious publications are *Svedok* (The witness; 1906–), the official monthly of the Synod of Slovak Evangelical Lutheran Churches in America, published in Pittsburgh and edited for many years by Reverend Jaroslav Pelikán, Sr. (father of Jaroslav Pelikán, Jr., the well-known Yale Divinity School professor); the *Sion* (Zion; 1920-), also a monthly published in Pittsburgh, by the rival Slovak Evangelical Zion Synod; and *Dobrý pastier* (Good shepherd; 1919-), a monthly publication of the Slovak Catholic Federation established in Munhall, Pennsylvania, and edited by Reverend Ján M. Liščinský. Many of these titles were copies of Old World publications. In keeping with their religious mission, these newspapers tended to avoid politics. Thus, only two were openly Magyarone and one espoused Slovak nationalism. The rest were neutral most of the time.[12]

The third major component of the Slovak-American press, fraternal publications, had its origin in 1891 and would eventually dominate the field in stability and duration. Reverend Štefan Furdek of Cleveland, Ohio, whom many consider to be the "father" of Slovak-American Catholics, founded the first weekly fraternal publication, the Catholic *Jednota* (Union; 1891-) as the official organ of the First Catholic Slovak Union, which Furdek helped to organize in Cleveland in 1890. Furdek also edited this newspaper until 1910, after which Jozef Hušek took over. Other fraternal organizations soon followed suit and began to publish newspapers that reflected their particular religious and national orientation: the weekly *Bratstvo* (Brotherhood; 1899-), official organ of the Pennsylvania Slovak Catholic Union headquartered in Wilkes-Barre, Pennsylvania; the *Slovenský hlásnik* (Slovak herald; 1900–1962; after that the *United Lutheran*), official weekly of the Slovak Evangelical Union headquartered in Pittsburgh (Ján Pankuch was one of its founders); the weekly *Slovenský Sokol* (Slovak falcon; 1905–1967; after that *Sokol Times*), official organ of the Slovak Gymnastic Union Sokol headquartered in Perth Amboy, N. J., and edited in its early years by Milan Getting; the *Slovenský Kalvín* (Slovak Calvin; 1907–1962; after that *Calvin*), official semimonthly, and later monthly, publication of the Slovak Calvin Presbyterian Union, headquartered in Pittsburgh; the monthly *Živena* (Giver of life; 1908-), official organ of the women's fraternal organization of the same name headquartered in Pittsburgh; *Národné noviny* (National news; 1910-), official weekly of the National Slovak Society headquartered in Pittsburgh (from 1890 to 1909 the official organ had been Rovnianek's *Amerikánsko-Slovenské noviny*); the weekly *Katolícky Sokol* (Catholic Sokol, headquartered in Passaic, N. J.); and *Ženská Jednota* (Women's Union; 1913–1975; after that *Fraternally yours*), official monthly of the First Catholic Slovak Ladies Union headquartered in Cleveland, Ohio.[13] While Slovak-Americans published only twenty-two fraternal organs between 1891 and the 1980s, they lasted an average of 40.5 years, which is the best record of survival of any of the eleven types of newspapers that Slovaks published. This record also disproves Robert E. Park's prediction that the independent commercial press would last the longest among ethnic publications in America.[14] Instead, among Slovak-Americans, the fraternal newspapers have shown the greatest resilience. They have also largely followed the nationalist line (self-determination or independence for the Slovaks) with the exception of *Slovenský Sokol* and *Slovenský Kalvín*, which have always been pro-Czechoslovak.

In addition to the three kinds of presses described above, Slovak-Americans have also had a tiny socialist (later communist) press. The first of this genre was the weekly *Robotník* (Worker; 1889) in Connellsville, Pennsylvania, but it did not survive the year and very little is known about it. The second attempt to publish a socialist newspaper was made in 1894 by the ex-Jesuit František Pucher-Čiernovodský. Entitled *Fakľa* (Torch) and printed in New York City, this monthly lasted only nine months. Finally, in 1906, a group of Slovak socialists led by Viktor Jesenský established *Rovnosť Ľudu* (Equality of the people; 1906–1935) in Chicago. It struggled to survive as a daily, monthly, and weekly, and after World War I it became a communist publication. It was succeeded by *Ľudový denník* (The people's daily; 1935–1945) and by the weekly *Ľudové noviny* (The people's news; 1945–1981). The latter two were edited by Koloman Brook.[15] Altogether, Slovak-Americans published ten socialist (after 1920 communist) newspapers between 1889 and 1981, which represent 4.6 percent of the titles published. This is hardly a number worth celebrating, and one that Marxist historians in the old country have failed to notice. They have also ignored the fact that the Slovak-American socialist/communist press has always gone counter to Slovak nationalism by stressing the "international workers' struggle."[16]

Besides those already discussed, six other types of newspapers merit attention—literary, family, humor, organizational, and youth and student publications.

Since 1885 Slovak-Americans have published eight literary journals, but only one has had a respectable run. The first was founded and edited by P. V. Rovnianek in 1894 and was entitled *Maják* (Lighthouse). Published in Pittsburgh, this monthly was patterned on an Old World model. It lasted for only six issues due to the almost complete absence of an intelligentsia among Slovak-Americans. More successful was Albert Mamatey's *Škola reči anglickej* (School of the English language; 1908–1909), published as a monthly in Pittsburgh by a self-educated mechanical engineer. It was later bound into one volume and sold as a practical grammar to Slovak immigrants. Among the six other literary journals, only *Most* (Bridge; 1954-) deserves mention. It was founded by the Reverend Ján J. Lach of Whiting, Indiana, and edited by the émigré poet-priest Mikuláš Šprinc of Cleveland, Ohio. It appears quarterly and chiefly serves a small group of intellectuals who fled Czech and communist rule of their homeland after 1945.[17] All these literary journals had a nationalist orientation; they have lasted an average of only 3.7 years. The Slovaks have yet to develop a strong literary tradition in the United States.

Family magazines have had an even worse record among American Slovaks. Only thirteen have appeared in the last century, and their average longevity has been nine months. The first was founded by Ján. A. Ferienčík in Cleveland and was entitled *Rodina* (Family). Patterned on Old World self-help and practical advice journals, this monthly did not survive a year. Ferienčik did not learn from this failure the lesson that Slovak-Americans, because of their poverty and the conditions of their lives—mothers too busy doing chores for family and boarders, and their husbands and children too exhausted after work in the mines and mills—were unlikely to subscribe to such middle-class publications. Thus, his monthly *Slovaktownské hlasy* (Slovaktown news; Pittsburgh, 1896) and his weekly *Osveta* (Enlightenment; Cleveland, 1913) also folded after less than a year. The only other such publication worthy of notice was *Úplná zdržanlivosť* (Complete abstinence; Hazleton, Pennsylvania, 1914); this temperance monthly, edited by Ján Jánošov, was the only journal of its kind ever to appear among Slovak-Americans. It died a quick death among immigrants who loved to frequent saloons and who were masters at making "home brew" during Prohibition.[18]

Humor magazines, with two exceptions, have also fared poorly among American Slovaks. Only fourteen have been published since 1896, and only two have had a long run. The first was *Rárášek* (Demon; 1896–1912), a monthly published by P. V. Rovnianek and patterned after a magazine of the same name in Slovakia. Rovnianek published it as a supplement to his *Amerikánsko-Slovenské noviny*; after he fled west in 1911, the magazine folded. The other successful humor magazine was *Zrkadlo* (Mirror; 1924–1965), a monthly supplement to *Slovenský Sokol*, published in Perth Amboy. Edited by Frank Čelko, it specialized in anti-Catholic and antinationalist humor.[19] The twelve other humor journals lasted an average of only 2.6 years. Most often the humor was too sophisticated for its working-class audience, and those magazines that were not supplements to larger newspapers did not long survive.

Organizational publications are another group of short-lived newspapers that have appeared in the last century among American Slovaks. Seventeen have seen the light of day, including two connected with workers' organizations: *Robotník* (Worker; 1904), a New York monthly, and *Pokroková Jednota* (Progressive union; 1924–1935), a weekly published by the Slovak Progressive Union of McKees Rocks, Pennsylvania. Much more important were eight publications of the Slovak League of America, the blanket organization for all the nationalist fraternal societies. They started with *Nové Slovensko* (The New Slovakia; 1918–1922), edited by Ján A. Ferienčík, among others; it was a weekly published in Pittsburgh. This, and subsequent Slovak League publications, such as *Bulletin Slovenskej Ligy v Amerike* (Bulletin of the Slovak League of America; 1935–1937), a monthly edited by its president, Peter P. Hletko, in Pittsburgh, and the monthly *Slovenská Liga* (Slovak league; 1948), edited by its president, Peter P. Yurchak, in Passaic, New Jersey, championed the right of Slovaks in Europe to self-determination and/or independence. Less important was the *Československý Legionár* (Czechoslovak legionnaire; 1920–1926), a monthly published by and for former members of the World War I Czechoslovak Legions, and *Roduverný Slovák* (The faithful Slovak; 1940–1942), published monthly in Chicago by the Slovak National Council (a "Pro-Czechoslovak" organization) and edited by Reverend Jaroslav Pelikán, Sr.[20] Since these seventeen periodicals lasted only an average of 2.3 years, they have had a minimal impact on Slovak-American journalism.

Finally, Slovak-Americans have also published fourteen periodicals for youth and students; these have shown a greater propensity for survival. The Slovak

Catholic Sokol, which was always a youth-oriented fraternal society, established the *Priateľ dietok* (Friend of children; 1911-) as a monthly supplement to its weekly newspaper in Passaic. The National Slovak Society followed suit with its own monthly, *Kruh mládeže* (Young folks' circle; 1915–1934 and intermittently thereafter), in Pittsburgh, as did the First Catholic Slovak Union with its weekly, *Jaro* (Spring 1921–1964), in Middletown, Pennsylvania. Similarly, the Slovak Evangelical Synod published a monthly, *Mladý Luterán* (Young Lutheran; 1918–1941), in Streator, Illinois.[21] These and four other youth papers had an average life of twenty years.

As the second generation of Slovak-Americans began to mature and attend school, newspapers for their benefit also appeared. Three high schools led the way in this venture. The first, St. Procopius College in Lisle, Illinois, which was run by Czech Benedictines, attracted Slovak boys starting in World War I; by 1922 they had established *Študentská horlivosť* (Student zeal; 1922–1923), which appeared ten times a year. It was replaced in 1923 by *Furdek* (named after Reverend Štefan Furdek), published by the Federation of Slovak Catholic Students in the United States, in Middletown, Pennsylvania, until 1941. Jozef Konuš, who later made his reputation as a compiler of Slovak-English dictionaries, was its first editor. The second, a Slovak girls' high school, run by the Sisters of Sts. Cyril and Methodius in Danville, Pennsylvania, published the quarterly *Fialky* (Violets) by and for students from 1923 to 1970. The third, a high school for boys, was run by a group of Slovak Benedictines in Cleveland; between 1931 and 1976 they published the monthly *Benedicitine* under the initial editorship of Reverend Andrew Pier.[22] These and other student newspapers lasted an average of thirty years. All of them had a nationalist orientation.

Having surveyed the eleven kinds of periodicals published by Slovak-Americans since 1885, we can now take a closer look at its editors and publishers. The first generation consisted partly of adults who had immigrated in the 1880s and early 1890s and who founded and built up the Slovak-American press. Among them were P. V. Rovnianek, Štefan Furdek, Gustáv Maršall-Petrovský, and Ján A. Ferienčík. Most of these pioneers, some of whose careers we have already traced, died in the early twentieth century. A second age cohort succeeded them—immigrants who had come as children in the 1890s or as adults after 1900. Among them were Ján Pankuch, Jozef Hušek, Ivan Bielek, Jaroslav Pelikán, Sr., and Milan Getting. The older cohort ceased to have much influence over the Slovak-American press after World War I, and was replaced by the younger cohort.

Although the fortunes of three members of the younger group have been discussed, more needs to be said about Jozef Hušek and Ivan Bielek. Hušek became editor of the Catholic fraternal weekly *Jednota* in 1911 and remained in this post until 1937. While editor he exerted an enormous influence over the First Catholic Slovak Union (FCSU), the Czecho-Slovak liberation movement of World War I, and the struggle for Slovak autonomy and independence between 1918 and his death in 1947. Hušek's fraternal society and his newspaper represented the largest single bloc of Slovak-Americans, and he personally had a hand in the drafting of the Pittsburgh Agreement of 1918 wherein T. G. Masaryk, the future president of Czechoslovakia, promised the Slovaks home rule in that state. After Masaryk went back on his word, Hušek waged a relentless editorial war against him and the centralist government of the interwar Czechoslovak Republic. In 1937 Hušek resigned as editor and ran for the presidency of the FCSU, hoping to steer it more purposefully toward the cause of Slovak autonomy in Czechoslovakia. After he lost the election he privately published an independent semimonthly named *Stráž* (Guard; Palmyra, Pennsylvania, 1938), but it folded after less than a year. He then became editor of the independent weekly *Obrana*, which took a pro-Slovak independence stand during World War II, a position it continued to champion until its demise in 1972.[23] Hušek is now revered by champions of Slovak independence, particularly by those who fled their homeland for the United States after 1945.

Ivan Bielek, in contrast, has not received the recognition that he has deserved among his countrymen. The son of a Slovak editor and patriot who was hounded into insanity by the Hungarian government, Ivan came to the United States in 1906 and by 1912 had become editor of *Národné noviny*, the newly established official organ of the National Slovak Society. He carefully edited this influential weekly throughout the war, participated in the Czechoslovak liberation movement, and became outraged when the centralist Czechoslovak government repudiated the Pittsburgh Agreement. He became president of the Slovak League of America in 1920 and for the next decade deluged Prague with memorandums demanding that T. G. Masaryk implement the home rule that he had promised the Slovaks. He continued to expound on this theme in the 1930s and 1940s when he edited the weekly *Bratstvo*, the official organ of the Pennsylvania Slovak Catholic Union. He died in 1943, rejoicing that the Slovaks had at last achieved their independence, albeit under German protection, in 1939.[24]

While both Hušek and Bielek were still active, a new generation of editors slowly began to take over the Slovak-American press. These were the sons of immigrants who, with one exception, were born in the United States and were fluent in both Slovak and English. Nationalists to a man, they gradually took the reins of the press; while they did not bring any new or radical philosophy to their profession, they did eventually bow to reality and begin to publish bilingual versions of their newspapers. Among them were John C. Sciranka, Edward Kováč, Jr., Peter P. Hletko, Filip Hrobak, Reverend Andrew V. Pier, and Joseph C. Krajsa.

John C. Sciranka (1902–1980) was the epitome of Slovak "ethnic" editors. Born in Pittsburgh, he began his journalistic career at age ten by sending letters to the editors of the youth magazines *Priateľ dietok* and *Jaro*. In 1922 he became an assistant editor of the weekly *Jednota* and in 1924 moved up to the editorship of the daily *Slovák v Amerike*. However, in the late 1920s and 1930s he became involved in some land speculation on Long Island and ended up in jail for a few years. In the 1940s he again became editor of *Slovák v Amerike*. In the 1950s he was assistant editor of *Katolícky Sokol*, becoming editor of this important weekly in the early 1960s. Meanwhile, he also published the occasional *Slovak Manor Obzor* (Slovak manor overview; New York, 1929), to publicize his land dealings, as well as a weekly independent, *Slovák* (New York, 1934), to try to defend his activities, and an occasional issue of *Slovak Democrat* (New York, 1933) to try to ingratiate himself with the party of the future. An inveterate joiner and fraternalist, he attended over seventy conventions and gave rousing speeches at many of them. His death ended a very colorful career in the world of Slovak-American journalism.[25]

Very different has been the life of his contemporary Edward Kováč, Jr. Born in Slovakia in 1901, he was brought to the United States in 1903 and educated here. He returned with his family to Slovakia in 1921 and came back to the United States in 1925. He became editor of *Slovák v Amerike* in 1926 and held that post until 1938, when he went to work for *New Yorský deník*. Disillusioned by that newspaper's "Czechoslovak" stand, he returned to the nationalist camp in 1943 as assistant editor of *Obrana*; he was its editor from 1947 to 1972. After it ceased publication he became editor of *Národné noviny*. The latter is now a bilingual monthly edited by the perfectly bilingual Kováč. He is also the author of several books and Slovak-English dictionaries and is now considered the dean of Slovak-American journalists.[26]

More politically active and controversial was Peter P. Hletko. Born in Chicago in 1902, he studied with the Czech Benedictines in Lisle, Illinois, and eventually received an M. D. from Loyola University in Chicago. His newspaper career began in 1927 as editor of the youth magazine *Jaro* (to 1936) and also as contributing editor of the Chicago weekly *Osadné hlasy* (Parish voices; 1927–1963). In 1935 he was elected president of the Slovak League of America, and in 1938 he brought the original of the Pittsburgh Agreement to Slovakia and helped his countrymen to achieve their long-sought autonomy. He published several pamphlets in defense of the Pittsburgh Agreement and, although he remained a champion of Slovak independence after World War II, he had a stormy relationship with post–World War II political émigrés. He was personally responsible for the dismissal in 1959 of Konštantín Čulen from the directorship of the Slovak Institute in Cleveland. This was a great blow to Slovak journalism and scholarship because Čulen, besides having been a first-rate journalist in Slovakia, was also the first historian of American Slovaks. He died in poverty in 1964, and his manuscript *Slovenské časopisy v Amerike* (Slovak newspapers in America), from which the bulk of the information in this account was taken, was published posthumously in an uneven version in 1970.[27]

Filip A. Hrobak became the patron of Slovak political émigrés after 1945. Born in Cleveland in 1904 and orphaned at an early age, he was the first orphan taken into the care of the newly established order of Sts. Cyril and Methodius in 1911. Educated at St. Procopius College and New York University, he became a teacher at Benedictine High School in Cleveland in 1929. While there he published a Slovak grammar and dictionary and in 1937 was elected editor of

Jednota. Having supported the Slovak Republic (1939–1945), he welcomed with open arms the political refugees from that state after it had been destroyed by the Red Army. He also served as president of the Slovak League of America from 1950 to 1964 and published the English-language quarterly (later annual) *Slovakia* (1950–) and the monthly English-language political tract *Slovak Newsletter* (Middletown, Pennsylvania, 1949–1958).[28] His death in 1964 was a severe loss to Slovak-American journalism, particularly to supporters of the Slovak independence movement.

A close friend and collaborator of Filip Hrobak was Reverend Andrew V. Pier. Born in Blandburg, Pennsylvania, in 1909, he was educated at St. Procopius College and joined the Slovak Benedictines in the early 1930s. He began his journalistic career in 1931 when he launched and edited the monthly *Benedictine* (Cleveland, 1931–1976) for students of his high school. During World War II he translated František Hrušovský's *History of the Slovaks* into English in the weekly *Jednota*. In 1949 he became editor of the weekly *Slovenské noviny* (Slovak news; Cleveland, 1949–1959), which also employed the talents of the historians František Hrušovský and Konštantín Čulen and the émigré poets Karol Strmeň and Mikuláš Šprinc. After the paper folded Pier began to edit the monthly *Ave Maria* (1917-) and contributed a column entitled "Slovak News and Views," first to *Katolícky Sokol*, and since 1960 to *Jednota*. With his acerbic comments, Pier has remained a gadfly in the world of Slovak-American journalism, particularly on the question of Slovak independence. He will not compromise on this point and has become more staunchly nationalist than many of the nationalists who fled their country in 1945.[29]

More tolerant of diversity, and, ironically, more religiously oriented than Reverend Pier, is Joseph C. Krajsa. Born in Allentown, Pennsylvania, in 1917, and educated at Pennsylvania State University, he taught high school and then worked in a savings and loan institution. In the 1950s he became an active fraternalist, particularly in the First Catholic Slovak Union. In 1964 he was elected editor of *Jednota*, a position which he still holds. Under his editorship this influential weekly has become completely bilingual and more Catholic and fraternal-oriented than nationalist. After the death of Jozef Paučo in 1975 Krajsa also assumed responsibility for *Slovák v Amerike*. Although Krajsa's son Michael is ostensibly the publisher, it is really Joseph Krajsa, with the help of Paučo's widow Draga, who is keeping this oldest Slovak newspaper in America, now a monthly, alive.[30]

A number of Slovak intellectuals immigrated to the United States after the collapse of the Slovak Republic in 1945. While they helped to inject new blood into Slovak-American journalism, they also brought with them a great deal of controversy. The most important of these political émigrés was Jozef Paučo. Holder of a Ph.D. in history from the Comenius University in Bratislava, and editor (1942–1945) of the daily *Slovák*, the official organ of the ruling Hlinka Slovak People's Party, Paučo was one of the most important supporters of Slovak independence from the Czechs to go into exile. From 1945 to 1950 he lived in

West Germany and published several pro-independence newspapers there. In 1950 he moved to the United States and immediately began to assist Filip Hrobak in the editing of *Jednota*. In 1958 Paučo became editor and in 1964 publisher of the weekly *Slovák v Amerike*, which remained in his control until 1975. Meanwhile, he also wrote a host of books, published a series of almanacs, organized the American branch of the Slovak National Council Abroad, and for two decades served as secretary of the Slovak League of America. Paučo reached the pinnacle of his influence when Richard Nixon, in his first term as president, appointed him Slovak advisor for the Ethnic Affairs Division of the Republican National Committee. However, the "muckraking" columnist Jack Anderson, prodded by Paučo's enemies, persuaded Nixon to drop him from this advisory body, accusing Paučo of having had a pro-Nazi past. Paučo denied these charges until his death in 1975.[31]

Paučo's major rivals and enemies included the émigrés Juraj Slávik and Martin Kvetko. Both of these proponents of "Czechoslovakism" fled to the West after the communist takeover of Czechoslovakia in 1948. They waged editorial war upon Paučo and his nationalists, Slávik in his semimonthly *Čas* (Time; Washington, D.C., 1950–1959) and Kvetko in his semimonthly *Naše snahy* (Our aspirations; Chicago, 1965-). To try to offset Paučo's pro-Slovak independence organizations they also established the Council for a Free Czechoslovakia.[32] Their overall influence on American Slovaks has been slight.

In the 1980s the Slovak-American press entered a new stage in its existence. The second generation began to die off or reach retirement age, and the third generation is about to take over. This has already happened with the *Katolícky Sokol* where, after John C. Sciranka's death in 1980, ex-seminarian Daniel F. Tanzone became editor. The émigré John F. Holy, who is also secretary-treasurer of the Slovak League of America, assists Tanzone with the ever-shrinking Slovak-language portion of the paper. The weekly *Jednota* and the now monthly *Národné noviny* are actively seeking new editors as their veterans prepare to retire. *Slovák v Amerike* has been without a full-time editor for many years. It appears likely that the Slovak-American press will soon become almost exclusively English-language because most members of the third generation cannot write in Slovak. It will probably survive in this altered form if it continues to report news from Slovak communities across the country, something which the mass-circulation English-language press has never done. As long as the Slovaks maintain some form of ethnic identity in the United States, they will continue to have their own press.

Having surveyed the kinds of newspapers that Slovak-Americans published and the people who published them, it may now be worthwhile to complete our demographic profile of this press.

Pennsylvania, and especially the Pittsburgh region, is the largest center of Slovak-American publishing. Twenty-six percent of all Slovak-American newspapers published since 1885 have originated in the Pittsburgh region, and 41 percent in the Commonwealth of Pennsylvania. Chicago is a distant second with

15.7 percent of the total (the region of Illinois, Wisconsin, and Minnesota totaled 20.3 percent); Cleveland, with 14.3 percent, third (Ohio, Indiana, and Michigan had 18.4 percent); and New York City, with 11 percent, fourth (New York, New Jersey, and Connecticut had 17.6 percent). These totals roughly correspond to the location of major Slovak settlements as revealed in the 1920 census, which recorded 619,866 first- and second-generation Slovaks living in the United States, with 296,219 (almost half) in Pennsylvania.[33]

In terms of the kinds of newspapers published by Slovak-Americans, weeklies and monthlies dominated. Of 217 newspapers for which information is available, 89 (41 percent) were monthlies; 87 (40 percent) were weeklies; 15 (7 percent) were dailies; 12 (5.5 percent) were semimonthlies; 12 (5.5 percent) were quarterlies or occasionals; and 2 (1 percent) were semiweekly. Weeklies and monthlies each lasted an average of 40 years; the dailies 7 years; the semimonthlies 5.6 years; the quarterlies or occasionals 5.6 years; and the semiweeklies less than a year. The most viable Slovak-American newspapers, therefore, were the weeklies and monthlies; these were, typically, the fraternal organs.

Moreover, looking at the duration of 217 Slovak-American newspapers for which information is available it quickly becomes apparent that the rate of survival has not been high. Seventy-three (33.6 percent) lasted less than one year; 36 (16.6 percent) lasted one to two years; 16 (7.4 percent) lasted two to three years; five (2.3 percent) lasted three to four years; and six (2.8 percent) lasted four to five years. In other words, 50 percent of all Slovak-American newspapers lasted less than two years and 66 percent lasted less than seven years. Only two newspapers (*Slovák v Amerike* and *Jednota*) have survived for more than ninety years.

Another interesting pattern emerges when the founding and folding dates of Slovak-American newspapers are examined. Of 217 newspapers for which information is available, more than half (56.2 percent) were founded before 1919, with the decade 1910–1919 producing the largest number: sixty-one, or 28.1 percent. Similarly, the largest number that folded (43, or 20 percent) also fell in the decade 1910–1919. Even though large numbers of papers folded, the numbers that were founded and survived kept ahead of those that folded until the decade of the 1960s, when six were founded and seven folded. Since then the number folding has kept ahead of the number founded and, therefore, a slow period of decline has set in.

This pattern is confirmed by the absolute number of Slovak-American newspapers, by decade, starting in 1885. That year there was only one Slovak-American newspaper. In 1895 there were twelve; in 1905 there were twelve; in 1915 there were thirty-four; in 1925 there were forty-three; in 1935 there were fifty (the peak year was 1936, when Slovak-Americans published fifty-one newspapers); in 1945 there were thirty-nine; in 1955 there were thirty-eight; in 1965 there were thirty-two; and in 1975 there were thirty-one. This pattern again diverges from Robert E. Park's contention that the ethnic press peaked in the 1920s and would then precipitously decline. Instead, the Slovak press grew and peaked in the 1930s and has since only very slowly declined. Joshua Fishman's observation that the ethnic press "would seem to have more lives than the proverbial cat" is more reflective of reality.[34]

A final comparison, with the Slovak press in Europe, is also instructive. In 1885, when Slovak-Americans established their first newspaper, Slovaks in Hungary had twelve. By 1914 Slovaks in Europe had sixty-one periodicals, while those in the United States had thirty. By 1918, however, due to war censorship, Slovaks had only thirty newspapers in their homeland, while their kinsmen in the New World had forty-one.[35] Furthermore, the total circulation of the Slovak press in America at this time was around 150,000, whereas in Hungary it was only around 40,000.[36] Since there were four times as many Slovaks in Europe as there were in America, these figures are surprising. They testify to the social, political, and economic oppression that the Slovaks suffered under Hungarian rule and also to the importance that the Slovak press (and Slovak people) in America would play as surrogates for their oppressed countrymen in the World War I liberation movement. How this situation partly corrected itself after the creation of Czechoslovakia in 1918 is evident in the fact that the Slovaks, in relative freedom, published 980 newspapers in the short period 1919–1938 (versus 220 in the United States between 1885 and 1984).[37]

Since 1885, therefore, the Slovak-American press has served the interests of most of the political, social, economic, religious, and generational groupings that have appeared in this ethnic group's principal areas of settlement. The press's greatest strength in terms of longevity lay in its fraternal, student, youth, and religious publications. So far two generations of editors have spawned and nourished the press, which had its greatest growth just before and during World War I, and which peaked in 1936. Pennsylvania, and especially Pittsburgh, formed the heartland of the Slovak-American press, with smaller concentrations in Illinois, Ohio, and the New York-New Jersey area. Moreover, the Slovak-American press played an important role in fostering the spirit of nationalism, both before and after World War I, and continues to do so today.

While Konštantín Čulen did an admirable job in gathering titles and writing an annotated bibliography of the Slovak-American press, much remains to be done. Historians need to read the extant newspapers and prepare a content analysis of them. While we know from Čulen what Slovak editors' political leanings were, we know little of what they had to say about American society in general. Slovak-American newspapers, therefore, need to be utilized as the valuable source of social history that they undoubtedly are. This task, like that of taking over the Slovak-American press itself, remains as a challenge for the third generation.

NOTES

1. I arrived at this number by counting the titles listed in Konštantín Čulen's *Slovenské časopisy v Amerike* (Cleveland: The First Catholic Slovak Union, 1970), which is the most authoritative work on the subject. Čulen listed 246 titles. However, I found that he

either did not verify or else listed some titles that should not have appeared, so I subtracted 39 titles from his list. I also discovered that Čulen had missed 13 titles listed by Michal Lacko in his *Bibliografica I* and *II*, published in *Slovak Studies* 7 (1967) and 17 (1975) (Rome; Slovak Institute). Therefore, I added Lacko's 13 titles to Čulen's 207 and arrived at the figure 220. There probably have been more than 220 titles since 1885 but they remain to be discovered and verified.

2. The classification of the Slovak-American press was done by its first historian, Konštantín Čulen, in the book cited above. He divided the press into the following categories: literary, independent, fraternal, organizational, religious, humor, family, student, youth, socialist, communist.

The numbers and percentages of the types of newspapers discussed throughout this essay come from my analysis of Čulen's book. Čulen died before he could properly sort and arrange his entries, and Jozef Paučo subsequently published the manuscript basically as he found it—in alphabetical order by title. I took the book apart and grouped it by the classification given above. Under each heading I listed every appropriate paper alphabetically, by place of origin, by date of founding and folding, by frequency of publication, by publisher and editor, and by political and religious orientation. I used these headings because they best reflected the kind of information that Čulen gave about each paper, when he could. I then turned this information over to an advanced graduate student of sociology at Temple University, Dale Drews. With the help of an SPSS program, he cross-tabulated the information for me on a computer.

3. Ján A. Ferienčík, "Slovenské prisťahovalectvo a slovenská spisba v Amerike," *Sborník Národného Slovenského Spolku* 1 (1915): 22; and Konštantín Čulen, *J. Slovenský: Životopis zakladateľa prvých slovenských novín v Amerike* (Winnipeg: Canadian Slovak Printing and Publishing Co., 1954), pp. 88–106.

4. Čulen, *J. Slovenský*, pp. 106–131; Čulen, *Slovenské časopisy*, p. 19: and Ladislav Tajták, "K začiatkam Amerikánsko-Slovenských novín," in Josef Polišensky, ed., *Začiatky českej a slovenskej emigrácie do USA* (Bratislava: Slovenská akadémia vied, 1970), pp. 186–196.

5. Čulen, *Slovenské časopisy*, pp. 83–84, 176–181.

6. Ibid., pp. 19–21; N. W. Ayer & Son, *Directory of Newspapers and Periodicals in the United States* (Philadelphia: N. W. Ayer & Son, 1889); Fraňo Ruttkay, *Prehľad dejín Slovenského novinárstva do Roku 1918* (Bratislava: Filozofická fakulta Univerzity Komenského, 1968 and 1979), p. 267; P. V. Rovnianek, *Zápisky za živa pochovaného* (Pittsburgh: P. V. Rovnianek, 1924). Ayer's *Directory*, 1910, gave the circulation of *Slovák v Amerike*, the principal rival of *Amerikánsko-Slovenské noviny*, as 36,000. From this figure I have estimated that it had a circulation of 40,000 because it was always just a bit larger than its closest rival.

7. Čulen, *Slovenské časopisy*, pp. 120–126.

8. Ibid. pp. 39, 44–46; Ján Pankuch, *Dejiny Clevelandských a Lakewoodských Slovákov* (Cleveland: Hlas Publishing Co., 1930); Jozef Paučo, *Slovenskí priekopníci v Amerike* (Cleveland: The First Catholic Slovak Union, 1972), pp. 299–308.

9. Čulen, *Slovenské časopisy*, p. 39; Paučo, *Slovenskí priekopníci*, pp. 64–71.

10. Čulen, *Slovenské časopisy*, pp. 63–65; Paučo, *Slovenskí priekopníci*, pp. 150–198.

11. Čulen, *Slovenské časopisy*, pp. 85–86; Paučo, *Slovenskí priekopníci*, pp. 137–138; see also Milan Getting, *Americkí Slováci a vývin československej myšlienky v rokoch 1914–1918* (New York: Slovenská Telocvičná Jednota Sokol v Amerike, 1933). Čulen

spelled the title of this newspaper correctly, according to the rules of Slovak grammar. The publishers, however, always misspelled it.

12. Čulen, *Slovenské časopisy*, pp. 55–56, 164, 113, 40.

13. Paučo, *Slovenskí priekopníci*, pp. 72–127; Čulen, *Slovenské časopisy*, pp. 51–54, 27–29, 151–152, 157–158, 152–153; 185, 75–77, 58–59, 183–184; Lacko, *Bibliografica I*, pp. 33, 32; *Bibliografica II*, pp. 25, 31.

14. Robert E. Park, *The Immigrant Press and Its Control* (1922; repr. Montclair, N. J.: Patterson Smith, 1971), p. 328.

15. Čulen, *Slovenské časopisy*, pp. 101, 41–42, 104–107, 68–69; *Encyklopédia Slovenská, II* (Bratislava: Slovenská akadémia vied, 1978), p. 518; (1981), p. 151; Miloš Gosiorovský, "František Pucher-Čiernovodský a robotnícke hnutie," in Polišensky, *Začiatky*, pp. 197–207.

16. Miloš Gosiorovský, "Americkí Slováci a vznik Československa," in *Slováci v zahraničí* 1 (1971): 19–30.

17. Čulen, *Slovenské časopisy*, pp. 70–71, 166–167, 72–74; Paučo, *Slovenskí priekopníci*, pp. 315–321, 269–275; *Literárny almanach Slováka v Amerike* (hereafter *Literárny almanach*), 1967, pp. 232–233.

18. Čulen, *Slovenské časopisy*, pp. 102, 127, 170.

19. Ibid., pp. 100–101, 183; Čulen gave the wrong date (1919) for its founding.

20. Ibid., pp. 101, 97, 92–93, 32–33, 128, 37–38, 102–104.

21. Ibid., pp. 99–100, 65, 51, 74–75.

22. Ibid., pp. 167–168, 44, 43; Lacko, *Bibliografica I*, p. 24.

23. Jozef Paučo, *75 rokov Prvej Katolíckej Slovenskej Jednoty* (Cleveland: First Catholic Slovak Union, 1965), pp. 93–364; Jozef Hušek, "Prehlad vážnejších udalostí v histórii I. Kat. Slovenskej Jednoty," *Kalendár Jednota* (1931), p. 68; Paučo, *Slovenskí priekopníci*, pp. 150–198; Čulen, *Slovenské časopisy*, pp. 163–164, 129–130, 51–54.

24. Paučo, *Slovenskí priekopníci*, pp. 25–28; Ivan Bielek, "Len tak letmo cez dejiny minulého roku," *Národný Kalendár* (1924), p. 167; Čulen, *Slovenské časopisy*, pp. 75–77, 27–29.

25. *Literárny almanach* (1967), pp. 218–219; Čulen, *Slovenské časopisy*, pp. 126, 58, 119, 118.

26. *Literárny almanach* (1967), pp. 174–175; Čulen, *Slovenské časopisy*, pp. 126, 129.

27. *Literárny almanach* (1967), pp. 154–155, 129–130; Čulen, *Slovenské časopisy*, pp. 51, 94–95; Konštantín Čulen, "V zajatí falošných legiend a nenávistneho srdca" (New York: author's mimeographed publication, 1961).

28. *Literárny almanach* (1967), pp. 157–158; Čulen, *Slovenské časopisy*, pp. 54, 192.

29. *Literárny almanach* (1967), pp. 206–207; Lacko, *Bibliografica I*, p. 24; Čulen, *Slovenské časopisy*, pp. 137–138, 25.

30. *Literárny almanach* (1967), pp. 175–176.

31. Ibid., pp. 200–202; Anderson's attacks on Paučo can be found in the *Evening Bulletin* (Philadelphia), September 24, 1971; October 25, 1971; and November 10, 1971. A forceful reply by Michael Krajsa appeared in *Slovák v Amerike*, May 12, 1976.

32. *Literárny almanach* (1967), pp. 223–224; Lacko, *Bibliografica I*, pp. 24–25; *Bibliografica II*, p. 29.

33. *U. S. Census, Fourteenth, 1920, Population* (Washington: United States Printing Office, 1922), 2:973.

34. Park, *Immigrant Press*, p. 326; Joshua A. Fishman, *Language Loyalty in the United States* (The Hague: Mouton & Co., 1966), p. 51.

35. Michal Potemra, *Bibliografia slovenských novín a časopisov do roku 1918* (Martin: Matica slovenská, 1958), pp. 119–120, 125, 126.

36. Ayer, *Directory*, 1910, listed only ten of the-then-existing 24 Slovak newspapers in America and it gave circulations for only five—*Slovák v Amerike* (36,000); *Jednota* (15,000); *Hlas* (6,000); *Slovenský denník* (5,000); *Slovenské noviny* (3,750). The total of these five was 67,750. For some unknown reason Ayer missed *Amerikánsko-Slovenské noviny* until 1920 when it had only 15,000 subscribers. As I pointed out in footnote 6, *Amerikánsko-Slovenské noviny* had an estimated 40,000 subscribers in 1910. If we add this figure to the 67,750 given above, we arrive at 107,750 for only five newspapers. It is safe to estimate that the rest of the 19 newspapers had a total circulation of 42,250 or more, making a grand total circulation of 150,000 or more in 1910. For the circulation of Slovak newspapers in Hungary in 1910 see Owen V. Johnson, "Sociocultural and National Development in Slovakia 1918–1938, Education and Its Impact," Ph.D. diss., University of Michigan, 1978.

37. Mári Kipsová et. al., *Bibliografia slovenských a inorečových novín a časopisov z rokov 1919–1938* (Martin: Matica slovenská, 1968), pp. 125–558.

BIBLIOGRAPHY

Ayer, N. W. & Son. *Directory of Newspapers and Periodicals in the United States.* Philadelphia: N. W. Ayer & Son, 1899–1984.

Čulen, Konštantín. *J. Slovenský: Životopis zakladateĺa prvých slovenských novín v Amerike.* Winnipeg: Canadian Slovak Printing and Publishing Co., 1954.

———. *Slovenské časopisy v Amerike.* Cleveland: The First Catholic Slovak Union, 1970.

Ferienčík, Ján A. "Slovenské prisťahovalectvo a slovenská spisba v Amerike." *Sborník Národného Slovenského Spolku* 2 (1915), pp. 20–39.

Fishman, Joshua A. *Language Loyalty in the United States.* The Hague: Mouton & Co., 1966.

Kipsová, Mária et al. *Bibliografia slovenských a inorečových novín a časopisov z rokov 1919–1938.* Martin: Matica slovenská, 1968.

Lacko, Michal, ed. *Bibliografica I and II. Slovak Studies* 7 (1967) and 17 (1975). Rome, Slovak Institute.

Park, Robert E. *The Immigrant Press and Its Control.* 1922. Reprint. Montclair, N. J.: Patterson Smith, 1971.

Paučo, Jozef. *Slovenskí priekopníci v Amerike.* Cleveland: The First Catholic Slovak Union, 1972.

Potemra, Michal. *Bibliografia slovenských novín a časopisov do roku 1918.* Martin: Matica slovenská, 1958.

Rovnianek, P. V. *Zápisky za živa pochovaného.* Pittsburgh: P. V. Rovnianek, 1924.

Ruttkay, Fraňo. *Prehĺad dejín Slovenského novinárstva do roku 1918.* Bratislava: Filozofická fakulta Univerzity Komenského, 1968 and 1979.

Tajták, Ladislav. "K začiatkam Amerikánsko-Slovenských novín." In Jozef Polišensky, ed., *Začiatky českej a slovenskej emigrácie do USA* (Bratislava: Slovenská akadémia vied, 1970).

25

The Slovene–American Press

JOSEPH D. DWYER

The Slovene people, one of the numerous Slavic nationalities, are a part of the South Slavic group.[1] Their homeland at the northeastern corner of the Adriatic Sea forms a small triangle wedged in between the Croatians, Italians, and Austrians. They have always been a relatively small national group, even today numbering somewhat less than 2 million persons. Presently they inhabit the territory of the Socialist Republic of Slovenia within the Socialist Federative Republic of Yugoslavia. In addition, the Slovenes are found as a minority group in adjacent areas of Italy and Austria.

Most Slovenes who migrated to the United States came either before 1918, when Slovene lands were a part of the Austro-Hungarian Empire, or between 1918 and 1925, when they formed a part of the Kingdom of Serbs, Croats, and Slovenes, later called the Kingdom of Yugoslavia.

The earliest Slovenes to reach North America arrived at the beginning of the nineteenth century. They were few in number (perhaps only a dozen or two) and consisted of missionaries, explorers, and merchants. There are only minimal traces left to document the presence of most of them. Certain of the missionaries, for example Reverend Friedrich (Frederik) Baraga (who eventually became bishop of Upper Michigan), Reverend Francis X. Pierz, and their followers, such as Reverend Joseph Buh, have left contributions which are more widely known. These pioneers were followed in the second half of the nineteenth century by small groups of settlers, primarily farmers, who found their way to Pennsylvania, Ohio, and Minnesota; some were also attracted to the early industries around Chicago. With the development of industry generally, and iron and coal mining specifically, the pattern began to change. At first the Slovene settlers already in the United States began moving from farms to mining and industrial centers. An example of this was the movement of Slovene farmers as a group from the area around St. Stephen in central Minnesota to the Mesabi iron range in the far north of the state in the early 1890s. Similar movements took place in Pennsylvania and other states. Before long, the news of employment opportunities spread back to the homeland, setting in motion a relatively large flow of Slovene immigrants, just as it did for most other Eastern and Southern European peoples. In fact, the vast majority of all Slovene immigrants came to the United States during the forty-four-year period between 1880 and 1924, when the quota system went into effect and decreased the possibilities for immigration.

Another, smaller wave of immigration followed World War II, when a few thousand Slovene refugees arrived from Europe. Though small in number, these refugees were generally more educated than previous immigrants, and therefore had a significant effect on the intellectual life of the ethnic community.

It is very difficult to estimate the actual number of Slovenes who came to America and stayed. For a thousand years Slovene lands had been under Germanic domination. As a result, ethnic consciousness, though present, was quite undefined in nature. The people usually referred to themselves as Austrians, Krainers (from the name of the province, Kranjska or Carniola, Krain, in German), or Slavonians, and only rarely as Slovenes. Early U. S. immigration statistics were kept according to country of origin, which for the Slovenes was Austria. In addition, the Slovenes were often grouped together with Croatians and other Slavs and labeled Croatians or Austrian Slavs. Beyond this problem of just how many Slovenes entered the United States, there is the further problem of exactly how many stayed. Again, the answer can never be known for sure. It is clear that a significant portion of the immigrants did return to the old country after a period of earning and saving in the United States.

During this era of industrial immigration Slovenes settled in the large cities of the eastern part of the country—New York, Pittsburgh, Cleveland, Toledo, Detroit, Chicago, and Milwaukee. Smaller numbers also settled in the new mining and industrial centers of the Midwest, in the Rockies, and in the West. They located in such areas as Upper Michigan, the iron range of Minnesota, and in the mining areas of Kansas, Colorado, Utah, Wyoming, Montana, California, and Washington. Seldom did they represent the majority of the population in any of these areas. Scattered communities developed in Calumet, Michigan; Ely and Chisholm, Minnesota; Leadville and Pueblo, Colorado; Frontenac, Kansas; Helper, Utah; and Rock Springs, Wyoming. Individual Slovene families could be found on farms in Michigan, Minnesota, Pennsylvania, Illinois, Kansas, and Colorado, but very rarely in the Dakotas or in the southern states.

A figure for the number of persons of Slovene heritage currently in the United States can only be a rough estimate. Such estimates range from 150,000 to over 500,000. They are based on several factors: emigration and immigration statistics, membership in fraternal organizations, church membership, subscriptions to Slovene publications, and pure guesswork. A figure of some 200,000 seems to be the most reasonable approximation.

Immigrants arriving in America in the late nineteenth century were often characterized as illiterate, uneducated, and basically unskilled workers. It was believed that they had neither desire nor ability for anything beyond manual labor and a decent wage. To be sure, they were outside the general English-language community, but the various ethnic communities, including that of the

Slovenes, each had its own life, consisting of family, religious, and cultural ties. One important manifestation of these close ties was the development of each group's own ethnic newspapers, periodicals, and other publications.

The places of publication of the Slovene-American press clearly reflect the geography of settlement. The birth of Slovene journalism in America took place in Chicago, where some of the earliest Slovene immigrants to the continent had settled. More than forty years passed, however, between the first such settlement in Chicago in the 1840s and the founding of the first newspaper in 1891.

The Slovenes who established the first newspaper on this side of the Atlantic, a weekly called *Amerikanski Slovenec* (The American Slovene), had themselves lived in Chicago for more than a decade. They were a group who came mostly from one Slovene town, Bela Krajina. As a result they regularly got together at one or another's home for entertainment and to exchange news and ideas. They were skilled craftsmen, some of whom had traveled a bit in Europe. Many were to some extent self-educated. Among them were Frank Zalokar from Metlika, his three daughters, who had married men from Črnomelj (near Bela Krajina), Ivan Lesar, Alojzij Skubic, and Jože Verščaj. Constantly in association with them were two others, Anton Murnik, a former Austrian officer from Gorenje who boasted of knowing how to write, and Ivan Grilec from Litija, who also had some secondary schooling in the old country and was considered educated.

At that time the Slovene colony in Chicago was located between Halsted and Centre along 18th Street and in the surrounding neighborhood. Murnik took charge of the editorship and management, while Grilec, who wrote articles and short stories, was designated as assistant editor. Frank Zalokar, his three daughters and sons-in-law, and many friends helped advertise the new publication by writing to all known addresses of other Slovenes across America.

Only ten numbers of *Amerikanski Slovenec* were published in Chicago, however. The field of journalism proved to be too difficult for Murnik and his small group. Murnik sold the paper to a Catholic missionary priest, a Slovene, Reverend Joseph F. Buh, of Tower, Minnesota, where four months later, in March 1892, the eleventh issue of *Amerikanski Slovenec* appeared. In Buh's hands the paper became strongly religious. The new owner and editor attempted to get as many members of the Slovene-American clergy as possible to write for his paper. For seven years the paper came out as a weekly in Tower, until toward the end of 1899, when Buhn sold it to a new owner in Joliet, Illinois.

In the meantime, in 1893, more than a year after the founding of *Amerikanski Slovenec*, the second Slovene weekly in America, *Glas Naroda* (The people's voice) began to appear in New York City. It was founded, edited, and financed from the beginning by Frank Sakser, who had studied printing at the National Printery (Narodna Tiskarna) in Ljubljana.

The two Slovene-American newspapers immediately became hostile competitors. *Glas Naroda* set out in a liberal and socially radical direction, and, as such, was very quickly in conflict with the strongly Catholic *Amerikanski Slovenec*. The Slovenes in the United States who were not satisfied with the first paper turned to *Glas Naroda*. One of the first correspondents for Sakser's paper was Ivan Grilec from Chicago, who had been involved in the founding of *Amerikanski Slovenec*. Later, both Grilec and his friend Anton Murnik worked with another newspaper, *Proletarec* (The proletarian).

In 1895 a group of Slovenian-American priests figured prominently in the planning of a utopian Slovene settlement in California. The settlement was to be called Rajska Dolina (Paradise Valley) and was staunchly supported by Reverend Buh and his *Amerikanski Slovenec*. The venture turned out to be a complete fiasco. This unfortunate affair gained hundreds of new subscribers for Sakser and did serious damage to *Amerikanski Slovenec*. It was one of the chief reasons that Buh sold his paper shortly thereafter. Anton Murnik, who had been postmaster for a short time in Rajska Dolina, was so disillusioned by the fate of *Amerikanski Slovenec* that several years later he went to Sakser and offered his services as assistant editor of *Glas Naroda*.

In 1899 Slovenes in Cleveland and in Pueblo, Colorado, who felt a need for their own press, founded three new papers. Anton Klinc in Cleveland began with a monthly, *Narodna Beseda* (The people's word). This title lasted only six months, but from its holdings a printing society was founded in the same city which began to publish the weekly *Nova Domovina* (New homeland). For some time the editor of the new paper was a priest, Reverend Francis Kerže. In Pueblo, Colorado, Martin Konda issued a weekly called *Mir* (Peace), which lasted only about four years.

The Chicago Slovene community, which after the failure of *Amerikanski Slovenec* was without a paper for a full ten years, made another attempt in the spring of 1901 with the weekly *Zora* (Dawn). This was the first Slovene-American newspaper specifically aimed at freethinkers, but it did not have great success, ceasing after only ten issues. The editor of *Zora* was Aleksander Toman, an adventurer who arrived in Chicago from Pueblo, where he had been editor of *Mir* for Martin Konda.

Several weeks after the death of *Zora*, Calumet, a mining settlement on the peninsula of Upper Michigan, became the center of Slovene-American journalism. An adventurer of the same type as Toman, Frank Schweiger, who was originally from Črnomelj, succeeded in organizing a printing society in Calumet and started to issue a weekly, *Glasnik od Gorenjega Jezera* (The herald of Lake Superior). Since most Americans could not pronounce this title, the title was changed after a few months to *Glasnik* (The herald).

The first decade of the twentieth century was probably the most fruitful for Slovene journalism in the United States. During those ten years twenty-one new newspapers and magazines were established. (Today only one of these is still being published.) The largest number of papers during that period were started in Pueblo, Colorado, where as many as ten were published simultaneously. Credit for this journalistic flood is owed mainly to four men: Maks Buh (a nephew of the missionary Buh), Rudolf Gregorič, E. J. Mencinger, and Zvonko Novak. None of the Pueblo papers has survived to this day.

Overall, during the first fifty years of Slovene-American journalism, between 1891 and 1941, Chicago had the largest number of publications, twenty-one newspapers and periodicals having been established there. During the same period Cleveland was second with fourteen titles, New York City third with nine, Calumet, Michigan, and Milwaukee tied for fourth with six each, followed by Pittsburgh with five titles.

The first Slovene magazine in America was put out by Ivan Mulaček. He published a monthly called *Nada* (Hope) in 1904 in Chicago, which appeared for five issues. Another attempt was made by Ivan Kaker. Published in the same city and called *Izobraževalna Knjižnica* (The educational library), it lasted for only four numbers. Bert Lakner in New York City, Zvonko Novak in Calumet, and Anton Šabec in Chicago also tried their luck with magazines, all without notable success.

Only about a dozen magazines managed to last ten years or more. Among them have been *Čas/Novi Čas* (Time/New time; 1915–1928), *Novi Svet* (New world; 1938–1965), *Ave Maria* (1909-), *Sloga* (Harmony; 1942-), and *Zarja* (Dawn; 1929-). The last two are issued by fraternal organizations.

The first Slovene monthly for young people, *Angelček* (The little angel), was published by the Grand Carniolian Slovenian Catholic Union (KSKJ) from 1921 until 1923. Reverend Kazimir Zakrajšek also issued a youth-oriented magazine, *Mali Ave Maria* (Little Ave Maria), which did not last long. However, the Slovene National Benefit Society (SNPJ) succeeded with *Mladinski List* (The youth journal), which has been published for some sixty-three years. Today *Mladinski List* is the only independent Slovene youth magazine in the United States, although it does appear for the most part in the English language.

Fraternal unions and societies were an important element in the lives of most immigrant ethnic communities, and the Slovenes were no exception in this respect. Slovene-American newspapers played a great part in the creation and operation of these societies. For example, with the assistance of *Amerikanski Slovenec* several of the oldest Slovene independent Catholic fraternal societies were formed and the first centralized Catholic fraternal union, the Grand Carniolian Slovenian Catholic Union (KSKJ) emerged in 1894. From the very beginning *Amerikanski Slovenec* served as the official organ of the KSKJ.

Four years later *Glas Naroda* provided the means for the establishment of a second union, the South Slavonic Catholic Union, which then chose *Glas Naroda* as its official organ. Soon every Slovene newspaper in the United States was trying to become the official organ of one local independent fraternal society or another. In 1903 *Glasnik*, in Calumet, became the organ of the Slovenian-Croatian Union, after having earlier served as the organ of the St. Joseph Society, the very first Slovene society in America.

The freethinkers' weekly, *Glas Svobode* (The voice of freedom), which was founded in 1902 by Martin Konda and Frank Medica in Pueblo, Colorado, moved to Chicago in 1903. There it was instrumental in the establishment of the Slovene National Benefit Society (SNPJ) and for three years thereafter it served as the organization's official organ. In Pennsylvania and Colorado, still other independent fraternal organizations emerged, and simultaneously local newspapers also appeared which wished to act as their organs.

In 1903 American Slovenes developed—again in Chicago—their first permanent political organization, a socialist one, which within three years set up the monthly *Proletarec* as its organ. *Proletarec* was the first Slovene paper in America to be the property of an organization and, in fact, the property of its readers. When in the fall of 1907 *Proletarec* became a weekly, a workers' committee was needed to get it on its feet, but within a few years it was back in the hands of a political organization, the Slovene section of the Yugoslav Socialist Federation.

Until 1908 all Slovene papers in America except *Proletarec* were the private property of individuals or stockholders. Even the official organs of the fraternal organizations were in private hands. The members of the Slovene National Benefit Society, at that time the youngest of the centralized fraternal unions, were the first to recognize that it would be best for large fraternal organizations to publish and control their own official organs. In 1908, as a result, it set up its own monthly, *Glasilo SNPJ* (The organ of SNPJ), which two years later was converted to a weekly. *Glas Svobode*, which then ceased to be the organ of the SNPJ, did not give up, however. It took an active part in establishing a new organization, the Slovene Freethinkers' Fraternal Society, of which it naturally became the official organ. All the larger fraternal societies one by one rejected the idea of privately owned official organs and established their own papers.

In 1925 the Slovene-American press reached its peak with twenty-six newspaper and periodical titles being published concurrently. From that point on there began a gradual but steady decline; in the mid–1980s only twelve titles are being produced. In 1924 restrictive immigration legislation went into effect which almost completely stopped the inflow of new Slovene immigrants. In the following decade the economic depression caused many Slovenes to return to Europe. Thereafter the inevitable assimilation of Slovenes into American life through American education and intermarriage slowly began to take its toll on the ethnic community.

As reflected in the two rival newspapers of the 1890s, *Amerikanski Slovenec* and *Glas Naroda*, ever since the early days of Slovene immigration to the United States there were two major groups within the community. One was the more conservative and religious group whose life centered around its church and the religiously oriented fraternal societies and press. The other group was more labor-oriented, pro-socialist, freethinking, and anticlerical in nature, and centered its life around the so-called progressive organizations and press. Of course, not every Slovene immigrant fell neatly into one of these two groups, but these two major orientations persisted from the 1890s through World War II. During World War II both groups tried to help their countrymen under Axis occupation. As one might expect, the more conservative group directed aid to clerical organizations in Slovenia and generally supported anticommunist resistance movements, such as that of General Draža Mihailović and his Chetniks. By the midpoint of the war the more progressive group, led by the best-known Slovene-American writer, Louis Adamič, was supporting Marshal Josip Broz Tito and his partisan resistance movement. After the war, especially during the McCarthy era, the stigma of having supported the communist, Tito, dealt a blow to the progressive group from which it never really recovered. Many of its organizations and publications, such as *Proletarec* and *Ameriški Družinski Koledar* (The American family almanac), came to an abrupt end, and today few groups or publications remain that could be called pro-socialist.

The end of World War II also brought a few thousand educated Slovene refugees to the United States, most of whom were conservative and anticommunist. A few experienced editors and publishers arrived in these years and the impact of their presence resulted in strengthening existing publications rather than producing many new ones. In spite of the greater education and perhaps better Slovene language skills of the new refugees, seldom did the post–World War II publications reach the quality or continuity of those of the interwar period.

Over the more than nine decades of Slovene publishing in the United States, newspapers appeared at twenty-four different geographic locations, with at most nine locations active simultaneously. Only ten had publications that lasted for any length of time: Chicago; New York; Cleveland; Joliet, Illinois; Pueblo, Colorado; Calumet, Michigan; Denver; Milwaukee; Bethlehem, Pennsylvania; and Lemont, Illinois. The locations which still have an active press are New York, Cleveland, Chicago, Denver, and Lemont. New York and Denver, however, produce only English-language titles; Chicago has five titles currently, Cleveland has three, and Lemont only one.

By region, places of publication correspond quite closely to the areas of Slovene settlement. The concentration of both settlement and publishing is greatest in the northeastern quarter of the United States, stretching eastward from Minnesota along the southern shore of the Great Lakes to New York and finally ending in Connecticut. The South had very few Slovene immigrants and no publications whatsoever. The West had a large scattering of Slovene immigrants, with only the Colorado enclaves producing any publications. Pueblo, which was a point of concentration for Slovene settlers from the late 1880s until World War I, was the home of a number of important Slovene ethnic publications, with a wide range of ideological viewpoints represented.

Chicago has definitely dominated in terms of the number of titles produced. While the Slovene population there was not large, Chicago attracted an unusual number of talented leaders. In addition, Chicago was home to sizeable groups of closely related ethnic peoples such as Czechs and Croations, who could share printing facilities. Also significant was the fact that Chicago was the site of the headquarters of numerous large ethnic fraternal unions, giving the city a natural edge in becoming a focal point for Slovene-American publishing. New York City was the second major publishing center. Papers there, especially Frank Sakser's *Glas naroda*, which published in New York for sixty years, served to help orient newcomers who so often entered the United States through the port of New York.

Cleveland also became a Slovene publishing center. It remained a chief source for Slovene ethnic publishing by producing *Ameriška Domovina* (American homeland), one of the last newspapers largely in the Slovene language. Cleveland has the greatest single concentration of Slovenes in the United States and has experienced a continuous immigration (albeit small in the 1980s).

Lemont, Illinois, became prominent for special reasons. Although there has never been a sizeable Slovene community there, it has been the site of the headquarters of the Slovene province of the Franciscan priests in America. In addition to having a school and seminary there, the Franciscans have long maintained their printing press and publishing facilities. As a result, for decades Lemont has been a center of Slovene Catholic publishing activities. Among the most prominent and most prolific of the leaders there over the years have been Reverend Kazimir Zakrajšek and Reverend Hugo Bren.

Industrial sites of settlement produced a number of durable publications. Pittsburgh, for example, had a number of successful ventures which lasted for considerable periods of time. Pueblo, Colorado, had a newspaper from 1900 to 1916, and Duluth, Minnesota, had one from 1911 until 1917. Even more successful in terms of longevity were efforts in Joliet, Illinois (1899–1926) and Milwaukee (1913–1946). Mining areas, in contrast, have produced papers which were often ephemeral. Leadville, Colorado, supported various Slovene newspapers periodically; Tower, Michigan, had one Slovene paper for eight years; and Calumet, Michigan published, with interruptions, one newspaper for twenty-five years.

A special subgroup of Slovenes were those called "Prekmurci," coming from the region of Prekmurje on the Hungarian border of Slovenia. They spoke a quite distinct dialect of the Slovenian language. A colony of these immigrants settled around Bethlehem, Pennsylvania, and produced four publications in their own dialect. The group never merged with the main body of Slovene immigrants. Another settlement of Prekmurci was established in Bridgeport, Connecticut, but never developed its own publications.

Over almost a century of Slovene-American publishing, only a relatively small number of writers and editors bore major responsibility for the development of the press. A few created long-lived papers, such as Frank Sakser, Anton Murnik, Charles Pogorelec of *Proletarec*, and Frank Zaitz of *Ameriški Družinski Koledar*. Others were involved in numerous publishing enterprises throughout long careers; among them were Martin Konda, Frank Kerže, Kazimir Zakrajšek, Ivan Molek, and Edward Mencinger. A third group comprised those who published only one or two titles over a short period. Regardless of the extent of their individual contributions, almost all of them were very dedicated.

For the past fifty years people have been predicting the imminent demise of the ethnic press in America, and yet it continues undaunted. Without doubt, assimilation is making inroads, and many ethnic publications have been forced to switch over partially or even completely to English as the younger generations begin to lose the knowledge of their ethnic language. This has been especially true of groups such as the Slovenes, who have not been radicalized in any political sense. Nevertheless, the Slovene press in the United States still continues to this day. The ethnic press, including that of the Slovene Americans, no longer holds the prominent position in social and political movements that it did in the period between 1895 and 1924, but the "renewed migration after World War II and ethnic revival, triggered by the Civil Rights movement and the drive for recognition of ethnic diversity," have helped to buy still more time for such small ethnic groups as the Slovenes in America.[2]

Even after the Slovene-American press has ceased to exist, which it some day undoubtedly will, one will be able to say that in its long life it has left a meaningful mark on history—the history of America, the history of the land of Slovenia, and the history of the Slovenes in America and their descendants.

NOTES

1. Major portions of this chapter are based on works by Joseph Velinjonka, Ivan Molek, and Jože Bajec, which are listed in the bibliography that follows.

2. Joseph Velijonka, "Slovene Newspapers and Periodicals in the United States," (paper presented at a meeting of the Society for Slovene Studies, New York, November 1979), p. 15.

BIBLIOGRAPHY

Ambrožič, Bernard. "Pridiga o katoliškem tisku." *Ave Maria Koledar*, 1930, pp. 105–108.

Bajec, Jože. "Biografije urednikov in publicistov slovenskega časopisja v Z. D. A." *Slovenski Izseljenski Koledar*, 1970, pp. 319–328.

———. "O bibliografijah ameriško-slovenskega izseljenskega tiska." *Slovenski Izseljenski Koledar*, 1969, pp. 272–277.

———. "Petinsedemdeset Let Slovenskega Časnikarstva v Z. D. A." Ljubljana: Slovenska Izseljenska Matica, 1966.

———. "Razvoj slovenskega izseljenskega časnikarstva v Evropi, Južni Ameriki in Kanadi." *Slovenski Izseljenski Koledar*, 1969, pp. 297–336.

———. *Slovenske Izseljenske Knjige, Brošure in Drobni Tiski*. Ljubljana: Slovenska Izseljenska Matica, 1966.

———. "Slovensko izseljensko časopisje, 1891–1945: seznam časnikov in časopisov, ki so v ljubljanskih knjižnicah." *Slovenski Izseljenski Koledar*, 1965, pp. 225–240.

———. *Slovensko Izseljensko Časopisje, 1891–1945*. Ljubljana: Slovenska Izseljenska Matica, 1980.

Chesarek, Joseph. "Začetek in konec slovenskega lista v Calumetu, Mich." *Ameriški Družinski Koledar*, 1944, pp. 97–107.

Dwyer, Joseph D. "Ninety Years of the Slovene Press in America." Paper presented at the Thirteenth National Convention of the American Association for the Advancement of Slavic Studies, Pacific Grove, California, October 1981.

————, comp., with Maurycy Czerworka. *Slovenes in the United States and Canada: A Bibliography*. St. Paul: Immigration History Research Center, University of Minnesota, 1981.

Grdina, Jože. "Naša kulturna revija." *Ameriški Družinski Koledar*, 1937, pp. 188–191.

Grill, Vatro. "Clevelandska 'Enakopravnost.' " *Slovenski Izseljenski Koledar*, 1974, pp. 288–293.

Jerič, John. "Shodi katoliškega tiska med Slovenci v Ameriki." *Ameriški Družinski Koledar*, 1938, pp. 141–145.

————. "Slovensko časopisje v Ameriki." *Ameriški Družinski Koledar*, 1927, pp. 117–119.

————. "Slovensko časopisje v Ameriki." *Ameriški Družinski Koledar*, 1930, pp. 126–128.

"Jugoslovansko časopisje v Ameriki."*Ameriški Družinski Koledar*, 1927, pp. 26–33.

Molek, Ivan. "Petdesetletnica slovenskega časnikarstva v Ameriki." *Ameriški Družinski Koledar*, 1941, pp. 28–36.

————. "Slovenski časniki in revije v Ameriki." *Ameriški Družinski Koledar*, 1941, pp. 118–122.

Novak, Zvonko A. "Časnikarstvo." *Ameriški Družinski Koledar*, 1942, pp. 86–95.

Oven, Joško. "Proletarec: glasilo Jugoslovanske Socialistične Zveze in Prosvetne Matice." *Slovenski Izseljenski Koledar*, 1955, pp. 121–124.

Prisland, Marie. "Ob 30-letnici 'Zarje,' glasila Slovenske Ženske Zveze v Ameriki." *Slovenski Izseljenski Koledar*, 1960, pp. 182–184.

"Še en srebrni jubilej: petindvajsetletnica naše proletarske knjige v Ameriki." *Ameriški Družinski Koledar*, 1930, pp. 60–61.

"Slovenski časopisi in listi." *Ameriški Družinski Koledar*, 1942, pp. 30–31.

"Slovensko časopisje v Ameriki" [an annual listing appears in the 1929, 1930, 1931, 1935, 1937, 1938, 1942, 1945, 1946, and 1948 volumes of the *Ameriški Družinski Koledar*].

"Socialistično gibanje med ameriškim jugoslovanskim delavstvom in Proletarec." *Ameriški Družinski Koledar*, 1923, pp. 183–187.

"Sotrudniki Ameriškega družinskega koledarja." *Ameriški Družinski Koledar*, 1944, pp. 128–225.

Spominska Knjiga Izdana Povodom Štiridesetletnice. *"Amerikanskega Slovenca,"* In *Prvega in Najstarejšega Slovenskega Časopisa v Ameriki, 1881–1931*. Chicago: N. p., 1931.

Spominska Knjiga Izdana za Zlati Jubilej Amerikanskega Slovenca, 1891–1941. Chicago: [Amerikanski Slovenec], 1941.

"Štiridesetletnica 'Proletarca,' " *Ameriski Druzinski Koledar*, 1945, p. 166.

Velijonka, Joseph. "Slovene Newspapers and Periodicals in the United States." Paper presented at a meeting of the Society for Slovene Studies, New York, November 1979.

Zaitz, Frank. "Četrtstoletja 'Ameriškega družinskega koledarja.' " *Ameriški Družinski Koledar*, 1939, pp. 46–57.

————. "Slovenske knjige in brošure, ki so izšle v Ameriki." *Ameriški Družinski Koledar*, 1928, pp. 30–34.

————. "Trideset let Ameriškega družinskega koledarja." *Ameriški Družinski Koledar*, 1944, pp. 194–217.

26

The Swedish Press

ULF A. BEIJBOM

During the migration epoch, 1846–1930, 1.2 million Swedes immigrated to the United States. The Swedish immigration was part of the "old" Western European wave—44 percent of the Swedes are recorded as having immigrated in the period 1879–1893, and 65 percent of them arrived before 1900. The nineteenth-century immigration was concentrated in the American Midwest, with Illinois as the first important immigration goal: approximately one out of three Swedish immigrants lived in Illinois from 1850 to 1870, a ratio which decreased to 21 percent in 1881; during the 1880s Minnesota took over as the leading "Swede state" of the United States.[1]

The rural majority of the Swedish immigrants settled on the prairies in Henry, Knox, Warren, Mercer, Rock Island, and Bureau counties in northwestern Illinois. In this agricultural region the utopian, hyperevangelical colony known as Bishop Hill was established in 1846 and the first Swedish-oriented Methodist, Lutheran, and Baptist congregations were founded. In 1860 the activities of the religious majority led to the founding of the Lutheran Augustana Synod, the most important Swedish organization in America. Meanwhile, the urbanized minority of the early Swedish immigrants concentrated in Chicago, where 10 percent of the Swedish-born Americans lived in 1890. Another urban stronghold was Rockford, Illinois, which received Swedish immigrants from the early 1850s and where 22 percent of the population in 1900 was born in Sweden. Accordingly, the prerequisites for a Swedish immigrant press presented themselves first in Illinois.[2]

EARLY PAPERS IN RURAL AND URBAN ILLINOIS

Due to the Swedish Lutheran state church and, from 1842, an elementary school system, almost all adult Swedish immigrants could read uncomplicated texts. In the mid-nineteenth century daily newspapers became common outside of Stockholm, and most adult immigrants had been confronted with modern papers, even if it was rare for an individual of rural or urban working-class background to have read newspapers regularly. The "father" of the Augustana

Synod, Pastor T. N. Hasselquist of Galesburg, Illinois, must have considered such factors when, on January 3, 1855, he launched *Hemlandet, det gamla och det nya* (The home land, old and new). This Christian newspaper, which soon became a weekly, was published at the editor's church and was first intended to serve the five Lutheran congregations in the nearby Swedish immigrant district. But since Hasselquist worked for the religious unity of all Swedish immigrants, the paper in reality had no territorial limitation. Considering the small number of Swedish immigrants in 1855, *Hemlandet* became an immediate success, with about 1,000 subscribers after one year. In order to make it a more devout medium, after July 1856 it was complemented by a religious periodical, *Det Rätta Hemlandet* (The true home land; from 1874 called *Augustana*), which became the pioneer for the overwhelmingly rich devotional press.[3] *Den Swenske Republikanen i Norra Amerika* (The Swedish republican in North America), a newspaper for Swedish immigrants who were indifferent to the Lutheran gospel, was issued in Galva, Illinois, near Bishop Hill, the same year and month as *Det Rätta Hemlandet*. Its radical editor, Svante Cronsioe, was backed by the anti-Lutheran circle of Bishop Hill. *Den Swenske Republikanen*, therefore, became an antagonist to Pastor Hasselquist and his papers. This forerunner of the radical wing of the secular press appealed especially to educated people of urban background. In January 1858 it was moved to the more sophisticated Swedish colony in Chicago, where it became the pioneering newspaper; however, it succumbed after only half a year.[4]

Galesburg was too remote for a paper intended as a "national" newspaper for Swedish-America. Accordingly, in January 1859, *Hemlandet* and its religious supplement were moved to Chicago, where a Swedish Lutheran publication society was formed. From this time until the final number was issued in 1914, *Hemlandet*, according to the principles of its founder, functioned as the popular organ of the Augustana Synod, which had more than 1,000 congregations from coast to coast. In addition to being the first Swedish-language newspaper in America, *Hemlandet* also served as a model for other church-oriented newspapers.

In this context a few words should be said about a Scandinavian newspaper started in New York City by a Swedish typesetter, Napoleon Berger, who used the name A. G. Öbom. This adventurer had mysteriously left Stockholm in 1838 and after a dozen years in Switzerland had been expelled "because of communistic intrigues." In 1851 Öbom appeared in New York, where in July he started the antireligious newspaper *Skandinaven*, printed in Swedish and Dano-Norwegian. It met with little response and ceased publication in 1853. Of much greater significance was Öbom's second newspaper venture, *Skandinavisk Post* (1863–1875), which appeared as both a daily and a weekly.[5]

SECULAR AND DEVOTIONAL PIONEERS

Chicago's numerous bourgeois immigrants with a nonreligious and liberal conception of the world provided a fertile ground for the secular press. A significant move to break the domination of church-influenced opinion in Swedish immigrant circles was taken in September 1866 by the leading group of the first social club in Chicago's Swede Town. It was no accident that *Svenska Ameri-kanaren* (The Swedish American) was launched on the threshold of the Swedish mass immigration. The liberal and mercantile orientation of the men behind this trailblazer for a secular Swedish immigrant press was expressed in the choice of the first editors, Herman Roos and Hans Mattson, the former a radical journalist and the latter a Civil War colonel with strong interests in immigration agencies. Its radical ideas and provocative style brought *Svenska Amerikanaren* instantly in conflict with *Hemlandet*. It became very popular and reported 5,000 sub-scribers in 1870. Losses during the Chicago fire and the economic panic of 1873 forced *Svenska Amerikanaren* to consolidate with another liberal paper in 1877, but its popular name was adopted by a new organ which still exists as *Svenska Amerikanaren Tribunen*.[6]

Another initiative of great significance to press development was taken in 1869 when *The Illinois Swede* started in Galva, Illinois. This weekly was established by a son of the founder of the Bishop Hill colony and opposed the prevailing Lutheran opinion. Its radical viewpoints were not just demonstrated in religious matters but also in its attitude to the assimilation question. *The Illinois Swede* argued for Americanization of the immigrants and was, as demonstrated by its name, printed partly in English. The readers were, however, not sufficiently mature for such a policy, forcing the paper to give up "our adopted language" and move to cosmopolitan Chicago, where the name was changed to *Nya Verlden* (The New World; 1870–1877). Edited by the prominent liberal jour-nalist C. F. Peterson, the paper continued its anti-Augustana line. The harsh economic times of the early 1870s forced a merger between *Nya Verlden* and *Svenska Amerikanaren* under the name *Svenska Tribunen* (The Swedish trib-une; 1877–1906), cited above. The new organ became the leading Swedish-American voice for middle-class liberalism and suspicion of rural hyperevangelism.[7]

The Swedish colony of Chicago also cradled a series of religious papers of denominations other than the Augustana Synod. When in 1864 the Methodist organ *Sändebudet* (The messenger; 1862–1965) moved from Rockford to Chi-cago, it was announced as a news weekly. The Swedish Covenant Church issued another successful weekly under the name *Missions-Vännen* (The mission friend; 1874–1960). In 1877 a still more hyperevangelical group, the Free Mission Friends, launched the *Chicago-Bladet* (Chicago-Herald; published until 1952). Such papers and their many successors in other places were primarily intended for their own religious groups, but a few of them shared *Hemlandet's* ambition to serve as a general news medium. The devotional non-Augustana press automatically became involved in a two-front war against the Augustana Lutherans on one side and the secular organs on the other. This, of course, hampered their capacity to mold opinion outside their own religious group.[8]

THE SWEDISH PRESS IN MINNESOTA

Minnesota became a greenhouse for the Swedish-language press, and papers were published in some thirty places. The pioneer newspaper, *Minnesota Posten* of Red Wing, lasted for only one year after its establishment in November 1857 by the extremely energetic Augustana pastor Eric Norelius; the paper was regarded as interfering with plans to make *Hemlandet* a national paper. Norelius was therefore forced to consolidate his paper with the main organ of the Swedish Lutherans. The unusually active Swedish colony in Red Wing in 1869 backed *Svenska Minnesota Bladet* (The Swedish Minnesota herald), which in January 1870 was absorbed by *Minnesota Tidning* (The Minnesota paper) of St. Paul. In July of the same year the name was changed to *Svenska Monitoren* (The Swedish monitor). This paper can be regarded as the pioneer of the secular Swedish-American press in Minnesota; it lasted until 1965. A more successful secular newspaper was started in 1877 by the immigrant agent and politician Hans Mattson, under the name *Minnesota Stats Tidning* (The Minnesota state paper). In 1882 it was bought out by its antagonist, the pro-Augustana *Skaffaren* (The harvester) which took the more salable name *Minnesota Stats Tidning* in 1895. This advocate of Augustana interests became one of the longest-lived Swedish-American newspapers (to 1939). Among the many successful secular papers of the Twin Cities worthy of mention were *Svenska Folkets Tidning* (The Swedish people's herald; 1881–1927) and *Svenska Amerikanska Posten* (Swedish-American post, 1885–1940). The latter started as a temperance organ but later became an independent liberal newspaper. Under the eminent leadership of Swan J. Turnblad, *Svenska Amerikanska Posten* developed into one of America's most popular Swedish newspapers.[9]

LEADING PAPERS IN THE EAST, WEST, AND SOUTH

The most successful Swedish paper in the Atlantic states, New York's *Nordstjernan* (The north star, 1872-), continued the liberal newspaper tradition initiated by A. G. Öbom in 1851 and 1863. *Nordstjernan* became extremely successful under three generations of Johansens who were the main owners from 1875 to 1952. A long series of outstanding editors such as Vilhelm Berger and Ernst Skarstedt as well as its close contacts with Sweden and the immigrant stream kept it more up-to-date than any other Swedish newspaper. *Nordstjernan* still appears as the leading representative of the Swedish-American press.[10]

Manhattan and Brooklyn, with a strong Swedish enclave around Atlantic Avenue, became the United States' leading Swedish press center next to Chicago and the Twin Cities, with some ninety newspapers and periodicals published from 1851 to 1910. Another stronghold for Swedish-language papers was the industrial settlement of Jamestown, New York, where Swedes published about twenty papers from 1874. The most important was *Vårt Land* (Our country;

1890–1920), a continuation of the Augustana paper *Österns Väktare* (The eastern guardian, 1888–1890) and the secular *Skandia* (1909–1946). The strong Swedish enclave in Worcester, Massachusetts, produced some thirty newspapers and periodicals, the secular *Svea* (Sweden; 1897–1966), owned by two generations of Trulsons, being the most popular news organ among the Swedes of the New England states.[11]

The three major urban centers of the West Coast provided bases for the Swedish press. After over ten years of premature newspaper enterprises in San Francisco, *Vestkusten* (The west coast, 1887-) appeared as California's leading Swedish paper. It began as an Augustana organ but soon adopted the secular profile that better fitted an urban settlement. Its persistence in a changing environment is explained by the purchase of *Vestkusten* in 1894 by the outstanding journalist Alexander Olsson, who ran the paper until his death in 1952. After fourteen years of newspaper failures in Los Angeles, *California Veckoblad* (California weekly) was launched in 1910. This liberal paper, like *Vestkusten*, was for many decades owned and edited by one person. Another similarity has been its ability to survive to the present, which, as in the case of *Nordstjernan* of New York, may be explained by the unbroken stream of immigrants to the East and West coasts.[12] The first Swedish papers in the state of Washington were started during the latter part of the 1880s but showed little ability to survive among a very unstable population of lumbermen, railroad workers, and day laborers. Two successful ventures were initiated around 1890 under the names *Vestra Posten* (The west post) and *Tacoma Tribunen*. In 1902 these nonsectarian organs merged into the *Westerns Tribun*, which in 1914 continued as *Svenska Pacific Tribunen* (1914–1946). The most successful of the newspapers in Seattle was *Svenska Posten* (The Swedish post, 1936–1976), a continuation of the *Puget Sound Posten* of Tacoma (1907–1935), which was owned and edited by the radical journalist Harry Fabbe during its last decades.

Unique both as a voice for a Swedish settlement in the Deep South and as a one-family enterprise was *Texas Posten* in Austin (1896–1982), owned and edited by three generations of the Knape family. This paper is interesting for its coverage of a peripheral but strong immigrant community. It also exemplifies the strengthening effects of one-family ownership.[13]

NUMBERS, PUBLICATION REGIONS, CATEGORIES, AND CIRCULATION

We have seen that the Swedish-American press was founded right after the first immigration wave. From the beginning of the Swedish mass immigration in the late 1860s the first "national" papers were published in Chicago, the urban center of Swedish-America. The following twenty years were characterized by diversification and competition as papers were started in new settlements all over the Midwest, in the New England states, and in the West. At least 173 Swedish-American newspapers and periodicals had been published before 1886.

The number of Swedish immigrants living in the United States peaked in 1910 (665,000), the year that marked the end of the "foundation period" of the Swedish-American press in which fifty-eight weeklies and 238 monthlies and annuals existed. Up to the same year 1,150 periodicals had been registered by the journalist Alfred Söderström. This high figure should be reduced by about 20 percent because of double registration (no consideration is given to the frequent changes of names and publication places).[14]

The most recent of the Swedish-American press indexes is based primarily on the collections at Augustana College, Rock Island, Illinois, and at the Royal Library in Stockholm. Due to duplications, the 832 titles listed by O. Fritjof Ander must be reduced to about 650. Thirty-five percent were newspapers, 54 percent periodicals, and 11 percent annuals, calendars, or Christmas magazines. According to Ander, Swedish papers had been published in twenty-seven states, Illinois (with 276), Minnesota (with 143), and New York (with 86) being the leading publication states. One-hundred-eighty-seven papers came out in Chicago and 87 in Minneapolis. No less than 75 percent of the papers had been founded in the period 1870–1910. One out of four lasted less than a year, while 36 percent had a life span of two to five years and 10 percent lived six to ten years. One out of three lasted ten years or more.

Most newspapers had a local character serving a town or a group of rural settlements. Only a dozen can be described as national, and those were published in Chicago, Minneapolis, or New York. Periodicals that were not published by a congregation or a local society often had a national character, geared as they were to a nonterritorial interest circle. The most important group of periodicals served church interests—130 in 1910, of which 71 were Lutheran papers. Publications by the temperance movement comprised another category. Fraternal organizations such as the Orders of Vikings, Svithiod, and Vasa published (and continue to publish) periodicals with impressive editions. A sophisticated group of periodicals was dedicated to literature, art, and music. Among the literary journals was *Valkyrian* (The Valkyrie; 1897–1909), one of Swedish-America's most popular monthlies and a literary supplement to *Nordstjernan* in New York. Women's interests were appealed to by a handful of magazines led by *Kvinnan och Hemmet* (The woman's home journal; Cedar Rapids, Iowa, 1893–1947). Specific religious, cultural, and political interests were met by various periodicals.

With the exception of a dozen periodicals, such as the weekly *Augustana* (with a circulation of 21,000 in 1915), *Ungdomsvännen* (The youth friend; 9,200 in 1913), and *Kvinnan och Hemmet* (78,500 in 1912), the magazines reached rather humble circulation levels. This holds true also for most newspapers, although a few reported impressive numbers. The Chicago papers *Svenska Amerikanaren*, *Svenska Kuriren* (Swedish courier), and *Svenska Tribunen-Nyheter* (Swedish-Tribune news) in 1915 had circulations of 47,000, 42,500, and 65,000, respectively. In the same year the Minneapolis weeklies *Minnesota Stats Tidning* and *Svenska Amerikanska Posten* claimed 12,500 and 56,000 subscribers, respectively. *Nordstjernan* of New York reported 12,500 and *Svea* of Worcester 19,000, while *Vestkusten* and *Texas Posten* each reported about 4,000. According to *Ayer's Newspaper Directory*, the combined circulation of seventy-two Swedish newspapers in 1915 was 651,000, or about one issue per Swedish-born American.[15]

THE PERIOD OF DECLINE

That such impressive figures were more than halved by 1932 can be explained by a fatal combination of factors: aggressive Americanism during World War I, the depressions at the beginning and the end of the 1920s, and decreasing immigration. In 1925 *Svenska Kuriren*, for instance, was very pessimistic about the future. Not only was emigration a closed chapter, but the Swedish immigrants were becoming Americanized faster than any other group, lamented the paper. In order to counter this negative pattern, several papers opened their columns to the English language. This proved unsuccessful in the case of newspapers, while journals such as *The Lutheran Companion* (1911–1962) from 1927 had a larger circulation than the Swedish-language weekly *Augustana*.

Most editors realized that a change of language hardly could be combined with a strong ethnic profile. Competition with American newspapers in their own language was out of the question, and a change from Swedish and local news would possibly attract people from the second generation, but it discouraged the only dedicated readers, the old-timers. For such reasons the Swedish-American newspapers have remained unchanged to the bitter end. Most surviving journals, however, such as *The Covenant Companion* (1923-), *Vasa Star* (formerly *Vasastjernan*, 1908-), or *Musiktidning* (Journal of music; 1906-), *Svithiod Journal* (1898-), and *Viking Journal* (1912-), are printed in English. With the exception of the modernized layout of *Nordstjernan-Svea*, the four last newspapers appear as they did fifty years ago. Fifteen-thousand seems to be a maximum figure for the combined circulation of those four: *California Veckoblad*, *Nordstjernan-Svea*, *Svenska Amerikanaren Tribunen*, and *Vestkusten*.[16]

SUBSCRIPTIONS, ADVERTISEMENTS, AND EDITING PRACTICES

A characteristic of all Swedish-American newspapers and most periodicals was that readers had to be recruited by subscription. In the case of the newspapers, subscriptions were canvassed by agents hired on a commission basis. Extended credits were usual, and a large share of the readers never paid their debts in full. A powerful but costly weapon in the war for readers was premiums such as books. In this way the leading papers also functioned as publishing houses. The most important source of income consisted of advertisements, also sold by agents. In times of political elections the newspapers, especially in big cities, drew incomes from the campaign treasurers (mostly the Republican ones). Abrupt swings between the political constellations could often be explained by the fact that the papers "sold their services to the highest bidder."[17]

A successful newspaper devoted at least 25 percent of its space to advertisements. The news columns were primarily filled with national and provincial news from Sweden and local Swedish-American material. In 1930 *Svenska Amerikanaren* and *Svenska Tribunen-Nyheter* of Chicago (80,000 and 60,000, respectively, in circulation) gave less than 5 percent of their news space to U. S. news, while 40–50 percent was devoted to Swedish-American news. The remainder (45–55 percent) was principally used for news from Sweden. With the readers' increasing age the ethnic orientation grew even stronger, with a concentration of news about families, church, and club life. A maximum of 4 percent of the total space was spent on editorials. Until the newspaper crisis of the 1920s, most papers retained an editorial column. The inability to hire qualified journalists and similarities in viewpoints, especially in political matters, led many papers to reproduce the editorials of the leading papers in Chicago and Minneapolis. More persistent was the ambition to retain a literary page, on which appeared Swedish novels or short stories; it was also an important forum for immigrant authors.[18]

THE JOURNALISTS

The many men and a dozen women behind the Swedish immigrant press represented the thin layer of immigrant intellectuals. Of 288 identified "scribblers," 55 percent had arrived in America with a theoretical education, at least fifty on the university level and thirty-two having journalistic experience. Another seventy-two attended college in the United States, and of these no less than fifty-two became pastors. One-third had emigrated from cities or towns, which indicates a slightly higher urbanization rate than among ordinary Swedish immigrants. These characteristics describe a group not representative of the average Swedish immigrant. Specialized as they were in communication in the Swedish language, one can presume that the journalists would have met serious difficulties outside the immigrant enclaves.[19] The ethnic press rescued this category of educated immigrants from social and economic catastrophe. The great influence of the churches is reflected among the journalists in the sixty-two pastors, of whom ten were ordained in Sweden. Many clergymen, like T. N. Hasselquist of *Hemlandet*, served as newspaper editors during important parts of their lives. Other journalists, like *Hemlandet*'s most famous chief editor, John Enander, were recruited from college. The man who was referred to as the founder of the liberal Swedish-American press, Herman Roos, represented the many journalists of upper-class background. Roos was a nobleman with a law degree and journalistic experience; he had been involved in a scandal which made it difficult to follow a career according to family traditions. Other prominent examples of journalists of upper-class background are Vilhelm Berger of *Nordstjernan* and Ernst Skarstedt of *Vestkusten* and other papers, who also made themselves known as authors. A large group of the editors were, however, entirely self-made, like the journalist and author C. F. Peterson, or Minneapolis's Swedish "newspaper king," S. J. Turnblad of *Svenska Amerikanska Posten*.[20]

PROMOTERS OF ETHNICITY AND ASSIMILATION

The role of the foreign-language press as a promoter of both ethnicity and cultural assimilation is clearly reflected in the Swedish-American press. Its ability to generate feelings of ethnic solidarity as well as loyalty to the adopted land can hardly be overestimated. The ethnic qualities were especially apparent in the informative function of the press. Through reporting and advertising, the newspapers secured support for Swedish organizations and business enterprises and functioned as communication lines between scattered immigrant enclaves. The life and mentality of Swedish America were recorded by the newspapers. At the end of the epoch, due to decreasing immigration and an aging public, its ethnocentric role became even more accentuated.

The strongest factor in the promotion of assimilation was the availability of information and advice about American society. Such guidance in one's own language eased the immigrant's feelings of dislocation and uprootedness. No other ethnic organization was closer to the society and its demands than the press, and few ethnic leaders were better equipped to analyze and interpret the United States than the journalists. This, for instance, was evident when readers were advised to apply for citizenship and assume voting power. With few exceptions, language adjustment was promoted by the most assiduous printers of the Swedish language. About a hundred papers were printed in English.[21]

THE DUALISM OF SWEDISH-AMERICA

Although unanimously conservative on most social, moral, and political questions, the editorials in the leading Swedish-American newspapers and religious periodicals reflected the breach between the religious and secular phalanxes of Swedish-America. The storm center for a half-century-long polemic was Chicago and its leading Swedish weeklies, above all the Lutheran *Hemlandet*, the two *Svenska Amerikanarens*, and their successors. The debate was generated by the differences between conservative rural-Lutheran viewpoints and the more cosmopolitan and open attitudes of the successful element in the urban settlements. The struggle over control of Swedish-American opinion was not entirely a debate about religion and morals but also concerned culture and politics. The Swedish theater of Chicago, for instance, became a topic of discussion in 1868 and again in 1877 when *Hemlandet* condemned theatrical activities as immoral. Related to this was the paper's negative attitude toward secular clubs and their social and cultural programs. Other Augustana papers joined in, and for a year a periodical dedicated to fighting so-called secret societies was published (*Schibboleth*; Chicago and Rock Island, Illinois, 1878–1879).

A more important issue was the assimilation question. The leading opinion molder of the Augustana Synod, editor John Enander, appears to have been convinced that the Swedish language and culture should live on in the Midwest. *Svenska Amerikanaren* also recognized the need to preserve the immigrant heritage but opposed Enander's filiopietistic approach. The paper placed the public schools before the parochial ones and turned against Enander's idea that Swedish should be taught in Chicago schools. That this issue had bearings on the situation on both sides of the Atlantic is expressed by the radical journalist Isidor Kjellberg, founder of the scandal sheet *Justitia* (1871), who held that ethnic schools hampered the advancement of the Swedes by keeping them ignorant of English. The cultural debate petered out at the end of the century and was brought to a conclusion by World War I. The 1914 merger between *Hemlandet* and *Svenska Amerikanaren* symbolized a new, more conciliatory epoch.[22]

POLITICAL ATTITUDES

The Republican orthodoxy of most nineteenth-century Swedes in America had a strong base in *Hemlandet* and its powerful editors, Hasselquist and Enander, who identified Swedishness with Luther and Lincoln. Secular and non-Augustana devotional papers were, with few exceptions, as Republican as *Hemlandet* but opposed Lutherism. Devotional and secular organs therefore often allied themselves with different Republican groups. This, of course, split the political front and made it difficult for a Swedish candidate to count on the votes of his own ethnic group. Political impotence, therefore, became a theme when the papers summed up the meager results of Swedish Republican activities in Chicago. The importance of politics in the newspaper world is nevertheless reflected in the fact that editors like John Enander and Alexander J. Johnson of Chicago, Hans Mattson and Herman Stockenström of Minneapolis, and Samuel A. Carlson of Jamestown, New York, obtained important political appointments.[23]

The Republican-conservative front was not monolithic. A handful of "scandal papers of blackest water" were published in the 1870s and 1880s, and socialist newspapers existed from May Day, 1895, when *Arbetaren* (The working man) started the longest run of any Swedish-American socialist weekly (to 1928). A total of about sixty socialist newspapers or periodicals have been published by the Swedes in America.[24]

Republican loyalty was especially shaken by the many crises of the 1890s. The populist movement became especially strong in Minnesota, and several Swedish-American editors in 1892 supported the Democratic Presidential candidate, Grover Cleveland. *Svenska Amerikanska Posten* followed the Swedish politician John Lind when he defected to the Democratic Party in his candidacy for governor of Minnesota in 1896. A combination of ethnicism and mistrust of the Republicans drew strong support also for the Swede John A. Johnson, who was on Minnesota's Democratic gubernatorial ticket in 1904, 1906, and 1908. Theodore Roosevelt's Progressive Republican movement attracted much sympathy from the Swedish press, which split nearly evenly for and against Roosevelt in 1912. Among its supporters were such powerful newspapers as *Svenska Amerikanaren* and *Svenska Tribunen-Nyheter*. Much of the third-party support in Minnesota was transferred to the radical Farmer-Labor Party during the 1920s.[25]

Scandinavian suspicion of the great powers and also its Midwest isolationism suited the conservatism of most Swedish-American editors. This became especially clear during World War I, which commonly was seen by them as initiated by the depraved European powers (*Svenska Tribunen-Nyheter*). When the isolationist viewpoints of Republican congressman Charles A. Lindbergh, Sr., were cheered by many Swedish newspapers, this was not entirely because of his Swedish nationality. The fact that Luther was a German, on the other hand, caused pro-German feelings to be voiced in the early war editorials even outside of Augustana circles. The most outspoken sympathies for Germany were articulated by such Augustana organs as *Hemlandet* and *Minnesota Stats Tidning*, while an opposing position was taken by the Methodist weekly *Sändebudet*. As the war continued and the United States became involved, pro-Germanism became too inconvenient and faded away.[26]

Democratic and socialist sentiments grew steadily during the economic crises of the 1920s and 1930s. Franklin D. Roosevelt's New Deal attracted some support from Republican newspapers, but only a handful of Swedish editors openly supported Roosevelt in 1932 and 1936. *Svenska Posten* in Seattle was the only paper to declare itself Democratic in the 1936 election.[27]

A defensive kind of ethnicity was generated by "100 percent Americanism" during and after the war and by the quota regulations of the 1920s which, although of little significance for the dwindling Swedish immigrant stream, badly hurt Swedish-American feelings. It was also felt that Swedish institutions were threatened by decreasing immigration. The negative forces of the time united the Swedish-American press in a defense of what remained a Swedish language and culture. This new debate on ethnicity was often addressed to the ethnically lukewarm second generation, which now was more numerous than the immigrants. The defenders of Swedishness got much support from the depressed times, especially after 1929, when many humanitarian actions were initiated by the ethnic organizations. The papers gained much goodwill by supporting the relief committees. It is, however, doubtful that this renaissance of ethnic solidarity brought many new names to the subscription lists.[28] At the same time a generation shift occurred among the editors, and by 1939 the old guard had been replaced by Americanborn or newly arrived journalists from Sweden. As the number of subscribers decreased, it became common for one person to both edit and own a paper, and this limited the time available for writing. Less original material appeared in the papers, and the attitude was to please as many readers as possible. Only major papers such as *Nordstjernan*, *Svenska Amerikanaren Tribunen*, and *Svenska Pressen* expressed individual opinions. In order to satisfy an aging readership the papers were edited in the traditional way and the ethnocentric profile was accentuated. With the exception of *Nordstjernan-Svea*, these characteristics hold true for those Swedish-American newspapers still in existence.[29]

NOTES

1. Ulf Beijbom, "Swedes," in Stephan Thernstrom ed., *Harvard Encyclopedia of American Ethnic Groups* (Cambridge, Mass.: Harvard University Press, 1980), pp. 971–981; Helge Nelson, *The Swedes and the Swedish Settlements in North America* (Lund, Sweden: Gleerup, 1943), 1: 390f.

2. Beijbom, pp. 973–976; Nelson, pp. 140, 155.

3. Oliver A. Linder, "The Swedish-American Press," in E. G. Westman and E. G. Johnson, eds., *The Swedish Element in America* (Chicago: Swedish-American Bibliographical Society, 1931–1934), 2: 324–343; J. Oscar Backlund, *A Century of the Swedish-American Press* (Chicago: Swedish American Newspaper Co., 1952), pp. 15–18.

4. Linder, p. 21; Ulf Beijbom, *Swedes in Chicago: A Demographic and Social Study of the 1846–1880 Immigration* (Växjö: Läromedelsförlagen, 1971), pp. 289, 294.

5. Beijbom, *Swedes in Chicago*, pp. 288–289; Erik Gamby, "Napoleon Berger alias Gustaf Öbom," *Swedish American Historical Quarterly* 34 (January 1983): 4–31.

6. Beijbom, *Swedes in Chicago*, pp. 289–290, 292–293.

7. Ibid., pp. 290–291; Backlund, pp. 27–29.

8. Beijbom, *Swedes in Chicago*, pp. 291–293; Backlund, pp. 77–88.

9. Backlund, pp. 18–20, 59–64; Linder, p. 337–338; Alfred Söderström, *Blixtar på tidningshorisonten* (Warroad, Minn.: Svenska Amerikanska Posten, 1910), pp. 26–32.

10. Backlund, pp. 43–46; Linder, pp. 333–334.

11. Backlund, pp. 48–51; Linder, pp. 338–339; Söderström, pp. 35–37.

12. Backlund, pp. 57–59; Söderström, pp. 38–39.

13. Backlund, pp. 51–56, 66; Söderström, p. 47; Nelson, pp. 301–309.

14. Bernhard Lundstedt, *Svenska Tidningar och Tidskrifter utgifna inom Nord-Amerikas Förenta Stater: Bibliografisk öfversigt* (Stockholm: Norstedt & Söner, 1886); Söderström, p. 55.

15. O. Fritjof Ander, *The Cultural Heritage of the Swedish Immigrant: Selected References* (Rock Island, Ill.: Augustana College Library Publications, No. 27, 1956), pp. 147–187; Söderström, pp. 16–55; Finis Herbert Capps, *From Isolationism to Involvement: The Swedish Immigrant Press in America. 1914–1945* (Chicago: Swedish Pioneer Historical Society, 1966), pp. 233–235; Marion T. Marzolf, *The Danish-Language Press in America* (New York: Arno Press, 1979), pp. 104–105; Sture Lindmark, *Swedish America, 1914–1932: Studies in Ethnicity with Emphasis on Illinois and Minnesota* (Uppsala: Läromedelsförlagen, 1971), p. 226.

16. Lindmark, pp. 226, 229–232; Nils Hasselmo, *Swedish America: An Introduction* (Minneapolis: Swedish Information Service, 1976), pp. 41–44.

17. Ernst Skarstedt, *Svensk-Amerikanska Folket i Helg och Söcken* (Stockholm: Björck och Börjesson, 1917), pp. 180–182; Söderström, pp. 220–223, 229–230; Beijbom, *Swedes in Chicago*, pp. 315–329; Capps, p. 23.

18. A. F. Schersten, *The Relation of the Swedish-American Newspapers to the Assimilation of Swedish Immigrants* (Rock Island, Ill.: Augustana College Library Publications, No. 15, 1935), especially pp. 36f.; Capps, pp. 23, 26–28; Marzolf, pp. 180–185, 210–211.

19. Ernst Skarstedt, *Pennfäktare: Svensk-Amerikanska författere och tidningsmän* (Stockholm: Åhlén & Åkerlund, 1930), pp. 15–212.

20. Beijbom, *Swedes in Chicago*, pp. 294–298; Skarstedt, *Pennfäktare* pp. 30–31, 169–170, 193.

21. Marzolf, pp. 3–19; Beijbom, *Swedes in Chicago*, p. 301; Schersten, pp. 54–98.

22. Beijbom, *Swedes in Chicago*, pp. 298–301; Capps, pp. 19–20, 23–24; Skarstedt, *Svensk-Amerikanska Folket*, pp. 182–183.

23. Beijbom, *Swedes in Chicago*, pp. 315–329; Capps, pp. 10–12, 23; Skarstedt, *Pennfäktare*, pp. 54–55, 126–127, 175; Allan Kastrup, *The Swedish Heritage in America* (St. Paul: Swedish Council of America, 1975), p. 547.

24. Michael Brook, "Radical Literature in Swedish America: A Narrative Survey," *Swedish Pioneer Historical Quarterly* 20 (July 1969): 111–132; letter from Michael Brook, December 9, 1983.

25. Capps, pp. 18–20; Sten Carlsson, "Scandinavian Politicians in the United States," in Ingrid Semmingsen and Per Seyersted, eds., *Scando-Americana: Papers on Scandinavian Emigration to the United States* (Oslo: American Institute, University of Oslo, 1980), pp. 153–166.

26. Capps, pp. 31–58, 225–226.

27. Ibid., pp. 105–132, 227–228; Lindmark, pp. 162–190.

28. Lindmark, pp. 137–190; Capps, pp. 25–26, 81–132.

29. Capps, pp. 25–28.

BIBLIOGRAPHY

Bibliographies of Swedish-American Presses and Journalists

Ander, O. Fritjof. *The Cultural Heritage of the Swedish Immigrant: Selected References*. Rock Island, Ill.: Augustana College Library Publications, No. 27, 1956.

Lundstedt, Bernhard. *Svenska Tidningar och Tidskrifter utgifna inom Nord-Amerikas Förenta Stater: Bibliografisk öfversigt*. Stockholm: Norstedt & Söner, 1886.

Setterdahl, Lilly. *Swedish-American Newspapers: A Guide to the Microfilms Held by SSIRC*. Rock Island, Ill.: Augustana College Library Publications, No. 35, 1981.

Skarstedt, Ernst. *Pennfäktare: Svensk-Amerikanska författare och tidningsmän*. Stockholm: Åhlén & Åkerlund, 1930.

Söderström, Alfred. *Blixtar på tidningshorisonten*. Warroad, Minn.: Svenska Amerikanska Posten, 1910.

Secondary Works

Backlund, J. Oscar. *A Century of the Swedish-American Press*. Chicago: Swedish American Newspaper Co., 1952.

Beijbom, Ulf. "The Printed Word in a Nineteenth Century Immigrant Colony: The Role of the Ethnic Press in Chicago's Swede Town." *Swedish Pioneer Historical Quarterly* 28 (April 1977): 82–96.

———. *Swedes in Chicago: A Demographic and Social Study of the 1846–1880 Immigration*. Växjö: Läromedelsförlagen, 1971.

Brook, Michael. "Radical Literature in Swedish America: A Narrative Survey." *Swedish Pioneer Historical Quarterly* 20 (July 1969): 111–132.

Capps, Finis Herbert. *From Isolationism to Involvement: The Swedish Immigrant Press in America, 1914–1945*. Chicago: Swedish Pioneer Historical Society, 1966.

Gamby, Erik. "Napoleon Berger alias Gustaf Öbom." *Swedish American Historical Quarterly* 34 (January 1883): 4–31.

Linder, Oliver A. "The Swedish-American Press." In *The Swedish Element in America*, Vol. 2. ed. E. G. Westman and E. G. Johnson. Chicago: Swedish-American Bibliographical Society, 1931–1934.

Lindmark, Sture. *Swedish America, 1914–1932: Studies in Ethnicity with Emphasis on Illinois and Minnesota*. Uppsala: Läromedelsförlagen, 1971.

Schersten, A. F. *The Relation of the Swedish-American Newspapers to the Assimilation of Swedish Immigrants*. Rock Island, Ill.: Augustana College Library Publications, No. 15, 1935.

27

The Ukrainian Press

BOHDAN P. PROCKO

This chapter is intended to provide the general reader with a historical survey of the Ukrainian press in America.[1] It does not claim to be comprehensive, and it is limited to serials which have had direct connection with the size, growth, and development of Ukrainian-American communities in the United States. Publications representing Russophile, Rusynophile, or Magyarophile viewpoints fall outside the scope of the account. Its primary concerns are newspapers and journals intended for general rather than local distribution issued at regular intervals. Calendars and almanacs, though extremely important, are not included, nor are the early educational booklets issued more or less at regular intervals.

BEGINNINGS TO 1920

Mass Ukrainian immigration to the United States began late in the 1870s when villagers from the mountainous border districts between Transcarpathia and Galicia in Austro-Hungary, where neither literacy nor national consciousness was commonplace, began arriving as laborers for the mining companies in the anthracite region of eastern Pennsylvania. The new immigrants became generally known as Ruthenians, a Latinization of the Slavic *Rusyny* (*Rusini*), which is derived from the Kievan *Rus'*.

Thrust into unfamiliar and hostile surroundings, these immigrants yearned for their own familiar institutions, in particular their own Greek Catholic (Uniate) church, the center of their social life in Europe. The handful of priests, the first intellectuals among these early immigrants, and the churches that they organized became the nuclei from which other institutions began to spread. From these emanated ethnic awareness and, eventually, future Ukrainian-American communities. The systematic attempt to arouse the immigrants' ethnic awareness really began with the appearance of the press. With the growth of national consciousness during the first two decades of the twentieth century the immigrants from the Austrian provinces of Galicia and Bukovina became generally known by their new national name: Ukrainians.

The early Ukrainian immigrants, most of whom were single males, settled primarily in the industrial Northeast. They congregated most numerously in the mining and mill towns of Pennsylvania with less dense settlements in New York and New Jersey. Even today, with the considerable upward movement that has occurred in the socioeconomic structure of the Ukrainian communities, 54 percent of Ukrainian-Americans still reside within the borders of these three states. In addition, over 90 percent of them continue to live in urban areas.[2] The largest Ukrainian-American communities today are located in the metropolitan areas of New York, Chicago, Philadelphia, Detroit, Pittsburgh, Cleveland, and Newark. A rough estimate of the number of Americans claiming to be of Ukrainian origin is about 700,000.[3]

The first Ukrainian newspaper in America was founded by Reverend John Volansky, the first Ukrainian Catholic (Uniate) priest to settle in the United States, who arrived in Shenandoah, Pennsylvania, in 1884, from Austria's Galicia. As he later stated in his recollections, Volansky decided to put out a newspaper to help his widely scattered flock preserve its religious and national identity and adjust more readily to its new surroundings.[4] He purchased an old hand-operated press in New York, imported Cyrillic type from Austria, and, working out of his own living quarters, brought out the first issue of his paper, which he named *Ameryka*, on August 15, 1886. Shortly thereafter, it proved more expeditious to transport the type, set in frames, for printing at the *Evening Herald*, the Shenandoah newspaper.

At first Volansky was his own editor, compositor, and proofreader for the four-page, small-format paper that he issued twice a month.[5] As with most early immigrant publications, news from the old country was an important feature in its chronicle-like character. The publication improved in 1887 with the arrival of Vladimir Simenovich, the first Ukrainian lay intellectual to settle in America, who became the paper's editor. *Ameryka* was further improved when Wasyl Sarich, a skilled printer, was hired; the paper then began to appear in a larger format.

When the capable and energetic Volansky was recalled to Galicia in June 1889,[6] he turned over control of *Ameryka* to Reverend Constantine Andrukhovich. The paper, in fact, became the property of St. Michael's Ukrainian Catholic Church in Shenandoah. Under Andrukhovich's management, *Ameryka*, in mid–1890, ceased publication and was replaced by the semimonthly *Ruskoie slovo* (Ruthenian word).[7] This second Ukrainian newspaper, which started in January 1891 and continued through December, was, from the standpoint of professional journalism, even poorer than the first. The dawn, however, was at hand.

In 1892 Reverend George Hrushka, who arrived in Jersey City, New Jersey, from Galicia late in 1889, apparently printed only a single issue of a small paper called *Novy svit* (New world). The first truly national Ukrainian newspaper to appear on American soil was *Svoboda* (Liberty), the first issue of which was published under the direction of Father Hrushka on September 15, 1893. *Svoboda*, which began as a biweekly, went through periods as a weekly and a triweekly before becoming a daily in 1921.[8] Its ownership changed several times after June 1895, as did the place of its publication. *Svoboda* remains the oldest, largest, and most prestigious Ukrainian newspaper in the United States.

The systematic attempt to educate and Americanize the mostly illiterate Ukrainian immigrants began with the appearance of Father Hrushka's *Svoboda*. In its first issue, Hrushka explained: "Our task is: to enlighten the Ukrainian [rus'kii] people, protect its honor from hostile attacks, point out the road to progress, to civilization, to well-being."[9] Though Hrushka remained its owner and editor, on May 30, 1894, *Svoboda* became the official organ of the Ruskyi Narodnyi Soyuz (which was to become the Ukrainian National Association), the fraternal mutual aid society which Hrushka and others had formally organized earlier that year in Shamokin, Pennsylvania.[10] Thus the Church and the Soyuz, which was founded by priests and in which they were to play the leading roles for many years, are the two institutions which educated the Ukrainian masses, preserved their national and religious heritage, and contributed to their Americanization.

Svoboda began its formal cultural and educational endeavors in 1894 with the publication, in Ukrainian and English, of *The Self-Teacher and Dictionary*:

We consider it our responsibility not only to encourage Ukrainians [Rusyniv] to appreciate learning, but also to provide them with all the tools at our disposal. One of the best means of enlightenment will be the *Self-Teacher*, which will make it possible for our workers to learn the English language, while at the same time it will help them to understand the conditions of life of the country in which they live; it will also teach them to be genuine citizens and not servile workers in the hands of politicians.[11]

As early as 1900 the political views proclaimed by the newspaper began to crystallize.[12] Generally, it might be said that the editors projected a future when all Ukrainians would be working toward the establishment of an independent and democratic Ukraine.

Beginning in 1895, when the so-called priest-radicals[13] purchased *Svoboda*, the paper became more radical in its outlook. The group of young priests who arrived from Galicia between 1895 and 1898 were imbued with the spirit of the Ukrainian national movement, which in the 1890s was characterized in part by anticlericalism and agrarian non-Marxist socialism. Between 1900 and 1907, when John Ardan, the most radical of the group, was the paper's owner and editor, *Svoboda* even leaned toward socialism.[14] In addition, because of the serious religious and national identity conflicts among the immigrants (inherited from political differences born in Europe), the first two decades of this century witnessed the spread of various highly partisan publications, which began competing with *Svoboda*, and with each other, for support for their respective ideologies from the expanding Ukrainian communities.[15] Most of these publications were short-lived; a few have continued their publications to the present.

The satirical *Osa* (The wasp), for example, made its appearance in October

1902 in Olyphant, Pennsylvania, under the editorship of Michael Strutynsky. The semimonthly directed its barbs primarily at the Russophile leaders, until its demise in March of the following year. The year 1905 witnessed the founding of the *Yevanhelskyj ranok* (Evangelical morning), which became the official organ of the Ukrainian Evangelical Alliance of North America, formerly located in Detroit, Michigan, currently in Dumwoody, Georgia. Today this oldest Ukrainian Protestant periodical in the United States, which includes an English section, lists a modest circulation of 600 and is edited by Reverend W. Borowsky. In January 1906 three Catholic priests, Leo Levytsky, Joseph Chaplynsky, and Alexander Ulytsky, published and edited in New York City a religious monthly pamphlet, *Pastyr* (The pastor). It ceased publication, however, after four issues. The same fate befell the weekly *Zirnytsia* (Little star), which Osyp Stemkevich began in June 1906 in Shamokin, Pennsylvania. In February 1907 a popular-educational monthly, *Nasha zhyzn* (Our life), appeared in booklet form in New York under the editorial guidance of Osyp Kosovyj, former compositor at *Svoboda*; it lasted till June 1908. In September of the same year, with the help of a group of Ukrainian Presbyterians in New York, Kosovyj was also instrumental in founding the *Amerykansky holos* (The American voice), a political weekly which directed its attack primarily at what it considered the intrusion of the excessive clericalism of the Ukrainian Catholic Church (Uniate) in national affairs. Although that paper lasted only until February 1908, it apparently influenced a considerable number of Ukrainians in New York and led to the organization of an independent church. With the financial support of the Presbyterian Mission, which was active among the newly arrived immigrants from Eastern Europe, Kosovyj initiated a third weekly, the *Soyuz* (The alliance), in August 1908. In June 1911, when Zigmont Bachynsky, a Ukrainian Presbyterian preacher from Pittsburgh, became the editor, the *Soyuz* became strictly a Presbyterian organ.

The same year was also an active one for the Ukrainian Catholics. In February, Reverend Peter Poniatishin began publishing a Catholic monthly in booklet form, the *Dushpaster* (Shepherd of souls), in New York City. It became the official organ of the first Ukrainian bishop, Soter Ortynsky, who had arrived in August 1907. In October, the *Dushpaster* was moved to Philadelphia, the bishop's see, where it was edited by Reverend Zakhar Orun. In 1912 it became a semimonthly edited by Reverend Zalitach from New Britain, Connecticut. Bishop Ortynsky's attempt in 1908 to transform the Ukrainian (Ruthenian) National Association into a purely Catholic organization resulted in much friction among the Ukrainians, leading to harsh exchanges in print between the supporters and opponents of the bishop.

The situation tended to further the spread of anticlericalism, radicalism, and socialism among the Ukrainians. Thus, for example, in January 1909, the *Khlopsky paragraf* (The commoner's paragraph), which claimed to be the organ of "Ukrainian free thinkers of America," made its appearance in Salem, Massachusetts. The twice-monthly publication, edited by John Sliuzar, expired at the end of the year. Also, early in 1909, the monthly *Hajdamaky* (The insurgents) appeared in New York under the editorial leadership of Mathew Khandola and Andrew Petrow. It was the organ of a workers' political organization of the same name which was linked with the American Socialist Party. Another New York semimonthly, *Meta* (The goal), organ of the "Progressive Ukrainians in America," appeared at about the same time and was discontinued in less than a year. Of the three, only *Hajdamaky* had a moderately long life span; it lasted until 1916.

The twice-monthly satirical *Szerszen* (The hornet), which appeared in New York in March 1908, and moved to Scranton, Pennsylvania, in November, was published and edited by Basil Hryshka. In October 1910 it was transformed into a popular literary-educational periodical. Following the split within the Soyuz in 1910, *Szerszen* became the organ of the radical "new" Soyuz. When the new Soyuz founded its own newspaper, *Narodna volya* (National freedom), in Oly-phant, Pennsylvania, in June 1911, under the editorship of Eugene Hvozdyk, *Szerszen* found it necessary to discontinue publication the following month. In June 1913 the *Narodna volya* was moved to Scranton, Pennsylvania, the home of the new Soyuz, where it was published in a libertarian anticlerical spirit, at times with strong socialist tendencies.[16] During World War I the new Soyuz changed its name to the Ukrainian Workingmen's Association and moderated its outlook; today it is one of the four leading Ukrainian national fraternal societies in the United States.

The newspaper *Ukrainske narodne slovo* (Ukrainian national word) made its initial appearance in 1914 as the organ of the Ukrainian National Aid Association. This fraternal society, which originated in McKees Rocks, Pennsylvania, started publishing its bimonthly organ in Pittsburgh in 1921. Due to economic diffi-culties, the society and its newspaper changed their headquarters to Chicago, Illinois, in October 1981. Since January 1983 further retrenchment has resulted in the transformation of *Narodne slovo* from a bimonthly into a sixteen-page quarterly newspaper, which usually includes a two- or three-page English section.[17]

The second decade of this century also marked the founding of several other important Ukrainian Catholic clerical newspapers. The *Rusin* (Ruthenian), a weekly founded in McKeesport, Pennsylvania, in 1910, was the organ of the Union of Greek Catholic Church Brotherhoods, a fraternal society organized by the priests from the Presov Region of Hungary who supported Bishop Ortynsky. It was edited by Reverend Joseph Hanula and printed in the Latin alphabet since most of the Presov immigrants were unfamiliar with Cyrillic. It lasted until 1914. Ortynsky himself founded the weekly *Zaokeanska Rus* (Ruthenia beyond the sea), which began pulication in Philadelphia in April 1911 with Reverend Val-dimir Derzyruka as its editor. It ended its existence, however, the following year. In 1912, when Ortynsky organized the Providence Association, a fraternal society for Ukrainian Catholics, an existing weekly, *America* (edited by Reverend Roman Zalitach in New Britain, Connecticut) became its organ. *America*, owned by Reverends Zalitach, Alexander Pavliak, Vladimir Dovhovich, and others, was originally published in Hartford, Connecticut. Shortly thereafter it was moved to New Britain, and after becoming the Providence Association's organ it was transferred to Philadelphia, where the new ownership and editorial committee made it the chief spokesman of Ortynsky.[18] *America* today remains the leading Ukrainian Catholic newspaper, and since 1951 it has been the only Catholic daily paper in the United States. Also in Philadelphia, the Sisters of St. Basil the Great began the publication in 1917 of a religious journal called *Misionar* (The missionary). The monthly journal's present circulation is 1,600.

In his classic work on Ukrainian immigration in the United States, published in Europe on the eve of World War I, Julian Bachynsky made some harsh observations about the nature of the early Ukrainian newspapers in America.[19] They were, in his view, frequently in the hands of unqualified editors, who were poorly educated and who came to the United States with fixed ideas about American society. The publications contained, he felt, excessive florifications of their own organizations and supporters at the expense of their opponents. Since, in the view of Bachynsky, the early immigrants were mostly illiterate, the newspapers did not have the influence and educational value that they might have had. In fact, the early press could not have existed if it had had to depend solely on voluntary subscription income from its readers. Since most papers were organs of fraternal-insurance societies, however, each member was required to subscribe to the association's newspaper. If he were illiterate, he might rely on someone who could read to him, and thus might fall slowly under the paper's influence.

But the greatest weakness of these newspapers, regardless of their journalistic competence, was, in Bachynsky's opinion, that all of them were concerned most with the internal life of the immigrants, their organizations, and events in the old country, and showed relatively little concern about American life. The Ukrainian newspapers needed to devote greater attention to the realities of immigrant life, to the conditions in which they lived and worked, and to explain for the immigrant the character of American society in its entirety. Bachynsky's sentiments, generally, were indeed valid.

After 1908, with the threat of a European war on the horizon, Ukrainian nationalist leaders in Galicia generally supported the Austrian cause. Russia's defeat would, they believed, lead to the liberation of Ukraine. Consequently, the entry of the United States into the war led it to regard the entire Ukrainian movement unfavorably. The attempt by the Ukrainian press to win U.S. support for the right of the Ukrainians to self-determination was therefore doomed to failure.

The status of the Ukrainian-American community was further confused during and after the war as a result of increased socialist influences in the Ukrainian press. For example, prior to U.S. entry into the war, *Robitnyk* (The worker), a small Ukrainian weekly in Cleveland, Ohio, affiliated with the American Socialist Party and edited by Miroslav Sichinsky since the summer of 1916, experienced extraordinary growth. It grew from a weekly with 300 subscribers in May 1916 to a daily with circulation of 3,000 in February 1917.[20] Sichinsky left *Robitnyk* in 1917 and became associate editor of a new weekly called *Narod* (The people), which was organized in New York by the Ukrainian Federation, of which Sichinsky was vice-president. The *Narod*, however, was discontinued before year's end, and the federation founded a new paper in January 1918 called *Ukrainska gazeta* (Ukrainian gazette), which Sichinsky also edited. It, too, expired that fall.

It seems that socialist and other radical papers generally represented a minority on the fringe of the Ukrainian community. They did not, as a rule, exhibit long life. The chief exception to this rule is the *Ukrainski visti* (Ukrainian news), founded as a daily in 1919 in New York. This labor-oriented paper published by the Ukrainian Daily News, Inc., and edited by Leon Tolopko, is no longer a daily but a weekly. Its circulation has dropped drastically from a high of 8,210 in 1952. It is the only Ukrainian newspaper in America with a communist orientation.

1920–1945

After World War I, new and more educated leadership, both Americanborn and political exiles from Europe, contributed to a general professional improvement of the Ukrainian press. One of the more visible of these changes was the earnest attention given to the use of the English language. It became clear that the needs of Ukrainian-American youth, whose everyday language was English, were not being provided for. Thus, in the 1920s, for example, more space in the pages of *Svoboda* was devoted to articles and other materials in the English language. From 1927 to mid–1933 a quarterly called the *Ukrainian Juvenile Magazine* was published by the Soyuz, edited by Emil Reviuk, who was also the editor of *Svoboda*. It was replaced on October 6, 1933, by an English-language weekly supplement of *Svoboda* called *The Ukrainian Weekly* whose first and longtime editor was Stephen Shumeyko. The *Weekly*'s basic goal was similar to that of *Svoboda*, to propagate the principles of Americanization and to acquaint its readers with Ukrainian culture and with the efforts of the Ukrainian people to gain freedom and independence. Many years later, Shumeyko expressed the subjective opinion that the characteristically high ethnic awareness of Ukrainian-American youth was due in large part to the influence of the *Weekly*.[21] The modern *Weekly*, in tabloid format, is edited today by Roma Hadzewyca and continues to be popular among young adults.

The early and mid–1930s witnessed the founding of a number of other English-language newspapers, among them *The Rising Star* (Detroit); the Catholic paper *Ukrainian Youth* (Philadelphia); an Orthodox periodical also titled *Ukrainian Youth* (New Britain, Connecticut); the *Ukrainian Chronicle* (Philadelphia); and the *Trident* (Chicago). *The Rising Star* was a weekly; the others were monthlies.

None of them, it should be noted, experienced the national success of *The Ukrainian Weekly*.

Trend, however, which began in 1938 as the quarterly organ of the Ukrainian Youth's League of North America, appealed to a wider national readership. The quarterly, in booklet format, originated in Union, New Jersey; it subsequently was moved to New York City and later to Detroit, Michigan. The league also published a monthly *Bulletin*, which was renamed *Trendette* in 1950. Both publications ceased in the 1950s.

Another obvious reason for the expansion of English-language publications within the Ukrainian press was the need to provide information about Ukraine to the English-speaking world. In 1939 the Organization for the Rebirth of Ukraine (ODWU) began publishing an English-language monthly, *The Trident*. That publication, which carried articles on the political aspirations of the Ukrainian people, did not last beyond 1941. Of the periodicals directed toward informing non-Ukrainians about Ukraine, the leading one is *The Ukrainian Quarterly*, a popular-educational journal founded in 1944 as the organ of the Ukrainian Congress Committee of America (UCCA). The editorial in the first issue of the *Quarterly*, which appeared in New York in October 1944, expressed its purpose thus:

The responsibility for the future rests on the English speaking world. It is therefore a duty of those Americans who are of Ukrainian birth or descent and have, as the most recent group of immigrants, very strong ties with their brethren in Europe on the one hand, and through their new American homeland ties with the Anglo-Saxon world on the other to inform the world of the true state of Ukrainian Affairs.[22]

The founder and guiding spirit of the *Quarterly* was Dr. Nicholas D. Chubaty, a Ukrainian historian who became an immigrant in 1939 when the outbreak of World War II prevented his return to his homeland. The measure of international success that the *Quarterly* has had in informing the world about Ukrainian nationalist affairs in particular, and East European and Asian affairs in general, was proudly summed up by Dr. Walter Dushnyck, the *Quarterly*'s editor since 1957, on the occasion of its thirteenth anniversary.

Indeed, perhaps the greatest compliment paid *The Ukrainian Quarterly* has come from a Communist source. The Czechoslovak Academy of Sciences in Prague listed *The Ukrainian Quarterly* and its publisher, the Ukrainian Congress Committee of America, among the 12 top American "Kremlinologist" centers in the United States. *Slovansky Prehled* (an article by Emil Sip in No. 3, 1966) ranked *The Ukrainian Quarterly* and the UCCA with such prestigious American institutions as the Foreign Policy Research Institute at the University of Pennsylvania, the Hoover Institution, The Russian Institute at Columbia, The Russian Institute at Harvard, the Institute for Sino-Soviet Studies at George Washington University, the Research Institute on Communist Affairs at Columbia, the Center for International Studies at M.I.T., The RAND Research and Development Organization, the International Institute at the University of California (Berkeley, Cal.), the Council on Foreign Relations and the "Free Europe Committee."[23]

The founding of English-language periodicals in the interwar period represented a new emphasis in the Ukrainian press. By the mid–1930s nearly every Ukrainian-language newspaper in America, including those published by smaller organizations, such as *Sichovyi klych* (The Sich call) of Newark, New Jersey, and *Natsionalyst* (Nationalist) of New York, also had an English section or supplement.[24] In addition, new Ukrainian-language serials continued to be established during the period. *Pislanets pravdy* (Messenger of truth), for example, organ of the Ukrainian Baptist Convention in the U.S.A., was founded in 1927. This bimonthly was published in Chester, Pennsylvania, until the mid–1970s.

A number of new publications appeared in the 1930s. The Pacific Press Publishing Association of Mountain View, California, founded *Oznaky nashoho chasu* (Signs of our times) in 1930. This monthly religious magazine, dedicated to the interpretation of the Bible, is presently edited by Nicholas Ilchuk. Moreover, there were the semimonthly newspaper *Dnipro* (Dnieper), published in Philadelphia by the Ukrainian Autocephalous Orthodox Church, and the semimonthly *Nove zhyttia* (New life), published in Olyphant by the small Concord Fraternal Association. Both ceased publication before World War II.

In 1944 the Ukrainian National Women's League of America founded the monthly *Nashe zhyttia* (Our life), in Philadelphia. Since 1976, both the league and its publication have had headquarters in New York City. *Nashe zhyttia*, which contains an English section, includes articles on literature, folk art, children's interests, and household hints. This serial, with a circulation of 4,000, is currently edited by Ulana Lubovych.

Despite the greater professionalism and apparent expansion of the Ukrainian press during the interwar period, its future was by no means assured. Historian Wasyl Halich, for example, in his pioneering study, *Ukrainians in the United States*, published in 1937, foresaw a bleak future for the Ukrainian press:

The prospect for the future of the Ukrainian press in the United States is not bright. As a matter of fact, it is dark, and its end may not be far off. Ever since the American government closed its doors to southeastern European immigration, it more or less signaled a death warning to the press of these peoples in America.[25]

The events of World War II, however, had consequences that were wholly unforeseen.

POST–WORLD WAR II

Following World War II the Ukrainian press experienced a period of unusual expansion and revitalization due to the arrival of between 85,000 and 100,000 Ukrainian displaced persons who had been forced to leave their homeland as a consequence of the war. Some intellectuals among the new political immigrants became associated with existing Ukrainian publications, while others, many intensely nationalistic, organized new publications, thus expanding considerably the content and outlook of the press. With few exceptions the new publications were subsidized, as were the old, by organizations. Because of the competition by so many publications for what was actually a fixed number of readers, many of the periodicals were short-lived. By 1952, when the immigration of displaced persons had begun to taper off, thirty-five Ukrainian periodicals were being published, with an overall circulation of close to 75,000.[26]

The number of publications is partially explained by the somewhat unique role that the Ukrainian press has had within American journalism as a whole. Not only does it provide a service to the newly arrived who are unfamiliar with the English language, but it provides a source of information about Ukraine and Ukrainians which can not be obtained in the English-language American press, or anywhere else for that matter. In a recent article, Anthony Dragan, the distinguished editor of *Svoboda* from 1955 to 1978, notes that there are two types of ethnic newspapers in the United States, each with its own special role and responsibilities: newspapers of groups that have free and independent states in the old country, and papers of groups that do not have free and independent homelands.[27] The first type serves primarily as a bridge between the new Americans and the land of their origin. The second type has an additional responsibility of aiding the people still in the homeland in their quest for freedom and independence, of spreading the truth about them, and frequently of being their voice.

Because the land of their origin remains under foreign domination and their kinsmen cannot control their own destiny, the Ukrainians in Diaspora (particularly those in North America, where more Ukrainians have settled than anywhere else in the world) consider it imperative for the continued existence of the Ukrainian people as a nation to inform the world about the history of their native land and the traditions of its people. The leaders of ethnic groups whose homelands have gained independent national states are less likely to feel a need to become the spokesmen of their kinsmen in the old country. The Ukrainian press, which from its beginnings had been oriented toward the homeland, had its Old World outlook reinforced in many of the new publications organized by the politicized postwar immigrant intellectuals.

One of the earliest of the highly political new periodicals was the monthly *Visnyk* (The herald), organ of the Organization for Defence of Four Freedoms for the Ukraine, which first made its appearance in typewritten format in New York City in 1947. It is edited today by Viacheslav Davydenko and has a circulation of 2,000. In February 1948 the Organization for the Rebirth of Ukraine issued a bulletin called *Samostiina Ukraina* (Independent Ukraine) in Chicago. Though primarily a political monthly, it also featured articles on the social and political life of the Ukrainians at home and abroad. It is of interest that in its August 1948, issue, V. Shemerdiak, in an article entitled "The New Ukrainain Emigration in America," foresaw and warned about the dangers to Ukrainian national interests should an unnatural division develop between the old and new emigrations. In his opinion, the "Ukrainian emigration in America must be only one and it must have a common language and a common goal."[28] That division nevertheless did occur, contributing to serious differences of opinion on many issues which are not yet entirely absent from the pages of the Ukrainian-American press. *Lysty do pryiateliv* (Letters to friends), another political publication of this period, was discontinued in 1968. In 1978 Smoloskyp Publishers in Ellicot, Maryland, introduced a quarterly, *Smoloskyp* (The torch), dealing with human rights affairs in Ukraine and Eastern Europe. The current interest in the issue of human rights probably has contributed to the tabloid's current circulation of 10,000.

The postwar period also witnessed the founding of new religious publications. The Ukrainian Catholic Church, for example, has published the bilingual weekly *Shlakh/The Way* in Philadelphia since 1949. The paper appears in two sections of eight pages each and is the organ of the Ukrainian Archdiocese in Philadelphia, the Diocese of Stamford, Connecticut, and the recently established St. Josaphat Diocese in Parma, Ohio. The Ukrainian section is edited by Mstyslaw B. Dolnycky, and the English section by Reverend Ronald D. Popivchak. The paper serves Ukrainian Catholics in the eastern part of the United States. It lists a circulation among its membership of 12,000; consequently, it is the largest Ukrainian religious newspaper in the country. St. Nicholas Ukrainian Catholic Diocese in Chicago, which serves the western half of the United States, introduced its organ, *Nova zoria* (The new star), in 1965. This Ukrainian and English biweekly newspaper, originally a weekly, has a current circulation of 4,520. And in 1967, in Philadelphia, the Society for Promotion of the Patriarchal System in the Ukrainian Catholic Church founded its quarterly newsletter *Za Patriarchat* (For the patriarchate).

The Ukrainian Orthodox Church in the U.S.A. established its organ, the *Ukrainske pravoslavne slovo* (Ukrainian Orthodox word), in South Bound Brook, New Jersey, in 1950. The monthly, in tabloid form, is currently edited by Reverend Joseph Kreta and lists its circulation as 950. In addition, an English edition has been published bimonthly since 1974, edited by Reverend Frank Estocin. Between 1952 and the mid–1970s, the Ukrainian Autocephalous Orthodox Church in the U.S.A. published an official quarterly, *Pravoslavnyi ukrainets* (Orthodox Ukrainian), in Chicago.

A number of new cultural periodicals made their initial appearance in the post–1945 period as well. In 1949, in Chicago, Mykola Denysiuk Publishing Company founded the quarterly journal *Ovyd* (Horizon), edited by Denysiuk himself and devoted primarily to cultural issues. By the mid–1970s it listed a circulation of 1,200. *Kyiw* (Kiev), the Ukrainian literary and art magazine, published by the Kyiw Publishing House for the Ukrainian Literary and Art Society of Philadelphia, was established in 1950. The need for the journal was made clear in the editorial statement of the July-August issue, its first: "At the present time Ukrainian literature and art can be represented only by Ukrainian writers and artists in exile."[29] It was issued bimonthly until 1964 with Bohdan Romanenchuk as its editor-in-chief. In addition, since 1954 Dr. Wasyl O. Luciv of State College, Pennsylvania, has been publishing and editing *Zhyttia i shkola*

(Life and school), an independent bimonthly cultural and educational journal with a circulation of 1,000. It frequently contains older material reprinted from various periodicals, and includes summaries in English. *Recenzija*, a semiannual review of Soviet Ukrainian scholarly publications, is edited by the students of Harvard's Ukrainian Research Institute, and began publication in 1970. In Philadelphia, since 1971, the Shevchenko Scientific Society and the Association of Ukrainian Librarians in America have sponsored a bibliographic quarterly named *Ukrainska knyha* (The Ukrainian book). It is edited by Bohdan Romanenchuk. A number of youth publications and professional periodicals were also introduced during this period.

Several other postwar publications deserve mention. *The Ukrainian Bulletin* has been published by the Ukrainian Congress Committee of America in New York since 1948. The English-language bimonthly, which provides information on the current life of the Ukrainian people, is edited by Walter Dushnyck. *Lys Mykyta* (The fox), a satirical magazine founded by the Ukrainian Publishing Company of Detroit, Michigan, in 1950, was published for about twenty years; it had a circulation of 2,800 in the mid–1960s. *Biblos*, a bibliographical trade magazine, was founded in New York in 1954. A quarterly edited by Nicholas Sydor-Czartorysky, it also lasted about twenty years. Another magazine, *Nash svit* (Our world), a bimonthly dealing with Ukrainian economic life in America, has been published since 1958 in New York by the Self-Reliance Association of American Ukrainians. This journal, which has a circulation of 5,000, is edited by V. Davydenko.

Although sixty-seven Ukrainian-language newspapers and journals were published in America in 1976, with total circulation of 50,000 among newspapers and 90,000 among magazines and journals,[30] the future of the Ukrainian press in the United States is uncertain. Circulation of the national papers and journals has generally declined from the highs of the 1950s and 1960s. In several instances the decline has been greater than 50 percent.[31] The assimilation of the postwar immigrants has obviously diminished their original reliance on Ukrainian-language publications. At the same time, it should be noted that part of the decline in circulation among Ukrainian-language periodicals must be balanced against the expansion in the number of English-language Ukrainian periodicals.

The leading national Ukrainian newspapers in America today, those that address themselves to the Ukrainian community as a whole, are those that were founded in the period before World War I by today's four leading fraternal societies: *Svoboda* (circulation 16,000), the daily published in Jersey City by the Ukrainian National Association and edited by Zenon Snylyk;[32] *America* (4,500), the Catholic daily published in Philadelphia by the Providence Association and edited by Mstyslav B. Dolnycky;[33] *Narodna volya* (3,500), the weekly published in Scranton by the Ukrainian National Workingmen's Association, edited by Dmytro Korbut; and *Ukrainske narodne slovo* (3,567), now a quarterly paper published in Chicago by the Ukrainian National Aid Association of America.[34] Its current editor is Leonid Poltava. Although the four are sponsored by fraternal societies, they are not aligned with any political party; all are devoted to supporting the ideal of a free and democratic Ukraine, an ideal which Americans of Ukrainian descent have associated with the traditional American love of freedom and democracy.

Of the four newspapers just mentioned, *Svoboda* is of greatest historical importance. It is the oldest existing newspaper in the history of the Ukrainian press anywhere in the world. To the present, *Svoboda* and its various publications remain the best sources of information about Ukrainian life in America. In the view of Luke Myshuha, lawyer, diplomat, and distinguished editor of *Svoboda* from 1933 to 1955, the early Ukrainian immigrants were not as lucky as many other ethnic groups. When others arrived in America, they came with their leaders. Furthermore, they did not have to struggle for their name, their language, their national identity. From its beginnings, *Svoboda* was in the forefront of the struggle that the Ukrainian immigrants had to face.[35]

To some, even today, the proliferation of English-language Ukrainian periodicals appears to be self-defeating. Others see it as a practical recognition that the language of everyday use for many Ukrainian-Americans is English. The position of the latter group was convincingly stated in an editorial in a new Ukrainian English-language newspaper established in 1977 in Canada. The statement would seem to be equally applicable to the American milieu:

We hope to be able to discuss and report development and opportunities which will allow individuals of Ukrainian origin or perhaps their children to foster their identity, to sensitize them to the problems affecting our community and to involve them in resolving the problems. We intend to reach those, who, due to their inability to communicate in Ukrainian, have lost touch with their community and the issues facing it, or have been unable to interact with and relate to it.[36]

The Ukrainian press will have to move beyond mere expansion of English-language publications, however, in order to remain viable in the future. Newspapers, in particular, must Americanize and modernize by providing their readers on a regular basis with far better coverage of entertainment, sports, fashion, and comics, as well as international and national news. By American standards Ukrainian newspapers are small in circulation and size (generally four to sixteen pages); consequently, they cannot expect to survive solely on the income produced by advertisements and subscriptions. That should not necessarily imply, however, that the Ukrainian press is near the point of extinction. From its beginnings, the Ukrainian press in America was not intended as a business venture. Subsidies from sponsoring institutions and private contributions have provided the necessary additional income for their continued existence. it seems likely, therefore, that as long as the ancestral homeland of the Ukrainian-Americans remains under the political domination of foreign regimes, a strong motivation for the maintenance of an ethnic Ukrainian press will also remain intact.

NOTES

1. For the best sources on the Ukrainian press in the United States as well as the most useful readings relevant to this chapter, see the bibliography that follows.

2. Paul R. Mogocsi, "Ukrainians," in Stephan Thernstrom, ed., *Harvard Encyclopedia of American Ethnic Groups* (Cambridge, Mass.: Harvard University Press, 1980), p. 999.

3. This estimate is based on the author's downgrading of figures provided in Volodomyr Kubijovic, ed., *Ukraine: A Concise Encyclopedia*, (Toronto: University of Toronto Press, 1971), 2: 1103–1104; and Michael Buryk, *Ukrainians in America* (Clifton, N. J.: Ukrainian National Bicentennial Committee, 1976), p. 14. The figures given in both sources include individuals and groups who do not consider themselves Ukrainians.

4. John Volansky, "Spomyny z davnykh lit," *Svoboda* (Jersey City, N. J.), September 5, 1912, p. 4. See also "A Progressive Enterprise," *Evening Herald* (Shenandoah, Pa.), November 26, 1886, p. 4.

5. Volansky was aided considerably in his editorial work by his wife, particularly during his extended visits to distant Ukrainian colonies. According to Byzantine-Slavic tradition, married as well as single men were ordained to the priesthood.

6. "A Noted Character: An American Priesthood of One and What He Has Accomplished," *Evening Herald*, May 30, 1887, p. 4.

7. In the opinion of at least some of his opponents, *Ruskoie slovo* was merely a cosmetic change from the name *Ameryka* rather than a new publication. See "Vyselenie halitsiiskikh i uhorskikh rusinov v Ameriku i ikh sorhanizovanie," *Amerikansky russky viestnik* (Scranton, Pa.), January 9, 1894, p. 2.

8. See Luke Myshuha's concise outline of the early history of *Svoboda* in *Propamiatna knyha Ukrainskoho Narodnoho Soyuza, 1894–1934* (Jersey City: Ukrainian National Association, 1937), pp. 45–46.

9. "Bratia rusyny," *Svoboda*, September 15, 1893, p. 1.

10. The Soyuz became the sole owner of *Svoboda* in 1908. In April 1911 the paper was relocated to Jersey City, the home of the Soyuz, where it is published to the present.

11. *Svovoda*, No. 13, 1894. Translated by the author.

12. "Do dila bratia," *Svoboda*, October 17, 1900.

13. Their arrival not only signified a radical leadership in Church matters, it also marked a rapid expansion of cultural and national development among the Ukrainian immigrants. Of that circle of priests, Nestor Dmytriv and Stephen Makar were two of the more noted *Svoboda* editors.

14. Ardan was excommunicated for his radical anti-Rome views in February 1902.

15. See Julian Bachynsky (Bachinskii), *Ukrainska immigratsiia v Ziedynenykh Derzhavakh Ameryky* (Lvov: J. Bachynsky and O. Harasevych, 1914), pp. 452–61, for a general survey of the various publications in this period.

16. Ibid., p. 457.

17. Correspondence with the main office in Chicago, January 16, 1984.

18. For a summary of the history of this paper, see the fifty-year jubilee edition of *America*, October 25, 1961.

19. Bachynsky, pp. 462–463.

20. Miroslav Sichinsky, "Editorial Experiences" (manuscript), excerpt quoted in Robert E. Park's classic work, *The Immigrant Press* (New York: Harper, 1922), p. 334.

21. Stephen Shumeyko, "Ukrainsky Schodennyk," in *Yuvileiny almanakh Svobody, 1893–1953* (Jersey City: Ukrainian National Association, 1953), p. 105.

22. "Introducing the Ukrainian Quarterly," *Ukrainian Quarterly* 1 (October 1944), quoted in Walter Dushnyck, ed., *Ukraine in a Changing World* (New York: Ukrainian Congress Committee of America, 1977), p. 1.

23. Dushnyck, pp. 5–6.

24. Wasyl Halich, *Ukrainians in the United States* (Chicago: University of Chicago Press, 1937), p. 117.

25. Ibid., p. 120.

26. Yaroslav Chyz, "Chuzhomovna presa v Amerytsi," in *Yuvileiny almanakh Svobody, 1893–1953* (Jersey City: Ukrainian National Association, 1953), p. 133. Chyz, for years editor of *Narodna volya* in Scranton, headed the Foreign Language Press Division of the Common Council for Nationalities Services in New York City from 1942 until his death in 1958. He was one of the best known and influential Ukrainian-American newspapermen in the country.

27. A Dragan, "Hazeta khrestonosnykh pokhodiv," in *Almanakh Ukrainskoho Narodnoho Soyuzu, 1983* (Jersey City: Svoboda Press, 1983), p. 69.

28. V. Shemerdiak, "Nova Ukrainska emihratsiia v Amerytsi," *Samostiina Ukraina* 1 (August 1948): 14–15.

29. *Kyiw* 1 (July-August 1950): 1.

30. Magocsi, "Ukrainians," p. 1004.

31. Circulation figures are very difficult to substantiate. Nevertheless, as an illustration of a general decline, the following example is offered. A U. S. Post Office statement listed the circulation of *Narodna volya* in 1952 as 7,500. By 1974 it had fallen drastically, to 3,750. That decline has continued, though at a far slower rate, to 3,500 in 1983. With a few exceptions, such as the religious newspaper *Shlakh/The Way* (which lists an exceptional increase in its controlled circulation from 4,525 in 1952 to 12,000 in 1983), the downward trend is characteristic.

32. *Svoboda* is published daily except on Sundays, Mondays, and holidays.

33. *America* is published five times a week except on holidays. The English edition appears each Monday and is also edited by Dolnycky.

34. *Narodne slovo* was published in Pittsburgh as a biweekly until 1981, when its sponsoring fraternal society moved its headquarters to Chicago.

35. Myshuha, p. 7.

36. Quoted in Lubomyr Luciuk, "Two English-Language Ukrainian Newspapers," *Polyphony: The Bulletin of the Multicultural History Society of Ontario* 4 (Spring-Summer 1982): 79.

BIBLIOGRAPHY

Bachynsky, Julian. *Ukrainska immigratsiia v Ziedynenykh Derzhavakh Ameryky*. Lvov: J. Bachynsky and O. Harasevych, 1914.

Doroshenko, V. "Reiestr ukrainskykh periodychnykh vydan u vilnomu sviti za rr. 1961–62." *Yuvileiny almanakh Svobody, 1963*. Jersey City: Ukrainian National Association, 1963.

Fedynskyj, Alexander. *Bibliografichnyi pokazhchyk ukrainskoi presy poza mezhamy Ukrainy*. Cleveland: Ukrainian Museum-Archives, 1975.

Halich, Wasyl. *Ukrainians in the United States*. Chicago: University of Chicago Press, 1937.

Ihnatiyenko, V. *Bibliografiia ukrainskoi presy, 1816–1916*. State College, Pa.: Wasyl D. Luciw, 1968.

Markus, V. "Press and Publishing." In Volodomyr Kubijovic, ed., *Ukraine: A Concise Encyclopedia*, vol. 2. Toronto: University of Toronto Press, 1971.

Miller, Wayne Charles, et al., eds. *A Comprehensive Bibliography for the Study of American Minorities*, vol. 1. New York: New York University Press, 1976.

Wynar, Lubomyr R. *Encyclopedic Directory of Ethnic Newspapers and Periodicals in the United States*. Littleton, Colo.: Libraries Unlimited, 1972.

About the Editor and Contributors

ARLOW W. ANDERSEN is Professor Emeritus of History, University of Wisconsin-Oshkosh. He holds a Ph.D. from Northwestern University and is the author of three books and many articles on the history of the Norwegian-American experience, including *The Norwegian-Americans*. He was a Fulbright Professor at the University of Oslo and is on the board of publications of the Norwegian-American Historical Association. He is currently working on a volume on political attitudes in the Norwegian-American press.

EDGAR ANDERSON is Professor of History at San Jose State University. A specialist in Latvian studies, he earned a Ph.D. at the University of Chicago after receiving an M.A. at Riga University and is the author of fifteen books and one hundred articles and chapters in anthologies. He has been a lecturer in Australia and New Zealand and has been awarded grants by the National Endowment for the Humanities and the Hoover Institution, among other honors.

ULF A. BEIJBOM is Director of the Emigrant Institute, Växjö, Sweden, where he has served since its establishment in 1966. He holds a Ph.D. from Växjö and has been on the faculty at the University of Uppsala and the University of Washington in Seattle. He has published six books, both scholarly and popular, on Swedish emigration and over one hundred articles in American and Swedish publications.

JAMES M. BERGQUIST is Associate Professor of History at Villanova University. He earned a Ph.D. at Northwestern University and has published several essays on German-Americans, including "People and Politics in Transition: The Illinois Germans, 1850–60," in Frederick C. Luebke, *Ethnic Politics and the Election of Lincoln*. He has served as president of the Ethnic Studies Association of Philadelphia.

GERALD J. BOBANGO had his Ph.D. dissertation, *The Emergence of the Romanian National State*, published by Columbia University Press in 1979. He is the author of four books on the history of Romanians in America as well as numerous essays, reviews, and articles. He has taught at the Pennsylvania State University and has been an International Research and Exchanges Board Fellow and a Fulbright Fellow to Romania. He is currently writing a book on the post–World War II Romanian immigration in North America.

CARLOS E. CORTÉS is Professor of History and Chair of the Department of History at the University of California, Riverside. He holds a Ph.D. from the University of New Mexico. Among his many publications are *Three Perspectives on Ethnicity: Blacks, Chicanos, and Native Americans*; *Understanding You and Them: Tips for Teaching about Ethnicity*; *Gaúcho Politics in Brazil*; and *A Filmic Approach to the Study of Historical Dilemmas*, and several book series. He is the recipient of numerous honors, including two book awards, his university's 1976 Distinguished Teaching Award, the California Council for the Humanities' 1980 Distinguished California Humanist Award, and the 1983 Bildner Fellowship of the Association of American Schools in South America.

LINDA PEGMAN DOEZEMA is presently a librarian and the college archivist at Houghton College, Houghton, New York. She is a graduate of Calvin College, Grand Rapids, Michigan, and received her Master's in Library Science and Master of Arts in Sociology from Kent State University, where she was formerly a librarian. She has written an annotated bibliography entitled *Dutch Americans: A Guide to Information Sources*.

JOSEPH D. DWYER is Deputy Curator of the Soviet and East European Collection at the Hoover Institution, Stanford University. He holds degrees in library science and in Slavic languages. He has published numerous books and articles including *Slovenes in the United States and Canada: A Bibliography*.

JOSEPH P. FITZPATRICK, S. J., is Professor Emeritus of Sociology at Fordham University. Father Fitzpatrick has written several studies of the Puerto Rican community, such as *Puerto Rican Americans: The Meaning of Migration to the Mainland*. He is vice-president of the Puerto Rican Family Institute and a member of the board of the Puerto Rican Legal and Education Defense Fund. He is an active member of the Research Exchange, an informal group of scholars dedicated to the study of the Puerto Rican experience.

ENYA P. FLORES-MEISER is a cultural anthropologist on the faculty of Ball State University. She holds degrees from the University of the Philippines, the University of Iowa, and the Catholic University of America. Her ethnographic fieldwork and related research includes that among Samal Moslems and Tagalogs of the Philippines; Japanese-Brazilians; and Filipinos in the United States. Flores-Meiser's publications include works on evil eye beliefs, comparative fieldwork techniques, and culture change.

ARTHUR A. GOREN is Head of American Studies at Hebrew University in Jerusalem. He holds a B.A. from Hebrew University and a Ph.D. from Columbia University. He has published a monograph and several articles on the Jewish-American experience. His honors include the Bancroft Award and a Charles Warren Fellowship, among others.

A. WILLIAM HOGLUND earned his Ph.D. at the University of Wisconsin and is on the faculty at the University of Connecticut. He is the author of *Finnish Immigrants in America, 1880–1920*, and numerous articles, and has been awarded a Scandinavian Area Fellowship.

HARRY H. L. KITANO is Professor of Social Welfare at UCLA. He holds a Ph.D. from the University of California, Berkeley. He has published over a half dozen books on Japanese-Americans, race relations, and other topics, and is the author of over three dozen articles. He has received numerous awards and has been visiting professor at the University of Bristol, England, the International Christian University, Tokyo, and the University of Hawaii-Manoa.

ANDREW T. KOPAN is Professor of Education at DePaul University in Chicago. He received his Ph.D. from the University of Chicago, and his dissertation received the Archbishop Iakovos Prize from the Center for Neo-Hellenic Studies of the University of Texas. He has written several books and monographs on Greek immigration and is currently writing the history of the Greeks of Chicago.

A. J. KUZNIEWSKI, S.J., is Associate Professor of History at the College of the Holy Cross. Father Kuzniewski earned his Ph.D. at Harvard University. He is the author of several articles on Polish immigration and of a book, *Faith and Fatherland*, which received the best manuscript award of the Center for the Study of American Catholicism at Notre Dame University and the Halecki Award of the Polish American Historical Association. He has served as president of the Polish American Historical Association.

H. M. LAI is a writer and researcher on Chinese-American history, and lecturer in Asian American Studies at San Francisco State University and the University of California at Berkeley. He is coauthor of *Island, Poetry and History of Chinese Immigrants on Angel Island, 1910–1940* and project director of "The Chinese of America, 1785–1980" exhibition. He is a past president of the Chinese Historical Society of America and of the Chinese Culture Foundation of San Francisco.

C. MICHAEL McADAMS is Director of the Sacramento, California, office of the University of San Francisco's College of Professional Studies. He earned an M.A. in Croatian history and a graduate certificate in Soviet and East European studies from John Carroll University and is completing an Ed.D. degree at the

University of San Francisco. He has published four monographs and over fifty articles and chapters in Croatian studies and has broadcast numerous radio series on Croatian affairs.

EILEEN McMAHON is currently completing her Ph.D. in Irish ᵀ ʹrish-American history. She is a reviewer for the *Irish Literary Supplement* and the Center for Migration Studies. In 1984 she delivered a paper at a conference on the Cultural Dimensions of American Catholicism entitled "The Church in Transition, 1945–60." Her dissertation is on an Irish community on the south side of Chicago during the late 1950s and early 1960s.

PAUL R. MAGOCSI is Professor of History and Political Science at the University of Toronto, where he is the holder of the first chair of Ukrainian studies in Canada. He received his Ph.D. from Princeton University and was a member of the Society of Fellows at Harvard University (1973–1976). He has published seven books, including *Shaping of a National Identity* and *Galicia*. His most recent work is a forthcoming history of Carpatho-Rusyns in America, entitled *Our People*.

MARION TUTTLE MARZOLF is an Associate Professor in the Department of Communication at the University of Michigan. She earned her Ph.D. at the University of Michigan. Her dissertation was published as *The Danish-Language Press in America* by Arno Press. She has also published *Up from the Footnote: A History of Women Journalists* and several articles. She has worked as a professional journalist and freelance writer.

SALLY M. MILLER is Professor of History at the University of the Pacific and Managing Editor of the *Pacific Historian*. A University of Toronto Ph.D., she has published four books, including *The Radical Immigrant, 1820–1920*, and many articles. Her honors include a Visiting Professorship at the University of Warwick, England, 1978–1979, and a Fulbright appointment to New Zealand in 1986. She is currently writing an essay on Milwaukee's political and ethnic history for a University of Notre Dame anthology.

HALYNA MYRONIUK was educated at the University of Minnesota and is a Senior Library Assistant at that university's Immigration History Research Center. She has published several articles on Ukrainian immigration, especially on Ukrainian immigrant bibliography. Her "Ukrainian Collections and Archives in America," in *The Ukrainian Heritage in America*, ed. Walter Dushnyck, is forthcoming.

ALIXA NAFF is currently on the staff of the Smithsonian Institute and was formerly with the National Center for Urban Ethnic Affairs. She holds a Ph.D. in history from UCLA with a Middle Eastern specialization through St. Anthony's

College at Oxford. She is the author of several articles on Arab-American history and of a new book *Becoming American: The Early Arab Immigrant Experience in America*.

LEO PAP, Ph.D., is Professor Emeritus of Linguistics at the State University of New York. His research on various aspects of Portuguese immigrant life started with a linguistic study, *Portuguese American Speech* (1949), and culminated in *The Portuguese-Americans* (1982). He is also the author of *The Portuguese in the United States: A Bibliography* (1976) and of several related articles.

ROBERT B. PERREAULT holds a Master's degree in French and French-American studies from Rhode Island College. He has published books and articles on the French-American experience in New England. He was research assistant and interviewer for the Amoskeag textile workers oral history project under Tamara K. Hareven, librarian-archivist of L'Association Canado-Américaine, and assistant editor of *Le Canado-Américain*.

BOHDAN P. PROCKO is Professor of History at Villanova University. He received his Ph.D. from the University of Ottawa, Canada. He is the author of *Ukrainian Catholics in America: A History*, and has contributed chapters on the Ukrainians to several books dealing with immigration and ethnicity.

GEORGE J. PRPIĆ is Professor of History and member of the Institute for Soviet and East European Studies at John Carroll University. He has a diploma from Croatian University and a Ph.D. from Georgetown University. He has published books, chapters, and studies on Croatians and South Slavs in North America and Europe in several languages. They include *The Croatian Immigrants in America*.

MILAN M. RADOVICH is a librarian at the University of Wisconsin-Madison. He holds an M.A. in History, an M.L.S., and a Russian Area Studies Certificate. He is the author of numerous articles and reviews and the compiler of the basic bibliography on Serbs in North America, and served as editor of *Serb World Magazine*.

M. G. SLAVENAS is on the faculty of Fredonia State University College and that of Buffalo State University College. She holds a Ph.D. from the University of New York at Buffalo. An editor, translator, and bibliographer, she has published and edited works on various aspects of Lithuanian studies and is a member of the Institute of Lithuanian Studies.

M. MARK STOLARIK is Executive Director of the Balch Institute for Ethnic Studies. He holds degrees from the University of Ottawa and the University of

Minnesota, where he earned a Ph.D. He has published three books and over twenty articles on aspects of immigration and ethnicity, and has produced an award-winning film on Slovaks in Canada. His newest book is *Growing Up on the South Side: Three Generations in Bethlehem, Pa., 1880–1976.*

Index